European treaties bearing on the history of the United States and its dependencies to 1648

D1606004

Editor

Frances Gardiner Davenport

Alpha Editions

This edition published in 2019

ISBN : 9789353703967

Design and Setting By
Alpha Editions
email - alphaedis@gmail.com

European Treaties bearing on the History of the United States and its Dependencies to 1648

EDITED BY

FRANCES GARDINER DAVENPORT

WASHINGTON, D. C.
PUBLISHED BY THE CARNEGIE INSTITUTION OF WASHINGTON
· 1917

CARNEGIE INSTITUTION OF WASHINGTON

PUBLICATION No. 254

PAPERS OF THE DEPARTMENT OF HISTORICAL RESEARCH

J. FRANKLIN JAMESON, EDITOR

The Lord Baltimore Press
BALTIMORE, MD., U. S. A.

PREFACE.

The colonial dependence of the American settlements upon various European governments brings it about, as a necessary consequence, that several of the treaties between European governments, and several of the bulls issued by the popes in virtue of their powers of international regulation, are fundamental documents for some of the earlier portions of American history. Other treaties, or individual articles in treaties, of the period before independence, though not of fundamental importance to that history, have affected it in greater or less degree. In the period since the United States became independent, though the treaties most important to their history have been those made by their own government, not a few of the treaties concluded between European powers have had an influential bearing on the course of their development and their public action.

Taken altogether, therefore, European treaties, and the earlier papal bulls, form an important portion of the original material for American history. Yet access to authentic and exact texts of them is far from easy. In a few cases, as the researches made for this volume have shown, they do not exist in print. Of those which have been printed, there are many which the student cannot possess except by buying several large and expensive series of volumes; and there are some which, though existing in print, are not to be found in these series, but in volumes which have escaped the attention of most students of American history.

In view of these considerations, it was a natural thought, to a department of historical research in an endowed institution, to serve the interests of historical scholars and of libraries by bringing together in one collection those treaties and parts of treaties, between European powers, which have a bearing on the history of the United States and of the lands now within their area or under their government as dependencies. Of this task, the first-fruits are presented in this volume, extending through the Treaty of Westphalia, 1648. The second volume, embracing treaties from that date to 1713, the date of the Treaties of Utrecht, is in preparation.

Extraordinary pains have been taken by Dr. Davenport to find, in European archives, all the treaties and articles which her volume, as defined in her introduction, ought to contain, and to secure perfect accuracy in texts. The index has been made by Mr. David M. Matteson.

J. FRANKLIN JAMESON.

WASHINGTON, OCTOBER 12, 1917.

iii

TABLE OF CONTENTS.

INTRODUCTION.

The documents printed in this volume illustrate the diplomatic aspect of the great struggle which, from the fifteenth century onwards, was in progress between the governments of the maritime powers of Europe, over the question of participation in the trade and territorial possession of the newly discovered lands.

The story which they tell has a dramatic interest, culminating in the diplomatic victory which, in 1648, the Dutch were able to wrest from Spain. The purpose of this introduction is, so to summarize this story that it may be readily grasped as a whole.

In 1455 and 1456 (Docs. 1 and 2), Portugal received from Pope Nicholas V. the exclusive right to trade and acquire territory in the region lying south of Cape Bojador, through and beyond Guinea. The further limit of the region thus set apart as a field of enterprise open to Portugal alone, was indicated by the phrase " all the way to the Indians " (p. 31), evidently the equivalent of the fuller phrase, " as far as to the Indians who are said to worship the name of Christ " (p. 22).

In spite of the papal letters Castile continued to claim Guinea. But in 1479 (Doc. 3), Castile agreed to leave Portugal in peaceable possession of the trade and territory acquired or to be acquired in Guinea, the Azores, Madeira, and the Cape Verde Islands, while Portugal, on the other hand, acknowledged that Castile had an exclusive right to the Canaries. This settlement was confirmed by the Pope (Doc. 4).

Columbus's discovery, in the western seas, of lands supposedly Asiatic, led to a renewal of the dispute between Castile and Portugal in respect to the newly found regions. The Spanish Pope, Alexander VI., decided the controversy in favor of Castile, assigning to that crown the exclusive right to acquire territory, to trade in, or even to approach the lands lying west of the meridian situated one hundred leagues west of any of the Azores or Cape Verde Islands. Exception was however made of any lands actually possessed by any other Christian prince beyond this meridian before Christmas, 1492 (Docs. 5, 6, 7). In September, 1493, the Pope extended his earlier grant by decreeing that if the Castilians, following the western route, should discover lands in Indian waters, these also should belong to them (Doc. 8). In 1494 (Doc. 9), Portugal succeeded in persuading Castile to push the line of demarcation further to the west—370 leagues west of the Cape Verde Islands; and both powers agreed that within ten months they would despatch caravels with pilots and astrologers to determine the location of the line. In the following year further provisions were made for determining the demarcation (Doc. **10**), but these, like the earlier arrangements, failed to be executed. The treaty of 1494 was confirmed by Pope Julius II. in 1506 (Doc. **11**).

The arrival of the Portuguese at the Moluccas, in 1512, and the doubt as to whether the Spice Islands lay on the Portuguese or on the Spanish side of the extended line of demarcation, seem to have been the occasion of the issue of the bull of 1514 (Doc. **12**), which assigned to the Portuguese all lands discovered by them in their voyages to the east, even those situated more than half-way around the earth, reckoning eastwards from the demarcation line. This bull also renewed the grants of 1455, 1456, and 1481, whose scope had been narrowed by the bull of September, 1493.

Although the Pope thus appeared to oppose the extension of the line of demarcation to the further side of the globe, yet the Spanish and Portuguese governments evidently considered that the line established by the Treaty of Tordesillas passed around the earth. This is assumed in the protracted negotiations concerning the possession and ownership of the Moluccas, and the determination of the position of the line, which, beginning in 1522, resulted in the indecisive conference at Badajoz in 1524 (Docs. **13, 14**), and finally in the treaties of 1529 (Docs. **15, 16**). By the treaty of Saragossa (Doc. **16**), the Emperor, in defiance of the wishes of the Castilian Cortes, pledged to the crown of Portugal, for the sum of 350,000 ducats, all rights of possession and trade in the Moluccas, and in all the lands and seas eastwards, as far as to the meridian situated 17 degrees east of the Spice Islands. According to the provisions of this treaty, the Philippines should have passed to Portugal, but Spain managed to retain them. *1565*

The Portuguese-French treaty of 1536 (Doc. **17**) is the earliest of those included in this volume to which a power situated outside the Iberian peninsula was party. The French were the first vigorously to make their way into the distant regions, from which the Pope, Portugal, and Spain desired to exclude them. In the early years of the sixteenth century Breton, Norman, and Gascon captains frequented the waters of Newfoundland, a region claimed by Portugal, cruised to the Antilles and to the mainland of America and Africa, and by 1529 had sailed to Sumatra. Before 1515 the French had instituted a regular trade with Brazil, where in 1530 they made a short-lived establishment. So formidable were the corsairs of this nation that in 1523 and 1525 the Cortes of Castile complained of their frequent and intolerable depredations, and their feeling appears to be reflected in the treaty of Madrid concluded between Spain and France in 1526, art. 33.

While the French mariners displayed great resolution, the policy of Francis I. fluctuated. He sanctioned the voyages of Verrazano and Cartier, despatched a galleon to Brazil, and in 1528 and 1533 affirmed the principle of free navigation. On the other hand, he did not consistently maintain this attitude, but shifted his position in accordance with his political necessities. During his long warfare with Charles V. he balanced the need of maintaining friendly relations with Portugal against the economic advantage derived from the capture of Portuguese ships. Moreover, he was influenced by the counsels of Admiral Brion-Chabot, who was in the pay of Portugal. In 1536, Portugal apparently sought to secure her own ships and colonies from French attack by permitting the French to use the harbors of Portugal, the Azores, and other Portuguese islands, as lurking-places whence they might prey upon the Spanish treasure-fleets and to which they might bring their prizes. The Portuguese-French treaty of this date was highly injurious to Spain.

Not only did the French corsairs plague the fleets and oversea settlements of Spain, but, as indicated by Cartier's voyages, they were bent on establishing themselves on the mainland of America. So alarming was this prospect to the Emperor Charles V. that he was apparently willing to conclude an agreement with the French, permitting them to trade in the Indies if they would not attempt any discoveries or other enterprises there. An article (Doc. **18**) to this effect was signed by the French commissioners, but it was not ultimately accepted by Spain, partly on account of the opposition of the King of Portugal.

Portuguese as well as Spanish shipping suffered terribly from the French privateers, and in 1552, when war between the Emperor and France was about to be renewed, articles (Doc. **19**) were concluded between Portugal and Spain, providing, *inter alia,* for the protection of their Indian fleets. In a truce, signed with Spain four years later, the French relinquished their navigation and trade in the Indies (Doc. **20**), but in the negotiations that resulted in the treaty of Cateau-Cambrésis, an oral agreement was made, apparently to the effect that the French would navigate west of the prime meridian and south of the tropic of Cancer at their own risk, and that what was done in those regions would not be regarded as violating international amity, since treaties would have no force beyond these lines (Doc. **21**).

For a long period after the settlement made at Cateau-Cambrésis, France was so distracted by civil strife that she was unable to carry on a vigorous policy abroad. Enterprises, like Coligny's Florida colony, or the Azores expedition whereby France planned to purchase the region of Brazil, by aiding the Prior of Crato to recover from Spain the Portuguese crown, failed grievously. So closely were the French Catholic leaders of the League bound to Spanish interests, that in their treaty of 1585 they promised Philip to put a stop to the French voyages to the Indies and Azores (Doc. **22**).

In 1595 Henry IV., having established himself on the French throne, declared war on Spain, and in 1596 he sought to form an alliance with the two great sea-powers, England and the United Provinces, against their common enemy (Doc. **23**).

The English mariners had been slower than the French to make their way into the distant regions. The comparatively few voyages undertaken by them in the early part of the sixteenth century to the West Indies and Brazil seem to have been usually made in association with French ship-owners and seamen.[1] In the latter half of the sixteenth century, however, England came to be the most formidable opponent of the monopolistic claims of Portugal and Spain. In 1553, a joint-stock company was founded in London for the Guinea trade; between 1562 and 1568 Hawkins made three slave-trading voyages between Africa and the West Indies; subsequently English privateers played havoc with Spanish shipping in West Indian waters, and by 1586, Drake had definitely proved England's mastery of the sea. Upon Spain's command of the sea, as Spain and England were perfectly aware, depended the maintenance not only of Spain's colonial monopoly, but also of her national strength, which was derived from the Indian trade; hence, the great potential importance of uniting the naval forces of the English and Dutch to co-operate against Spain's American fleets. At this time France, on the other hand, had little strength upon the ocean, and sought to defeat Spain on land. For this purpose she received small aid from her allies, and therefore in 1598 she made a separate and advantageous peace with Spain, but was able to arrive at no better understanding in respect to navigation beyond the lines of amity than she had reached in 1559 (Doc. **23**, end of introduction).

In the last decade of the sixteenth century, the Dutch were beginning to send out their ships to Guinea and both the Indies. Their well-founded hopes for the future expansion of this commerce strengthened their aversion to reunion with the southern provinces, or Spanish Netherlands, when these, upon receiving from Philip II. in 1598 a quasi-independent status, were prohibited from engaging in the East and West Indian trade (Doc. **24**). In the same year, despite some jealousy aroused by the commercial successes of the Dutch, England concluded an alliance with the States General (Doc. **25**) which provided for joint aggressive action on the part of their naval forces against the Azores and the Indies.

But the death of Elizabeth, and James's accession, foreshadowed an Anglo-Spanish peace. This Henry IV. endeavored to prevent, urging England to continue her offensive action against the Spanish coasts and colonies. He succeeded only in drawing her into a defensive alliance (Doc. **26**), which provided only contingently for such naval operations. Conformably with Henry's expectation, in the following year (1604), James made peace with Spain (Doc. **27**).

In the discussions preliminary to the treaty of 1604, the right of Englishmen to engage in the Indian trade was argued at length. The question had previously been debated with representatives of Portugal or Spain in 1555,

---

[1] R. G. Marsden, in *English Historical Review*, XXIV. (1909), p. 100.

1561, 1562, 1569-1576, 1587, 1588, and 1600. Since 1555 the claim that Englishmen had a right to visit such parts of the Indies as were not actually held by Spain had been maintained. It may have been due to Robert Cecil's characteristic subtlety that in 1604 an ambiguous article was finally agreed on, which, according to England, admitted Englishmen to the Indies; according to Spain, excluded them. On account of this difference in interpretation, the status of Englishmen beyond the line was the same as that of the French— right made might in those distant regions.

In the negotiations, for a peace or truce, conducted between the United Provinces of the Netherlands and Spain in the years 1607-1609, no question was debated with greater vehemence than that of Dutch participation in the Indian trade. In fact, the Dutch were already profiting by their trade in the East Indies. Spain ardently desired to keep them out of the West Indies, at least, but she was finally obliged to make the great concession, for a limited time. In the twelve years' truce concluded on April 9, 1609, an obscurely worded article permitted the Dutch to trade in both Indies, during the period of the truce, in places not actually held by Spain (Doc. **28**). Furthermore, it was certified by the French and English ambassadors at the Hague that it had been agreed that Spaniards should refrain from traffic in places held by the Dutch in the Indies. France and England also guaranteed that, during the truce, Spain would not molest the Dutch in the Indian trade (Doc. **29**).

In 1621 the twelve years' truce expired, and Spain declared war on the United Netherlands. Within the period from 1621 to 1625 the Dutch were conducting various negotiations with Denmark, France, and England, as well as with other powers, for the purpose of securing their alliance against Spain. The States General were very desirous that Danes, French, and English should co-operate with the Dutch West India Company, chartered in 1621 for the purpose of attacking Spain's American possessions and treasure-fleets, as well as for trade. The Danes and French, on the other hand, desired rather to share in the profitable East India commerce. In 1621 the Dutch and Danish commissioners signed an agreement that in their journeys, trade, and navigation in the East and West Indies, Africa, and Terra Australis, subjects of either party should befriend subjects of the other (Docs. **30, 31**). The Dutch treaty with France in 1624 merely stipulated that the question of traffic to the East and West Indies should be treated later by the French ambassador (Doc. **32**). The defensive alliance formed with England in 1624 did not refer to the Indies; but the offensive alliance of the following year (Doc. **33**) enjoined attacks by both parties on Spain's dominions on both sides of the line, and especially on the treasure-fleets. One of the results of this treaty was the opening of trade between the Dutch and the English colonists in North America.

The treaty which France made with Spain in 1626, and English interference with the French trade with Spain, were among the most important causes of the war between England and France which broke out in 1627. During this war the English, operating in the St. Lawrence River, captured the first fleet sent out by the trading Company of New France, and devastated some French settlements. They also seized some posts occupied by the French in the region of Acadia, but did not capture Quebec until after peace had been proclaimed between England and France in 1629 (Doc. **34**).

In the following year, when England made peace with Spain, under circumstances of domestic dissension that made it impossible for her to compel large concessions, the article respecting trade with the Indies was left in practically the same ambiguous form as in the previous Anglo-Spanish treaty of 1604. An article, which stipulated the return of prizes made south of the Equator, marked a departure from the ancient principle that, between Spain and other nations, might made right beyond the line·(Doc. **35**).

The seizure of the fort of Quebec, together with a quantity of furs and merchandise, effected after the conclusion of the Franco-English peace, led to protracted negotiations between the English and French. These finally bore fruit in the treaty of 1632 (Doc. **36**), which provided for the restitution to France of all places occupied by the English in " New France, Acadia, and Canada ". Subsequently, a long and bitter quarrel between two lieutenant-governors of Acadia threatened seriously to involve the English of Massachusetts Bay. But the danger was averted by the conclusion of a treaty between D'Aulnay of Acadia and the magistrates of Massachusetts (Doc. **39**), stipulating peace and mutual liberty of trade.

The liberation of Portugal from Spain in 1640 gravely affected the commercial interests of those nations which, in the course of their wars against Spain, or at other times, had acquired territory in both Indies and Africa, or had seized Spanish-Portuguese colonies, or were developing the slave-trade. Nevertheless, it was to these nations that Portugal turned for friendly recognition or aid. In 1641 and 1642 she signed treaties with France, the United Provinces, and England (Doc **37**, Doc. **38**, and Doc. **38**, note 24). By these treaties France and the Provinces agreed to send ships to co-operate with those of Portugal in attacking the silver fleet on the seas and the naval fleet at Cadiz; and it was further arranged that neither Dutch nor Portuguese should send any ships, negroes, or merchandise to the Spanish Indies, and that conquests made there should be divided or enjoyed by common consent. The right of the English and Dutch to continue in the African trade and possessions was recognized.

This separation of Portuguese from Spanish colonial interests made possible a peace between Spain and the Dutch. In the treaty of Münster, 1648 (Doc. **40**), Spain, for the first time, in a public treaty, and with express mention of the Indies, recognized the right of the subjects of another nation to trade and hold territory in both the Indies.

Thus by the middle of the seventeenth century the two Iberian powers were compelled to admit other nations to trade and territorial dominion in those oversea regions which they had hoped to monopolize. But as old barriers fell new ones were erected. The successful intruders, French, English, Dutch, and others, also sought exclusive rights for their respective peoples or even for certain of their own trading companies in the newly acquired commerce and land. So the ideal of free ocean commerce and navigation, championed by some Frenchmen and Englishmen in the sixteenth century, and brilliantly expounded by Grotius near the beginning of the seventeenth century, remained unrealized.

In selecting the texts for this volume the aim has been to include all treaties, or parts of treaties, that bear upon the history of the present territory of the United States, or of its outlying possessions. Some drafts of treaties, and the papal bulls which formed a basis for the claims of Portugal or Spain to the aforesaid territory, are also included.

Of the texts contained in this volume, numbers **14, 15, 17,** and **18,** are, it is believed, here printed for the first time. Of those previously printed, some are drawn from more authoritative manuscripts than those formerly published; others, it is believed, are reproduced with greater accuracy. All of the texts but one [1] have been collated, either with the manuscripts from which they are derived, or with photographs, or, in a few cases, with official transcripts of these manuscripts. The spelling but not always the capitalization or punctuation of the originals has been followed. A large proportion of the texts of treaties have already been printed in Dumont's *Corps Diplomatique,* but that great and valuable collection, it is well known, is lacking in verbal exactitude. The same is true of most of the other collections, with some modern exceptions.

The translations have, in most instances, been made by the editor. When this is not the case, the fact has been stated.

In compiling the bibliographies, the needs of less advanced students, and also the needs of scholars and investigators, have been kept in mind; for the purpose of the work is not merely to present a body of texts in convenient form, but also to stimulate further research into the history of European-American relations.

In collecting the material for this and later volumes, the editor has received generous assistance from many sources. The unfailing courtesy of the officials of the London Public Record Office, of the British Museum, and of the Library of Congress, where most of the editorial work has been done, calls for special recognition. It is a pleasure also to acknowledge the aid

[1] Doc. **19,** of which no complete manuscript was found.

received from the director and officials of the archives at Paris, Lisbon, Seville, the Hague, Copenhagen, and Mons. Particular mention must be made of kind help given by Mr. Hubert Hall, by Mr. Henry P. Biggar, and by Miss Ruth Putnam, and by the editor's colleagues, especially by Mr. Waldo G. Leland in Paris, and Mr. Roscoe R. Hill in Seville. The editor is also indebted to the Arthur H. Clark Company of Cleveland and to Dr. James A. Robertson for kind permission to make use, so far as was desired, in connection with Docs. **5, 6, 7, 8, 9, 10, 13,** and **16,** of translations from the first volume of Blair and Robertson's *The Philippine Islands.* Dr. Robertson has also made valuable suggestions respecting other of the translations.

FRANCES GARDINER DAVENPORT.

1.

The Bull Romanus Pontifex (*Nicholas V.*). *January 8, 1455.*

Columbus, returning from his first voyage to America, was driven by storms into the river Tagus. On March 9, 1493, he was received by the King of Portugal, who "showed that he felt disgusted and grieved because he believed that this discovery [of the lands found by Columbus] was made within the seas and bounds of his lordship of Guinea which was prohibited and likewise because the said Admiral was somewhat raised from his condition and in the account of his affairs always went beyond the bounds of the truth ".[1] The king said "that he understood that, in the capitulation[2] between the sovereigns [of Castile] and himself, that conquest [which Columbus had made] belonged to him.[3] The admiral replied that he had not seen the capitulation, nor knew more than that the sovereigns had ordered him not to go either to La Mina[4] or to any other port of Guinea, and that this had been ordered to be proclaimed in all the ports of Andalusia before he sailed ".[5] Thus, before Columbus had arrived in Spain, his discoveries in the New World threatened to create an international difficulty. To explain this difficulty it is necessary to consider the earlier history of the conflicting claims of Portugal and Castile to the newly discovered lands.

The first such conflict concerned the Canary Islands, rediscovered in the latter part of the thirteenth century. In 1344, on the ground that he wished to Christianize these islands, Don Luis de la Cerda, admiral of France and great-grandson of Alfonso the Wise, obtained a bull of investiture from Pope

---

[1] The whole passage from Ruy de Pina, *Chronica d'El Rei Dom Joaõ II.*, in J. F. Corrêa da Serra, *Collecçaõ de Livros Ineditos de Historia Portugueza*, pub. by the Academia Real das Sciencias, Lisbon, II. 178-179, is translated in a foot-note to the translation of the " Journal of the First Voyage of Columbus ", in J. E. Olson and E. G. Bourne, *The Northmen, Columbus, and Cabot* (1906), pp. 255-256, in J. F. Jameson's series of *Original Narratives of Early American History*.

[2] The treaty of Alcaçovas. See below, Doc. **3**.

[3] According to Ruy de Pina, " that conquest" was the " islands of Cipango and Antilia ". Vignaud points out (*Histoire Critique*, I. 368 ff.) that there is no evidence that the Indies were mentioned in this interview, but, as Vander Linden remarks, Columbus placed the island of Cipango in the " sea of the Indies ". *American Historical Review*, XXII. 12, note 30.

[4] Elmina, on the Gold Coast; known also as S. Jorge da Mina, or, in English, St. George of the Mine. In 1482 Diogo d'Azambuja, acting under royal orders, built a fort there to protect Portuguese commerce. J. de Barros, *Da Asia*, I. (1778), dec. I., liv. III., cc. 1, 2. *Cf.* Doc. **4**, introduction.

[5] "Journal of the First Voyage of Columbus ", in Olson and Bourne, *The Northmen, Columbus, and Cabot*, p. 254. The royal letter prohibiting Columbus from going to the Mine is in Navarrete, *Coleccion de Viages* (1825-1837), tom. III., no. 11, pp. 483-484.

Clement VI., and was crowned Prince of Fortunia[6] at Avignon. At this time
the kings of Portugal and Castile agreed to set aside their own opposing
claims to the archipelago and to help Luis in the enterprise to which the Pope
had thus lent his support.[7] But Luis never entered into possession, and
Portugal and Castile kept up the struggle for the islands. Papal bulls were
issued, favorable now to one and now to the other party, and the question of
ownership, which was argued before the Council of Basel in 1435, was not
finally settled until 1479, when, by the treaty of Alcaçovas, Portugal ceded
the islands to Castile.[8]

The second Castilian-Portuguese controversy concerned Africa, where
Portugal was following up her conquest of Ceuta (1415) by other military
expeditions in Morocco, and by sending caravels southward along the western
coast and opening up a trade with Guinea. In 1441 slaves and gold-dust
were first brought back to Portugal from beyond Cape Bojador. By 1454
trade with that region had greatly developed[9] so that Cadamosto, the Venetian, wrote that " from no traffic in the world could the like [gain] be had ".[10]

The kings of Castile, basing their claims on the same grounds that they had
employed in respect to the Canaries—possession by their ancestors, the Visi-
gothic kings—asserted their right to the conquest of the lands of Africa[11]
and to Guinea and the Guinea trade. They even imposed a tax upon the
merchandise brought from those parts.[12]

The Castilian-Portuguese controversy over the Guinea trade began as early
as 1454. On April 10 of that year the King of Castile, John II., wrote a
letter[13] to the King of Portugal, Alfonso V., containing complaints and demands in respect to the Canaries, and also in respect to the seizure by a Portu-

---

[6] The Canary Islands were believed to be the Fortunatae Insulae of the ancients.
[7] An incomplete text of the bull and the letters from the kings of Portugal and
Castile to the Pope are in Raynaldus, *Annales Ecclesiastici*, VI. 359-364. The full
text of the bull is in C. Cocquelines, *Bullarum Collectio*, tom. III. (1741), pt. II.
pp. 296 ff. A French translation (incomplete) is in M. A. P. d'Avezac, *Iles de l'Afrique*
(1848), pt. II., pp. 152-153. A facsimile and transliteration of the letter of the King
of Portugal to the Pope have been printed by Eugenio do Canto (Lisbon, 1910). The
sermon preached by Clement VI. on the occasion of the appointment of Luis to the
lordship of the Canaries is extant, see L. von Pastor, *Geschichte der Päpste*, I. (1901)
91, note. For other references, see Ch. de La Roncière, *Histoire de la Marine Française*, II. (1900), 104-106.
[8] Summaries of the statement of the Bishop of Burgos at the Council of Basel, and
of the bull of July 31, 1436, are in *Alguns Documentos*, pp. 3, 4. The article of the
treaty of Alcaçovas by which the Canaries were awarded to Castile is to be found *ibid.*,
pp. 44-45, and see Doc. 3, introduction.
[9] Ch. de Lannoy and H. Vander Linden, *L'Expansion Coloniale: Portugal et Espagne*
(1907), pp. 43, 44.
[10] Quoted in the introduction to Azurara, *Guinea*, II. xxii (ed. Beazley and Prestage,
Hakluyt Soc., vol. C., 1899).
[11] Bull of July 31, 1436, *Algs. Docs.*, p. 4; bull of Jan. 5, 1443, *ibid.*, p. 7.
[12] Navarrete, *Viages*, I. xxxvii-xxxix. *Cf.* Doc. 3, note 2.
[13] The letter is printed in Las Casas, *Historia de las Indias*, I. 141-151. A Portuguese translation made from the manuscript of the *Historia* is in Viscount de Santarem,
Quadro Elementar (1842-1876), II. 352-367.

guese captain of an Andalusian vessel which, together with others also belonging to the citizens of Seville and Cadiz, had arrived within a league of Cadiz on its return from a trading voyage to Guinea." The King of Castile, or rather the two ecclesiastics who a few months before had begun their energetic management of his affairs," demanded the restitution of the captured subjects of the Castilian crown and of the caravel and her cargo of Guinea merchandise. At the same time " these virtual rulers of Castile sent ambassadors to the King of Portugal to threaten war unless he should desist from the "conquest" of Barbary and of Guinea, which belonged to Castile. The King of Portugal, although greatly vexed, replied with much moderation that it was certain that that "conquest" belonged to him and to the kingdom of Portugal, and urged that the peace should not be broken until the truth as to the proprietorship were ascertained. Before this reply had reached the King of Castile he had fallen ill and he died in July of this year."' His successor, Henry IV., a king of weak character, was little fitted to oppose the pretensions of Portugal. Moreover, by August, 1454, he was already engaged in negotiating a marriage with the sister of the Portuguese king."

It is probable that King Alfonso deemed the time especially propitious for a settlement of the dispute over the proprietorship of Morocco, Guinea, and the Guinea trade. In attempting to establish his claims, he would naturally seek aid from the Pope, for that potentate's independent position made him the arbitrator between nations, while his spiritual authority, in particular his powers of excommunication and interdict, gave weight to his decisions." Moreover, as spiritual fathers of all the peoples of the earth, the popes had long undertaken to regulate the relations—including the commercial relations—between Christians and unbelievers. The Lateran Council of 1179 prohibited the sale to the Saracens of arms, iron, wood to be used in construction, and anything else useful for warfare. Certain later popes prohibited all commerce with the infidels." These prohibitions were, however, tempered by papal licenses to trade, which were on occasion granted to monarchs, communities, or individuals, or by the absolutions sometimes purchased by re-

---

" "La tierra que llaman Guinea, que es de nuestra conquista." Las Casas, *op. cit.,* I. 150.

" Nunes de Leão (do Liam), *Cronicas*, p. 221.

" Nunes do Liam does not give the precise date of the sending of the embassy but places it after the beginning of the year 1454 and before June of that year. He names Juan de Guzman and Fernando Lopez of Burgos as the ambassadors, whereas the letter of Apr. 10. 1454. names Juan de Guzman and Juan Alfonso of Burgos as the ambassadors who will bear the letter to the King of Portugal. Fernando Lopez was sent by Henry IV. as ambassador to Portugal in Aug., 1454. Santarem, *Quadro Elementar,* I. 354.

" Nunes do Liam, *Cronicas*, p. 222.

" Santarem, *Quadro Elementar,* I. 353, 354.

" On the papacy as an international power, see R. de Maulde-la-Clavière, *La Diplomatie au Temps de Machiavel* (1892), tom. I., ch. 2.

" The canon law on the subject is in *Decretal. Gregor. IX.,* lib. V., tit. VI., cc. 6, 11, 12, and 17; *Extravag. Joann. XXII.,* tit. VIII., c. 1; *Extravag. Commun.,* lib. V., tit. II., c. 1.

turning merchants. In order the more readily to obtain these favors, the applicant sometimes pointed out to the Pope how commerce tended to the spread of the Christian faith.[21]

On January 8, 1455, doubtless in accordance with the request of King Alfonso, Nicholas V. issued the bull *Romanus pontifex*, which marks a definite stage in the colonial history of Portugal. By the bull *Rex regum*, January 5, 1443, Eugenius IV. had taken neutral ground in the dispute between Portugal and Castile concerning their rights in Africa ; by the bull *Dum diversas*, June 18, 1452, Nicholas V. granted King Alfonso general and indefinite powers to search out and conquer all pagans, enslave them and appropriate their lands and goods.[22] The bull *Romanus pontifex*, on the other hand, settled the dispute between Portugal and Castile in favor of the former, and. apparently for the first time,[23] granted Portugal *exclusive* rights in a vast southerly region. It confirmed the bull *Dum diversas*, specified the district to which it applied—Ceuta, and the district from Capes Bojador and Não through all Guinea, and " beyond towards that southern shore "—and declared that this, together with all other lands acquired by Portugal from the infidels before or after 1452, belonged to King Alfonso, his successors, and Prince Henry, and *to no others*. It further declared that King Alfonso, his successors, and Prince Henry might make laws or impose restrictions and tribute in regard to these lands and seas, and that they and persons licensed by them might trade there with the infidels, except in the prohibited articles, but that no other Catholics should trade there or enter those seas or harbors under pain of excommunication or interdict.

---

[21] On the relations of the Church to commerce, see E. Nys, *Les Origines du Droit International* (1894), pp. 284-286, and especially G. B. Depping, *Histoire du Commerce* (1830), ch. 10. Depping mentions a king of Aragon's attempt to persuade the Pope that his trade with the infidels was in the interest of the Christian faith. In 1485 the orator of the Portuguese embassy of obedience to Pope Innocent VIII. argued that commercial intercourse led to the conversion of the Ethiopians, and that the trade established with the Ethiopians at Elmina had prevented them from furnishing supplies to the Moors (see below, Doc. **1**, note 30). An interesting passage in the bull *Sedis apostolicae*, issued by Julius II. on July 4, 1505, shows that the then King of Portugal was using the same kind of argument to persuade the Pope to absolve from excommunication such Portuguese as might have traded unlawfully in Guinea or India. L. A. Rebello da Silva, *Corpo Diplomatico Portuguez* (Acad. Real das Sciencias, Lisbon, 1862), I. 59-61.

[22] The bull *Rex regum* is printed in *Algs. Docs.*, pp. 7, 8. The entire bull *Dum diversas* is printed in Jordão, *Bullarium*, pp. 22 ff. ; a part is printed below, Doc. **1**, note 37.

[23] Barros states that upon petition of Prince Henry, Martin V. (1417-1431) granted to the crown of Portugal the land that should be discovered from Cape Bojador to and including the Indies. (*Da Asia*, I., dec. I., lib. I., cap. 7.) No such bull is known, but *cf.* below, note 42.

A grant by Pope Nicholas V., dated Jan. 8, 1450, conceding to Alfonso V. all the territories which Henry had discovered, has been said to be preserved in the National Archives at Lisbon, Coll. de Bullas, maço 32, no. 1, or no. 10. (Santarem, *Prioridade*, p. 26, and Azurara, *Guinea*, ed. Carreira and Santarem, 1841, p. 92, note 1 ; and, in Beazley and Prestage's edition, II. 318, note 67). The editor looked up both these manuscripts and found that one is the *executoria* of the bull of Jan. 8, 1455 (see below, note 43), and that the other is a bull issued by Paul III. toward the middle of the following century.

BIBLIOGRAPHY.

Text: MS. The original manuscript of the promulgated bull is in the National Archives in Lisbon, Coll. de Bullas, maço 7, no. 29.
Text: Printed. J. Ramos-Coelho, *Alguns Documentos* (1892), pp. 14-20; L. M. Jordão, *Bullarium Patronatus Portugalliae Regum* (1868), pp. 31-34; J. Dumont, *Corps Diplomatique* (1726-1731), tom. III., pt. I., pp. 200-202; O. Raynaldus (continuing Baronius), *Annales Ecclesiastici* (1747-1756), X. 17-20; and in various *bullaria* and other works.
Translation: English. William Bollan, *Coloniae Anglicanae Illustratae* (1762), pp. 117-136. **Spanish.** *Boletín del Centro de Estudios Americanistas de Sevilla,* año III., núm. 7 (March-April, 1915).
References: Contemporary and early writings. Gomes Eannes de Azurara, *Conquest of Guinea* (trans. and ed. by C. R. Beazley and E. Prestage, Hakluyt Soc., vols. XCV. and C., 1896, 1899); Nunes de Leão (do Liam), *Cronicas dos Reys* (1780), tom. IV., p. 222; B. de Las Casas, *Historia de las Indias* (1875), tom. I., c. 18, in M. F. de Navarrete *et al., Coleccion de Documentos Inéditos para la Historia de España* (1842—), tom. LXII.
References: Later writings. R. H. Major, *Life of Prince Henry* (1868); H. Schäfer, *Geschichte von Portugal* (1838-1854), II. 477 ff., and III. 144-148, in Heeren and Ukert, *Geschichte der Europäischen Staaten*; H. Harrisse, *Diplomatic History of America* (1897), pp. 6, 7; H. Vignaud, *Toscanelli and Columbus* (1903), pp. 58-61; *id., Histoire Critique de la Grande Entreprise de Christophe Colomb* (1911), I. 200-206; E. G. Bourne, *Essays in Historical Criticism* (1901), "Prince Henry the Navigator"; C. R. Beazley, "Prince Henry of Portugal and the African Crusade of the Fifteenth Century", *American Historical Review,* XVI. 11-23; *id.,* "Prince Henry of Portugal and his Political, Commercial, and Colonizing Work", *ibid.,* XVII. 252-267; J. P. Oliveira Martins, *The Golden Age of Prince Henry the Navigator,* translated, with additions, by J. J. Abraham and W. E. Reynolds (1914). For other references to the period of Prince Henry's voyages, see the "Critical Essay on Authorities" in E. P. Cheyney, *European Background of American History* (1904), in A. B. Hart, *The American Nation.*

TEXT.[24]

Nicolaus episcopus, servus servorum Dei. Ad perpetuam rei memoriam. Romanus pontifex, regni celestis clavigeri successor et vicarius Jhesu Christi, cuncta mundi climata omniumque nationum in illis degentium qualitates paterna consideratione discutiens, ac salutem querens et appetens singulorum, illa propensa deliberatione salubriter ordinat et disponit que grata Divine Majestati fore conspicit et per que oves sibi divinitus creditas ad unicum ovile dominicum reducat, et acquirat eis felicitatis eterne premium, ac veniam impetret animabus; que eo certius auctore Domino provenire credimus, si condignis favoribus et specialibus gratiis eos Catholicos prosequamur reges et principes, quos, veluti Christiane fidei athletas et intrepidos pugiles, non

---

[24] The text is from the original manuscript of the bull, preserved in the National Archives at Lisbon, Coll. de Bullas, maço 7, no. 29.

modo Saracenorum ceterorumque infidelium Christiani nominis inimicorum feritatem reprimere, sed etiam ipsos eorumque regna ac loca, etiam in long- issimis nobisque incognitis partibus consistentia, pro defensione et augmento fidei hujusmodi debellare, suoque temporali dominio subdere, nullis parcendo laboribus et expensis facti evidentia cognoscimus, ut reges et principes ipsi, sublatis quibusvis dispendiis, ad tam saluberrimum tamque laudabile prose- quendum opus peramplius animentur. Ad nostrum siquidem nuper, non sine ingenti gaudio et nostre mentis letitia, pervenit auditum, quod dilectus filius nobilis vir, Henricus,[25] infans Portugalie, carissimi in Christo filii nostri Alfonsi[26] Portugalie et Algarbii regnorum regis illustris patruus, inherens vestigiis clare memorie Johannis,[27] dictorum regnorum regis, ejus genitoris, ac zelo salutis animarum et fidei ardore plurimum succensus, tanquam Ca- tholicus et verus omnium Creatoris Christi miles, ipsiusque fidei acerrimus ac fortissimus defensor et intrepidus pugil, ejusdem Creatoris gloriosissimum nomen per universum terrarum orbem etiam in remotissimis et incognitis locis divulgari, extolli, et venerari, nec non illius ac vivifice qua redempti sumus Crucis inimicos perfidos, Sarracenos videlicet ac quoscunque alios infideles, ad ipsius fidei gremium reduci, ab ejus ineunte etate totis aspirans viribus post Ceptensem[28] civitatem, in Affrica consistentem, per dictum Johannem Regem ejus subactam dominio, et post multa per ipsum infantem nomine tamen dicti regis contra hostes et infideles predictos, quandoque etiam in propria persona, non absque maximis laboribus et expensis, ac rerum et personarum periculis et jactura, plurimorumque naturalium suorum cede, gesta bella, ex tot tantisque laboribus, periculis, et damnis non fractus nec territus, sed ad hujusmodi laudabilis et pii propositi sui prosecutionem in dies magis atque magis exardescens, in oceano mari quasdam solitarias insulas fidelibus populavit, ac fundari et construi inibi fecit ecclesias et alia loca pia, in quibus divina celebrantur officia. Ex dicti quoque infantis laudabili opera et industria, quamplures diversarum in dicto mari existentium insu- larum incole seu habitatores ad veri Dei cognitionem venientes, sacrum bap- tisma susceperunt ad ipsius Dei laudem et gloriam, ac plurimorum animarum salutem, orthodoxe quoque fidei propagationem, et divini cultus augmentum.[29] Preterea cum olim ad ipsius infantis pervenisset notitiam, quod nunquam vel saltem a memoria hominum non consuevisset per hujusmodi occeanum mare versus meridionales et orientales plagas navigari, illudque nobis occiduis

[25] Prince Henry the Navigator (b. 1394–d. 1460).

[26] Alfonso V., surnamed "the African" from his conquests in Morocco, ruled from 1438 to 1481. He stood high in the favor of Pope Nicholas because, after the fall of Constantinople and in response to the Pope's summons, he alone, of all the western monarchs, seriously prepared to aid in resisting the Turks. In April, 1454, in recognition of his efforts, the Pope sent him the consecrated golden rose. L. von Pastor, *Geschichte der Päpste*, I. (1901), 608; Jordão, *Bullarium*, p. 35.

[27] John I., surnamed "the Great", the founder of the house of Aviz, ruled from 1385 to 1433.

[28] The conquest of Ceuta in 1415, in which Prince Henry played a leading part, marks the beginning of the colonial expansion of Portugal. An account of the crusade against the city is given in Major, *Life of Prince Henry*, ch. 3.

[29] The Madeira Islands were rediscovered in 1418-1420; the Azores, in 1427 or 1432 or 1437. J. Mees argues for the last date in his *Histoire de la Découverte des Îles Açores* in *Recueil de Travaux publiés par la Faculté de Philosophie et Lettres*, University of Ghent (1901), fasc. 27. The Cape Verde Islands were discovered in 1456, shortly after the issue of this bull. Azurara, *Guinea* (ed. Beazley and Prestage), II. ix, lxxxv, lxxxvi, xcii-xcvi.

adeo foret incognitum, ut nullam de partium illarum gentibus certam notitiam
haberemus, credens se maximum in hoc Deo prestare obsequium, si ejus opera
et industria mare ipsum usque ad Indos qui Christi nomen colere dicuntur,[20]
navigabile fieret, sicque cum eis participare, et illos in Christianorum auxilium
adversus Sarracenos et alios hujusmodi fidei hostes commovere posset, ac
nonnullos gentiles seu paganos nefandissimi Machometi secta minime infectos
populos inibi medio existentes continuo debellare, eisque incognitum sacra-
tissimum Christi nomen predicare ac facere predicari, regia tamen semper
auctoritate munitus, a viginti quinque annis, citra exercitum ex dictorum
regnorum gentibus, maximis cum laboribus, periculis, et expensis in velo-
cissimis navibus, caravelis[21] nuncupatis, ad perquirendum mare et provincias
maritimas versus meridionales partes et polum antarticum, annis singulis fere
mittere non cessavit; sicque factum est, ut cum naves hujusmodi quamplures
portus, insulas, et maria perlustrassent, et occupassent, ad Guineam provinciam[22] tandem pervenirent, occupatisque nonnullis insulis, portibus, ac
mari eidem provincie adjacentibus, ulterius navigantes ad hostium cujusdam
magni fluminis Nili[23] communiter reputati pervenirent, et contra illarum

[20] The early voyages sent out by Prince Henry along the west coast of Africa were
connected with the crusade which after the conquest of Ceuta the Portuguese carried
on against tĥe Saracens in Morocco (see Beazley, "Prince Henry of Portugal and the
African Crusade of the Fifteenth Century", in the *American Historical Review*, XVI.
11-23). They were undertaken partly to learn whether there were any Christian princes
in the interior who would aid the prince against the Moors, and because the infante
desired to have knowledge not only of Guinea "but also of the Indies and the land of
Prester John" (Azurara, *Guinea*, chs. 7, 16; ed. Beazley and Prestage, I. 55). The "Indians who are said to worship Christ" are clearly the subjects of Prester John. The
question where the Portuguese supposed these Christian Indians to dwell—whether
in Abyssinia or Asia—has aroused a controversy, which is summed up in Vignaud,
Histoire Critique, I. 195 ff. A bit of evidence, apparently not noticed hitherto but
conclusive for its date, is in the oration of obedience, delivered on Dec. 9, 1485, before
Innocent VIII., by the Portuguese ambassador, Vasco Fernandes de Lucena. A copy
of this oration, printed at Rome, probably in 1485, is in the British Museum. The passage is as follows: "Accedit tandem hiis omnibus haud dubia spes Arabici sinus
perscrutandi, ubi Asiam incolentium regna et nationes, vix apud nos obscurissima fama
cognite, sanctissimam Salvatoris fidem religiosissime colunt: a quibus jam si modo vera
probatissimi geographi tradunt paucorum dierum itinere Lusitanorum navigatio abest."
This statement concerning the goal of the Portuguese is opposed to Vignaud's conclusion
that up to 1486 the Portuguese were seeking the Indies of Prester John in Africa.

[21] Cadamosto, the Venetian, called the Portuguese caravels the best sailing ships at
sea. "They were usually 20-30 metres long, 6-8 metres in breadth; were equipped with
three masts, without rigging-tops, or yards; and had lateen sails stretched upon long
oblique poles, hanging suspended from the mast-head. . . . They usually ran with all
their sail, turning by means of it, and sailing straight upon a bow-line driving before
the wind. When they wished to change their course it was enough to trim the sails."
Beazley's introduction to Azurara, *Guinea*, II. cxii-cxiii.

[22] A vague knowledge of a land called Guinea ("Ganuya", "Ginuia"), south of the
great desert, inhabited by negroes and rich in gold, existed in Europe long before the
time of Prince Henry. The name "provincia Ganuya" appears on the *mappemonde*
of the Medicean or Laurentian atlas of 1351, reproduced in facsimile in T. Fischer,
Raccolta di Mappamondi, pt. V. (1881), and, with clearer lettering, in Santarem, *Atlas
de Mappemondes* (1849-1852), no. 24, and is fully discussed in T. Fischer, *Sammlung
Mittelalterlicher Welt- und Seekarten* (1886), pp. 127-147. "Ginuia" is indicated on the
Catalan *mappemonde* of 1375, of which an available reproduction is opposite p. 78 in
S. Ruge, *Zeitalter der Entdeckungen* (1881), in W. Oncken, *Allgemeine Geschichte*.

[23] The Senegal, or Western Nile, or Nile of the Negroes. When this river was discovered in 1445 it was believed to be a branch of the Nile. The maps referred to in the
preceding note show a water connection between the Atlantic, Guinea, and the Nubian
Nile. *Hostium* is for *ostium*.

partium populos nomine ipsorum Alfonsi Regis et infantis, per aliquos annos guerra habita extitit, et in illa quamplures inibi vicine insule debellate ac pacifice possesse fuerunt, prout adhuc cum adjacenti mari possidentur. Ex inde quoque multi Guinei et alii nigri vi capti, quidam etiam non prohibitarum rerum permutatione, seu alio legitimo contractu emptionis ad dicta sunt regna transmissi; quorum inibi in copioso numero ad Catholicam fidem conversi extiterunt, speraturque, divina favente clementia, quod si hujusmodi cum eis continuetur progressus, vel populi ipsi ad fidem convertentur, vel saltem multorum ex eis anime Christo lucrifient.[34] Cum autem sicut accepimus, licet rex et infans prefati, qui cum tot tantisque periculis, laboribus. et expensis, nec non perditione tot naturalium regnorum hujusmodi, quorum inibi quamplures perierunt, ipsorum naturalium duntaxat freti auxilio provincias illas perlustrari fecerunt ac portus, insulas, et maria hujusmodi acquisiverunt et possederunt, ut prefertur, ut illorum veri domini, timentes ne aliqui cupiditate ducti, ad partes illas navigarent, et operis hujusmodi perfectionem, fructum, et laudem sibi usurpare vel saltem impedire cupientes, propterea seu lucri commodo, aut malitia, ferrum, arma, ligamina,[35] aliasque res et bona ad infideles deferri prohibita portarent, vel transmitterent, aut ipsos infideles navigandi modum edocerent, propter que eis hostes fortiores ac duriores fierent, et hujusmodi prosecutio vel impediretur, vel forsan penitus cessaret, non absque Dei magna offensa et ingenti totius Christianitatis obprobrio, ad obviandum premissis ac pro suorum juris et possessionis conservatione, sub certis tunc expressis gravissimis penis prohibuerint et generaliter statuerint quod nullus, nisi cum suis nautis et navibus et certi tributi solutione obtentaque prius desuper expressa ab eodem rege vel infante licentia, ad dictas provincias navigare aut in earum portibus contractare seu in mari piscari presumeret;[36] tamen successu temporis evenire posset, quod aliorum regnorum seu nationum persone, invidia, malitia, aut cupiditate ducti, contra prohibitionem predictam, absque licentia et tributi solutione hujusmodi, ad dictas provincias accedere, et in sic acquisitis provinciis, portibus, insulis, ac mari, navigare, contractare, et piscari presumerent, et exinde inter Alfonsum Regem ac infantem, qui nullatenus se in hiis sic deludi paterentur, et presumentes predictos quamplura odia, rancores, dissensiones, guerre, et scandala in maximam Dei offensam et animarum periculum verisimiliter subsequi possent et subsequerentur—Nos, premissa omnia et singula debita meditatione pensantes, ac attendentes quod cum olim prefato Alfonso Regi quoscunque Sarracenos et paganos aliosque Christi inimicos ubicunque constitutos, ac regna, ducatus, principatus, dominia, possessiones, et mobilia ac immobilia bona quecunque per eos detenta ac possessa invadendi, conquirendi, expugnandi, debellandi, et subjugandi, illorumque personas in perpetuam servitutem redigendi, ac regna, ducatus, comitatus, principatus, dominia, possessiones, et bona sibi et successoribus suis applicandi. appropriandi, ac in suos successorumque suorum usus et utilitatem convertendi, aliis nostris

---

[34] The first natives captured beyond Cape Bojador were brought to Portugal by Antam Gonçalves in 1441 or 1442. Azurara, *Guinea*, chs. 12 and 13.

[35] This word appears in this same form in the *Corpus Juris Canonici*, Decretal. Gregor. IX., lib. V., tit. VI., c. 6, ed. E. Friedberg, who gives as variant forms *lignamina* and *ligneamina.*

[36] A royal charter, dated Oct. 22, 1443, forbidding any one to pass beyond Cape Bojador without a license from Prince Henry, is printed in *Algs. Docs.*, pp. 8-9.

litteris [37] plenam et liberam inter cetera concesserimus facultatem, dicte facultatis obtentu idem Alfonsus Rex, seu ejus auctoritate predictus infans, juste et legitime insulas, terras, portus, et maria hujusmodi acquisivit ac possedit et possidet, illaque ad eundem Alfonsum Regem et ipsius successores de jure spectant et pertinent, nec quisvis alius etiam Christifidelis absque ipsorum Alfonsi Regis et successorum suorum licentia speciali de illis se hactenus intromittere licite potuit nec potest quoquomodo, ut ipsi Alfonsus Rex ejusque successores et infans eo ferventius huic tam piissimo ac preclaro et omni evo memoratu dignissimo operi, in quo cum in illo animarum salus, fidei augmentum, et illius hostium depressio procurentur, Dei ipsiusque fidei ac reipublice, universalis ecclesie rem agi conspicimus, insistere valeant et insistant, quo, sublatis quibusvis dispendiis amplioribus, se per nos et Sedem Apostolicam favoribus ac gratiis munitos fore conspexerint, de premissis omnibus et singulis plenissime informati, motu proprio,[38] non ad ipsorum Alfonsi Regis et infantis vel alterius pro eis nobis super hoc oblate petitionis instantiam, maturaque prius desuper deliberatione prehabita, auctoritate apostolica et ex certa scientia, de apostolice potestatis plenitudine, litteras facultatis prefatas, quarum tenores de verbo ad verbum presentibus haberi volumus pro insertis, cum omnibus et singulis in eis contentis clausulis, ad

[37] The bull of June 18, 1452 (Nicholas V.). The provisions of this bull are as follows:
". . . Nos igitur considerantes, quod contra Catholicam fidem insurgentibus, Christianamque religionem extinguere molientibus, ea virtute, et alia constantia a Christi fidelibus est resistendum, ut fideles ipsi fidei ardore succensi virtutibusque pro posse succincti detestandum illorum propositum, non solum obice intentionis contraire impediant, si ex oppositione roboris iniquos conatus prohibeant, et Deo, cui militant, ipsis assistente, perfidorum substernant molimenta, nosque divino amore communiti, Christianorum charitate invitati, officiique pastoralis astricti debito, ea, quae fidei, pro qua Christus Deus noster sanguinem effudit, integritatem, augmentumque respiciunt nobis fidelium animis vigorem, tuamque Regiam Magestatem in hujusmodi sanctissimo proposito confovere merito cupientes, tibi Sarracenos, et paganos, aliosque infideles, et Christi inimicos quoscunque, et ubicunque constitutos regna, ducatus, comitatus, principatus aliaque dominia, terras, loca, villas, castra, et quaecunque alia possessiones, bona mobilia et immobilia in quibuscunque rebus consistentia, et quocunque nomine censeantur, per eosdem Sarracenos, paganos, infideles, et Christi inimicos detenta, et possessa, etiam cujuscunque seu quorumcunque regis, seu principis, aut regum, vel principum regna, ducatus, comitatus, principatus, aliaque dominia, terrae, loca, villae, castra, possessiones, et bona hujusmodi fuerint, invadendi, conquerendi, expugnandi, et subjugandi, illorumque personas in perpetuam servitutem redigendi, regna quoque, ducatus, comitatus, principatus, aliaque dominia, possessiones, et bona hujusmodi, tibi et successoribus tuis Regibus Portugalliae, perpetuo applicandi, et appropriandi, ac in tuos, et eorundem successorum usus et utilitates convertendi plenam et liberam, auctoritate apostolica, tenore praesentium concedimus facultatem. . . ." Jordão, *Bullarium*, p. 22. It will be noticed that this bull sanctions the enslaving of the infidels. Two interesting bulls respecting slaves from the Canary Islands, printed in appendix II. of *Carácter de la Conquista y Colonización de las Islas Canarias: Discursos leídos ante la Real Academia de la Historia* (1901) by Don Rafael Torres Campos, show that Eugenius IV., the immediate predecessor of Nicholas V., not only wished to protect from slavery and annoyance those aborigines who had embraced the faith, but also expressed a fear that dread of captivity would deter others from conversion.

[38] The phrase *motu proprio*, etc., had long been a mere form, which exempted the recipient of the bull from the ordinary taxes. J. Haller, " Die Ausfertigung der Provisionen ", *Quellen und Forschungen*, II. (1), (1899), p. 3. " Eine päpstliche Verleihung erfolgt fast immer nur auf Grund einer eingereichten Supplik. Der Empfänger also hat die Initiative zu ergreifen auch da, wo es sich scheinbar um einen spontanen Act des Papstes, ein *motu proprio* handelt. Denn auch diese Art der Verleihung ist schon früh eine blosse Form geworden, bestimmt, dem Empfänger Abgabenfreiheit und andere Vorrechte zu verschaffen."

Ceptensem et predicta ac quecunque alia etiam ante data dictarum facultatis litterarum acquisita, et ad ea, que imposterum nomine dictorum Alfonsi regis suorumque successorum et infantis, in ipsis ac illis circumvicinis et ulterioribus ac remotioribus partibus, de infidelium seu paganorum manibus acquiri poterunt provincias, insulas, portus, et maria quecunque extendi et illa sub eisdem facultatis litteris comprehendi, Ipsarumque facultatis et presentium litterarum vigore jam acquisita et que in futurum acquiri contigerit, postquam acquisita fuerint, ad prefatos regem et successores suos ac infantem, ipsamque conquestam quam a capitibus de Bojador [39] et de Nam [40] usque per totam Guineam et ultra versus illam meridionalem plagam [41] extendi harum serie declaramus etiam ad ipsos Alfonsum Regem et successores suos ac in- fantem et non ad aliquos alios spectasse et pertinuisse ac imperpetuum spectare et pertinere de jure, Necnon Alfonsum Regem et successores suos ac infantem predictos in illis et circa ea quecunque prohibitiones, statuta, et man- data, etiam penalia, et cum cujusvis tributi impositione facere, ac de ipsis ut de rebus propriis et aliis ipsorum dominiis disponere et ordinare potuisse ac nunc et in futurum posse libere ac licite tenore presentium decernimus et declaramus. Ac pro potioris juris et cautele suffragio, jam acquisita et que imposterum acquiri contigerit, provincias, insulas, portus, loca, et maria, quecunque, quotcunque, et qualiacunque fuerint, ipsamque conquestam a capitibus de Bojador et de Nom predictis Alfonso Regi et successoribus suis, regibus dictorum regnorum, ac infanti prefatis, perpetuo donamus, con- cedimus, et appropriamus per presentes. Preterea cum id ad perficiendum opus hujusmodi multipliciter sit oportunum [concedimus] quod Alfonsus Rex et successores ac infans predicti, nec non persone quibus hoc duxerint, seu aliquis eorum duxerit committendum, illius dicto Johanni Regi per felicis recordationis Martinum V., et alterius indultorum etiam inclite memorie Eduardo eorumdem regnorum regi, ejusdem Alfonsi Regis genitori, per pie memorie Eugenium IV., Romanos pontifices, predecessores nostros, conces- sorum versus dictas partes cum quibusvis Sarracenis et infidelibus, de qui- buscunque rebus et bonis ac victualibus, emptiones et venditiones prout con- gruerit facere, nec non quoscunque contractus inire, transigere, pacisci, mercari, ac negociari, et merces quascunque ad ipsorum Sarracenorum et infidelium loca, dummodo ferramenta, ligamina, funes, naves, seu armatura- rum genera non sint, deferre, et ea dictis Sarracenis et infidelibus vendere, omnia quoque alia et singula in premissis et circa ea oportuna vel necessaria facere, gerere, vel exercere: [42] ipsique Alfonsus Rex, successores, et infans

[39] Cape Bojador, in 26° 7′ N., was rounded by Gil Eannes in 1434. Azurara, *Guinea* (ed. Beazley and Prestage), II. x.

[40] During a long period prior to Prince Henry's expeditions, Cape Na or Nam was the southern limit of Portuguese coast navigation. This cape was therefore probably not the Cape Non situated to the north of the Canary Islands, in 28° 47′ N., but must have been south of Cape Bojador, where, indeed, it is placed on some maps of the early fifteenth century. See the article on "España en Berbería" by M. Jiménez de la Espada in the *Boletín de la Sociedad Geográfica de Madrid*, tom. IX. (1880), p. 316. The fact that throughout this and the following text Cape Nam is mentioned after Cape Bojador may indicate that it lay to the south of it.

[41] Probably no definite locality is intended.

[42] The reference is to the bull *Praeclaris tuae*, issued by Eugenius IV. on May 25, 1437, and summarized in *Algs. Docs.*, p. 5. The bull of Martin V. here mentioned may have been issued in 1424 or 1425 in connection with the Spanish-Portuguese controversy over the Canaries. Such a bull is referred to in Cod. Vatic. 4151, f. 18 (Kretschmer, *Entdeckung Amerika's*, 1892, p. 220 note) and in *Algs. Docs.*, p. 3. *Cf.* above, note 23.

in jam acquisitis et per cum acquirendis provinciis, insulis, ac locis, quascunque
ecclesias, monasteria, et alia pia loca fundare ac fundari et construi [curare],
nec non quascunque voluntarias personas ecclesiasticas, seculares, quorumvis
etiam mendicantium ordinum regulares, de superiorum tamen suorum licentia,
ad illa transmittere, ipseque persone inibi etiam quoad vixerint commorari,
ac quorumcunque in dictis partibus existentium vel accedentium confessiones
audire, illisque auditis in omnibus preterquam sedi predicte reservatis, casibus,
debitam absolutionem impendere, ac penitentiam salutarem injungere, nec
non ecclesiastica sacramenta ministrare valeant libere ac licite decernimus,
ipsique Alfonso et successoribus suis Regibus Portugalie, qui erunt imposterum et infanti prefato concedimus et indulgemus; ac universos et singulos
Christi fideles ecclesiasticos, seculares, et ordinum quorumcunque regulares,
ubilibet per orbem constitutos, cujuscunque status, gradus, ordinis, conditionis, vel preeminentie fuerint, etiamsi archiepiscopali, episcopali, imperiali,
regali, reginali, ducali, seu alia quacunque majori ecclesiastica vel mundana
dignitate prefulgeant, obsecramus in Domino et per aspersionem sanguinis
Domini nostri Jhesu Christi, cujus ut premittitur res agitur, exhortamur,
eisque in remissionem suorum peccaminum injungimus, nec non hoc perpetuo
prohibitionis edicto districtius inhibemus, ne ad acquisita seu possessa nomine
Alfonsi Regis aut in conquesta hujusmodi consistentia provincias, insulas,
portus, maria, et loca quecunque seu alias ipsis Sarracenis, infidelibus, vel
paganis arma, ferrum, ligamina, aliaque a jure Sarracenis deferri prohibita
quoquomodo, vel etiam absque spetiali ipsius Alfonsi Regis et successorum
suorum et infantis licentia, merces et alia a jure permissa deferre, aut per
maria hujusmodi navigare, seu deferri vel navigari facere, aut in illis
piscari, seu de provinciis, insulis, portibus, maribus, et locis, seu aliquibus
eorum, aut de conquesta hujusmodi se intromittere, vel aliquid per quod
Alfonsus Rex et successores sui et infans predicti quo minus acquisita et
possessa pacifice possideant, ac conquestam hujusmodi prosequantur et
faciant, per se vel alium seu alios, directe vel indirecte, opere vel consilio,
facere, aut impedire quoquo modo presumant. Qui vero contrarium fecerint,
ultra penas contra deferentes arma et alia prohibita Sarracenis quibuscunque
a jure promulgatas, quas illos incurrere volumus ipso facto, si persone fuerint,
singulares excommunicationis sententiam incurrant, si communitas vel uni-
versitas civitatis, castri, ville, seu loci, ipsa civitas, castrum, villa, seu locus
interdicto subjaceant eo ipso; nec contrafacientes ipsi vel aliqui eorum ab
excommunicationis sententia absolvantur, nec interdicti hujusmodi relaxa-
tionem, apostolica vel alia quavis auctoritate obtinere possint, nisi ipsis Alfonso et successoribus suis ac infanti prius pro premissis congrue satisfecerint,
aut desuper amicabiliter concordaverint cum eisdem. Mandantes per apostolica scripta venerabilibus fratribus nostris Archiepiscopo Ulixbonensi et
Silvensi ac Ceptensi Episcopis,[43] quatenus ipsi vel duo aut unus eorum, per se
vel alium seu alios, quotiens pro parte Alfonsi Regis et illius successorum ac
infantis predictorum vel alicujus eorum desuper fuerint requisiti, vel aliquis
ipsorum fuerit requisitus, illos quos excommunicationis et interdicti sententias hujusmodi incurrisse constiterit, tamdiu dominicis aliisque festivis diebus

---

[43] The executory instrument (*executoria*) issued by Dom Jayme, archbishop of
Lisbon, and Alvaro, bishop of Silves, as executors (*juizes executores*) of this bull, is
preserved in the National Archives at Lisbon, Coll. de Bullas, maço 32, no. 10. The
similar instrument issued by João, bishop of Ceuta, is in the same archives, Coll. de
Bullas, maço 33, no. 14. Both instruments include the text of the bull.

in ecclesiis, dum inibi major populi multitudo convenerit ad divina, excommunicatos et interdictos aliisque penis predictis innodatos fuisse et esse, auctoritate apostolica declarent et denuntient; nec non ab aliis nuntiari et ab omnibus arctius evitari faciant, donec pro premissis satisfecerint seu concordaverint, ut prefertur; contradictores per censuram ecclesiasticam, appellatione postposita, compescendo, non obstantibus constitutionibus et ordinationibus apostolicis ceterisque contrariis quibuscunque. Ceterum, ne presentes littere, que a nobis de nostra certa scientia et matura desuper deliberatione prehabita emanarunt, ut prefertur, de surreptionis vel obreptionis aut nullitatis vitio a quoquam imposterum valeant impugnari, volumus, et auctoritate, scientia, ac potestate predictis, harum serie decernimus pariter et declaramus, quod dicte littere et in eis contenta de surreptionis, obreptionis, vel nullitatis, etiam ex ordinarie vel alterius cujuscunque potestatis, aut quovis alio defectu, impugnari, illarumque effectus retardari vel impediri nullatenus possint, sed imperpetuum valeant, ac plenam obtineant roboris firmitatem; irritum quoque sit et inane si secus super hiis a quoquam quavis auctoritate, scienter vel ignoranter, contigerit attemptari. Et insuper, quia dificile foret presentes nostras litteras ad quecunque lòca deferre, volumus, et dicta auctoritate harum serie decernimus, quod earum transumpto, manu publica et sigillo episcopalis vel alicujus superioris ecclesiastice curie munito, plena fides adhibeatur et perinde stetur, ac si dicte originales littere forent exhibite vel ostense; et excommunicationis alieque sententie in illis contente infra duos menses, computandos a die qua ipse presentes littere seu carte vel membrane earum tenorem in se continentes valvis ecclesie Ulixbonensi affixe fuerint, perinde omnes et singulos contra facientes supradictos ligent, ac si ipse presentes littere eis personaliter et legitime intimate ac presentate fuissent. Nulli ergo omnino hominum liceat hanc paginam nostre declarationis, constitutionis, donationis, concessionis, appropriationis, decreti, obsecrationis, exhortationis, injunctionis, inhibitionis, mandati, et voluntatis infringere, vel ei ausu temerario contraire. Si quis autem hoc attemptare presumpserit, indignationem Omnipotentis Dei et beatorum Petri et Pauli apostolorum ejus se noverit incursurum. Datum Rome apud Sanctum Petrum, anno Incarnationis Dominice millessimo quadringentesimo quinquagesimo quarto,[44] sexto idus Januarii, pontificatus nostri anno octavo.

PE. DE NOXETO.[45]

TRANSLATION.[46]

Nicholas, bishop, servant of the servants of God. For a perpetual remembrance.

The Roman pontiff, successor of the key-bearer of the heavenly kingdom and vicar of Jesus Christ, contemplating with a father's mind all the several climes of the world and the characteristics of all the nations dwelling in them

[44] In the dating of papal bulls, up to the pontificate of Innocent XII. (1691-1700), the 25th of March was usually reckoned as the beginning of the year. A. Giry, *Manuel de Diplomatique* (1894), p. 696. According to our present reckoning, therefore, this bull dates from the year 1455.

[45] Pietro da Noceto was the private secretary and confidant of Nicholas V. L. von Pastor, *Geschichte der Päpste*, I. (1901), 365.
The bull bears the usual official endorsement "Registrata in camera apostolica".

[46] In this translation the editor has been aided by Bollan's translation, mentioned in the bibliography, and by valuable suggestions from C. G. Bayne, C. S. I.

and seeking and desiring the salvation of all, wholesomely ordains and disposes upon careful deliberation those things which he sees will be agreeable to the Divine Majesty and by which he may bring the sheep entrusted to him by God into the single divine fold, and may acquire for them the reward of eternal felicity, and obtain pardon for their souls. This we believe will more certainly come to pass, through the aid of the Lord, if we bestow suitable favors and special graces on those Catholic kings and princes, who, like athletes and intrepid champions of the Christian faith, as we know by the evidence of facts, not only restrain the savage excesses of the Saracens and of other infidels, enemies of the Christian name, but also for the defense and increase of the faith vanquish them and their kingdoms and habitations, though situated in the remotest parts unknown to us, and subject them to their own temporal dominion, sparing no labor and expense, in order that [47] those kings and princes, relieved of all obstacles, may be the more animated to the prosecution of so salutary and laudable a work.

We have lately heard, not without great joy and gratification, how our beloved son, the noble personage Henry, infante of Portugal, uncle of our most dear son in Christ, the illustrious Alfonso, king of the kingdoms of Portugal and Algarve, treading in the footsteps of John, of famous memory, king of the said kingdoms, his father, and greatly inflamed with zeal for the salvation of souls and with fervor of faith, as a Catholic and true soldier of Christ, the Creator of all things, and a most active and courageous defender and intrepid champion of the faith in Him, has aspired from his early youth with his utmost might to cause the most glorious name of the said Creator to be published, extolled, and revered throughout the whole world, even in the most remote and undiscovered places, and also to bring into the bosom of his faith the perfidious enemies of him and of the life-giving Cross by which we have been redeemed, namely the Saracens and all other infidels whatsoever, [and how] after the city of Ceuta, situated in Africa, had been subdued by the said King John to his dominion, and after many wars had been waged, sometimes in person, by the said infante, although in the name of the said King John, against the enemies and infidels aforesaid, not without the greatest labors and expense, and with dangers and loss of life and property, and the slaughter of very many of their natural subjects, the said infante being neither enfeebled nor terrified by so many and great labors, dangers, and losses, but growing daily more and more zealous in prosecuting this his so laudable and pious purpose, has peopled with orthodox Christians certain solitary islands in the ocean sea, and has caused churches and other pious places to be there founded and built, in which divine service is celebrated. Also by the laudable endeavor and industry of the said infante, very many inhabitants or dwellers in divers islands situated in the said sea, coming to the knowledge of the true God, have received holy baptism, to the praise and glory of God, the salvation of the souls of many, the propagation also of the orthodox faith, and the increase of divine worship.

Moreover, since, some time ago, it had come to the knowledge of the said infante that never, or at least not within the memory of men, had it been customary to sail on this ocean sea toward the southern and eastern shores, and that it was so unknown to us westerners that we had no certain knowledge of the peoples of those parts, believing that he would best perform his

---

[47] *I. e.*, if we bestow these favors, in order that.

duty to God in this matter, if by his effort and industry that sea might become navigable as far as to the Indians who are said to worship the name of Christ, and that thus he might be able to enter into relation with them, and to incite them to aid the Christians against the Saracens and other such enemies of the faith, and might also be able forthwith to subdue certain gentile or pagan peoples, living between, who are entirely free from infection by the sect of the most impious Mahomet, and to preach and cause to be preached to them the unknown but most sacred name of Christ, strengthened, however, always by the royal authority, he has not ceased for twenty-five years past [48] to send almost yearly an army of the peoples of the said kingdoms, with the greatest labor, danger, and expense, in very swift ships called caravels, to explore the sea and coast lands toward the south and the Antarctic pole. And so it came to pass that when a number of ships of this kind had explored and taken possession of very many harbors, islands, and seas, they at length came to the province of Guinea, and having taken possession of some islands and harbors and the sea adjacent to that province, sailing farther they came to the mouth of a certain great river commonly supposed to be the Nile, and war was waged for some years against the peoples of those parts in the name of the said King Alfonso and of the infante, and in it very many islands in that neighborhood were subdued and peacefully possessed, as they are still possessed together with the adjacent sea. Thence also many Guineamen and other negroes, taken by force, and some by barter of unprohibited articles, or by other lawful contract of purchase, have been sent to the said kingdoms. A large number of these have been converted to the Catholic faith, and it is hoped, by the help of divine mercy, that if such progress be continued with them, either those peoples will be converted to the faith or at least the souls of many of them will be gained for Christ.

But since, as we are informed, although the king and infante aforesaid (who with so many and so great dangers, labors, and expenses, and also with loss of so many natives of their said kingdoms, very many of whom have perished in those expeditions, depending only upon the aid of those natives, have caused those provinces to be explored and have acquired and possessed such harbors, islands, and seas, as aforesaid, as the true lords of them), fearing lest strangers induced by covetousness should sail to those parts, and desiring to usurp to themselves the perfection, fruit, and praise of this work, or at least to hinder it, should therefore, either for the sake of gain or through malice, carry or transmit iron, arms, wood used for construction, and other things and goods prohibited to be carried to infidels, or should teach those infidels the art of navigation, whereby they would become more powerful and obstinate enemies to the king and infante, and the prosecution of this enterprise would either be hindered, or would perhaps entirely fail, not without great offense to God and great reproach to all Christianity, to prevent this and to conserve their right and possession, [the said king and infante] under certain most severe penalties then expressed, have prohibited and in general have ordained that none, unless with *their* sailors and ships and on payment of a certain tribute and with an express license previously obtained from the said king or infante, should presume to sail to the said provinces or to trade in their ports or to fish in the sea,

---

[48] It is probable that *a viginti quinque annis* should be translated " from twenty-five years [of age]", *i. e.*, from 1419. *Cf.* Bourne, *Essays*, p. 178.

[although the king and infante have taken this action, yet] in time it might happen that persons of other kingdoms or nations, led by envy, malice, or covetousness, might presume, contrary to the prohibition aforesaid, without license and payment of such tribute, to go to the said provinces, and in the provinces, harbors, islands, and sea, so acquired, to sail, trade, and fish : and thereupon between King Alfonso and the infante, who would by no means suffer themselves to be so trifled with in these things, and the presumptuous persons aforesaid, very many hatreds, rancors, dissensions, wars, and scandals, to the highest offense of God and danger of souls, probably might and would ensue—We [therefore] weighing all and singular the premises with due meditation, and noting that since we had formerly by other letters of ours granted among other things free and ample faculty to the aforesaid King Alfonso—to invade, search out, capture, vanquish, and subdue all Saracens and pagans whatsoever, and other enemies of Christ wheresoever placed, and the kingdoms, dukedoms, principalities, dominions, possessions, and all movable and immovable goods whatsoever held and possessed by them and to reduce their persons to perpetual slavery, and to apply and appropriate to himself and his successors the kingdoms, dukedoms, counties, principalities, dominions, possessions, and goods, and to convert them to his and their use and profit—by having secured the said faculty, the said King Alfonso, or, by his authority, the aforesaid infante, justly and lawfully has acquired and possessed, and doth possess, these islands, lands, harbors, and seas, and they do of right belong and pertain to the said King Alfonso and his successors, nor without special license from King Alfonso and his successors themselves has any other even of the faithful of Christ been entitled hitherto, nor is he by any means now entitled lawfully to meddle therewith—in order that King Alfonso himself and his successors and the infante may be able the more zealously to pursue and may pursue this most pious and noble work, and most worthy of perpetual remembrance (which, since the salvation of souls, increase of the faith, and overthrow of its enemies may be procured thereby, we regard as a work wherein the glory of God, and faith in Him, and His commonwealth, the Universal Church, are concerned) in proportion as they, having been relieved of all the greater obstacles, shall find themselves supported by us and by the Apostolic See with favors and graces—we, being very fully informed of all and singular the premises, do, *motu proprio,* not at the instance of King Alfonso or the infante, or on the petition of any other offered to us on their behalf in respect to this matter, and after mature deliberation, by apostolic authority, and from certain knowledge, in the fullness of apostolic power, by the tenor of these presents decree and declare that the aforesaid letters of faculty (the tenor whereof we wish to be considered as inserted word for word in these presents, with all and singular the clauses therein contained) are extended to Ceuta and to the aforesaid and all other acquisitions whatsoever, even those acquired before the date of the said letters of faculty, and to all those provinces, islands, harbors, and seas whatsoever, which hereafter, in the name of the said King Alfonso and of his successors and of the infante, in those parts and the adjoining, and in the more distant and remote parts, can be acquired from the hands of infidels or pagans, and that they are comprehended under the said letters of faculty. And by force of those and of the present letters of faculty the acquisitions already made, and what hereafter shall happen to be acquired, after they shall have been acquired, we do by the

tenor of these presents decree and declare have pertained, and forever of
right do belong and pertain, to the aforesaid king and to his successors and
to the infante, and that the right of conquest which in the course of these
letters we declare to be extended from the capes of Bojador and of Não, as
far as through all Guinea, and beyond toward that southern shore,[19] has belonged and pertained, and forever of right belongs and pertains, to the said
King Alfonso, his successors, and the infante, and not to any others. We
also by the tenor of these presents decree and declare that King Alfonso
and his successors and the infante aforesaid might and may, now and henceforth, freely and lawfully, in these [acquisitions] and concerning them make
any prohibitions, statutes, and decrees whatsoever, even penal ones, and with
imposition of any tribute, and dispose and ordain concerning them as concerning their own property and their other dominions. And in order to confer a more effectual right and assurance we do by these presents forever
give, grant, and appropriate to the aforesaid King Alfonso and his successors, kings of the said kingdoms, and to the infante, the provinces, islands,
harbors, places, and seas whatsoever, how many soever, and of what sort
soever they shall be, that have already been acquired and that shall hereafter come to be acquired, and the right of conquest also from the capes of
Bojador and of Não aforesaid.

Moreover, since this is fitting in many ways for the perfecting of a work
of this kind, we allow that the aforesaid King Alfonso and [his] successors
and the infante, as also the persons to whom they, or any one of them, shall
think that this work ought to be committed, may (according to the grant
made to the said King John by Martin V., of happy memory, and another
grant made also to King Edward of illustrious memory, king of the same
kingdoms, father of the said King Alfonso, by Eugenius IV., of pious
memory, Roman pontiffs, our predecessors) make purchases and sales of
any things and goods and victuals whatsoever, as it shall seem fit, with
any Saracens and infidels, in the said regions; and also may enter into any
contracts, transact business, bargain, buy and negotiate, and carry any commodities whatsoever to the places of those Saracens and infidels, provided
they be not iron instruments, wood to be used for construction, cordage,
ships, or any kinds of armor, and may sell them to the said Saracens and
infidels; and also may do, perform, or prosecute all other and singular things
[mentioned] in the premises, and things suitable or necessary in relation to
these; and that the same King Alfonso, his successors, and the infante, in the
provinces, islands, and places already acquired, and to be acquired by him,
may found and [cause to be] founded and built any churches, monasteries,
or other pious places whatsoever; and also may send over to them any ecclesiastical persons whatsoever, as volunteers, both seculars, and regulars of any
of the mendicant orders (with license, however, from their superiors), and
that those persons may abide there as long as they shall live, and hear confessions of all who live in the said parts or who come thither, and after the
confessions have been heard they may give due absolution in all cases, except
those reserved to the aforesaid see, and enjoin salutary penance, and also
administer the ecclesiastical sacraments freely and lawfully, and this we
allow and grant to Alfonso himself, and his successors, the kings of Portugal,

---

[19] Vignaud, *Toscanelli*, p. 61, translates " extending thence beyond towards the distant shores of the south ".

who shall come afterwards, and to the aforesaid infante. Moreover, we entreat in the Lord, and by the sprinkling of the blood of our Lord Jesus Christ, whom, as has been said, it concerneth, we exhort, and as they hope for the remission of their sins enjoin, and also by this perpetual edict of prohibition we more strictly inhibit, all and singular the faithful of Christ, ecclesiastics, seculars, and regulars of whatsoever orders, in whatsoever part of the world they live, and of whatsoever state, degree, order, condition, or pre-eminence they shall be, although endued with archiepiscopal, episcopal, imperial, royal, queenly, ducal, or any other greater ecclesiastical or worldly dignity, that they do not by any means presume to carry arms, iron, wood for construction, and other things prohibited by law from being in any way carried to the Saracens, to any of the provinces, islands, harbors, seas, and places whatsoever, acquired or possessed in the name of King Alfonso, or situated in this conquest or elsewhere, to the Saracens, infidels, or pagans; or even ,without special license from the said King Alfonso and his successors and the infante, to carry or cause to be carried merchandise and other things permitted by law, or to navigate or cause to be navigated those seas, or to fish in them, or to meddle with the provinces, islands, harbors, seas, and places, or any of them, or with this conquest, or to do anything by themselves or another or others, directly or indirectly, by deed or counsel, or to offer any obstruction whereby the aforesaid King Alfonso and his successors and the infante may be hindered from quietly enjoying their acquisitions and possessions, and prosecuting and carrying out this conquest.

And we decree that whosoever shall infringe these orders [shall incur the following penalties], besides the punishments pronounced by law against those who carry arms and other prohibited things to any of the Saracens, which we wish them to incur by so doing; if they be single persons, they shall incur the sentence of excommunication; if a community or corporation of a city, castle, village, or place, that city, castle, village, or place shall be thereby subject to the interdict; and we decree further that transgressors, collectively or individually, shall not be absolved from the sentence of excommunication, nor be able to obtain the relaxation of this interdict, by apostolic or any other authority, unless they shall first have made due satisfaction for their transgressions to Alfonso himself and his successors and to the infante, or shall have amicably agreed with them thereupon. By [these] apostolic writings we enjoin our venerable brothers, the archbishop of Lisbon, and the bishops of Silves and Ceuta, that they, or two or one of them, by himself, or another or others, as often as they or any of them shall be required on the part of the aforesaid King Alfonso and his successors and the infante or any one of them, on Sundays, and other festival days, in the churches, while a large multitude of people shall assemble there for divine worship, do declare and denounce by apostolic authority that those persons who have been proved to have incurred such sentences of excommunication and interdict, are excommunicated and interdicted, and have been and are involved in the other punishments aforesaid. And we decree that they shall also cause them to be denounced by others, and to be strictly avoided by all, till they shall have made satisfaction for or compromised their transgressions as aforesaid. Offenders are to be held in check by ecclesiastical censure, without regard to appeal, the apostolic constitutions and ordinances and all other things whatsoever to the contrary notwithstanding. But in order that the present letters, which have been issued by us of our certain knowledge and after mature deliberation thereupon, as is aforesaid, may not hereafter be impugned by anyone as fraudulent, secret, or void, we will, and by the authority, knowledge, and power aforementioned, we do likewise by these letters, decree and declare that the said letters and what is contained therein cannot in any wise be impugned, or the effect thereof hindered or obstructed, on account of any defect of fraudulency, secrecy, or nullity, not even from a defect of the ordinary, or of any other authority, or from any other defect, but that they shall be valid forever and shall obtain full authority.   And if anyone, by whatever authority, shall, wittingly or unwittingly, attempt anything inconsistent with these orders we decree that his act shall be null and void.   Moreover, because it would be difficult to carry our present letters to all places whatsoever, we will, and by the said authority we decree by these letters, that faith shall be given as fully and permanently to copies of them, certified under the hand of a notary public and the seal of the episcopal or any superior ecclesiastical court, as if the said original letters were exhibited or shown ; and we decree that within two months from the day when these present letters, or the paper or parchment containing the tenor of the same, shall be affixed to the doors of the church at Lisbon, the sentences of excommunication and the other sentences contained therein shall bind all and singular offenders as fully as if these present letters had been made known and presented to them in person and lawfully.   Therefore let no one infringe or with rash boldness contravene this our declaration, constitution, gift, grant, appropriation, decree, supplication, exhortation, injunction, inhibition, mandate, and will. But if anyone should presume to do so, be it known to him that he will incur the wrath of Almighty God and of the blessed apostles Peter and Paul. Given at Rome, at Saint Peter's, on the eighth day of January, in the year of the incarnation of our Lord one thousand four hundred and fifty-four, and in the eighth year of our pontificate.

P. DE NOXETO.

2.

The Bull Inter Caetera (*Calixtus III.*). *March 13, 1456.*

INTRODUCTION.

Calixtus III., who succeeded Nicholas V. on April 8, 1455, was a Spaniard of fiery spirit and religious zeal, who exerted himself to the utmost to rouse the nations of Europe to a crusade against the Turk. For this purpose he despatched legates to many countries,[1] and among them he sent Alvaro, bishop of Silves, an executor of the bull *Romanus pontifex*[2] and a man of great authority in the Roman Court,[3] as legate *a latere* to King Alfonso V. of Portugal. At the same time (February-March, 1456) he granted that monarch a number of concessions,[4] including the following bull, for which Prince Henry and Alfonso had petitioned.

Besides confirming the bull *Romanus pontifex,* this bull conferred upon the Portuguese military Order of Christ,[5] of which Prince Henry was governor,[6] the spiritualities in all the lands acquired and to be acquired " from Capes Bojador and Nam through the whole of Guinea and beyond its southern shore as far as to the Indians ". Whether the phrase " usque ad Indos " referred to the subjects of Prester John or to the East Indians remains a point of controversy.[7]

BIBLIOGRAPHY.

Text: MS. An official copy of the bull, made on August 16, 1456, in the house of King Alfonso's master of requests, at the instance of the king's procurator, is in the National Archives in Lisbon, gav. 7ª, maço 13, no. 7.

Text: Printed. J. Ramos-Coelho, *Alguns Documentos* (1892), pp. 20-22; L. M. Jordão, *Bullarium*,[8] pp. 36-37.

References. L. von Pastor, *Geschichte der Päpste*, I. (1901) 655 ff.; H. Vignaud, *Histoire Critique*,[8] I. 205-206.

[1] Pastor, *Geschichte der Päpste*, I. (1901) 660 ff.
[2] Doc. **1**, note 43.
[3] Damião de Goes, *Chronica de Joam II.* (1567), c. 10.
[4] Santarem, *Quadro Elementar* (1842-1876) X. 59-64.
[5] See below, note 14.
[6] *Cf.* note 3 in Beazley, " Prince Henry of Portugal and the African Crusade ", *Am. Hist. Rev.*, XVI. 11-23.
[7] Vignaud, *Histoire Critique*, I. 205, 206; and *cf.* Doc. **1**, note 30.
[8] For fuller title, see the bibliography of Doc. **1**.

TEXT.[*]

In nomine Domini, Amen. Noverint universi presens publicum instrumentum inspecturi, quod anno a nativitate Domini millesimoquatuorcentesimoquinquagesimo sexto, decimasexta mensis Augusti, coram egregio legum Doctore Lupo Valasci[10] de Serpa, illustrissimi domini nostri domini Alfonsi, Portugalie et Algarbii regis Cepteque domini, et in ejus sacro pallacio supplicacionum expeditore, in presencia mei, notarii et testium infrascriptorum, in domo habitacionis ejusdem doctoris, comparuit Alvarus Petri legum licenciatus et ejusdem Serenissimi Regis generalis et legitimus procurator et ejus nomine presentavit dicto doctori quasdam litteras apostolicas Calisti Pape Tercii, quasdam alias Nicolai Pape Quinti in se continentes, non viciosas, non rasas, non cancellatas, set omni suspicione carentes et sigillo plumbeo[11] sigillatas, quarum tenor de verbo ad verbum sequitur et est talis:

Calistus episcopus, servus servorum Dei. Ad perpetuam rei memoriam. Inter cetera que nobis, divina disponente clementia, incumbunt peragenda, ad id nimirum soliciti corde reddimur, ut singulis locis et presertim que Sarracenis sunt finitima, divinus cultus ad laudem et gloriam Omnipotentis Dei et fidei Christiane exaltacionem vigeat et continuum suscipiat incrementum, et, que regibus et principibus per predecessores nostros, Romanos pontifices, bene merito concessa sunt, [et][12] ex causis legitimis emanarunt, ut, omnibus sublatis dubitacionibus, robur perpetue firmitatis obtineant, apostolico munimine solidemus. Dudum siquidem felicis recordationis Nicolaus Papa V., predecessor noster, litteras concessit tenoris subsequentis:

[Here follows the bull *Romanus pontifex*, printed above, Doc. **1**.]

Cum autem sicut [nobis relatum est][12] pro parte Alfonsi Regis et Henrici Infantis predictorum ipsi supra modum affectent quod espiritualitas in eisdem solitariis insulis,[13] terris, portubus, et locis in mari occeano versus meridionalem plagam in Guinea consistentibus, quas idem infans de manibus Sarracenorum manu armata extraxit, et Christiane religioni, ut prefertur, conquesivit, prefate Militiae Jhesu Christi,[14] cujus reddituum suffragio idem infans hujusmodi conquestam fecisse perhibetur, per Sedem Apostolicam perpetuo concedatur, ac declaratio, constitutio, donatio, concessio, appropriatio, decretum, obsecratio, exhortatio, injunctio, inhibitio, mandatum, et

[*] The text is from a copy of the bull made in the house of King Alfonso's master of requests at the instance of the king's procurator, on Aug. 16, 1456, and preserved in the National Archives at Lisbon, gav. 7ª, maço 13, no. 7.

[10] Lopo Vasques, a native of Serpa, stood high in the favor of King Alfonso, by whose order he translated from Latin into the vernacular a work entitled *Tomada de Constantinopla pelo Graõ Turco*. D. Barbosa Machado, *Bibliotheca Lusitana*, III. (1752) 21.

[11] In MS., *pumblio*.

[12] Not in the MS.

[13] In MS., *insolis*.

[14] The Order of Christ was founded in 1319 by King Diniz in conjunction with Pope John XXII. and was endowed with the greater part of the wealth of the recently dissolved Order of the Templars. Prince Henry's African expeditions were made under its banner, and it was granted ecclesiastical and other revenues from many of the newly found lands, in the islands of the Atlantic, Africa, and the Far East. Since its growing wealth threatened to make it a danger to the kingdom, its grandmastership was permanently united with the crown of Portugal in 1551. In 1789 it was secularized. For an account of this order to 1551 see H. da Gama Barros, *Historia da Administração Publica em Portugal nos Seculos XII. a XV.*, I. (1885) 382-388.

voluntas, nec non littere Nicolai predecessoris hujusmodi, ac omnia et singula [14] in eis contenta confirmentur, quare pro parte regis et infantis predictorum nobis fuit humiliter supplicatum, ut declarationi, constitutioni, donationi, concessioni, appropriationi, decreto, obsecrationi, exhortationi, injunctioni, inhibitioni, mandato et voluntati, ac litteris hujusmodi et in eis contentis pro illorum subsistentia firmiori, robur apostolice confirmationis adjicere, nec non spiritualitatem ac omnimodam jurisdictionem ordinariam tam in predictis acquisitis quam aliis insulis, terris, et locis per eosdem regem et infantem seu eorum successorem, in partibus dictorum Sarracenorum in futurum acquirendis, prefate militie et ordini hujusmodi perpetuo concedere, aliasque in premissis oportune providere de benignitate apostolica dignaremur.

Nos igitur attendentes religionem dicte militie in eisdem insulis, terris, et locis, fructus afferre posse in Domino salutares, hujusmodi suplicationibus inclinati, declarationem, constitutionem, donationem, appropriationem, decretum, obsecrationem, exhortationem, injunctionem, inhibitionem, mandatum, voluntatem, litteras, et contenta hujusmodi et inde secuta quecunque rata et grata habentes, illa omnia et singula auctoritate apostolica tenore presentium, ex certa scientia, confirmamus et approbamus, ac robori perpetue firmitatis subsistere decernimus, supplentes omnes defectus, si qui forsan intervenerint in eisdem. Et nichilominus auctoritate et scientia predictis, perpetuo decernimus, statuimus, et ordinamus, quod spiritualitas et omnimoda jurisdictio ordinaria, dominium, et potestas, in spiritualibus duntaxat in insulis, villis, portubus, terris, et locis a capitibus de Bojador et de Nam usque per totam Guineam et ultra illam meridionalem plagam usque ad Indos, acquisitis et acquirendis, quorum situs, numerum, qualitas, vocabula, designationes, confines, et loca presentibus pro expressis haberi volumus ad militiam et ordinem hujusmodi perpetuis futuris temporibus spectent atque pertineant; illaque eis ex nunc tenore, auctoritate, et scientia predictis concedimus et elargimur. Ita quod prior major pro tempore existens ordinis dicte militie [15] omnia et singula beneficia ecclesiastica, cum cura et sine cura, secularia et ordinum quorumcunque regularia, in insulis, terris, et locis predictis fundata et instituta, seu fundanda et instituenda, cujuscunque qualitatis et valoris existant seu fuerint, quotiens illa in futurum vacare contigerit, conferre et de illis providere; nec non excommunicationis, suspensionis, privationis, et interdicti, aliasque ecclesiasticas sententias, censuras, et penas, quociens opus fuerit ac rerum et negotiorum pro tempore ingruentium qualitas id exegerit proferre; omniaque alia et singula que locorum ordinarii in locis in quibus spiritualitatem habere censentur de jure vel consuetudine facere, disponere, et exequi possunt et consueverunt pariformiter, absque ulla differentia facere, disponere, ordinare, et exequi possit et debeat, super quibus omnibus et singulis ei plenam et liberam tenore presentium concedimus facultatem, decernentes insulas, terras, et loca acquisita et acquirenda hujusmodi nullius [16] diocesis existere, ac irritum et inane si secus super hiis a quoquam quavis auctoritate scienter vel ignoranter contigerit attemptari, non obstantibus constitutionibus et ordinationibus apostolicis nec non statutis, consuetudinibus, privilegiis, usibus, et naturis dicte militie, [17] juramento confirmatione apostolica vel quavis alia firmitate roboratis, ceterisque contrariis quibuscunque. Nulli ergo omnino hominum liceat hanc paginam nostrorum confirmationis, approbationis, constitutionis, supplectionis, decreti, statuti,

---

[14] In MS., *singulla*.   [15] In MS., *millitie*.   [16] In MS., *nullus*.   [17] In MS., *millitie*.

ordinationis, voluntatis, concessionis, et elargitionis infringere vel ei ausu temerario contraire. Si quis autem hoc attemptare presumpserit, indignationem Omnipotentis Dei ac beatorum Petri et Pauli apostolorum ejus se noverit incursurum. Datum Rome apud Sanctum Petrum, anno Incarnationis Dominice millesimo quadringentesimo quinquagesimo quinto," tertio idus Martii, pontificatus nostri anno primo.

Quibus quidem litteris sic presentatis, prefatus procurator, nomine dicti Serenissimi Regis dicto doctori exposuit quod pro servicio ejusdem regis oportebat ipsum habere unum vel plura transunta dictarum litterarum apostolicarum. Iccirco petebat per me notarium publicum infrascriptum, cum autoritate predicti doctoris sibi in publica forma concedi. Prefatus vero doctor, auctoritate sui publici officii, sibi fieri mandavit. Acta fuerunt hace in civitate Ulixbonense, in predicta domo habitationis ejusdem doctoris, anno, mense, et die quibus supra, presentibus ibidem venerabilibus viris, ALFONSO JOHANNIS, DIDACO ALFONSI, PHILIPPO ALFONSI, et ALVARO MARTINI scriptoribus in curia prefati Serenissimi Regis, testibus ad hoc vocatis specialiter et rogatis.

Et ego, DIDACUS GONSALVI, regali auctoritate publicus notarius, predictarum litterarum, apostolicarum presentacioni, requisicioni, et auctoritatis prestationi, dum sic fierent et agerentur cum prenominatis testibus presens fui, et hoc presens publicum instrumentum manu propria scripsi, et me subscripsi et signo meo signavi.

[Notarial sign.]

TRANSLATION.

In the name of God, amen. Be it known to all who shall examine the present public instrument that in the fourteen hundred and fifty-sixth year from the nativity of our Lord, on the sixteenth day of the month of August, in the presence of the eminent doctor of laws, Lopo Vasques de Serpa, master of requests in his sacred palace of the most illustrious lord, our lord Alfonso, king of Portugal and Algarve and lord of Ceuta, in the presence of me, the notary, and of the witnesses whose names are written below, Alvaro Pirez, licentiate of laws and general and lawful procurator of the said Most Serene King, appeared in the dwelling-house of the said doctor and in the king's name presented to the said doctor certain apostolic letters of Pope Calixtus III., containing within them certain others of Pope Nicholas V., not defective, erased, or cancelled, but free from all suspicious indication, and sealed with a leaden seal, the tenor of which, word for word, is as follows:

Calixtus, bishop, servant of the servants of God. For an abiding memorial. Among other works, which, by the merciful dispensation of Providence, it is incumbent upon us to accomplish, we are rendered deeply solicitous at heart with respect to this—that in all places, and especially in those bordering upon the Saracens, divine worship may flourish to the praise and glory of Almighty God and the exalting of the Christian faith, and may obtain continual increase, and that by means of apostolic protection we may establish those grants to

" Doc. 1, note 44. According to our present reckoning, 1456.

kings and princes, justly made by our predecessors the Roman pontiffs, and based on legitimate grounds, so that through the removal of all doubts they may possess perpetual validity. Indeed a short while ago Pope Nicholas V., of happy memory, our predecessor, granted letters of the following tenor:

[Here follows the bull *Romanus pontifex*, Doc. **1.**]

Since, however, as has been reported to us on behalf of the aforesaid King Alfonso and the Infante Henry, they are extremely eager that ecclesiastical jurisdiction in the said solitary islands, lands, harbors, and places, situated in the ocean toward the southern shore in Guinea, which the said infante withdrew with mailed hand from the hands of the Saracens, and conquered for the Christian religion, as is stated, may be granted forever by the Apostolic See to the aforesaid Order of Jesus Christ, by the support of whose revenues the said prince is asserted to have made this conquest; and that the declaration, constitution, gift, grant, appropriation, decree, entreaty, exhortation, injunction, inhibition, mandate, and will, and the letters of the said Nicholas, our predecessor, and all and singular contained therein, may be confirmed; therefore, on the part of the said king and infante we were humbly besought that we might be graciously pleased of our apostolic good-will to add the support of the apostolic confirmation to the declaration, constitution, gift, grant, appropriation, decree, entreaty, exhortation, injunction, inhibition, mandate, and will, and to the said letters and what is contained therein, in order to establish them more firmly; and to grant in perpetuity to the military order aforesaid, ecclesiastical and all kinds of ordinary jurisdiction, both in the acquired possessions aforesaid, and in the other islands, lands, and places, which may hereafter be acquired by the said king and prince or by their successor, in the territories of the said Saracens; and otherwise, in respect to the premises, to make convenient provision. We, therefore, longing that the religion of the said order may be able in the Lord to bear wholesome fruit in the said islands, lands, and places, influenced by these supplications, and considering as valid and acceptable the above-mentioned declaration, constitution, gift, appropriation, decree, entreaty, exhortation, injunction, inhibition, mandate, will, letters, and contents, and everything done by virtue thereof, through our apostolic authority and of our certain knowledge, do confirm and approve them, all and singular, by the tenor of these presents, and supplying all defects, if there should be any therein, we decree that they remain perpetually valid. And moreover by the authority and with the knowledge aforesaid, we determine, ordain, and appoint forever that ecclesiastical and all ordinary jurisdiction, lordship, and power, in ecclesiastical matters only, in the islands, villages, harbors, lands, and places, acquired and to be acquired from capes Bojador and Nam as far as through all Guinea, and past that southern shore all the way to the Indians, the position, number, nature, appellations, designations, bounds, and localities of which we wish to be considered as expressed by these presents, shall belong and pertain to the said military order for all time; and in accordance with the tenor of these presents, by the authority and knowledge aforesaid, we grant and give them these. So that the prior major, for the time being, of the said military order may and ought to collate and provide to all and singular ecclesiastical benefices, with or without cure of souls, and whether tenable by seculars or by regulars of whatsoever orders, founded and instituted, or to be founded or instituted, in the said islands, lands, and places, of whatever nature and

value the benefices are or shall be, as often as they may fall vacant in the
future. Also, he may and ought to pronounce ecclesiastical sentences, censures, and penalties of excommunication, suspension, deprivation, interdict,
and other sentences, whenever the necessity may arise and the nature of
affairs and the course of circumstances may require. And all and singular
other acts which, in the places wherein the local ordinaries are held to possess
ecclesiastical jurisdiction by law or custom, they are able or are accustomed
to perform, determine, and execute, the prior major may and ought to perform, determine, order, and execute, in like manner and without any difference. In respect to all and singular these things, we grant him full and free
faculty by virtue of these presents, decreeing that these islands, lands, and
places, acquired and to be acquired, are included in no diocese and that, if
it shall happen that anyone, by whatever authority, shall wittingly or unwittingly attempt anything in respect to these matters which is inconsistent
with these provisions, it shall be null and void; the apostolical constitutions
and ordinances, also the statutes, customs, privileges, use, and natural rights
of the said military order, though strengthened by oath, by apostolical confirmation, or by any other binding force, and any other things whatsoever, to the
contrary notwithstanding. Let no one, therefore, infringe or with rash
boldness contravene this our confirmation, approbation, constitution, completion, decree, statute, order, will, grant, and gift. Should anyone presume to
attempt this, be it known to him that he will incur the wrath of Almighty God
and of the blessed apostles Peter and Paul. Given at Rome, at St. Peter's, on
the thirteenth day of March, in the year of the incarnation of our Lord one
thousand four hundred and fifty-five, in the first year of our pontificate.

These letters having been thus presented, the aforesaid procurator, in the
name of the said Most Serene King, explained to the said doctor that for the
service of the said king it was necessary that he should have one or more
copies of the said apostolic letters; therefore he asked that they be granted
to him in public form, by me the undersigned notary public, with the authority
of the aforesaid doctor. The aforesaid doctor by authority of his public
office ordered it to be done.

These things were transacted in this very city of Lisbon, in the aforesaid
dwelling-house of the said doctor, in the year, month, and day above-mentioned, there being present the venerable men: ALFONSO YÁÑES, DIOGO
ALFONSO, FILIPPO ALFONSO, and ALVARO MARTINES, scribes in the court of
the aforesaid Most Serene King, especially called and summoned to witness
this; and I, DIOGO GONÇALVES, notary public, by royal authority, was present
with the aforenamed witnesses at the presentation, examination, and guaranty
of authority of the aforesaid apostolic letters, while they were thus made
and prepared, and I wrote this present public instrument with my own hand,
and I subscribed myself and signed it with my sign.

3.

Treaty between Spain and Portugal, concluded at Alcaçovas,
September 4, 1479. Ratification by Spain, March 6, 1480.
[Ratification by Portugal, September 8, 1479.]

INTRODUCTION.

In 1460 the Infante Henry died and the sovereignty of the newly discovered lands became vested in the crown of Portugal. King Alfonso V., however, whose chief ambitions were to extend his Moorish conquests and annex Castile, did not directly concern himself with continuing the work of exploration. This was left to private enterprise, and the impetus given by the infante gradually wore itself out, although the Guinea trade was actively prosecuted.

In 1475 Alfonso invaded Castile, and, to strengthen his pretensions to that country, became betrothed to the Princess Joanna, Queen Isabella's rival for the Castilian crown. The resulting War of Succession extended beyond the limits of the peninsula into the Canary Islands, where the Portuguese aided the natives against the Castilians;[1] and it gave the Castilians the chance to engage vigorously in trade with Guinea—a country which, in spite of the bull *Romanus pontifex,* they continued to claim.[2] As the result of preliminary negotiations held at Alcántara in March, 1479, between Queen Isabella of Castile and her aunt, the Infanta Beatrice of Portugal, the bases for a settlement were laid, and it was agreed that a peace should be negotiated and concluded in Portugal.[3]

In the following June, in pursuance of this agreement, Queen Isabella despatched Dr. Rodrigo Maldonado, of Talavera, a lawyer in whom she had

---

[1] J. de Viera y Clavijo, *Historia General de las Islas Canarias* (1858-1863), II. 37.
[2] Pulgar, *Crónica,* pt. II., cc. 62, 88. The Catholic sovereigns declared (1475) that "los Reyes de España tuvieron siempre la conquista de Africa y Guinea, y llevaron el quinto de cuantas mercaderias en aquellas partes se resgataban". Navarrete, *Viages* (1825-1837), I. xxxvii-xxxix, with which, however, compare Santarem, *Recherches sur la Priorité* (1842), p. 199. A few years later, but before the end of the war, they instructed their ambassadors in Rome to procure permission for themselves and those to whom they should give license "para que puedan contratar con los infieles que tienen la mina del oro e de la Guinea sin incurrir por ello en sentencia de excomunion." M. F. de Navarrete *et al., Coleccion de Documentos Inéditos para la Historia de España* (1842—), VII. 552.
[3] For accounts of the peace negotiations, see the chronicles of Nunes do Liam, Ruy de Pina, and Pulgar, and J. B. Sitges, *Enrique IV. y Doña Juana la Beltraneja.*

33

great confidence, as ambassador to Portugal with full powers to treat.[4] On the side of Portugal, D. João da Silveira, baron d'Alvito, was appointed plenipotentiary,[5] but negotiations were principally directed by Prince John.

On September 4 the plenipotentiaries concluded two treaties at Alcaçovas. One, called the Tercerías, dealt mostly with dynastic matters;[6] the second, a treaty of perpetual peace, incorporated and ratified the treaty of peace concluded on October 30, 1431, between John I. of Portugal and John II. of Castile, and also included a number of additional articles. These related mostly to such matters as the restitution of places, release of prisoners, pardoning of offenders, demolition of fortresses, and suppression of robberies committed on land or sea by the subjects of one crown against those of the other. But by the eighth of these additional articles,[7] Ferdinand and Isabella bound themselves not to disturb Portugal in her possession of the trade and lands of Guinea,[8] or of the Azores, Madeira, or Cape Verde Islands, or of any other islands in the region from the Canaries towards Guinea, and not to interfere in the conquest of Morocco. On the other hand, by the ninth article,[9] King Alfonso and Prince John ceded the Canaries to Castile.

The treaty was apparently ratified by Alfonso and Prince John at Evora on September 8, 1479.[10] It was ratified by Queen Isabella (King Ferdinand being absent in his kingdoms of Aragon) at Trujillo, on September 27, 1479;[11] proclaimed and published in the frontier cities of Badajoz and Elvas on September 15, and at Evora on September 30;[12] and was ratified by Ferdinand and Isabella at Toledo on March 6, 1480.

Portugal at once took measures to secure her rights. On April 6, 1480, Alfonso ordered the captains of ships sent by Prince John to Guinea to capture such foreign ships as they might encounter within the limits laid down by the treaty of Alcaçovas (" das Canarias pera baixo e adjante contra Guinea ") and to cast their crews into the sea.[13] In the following year the Pope confirmed the clause of the treaty that excluded foreigners from Guinea.[14]

---

[4] His powers are dated July 2, 1479. Santarem, *Quadro Elementar*, I. 380. On the part taken by him in the negotiations, see Pulgar, *Crónica*, pt. II., c. 90. He was one of the signers of the treaty of Tordesillas, Doc. **9**.
[5] His powers are dated Aug. 19, 1479. Santarem, *loc. cit.*
[6] This treaty is printed in full in J. B. Sitges, *op. cit.*, app. 2.
[7] This is the article printed below.
[8] It is interesting to notice that in summarizing the treaty the chroniclers, Ruy de Pina and Nunes do Liam, describe Guinea as extending as far as the Indies—" O Senhorio de Guinee, que he dos cabos de Nam e do Bojador atée os Yndios inclusivamente ", although no reference to the Indies is found in the treaty itself.
[9] *Cf.* Doc. **1**, note 8.
[10] This seems to be the correct interpretation of the evidence given in Harrisse, *Diplomatic History*, p. 2, and notes.
[11] A late copy of this ratification, preserved in the Biblioteca Nacional at Madrid, has been brought to the editor's attention by Professor R. B. Merriman. *Cf.* also Navarrete, *Viages*, I. xxxix, and Pulgar, *op. cit.*, c. 91.
[12] Santarem, *Quadro Elementar*, II. 377-378.
[13] *Algs. Docs.*, p. 45.
[14] Doc. **4**.

It was pursuant to this treaty that, in 1492, the Catholic sovereigns ordered Columbus not to go to La Mina; and that, in 1493, the King of Portugal claimed the lands discovered by Columbus as his own.

BIBLIOGRAPHY.

Text: MS. The original manuscript of the ratification, signed by Ferdinand and Isabella at Toledo, March 6, 1480, is in the National Archives at Lisbon, gav. 17, maço 6, no. 16. See also above, note 11 of this document.

Text: Printed. Spanish. The whole of the treaty, except the formal preliminary part, is printed in Joseph Soares da Sylva, *Collecçam dos Documentos, com que se Authorizam as Memorias para a Vida del Rey D. João o I.,* tom. IV. of *Memorias para a Historia de Portugal, que comprehendem o Governo del Rey D. Joaõ o I.* (1730-1734), doc. no. 36, pp. 270 ff. That Soares printed this treaty by mistake appears from a collation of his "doc. no. 36" with the manuscript register entitled "Demarquacoës e Contractos", preserved in the National Archives at Lisbon. Soares intended to print the treaty concluded on October 30, 1431, between John I. (d. 1433) and the King of Castile, a copy of which covers ff. 142-165 of the above-mentioned register. Preceding this treaty, on ff. 113-140, is the treaty of Alcaçovas which confirms and partially incorporates the treaty of 1431. Soares's "doc. no. 36" begins with f. 117 of the register, *i. e.,* with the treaty of 1431 *as it stands in the treaty of Alcaçovas*; it continues through the treaty of Alcaçovas and through the first part of the original treaty of 1431, and ends at f. 146 of the register. The eighth and ninth articles of the "new articles" of the treaty of Alcaçovas are printed in *Alguns Documentos,* pp. 42-45, from the above-mentioned register.

Text: Printed. Portuguese. A Portuguese version of a portion of the eighth article is printed by H. Harrisse, *Diplomatic History of America* (1897), p. 156.

Text: Printed. Latin. A Latin version of the eighth article is in the bull of June 21, 1481, Doc. **4.**

References: Contemporary and early writings. Ruy de Pina, *Chronica do Rey Dom Affonso V.* (1790), in J. F. Corrêa da Serra, *Collecçaõ de Livros Ineditos de Historia Portugueza,* pub. by the Acad. Real das Sciencias, Lisbon, tom. I., c. 206; Nunes do Liam, *Cronicas dos Reys* (1780), tom. IV., c. 66; H. del Pulgar, *Crónica de los Reyes Católicos* (1878), pt. II., cc. 89, 90, 91, in B. C. Aribau, *Biblioteca de Autores Españoles,* tom. LXX.; G. Zurita, *Anales de Aragon* (1578-1585), pt. II., lib. XX., c. 34, IV. 306-307; Viscount de Santarem (M. F. de Barros e Sousa), *Quadro Elementar* (1842-1876), I. 379-382, II. 368-378.

References: Later writings. H. Schäfer, *Geschichte von Portugal* (1836-1854), II. 580-582, in Heeren and Ukert, *Geschichte der Europäischen Staaten*; H. Vignaud, *Toscanelli and Columbus* (1903), pp. 62-64; *id., Histoire Critique de la Grande Entreprise de Christophe Colomb* (1911), I. 207-211; Harrisse, *Diplomatic History* (1897), pp. 2-5; J. B. Sitges, *Enrique IV. y la Excelente Señora Doña Juana la Beltraneja, 1425-1530* (1912), pp. 331 ff.

Don Ferrando e Dona Ysabel, por la gracia de Dios rrey e rreyna de
Castilla, de Leon, de Aragon, de Cecilia, de Toledo, de Valençia, de Gallizia,
de Mallorcas, de Sevilla, de Çerdeña, de Cordova, de Corçega, de Murçia, de
Jahen, de los Algarbeś, de Algezira, et de Gibraltar, conde e condesa de Barcelona, señores de Viscaya et de Molina, duques de Atenas, e de N[e]opatria,
condes de Ruysellon et de Çerdania, marqueses de Oristan e de Goçiano,
fazemos saber a quantos la presente carta bieren, que por el Doctor Rodrigo
Maldonado, oydor de la nuestra audiencia e del nuestro consejo, como nuestro
procurador e enbaxador fueron por nuestro mandado tratadas pazes perpetuas
entre nos e los dichos nuestros rreynos e señorios e el muy ylustre Rey de
Portogal e de los Algarbes de aquen e allen mar en Africa, nuestro primo, e
el ylustre principe Don Juan, su fijo, e entre los dichos sus rreynos e señorios,
las quales dichas pazes fueron primeramente tratadas ̀por Don Juan de
Silveyra, Varon Dalvito, del consejo del dicho Rey de Portogal, e escrivano
de la poridat e veedor de la fazienda e chançeller mayor del dicho Principe de
Portogal, e por Pero Botello e Rodrigo Alfonso, cavalleros e del consejo del
dicho Rey de Portogal, e despues fueron asentadas, firmadas, e juradas por
el dicho Varon Dalvito, como procurador bastante e sufiçiente delos dichos
Rey e Prinçipe de Portogal, e como su procurador e enbaxador, segund que
mas conplidamente es contenido en la escritura de capitulaçion e asiento de
las pazes que sobre ello fue fecha, en la qual entre otras cosas se contiene que
cada e quando fuesemos requeridos por parte del dicho muy ylustre Rey de
Portogal e del ylustre principe, su fijo, otorgariamos, confirmariamos, e
jurariamos las dichas pazes por nuestras personas, e porque por Ferrando
de Silva, del consejo delos dichos Rey e Prinçipe de Portogal e su enbaxador
e procurador, fuesemos requeridos, que otorgasemos e jurasemos e firmase-
mos las dichas pazes segunt' que por el dicho doctor, nuestro procurador e
enbaxador, fueron otorgadas, firmadas, e juradas, nos mandamos venir para
ante nos la dicha escritura dela dicha capitulacion e asiento delas dichas
pazes para las ver e esaminar.   El tenor de la qual de verbo ad verbo es este
que se sigue:

En el nombre de Dios Todo Poderoso, Padre, e Fijo, e Sp[irit]u Santo, tres
personas rrealmente distintas e apartadas e una sola esençia divina, manifiesto
e notorio sea a quantos este publico ymstrumento de confirmaçion e asiento,
rreformaçion et rreteficacion de pazes perpetuas vieren, que en el año del
nascimiento de Nuestro Señor Jhesu Christo de mill e quatroçientos e setenta
e nueve años, a quatro dias del mes de Setienbre, en la villa de los Alcaçovas,
en las casas donde posava la muy ylustre Señora Ynfante Doña Beatris, en
presençia de mi, el notario publico e general abaxo nonbrados e de los testigos
aqui escritos, estando y el honrrado e discreto Doctor Rodrigo Maldoñado,
oydor del audiencia e del consejo de los muy altos e muy poderosos señores
Don Ferrando e Doña Ysabel, rrey e rreyna de Castilla, de Leon, de Aragon,
de Ceçilia, de Toledo, de Valencia, de Gallizia, de Mallorcas, de Sevilla, de
Çerdeña, de Cordova, de Corçega, de Murcia, de Jahen, del Algarbe, e de
Algezira, de Gibraltar, conde e condesa de Barceloña, señores de Viscaya e de

[15] This text is from the original manuscript of the ratification, signed by Ferdinand
and Isabella, Mar. 6, 1480, preserved in the National Archives in Lisbon, gav. 17,
maço 6, no. 16.

Molina, duques de Atenas e de Neopatria, condes de Ruysellon e de Cerdania, marqueses de Oristan e de Goçiano e del su consejo e su enbaxador e procurador suficiente para lo abaxo escrito, e el honrrado Don Juan de Silveyra, varon Dalvito, del consejo del muy alto e muy poderoso señor Don Alfonso, por la gracia de Dios rrey de Portogal e de los Algarbes de aquen e allen mar en Africa, escrivano de la poridad, veedor de la fazienda e chançeller mayor del muy ylustre Principe Don Juan, su fijo prymogenito, heredero de los dichos rreynos e senorios, procurador bastante de los dichos señores de la otra parte, segunt amos mostraron por las procuraciones de los dichos señores sus costituyentes.

[Here follow the powers granted by Ferdinand and Isabella to Rodrigo Maldonado, dated July 2, 1479, and the powers granted by King Alfonso and Prince Dom João, his son, to João, Baron d'Alvito, dated August 19, 1479. The ratification then continues:]

E luego el dicho procurador de los dichos señores Don Ferrando e Doña Ysabel, rrey e rreyna de Castilla e dAragon, etc. dixe que por quanto entre los dichos señores sus costituyentes de la una parte e el dicho procurador de los dichos señores Rey e Principe de la otra, despues del fallescimiento del senor Rey Don Enrrique de gloriosa memoria, rrey que fue de Castilla e de Leon etc., fuera e al presente son grandes debates e quistiones, desençiones, e diferençias yntitulandose los dichos señores Rey Don Ferrando e Reyna Doña Ysabel, rrey e rreyna de Castilla de Leon de Portogal e de los Algarbes etc., e el dicho señor Rey Don Alfonso, rrey de Castilla e de Leon etc., lo qual diera principalmente causa a muy grandes e muy crudas guerras que oviere del dicho tienpo aca entre los dichos señores de que sesiguieran muchas muertes de oñes, quemas, incendios e innumerables rrobos, fuerças, prisiones, rrescates, e otras ynjurias, ofensas de diversas calidades e tomamientos de cibdades e villas e lugares e fortalezas e muchas perdidas e daños, gastos e despensas e yntolerables males, en grande deservicio de Dios Nuestro Señor e delos dichos señores, e grant daño e detrimento de los dichos sus rreynos e senorios e subditos e naturales dellos, e que agora por que a nuestro señor provera por su ynfinita bondat de clemencia, como autor de paz. El qual el sienpre sobre todas cosas encomendo e mando procurar e guardar que la dicha señora Ynfante Dona Beatris por servicio suyo e delos dichos señores, e por la naturaleza e grandes deudos que con ellos tiene, trato e procuro con todas sus fuerças de tratar paz e conformidad entre ellos, e moviera e praticara algunos medios para los tirar de los dichos debates e diferencias, guerras e males, e dar asiento e paz entre ellos e los dichos señores movidos con zelo del servicio de Dios e del bien publico de los dichos rreynos e señorios e subditos e naturales dellos, queriendo seguir las pazes de los bien aventurados rreyes de gloriosa memoria, sus progenitores, los quales tovieran de muy luengos e antiguos tiempos aca pazes ynviolablemente guardadas porsy e por los dichos sus rreynos e señorios e por conservar los grandes deudos que entre ellos ha e el mucho amor e conformidad que entresy e los dichos sus rreynos eran ante de las dichas guerras, e escusar que se non fagan mas males nin daños de aqui adelante, los quales de cada dia se yvan acrecentando, deliberan de confirmar e reformar e asentar porsi e por sus subcesores e por los dichos sus rreynos e señorios entre ellos las pazes antiguas, con algunos nuevos capitulos e condiçiones que para mejor guarda dellas eran nescesarias. Del qual contrato de las pazes antiguas, con la rreteficacion e rreformacion e adiçiones agora nuevamente fechas, el tenor es este que se sigue:

[Here follows the ancient treaty of peace concluded in 1431 between John I. of Portugal and the Infante Dom Duarte his son, and the other infantes, and King John of Castile.]

Comiençan los capitulos que nuevamente fueron fechas e añadydos e acrecētadas a este trato de las pazes.

.   .   .   .

[8.] Otrosy, quisieron mas los dichos señores Rey e Reyna de Castilla e de Aragon e de Seçilia, etc., e les plogo para que esta paz sea firme, estable, e para sienpre duradera, e prometieron, de agora para en todo tienpo, que por si nin por otro, publico nin secreto, nin sus herederos e subcesores, non turbaran, molestaran, nin ynquietaran, de fecho nin de derecho, en juyzio nin fuera de juyzio, los dichos señores Rey e Prinçipe de Portogal, nin los rreyes que por tienpo fueren de Portogal, nin sus rreynos, la posesion e casi posesion en que estan en todos los tractos, tierras, rrescates de Guinea, con sus minas de oro, e qualesquier otras yslas, costas, tierras, descubiertas e por descobrir, falladas e por fallar, yslas de la Madera, Puerto Santo, e Desierta, e todas las yslas de los Açores, e yslas de las Flores, e asy las yslas de Cabo Verde, e todas las yslas que agora tiene descubiertas, e qualesquier otras yslas que se fallaren o conquirieren de las yslas de Canaria para baxo contra Guinea, porque todo lo que es fallado e se fallare, conquerir o descobrir en los dichos terminos, allende de lo que ya es fallado, ocupado, descubierto, finca a los dichos Rey e Prinçipe de Portogal e sus rreynos, tirando solamente las yslas de Canaria, a saber, Lançarote, Palma, Fuerte Ventura, la Gomera, el Fierro, la Graciosa, la Grant Canaria, Tenerife, e todas las otras yslas de Canaria, ganadas o por ganar, las quales fincan a los reynos de Castilla; e bien asy non turbaran, moslestaran, nin inquietaran qualesquier personas que los dichos tractos de Guinea, nin las dichas costas, tierras descobiertas e por descobrir, en nonbre o de la mano de los dichos señores rreys e prinçipe, o de sus subçesores, negoçiaren, trataren, o conquirieren, por qualquier titulo, modo, o manera que sea o ser pueda. Antes, por esta presente, prometen e seguran, a buena fee, syn mal engaño, a los dichos señores rrey e prinçipe e a sus subcesores, que non mandaran por sy, nin por otro, nin consyntiran, ante defenderan que syn liçencia de los dichos señores Rey e Prinçipe de Portogal non vayan a negoçiar a los dichos tractos, nin yslas, tierras de Guinea, descobiertas e por descobrir, sus gentes naturales o subditos, en todo logar o tienpo, e en todo caso, cuydado o non cuydado, nin otras qualesquier gentes estrangeras que estovieren en sus reynos e señorios, o en sus puertos, armaren o se abitullaren, nin daran a ello alguña ocasion, favor, logar, ayuda, nin consentimiento, direte nin yndirete, nin consentiran armar nin cargar para alla en manera alguna. E sy alguno de los naturales o suditos de los rreynos de Castilla, o estranjeros, qualesquier que sean, fueren tratar, ympedir, danificar, rrobar, o conquirir la dicha Guinea, tractos, rrescates, minas, tierras, yslas della descobiertas o por descubrir, syn licencia e consentimiento espreso de los dichos señores rrey e prinçipe, o de sus subçesores, que los tales sean pugnidos en aquella manera, logar, e forma, que es ordenado por el dicho capitulo desta nueva reformacion e rretificaçion de los tractos de las pazes que se tenia e deve tener en las cosas de la mar, contra los que salen a tierra en las costas, prayas, puertos, abras, a rrobar, danificar, o mal fazer, o en el mar largo las dichas cosas fazen.[19]

Otrosi, los dichos señores Rey e Reyna de Castilla e de Leon, etc., prometieron, otorgaron, por el modo sobredicho, por sy e por sus subcesores, que non se entremeteran de querer entender, nin entenderan en manera alguna, en la conquista del rreyno de Fez, como se en ello non enpacharan, nin entremeteran, los Reyes pasados de Castilla, ante libremente los dichos señores Rey e Prinçipe de Portogal e sus reynos e subcesores, podran proseguir la dicha conquista, e la defenderan, como les ploguiere. E prometieron e otorgaron en todos los dichos señores rrey e rreyna, que por sy nin por otro, en juyzio nin fuera del, de fecho nin de derecho, non moveran sobre todo lo que dicho es, nin parte dello, nin sobre cosa alguna que a ello pertenesca, pleito, dubda, question, nin otra contienda alguna, ante todo guardaran, conpliran muy enteramente e faran guardar e complir syn menguamiento alguno. E, porque adelante non se pueda alegar ynorançia de las dichas cosas vedadas e penas, los dichos señores rrey e rreyna mandaron luego a las justiçias e ofiçiales de los puertos de los dichos sus rreynos, que todo asy guarden, e cunplan, e esecuten fielmente, e asy lo mandaran pregonar e publicar en su corte e en los dichos puertos de mar de los dichos sus rreynos e señorios, para que a todos venga en notiçia.

E el dicho Doctor Rodrigo Maldonado, en nombre y como procurador y enbaxador de los dichos señores Rey Don Fernando y Reyna Dona Ysabel, rrey y rreyna de Castilla, de Leon, d'Aragõ, etc., sus señores, y el dicho Don Juan de Silveyra, baron d'Alvito, en nombre y como procurador de los dichos señores Rey Don Alfonso, rrey de Portogal y de los Algarbes de aquen y de allen mar em Africa, y del dicho señor Principe Don Juan, su fijo, sus señores, por virtud del dicho poder que para ello tienen, que encima va encorporado, dixeron que asentavan y otorgavan y asentaron y otorgaron pases perpetuas entre los dichos señores, sus constituyentes, y sus rreynos y señorios, para que serã guardadas entre ellos perpetuamente, segund es contenido en el tracto de las pases antiguas con las dichas condiciones, segund y por la forma y manera que en esta escritura y capitulacion se contiene; y dixeron que sy neçessario y complidero hera pera mayor validacion que aprovavan y reformavan y ennovavan, como de fecho aprovavan y reformavan y rrectificavan y ennovavan el dicho tracto de las pases antiguas como en el se contiene, enquanto es necessario y complidero o conviniente al tienpo presente con las dichas adiciones a ellas por ellos fechas. E prometieron y se obligaron, uno a otro y otro a otro, en nombre de los dichos señores sus constituientes, que ellos y sus [sub]cessores en los dichos sus rreynos y señorios ternan y guardaran para agora y para siempre jamas las dichas pases segund y por la forma y manera que en esta escritura se contiene syn arte y sin engaño y sin cautela alguna, y nõ yran nyn vernan nyn consentyran nyn permitiran que sea ydo nyn venido contra lo en ella contenido nyn parte alguna dello direte ny indirete por nynguna causa, color, ny rason alguno que sea o ser pueda, pensado o por pensar, y sy lo contrario fisieren, lo que Dios no quiera, que por el mesmo fecho yncurra la parte que lo fisiere en pena de tresientas mil doblas

[19] The treaties of Oct. 30, 1431. The article referred to is art. 7 of the "new articles". It is printed in Sylva, *Memorias*, tom. IV., doc. no. 36, pp. 327-329, and in abstract in Santarem, *Quadro Elementar*, II. 372-374. In the latter work, article 7 includes also article 8, according to the numbering adopted above. In the manuscript treaty the articles are not numbered.

de oro de la vanda de buen oro y justo peso para la otra parte obediente. Las quales prometieron y se obligaron que pagaran rrealmente y con efecto a la parte que en la dicha pena encurriese a la otra parte obediente luego tanto que en ella cayere syn contienda de juizio. E pagada la dicha pena o non pagada o remetida sinque poende[17] el dicho contracto de las dichas pases firme e valedero para syempre jamas.

Otrosy dixeron que rrenunciavan y rrenunciaron en nonbre de los dichos señores sus constituyentes todas alegaciones, excepciones, y todos rremedios juridicos y beneficios, auxilios ordinarios y extra ordinarios, que a los dichos señores constituyentes y a cada uno d'ellos compete podrian pertenescer agora y en qualquier tiempo de aqui adelante para anular o rrevocar o enfrengir, en todo o en parte, esta dicha escritura de tracto, assyento, y rreformacion y rretificacion de las dichas pases con las dichas adiciones por ellos fechas o por difirir o impedir el efecto dellas. E asy mismo rrenunciaron todos los derechos, leyes, costumbres, estilos, y fasañas y opiniones de doctores que para ello les pudiesen aprovechar en qualquier manera, especialmente renunciaron la ley y derecho que diz que general renunciaciõ non vala. Para lo qual todo asy tener y guardar y complir y pagar la dicha pena, sy en ella cayeren, obligaron los dichos procuradores los bienes patrimoniales y fiscales, muebles y raizes, avidos y por aver, de los dichos señores sus constituyentes y de sus subditos y naturales. E por mayor firmesa los dichos procuradores dixeron que juravan y juraron a Dios y a Santa Maria y a la señal de la cruz que tocaron con sus manos derechas, y a los Sanctos Evangelios do quier que estan, en nonbre y en las almas de los dichos señores sus constituyentes, por virtud de los dichos poderes que para ello especialmente tienen, que ellos y cada uno d'ellos, por sy y por sus subcessores y rreynos y señorios, ternan y guardaran y faran tener y guardar perpetua y inviolablemente las dichas pases, segund que en esta escritura se contiene, a buena fé y sin mal engaño, syn arte y syn cautela alguna. E que los dichos señores sus constituyentes, nyn alguno dellos, non pidiran por sy nyn por interpuestas personas absolucion, relaxacion, dispensacion, nyn comutacion del dicho juramento a nuestro muy Sancto Padre ny a otra persona alguna que poder tenga para lo dar y conceder. E puesto que proprio motu, o en otra qualquier manera le sea dado non usaran del. Ante aquello nõ embargante ternan y guardaran y compliran y faran tener y complir todo lo contenido en este dicho contracto de las dichas pases con las dichas adiciones y cada cosa y parte dello segund que en el se contiene fiel y verdaderamente y con efecto, y en testimonio de verdat otorgaron los dichos procuradores esta escritura y contracto de las dichas pases y pidieron a my el notario dello sendos instrumentos cõ mi publico signo y mas los que complideros fuesen para guarda del servicio de los dichos señores sus constituyentes. Testigos que a ello fueron presentes Fernando de Silvera del consejo del dicho señor Rey de Portogal y covdelmayor de sus rreynos y el doctor Juan Texera del consejo y desembargo y de las peticiones y su vice chanceller y Pero Botello y Rodrigo Alfonso, cavalleros del dicho señor rrey y del su consejo, y otros. E yo, Juan Garcez, cavallero de la casa del dicho señor principe y su escrivano de su fasienda y de la fasienda del rregno del Algarve de allen mar en Africa, notario general y publico en todos los rreynos y señorios del dicho señor rrey, que juntamente com Benito Royz de Castro, escrivano de camara de los dichos señores Rey

[17] Quede porende?

y Reyna de Castilla y de Aragon y etc., y con los dichos testigos a todo fue presente quando los dichos procuradores otorgaran esta escritura de capitulacion y todas las cosas particularmente en ella contenidas. E fisieron el dicho juramento poniendo sus manos derechas sobre una crus y sobre un libro de los Santos Evangelios. La qual dicha capitulacion y escritura yo, el dicho Juan Garces, fielmente fis escrevir en estas treynta y tres fojas atras escritas contando esta y fue fielmente emendada y corregida y reformada por ante los dichos procuradores segund se contiene en cada una foja signada por my y por el dicho Benito Roys de nuestros nonbres al pié della y por mi mano la sobre escrevi y sygne de mi publico señal que es tal. E yo Benito Roys de Castro, escrivano de camara de los dichos señores Rey y Reyna de Castilla y de Aragon etc. y notario publico en la su corte y en todos los sus rreynos y señorios, que por licençia y poder autoridad que me fue dada y otorgada por el dicho señor Rey de Portogal para dar fee y testimonio de verdad en el tracto de las pases y en todas las otras cosas que a ella pertenescen, fui presente con el dicho Juan Garces y testigos ençima nonbrados quando los dichos procuradores de los dichos señores otorgaram esta escritura y fisieron el dicho juramento, poniendo sus manos derechas en una crus y en un libro de los Santos Evangelios, y lo fis emendar en uno con el dicho Juan Garces segund suso va emendado. La qual va escrita en treynta y quatro fojas con esta en que va puesto esta my señal, y enfin de cada plana va puesto mi nonbre acostumbrado y lo signe de my señal que es tal.

La qual escritura de assyento y capitulacion de pases vista y entendida por nós y por los del nuestro consejo y por los grandes y cibdades y villas de nuestros rreynos, la aprovamos, otorgamos, y confirmamos, y prometemos y juramos a la señal de la crus y a los Santos Evangelios por nuestras manos corporalmente tangidas, presente el dicho Fernando de Silva, enbaxador de los dichos señores Rey y Principe de Portogal, de complir y mantener y guardar esta dicha escritura de contracto de pases y todos los capitulos en ella contenidos y cada uno dellos a buena fee y syn mal engaño, syn arte y syn cautela alguna, por nos y por nuestros herderos y subsessores y por nuestros rreynos y señorios, tierras, gentes, subditos naturales dellos, solas clausulas, pactos, obligaciones, penas, vinculos, renunciaciones en este dicho contracto y assyento de pases contenidos, y por certenidat, corroboracion, y convalidacion de todo mandamos faser esta carta y la dar al dicho Fernando de Silva para la dar a los dichos señores Rey y Principe de Portogal. La qual firmamos de nuestros nonbres y mandamos sellar con nuestro sello de plomo pendiente en filos de seda a colores. Dada en la muy noble cibdad de Toledo, a seys dias del mes de março, año del nascimiento del nuestro Señor Jesu Christo de mill y quatrocientos y ochenta años. Non sea dubda onde dise en la segunda foja sobre raydo onde poz que las assentaredes y firmaredes. E en la tercera foja donde dise diez y nueve. E en la setena foja en la margem donde dise que destos nuestros rreynos viniere con el procurador del dicho Rey de Castilla. E en la tresena foja sobre raydo onde dise tractos. E en la catorzena entre renglones onde dis sus reynos. Lo qual todo fue emendado y corregido presente el dicho Fernando de Silva. E en la dosena foja sobre raydo onde dis sentencias.

Yo, EL REY.   YO, LA REYNA.

Yo, FERNAND ALVARES de Toledo, secretario del Rey y de la Reyna, nuestros señores, lo fise escrevir por su mandado. Registrada. ALFONSO SANCHES de Logroño, chanceller.

TRANSLATION.[13]

We, Don Ferdinand and Doña Isabella, by the grace of God, king and queen of Castile, Leon, Aragon, Sicily, Toledo, Valencia, Galicia, Majorca, Seville, Sardinia, Cordova, Corsica, Murcia, Jaen, the Algarves, Algeciras, and Gibraltar; count and countess of Barcelona; lord and lady of Biscay and Molina; duke and duchess of Athens and Neopatras; count and countess of Roussillon and Cerdagne; marquis and marchioness of Oristano and Gociano: make known to all who shall see the present letter that perpetual peace between us and the said our kingdoms and lordships, and our cousin, the very illustrious king of Portugal and the Algarves on this side and beyond the sea in Africa, and his son, the illustrious prince, Dom John, and the said their kingdoms and lordships, was negotiated, at our command, by Doctor Rodrigo Maldonado, *oidor* of our audiencia and member of our council, acting as our representative and ambassador.   The said peace was first negotiated by Dom João da Silveira, baron d'Alvito, member of the council of the said king of Portugal and his private secretary, inspector of the treasury, and chancellor-in-chief of the said prince of Portugal, and by Pero Botello and Rodrigo Alfonso, knights and members of the council of the said king of Portugal.   Afterward the peace was affirmed, signed, and sworn to by the said Baron d'Alvito acting as a competent and qualified representative of the said king and prince of Portugal, and as their representative and ambassador, as is set forth more fully in the instrument of agreement and treaty of peace which was made in regard to it. Among other things that instrument sets forth that whenever we should be notified on the part of the said very illustrious king of Portugal, and by his son, the illustrious prince, we should authorize, confirm, and swear to the said peace in our own person.   And inasmuch as we have been notified by Ferrando de Silva, member of the council of the said king and prince of Portugal, and their representative and ambassador, to authorize, swear to, and sign the said peace, as it was authorized, signed, and sworn to by the said doctor, our representative and ambassador, we ordered the said instrument of agreement and treaty of the said peace to be brought before us, in order that we might see and examine it.   Its tenor, word for word, is as follows:

In the name of God Almighty, Father, Son, and Holy Ghost, three persons really distinct and separate, and one sole divine essence.   Be manifest and publicly known to all who shall see it this public instrument of confirmation and agreement, revision, and rectification of perpetual peace which [was made] in the year of the nativity of our Lord Jesus Christ, 1479, on the fourth day of the month of September, in the city of Alcaçobas, in the houses where the very illustrious infanta, Doña Beatrice, was lodging, in the presence of me, the notary public and general, below named, and of the undersigned witnesses, and being there the honorable and prudent doctor, Rodrigo Maldonado, *oidor* of the audiencia and member of the council of the very exalted and very powerful lord and lady, Don Ferdinand and Doña Isabella, king and queen of Castile, Leon, Aragon, Sicily, Toledo, Valencia, Galicia, Majorca, Seville, Sardinia, Cordova, Corsica, Murcia, Jaen, the Algarve, Algeciras, and Gibraltar, count and countess of Barcelona, lord and lady of Biscay and Molina, duke and duchess of Athens and Neopatras, count and countess of Roussillon and Cerdagne, marquis and marchioness of Oristano and Gociano, member of

[13] The translation is by Dr. J. A. Robertson.

their council, and their ambassador and representative qualified to act in what is below written, and the honorable Dom João da Silveira, baron d'Alvito, member of the council of the very exalted and very powerful lord, Dom Alfonso, by the grace of God, king of Portugal and the Algarves on this side and beyond the sea in Africa, private secretary to the king, inspector of the treasury, chancellor-in-chief of his firstborn son, the very illustrious prince, Dom John, heir of the said kingdoms and lordships, and qualified representative of the said lords of the other part—as both showed by the procurations of their constituents the said lords.

[Here follow the powers granted by Ferdinand and Isabella to Rodrigo Maldonado, dated July 2, 1479, and the powers granted by King Alfonso and Prince John, his son, to João, baron d'Alvito, dated August 19, 1479. The ratification then continues :]

And thereupon the said representative of the said lord and lady, Don Ferdinand and Doña Isabella, king and queen of Castile, Aragon, etc., declared that inasmuch as since the death of the lord king Don Henry of glorious memory, former king of Castile, Leon, etc., there have been and are at present serious disputes, questions, discussions, and differences between his constituents, the said lord and lady of the one part, and the said representative of the said lords, the king and prince, of the other part, because the said lord and lady, King Don Ferdinand and Queen Doña Isabella called themselves king and queen of Castile, Leon, Portugal, and the Algarves, etc., and the said lord, King Dom Alfonso, called himself king of Castile, Leon, etc., which furnished the chief cause for very serious and very cruel wars that were waged here during the said time between the said lords, and from which resulted the deaths of many men, conflagrations, fires, innumerable acts of violence, imprisonments, ransoms and other injuries, offenses of different kinds, the capture of cities, towns, villages, and fortresses, many losses and injuries, waste and expenses, and intolerable evils, to the great disservice of God our Lord, and of the said lords, and grave injury and detriment to the said their kingdoms and lordships, and the subjects and natives of the latter (and may this now be adjusted by our Lord, through His infinite goodness and clemency, as the Author of peace, for He always recommended and ordered that peace be procured and kept) and the said lady, Infanta Doña Beatrice, for His service and that of the said lord and lady, because of her relationship and great obligations toward them, tried and endeavored with all her might to obtain peace and harmony between them, and will set in motion and make use of any means whatsoever to free them from the said disputes and differences, and wars and evils, and cause agreement and peace between them—the said lord and lady, moved with zeal for the service of God and for the public welfare of the said kingdoms and lordships, and the subjects and natives of them, and desirous of continuing the peace of their progenitors, the very fortunate kings of glorious memory, who had observed here an inviolable peace for themselves and for the said their kingdoms and lordships from very remote and ancient times, and in order to preserve the close relationship that exists between them, and the great love and harmony which reigned between themselves and the said their kingdoms before the said wars, and in order to avoid the occurrence of other evils and injuries from this time forward, and which are increasing daily, do determine to confirm, revise, and agree to, for themselves and their successors, and for the said their kingdoms and

4

lordships, between them, the ancient peace, with certain new articles and conditions, which were necessary for the better keeping of it. Of that contract of the ancient peace, with the rectification, revision, and additions now newly made, the tenor is this which follows:

[Here follows the ancient treaty of peace concluded in 1431 between John I. of Portugal and his son, the infante Dom Duarte, and the other infantes, and King John of Castile.]

The articles which were newly made, added, and appended to this treaty of peace commence:

.   .   .   .

[8.] Moreover, the aforesaid King and Queen of Castile, Aragon, Sicily, etc., willed and resolved, in order that this peace be firm, stable, and everlasting, and promised, henceforth and forever, that neither of themselves nor by another, publicly or secretly, or by their heirs and successors, will they disturb, trouble, or molest, in fact or in law, in court or out of court, the said King and Prince of Portugal or the future sovereigns of Portugal or their kingdoms, in their possession or quasi possession in all the trade, lands, and barter in Guinea, with its gold-mines, or in any other islands, coasts, or lands, discovered or to be discovered, found or to be found, or in the islands of Madeira, Porto Santo, and Desierta, or in all the islands of the Azores, or the islands of Flores, as well as the islands of Cape Verde, or in all the islands hitherto discovered, or in all other islands which shall be found or acquired by conquest [in the region] from the Canary Islands down toward Guinea. For whatever has been found or shall be found, acquired by conquest, or discovered within the said limits, beyond what has already been found, occupied, or discovered, belongs to the said King and Prince of Portugal and to their kingdoms, excepting only the Canary Islands, to wit: Lançarote, Palma, Forteventura, Gomera, Ferro, Graciosa, Grand Canary, Teneriffe, and all the other Canary Islands, acquired or to be acquired, which belong to the kingdoms of Castile. And in like manner, [they promised] not to disturb, trouble, or molest any persons whomsoever, who, under any title or in any way or manner whatsoever, shall trade or traffic in or acquire by conquest the said trade of Guinea or that of the said coasts or lands, discovered or to be discovered, in the name or under the authority of the said king and prince or their successors. On the contrary, by these presents, they do promise and assure, in good faith and without deceit, the said king and prince and their successors, that they will not, of themselves or through others, order or consent, but rather forbid, that any of their people, native or subject, in any place or at any time, or in any case, specified or not specified, or any other foreign people who might be within their kingdoms and dominions, or who shall be equipped or provisioned in their ports, go to traffic in the said trade or in the islands or lands of Guinea discovered or to be discovered. Neither will they give any occasion, favor, opportunity, aid, or consent, direct or indirect, for such trade, nor consent to equip or freight for those regions in any manner. And if any of the natives or subjects of the kingdoms of Castile, or any foreigners whosoever, shall traffic in, obstruct, injure, plunder, or acquire by conquest the said Guinea, or its trade, barter, mines, lands, and islands, discovered or to be discovered, without the express license and consent of the said king and prince or of their successors, [they do promise] that all such shall be punished in the manner, place, and form ordained by the said article of this new revision and correction of the treaties of peace which hold and ought to hold in maritime affairs, against those who go by land along the coasts and shores, or in the ports and bays, to plunder, commit depredations, or do evil, or who shall do such things on the high seas.

Moreover, the said King and Queen of Castile, Leon, etc., promised and agreed, in the manner abovesaid, of themselves and for their successors, not to presume to meddle, nor will they meddle in any manner, with the conquest of the kingdom of Fez, just as the former sovereigns of Castile did not obstruct it or meddle with it; but the said King and Prince of Portugal and their kingdoms and successors shall be freely allowed to prosecute the said conquest and to defend it as they please. And the said king and queen promised and agreed faithfully that, neither of themselves nor by any other, in court or out of court, in fact or in law, will they raise against the abovesaid, nor any part of it, nor anything that pertains to it, any suit, doubt, question, or any other contention, but that, on the contrary, they will observe and fulfill everything strictly to the letter, and will have it observed and fulfilled without any diminution. And in order that no one in the future may allege ignorance of the said prohibitions and penalties, the said king and queen immediately ordered the justices and officials of the ports of the abovesaid their kingdoms faithfully to observe, fulfill, and execute everything as herein ordained, and such justices and officers shall so proclaim and publish it in their courts and in the said seaports of the abovesaid their kingdoms and dominions, so that all people may have notice of it.

.   .   .   .

And the said Doctor Rodrigo Maldonado, in the name of, and acting as the representative and ambassador of the said lord and lady, King Don Ferdinand and Queen Doña Isabella, king and queen of Castile, Leon, Aragon, etc., his master and mistress, and the said Dom João da Silveira, baron d'Alvito, in the name of, and acting as the representative of his masters, the said lords, King Dom Alfonso, king of Portugal and of the Algarves on this side and beyond the sea in Africa, and of the said lord, his son, Prince Dom John, by virtue of the said power conceded to them for that purpose (as is above incorporated), declared that they agreed to and authorized, and they did agree to and authorize, perpetual peace between their constituents, the said lords, and their kingdoms and lordships, so that it may be kept perpetually between them, as was set forth in the treaty of the ancient peace, with the said conditions, according to and in the form and manner as is set forth in this instrument and agreement. They declared that if it were necessary and obligatory for its greater validation, they approved, revised, and renewed, as in fact they did approve, revise, rectify, and renew, the said treaty of the ancient peace as is set forth in it, in so far as may be necessary, obligatory, and advisable at the present time, with the said additions made therein by them. They promised, and each bound the other mutually, in the name of their constituents, the said lords, that the latter and their successors, and the said their kingdoms and lordships will keep and observe for the present and for evermore the said peace according to and in the form and manner which is set forth in this instrument, without any deception, evasion, or mental reservation whatsoever. They will not oppose or violate, nor consent, nor permit that what is set forth in it be opposed or violated, or any part of it, directly or indirectly, under any motive, pretext, or reason whatsoever, or that may be imagined or that can be imagined. And should they do the contrary (which may God not permit), then by that very fact, the guilty party shall incur a fine of 300,000 gold *doblas* of the grade of good gold and of just weight [which shall be given] to the other, obedient, party. They promised and bound themselves to really and truly pay this sum—the party which should incur the said fine to the other, obedient, party—as soon as the fine should be incurred, without constraint of judgment; and whether the said fine be paid or not, or whether it be remitted, the said contract of the said peace would still be firm and valid forever.

Furthermore, they declared that they renounced, and they did renounce, in the name of their constituents, the said lords, all allegations, exceptions, and all legal remedies and beneficial aids, ordinary and extraordinary, which might rightly belong to their constituents, the said lords, or to any one of them, now or at any time hereafter, to annul, revoke, or infringe, in whole or in part, this said instrument of treaty, agreement, revision, and rectification of the said peace, with the said additions made by them, or to postpone or prevent its operation. Likewise they renounced all rights, laws, customs, usages, actions, and opinions of doctors of which they might avail themselves for it in any way. Especially did they renounce the law and right which declares a general renunciation invalid. In order to keep, perform, and comply with all the above, and in order to pay the said fine, should it be incurred, the said representatives pledged the property, both patrimonial and fiscal, the chattels and the landed property owned or to be owned, of their constituents, the said lords, and of their subjects and natives. And for greater assurance, the said representatives, by virtue of the said powers which they have especially for it, declared that they took oath, and they did take oath, before God and Holy Mary, and on the sign of the cross, on which they placed their right hands, and on the holy gospels, wherever they may be, in the names and on the consciences of their constituents, the said lords, that they, and each one of them, for themselves and for their successors, and their kingdoms and lordships, will keep and observe the said peace, and cause it to be kept and observed, perpetually and inviolably, according as it is set forth in this instrument, in good faith, and without any evasion, deception, or mental reservation whatsoever. Their constituents, the said lords, or any one of them, will not ask of our very Holy Father, or of any other person who may have the power to grant and concede it, in their own name, or by means of persons acting as their agents, absolution, remission, dispensation, or commutation of the said oath. And even should this be granted *proprio motu,* or in any other manner, they will not avail themselves of it. But the rather, notwithstanding that, they will keep, observe, and perform, and cause to be kept and performed, all that is set forth in this said contract of the said peace with the said additions, and each and every part of it, as it is set forth therein, faithfully and truly, and actually. In testimony of the truth, the said representatives approved this instrument and contract of the said peace, and each requested of me, the notary who drew it, writs of it, with my public seal, and whatever else might be suitable for the observance of the service of their constituents, the said lords. Witnesses of it, who were present, were Fernando de Silveira, member of the council of the said lord king of Portugal and master of the horse of his kingdoms, Doctor João Texera, member of the council and *disembargo* and of petitions, and his vice-chancellor, Pero Botello and Rodrigo Alfonso, knights of the said lord king and members of his council, and others. And I, João Garces, knight of the household of the said lord prince and his notary of his treasury and of the treasury of the kingdom of the Algarve beyond the sea in Africa, notary general and public throughout the kingdoms and lordships of the said lord king, who together with Benito Roys de Castro, notary of the high court of justice of the said lord and lady, king and queen of Castile, Aragon, etc., and with the said witnesses, was present throughout when the said representatives approved this instrument of agreement and all the things particularly set forth in it. And they took the said oath by placing their right hands on a cross and on a book of the holy gospels. I, the said João Garces, caused this said agreement and instrument to be written down faithfully on these thirty-three leaves above written counting this leaf. It was faithfully amended and corrected and revised in the presence of the said representatives, just as it is set forth on each single leaf, which was signed by me and the said Benito Roys with our names at the foot of it. With my hand I wrote the wrapper and sealed it with my public seal, which is as follows. And I, Benito Roys de Castro, notary of the high court of justice of the said lord and lady, king and queen of Castile, Aragon, etc., and notary public in their court and throughout their kingdoms and lordships, by the permission, power, and authority, which was granted and conceded to me by the said lord king of Portugal to attest and witness the truth of the treaty of peace and of all the other things which pertain to it, was present, together with the said João Garces and the witnesses abovementioned, when the said representatives of the said lords approved this instrument and took the said oath by placing their right hands on a cross and on a book of the holy gospels. I caused it to be corrected, together with the said Juan Garces, just as it is corrected above. It is written on thirty-four leaves, counting this leaf on which this my seal is placed. Finally on each leaf is written my customary name and I sealed it with my seal which is as follows.

This instrument of agreement and treaty of peace having been seen and examined by us, by the members of our council, and by the grandees, cities, and towns of our kingdoms, we approve, assent to, and confirm it, and promise and swear, on the sign of the cross and on the holy gospels, on which we actually placed our hands in the presence of the said Fernando de Silva, ambassador of the said lords, king and prince of Portugal, to perform, maintain, and observe this said instrument of contract of peace, and all the articles contained in it, and each one of them, in good faith, and without any evasion, deception, or mental reservation whatsoever, by us and by our heirs and successors, and by our kingdoms and lordships, lands, peoples, and subjects natives of them, under the stipulations, agreements, obligations, fines, bonds, and renunciations contained in this said contract and treaty of peace. For the assurance, corroboration, and validation of all, we caused this letter to be written and delivered to the said Fernando de Silva, in order that he might give it to the said lords, the king and prince of Portugal. We signed the same with our names, and ordered it sealed with our leaden seal hanging from colored silken threads. Given in the very noble city of Toledo, on the sixth day of the month of March, in the year of the nativity of our Lord Jesus Christ, 1480. Let there be no doubt where it says on the second leaf above the erasure " onde poz que las assentaredes y firmaredes " ; on the third leaf where it says " diez y nueve " ; on the seventh leaf, where it says in the margin " que destos nuestros rreynos viniere con el procurador del dicho Rey de Castilla " ; on the thirteenth leaf, where it says above the erasure " tractos " ; and on the fourteenth leaf, where it says between the lines " sus reynos ". It was thoroughly corrected and revised in the presence of the said Fernando de Silva. And on the twelfth leaf, where it says above the erasure " sentencias ".

I, THE KING.   I, THE QUEEN.

I, FERNANDO ALVAREZ de Toledo, secretary of the king and of the queen, our lord and lady, had it written by his command. Registered. ALFONSO SANCHEZ de Logroño, chancellor.

4.

The Bull Aeterni Regis (Sixtus IV.). June 21, 1481.

INTRODUCTION.

This bull is a confirmation by Pope Sixtus IV. of the bulls *Romanus pontifex* (1455)[1] and *Inter caetera* (1456),[2] sanctioning Portugal's claims to exclusive rights in Guinea; and it also includes an important new concession, since it confirms that article in the recently ratified treaty of Alcaçovas[3] whereby the sovereigns of Castile promised not to disturb Portugal in Guinea or in certain of the Atlantic islands or in Morocco. The weight of papal authority was thus brought to bear against any attempt on the part of Castile to evade her agreement.

Such a bull was of particular value to Prince John at this juncture. Apparently the first bull of this kind issued since the death of the Infante Henry in 1460, it marks the beginning of a new stage in the history of African exploration. The Portuguese government had for a long time ceased to push forward the southern expeditions, but in 1481 they were energetically resumed by Prince John, who, even in the lifetime of his father, was charged with the government of the places in Africa and received the revenues from the Guinea trade.[4] Upon the death of Alfonso in August, 1481, the prince succeeded to the throne under the title of John II., and before the end of the year he despatched an expedition under Diogo d'Azambuja to build the fort at Elmina, on the Gold Coast.[5]

In 1482 he sent ambassadors to urge King Edward IV. of England to prevent his subjects from sailing to Guinea. At about the same time Edward petitioned the Pope to permit Englishmen to trade in any part of Africa.[6]

BIBLIOGRAPHY.

Text: **MS.** The original manuscript of the promulgated bull is in the National Archives in Lisbon, Coll. de Bullas, maço 26, no. 10.

Text: **Printed.** J. Ramos-Coelho, *Alguns Documentos* (1892), pp. 47-55 (from the text inserted in the confirmatory bull of 1514); L. M. Jordão, *Bullarium Patronatus Portugalliae Regum* (1868), pp. 47-52.

[1] Doc. **1.**   [2] Doc. **2.**   [3] Doc. **3.**
[4] On May 4, 1481, Alfonso V. granted the prince the trade and fisheries of Guinea, and prohibited anyone from going or sending there without license from the prince. *Algs. Docs.*, p. 46.
[5] Ruy de Pina, *Chronica d'El Rei D. Ioaõ II.*, c. 2; cf. Doc. **1**, note 4.
[6] R. Hakluyt, *Principal Navigations* (ed. 1903-1905), VI. 122-124; *Cal. State Papers, Venice* (1864), I. 142.

References: Contemporary and early writings. J. de Barros, *Da Asia*, I.
(1778), dec. I., liv. III., cc. 1, 2.
References: Later writings. H. Schäfer, *Geschichte von Portugal* (1836-
1854), III. 148, in *Geschichte der Europäischen Staaten* (ed. Heeren
and Ukert).

Text.[1]

Sixtus episcopus, servus servorum Dei.   Ad perpetuam rei memoriam.
Eterni Regis clementia, per quam reges regnant, in suprema Sedis Apostolice
specula collocati, regum Catholicorum omnium, sub quorum felici gubernaculo
Christifideles in justitia et pace foventur, statum et prosperitatem ac quietem
et tranquillitatem sinceris desideriis appetimus, et inter illos pacis dulcedinem
vigere ferventer exoptamus; ac hiis que per predecessores nostros, Romanos
pontifices, et alios propterea provide facta fuisse comperimus, ut firma
perpetuo et illibata permaneant, et ab omni contentionis scrupulo procul
existant, apostolice confirmationis robur favorabiliter adhibemus.

Dudum siquidem ad audientiam felicis recordationis Nicolai Pape V.,
predecessoris nostri, deducto quod quondam Henricus, infans Portugalie,
carissimi in Christo filii nostri, Alfonsi Portugalie et Algarbii regnorum regis
illustris patruus—

[Here follows the rest of the confirmation of the bulls of January 8,
1455, and of March 13, 1456, Docs. 1 and 2.]

Postmodum vero, cum inter prefatum Alfonsum Regem et charissimum in
Christo filium nostrum Ferdinandum Castelle et Legionis Regem illustrem,
eorumque subditos, humani generis hostis causante versutia, guerre ali-
quandiu viguissent, tandem, divina operante clementia, ad pacem et concordiam devenerunt, et pro pace inter ipsos firmanda et stabilienda nonnulla
capitula[2] inter se fecerunt, inter que unum capitulum fore dinoscitur
hujusmodi tenoris:[3]

"Item voluerunt prefati Rex et Regina Castelle, Aragonie, et Sicilie, et
illis placuit, ut ista pax sit firma et stabilis ac semper duratura, [et] promiserunt ex nunc et in futurum quod nec per se nec per alium, secrete seu
publice, nec per suos heredes et successores, turbabunt, molestabunt, nec
inquietabunt, de facto vel de jure, in judicio vel extra judicium, dictos dominos
Regem et Principem Portugalie nec reges qui in futurum in dicto regno
Portugalie regnabunt nec sua regna, super possessione et quasi possessione,
in qua sunt, in omnibus commerciis, terris, et permutationibus sive resignatis
Guinee, cum suis mineriis seu aurifodinis, et quibuscunque aliis insulis,
littoribus, seu costis maris, terris, detectis seu detegendis, inventis et inveniendis, insulis de la Madera, de Portu Sancto, et Insula Deserta, et omnibus
insulis dictis de los Açores, id est, Ancipitrum, et insulis Florum, et etiam
insulis de Cabo Verde, id est, Promontorio Viridi, et insulis quas nunc
invenit, et quibuscunque insulis que deinceps invenientur aut acquirentur, ab
insulis de Canaria ultra et citra et in conspectu Guinee, ita quod quicquid

---

[1] The text is from the original manuscript of the bull, in the National Archives at
Lisbon, Coll. de Bullas, maço 26, no. 10.
[2] The treaty of Alcaçovas.
[3] The eighth of the "new articles" of the treaty of Alcaçovas. The Spanish text of
this article is printed above, Doc. 3.

est inventum vel invenietur et acquiretur ultra in dictis terminis, id quod est
inventum et detectum remaneat dictis Regi et Principi de Portugallia et suis
regnis, exceptis duntaxat insulis de Canaria, Lanzarote, Lapalma, Forteventura, Lagomera, Ho Fierro, Ha Gratiosa, Ha Gran Canaria, Tanarife,
et omnibus aliis insulis de Canaria, acquisitis aut acquirendis, que remanent
regnis Castelle; et ita non turbabunt nec molestabunt nec inquietabunt quascunque personas, que dicta mercimonia et contractus Guinee nec dictas terras
et littora aut costas, inventas et inveniendas, nomine aut potentia et manu
dictorum dominorum Regis et Principis Portugallie vel suorum successorum
tractabunt, negociabuntur, vel acquirent, quocunque titulo, modo, vel manerie
quod sit aut esse possit. Immo, per istam presentem, promittunt et assecurant
bona fide, sine dolo malo, dictis dominis regi et principi Portugalie et successoribus suis, quod non mittent per se nec per alios nec consentient, immo
defendent, quod sine licentia dictorum dominorum regis et principis Portugalie, non vadent ad negociandum dicta commercia et tractus nec in insulis,
terris Guinee, inventis vel inveniendis, gentes suas naturales vel subditos in
quocunque loco et in quocunque tempore et in quocunque casu, opinato vel
inopinato, nec quascunque alias gentes exteras que morarentur in suis regnis
et dominiis, vel in suis portubus armarent vel caperent victualia et necessaria
ad navigandum, nec dabunt illis aliquam occasionem, favorem, locum,
auxilium nec assensum, directe vel indirecte, nec permittant armari nec
onerari ad eundum illuc, aliquo modo. Et si aliqui ex naturalibus vel subditis
regnorum Castelle vel extranei quicunque sint, irent ad tractandum, impedien-
dum, damnificandum, depredandum, acquirendum in dicta Guinea et in
dictis locis mercimoniorum et permutationum et mineriorum seu aurifodi-
norum et terris et insulis que sunt invente et in futurum inveniende, sine
licentia et expresso consensu dictorum dominorum, regis et principis Portugalie, vel suorum successorum, quod tales sint puniendi eo modo, loco, et
forma quod ordinatum est per dictum capitulum istius nove reformationis
tractatus pacis, que servabuntur et debent servari in rebus maritimis contra
eos qui descendunt in littora, sin[us], et portus ad depredandum, damnificandum, vel ad male agendum, vel in mari medio dictas res faciant.[10] Preterea,
Rex et Regina Castelle et Legionis promiserunt et concesserunt, modo supra-
dicto, pro se et suis successoribus, ut se non intromittant ad inquirendum et
intendendum aliquo modo in conquesta regni de Fez, sicuti se non intro-
miserunt reges antecessores sui preteriti Castelle, immo libenter dicti domini,
rex et princeps Portugalie, et sua regna et sui successores poterunt prosequi
dictam conquestam et eam defendant quomodo illis placuerit, et promiserunt
et consenserunt in omnibus dicti domini, rex et regina Castelle, nec per se
nec per alios, nec in judicio nec extra judicium, nec de facto nec de jure,
non movebunt super premissis, nec in parte, nec super re que ad illud pertineat,
litem, dubium, questionem, nec aliquam contemptionem, immo, totum pre-
servabunt, complebunt integre et faciant observari et compleri sine aliquo
defectu; et ne im posterum possit allegari ignorantia de vetatione et penis
dictarum rerum contractarum, dicti domini miserunt illico justitiis et offi-
cialibus portuum dictorum suorum regnorum, ut totum quod dictum est
servent, compleant, et fideliter exequantur, et mittant ad preconizandum et
publicandum in sua curia et in dictis portubus maris eorum supradictorum
regnorum et dominiorum, ut id perveniat ad eorum notitiam."

[10] *Cf.* Doc. **3**, note 16.

Nos igitur, quibus cura universalis Dominici gregis celitus est commissa, quique ut tenemur inter principes et populos Christianos pacis et quietis suavitatem vigere et perpetuo durare desideramus, cupientes ut littere ,Nicolai[11] et Calixti,[12] predecessorum hujusmodi, ac preinsertum capitulum[13] necnon omnia et singula in eis contenta, ad Divini Nominis laudem et principum et populorum singulorum regnorum predictorum perpetuam pacem firma perpetuo et illibata permaneant, motu proprio,[14] non ad alicujus nobis super hoc oblate petitionis instantiam, sed de nostra mera liberalitate ac providentia et ex certa scientia, necnon de apostolice potestatis plenitudine, litteras Nicolai et Calixti predecessorum hujusmodi, ac capitulum predicta rata et grata habentes, illa, necnon omnia et singula in eisdem contenta, auctoritate apostolica, tenore presentium approbamus et confirmamus, ac presentis scripti patrocinio communimus, decernentes illa, omnia et singula, plenum firmitatis robur obtinere ac perpetuo observari debere. Et nichilominus venerabilibus fratribus, Elborensi[15] et Silvensi[16] ac Portugaliensi[17] Episcopis, per apostolica scripta, motu et scientia similibus, mandamus, quatinus ipsi vel duo aut unus eorum, per se vel alium seu alios, singulas litteras ac capitulum predicta, ubi et quando opus fuerit, solemniter publicantes, ac eisdem Regi et Principi Portugalie eorumque successoribus in omnibus et singulis premissis efficacis defensionis presidio assistentes, non permittant eosdem regem et principem et successores, contra premissa vel eorum aliquod, per quoscunque cujuscunque dignitatis, status, gradus, vel conditionis fuerint, molestari seu etiam impediri, molestatores et impedientes necnon contradictores quoslibet et rebelles, auctoritate nostra per censuram ecclesiasticam et alia juris remedia, appellatione postposita compescendo, non obstantibus, omnibus supradictis, aut si aliquibus, communiter vel divisim, ab Apostolica sit Sede indultum, quod interdici, suspendi, vel excommunicari non possint per litteras apostolicas non facientes plenam et expressam ac de verbo ad verbum de indulto hujusmodi mentionem. Nulli ergo omnino hominum liceat hanc paginam nostre confirmationis, approbationis, communitionis, constitutionis, et mandati infringere, vel ei ausu temerario contraire. Siquis autem hoc attemptare presumpserit, indignationem Omnipotentis Dei ac beatorum Petri et Pauli apostolorum ejus se noverit incursurum.

Datum Rome apud Sanctum Petrum, anno Incarnationis Dominice millesimo quadringentesimo octuagesimo primo, undecimo kalendas Julii, pontificatus nostri anno decimo.

Jo. DE SALOS.[18]
P. DE MONTE.[19]   Jo. HORN.[20]   L. GRIFUS.[21]

[11] The bull of Jan. 8, 1455, Doc. **1**.   [12] The bull of Mar. 13, 1456, Doc. **2**.
[13] The eighth of the "new articles" of the treaty of Alcaçovas, Doc. **3**.
[14] *Cf.* Doc. **1**, note 38.
[15] In 1481 Garcia Menezes was Bishop of Evora, the capital of the province of Alemtejo. C. Eubel, *Hierarchia Catholica Medii Aevi*, II. (1901).
[16] In June, 1481, João de Mello was Bishop of Silves, the ancient capital of the Moorish kingdom of Algarve. *Ibid.*
[17] In 1481 João de Azevedo was Bishop of Oporto. *Ibid.*
[18] The *rescribendarius*. An account of the functions of this and other officers of the papal chancery is given in L. Schmitz-Kallenberg, *Practica Cancellariae Apostolicae Saeculi XV. exeuntis* (Münster, 1904).
[19] The *computator*. This official and the *rescribendarius* were concerned with the charge made for the instrument. *Ibid.*, pp. 25 ff.
[20] The *summista* or *summator*, who noted any defects in the instrument. *Ibid.*, pp. 36, 37.
[21] Leonardo Griffo, bishop of Gubbio, and papal secretary. *Ibid.*, p. 37. The bull is endorsed "Registrata in Camera Apostolica".

TRANSLATION.

Sixtus, bishop, servant of the servants of God. For a perpetual remembrance.

Since, through the Eternal King's clemency, whereby kings reign, we have been placed in the most lofty watchtower of the Apostolic See, we earnestly seek the stability, prosperity, quiet, and tranquillity of all Catholic kings, under whose auspicious guidance Christ's faithful ones are cherished in justice and peace, and we fervently desire that sweet peace may thrive among them. Moreover we graciously apply the strengthening power of apostolic confirmation to what we find to have been done with that object by our predecessors, the Roman popes, and others, in order that it may remain forever firm, unshaken, and far removed from any risk of controversy.

A short while ago, when it was brought to the hearing of our predecessor, Pope Nicholas V., of happy memory, that formerly Henry, the infante of Portugal, uncle of our most dear son in Christ, Alfonso, the illustrious king of the kingdoms of Portugal and Algarve—

[Here follows the confirmation of the bull of January 8, 1455, and the bull of March 13, 1456, Docs. 1 and 2.]

Afterwards, however, when, through the craftiness of the enemy of humankind, war had raged for some time between the aforesaid King Alfonso and our dearest son in Christ, Ferdinand, the illustrious king of Castile and Leon, and their subjects, at length through the operation of divine clemency they reached peace and concord, and, for the purpose of strengthening and establishing peace between them, they concluded certain articles, one of which was to the following effect:

" Item, the aforesaid King and Queen of Castile, Aragon, and Sicily, willed and resolved that this peace shall be firm and stable and everlasting, and they promised henceforth and forever that neither directly nor indirectly, neither secretly nor publicly, nor by their heirs and successors, will they disturb, trouble, or molest, in fact or in law, in court or out of court, the said King and Prince of Portugal or the future sovereigns of Portugal or their kingdoms in the status of possession or quasi-possession which they hold over all the trade, lands, and barter of Guinea, with its gold-mines, or over any other islands, shores, sea-coasts, or lands, discovered or to be discovered, found or to be found, or over the islands of Madeira, Porto Santo, and Desierta, or over all the islands called the Azores, that is, Hawks, and the islands of Flores, nor over the islands of Cape Verde (the Green Cape), nor over the islands already discovered, nor over whatever islands shall be found or acquired from beyond the Canaries, and on this side of and in the vicinity of Guinea, so that whatever has been or shall be found and acquired further in the said limits, shall belong to the said King and Prince of Portugal and to their kingdoms, excepting only the Canary Islands, [namely] Lanzarote, Palma, Forteventura, Gomera, Ferro, Graciosa, Grand Canary, Teneriffe, and all the other Canary Islands, acquired or to be acquired, which remain the possession of the kingdoms of Castile. And in like manner they will not disturb, trouble, or molest any persons whomsoever, who, under any title or in any way or manner whatsoever, shall trade or traffic in or acquire the said merchandise or trade of Guinea or the said lands, shores, or coasts, discovered or to be discovered, in the name or under the authority of the said

lords, king and prince of Portugal, or of their successors. On the contrary,
by these presents, they do promise and assure, in good faith and without
deceit, the said lords, king and prince of Portugal, and their successors, that
they will not, of themselves or through others, order or consent, but rather
forbid that any of their people, native or subject, in any place or at any
time, or in any case, imagined or not imagined, or any other foreign people
who might be within their kingdoms and dominions, or who might be
equipped or provisioned in their ports, go to traffic in the said trade, or in
the islands or lands of Guinea, discovered or to be discovered, without the
permission of the said King and Prince of Portugal. Neither will they give
any occasion, favor, opportunity, aid, or consent, direct or indirect, for such
trade, nor permit the equipment or freighting of expeditions for those regions
in any manner. And if any of the natives or subjects of the kingdoms of
Castile, or any foreigners whosoever, shall set about trafficking in, obstruct-
ing, injuring, plundering, or acquiring by conquest the said Guinea or its
trade, barter, or mines, or the lands and islands, discovered or to be discovered, without the express license and consent of the said lords, king and
prince of Portugal, or of their successors, all such shall be punished in the
manner, place, and form ordained by the said article of this new revision of
the treaties of peace which will and ought to be observed in maritime affairs
against those who land upon the shores, bays, or ports in order to plunder,
commit depredations, or do evil, or who shall do such things on the high
seas.

"Moreover, the King and Queen of Castile and Leon, promised and
agreed, in the manner abovesaid, for themselves and for their successors,
not to concern themselves to interfere in any manner with the conquest of
the kingdom of Fez, just as the former sovereigns of Castile, their predecessors, abstained from meddling with it; but the said lords, king and prince
of Portugal, and their kingdoms and successors shall have a free hand to
prosecute the said conquest and to defend it as they please. And the said
lord and lady, king and queen of Castile, promised and agreed faithfully
that, neither of themselves nor by any other, in court or out of court, in fact
or in law, will they raise against this agreement, nor any part of it, nor
anything that pertains to it, any suit, doubt, question, or any other contention, but that, on the contrary, they will observe and fulfill everything
strictly, and will cause it to be observed and fulfilled without any diminution.
And in order that in the future ignorance might not be alleged of the prohibition and penalties involved in the said matters, the said king and queen
immediately ordered the justices and officials of the ports of their aforesaid
kingdoms faithfully to observe, fulfill, and execute everything herein ordained, and to proclaim and publish it in their courts and in the said seaports
of their aforesaid kingdoms and dominions, so that it might be universally
known."

We, therefore, to whom the care of all the Lord's flock is committed by
Heaven, and who, as we are bound, desire sweet peace and tranquillity to
flourish and endure forever between Christian princes and peoples, earnestly
wishing that the letters of Nicholas and of Calixtus, our predecessors, and the
article inserted above, and all and singular their contents, may remain stable
and unimpaired forever, to the praise of the Divine Name and the lasting
peace of the princes and peoples of each of the aforesaid realms: of our

own motion, not in compliance with any petition offered to us on this subject, but of our spontaneous liberality, foresight, and certain knowledge,
and from the plenitude of apostolic power, considering the letters of Nicholas
and of Calixtus, our predecessors, and the article aforesaid, as valid and
acceptable, do, by apostolic authority and the tenor of these presents, approve
and confirm them and everything contained in them and secure them by the
protection of this present writing, decreeing that they, all and singular, ought
to possess full authority and be observed forever. And, moreover, by our
apostolic writings and on our motion and knowledge aforesaid, we command
our venerable brothers, the bishops of Evora and of Silves and of Portugal,
that they themselves, or two or one of them, by himself, or another or others,
solemnly publishing each of the aforesaid letters and the article, where and
when it shall be necessary, and assisting with efficacious protection the said
King and Prince of Portugal and their successors, in all and singular the
aforesaid, shall not permit the said king and prince and their successors to
be molested or even hindered, contrary to the aforesaid, or any part of it,
by anyone of whatsoever rank, position, degree, or condition he may be,
restraining in our name all persons soever who obstruct, hinder, oppose, or
rebel against the aforesaid, by ecclesiastical censures and other legal remedies,
without permitting appeals, all [apostolic constitutions] to the contrary
notwithstanding, even though an indult shall have been granted by the Apostolic See to any persons, jointly or singly, declaring them to be exempt from
interdiction, suspension, or excommunication by apostolic letters that do
not make full and express and verbatim mention of the said indult. Let no
one, therefore, infringe or with rash boldness contravene this our confirmation, approbation, reinforcement, regulation, and mandate. Should anyone
presume to do so, be it known to him that he will incur the wrath of Almighty
God and of the blessed apostles Peter and Paul. Given at Rome, at St.
Peter's, on the twenty-first day of June, in the year of the incarnation of our
Lord one thousand four hundred and eighty-one, in the tenth year of our
pontificate.

> J. DE SALOS.
> P. DE MONTE.   J. HORN.   L. GRIFUS.

5.

The Bull Inter Caetera (*Alexander VI.*). May 3, 1493.

INTRODUCTION.

Immediately upon learning of the discoveries made by Columbus and of the claims of Portugal thereto,[1] Ferdinand and Isabella appear to have despatched an account of the same to the court at Rome. In consequence of these and later representations, Pope Alexander VI., a native of Valencia, and a friend of King Ferdinand,[2] issued three bulls, dated May 3 and May 4, which were highly favorable to Spain. By the first, the bull *Inter caetera* of May 3, the pope assigned to the present and future sovereigns of Castile the lands discovered and to be discovered by their envoys and not previously possessed by any Christian owner. On the other hand, he safeguarded the concessions already made to Portugal with the proviso that by this gift " no right conferred on any Christian prince is hereby to be understood as withdrawn or to be withdrawn ". The pope also commanded Ferdinand and Isabella to send men to instruct the inhabitants of these newly discovered lands in the Catholic faith and in good morals, and, following the precedent of the bull *Romanus pontifex*,[3] forbade anyone to go to them for trade or other purposes without special permit from the rulers of Castile.[4] He empowered the sovereigns of Castile to enjoy in respect to their discoveries the rights previously granted to Portugal in respect to hers, as if the terms of the grants to Portugal were repeated in this bull.

BIBLIOGRAPHY.

Text: MS. and facsimile. The original manuscript of the promulgated bull is in the Archives of the Indies at Seville, Patronato 1-1-1, no. 1,

---

[1] See above, p. 9.

[2] There are many evidences of this pope's friendliness to Spain. *Cf.* Pastor, *Geschichte der Päpste*, III. 515. H. Rossbach, *Das Leben und die Politisch-Kirchliche Wirksamkeit des Bernaldino Lopez de Carvajal* (1892). See also Vander Linden, " Alexander VI.", etc., *American Historical Review*, XXII. 13-15.

[3] Doc. 1.

[4] It is noteworthy that the restrictions in respect to trade in the prohibited articles, which are emphasized in the bull *Romanus pontifex* (Doc. 1), are omitted here. There is plenty of evidence that about this time the Portuguese were finding the commercial restrictions imposed by the Church very onerous. *Cf.* the bulls of Sept. 13, 1496; July 4, 1505 (see Doc. 1, note 21) ; and Apr. 2, 1506. L. A. Rebello da Silva, *Corpo Diplomatico Portuguez* (Acad. Real das Sciencias, Lisbon, 1862—), I. 59 ff., 97 ff.

but it is not now kept in this bundle but is framed and hanging on the wall. Photographs of this manuscript are reproduced in the *Am. Hist. Rev.*, vol. XIV., opp. p. 776; and in the *Boletin del Centro de Estudios Americanistas de Sevilla,* año III., núm. 7 (March-April, 1915). The text, as entered in the secret register of Alexander VI. in the Vatican Archives, is published in photographic facsimile in J. C. Heywood, *Documenta Selecta e Tabulario Secreto Vaticano* (1893), whence it is reproduced in J. B. Thacher, *Columbus* (1903-1904), II. 124-136.

Text: Printed. The Vatican text is printed in Heywood, *op. cit.*; Thacher, *op. cit.*, II. 125-137; and G. Berchet, *Fonti Italiane* (1892-1893), I. 5-7 (pt. III. of the *Raccolta di Documenti* published by the Reale Commissione Colombiana). A text from the Simancas Archives, where, in 1797, Muñoz discovered a copy of this previously unknown bull, is in Navarrete, *Coleccion de Viages* (1825-1837), tom. II., no. 17, pp. 23-27.

Translations: English. Thacher, *op. cit.*, II. 125-137; E. H. Blair and J. A. Robertson, *Philippine Islands* (1903-1909), I. 97-103. **Spanish.** *Boletin del Centro de Estudios Americanistas de Sevilla,* año III., núm. 7 (March-April, 1915).

References:[*] Contemporary and early writings. F. Colon, *Historie del S. D. Fernando Colombo* (1571, etc.), trans. in Churchill, *Collection of Voyages* (1732), vol. II., pp. 501 ff., chs. 42, 43; B. de Las Casas, *Historia de las Indias* (1875), tom. I., c. 79, in Navarrete *et al., Coleccion de Documentos Inéditos para la Historia de Espqña* (1842—), LXII.; G. Zurita, *Historia del Rey Don Hernando* (1580), lib. I., c. 29; A. de Herrera, *Historia General de los Castellanos* (1730), dec. I., lib. II., c. 4.

References: Later writings. J. B. Muñoz, *Historia del Nuevo Mundo* (1793), tom. I., lib. IV., § 18 f. (an English translation of the *Historia* was published in London in 1797); O. F. Peschel, *Theilung der Erde unter Papst Alexander VI. und Julius II.* (1871); F. Ehrle, " Historische Gehalt der Päpstlichen Abtheilung", in *Stimmen aus Maria-Laach*, XLVI. (1894), 383-388; E. G. Bourne, *Essays in Historical Criticism* (1901), " Demarcation Line of Alexander VI."; H. Harrisse, *Diplomatic History of America* (1897), ch. III.; S. E. Dawson, " Lines of Demarcation of Pope Alexander VI." (1899), in the *Transactions* of the Royal Society of Canada, 2d ser., 1899, vol. V., § 2, pp. 467 ff.; J. B. Thacher, *Columbus* (1903-1904), II. 84 ff.; A. Baum, *Demarkationslinie Papst Alexanders VI. und ihre Folgen* (dissertation, Cologne, 1890); K. Kretschmer, *Die Entdeckung Amerika's* (1892), pp. 300 ff.; L. von Pastor, *Geschichte der Päpste,* III. (1899), pp. 517-521; H. Vignaud, *Histoire Critique de la Grande Entreprise de Christophe Colomb* (1911), II. 276 ff.; H. Vander Linden, " Alexander VI. and the Demarcation of the Maritime and Colonial Domains of Spain and Portugal", *Am. Hist. Rev.*, XXII. 1-20. For further references, see J. Winsor, *Narrative and Critical History,* II. (1886) 45, etc., and E. G. Bourne, *Spain in America* (1904), " Critical Essay on Authorities", in A. B. Hart, *American Nation.*

[*] These are also the references for Docs. **6** and **7.**

TEXT.[a]

Alexander episcopus, servus servorum Dei: carissimo in Christo filio Fernando regi et carissime in Christo filie Elisabeth regine Castelle, Legionis, Aragonum, et Granate illustribus, salutem et apostolicam benedictionem. Inter cetera Divine Majestati beneplacita opera et cordis nostri desiderabilia, illud profecto potissimum existit, ut fides Catholica et Christiana religio nostris presertim temporibus exaltetur, ac ubilibet amplietur et dilatetur, animarumque salus procuretur, ac barbare nationes deprimantur, et ad fidem ipsam reducantur. Unde cum ad hanc Sacram Petri Sedem, divina favente clementia, meritis licet imparibus, evocati fuerimus, cognoscentes vos, tanquam veros Catholicos reges et principes, quales semper fuisse novimus, et a vobis preclare gesta toti pene jam orbi notissima demonstrant, nedum id exoptare, sed omni conatu, studio, et diligentia, nullis laboribus, nullis impensis, nullisque parcendo periculis, etiam proprium sanguinem effundendo, efficere, ac omnem animum vestrum omnesque conatus ad hoc jam dudum dedicasse—quenadmodum recuperatio regni Granate a tyrannide Sarracenorum hodiernis temporibus per vos, cum tanta Divini Nominis gloria facta, testatur—[7] digne ducimur non immerito, et debemus illa vobis etiam sponte et favorabiliter concedere, per que hujusmodi sanctum et laudabile ac immortali Deo acceptum propositum in dies ferventiori animo ad ipsius Dei honorem et imperii Christiani propagationem prosequi valeatis. Sane accepimus quod vos, qui dudum animo proposueratis aliquas terras et insulas, remotas et incognitas ac per alios hactenus non repertas, querere et invenire, ut illarum incolas et habitatores ad colendum Redemptorem nostrum et fidem Catholicam profitendum reduceretis, hactenus in expugnatione et recuperatione ipsius regni Granate plurimum occupati, hujusmodi sanctum et laudabile propositum vestrum ad optatum finem perducere nequivistis; sed tandem, sicut Domino placuit, regno predicto recuperato, volentes desiderium vestrum adimplere, dilectum filium, Christoforum Colon, cum navigiis et hominibus ad similia instructis, non sine maximis laboribus et periculis ac expensis, destinastis, ut terras remotas et incognitas hujusmodi, per mare ubi hactenus navigatum non fuerat, diligenter inquirerent; qui tandem, divino auxilio, facta extrema diligentia, *per partes occidentales, ut dicitur, versus Indos,* in mari occeano navigantes, certas insulas remotissimas, et etiam terras firmas,[8] que per alios hactenus reperte non fuerant, invenerunt, in quibus quamplurime gentes, pacifice viventes, et, ut asseritur, nudi incedentes, nec carnibus vescentes, inhabitant; et, ut prefati nuntii vestri

---

[a] The text is from the original manuscript of the bull, preserved in the Archives of the Indies at Seville. The pressmark is Patronato, 1-1-1; but the manuscript is not in this legajo, but framed and hanging on the wall. To facilitate comparison with the bull *Inter caetera* of May 4, words in this bull which are not in the latter are printed in italics. The variant readings in the Vatican text are few and insignificant.

[7] The conquest of the kingdom of Granada was completed by the capitulation of the city of Granada on Jan. 2, 1492.

[8] Columbus at first supposed Cuba to be part of the mainland, but he describes it as an island in the letter written on his homeward voyage, of which one copy was sent to Luis de Santángel, steward of King Ferdinand's household, and another to Gabriel Sanchez, treasurer of Aragon. Nearly all the data for the following description might have been taken from this letter, which was known in Rome before April 18. Harrisse, *Diplomatic History*, p. 160. A translation of the Santangel letter is given in J. E. Olson and E. G. Bourne, *The Northmen, Columbus, and Cabot* (1906), pp. 263-272, in J. F. Jameson's series of *Original Narratives of Early American History*.

possunt opinari, gentes ipse in insulis et terris predictis habitantes, credunt
unum Deum Creatorem in celis esse, ac ad fidem Catholicam amplexandum
et bonis moribus imbuendum satis apti videntur, spesque habetur quod, si
erudirentur, nomen Salvatoris Domini nostri Jesu Christi in terris et insulis
predictis facile induceretur; ac prefatus Christoforus in una ex principalibus
insulis predictis jam unam turrim* satis munitam, in qua certos Christianos
qui secum iverant, in custodiam, et ut alias insulas et terras remotas et
incognitas inquirerent, posuit, construi et edificari fecit; in quibus quidem
insulis et terris jam repertis, aurum, aromata, et alie quamplurime res
preciose diversi generis et diverse qualitatis repperiuntur. Unde omnibus
diligenter, et presertim fidei Catholice exaltatione et dilatatione, prout decet
Catholicos reges et principes, consideratis, more progenitorum vestrorum,
clare memorie regum, terras et insulas predictas illarumque incolas et
habitatores, vobis, divina favente clementia, subjicere et ad fidem Catholicam
reducere [proposuistis].[10] Nos igitur hujusmodi vestrum sanctum et laudabile propositum plurimum in Domino commendantes, ac cupientes ut illud
ad debitum finem perducatur, et ipsum nomen Salvatoris nostri in partibus
illis inducatur, hortamur vos plurimum in Domino, et per sacri lavacri susceptionem, qua mandatis apostolicis obligati estis, et viscera misericordie
Domini nostri Jhesu Christi attente requirimus, ut cum expeditionem
hujusmodi omnino prosequi et assumere prona mente orthodoxe fidei zelo
intendatis, populos in hujusmodi insulis degentes ad Christianam *professionem*
suscipiendam inducere velitis et debeatis, nec pericula, nec labores ullo
unquam tempore vos deterreant, firma spe fiduciaque conceptis, quod Deus
Omnipotens conatus vestros feliciter prosequetur. Et, ut tanti negotii provinciam apostolice gratie largitate donati, liberius et audacius assumatis,
motu proprio,[11] non ad vestram vel alterius pro vobis super hoc nobis oblate
petitionis instantiam, sed de nostra mera liberalitate, et ex certa scientia, ac
de apostolice potestatis plenitudine, omnes *et singulas terras et insulas
predictas, sic incognitas, et hactenus per nuntios vestros repertas et reperiendas in posterum, que sub dominio actuali temporali aliquorum dominorum
Christianorum constitute non sint,* auctoritate Omnipotentis Dei nobis in
beato Petro concessa, ac vicariatus Jhesu Christi, qua fungimur in terris,
cum omnibus illarum dominiis, *cum* civitatibus, castris, locis, et villis, juribusque et jurisdictionibus ac pertinentiis universis, vobis heredibusque et
succesoribus vestris, Castelle et Legionis regibus, in perpetuum *auctoritate
apostolica,* tenore presentium donamus, concedimus, et assignamus, vosque
ac heredes et succesores prefatos *de illis investimus,* illarumque dominos cum
plena, libera, et omnimoda potestate, auctoritate, et jurisdictione, facimus,
constituimus, et deputamus; decernentes nichilominus per hujusmodi donationem, concessionem, assignationem, *et investituram* nostram, nulli Christiano principi jus quesitum sublatum intelligi posse aut aufferri debere.
Et insuper mandamus vobis in virtute sancte obedientie, ut, sicut etiam
pollicemini et non dubitamus pro vestra maxima devotione et regia magnanimitate vos esse facturos, ad terras et insulas predictas viros probos et Deum
timentes, doctos, peritos, et expertos, ad instruendum incolas et habitatores

---

* In the town of Navidad, in Hispaniola. *Cf.* Olson and Bourne, *Northmen, Columbus, and Cabot* (1906), p. 268.
[10] In the bull *Inter caetera* of May 4, the word *proposuistis* appears here, but it is not
in either text of the bull *Inter caetera* of May 3.
[11] *Cf.* Doc. 1, note 38.

prefatos in fide Catholica et bonis moribus imbuendum, destinare debeatis, omnem debitam diligentiam in premisis adhibentes;[12] ac quibuscumque personis, *etiam* cujuscumque dignitatis, status, gradus, ordinis, vel condictionis, sub excomunicationis late sententie[13] pena, quam eo ipso, si contrafecerint, incurrant, districtius inhibentes, ne ad insulas et terras *predictas, postquam per vestros nuntios seu ad id missos invente et recepte fuerint,* pro mercibus habendis vel quavis alia de causa, accedere presumant, absque vestra ac heredum et succesorum vestrorum predictorum licentia speciali. *Et*[14] *quia etiam nonnulli Portugallie Reges in partibus Affrice, Guinee, et Minere Auri, ac alias, insulas, similiter, etiam ex concesione apostolica eis facta, reppererunt et acquisiverunt et per Sedem Apostolicam eis diversa privilegia, gratie, libertates, immunitates, exemptiones, et indulta concessa fuerunt,*[15] *nos, vobis ac heredibus et succesoribus vestris predictis, ut in insulis et terris per vos repertis et reperiendis hujusmodi, omnibus et singulis gratiis, privilegiis, exemptionibus, libertatibus, facultatibus, inmunitatibus, et indultis hujusmodi, quorum omnium tenores, ac si de verbo ad verbum presentibus insererentur, haberi volumus pro sufficienter expresis et insertis, uti, potiri, et gaudere libere et licite, possitis ac debeatis in omnibus et per omnia, perinde ac si vobis ac heredibus et succesoribus predictis specialiter concessa fuissent, motu, auctoritate, scientia, et apostolice potestatis plenitudine similibus, de specialis dono gratie, indulgemus, illaque in omnibus et per omnia ad vos, heredes ac succesores vestros predictos extendimus pariter, et ampliamus,* non obstantibus constitutionibus et ordinationibus apostolicis, *nec non omnibus illis que in litteris desuper editis concessa sunt, non obstare,* ceterisque contrariis quibuscunque; in Illo a quo imperia et dominationes ac bona cuncta procedunt confidentes, quod, dirigente Domino actus vestros, si hujusmodi sanctum et laudabile *negotium* prosequamini, brevi tempore, cum felicitate et gloria totius populi Christiani, vestri labores et conatus exitum felicissimum consequentur. Verum, quia difficile foret presentes litteras ad singula queque loca in quibus expediens fuerit deferre, volumus, ac motu et scientia similibus decernimus, quod illarum transumptis, manu publici notarii inde rogati subscriptis, et sigillo alicujus persone in ecclesiastica dignitate constitute seu curie ecclesiastice munitis, ea prorsus fides in judicio et extra ac alias ubilibet adhibeatur, que presentibus adhiberetur, si essent exhibite *et* ostense. Nulli ergo omnino hominum liceat hanc paginam nostre exhortationis, requisitionis, donationis, concessionis, assignationis, *investiture, facti,* constitutionis, deputationis, mandati, inhibitionis, *induiti, extensionis, ampliationis,* voluntatis, *et decreti,* infringere, vel ei ausu temerario contraire. Siquis autem hoc attemptare presumpserit, indignationem Omnipotentis Dei ac beatorum Petri et Pauli apostolorum ejus se noverit incursurum.

[12] In their instructions for Columbus's second voyage, dated May 29, 1493, the Spanish sovereigns showed their anxiety to comply with the papal injunction to Christianize the islands. With this in view, they appointed Fray Bernardo Boyl to accompany Columbus. Navarrete, *Viages*, tom. II., no. 45, p. 66.

[13] Excommunication is either *latae* or *ferendae sententiae.* "The first is incurred as soon as the offence is committed and by reason of the offence itself (*eo ipso*) without intervention of any ecclesiastical judge." *The Catholic Encyclopedia.*

[14] The following italicized passage, which is omitted from the bull *Inter caetera* of May 4 (Doc. 7), corresponds closely to the passage in the bull *Eximiae devotionis* (Doc. 6), beginning *Cum autem* and ending *ampliamus.* See below, pp. 66, 75.

[15] The reference is to the bulls of 1455, 1456, and 1481, Docs. 1, 2, and 4.

Datum Rome apud Sanctum Petrum, anno Incarnationis Dominice millesimo quadrigentesimo nonagesimo tertio, quinto nonas Maii, pontificatus nostri anno primo.

Gratis de mandato sanctissimi Domini nostri Pape.

    B. Capotius.[16]   L. Podocatharus.[17]
    D. Serrano.[16]
         Ferrariis.[18]

Ap[ril]i.

Translation.[19]

Alexander, bishop, servant of the servants of God, to the illustrious sovereigns, our very dear son in Christ, Ferdinand, king, and our very dear daughter in Christ, Isabella, queen, of Castile, Leon, Aragon, and Granada, health and apostolic benediction. Among other works well pleasing to the Divine Majesty and cherished of our heart, this assuredly ranks highest, that in our times especially the Catholic faith and the Christian religion be exalted and everywhere increased and spread, that the health of souls be cared for and that barbarous nations be overthrown and brought to the faith itself. Wherefore inasmuch as by the favor of divine clemency, we, though of insufficient merits, have been called to this Holy See of Peter, recognizing that as true Catholic kings and princes, such as we have known you always to be, and as your illustrious deeds already known to almost the whole world declare, you not only eagerly desire but with every effort, zeal, and diligence, without regard to hardships, expenses, dangers, with the shedding even of your blood, are laboring to that end; recognizing also that you have long since dedicated to this purpose your whole soul and all your endeavors—as witnessed in these times with so much glory to the Divine Name in your recovery of the kingdom of Granada from the yoke of the Saracens—we therefore are rightly led, and hold it as our duty, to grant you even of our own accord and in your favor those things, whereby with effort each day more hearty you may be enabled for the honor of God himself and the spread of the Christian rule to carry forward your holy and praiseworthy purpose so pleasing to immortal God. We have indeed learned that you, who for a long time had intended to seek out and discover certain lands and islands remote and unknown and not hitherto discovered by others, to the end that you might bring to the worship of our Redeemer and profession of the Catholic faith their residents and inhabitants, having been up to the present time greatly engaged in the siege and recovery of the kingdom itself of Granada, were unable to accomplish this holy and praiseworthy purpose; but the said kingdom having at length been regained, as was pleasing to the Lord, you, with the wish to fulfill your desire, chose our beloved son Christopher Columbus,

[16] Capotius was the *rescribendarius,* Serrano the *computator.* For some particulars concerning these and the other signatories of this bull see Vander Linden, *op. cit.*

[17] Lodovico Podocatharo, bishop of Capaccio and archbishop of Benevento, was physician to Pope Innocent VIII. and secretary to Alexander VI. In 1500 he was made a cardinal. M. Buchberger, *Kirchliches Handlexikon.* The bull bears the official endorsement "Registrata in Camera Apostolica". The names in the register are: B. Capotius, D. Serrano, A. de Campania, N. Casanova.

[18] The deciphering of the name of this abbreviator is due to Professor H. Vander Linden.

[19] In translating Docs. **5, 6, 7,** and **8,** free use has been made of the translations in Blair and Robertson, *Philippine Islands,* I. 97-114.

whom you furnished with ships and men equipped for like designs, not without the greatest hardships, dangers, and expenses, to make diligent quest for these remote and unknown countries through the sea, where hitherto no one had sailed ; and they at length, with divine aid and with the utmost diligence sailing in the ocean sea, through western waters, as is said, toward the Indians, discovered certain very remote islands and even mainlands, that hitherto had not been discovered by others ; and therein dwell very many peoples living in peace, and, as reported, going unclothed, and not eating flesh. Moreover, as your aforesaid envoys are of opinion, these very peoples living in the said islands and countries believe in one God, the Creator in heaven, and seem sufficiently disposed to embrace the Catholic faith and be trained in good morals. And it is hoped that, were they instructed, the name of the Savior, our Lord Jesus Christ, would easily be introduced into the said countries and islands. Also, on one of the chief of these aforesaid islands the above-mentioned Christopher has already caused to be put together and built a fortress fairly equipped, wherein he has stationed as garrison certain Christians, companions of his, who are to make search for other remote and unknown islands and countries. In the islands and countries already discovered are found gold, spices, and very many other precious things of divers kinds and qualities. Wherefore, after earnest consideration of all matters, as becomes Catholic kings and princes, and especially of the rise and spread of the Catholic faith, as was the fashion of your ancestors, kings of renowned memory, you have purposed with the favor of divine clemency to bring under your sway the said countries and islands with their residents and inhabitants, and to bring them to the Catholic faith. Hence, heartily commending in the Lord this your holy and praiseworthy purpose, and desirous that it be duly accomplished, and that the name of our Savior be carried into those regions, we exhort you very earnestly in the Lord and by your reception of holy baptism, whereby you are bound to our apostolic commands, and by the bowels of the mercy of our Lord Jesus Christ, enjoin strictly, that inasmuch as with eager zeal for the true faith you design to equip and despatch this expedition, you purpose also, as is your duty, to lead the peoples dwelling in those islands to embrace the Christian profession ; nor at any time let dangers or hardships deter you therefrom, with the stout hope and trust in your hearts that Almighty God will further your undertakings. And, in order that you may enter upon so great an undertaking with greater readiness and heartiness endowed with the benefit of our apostolic favor, we, of our own accord, not at your instance nor the request of anyone else in your regard, but of our own sole largess and certain knowledge and out of the fullness of our apostolic power, by the authority of Almighty God conferred upon us in blessed Peter and of the vicarship of Jesus Christ which we hold on earth, do by tenor of these presents give, grant, and assign forever to you and your heirs and successors, kings of Castile and Leon, all and singular the aforesaid countries and islands thus unknown and hitherto discovered by your envoys and to be discovered hereafter, provided however they at no time have been in the actual temporal possession of any Christian owner, together with all their dominions, cities, camps, places, and villages, and all rights, jurisdictions, and appurtenances of the same. And we invest you and your aforementioned heirs and successors with them, and make, appoint, and depute you lords of them with full and free power, authority, and jurisdiction of every kind, with this proviso however, that by this our gift, grant, assignment, and investiture

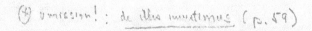

no right acquired by any Christian prince is hereby to be understood to be withdrawn or taken away. Moreover we command you in virtue of holy obedience, that, employing all due diligence in the premises, as you also promise—nor do we doubt that you will act in accordance with your devoted loyalty and royal greatness of spirit—you should appoint to the aforesaid countries and islands worthy and God-fearing, learned, skilled, and experienced men to instruct the aforesaid inhabitants and residents in the Catholic faith, and to train them in good morals. And under penalty of excommunication *late sententie* to be incurred *ipso facto,* should any thus contravene, we strictly forbid all persons of no matter what rank, estate, degree, order, or condition, to dare, without your special permit or that of your aforesaid heirs and successors, to go for the sake of trade or any other reason whatever to the said islands and countries after they have been discovered and found by your envoys or persons sent out for that purpose. And inasmuch as some kings of Portugal, likewise by apostolic grant made to them, have similarly discovered and taken possession of islands in the regions of Africa, Guinea, and the Gold Mine, and elsewhere, and divers privileges, favors, liberties, immunities, exemptions, and indults have been granted to them by the Apostolic See, we through similar accord, authority, knowledge, and fullness of apostolic power, by a gift of special favor, do grant to you and your aforesaid heirs and successors, that in the islands and countries thus discovered and to be discovered by you, you may and rightly can use, employ, and enjoy freely and legally, in all things and through all things, just as if they had been especially granted to you and your aforesaid heirs and successors, all and singular these favors, privileges, exemptions, liberties, faculties, immunities, and indults, the terms of all of which we wish to be understood as being sufficiently expressed and inserted, as if they were inserted word for word in these presents. Moreover we similarly extend and enlarge them in all things and through all things to you and your aforesaid heirs and successors, apostolic constitutions and ordinances as well as all those things that have been granted in the letters set forth above or other things whatsoever to the contrary notwithstanding. We trust in Him from whom empires and governments and all good things proceed, that should you with the Lord's guidance pursue this holy and praiseworthy undertaking, in a short while your hardships and endeavors will attain the most felicitous result, to the happiness and glory of all Christendom. But inasmuch as it would be difficult to have these present letters sent to all places where desirable, we wish, and with similar accord and knowledge do decree that to copies of them, signed by the hand of a notary public commissioned therefor and sealed with the seal of any ecclesiastical officer or ecclesiastical court, the same respect is to be shown in court and outside as well as anywhere else, as would be given to these presents should they be exhibited or shown. Let no one, therefore, infringe, or with rash boldness contravene this our exhortation, requisition, gift, grant, assignment, investiture, deed, constitution, deputation, mandate, inhibition, indult, extension, enlargement, will, and decree. Should anyone presume to do so, be it known to him that he will incur the wrath of Almighty God and of the blessed apostles Peter and Paul. Given in Rome, at St. Peter's, on the third day of May in the year one thousand four hundred and ninety-three of the incarnation of our Lord, in the first year of our pontificate.

Gratis by order of our most holy lord the Pope.

B. CAPOTIUS.   L. PODOCATHARUS.

D. SERRANO.

April.   FERRARIIS.

6.

The Bull Eximiae Devotionis (*Alexander VI.*). *May 3, 1493.*[1]

INTRODUCTION.

Although this bull bears the same date as the preceding,[2] it would seem that its expediting was not begun until July. In somewhat more precise and emphatic terms it repeats that concession of the earlier bull, which extended to the Catholic kings in respect to the lands discovered by Columbus the privileges previously granted to the kings of Portugal in respect to their discoveries in " Africa, Guinea, and the Gold Mine ".

BIBLIOGRAPHY.

Text: MS. and facsimile. An official copy of the promulgated bull, made in 1515, is in the Archives of the Indies at Seville, Patronato, 1-1-1, no. 4. A facsimile of the text preserved in the Vatican registers is in J. C. Heywood, *Documenta Selecta e Tabulario Secreto Vaticano* (1893), and is reproduced thence in J. B. Thacher, *Columbus* (1903-1904), II. 155, 159.

Text: Printed. The Vatican text is in Heywood, *op. cit.*; Thacher, *op. cit.*, II. 156, 160; G. Berchet, *Fonti Italiane* (1892-1893), I. 3, 4 (pt. III. of the *Raccolta di Documenti* published by the Reale Commissione Colombiana) ; S. E. Dawson, " Lines of Demarcation of Pope Alexander VI.", etc. (1899), pp. 535-536, in the *Transactions* of the Royal Society of Canada, 2d ser., 1899-1900, vol. V., § 2 ; and, except the formal concluding clauses, O. Raynaldus (continuing Baronius), *Annales Ecclesiastici* (1747-1756), XI. 213-214. The text of the promulgated bull is in J. de Solorzano Pereira, *De Indiarum Jure* (1629-1639), I. 612.

Translations. H. Harrisse, *Diplomatic History of America* (1897), pp. 20-24 ; Dawson, *op. cit.*, pp. 536-537; Thacher, *op. cit.*, II. 157-161 ; Blair and Robertson, *Philippine Islands* (1903-1909), I. 103-105.

References: See under Doc. 5.

TEXT.[3]

In nomine Domini, Amen. Universis et singulis presentes licteras sive presens publicum transumpti instrumentum visuris, lecturis, et audituris: quod nos, reverendus dominus, Don Didacus Hernandez, thesaurarius

---

[1] The bull as printed by Solorzano Pereira, *De Indiarum Jure*, I. 612, is dated May 4 (*quarto nonas Maii*), and some historians have accepted this as the date of the promulgated bull. The text in the Vatican Register is dated May 3 (*quinto nonas Maii*), which the text here printed proves to be that of the promulgated bull. In regard to the expediting of the bull see Vander Linden, " Alexander VI. and the Demarcation of the Maritime and Colonial Domains of Spain and Portugal", *American Historical Review*, XXII. 3-7.

[2] Doc. 5.

[3] The following text is from an official copy, made in 1515, and preserved in the Archives of the Indies, Patronato, 1-1-1, no. 4.

ecclesie collegialis Sancti Antolini de Medina Campi,[4] et reverendi in Christo patris et domini, Domini Belnardini Gutterez, prothonotarii apostolici et abbatis dicte ville Medine, provisor offitialis et vicarius generalis in temporalibus et spiritualibus, salutem in Domino et presentibus fidem indubiam adhibere placeat. Noveritis quod nos, ad spectabilis viri Domini Didaci Salmeron, in jure civili bachalarii, licterarum apostolicarum aliorumque jurium et instrumentorum Serenissime Domine nostre domine Joanne, divina favente clementia Castelle, Legionis, et Granate regnorum, etc. regine Catholice ad suumque regium patrimonium statum, jurisdictionem, facultates, et preheminentias concernentium custodis petitionis instantiam et requisitionem, vidimus et diligenter inspeximus quasdam licteras apostolicas felicis recordationis domini, Domini Alexandri Pape Sexti, in forma ejus vere bulle sigilli plumbei in cordula sirici rubei croceique coloris, more Romane curie, pendentis bullatas, im pergameno et lingua Latina scriptas, coram nobis in juditio per eumdem dominum, bachalarium Didacum Salmeron, in sua originali forma productas et presentatas. Et quia per hujusmodi visionem et inspectionem prefatas litteras apostolicas sanas, integras, et illesas, omnique prorsus vitio et suspitione carere, ut apparebat, reperimus. Ideo, eas, ad prefati domini bachalarii, Didaci Salmeron, ulteriorem instantiam, per notarium publicum infrascriptum, transumi et exemplari ac in hujusmodi transumpti publici formam redegi fecimus et mandavimus, volentes, et ordinaria auctoritate qua fungimur decernentes, quod hujusmodi transumpto publico illa et eadem ac similis et tanta fides ubique locorum et terrarum ubi illud exhibitum fuerit et productum, tam in juditio quam extra, adhibeatur, que et qualis et quanta eisdem originalibus litteris apostolicis, unde presens transumptum sive exemplar extractum fuit, adhiberetur, si in medium exhiberentur aut obstenderentur. Tenor vero licterarum apostolicarum predictarum de quibus supra fit mentio, sequitur et est hujusmodi:

Alexander episcopus, servus servorum Dei, carissimo in Christo filio Ferdinando regi et carissime in Christo filie Elisabeth, regine Castelle, Legionis, Aragonum, et Granate, illustribus, salutem et apostolicam benedictionem.

Eximie devotionis sinceritas et integra fides quibus nos et Romanam reveremini ecclesiam non indigne merentur ut illa vobis favorabiliter concedamus per que sanctum et laudabile propositum vestrum et opus inceptum in querendis terris et insulis remotis ac incognitis in dies melius et facilius ad honorem Omnipotentis Dei et imperii Christiani propagationem ac fidei Catholice exaltationem prosequi valeatis. Hodie siquidem omnes et singulas terras firmas et insulas remotas et incognitas, versus partes occidentales et mare oceanum consistentes, per vos seu nuncios vestros, ad id propterea non sine magnis laboribus, periculis, et impensis destinatos, repertas et reperiendas imposterum, que sub actuali dominio temporali aliquorum dominorum Christianorum constitute non essent, cum omnibus illarum dominiis, civitatibus, castris, locis, villis, juribus, et[5] jurisdictionibus universis, vobis, heredibusque et successoribus vestris, Castelle et Legionis regibus, imperpetuum, motu proprio et ex certa scientia ac de apostolice potestatis plenitudine donavimus,

[4] A bull of Sixtus IV. creating the collegiate church of Saint Antolin is printed in C. Pérez Pastor, *La Imprenta en Medina del Campo* (1895), pp. 183 ff.
[5] The words *juribus et* are struck out. They appear in the Vatican text, but not in Solorzano.

concessimus, et assignavimus, prout in nostris inde confectis litteris plenius
continetur.* Cum ⁷ autem alias nonnullis Portugallie regibus qui impartibus
Africe, Guinee, et Minere Auri, ac alias, insulas etiam ex ⁸ similibus con-
cessione et donatione apostolica eis facta repererunt et acquisiverunt, per
Sedem Apostolicam diversa privilegia, gratie, libertates, immunitates, exemptiones, facultates, littere, et indulta concessa fuerint; nos volentes etiam,
prout dignum et conveniens existit, vos, heredesque et successores vestros
predictos, non minoribus gratiis, prerogativis, et favoribus prosequi, motu
simili, non ad vestram vel alterius pro vobis super hoc oblate petitionis
instantiam sed de nostra mera liberalitate ac eisdem scientia et apostolice
potestatis plenitudine, vobis et heredibus et successoribus vestris predictis,
ut in insulis et terris per vos seu nomine vestro hactenus repertis hujusmodi et
reperiendis imposterum, omnibus et singulis gratiis et privilegiis, exemptionibus, libertatibus, facultatibus, immunitatibus, litteris, et indultis regibus
Portugallie concessis hujusmodi, quorum omnium tenores, ac si de verbo ad
verbum presentibus insererentur, haberi volumus pro sufficienter expressis
et insertis, uti, potiri, et gaudere libere et licite possitis et debeatis in omnibus
et per omnia perinde ac si illa omnia vobis ac heredibus et successoribus
vestris prefatis specialiter concessa [fuissent],* auctoritate apostolica, tenore
presentium de specialis dono gratie indulgemus, illaque in omnibus et per
omnia ad vos heredesque ac successores vestros predictos extendimus pariter
et ampliamus, ac eisdem modo et forma perpetuo concedimus, non obstantibus
constitutionibus et ordinationibus apostolicis, nec non omnibus illis que in
litteris Portugallie regibus concessis hujusmodi concessa sunt, non obstare
ceterisque contrariis quibuscunque. Verum, quia difficile foret presentes
litteras ad singula queque loca in quibus expediens fuerit, deferri, volumus,
ac motu et scientia similibus decernimus, quod illarum transumptis, manu
publici notarii inde rogati subscriptis et sigillo alicujus persone in ecclesiastica
dignitate constitute, seu curie ecclesiastice, munitis, ea prorsus fides indubia
in judicio et extra, ac alias ubilibet, adhibeatur, que presentibus adhiberetur,
si essent exhibite vel ostense. Nulli ergo omnino hominum liceat hanc
paginam nostrorum indulti, extensionis, ampliationis, concessionis, voluntatis,
et decreti infringere, vel ei ausu temerario contraire. Siquis autem hoc
attemptare presumpserit, indignationem Omnipotentis Dei ac beatorum Petri
et Pauli apostolorum ejus se noverit incursurum. Datum Rome apud Sanctum
Petrum, anno Incarnationis Dominice millesimo quadrigentesimo nonagesimo
tertio, quinto nonas Maii, pontificatus nostri anno primo. L. Podocatharus.¹⁰
D. Gallettus.¹¹ Registrata in secretaria apostolica. Crothonien[sis].¹²
Jul[io].¹³ Gratis de mandato b[eati] d[omini] nostri pape. Jo[hannes]
Nilis.¹⁴

---

* The bull *Inter caetera* of May 3 (Doc. **5**) is here referred to.
⁷ Compare with the passage that begins here and ends with the word *ampliamus*,
twenty lines below, the corresponding italicized passage in the bull *Inter caetera*, of
May 3 (Doc. **5**), which begins with the words *Et quia*, p. 60.
⁸ The Vatican text has *in* instead of *ex*.
⁹ The word *fuissent*, which appears in the Vatican text, is omitted from the copy
of the year 1515 and from Solorzano.
¹⁰ Papal secretary. See Doc. **5**, note 17.
¹¹ D. Galetti is mentioned in J. Burchard, *Diarium* (ed. Thuasne, 1883-1885), II. 285,
as an apostolic scribe.
¹² In 1493 Giovanni Ebu was Bishop of Cotrone.
¹³ This date is the same as that in the margin of the copy of this bull entered in the
Vatican register. It indicates the month in which the expediting of the bull began.
See above, note 1.
¹⁴ *Rescribendarius* in the third quarter of the year 1493. *Cf.* Doc. **8**, p. 81; and
Vander Linden, *op. cit.*, p. 7, note 19.

Nos, vero, provisor officialis et vicarius predictus, pro tribunali sedentes ad nostrum solitum banchum juris, hora solita causarum consueta im publica audientia, sit[uata] in dicta villa Medine, juxta[15] sua manifesta confinia, omnibus et singulis premissis, tamquam rite et recte factis, auctoritatem nostram judiciariam et ordinariam pariter et decretum interponendum duximus, et interposuimus presentium per tenorem. In quorum omnium et singulorum fidem et testimonium premissorum, presentes litteras sive presens publicum exemplar aut transumpti instrumentum ex inde fieri et per notarium publicum infrascriptum subscribi et publicari mandavimus, sigillique dicti domini abbatis, quo in similibus utimur, jussimus et fecimus impressione com[m]uniri, ac manibus nostris roboravimus. Datum et actum in dicta villa de Medina, in publica audientia nobis inibi, ut supra pro tribunali hora solita causarum consueta sedentes, anno nativitatis Domini millesimo quingentesimo quintodecimo, indictione tertia, die vero vigesima secunda mensis Martii, pontificatus santissimi in Christo patris et domini nostri Domini Leonis, divina providentia Pape Decimi anno tertio, presentibus Aloysio Hernandez de Medina et Johanne Garzia de Burgo, notariis audientie abbatialis predicte, et Stefano Saline procuratore causarum dicte ville, et Francisco Rodregez clerico benefitiato in logare Carpi, testibus ad premissa habitis, vocatis, et rogatis.

Datharius et prodatarius. Ego, Felecissimus de Mugnonibus de Crevio, Spoletane diocesis, publicus imperiali apostolicaque auctoritate notarius et judex ordinarius, et ad presens Catholice Majestatis curiam sequens, et spetialiter per dictum dominum, provisorem officialem et vicarium, ad hunc actum, electus, assumptus, et deputatus, quia, premissis omnibus et singulis dum sic ut premittitur, coram prefato domino provisore, ac que per eum fierent et dicerentur, una cum prenominatis testibus presens fui, eaque in notam sumpsi et recepi, ideo supra insertas apostolicas licteras transumpsi et exemplatus sum, et cum suis originalibus comprobavi ac in omnibus concordare reperi et presens publicum transumpti instrumentum subscripsi et publicavi, signoque et nomine meis solitis et consuetis una cum dicti domini provisoris manus appositione, et sigilli dicti domini abbatis impressione, signavi, in fidem et robur et testimonium omnium et singulorum premissorum, rogatus et requisitus.

Signum [*Here follows the*] mei FELECISSIMI
notarii [*notarial sign*] predicti.

TRANSLATION.

In the name of the Lord, Amen. To all and singular who shall see, read, or hear the present letters, or the present public transumpt, we the reverend lord, Don Diego Hernandez, treasurer of the collegiate church of Saint Antolin of Medina del Campo, and official provisor and vicar general in temporalities and spiritualities of the reverend father and lord in Christ, Don Bernardo Gutterez, apostolic protonotary and abbot of the said town of Medina, health in the Lord, and let certain credence be given to these presents.

Be it known that, at the instance and request of the petition of the honorable Don Diego Salmeron, bachelor in civil law and keeper of the apostolic letters

---

[15] *Justa* in MS.

and of other privileges and instruments concerning the status, jurisdiction, faculties, and pre-eminences of the Most Serene Lady, our Lady Joanna, by the favor of divine mercy Catholic queen of the kingdoms of Castile, Leon, and Granada, and in respect to her royal patrimony, we have seen and diligently inspected certain apostolic letters of our lord, of happy memory, the lord Pope Alexander VI., sealed in the form of his true bull, with a leaden seal hanging on a red and yellow cord of silk, in the manner of the Roman court, written on parchment and in the Latin tongue, produced and presented in its original form before us in judgment by the said lord, the bachelor, Diego Salmeron. And because, upon this view and inspection, we found the aforesaid apostolic letters whole, entire, and unimpaired, and, as it seemed, utterly without blemish or suspicious appearance, therefore, at the further instance of the aforesaid lord bachelor, Diego Salmeron, we have caused and ordered these letters to be copied and transcribed and brought into the form of this public transumpt by the notary public aforesaid, wishing and, by the ordinary authority which we enjoy, decreeing, that that and the same and similar and as great credence be given to this public transumpt, in whatever places or lands it shall be exhibited and produced, in court or out, as any of the same kind and degree as would adhere to the same original apostolic letters from which the present transumpt or exemplar was drawn, if they should be publicly exhibited or displayed. The tenor of the aforesaid apostolic letters of which mention was made above, follows, and is this:

Alexander,[16] bishop, servant of the servants of God, to the illustrious sovereigns, our very dear son in Christ, Ferdinand, king, and our very dear daughter in Christ, Isabella, queen of Castile, Leon, Aragon, and Granada, health and apostolic benediction. The sincerity and whole-souled loyalty of your exalted attachment to ourselves and the Church of Rome deserve to have us grant in your favor those things whereby daily you may the better and more easily be enabled to the honor of Almighty God and the spread of Christian government as well as the exaltation of the Catholic faith to carry out your holy and praiseworthy purpose and the work already undertaken of making search for far-away and unknown countries and islands. For this very day of our own accord and certain knowledge, and out of the fullness of our apostolic power, we have given, granted, and assigned forever, as appears more fully in our letters drawn up therefor, to you and your heirs and successors, kings of Castile and Leon, all and singular the remote and unknown mainlands and islands lying towards the western parts and the ocean sea, that have been discovered or hereafter may be discovered by you or your envoys, whom you have equipped therefor not without great hardships, dangers, and expense—and with them all their lordships, cities, castles, places, villages, rights, and jurisdictions; provided however these countries have not been in the actual temporal possession of any Christian lords. But inasmuch as at another time the Apostolic See has granted divers privileges, favors, liberties, immunities, exemptions, faculties, letters, and indults to certain kings of Portugal, who also by similar apostolic grant and donation in their favor, have discovered and taken possession of islands in the regions of Africa, Guinea, and the Gold Mine, and elsewhere, with the desire to empower by our apostolic authority, as also is right and fitting, you and your aforesaid heirs and successors with graces, prerogatives, and favors of no

---

[16] See Doc. **5**, note 19.

less character; moved also thereto wholly of our similar accord, not at your instance nor the petition of anyone else in your favor, but of our own sole liberality and out of the same knowledge and fullness of apostolic power, we do by tenor of these presents, as a gift of special favor, grant to you and your aforesaid heirs and successors that in the islands and countries, already thus discovered by you or in your name and to be discovered hereafter, you may freely and legally, as is proper, use, employ, and enjoy in all things and through all things, exactly the same as if they had been granted especially to you and your aforesaid heirs and successors, all and singular the graces and privileges, exemptions, liberties, faculties, immunities, letters, and indults that have been thus granted to the kings of Portugal, the terms whereof we wish to be understood as sufficiently expressed and inserted, as if they had been inserted word for word in these presents. Moreover we extend similarly and enlarge these powers in all things and through all things to you and your aforesaid heirs and successors, to whom in the same manner and form we grant them forever, apostolic constitutions and ordinances as well as all grants of similar kind made by letters to the kings of Portugal, as well as other things whatsoever to the contrary notwithstanding. But as it would be difficult to have these present letters sent to all places where desirable, we wish and with similar accord and knowledge do decree that to copies of them, signed by the hand of a public notary commissioned therefor, and sealed with the seal of any ecclesiastical officer or ecclesiastical court, the same respect is to be shown in court and outside as well as anywhere else as would be given to these presents should they be exhibited or shown. Let no one, therefore, infringe or with rash boldness contravene this our indult, extension, enlargement, grant, will, and decree. Should any one presume to do so, be it known to him that he will incur the wrath of Almighty God and of the blessed apostles Peter and Paul. Given at Rome, at St. Peter's, in the year of our Lord's incarnation one thousand four hundred and ninety-three, the third day of May, the first year of our pontificate. L. Podocatharus. D. Gallettus. Registered in the apostolic secretariate. The Bishop of Co-trone. July. Gratis, by command of our blessed lord, the pope. Jo. Nilis.

We, the official provisor and vicar aforesaid, sitting before the tribunal at our accustomed law bench at the hour when law suits are usually heard in the public *audiencia* situated in the said town of Medina, near its manifest boundaries, have thought that to all and singular the aforesaid, as rightly and correctly made, our authority and decree as judge and ordinary ought to be interposed, and we have interposed them by the tenor of these presents. In faith and testimony of these premises, all and singular, we have ordered the present letters or the present public exemplar or transumpt to be made therefrom, and to be subscribed and published by the notary public whose name is signed below, and we have ordered and caused them to be secured with the impression of the seal of the said lord abbot, which we use in such cases, and we have confirmed them with our hand. Given and done by us in the said town of Medina, as we sat in the public *audiencia* (as above) before our tribunal at the hour when causes are usually heard, in the year of the nativity of our Lord one thousand five hundred and fifteen, in the third indiction, on the twenty-second day of the month of March, in the third year of the pontificate of the most Holy Father and lord in Christ, our lord, by divine providence, Pope Leo X., there being present Luis Hernandez of Medina and Juan Garcia of Burgos, notaries of the *audiencia* of the abbey aforesaid, and Estevan de Salinas, attorney in legal proceedings of the said town, and Francisco Rodriguez, beneficed clerk in the village of Carpio, had, called, and summoned as witnesses to the aforesaid.

Datary and prodatary. I, Felecissimo di Mugnano of Crevio in the diocese of Spoleto, by imperial and apostolic authority notary public and ordinary judge, at present following the court of his Catholic Majesty, and especially elected, chosen, and deputed for this act by the said lord, the official provisor and vicar, because (in the manner aforesaid in the premises, all and singular) I, together with the aforenamed witnesses, was present before the said lord provisor and took notes of those things that were done and said by him, therefore I have transcribed the apostolic letters inserted above, and I have copied them and have compared them with the originals and have found them to agree in all respects, and I have subscribed and published the present public transumpt, and having been summoned and required, in faith and confirmation and testimony of all and singular the aforesaid, I have marked it with my usual customary sign and name, together with the apposition of the sign manual of the said lord provisor and the impression of the seal of the said lord abbot.

Sign [here follows the notarial sign] of
   me, FELECISSIMO, the notary aforesaid.

7.

The Bull Inter Caetera (*Alexander VI.*). May 4, 1493.

INTRODUCTION.

Like the bull *Eximiae devotionis* of May 3,[1] the bull *Inter caetera* of May 4 is a restatement of part of the bull *Inter caetera* of May 3.[2] Taken together the two later bulls cover the same ground as the bull *Inter caetera* of May 3, for which they form a substitute. The changes introduced into the bull *Inter caetera* of May 4, are, however, of great importance, and highly favorable to Spain. Instead of merely granting to Castile the lands discovered by her envoys, and not under Christian rule, the revised bull draws a line of demarcation one hundred leagues west of any of the Azores or Cape Verde Islands, and assigns to Castile the exclusive right to acquire territorial possessions and to trade in all the lands west of that line, which at Christmas, 1492, were not in the possession of any Christian prince. The general safeguard to the possible conflicting rights of Portugal is lacking. All persons are forbidden to approach the lands west of the line without special license from the rulers of Castile.

It is not probable that by this bull Alexander VI. intended to secure to Portugal an eastern route to the Indies, as some writers have maintained. In the bulls of May 3, the earlier papal grants to Portugal are said to have given her rights in the region of Guinea and the Gold Mine, but the Indies are not mentioned. The bull of May 4 does not name Portugal and refers to her only in the clause which excepts from the donation any lands west of the demarcation line, which at Christmas, 1492, might be in the possession of any Christian prince.

BIBLIOGRAPHY.

Text: **MS. and facsimile.** The original manuscript of the promulgated bull is in the Archives of the Indies at Seville, Patronato, 1-1-1, no. 3. A photograph of this manuscript is reproduced in the *Boletín del Centro de Estudios Americanistas de Sevilla,* año III., núm. 7 (March-April, 1915). A facsimile of the text found in the Vatican registers is in J. C. Heywood, *Documenta Selecta e Tabulario Secreto Vaticano* (1893),

---

[1] Doc. 6.
[2] Doc. 5. For some unknown reason the bull of May 4 was antedated by several weeks. It was expedited in June, and thus is actually prior to the bull *Eximiae devotionis*, which, also antedated, was expedited in July. Vander Linden, " Alexander VI. and the Demarcation", *American Historical Review*, XXII. 3-8.

whence it is reproduced in J. B. Thacher, *Columbus* (1903-1904), II.
139-151. An authenticated transcript of the bull, belonging to Columbus,
is partly reproduced in facsimile in the *Autógrafos de Cristóbal Colón*
(1892), opp. p. 20, published by the Duchess of Berwick and Alba ; and
the copy entered in Columbus's *Book of Privileges* is reproduced in the
facsimiles of that work.   (See F. G. Davenport, " Texts of Columbus's
Privileges ", *American Historical Review*, XIV. 764.)

Text: Printed.   The Vatican text is in Heywood, *op. cit.*; Thacher, *op. cit.*,
II. 140-153 ; G. Berchet, *Fonti Italiane* (1892-1893), I. 8-11 (pt. III. of
the *Raccolta di Documenti* published by the Reale Commissione Colom-
biana) ; S. E. Dawson, " Line of Demarcation of Pope Alexander VI.",
etc. (1899), pp. 529-531, in the *Transactions* of the Royal Society of
Canada, 2d ser., 1899, vol. V., § 2, pp. 467 ff. The text of the promulgated
bull, preserved in the Archives of the Indies, is printed in J. de Solorzano
Pereira, *De Indiarum Jure* (1629-1639), I. 608-610, and in Navarrete,
Coleccion de Viages (1825-1837), II. 28-34. The text in J. Ramos-
Coelho, *Alguns Documentos* (1892), pp. 66-68, is from a manuscript
in the National Archives at Lisbon. One or another of the above-
mentioned texts will be found in various *bullaria* and other printed works.

Translations:̄ English.   The earliest English rendering is doubtless that
published in 1555 in R. Eden's translation of Peter Martyr (Pietro
Martire d'Anghiera), *Decades of the Newe Worlde or West India*.
This version (together with the Latin text) is in J. Fiske, *Discovery of
America* (1892), II. 580-593, and in A. B. Hart, *American History
told by Contemporaries* (1897-1901), I. 40-43. Other translations are
in the *Memorials of Columbus* (1823), pp. 172-183, a translation of
G. B. Spotorno, *Codice Diplomatico Colombo-Americano* (1823) ; B. F.
Stevens, *Christopher Columbus; his Own Book of Privileges, 1502*
(1893), pp. 182-197; Dawson, *op. cit.*, pp. 532-534; Thacher, *op. cit.*,
II. 141-153; and in Blair and Robertson, *Philippine Islands* (1903-
1909), I. 105-111. Spanish. *Boletín del Centro de Estudios Americanistas de Sevilla*, año III., núm. 7 (March-April, 1915) ; Navarrete,
op. cit., II. 29-35.

References. Same as for Doc. 5.

TEXT.[1]

Alexander episcopus, servus servorum Dei: carissimo in Christo filio
Fernando regi, et carissime in Christo filie Elisabeth regine Castelle, Legionis,
Aragonum, Sicilie, et Granate, illustribus, salutem et apostolicam benedic-
tionem.

Inter cetera Divine Majestati beneplacita opera et cordis nostri[2] desiderabilia, illud profecto potissimum existit, ut fides Catholica et Christiana
religio[3] nostris presertim temporibus exaltetur, ac ubilibet amplietur et

---

[1] The following text is from the original manuscript of the promulgated bull, preserved in the Archives of the Indies at Seville, Patronato, 1-1-1, no. 3. Variant readings
are given from the text of the Vatican register, reproduced in facsimile in Heywood,
Documenta Selecta. Words in this bull, not in the bull *Inter caetera* of May 3, 1493,
are printed in italics.

[2] The Vatican text reads *vestri*.   [3] The Vatican text reads *lex*.

dilatetur, animarumque salus procuretur, ac barbare nationes deprimantur et ad fidem ipsam reducantur.[*] Unde cum ad hanc[†] Sacram Petri Sedem, divina favente clementia, meritis licet imparibus, evocati fuerimus, cognoscentes vos, tanquam veros Catholicos reges et principes, quales semper fuisse novimus, et a vobis preclare gesta toti pene jam orbi notissima demonstrant, nedum id exoptare, sed omni conatu, studio, et diligentia, nullis laboribus, nullis impensis, nullisque parcendo periculis, etiam proprium sanguinem effundendo, efficere, ac omnem animum vestrum omnesque conatus ad hoc jam dudum dedicasse—quemadmodum recuperatio regni Granate a tyrannide Saracenorum hodiernis temporibus per vos, cum tanta Divini Nominis gloria facta, testatur[†]—digne ducimur[‡] non immerito, et debemus illa vobis etiam sponte et favorabiliter concedere, per que hujusmodi sanctum et laudabile ac immortali Deo acceptum propositum in dies ferventiori animo ad ipsius Dei honorem et imperii Christiani propagationem prosequi valeatis. Sane accepimus quod vos, qui dudum animo proposueratis aliquas insulas et terras *firmas*,[10] remotas et incognitas ac per alios hactenus non repertas, querere et invenire, ut illarum incolas et habitatores ad colendum Redemptorem nostrum et fidem Catholicam profitendum reduceretis, hactenus in expugnatione et recuperatione ipsius regni Granate plurimum occupati, hujusmodi sanctum et laudabile propositum vestrum ad optatum finem perducere nequivistis; sed tandem, sicut Domino placuit, regno predicto recuperato, volentes desiderium adimplere vestrum, dilectum filium Cristophorum Colon, *virum utique dignum et plurimum commendandum, ac tanto negotio aptum,* cum navigiis et hominibus ad similia instructis, non sine maximis laboribus et periculis ac expensis, destinastis, ut terras *firmas et insulas* remotas et incognitas hujusmodi per mare, ubi hactenus navigatum non fuerat, diligenter inquireret; qui tandem, divino auxilio, facta extrema diligentia, in mari oceano navigantes, certas insulas remotissimas, et etiam terras firmas,[11] que per alios hactenus reperte non fuerant, invenerunt, in quibus quamplurime gentes, pacifice viventes, et, ut asseritur, nudi incedentes, nec carnibus vescentes, inhabitant; et, ut prefati nuntii vestri possunt opinari, gentes ipse in insulis et terris predictis habitantes credunt unum Deum Creatorem in celis esse, ac ad fidem Catholicam amplexandum et bonis moribus imbuendum satis apti videntur, spesque habetur quod, si erudirentur, nomen Salvatoris, Domini nostri Jhesu Christi, in terris et insulis predictis facile induceretur; ac prefatus Cristophorus in una ex principalibus insulis predictis jam unam turrim[12] satis munitam, in qua certos Christianos qui secum iverant, in custodiam, et ut alias insulas et terras *firmas* remotas et incognitas inquirerent, posuit, construi et edificari fecit; in quibusquidem[13] insulis et terris jam repertis, aurum, aromata, et alie quamplurime res preciose diversi generis et diverse qualitatis reperiuntur. Unde omnibus diligenter, et presertim fidei Catholice exaltatione et dilatatione, prout decet Catholicos reges et principes, consideratis, more progenitorum vestrorum, clare memorie regum, terras *firmas* et insulas predictas illarumque incolas et habitatores, vobis, divina favente clementia, subjicere et ad fidem Catholicam reducere proposuistis. Nos igitur hujusmodi vestrum sanctum et laudabile propositum plurimum in Domino commendantes, ac cupientes ut illud ad debitum finem perducatur, et ipsum nomen

---

[*] The Vatican text reads *deducantur.*   [†] The Vatican text reads *tam.*
[‡] *Cf.* Doc. **5**, note 7.   [*] The Vatican text reads *duximus.*
[10] Note the several instances of the introduction of this adjective.
[11] *Cf.* Doc. **5**, note 8.   [12] *Cf. ibid.*, note 9.   [13] The Vatican text reads *quibusdam.*

Salvatoris nostri in partibus illis inducatur, hortamur vos plurimum in Domino, et per sacri lavacri susceptionem, qua mandatis apostolicis obligati estis, et viscera misericordie Domini nostri Jhesu Christi attente requirimus, ut [14] cum expeditionem hujusmodi omnino prosequi et assumere prona mente orthodoxe fidei zelo intendatis, populos in hujusmodi insulis *et terris* degentes ad Christianam *religionem* suscipiendam inducere velitis et debeatis, nec pericula, nec labores ullo unquam tempore vos deterreant, firma spe fiduciaque conceptis, quod Deus Omnipotens conatus vestros feliciter prosequetur. Et, ut tanti negotii provinciam apostolice gratie largitate donati liberius et audacius assumatis, motu proprio,[15] non ad vestram vel alterius pro vobis super hoc nobis oblate petitionis instanciam, sed de nostra mera liberalitate et ex certa scientia ac de apostolice potestatis plenitudine, omnes *insulas et terras firmas inventas et inveniendas, detectas et detegendas versus occidentem et meridiem,*[16] *fabricando et constituendo unam lineam*[17] *a polo Arctico scilicet septentrione ad polum Antarcticum scilicet meridiem, sive terre firme et insule invente et inveniende sint versus Indiam aut versus aliam quancunque partem, que linea distet a qualibet insularum, que vulgariter nuncupantur de los Azores et Caboverde, centum leucis*[18] *versus occidentem et meridiem, ita quod omnes insule et terre firme reperte et reperiende, detecte et detegende, a prefata linea versus occidentem et meridiem, per alium regem aut principem Christianum non fuerint actualiter possesse usque ad diem nativitatis domini nostri Jhesu Christi proxime preteritum a*[19] *quo incipit annus presens millesimus quadringentesimus nonagesimus tertius, quando fuerunt per nuntios et capitaneos vestros invente alique predictarum insularum,* auctoritate Omnipotentis Dei nobis in beato Petro concessa, ac vicariatus Jhesu Christi, qua fungimur in terris, cum omnibus illarum dominiis, civitatibus, castris, locis et villis, juribusque et jurisdictionibus ac pertinentiis universis, vobis heredibusque et successoribus vestris, Castelle et Legionis regibus, in perpetuum tenore presentium donamus, concedimus, et assignamus, vosque et heredes ac successores prefatos illarum dominos cum plena, libera, et omnimoda potestate, auctoritate, et jurisdictione, facimus, constituimus, et deputamus; decernentes nichilominus per hujusmodi donationem, concessionem, *et* assignationem nostram nulli Christiano principi, *qui actualiter prefatas insulas aut terras firmas possederit usque ad predictum diem Nativitatis Domini nostri Jhesu Christi,* jus quesitum sublatum intelligi posse aut auferri debere. Et insuper mandamus vobis in virtute sancte obedientie, ut, sicut etiam pollicemini et non dubitamus pro vestra maxima devotione et regia magnanimitate vos esse facturos, ad terras *firmas* et insulas predictas viros probos et Deum timentes, doctos, peritos, et expertos, ad instruendum incolas et habitatores prefatos in fide Catholica et bonis moribus imbuendum destinare

[14] The Vatican text reads *et.*   [15] *Cf.* Doc. **1**, note 38.
[16] Of the many commentaries on the phrase, "versus occidentem et meridiem", the best appears to be that of Vander Linden, in his article on "Alexander VI. and the Demarcation" in the *American Historical Review,* XXII. 1-20.
[17] It is highly probable that this line was suggested by Columbus. *Cf.* Dawson, *Lines of Demarcation,* pp. 491-493; and Vander Linden, *op cit.*
[18] A discussion of ancient and medieval measures of length, including the marine league, is in Dawson, *Lines of Demarcation,* pp. 502-517, 545, 546. Kretschmer calculates that, reckoning a league as equal to four Roman or Italian miles, each equal to about 1480 metres, and counting from San Antonio, the most westerly of the Cape Verde Islands, the longitude of the first demarcation line was 31° west. *Entdeckung,* p. 303.
[19] The Vatican text reads *in.*

debeatis, omnem debitam diligentiam in premissis adhibentes, ac quibuscunque personis cujuscunque dignitatis, *etiam imperialis et regalis*, status, gradus, ordinis, vel conditionis, sub excommunicationis late sententie pena, quam eo ipso si contrafecerint, incurrant, districtius inhibemus, ne ad insulas et terras *firmas, inventas et inveniendas, detectas et detegendas versus occidentem et meridiem, fabricando et constituendo lineam a polo Arctico ad polum Antarcticum, sive terre firme et insule invente et inveniende sint versus Indiam aut versus aliam quancunque partem, que linea distet a qualibet insularum, que vulgariter nuncupantur de los Azores et Caboverde, centum leucis versus occidentem et meridiem, ut prefertur,* pro mercibus habendis vel quavis alia de causa, accedere presumant absque vestra ac heredum et successorum vestrorum predictorum licentia speciali, non obstantibus constitutionibus et ordinationibus apostolicis, ceterisque contrariis quibuscunque, in Illo a quo imperia et dominationes ac bona cuncta procedunt confidentes, quod, dirigente Domino [20] actus vestros, si hujusmodi sanctum et laudabile *propositum* prosequamini, brevi tempore, cum felicitate et gloria totius populi Christiani, vestri labores et conatus exitum felicissimum consequentur. Verum, quia difficile foret presentes litteras ad singula queque loca in quibus expediens fuerit deferri, volumus, ac motu et scientia similibus decernimus, quod illarum transumptis manu publici notarii inde rogati subscriptis, et sigillo alicujus persone in ecclesiastica dignitate constitute, seu curie ecclesiastice munitis, ea prorsus fides in judicio et extra ac alias ubilibet adhibeatur, que presentibus adhiberetur, si essent exhibite vel ostense. Nulli ergo omnino hominum liceat hanc paginam nostre *commendationis*, ortationis, requisitionis, donationis, concessionis, assignationis, constitutionis, deputationis, *decreti*, mandati, inhibitionis, *et* voluntatis, infringere, vel ei ausu temerario contraire. Si quis autem hoc attemptare presumpserit, indignationem Omnipotentis Dei ac beatorum Petri et Pauli apostolorum ejus se noverit incursurum.

Datum Rome apud Sanctum Petrum, anno Incarnationis Dominice millesimo quadringentesimo nonagesimo tertio, quarto nonas Maii, pontificatus nostri anno primo.

Gratis de mandato sanctissimi Domini nostri pape.

Jun[io]. Pro r[eferenda]rio,   Pro Jo. Buf[olinus],[21]
      A. de Mucciarellis.   A. Santoseverino.[21]
            L. Podocatharus.

TRANSLATION.[22]

Alexander, bishop, servant of the servants of God, to the illustrious sovereigns, our very dear son in Christ, Ferdinand, king, and our very dear daughter in Christ, Isabella, queen of Castile, Leon, Aragon, Sicily, and Granada, health and apostolic benediction. Among other works well pleasing to the Divine Majesty and cherished of our heart, this assuredly ranks highest, that in our times especially the Catholic faith and the Christian religion be exalted and be everywhere increased and spread, that the health of souls be

---

[20] The Vatican text omits *Domino*.
[21] The reading of these names is due to Professor Vander Linden, whose article in the *American Historical Review*, XXII. 1-20, contains information concerning the signatories of this bull.
[22] See Doc. **5**, note 19.

cared for and that barbarous nations be overthrown and brought to the faith itself. Wherefore inasmuch as by the favor of divine clemency, we, though of insufficient merits, have been called to this Holy See of Peter, recognizing that as true Catholic kings and princes, such as we have known you always to be, and as your illustrious deeds already known to almost the whole world declare, you not only eagerly desire but with every effort, zeal, and diligence, without regard to hardships, expenses, dangers, with the shedding even of your blood, are laboring to that end; recognizing also that you have long since dedicated to this purpose your whole soul and all your endeavors—as witnessed in these times with so much glory to the Divine Name in your recovery of the kingdom of Granada from the yoke of the Saracens—we therefore are rightly led, and hold it as our duty, to grant you even of our own accord and in your favor those things whereby with effort each day more hearty you may be enabled for the honor of God himself and the spread of the Christian rule to carry forward your holy and praiseworthy purpose so pleasing to immortal God. We have indeed learned that you, who for a long time had intended to seek out and discover certain islands and mainlands remote and unknown and not hitherto discovered by others, to the end that you might bring to the worship of our Redeemer and the profession of the Catholic faith their residents and inhabitants, having been up to the present time greatly engaged in the siege and recovery of the kingdom itself of Granada were unable to accomplish this holy and praiseworthy purpose; but the said kingdom having at length been regained, as was pleasing to the Lord, you, with the wish to fulfill your desire, chose our beloved son, Christopher Columbus, a man assuredly worthy and of the highest recommendations and fitted for so great an undertaking, whom you furnished with ships and men equipped for like designs, not without the greatest hardships, dangers, and expenses, to make diligent quest for these remote and unknown mainlands and islands through the sea, where hitherto no one had sailed; and they at length, with divine aid and with the utmost diligence sailing in the ocean sea, discovered certain very remote islands and even mainlands that hitherto had not been discovered by others; wherein dwell very many peoples living in peace, and, as reported, going unclothed, and not eating flesh. Moreover, as your aforesaid envoys are of opinion, these very peoples living in the said islands and countries believe in one God, the Creator in heaven, and seem sufficiently disposed to embrace the Catholic faith and be trained in good morals. And it is hoped that, were they instructed, the name of the Savior, our Lord Jesus Christ, would easily be introduced into the said countries and islands. Also, on one of the chief of these aforesaid islands the said Christopher has already caused to be put together and built a fortress fairly equipped, wherein he has stationed as garrison certain Christians, companions of his, who are to make search for other remote and unknown islands and mainlands. In the islands and countries already discovered are found gold, spices, and very many other precious things of divers kinds and qualities. Wherefore, as becomes Catholic kings and princes, after earnest consideration of all matters, especially of the rise and spread of the Catholic faith, as was the fashion of your ancestors, kings of renowned memory, you have purposed with the favor of divine clemency to bring under your sway the said mainlands and islands with their residents and inhabitants and to bring them to the Catholic faith. Hence, heartily commending in the Lord this your holy and praiseworthy purpose, and desirous that it be duly accomplished, and that the name of our Savior be carried into those regions, we exhort you very earnestly in the Lord and by your reception of holy baptism, whereby you are bound to our apostolic commands, and by the bowels of the mercy of our Lord Jesus Christ, enjoin strictly, that inasmuch as with eager zeal for the true faith you design to equip and despatch this expedition, you purpose also, as is your duty, to lead the peoples dwelling in those islands and countries to embrace the Christian religion; nor at any time let dangers or hardships deter you therefrom, with the stout hope and trust in your hearts that Almighty God will further your undertakings. And, in order that you may enter upon so great an undertaking with greater readiness and heartiness endowed with the benefit of our apostolic favor, we, of our own accord, not at your instance nor the request of anyone else in your regard, but of our own sole largess and certain knowledge and out of the fullness of our apostolic power, by the authority of Almighty God conferred upon us in blessed Peter and of the vicarship of Jesus Christ, which we hold on earth, do by tenor of these presents, should any of said islands have been found by your envoys and captains, give, grant, and assign to you and your heirs and successors, kings of Castile and Leon, forever, together with all their dominions, cities, camps, places, and villages, and all rights, jurisdictions, and appurtenances, all islands and mainlands found and to be found, discovered and to be discovered towards the west and south, by drawing and establishing a line from the Arctic pole, namely the north, to the Antarctic pole, namely the south, no matter whether the said mainlands and islands are found and to be found in the direction of India or towards any other quarter, the said line to be distant one hundred leagues towards the west and south from any of the islands commonly known as the Azores and Cape Verde. With this proviso however that none of the islands and mainlands, found and to be found, discovered and to be discovered, beyond that said line towards the west and south, be in the actual possession of any Christian king or prince up to the birthday of our Lord Jesus Christ just past from which the present year one thousand four hundred and ninety-three begins. And we make, appoint, and depute you and your said heirs and successors lords of them with full and free power, authority, and jurisdiction of every kind; with this proviso however, that by this our gift, grant, and assignment no right acquired by any Christian prince, who may be in actual possession of said islands and mainlands prior to the said birthday of our Lord Jesus Christ, is hereby to be understood to be withdrawn or taken away. Moreover we command you in virtue of holy obedience that, employing all due diligence in the premises, as you also promise—nor do we doubt your compliance therein in accordance with your loyalty and royal greatness of spirit—you should appoint to the aforesaid mainlands and islands worthy, God-fearing, learned, skilled, and experienced men, in order to instruct the aforesaid inhabitants and residents in the Catholic faith and train them in good morals. Furthermore, under penalty of excommunication *late sententie* to be incurred *ipso facto,* should anyone thus contravene, we strictly forbid all persons of whatsoever rank, even imperial and royal, or of whatsoever estate, degree, order, or condition, to dare, without your special permit or that of your aforesaid heirs and successors, to go for the purpose of trade or any other reason to the islands or mainlands, found and to be found, discovered and to be discovered, towards the west and south, by drawing and establishing a line from the Arctic pole to the Antarctic pole, no matter whether the mainlands and islands, found and to be found, lie in the direction of India or toward any other quarter whatsoever, the said line to be distant one hundred leagues towards the west and south, as is aforesaid, from any of the islands commonly known as the Azores and Cape Verde; apostolic constitutions and ordinances and other decrees whatsoever to the contrary notwithstanding. We trust in Him from whom empires and governments and all good things proceed, that, should you, with the Lord's guidance, pursue this holy and praiseworthy undertaking, in a short while your hardships and endeavors will attain the most felicitous result, to the happiness and glory of all Christendom. But inasmuch as it would be difficult to have these present letters sent to all places where desirable, we wish, and with similar accord and knowledge do decree, that to copies of them, signed by the hand of a public notary commissioned therefor, and sealed with the seal of any ecclesiastical officer or ecclesiastical court, the same respect is to be shown in court and outside as well as anywhere else as would be given to these presents should they thus be exhibited or shown. Let no one, therefore, infringe, or with rash boldness contravene, this our recommendation, exhortation, requisition, gift, grant, assignment, constitution, deputation, decree, mandate, prohibition, and will. Should anyone presume to attempt this, be it known to him that he will incur the wrath of Almighty God and of the blessed apostles Peter and Paul. Given at Rome, at St. Peter's, in the year of the incarnation of our Lord one thousand four hundred and ninety-three, the fourth of May, and the first year of our pontificate.

Gratis by order of our most holy lord, the pope.

June. For the referendary,   For J. Bufolinus,
       A. de Mucciarellis.   A. Santoseverino.
                L. Podocatharus.

8.

The Bull Dudum Siquidem (*Alexander VI.*). *September 26, 1493.*

INTRODUCTION.

Not long after the interview of March 9, 1493, between Columbus and John II. of Portugal,[1] the latter caused an armada to be fitted out to take possession of the lands found by Columbus. A report[2] of these hostile preparations having reached the Spanish sovereigns they at once despatched Lope de Herrera to the Portuguese court to request that ambassadors be sent them, and that the caravels should not sail, or Portuguese subjects go to those parts, until it should be determined within whose seas the discoveries lay.

Meanwhile the King of Portugal had sent Ruy de Sande to the Spanish sovereigns to entreat them (among other things) to prohibit their subjects from fishing south of Cape Bojador till the limits of the possessions of both kingdoms should be fixed, and to make these limits the parallel of the Canaries, leaving the navigation south of this line to the Portuguese.[3] In the middle of August the Portuguese ambassadors, Pero Diaz and Ruy de Pina, arrived in Barcelona, and an attempt at settlement was made. In the midst of the negotiations the Spanish sovereigns appealed to the Pope, who, on September 26, granted them a fourth bull, which confirmed the bull *Inter caetera* of May 4,[4] extended it so as to secure to Spain any lands discovered by her in her westward navigations, even though they should be in the eastern regions and belong to India, excluded the subjects of all other crowns from navigating or fishing or exploring in those parts, without license from Spain, and revoked all the earlier papal grants to Portugal which might seem to give her a claim to lands not already actually possessed by her in those regions.

BIBLIOGRAPHY.

Texts: **MS.** Two original manuscripts of the promulgated bull, written on parchment and with the leaden seal affixed, are in the Archives of the Indies at Seville, Patronato, 1-1-1, nos. 2 and 5. A manuscript copy,

[1] See introduction to Doc. **1.**
[2] The report came from the Duke of Medina-Sidonia. A letter in respect to this from the sovereigns to the duke, dated May 2, 1493, is printed in Navarrete, *Viages*, tom. II., no. 16, pp. 22-23.
[3] Las Casas quotes Columbus as stating that King John " said that there was mainland to the south ". J. E. Olson and E. G. Bourne, *Northmen, Columbus, and Cabot* (1906), p. 326. For these negotiations see Herrera, *Historia General*, dec. I., lib. II., c. 5; Zurita, *Historia*, tom. I., lib. I., c. 25; Muñoz, *Historia*, tom. I., lib., IV., § 26.
[4] Doc. **7.**

probably dating from the first years of the sixteenth century, is inserted at the beginning of a manuscript of the Columbus Codex, preserved in the Library of Congress. This bull has not been found in the Vatican registers, and it is a curious fact that neither of the original manuscripts of the promulgated bull bears the customary endorsement " Registrata ".

Texts: Printed. The text of the promulgated bull has been printed by J. de Solorzano Pereira, *De Indiarum Jure* (1629-1639), I. 613, and from this source in G. Berchet, *Fonti Italiane* (1892-1893), I. 15-16 (pt. III. of the *Raccolti di Documenti* published by the Reale Commissione Colombiana) ; S. E. Dawson, "Line of Demarcation of Pope Alexander VI.", etc. (1899), pp. 538-539, in the *Transactions* of the Royal Society of Canada, 2d ser., 1899-1900, vol. V., § 2 ; and J. B. Thacher, *Columbus* (1903-1904), II. 162-164. It has also been printed in the *Colección de Documentos Inéditos . . . de Ultramar*, 2d ser., tom. V., *Documentos Legislativos* (ed. A. M. Fabié, 1890-1897), I. 1-4.

Translations: A Spanish translation of the bull, made in 1554 by Gracian de Aldrete, secretary of Philip II., and printed in Navarrete, *Coleccion de Viages* (1825-1837), tom. II., app., pp. 404-406, has been erroneously supposed by several modern historians to be the basis of Solorzano's Latin text. The English translation in Blair and Robertson, *Philippine Islands* (1903-1909), I. 111-114, is from the Spanish version. Thacher's (*op. cit.*, II. 163-164) and Dawson's (*op. cit.*, pp. 539-540) are from Solorzano's text.

References: See under Doc. **9.**

TEXT.[a]

Alexander episcopus, servus servorum Dei: carissimo in Christo filio Ferdinando regi et carissime in Christo filie Elisabeth regine Castelle, Legionis, Aragonum, et Granate, illustribus, salutem et apostolicam benedictionem.

Dudum siquidem omnes et singulas insulas et terras firmas, inventas et inveniendas versus occidentem et meridiem, que sub actuali dominio temporali aliquorum dominorum Christianorum constitute non essent, vobis heredibusque et subcessoribus vestris Castelle et Legionis regibus, imperpetuum, motu proprio et ex certa scientia ac de apostolice potestatis plenitudine donavimus, concessimus, et assignavimus, vosque ac heredes et successores prefatos de illis investivimus, illarumque dominos cum plena, libera, et omnimoda potestate, auctoritate, et jurisdictione, constituimus et deputavimus, prout in nostris inde confectis litteris, quarum tenores, ac si de verbo ad verbum, presentibus insererentur haberi volumus pro sufficienter expressis, plenius continetur.[b] Cum autem contingere posset quod nuntii et capitanei aut vassalli vestri, versus occidentem aut meridiem navigantes, ad partes orientales applicarent, ac insulas et terras firmas que Indie fuissent vel essent, repperirent, nos, volentes etiam vos favoribus prosequi gratiosis, motu et scientia ac potestatis plenitudine similibus, donationem, concessionem, assignationem, et litteras predictas, cum omnibus et singulis in eisdem litteris contentis

---

[a] The text is from the original manuscript of the bull, preserved in the Archives of the Indies at Seville, Patronato, 1-1-1, no. 5.
[b] The reference is to the bull *Inter caetera* of May 4, Doc. **7.**

clausulis, ad omnes et singulas insulas et terras firmas, inventas et inveniendas ac detectas et detegendas, que navigando aut itinerando versus occidentem aut meridiem hujusmodi sint vel fuerint aut apparuerint, sive in partibus occidentalibus vel meridionalibus et orientalibus et Indie existant, auctoritate apostolica, tenore presentium, in omnibus et per omnia, perinde ac si in litteris predictis de eis plena et expressa mentio facta fuisset, extendimus pariter et ampliamus, vobis ac heredibus et successoribus vestris predictis, per vos vel alium seu alios, corporalem insularum ac terrarum predictarum possessionem, propria auctoritate libere apprehendendi ac perpetuo retinendi, illasque adversus quoscunque impedientes etiam defendendi, plenam et liberam facultatem concedentes, ac quibuscunque personis etiam cujuscunque dignitatis, status, gradus, ordinis, vel condicionis, sub excommunicationis late sententie pena, quam contrafacientes eo ipso incurrant, districtius inhibentes, ne ad partes predictas ad navigandum, piscandum,[1] vel inquirendum insulas vel terras firmas aut quovis alio respectu seu colore ire vel mittere quoquo modo presumant absque expressa et spetiali vestra ac heredum et successorum predictorum licentia, Non obstantibus constitutionibus et ordinationibus apostolicis, ac quibusvis donationibus, concessionibus, facultatibus, et assignationibus per nos vel predecessores nostros quibuscunque regibus, principibus, infantibus, aut quibusvis aliis personis aut ordinibus et miliciis,[2] de predictis partibus, maribus, insulis, atque terris, vel aliqua eorum parte, etiam ex quibusvis causis, etiam pietatis vel fidei aut redemptionis captivorum, et aliis quantuncunque urgentissimis, et cum quibusvis clausulis etiam derogatoriarum derogatoriis, fortioribus, efficacioribus, et insolitis, etiam quascunque sententias, censuras, et penas in se continentibus, que suum per actualem et realem possessionem non essent sortite effectum, licet forsan aliquando illi quibus donationes et concessiones hujusmodi facte fuissent, aut eorum nuntii, ibidem navigassent, quas tenores illarum etiam presentibus pro sufficienter expressis et insertis habentes, motu, scientia, et potestatis plenitudine similibus, omnino revocamus, ac quo ad terras et insulas per eos actualiter non possessas pro infectis haberi volumus, nec non omnibus illis que in litteris predictis voluimus non obstare, ceterisque contrariis quibuscunque. Datum Rome apud Sanctum Petrum, anno Incarnationis Dominice millesimo quadringentesimo nonagesimo tertio, sexto kalendas Octobris, pontificatus nostri anno secundo. Gratis de mandato sanctissimi domini nostri pape.

Jo[HANNES] NILIS.[9]   P. GORMAZ.[10]

Sept[embri].

---

[1] The reference to fishing is doubtless explained by the fact that Spain, yielding to the demands of Portugal, had just agreed to forbid her subjects to fish south of Cape Bojador. One of the two treaties between Spain and Portugal, concluded at Tordesillas on June 7, 1494, relates to the fisheries from Cape Bojador to the Rio do Ouro. This treaty is printed in J. Ramos-Coelhos, *Algs. Docs.* (1892), pp. 80 ff.

[2] This refers to the Portuguese military Order of Christ, to which Pope Calixtus had granted the spiritualities of Guinea, and beyond, as far as to the Indians. See Doc. **2**.

[9] *Cf.* Doc. **6**, note 14.

[10] In the second copy of the bull the name of L. Alvarus is substituted. The name of the pontifical secretary, L. Podocatharus, appears on the dorse of both copies of the bull.

TRANSLATION.[11]

Alexander, bishop, servant of the servants of God, to the illustrious sovereigns, his very dear son in Christ, Ferdinand, king, and his very dear daughter in Christ, Isabella, queen of Castile, Leon, Aragon, and Granada, health and apostolic benediction.

A short while ago of our own accord, and out of our certain knowledge, and fullness of our apostolic power, we gave, conveyed, and assigned forever to you and your heirs and successors, kings of Castile and Leon, all islands and mainlands whatsoever, discovered and to be discovered, toward the west and south, that were not under the actual temporal dominion of any Christian lords. Moreover, we invested therewith you and your aforesaid heirs and successors, and appointed and deputed you as lords of them with full and free power, authority, and jurisdiction of every kind, as more fully appears in our letters given to that effect, the terms whereof we wish to be understood as if they were inserted word for word in these presents. But since it may happen that your envoys and captains, or vassals, while voyaging toward the west or south, might bring their ships to land in eastern regions and there discover islands and mainlands that belonged or belong to India, with the desire moreover to bestow gracious favors upon you, through our similar accord, knowledge, and fullness of power, by apostolic authority and by tenor of these presents, in all and through all, just as if in the aforesaid letters full and express mention had been made thereof, we do in like manner amplify and extend our aforesaid gift, grant, assignment, and letters, with all and singular the clauses contained in the said letters, to all islands and mainlands whatsoever, found and to be found, discovered and to be discovered, that are or may be or may seem to be in the route of navigation or travel toward the west or south, whether they be in western parts, or in the regions of the south and east and of India. We grant to you and your aforesaid heirs and successors full and free power through your own authority, exercised through yourselves or through another or others, freely to take corporal possession of the said islands and countries and to hold them forever, and to defend them against whosoever may oppose. With this strict prohibition however to all persons, of no matter what rank, estate, degree, order or condition, that under penalty of excommunication *latae sententiae*, which such as contravene are to incur *ipso facto*, no one without your express and special license or that of your aforesaid heirs and successors shall, for no matter what reason or pretense, presume in any manner to go or send to the aforesaid regions for the purpose of navigating or of fishing, or of searching for islands or mainlands—notwithstanding apostolic constitutions and ordinances, and any gifts, grants, powers, and assignments of the aforesaid regions, seas, islands, and countries, or any portion of them, made by us or our predecessors to any kings, princes, infantes, or any other persons, orders, or knighthoods, for no matter what reasons, even for motives of charity or the faith, or the ransom of captives, or for other reasons, even the most urgent; notwithstanding also any repealing clauses, even though they are of the most positive, mandatory, and unusual character; and no matter what sentences, censures, and penalties of any kind they may contain; providing however these grants have not gone into effect through actual and real possession, even though it may have happened that

[11] See Doc. **5**, note 19.

the persons to whom such gifts and grants were made, or their envoys, sailed thither at some time through chance. Wherefore should any such gifts or grants have been made, considering their terms to have been sufficiently expressed and inserted in our present decree, we through similar accord, knowledge, and fullness of our power do wholly revoke them and as regards the countries and islands not actually taken into possession, we wish the grants to be considered as of no effect, notwithstanding what may appear in the aforesaid letters, or anything else to the contrary. Given at Rome, at St. Peter's, on the twenty-sixth day of September, in the year of the incarnation of our Lord one thousand four hundred and ninety-three, the second year of our pontificate.

Gratis by order of our most holy lord the Pope.

JOHANNES NILIS.   P. GORMAZ.

September.

9.

Treaty between Spain and Portugal concluded at Tordesillas, June 7, 1494. Ratification by Spain, July 2, 1494. [Ratification by Portugal, September 5, 1494.]

INTRODUCTION.

In the negotiations begun at Barcelona in the middle of August, 1493,[1] Spain insisted that just as her navigators would refrain from visiting the regions reserved to Portugal—which Spain described as the Madeiras, Azores, Cape Verde, and other islands discovered prior to 1479, and the region from the Canaries down towards Guinea—so the Portuguese must keep away from Spain's discoveries.[2] No agreement, however, could be reached, because, as the Spanish sovereigns wrote to Columbus, the Portuguese ambassadors were not informed as to what belonged to Spain.[3] Accordingly, in November, 1493, a magnificent embassy, headed by Garcia de Carvajal, brother of the Spanish ambassador in Rome, and Pedro de Ayala, was despatched to the Portuguese court; but it accomplished nothing. In March, 1494, the Portuguese commissioners, Ruy de Sousa, João de Sousa, his son, and Ayres de Almada, treated directly with the Spanish sovereigns in Medina del Campo. Portugal felt aggrieved by the papal bull,[4] which designated as the eastern limit of the Spanish demarcation a meridian only one hundred leagues west of the Azores or Cape Verde Islands. As their ships were continually sailing to these islands, the Portuguese considered the limits too narrow. They therefore wished another meridian to be agreed on, farther to the west, half-way between the Cape Verde Islands and the lands discovered by Columbus.[5] King John " was certain that within those limits famous lands and things must be found." This new line of demarcation was agreed to by Ferdinand and Isabella, and on June 7, at Tordesillas

---

[1] See introduction to Doc. **8**.   [2] Zurita, *Historia*, lib. I., c. 25.
[3] " Porque ellos no vienen informados de lo que es nuestro." Navarrete, *Viages*, tom. II., no. 71, p. 108.
[4] Doc. **7**.
[5] Zurita, *op. cit.*, lib. I., c. 29, ff. 35, 36. Harrisse suggests that the Portuguese had in view the acquisition of those islands in the northwest Atlantic fancifully displayed on the maps of Fra Mauro and other early cartographers. *Discovery of North America* (1892), pp. 57, 58. The voyages of Gaspar Corte-Real to the northwest lend some support to this suggestion but, according to Las Casas, the southwest was the special region in which at this time King John hoped to discover new lands. J. E. Olson and E. G. Bourne, *Northmen, Columbus, and Cabot* (1906), p. 326. There are a number of indications that both Spaniards and Portuguese coveted particularly the south Atlantic.

near Valladolid, the Spanish representatives, Don Enrique Enriques, Don Gutierre de Cardenas, and Dr. Rodrigo Maldonado, concluded a treaty with the above-mentioned plenipotentiaries of Portugal. According to this treaty all lands lying east of a meridian located 370 leagues west of the Cape Verde Islands, and discovered by Portugal, were to pertain to that country and all lands west of the line, discovered by Spain, were to pertain to Spain. If the sovereign of either country discovered lands within the bounds assigned to the other, he must surrender them to the other monarch. Within ten months after the date of the treaty each party was to send one or two caravels with pilots, astrologers, and mariners (the same number on each side) to assemble at the Grand Canary, sail to the Cape Verde Islands and thence west to determine the boundary; if the line should intersect land, boundary towers or marks were to be erected. Spanish ships crossing the Portuguese seas east of the line must follow the most direct route to their destination. Lands discovered by Spain within the twenty days next following the conclusion of the treaty were to belong to Portugal if situated within the first 250 leagues west of the Cape Verde Islands, otherwise to Spain. The pope was asked to confirm the treaty upon the request of either or both parties thereto.

Since in the then existing state of knowledge it was impossible to determine the position of the delimiting meridian, the treaty led to further disagreements and its interpretation has been a matter of dispute down to modern times. At different periods, in accordance with her changing interests, Portugal claimed now one and now another of the Cape Verde group as the point of departure for measurement westwards. Another debated question was the number of leagues in a degree.[*]

BIBLIOGRAPHY.

Text: MS. The original manuscript of the ratification signed by Ferdinand and Isabella at Arévalo, July 2, 1494, is in the National Archives at Lisbon, gav. 17, maço 2, no. 24. The original manuscript of the ratification signed by John II. at Setubal on September 5, 1494, is in the Archives of the Indies, " Legajo escogido ".

Text: Printed. J. Ramos-Coelho, *Alguns Documentos* (1892), pp. 69-80; G. F. von Martens, *Supplément au Recueil des Traités* (1802, etc.), I. 372-388; C. Calvo, *Receuil des Traités* (1862-1866), I. 19-36; J. F. Pacheco *et al.*, *Coleccion de Documentos Inéditos* (1864-1884), XXX. 258-285; M. Fernandez de Navarrete, *Coleccion de Viages* (1825-1837), II. 130-143, and thence in J. B. Thacher, *Columbus* (1903-1904), II. 165-175; *Boletín del Centro de Estudios Americanistas*, año III., no. 7. This treaty is also contained in the official collections of treaties of some

---

[*] For an account of the knowledge of nautical astronomy in Portugal at this time, see J. Bensaude, *L'Astronomie Nautique au Portugal à l'Époque des Grandes Découvertes* (1912), and the *Collection de Documents*, relative to this subject, now being published under his direction by order of the Portuguese ministry of public instruction.

of the South American states, and in various publications of those states dealing with boundary disputes. There are many differences between these abovementioned texts, due in some cases to the modernizing of the language, and in some cases, apparently, to the fact that they are translations from Portuguese into Spanish.

Translation: English. Thacher, *op. cit.*, II. 175-186; Argentine Republic, *Arbitration upon a Part of the National Territory of Misiones*, I. *Argentine Evidence* (1893), pp. 13-24, and thence in the *Report* of the American Historical Association for 1895, pp. 524-534. The most important parts of the treaty are translated in E. H. Blair and J. A. Robertson, *Philippine Islands* (1903-1909), I. 115-129.

References: Contemporary and early writings. Documents in Navarrete, *op. cit.*, tom. II., nos. 16 (p. 22), 50 (p. 76), 54 (p. 78), 63 (p. 91), 67 (p. 96), 68 (p. 97), 69 (p. 106), 71 (p. 108), 79 (p. 154). Ruy de Pina, *Chronica d'El Rei Joaõ II.*, in J. F. Corrêa da Serra, *Collecçaõ de Livros Ineditos de Historia Portugueza* (pub. by the Acad. Real das Sciencias, Lisbon, 1790, etc.), tom. II., c. 66; Garcia de Resende, *Chronica de D. Joam II.* (1752), cc. 166-168; J. de Barros, *Da Asia*, I. (1778), dec. I., liv. III., c. 11 ; G. Zurita, *Historia del Rey Don Hernando* (1580), tom. I., lib. I., cc. 25, 29 ; A. de Herrera, *Historia General de los Hechos de los Castellanos* (1730), tom. I., dec. I., lib. II., cc. 5, 8, 10 ; Viscount de Santarem, *Quadro Elementar* (1842-1876), I. 392-393.

References: Later writings. J. B. Muñoz, *Historia del Nuevo-Mundo* (1793), tom. I., lib. IV., §§ 26-30; H. Schäfer, *Geschichte von Portugal* (1836-1854), III. 162-163, in Heeren and Ukert, *Geschichte der Europäischen Staaten*; H. Harrisse, *Diplomatic History of America* (1897), chs. 7 and following ; S. E. Dawson, " Line of Demarcation of Pope Alexander VI.", etc. (1899), pp. 496-526, in the *Transactions* of the Royal Society of Canada, 2d ser., 1899-1900, vol. V., § 2 ; E. G. Bourne, *Essays in Historical Criticism* (1901), pp. 201-203 ; H. Vander Linden, " Alexander VI. and the Demarcation of the Maritime and Colonial Domains of Spain and Portugal ", *Am. Hist. Rev.*, XXII. 1-20.

TEXT.[1]

Don Fernando e Doña Ysabel, por la graçia de Dios rrey e rreyna de Castilla, de Leon, de Aragon, de Seçilia, de Granada, de Toledo, de Valençia, de Galizia, de Mallorcas, de Sevilla, de Cerdeña, de Cordova, de Corçega, de Murçia, de Jahen, del Algarbe, de Algezira, de Gibraltar, de las yslas de Canaria, conde e condesa de Barçelona e señores de Vizcaya e de Molina, duques de Atenas e de Neopatria, condes de Rosellon e de Çerdania, marqueses de Oristan e de Goçeano, en uno con el Prinçipe Don Juan, nuestro muy caro e muy amado hijo primogenito, heredero de los dichos nuestros rreynos e señorios. Por quanto por Don Enrrique Enrriques,[2] nuestro mayordomo

---

[1] The text is from the original manuscript of the ratification by Ferdinand and Isabella, in the National Archives at Lisbon, gav. 17, maço 2, no. 24.

[2] Son of the Admiral Don Fadrique Enriques. His family history is given by Dr. Lorenzo Galindez de Carvajal (*cf.* Doc. **13**, note 17) in his *Adiciones Genealógicas*, published in Navarrete's *Coleccion de Documentos Inéditos para la Historia de España*, tom. XVIII., pp. 454 ff.

mayor, e Don Gutierre de Cardenas, commisario mayor de Leon, nuestro
contador mayor,⁹ y el Doctor Rodrigo Maldonado,¹⁰ todos del nuestro consejo,
fue tratado, asentado, e capitulado por nos y en nuestro nonbre e por virtud
de nuestro poder, con el Serenisimo Don Juan, por la graçia de Dios rrey de
Portugal e de los Algarbes de aquende e alende el mar en Africa, señor de
Guinea, nuestro muy caro e muy amado hermano, e con Ruy de Sosa, señor
de Usagres e Berengel, e Don Juan de Sosa su hijo, almotaçen mayor ¹¹ del
dicho Serenisimo Rey, nuestro hermano, e Arias de Almadana, corregidor
de los fechos çeviles de su corte ¹² e del su desenbargo,¹³ todos del consejo
del dicho Serenisimo Rey nuestro hermano, en su nonbre e por virtud de su
poder sus enbaxadores, que a nos vinieron sobre la diferençia de lo que a
nos y al dicho Serenisimo Rey nuestro hermano pertenesçe de lo que hasta
siete dias deste mes de Junio, en que estamos, de la fecha desta escriptura,
esta por descubrir en el mar oçeano; en la qual dicha capitulaçion los dichos
nuestros procuradores, entre otras cosas, prometieron que dentro de çierto
termino en ella contenido, nos ·otorgariamos, confirmariamos, jurariamos,
ratificariamos, e aprovariamos la dicha capitulaçion por nuestras personas ;
e nos, queriendo complir e cunpliendo todo lo que asi en nuestro nonbre fue
asentado e capitulado e otorgado çerca de lo suso dicho, mandamos traer
ante nos la dicha escriptura de la dicha capitulaçion e asiento para la ver e
esaminar, e el tenor della *de verbo ad verbum* es este que se sigue:

En el nonbre de Dios Todo poderoso, Padre e Fijo e Espiritu Santo, tres
personas rrealmente distintas e apartadas e una sola esençia divina. Manifiesto e notorio sea a todos quantos este publico ynstrumento vieren, como
en la villa de Tordesillas, a siete dias del mes de Junio, año del nasçimiento
de nuestro Señor Jhesu Christo de mill e quatroçientos e noventa e quatro
años, en presençia de nos, los secretarios y escrivanos e notarios publicos de
, yuso escriptos, estando presentes los honrrados Don Enrrique Enrriques,
mayordomo mayor de los muy altos e muy poderosos prinçipes, los señores
Don Fernando e Doña Isabel, por la graçia de Dios rrey e rreyna de Castilla,
de Leon, de Aragon, de Seçilia, de Granada, etc., Don Gutierre de Cardenas,
contador mayor de los dichos señores rrey e rreyna, e el Doctor Rodrigo
Maldonado, todos del consejo de los dichos señores Rey e Reyna de Castilla,
e de Leon, de Aragon, de Seçilia e de Granada, etc., sus procuradores bastantes
de la una parte, e los honrrados Ruy de Sosa, señor de Usagres e Berengel,

---

⁹ The *contadores mayores,* who at this time numbered two, were the heads of the
financial administration of Spain. For a full account of their functions see " Organi-
zación de la Hacienda en la Primera Mitad del Siglo XVI°" in F. de Laiglesia,
Estudios Históricos, 1515-1555 (Madrid, 1908).

¹⁰ He had been sent to Portugal in 1479 to negotiate the treaty of Alcaçovas. See Doc.
3, introduction.

¹¹ It was the business of the *almotacé mór* to supply the Portuguese court with provisions, and to see that the roads over which the sovereign had to travel were in order.
H. da Gama Barros, *Historia da Administração Publica em Portugal nos Seculos XII.
a XV.* (1885-1896), I. 602-603.

¹² The *corregedor da corte* was a magistrate who exercised in the place where the King
of Portugal was, the police, administrative, and judicial functions exercised by the
local *corregedores.* A few years before the date of this treaty, the single *corregedor da
corte* was replaced by two *corregedores,* of whom one took cognizance of civil, the other
of criminal, causes. Gama Barros, *op. cit.,* I. 603, 604.

¹³ The *desembargo d'el rei* was a kind of privy-council, whose members were generally
lawyers. *Ibid.,* p. 593.

e Don Juan de Sosa, su hijo, almotaçen mayor del muy alto e muy exçelente
señor, el señor Don Juan, por la graçia de Dios rrey de Portugal e de los
Algarbes de aquende e de allende el mar en Africa, e señor de Guinea, e
Arias de Almadana, corregidor de los fechos çeviles en su corte, e del su
desenbargo, todos del consejo del dicho señor Rey de Portugal, e sus enbaxadores e procuradores bastantes, segund amas las dichas partes lo mostraron
por las cartas de poderes e procuraçiones de los dichos señores sus constituyentes, de las quales su tenor *de verbo ad verbum* es este que se sigue:

[Here follow the full powers granted by Ferdinand and Isabella to
Don Enrique Enriques, Don Gutierre de Cardenas, and Dr. Rodrigo
Maldonado on June 5, 1494; and the full powers granted by João II. to
Ruy de Sousa, João de Sousa, and Arias d'Almadana on March 8, 1494.]

E luego los dichos procuradores de los dichos señores Rey e Reyna de
Castilla, de Leon, de Aragon, de Seçilia, de Granada, etc., e del dicho señor
Rey de Portugal e de los Algarbes, etc., dixeron:

[1.] Que, por quanto entre los dichos señores, sus constituyentes, ay
çierta diferençia sobre lo que a cada una de las dichas partes perteneçe de lo
que fasta oydia, de la fecha desta capitulaçion, esta por descubrir en el mar
oçeano, porende que ellos por bien de paz e concordia, e por conservaçion del
debdo e amor quel dicho señor Rey de Portugal tiene con los dichos señores
Rey e Reyna de Castilla e de Aragon, etc., a sus Altezas plaze, e los dichos
sus procuradores en su nonbre e por virtud de los dichos sus poderes otorgaron
e consintieron que se haga e señale por el dicho mar oçeano una rraya o linea
derecha de polo a polo, conviene a saber, del polo Artico al polo Antartico,
que es de norte a sul, la qual rraya o linea se aya de dar e de derecha, como
dicho es, a tresientas e setenta leguas de las Yslas del Cabo Verde, hasia la
parte del poniente,[14] por grados o por otra manera, como mejor y mas presto
se pueda dar, de manera que no sean mas, e que todo lo que hasta aqui se ha
fallado e descubierto e de aqui adelante se hallare e descubriere por el
dicho señor Rey de Portugal y por sus navios, asy yslas, como tierra firme,
desde la dicha rraya e linea, dada en la forma suso dicha, yendo por la dicha
parte del levante dentro de la dicha rraya a la parte del levante, o del norte,
o del sul della, tanto que no sea atravesando la dicha rraya, que esto sea
e finque e pertenesca al dicho señor Rey de Portugal e a sus subçesores para
sienpre jamas; e que todo lo otro, asi yslas, como tierra firme, halladas y
por hallar, descubiertas y por descubrir, que son o fueren halladas por los
dichos señores Rey e Reyna de Castilla e de Aragon, etc., e por sus navios,
desde la dicha rraya, dada en la forma susodicha, yendo por la dicha parte
del poniente, despues de pasada la dicha rraya, hasia el poniente, o el norte,

---

[14] A meridian 370 leagues west of San Antonio, the most westerly of the Cape Verde
Islands, is in about 46° W. longitude; *i. e.*, east of the mouth of the Gurupy River. The
question where, in 1494, the Spanish and Portuguese governments supposed the line
to fall is elaborately discussed by Harrisse, *Diplomatic History*, and Dawson, *Line of
Demarcation*. From both the Portuguese and the Spanish maps of the early sixteenth
century, it appears that it was then believed that the line passed west of Newfoundland
(Baccallaos). Columbus and his heirs never assented to the new line, which, on account
of its more westerly position, deprived him of part of the region in which he had been
granted important rights. See Harrisse's introduction to B. F. Stevens, *Christopher
Columbus: his own Book of Privileges, 1502* (1893), pp. lviii, lix. For the methods
employed at this time to determine latitude and longitude, see the works edited and
written by J. Bensaude, and referred to above, note 6.

o el sul della, que todo sea e finque e pertenesca a los dichos señores Rey e Reyna de Castilla e de Leon, etc., e a sus subçesores para sienpre jamas.

[2.] Yten, los dichos procuradores prometieron e seguraron, por virtud de los dichos poderes, que de oy en adelante no enbiaran navios algunos, conviene a saber : los dichos señores Rey e Reyna de Castilla, e de Leon, e de Aragon, etc., por esta parte de la rraya a la parte del levante aquende de la dicha rraya, que queda para el dicho señor Rey de Portugal e de los Algarbes, etc., ni el dicho señor Rey de Portugal a la otra parte de la dicha rraya que queda para los dichos señores Rey e Reyna de Castilla, e de Aragon, etc., a descubrir e buscar tierras ni yslas algunas, ni a contratar, ni rrescatar, ni conquistar en manera alguna ; pero que, si acaesçiere que, yendo asi aquende de la dicha rraya, los dichos navios de los dichos señores Rey e Reyna de Castilla, de Leon, de Aragon, etc., hallasen qualesquier yslas o tierras en lo que asi queda para el dicho señor Rey de Portugal, que aquello tal sea e finque para el dicho señor Rey de Portugal e para sus herederos para sienpre jamas ; e sus Altezas gelo ayan de mandar luego dar e entregar. E si los navios del dicho señor Rey de Portugal hallaren qualesquier yslas e tierras en la parte de los dichos señores Rey e Reyna de Castilla, e de Leon, e Aragon, etc., que todo lo tal sea e finque para los dichos señores Rey e Reyna de Castilla, de Leon, e de Aragon, etc., e para sus herederos para sienpre jamas ; e que el dicho señor Rey de Portugal gelo aya luego de mandar dar e entregar.

[3.] Yten, para que la dicha linea o rraya de la dicha partiçion se aya de dar e de derecha e la mas çierta que ser pudiere por las dichas tresientas e setenta leguas de las dichas yslas del Cabo Verde hasia la parte del poniente, como dicho es, es concordado e asentado por los dichos procuradores de anbas las dichas partes, que dentro de diez meses primeros siguientes, contados desde el dia de la fecha desta capitulaçion, los dichos señores sus constituyentes ayan de enbiar dos o quatro caravelas, conviene a saber, una o dos de cada parte, o mas o menos, segund se acordare por las dichas partes que son neçesarias, las quales para el dicho tienpo sean juntas en la ysla de la Grand Canaria, y enbien en ellas cada una de las dichas partes, personas, asi pilotos como astrologos y marineros y qualesquier otras personas que convengan, pero que sean tantos de una parte, como de otra ; y que algunas personas de los dichos pilotos e astrologos e marineros e personas que sepan que enbiaren los dichos señores Rey e Reyna de Castilla e de Leon, de Aragon, etc., vayan en el navio o navios, que enbiare el dicho señor Rey de Portugal e de los Algarbes, etc.; e asi mismo algunas de las dichas personas que enbiare el dicho señor Rey de Portugal vayan en el navio o navios, que enbiaren los dichos señores Rey e Reyna de Castilla e Aragon, tantos de una parte como de otra, para que juntamente puedan mejor ver e rreconoscer la mar e los rrumos e vientos e grados de sol e norte e señalar las leguas sobredichas, tanto que para faser el señalamiento e limite convirran todos juntos los que fueren en los dichos navios que enbiaren amas las dichas partes e llevaren sus poderes ; [19] los quales dichos navios todos juntamente continuen su camino a las dichas yslas del Cabo Verde, e desde alli tomaran surrota derecha al poniente hasta las dichas tresientas e setenta leguas, medidas como las dichas personas, que asi fueren, acordaren que se deven medir, sin perjuisio de las dichas partes ; y alli donde se acabaren se haga el punto e señal que convenga por grados de sol o de norte, o por singradura de leguas, o como mejor se

---

[19] This stipulation was not carried out. See introduction to Doc. **10.**

pudieren concordar. La qual dicha rraya señalen desde el dicho polo artico
al dicho polo antartico, que es de norte a sul, como dicho es, y aquello que
señalaren lo escrivan e firmen de sus nonbres las dichas personas, que asi
fueren embiadas por amas las*dichas partes, las quales han de llevar facultad
e poderes de las dichas partes, cada uno de la suya, para haser la dicha señal
e limitaçion y fecha por ellos, seyendo todos comformes que sea avida por
señal e limitaçion perpetuamente para sienpre jamas, para que las dichas
partes, ni alguna dellas, ni sus subçesores para sienpre jamas no la puedan
contradezir, ni quitar, ni rremover en tiempo alguno, ni por alguna manera
que sea o ser pueda. E sy caso fuere que la dicha rraya e limite de polo a
polo, como dicho es, tocare en alguna ysla o tierra firme, que al comienço de
la tal ysla o tierra, que asi fuere hallada, donde tocare la dicha rraya, se
haga alguna señal o torre, e que en derecho de la tal señal o torre se continue
dend en adelante otras señales por la tal ysla o tierra, en derecho de la dicha
rraya, las quales partan lo que a cada una de las partes pertenesçiere della,
e que los subditos de las dichas partes no sean osados los unos de pasar a la
parte de los otros, ni los otros de los otros pasando la dicha señal o limite en
la tal ysla o tierra.

[4.] Yten, por quanto para yr los dichos navios de los dichos señores
Rey e Reyna de Castilla, de Leon, de Aragon, etc., desde sus rreynos e señorios
a la dicha su parte allende de la dicha rraya, en la manera que dicho es, es
forçado que ayan de pasar por las mares desta parte de la rraya que quedan
para el dicho señor Rey de Portugal, porende es concordado y asentado que
los dichos navios de los dichos señores Rey e Reyna de Castilla, de Leon,
de Aragon, etc., puedan yr e venir e vayan e vengan libre, segura, e paçifi-
camente, sin contradiçion alguna por las dichas mares que quedan con el
dicho señor Rey de Portugal dentro de la dicha rraya, en todo tiempo, y
cada e quando sus Altezas y sus subçesores quisieren, e por bien tovieren; los
quales vayan por sus caminos derechos e rrotas desde sus rreynos para
qualquier parte de lo que esta dentro de su rraya e limite, donde quisieren
enbiar a descobrir e conquistar, e a contratar, e que lleven sus caminos
derechos por donde ellos acordaren de yr, para qualquier cosa de la dicha su
parte, e de aquellos no puedan apartarse, salvo lo que el tienpo contrario
les fisiere apartar, tanto que no tomen ni ocupen, antes de pasar la dicha rraya,
cosa alguna de lo que fuere fallado por el dicho señor Rey de Portugal en la
dicha su parte; e si alguna cosa hallaren los dichos sus navios antes de pasar
la dicha rraya, como dicho es, que aquello sea para el dicho señor Rey de
Portugal e sus Altezas gelo ayan de mandar luego dar e entregar. E porque
podria ser que los navios e gentes de los dichos señores Rey e Reyna de
Castilla, e de Aragon, etc., o por su parte, avran hallado hasta veynte dias
deste mes de Junio, en que estamos, de la fecha desta capitulaçion, algunas
yslas e tierra firme dentro de la dicha rraya que se ha de faser de polo a
polo, por linea derecha, en fin de las dichas tresientas e setenta leguas,
contadas desde las dichas yslas del Cabo Verde al poniente, como dicho es,
es concordado e asentado, por quitar toda dubda, que todas las yslas e tierra
firme que sean halladas e descubiertas en qualquier manera hasta los dichos
veynte dias deste dicho mes de Junio, aun que sean halladas por los navios
e gentes de los dichos señores Rey e Reyna de Castylla e de Aragon, etc.,
con tanto que sea dentro de las dosientas e çinquenta leguas primeras de las
dichas trezientas e setenta leguas, contandolas desde las dichas yslas del Cabo
Verde al poniente hasia la dicha rraya, en qualquier parte dellas para los

dichos polos que sean halladas dentro de las dichas dosientas e çinquenta leguas hasiendose una rraya, o linea derecha de polo a polo donde se acabaren las dichas dosientas e çinquenta leguas, queden e finquen para el dicho señor Rey de Portugal e de los Algarbes, etc., e para sus subçesores e rreynos para sienpre jamas. E que todas las yslas e tierra firme que hasta los dichos veynte dias deste mes de Junio, en que estamos, sean falladas e descubiertas por los navios de los dichos señores Rey e Reyna de Castilla e de Aragon, etc., e por sus gentes, o en otra qualquier manera, dentro de las otras çiento e veynte leguas, que quedan para cunplimiento de las dichas trezientas e setenta leguas, en que ha de acabar la dicha rraya que se ha de faser de polo a polo, como dicho es, en qualquier parte de las dichas çiento e veynte leguas para los dichos polos, que sean halladas fasta el dicho dia, queden e finquen para los dichos señores Rey e Reyna de Castilla e de Aragon, etc., e para sus subçesores e sus rreynos para sienpre jamas, como es e ha de ser suyo lo que es o fuere hallado, allende de la dicha rraya de las dichas trezientas e setenta leguas que quedan para sus Altezas, como dicho es, aun que las dichas çiento e veynte leguas son dentro de la dicha rraya de las dichas trezientas e setenta leguas que quedan para el dicho señor Rey de Portugal e de los Algarbes, etc., como dicho es. E si fasta los dichos veynte dias deste dicho mes de Junio no son hallados por los dichos navios de Sus Altezas cosa alguna dentro de las dichas çiento e veynte leguas, y de alli adelante lo hallaren, que sea para el dicho señor Rey de Portugal, como en el capitulo suso escripto es contenido.

Lo qual todo que dicho es, e cada una cosa e parte dello, los dichos Don Enrrique Enrriques, mayordomo mayor, e Don Gutierre de Cardenas, contador mayor, e Doctor Rodrigo Maldonado, procuradores de los dichos muy altos e muy poderosos prinçipes, los señores el Rey e la Reyna de Castilla, de Leon, de Aragon, de Seçilia, e de Granada, etc., e por virtud del dicho su poder que de suso va encorporado, e los dichos Ruy de Sosa e Don Juan de Sosa su hijo e Arias de Almadana, procuradores e enbaxadores del dicho muy alto e muy exçelente prinçipe el señor Rey de Portugal e de los Algarbes de aquende e allende en Africa, señor de Guinea, e por virtud del dicho su poder, que de suso va encorporado, prometieron e seguraron, en nonbre de los dichos sus constituyentes, que ellos e sus subçesores e rreynos e señorios para sienpre jamas ternan e guardaran e conpliran rrealmente e con efecto, çesante todo fraude e cautela, engaño, ficçion, e simulaçion, todo lo contenido en esta capitulaçion, e cada una cosa e parte dello, e quisieron e otorgaron que todo lo contenido en esta dicha capitulaçion, e cada una cosa e parte dello, sea guardado e conplido e esecutado, como se ha de guardar e conplir e esecutar todo lo contenido en la capitulaçion de las pases fechas e asentadas entre los dichos señores Rey e Reyna de Castilla e de Aragon, etc., e el señor Don Alfonso Rey de Portugal, que santa gloria aya, e el dicho señor Rey, que agora es de Portugal, su fijo, seyendo prinçipe, el año que paso, de mill e quatroçientos e setenta e nueve años ; [16] e so aquellas mismas penas, vinculos, e firmezas e obligaçiones, segund e de la manera que en la dicha capitulaçion de las dichas pazes se contiene, e obligaronse que las dichas partes ni alguna dellas, ni sus subçesores para sienpre jamas, no yran ni vernan contra lo que de suso es dicho y espaçificado ; ni contra cosa alguna ni parte dello, directe ni yndirecte, ni por otra manera alguna en tienpo alguno, ni por alguna manera, pensada o no pensada, que sea o ser pueda, so las penas contenidas en la dicha capitulaçion de las dichas pases, e la pena pagada o non pagada, o

---

[16] The treaty of Alcaçovas, Doc. **3**.

7

graçiosamente rremetida, que esta obligaçion e capitulaçion e asiento quede
e finque firme, estable, e valedera para sienpre jamas; para lo qual todo asy
tener e guardar e cunplir e pagar los dichos procuradores, en nonbre de los
dichos sus constituyentes, obligaron los bienes, cada uno de la dicha su parte,
muebles e rrayes, patrimoniales e fiscales, e de sus subditos e vasallos, avidos
e por aver; e renunçiaron qualesquier leys e derechos de que se puedan
aprovechar las dichas partes e cada una dellas, para yr o venir contra lo
suso dicho o contra alguna parte dello, e por mayor seguridad e firmeza de
lo susodicho, juraron a Dios e a Santa Maria e a la señal de la Cruz, en que
pusieron sus manos derechas, e a las palabras de los Santos Evangelios do
quiere que mas largamente son escriptos, en anima de los dichos sus constituyentes, que ellos y cada uno dellos ternan e guardaran e cunpliran todo
lo suso dicho, y cada una cosa e parte dello, rrealmente e con efeto, cesante
todo fraude, cautela, e engaño, ficçion, e simulaçion, e no lo contradiran en
tienpo alguno, ni por alguna manera. So el qual dicho juramento juraron
de no pedir absoluçion ni rrelaxaçion del a nuestro muy Santo Padre, ni a
otro ningund legado ni prelado que gela pueda dar, e aun que propio motu
gela den, no usaran della, antes por esta presente capitulaçion suplican en el
dicho nonbre a nuestro muy Santo Padre, que a Su Santidad plega confirmar
e aprovar esta dicha capitulaçion, segund en ella se contiene e mandando
expedir sobre ello sus bullas a las partes, o a qualquier dellas que las pidieren;
e mandando encorporar en ellas el tenor desta capitulaçion, poniendo sus
çensuras a los que contra ella fueren o pasaren en qualquier tienpo que sea
o ser pueda; [17] e asi mismo los dichos procuradores en el dicho nonbre se
obligaron so la dicha pena e juramento, que dentro de çiento dias primeros
siguientes, contados desde el dia de la fecha desta capitulaçion, daran la
una parte a la otra, y la otra a la otra, aprovaçion e rratificaçion desta dicha
capitulaçion, escriptas en pergamino e firmadas de los nonbres de los dichos
señores sus constituyentes e selladas con sus sellos de plomo pendiente; e
en la escriptura que ovieren de dar los dichos señores Rey e Reyna de Castilla
e Aragon, etc., aya de firmar e consentir e otorgar el muy esclarescido e
yllustrisimo señor el señor prinçipe Don Juan su hijo, de lo qual todo que
dicho es, otorgaron dos escripturas de un tenor, tal la una como la otra, las
quales firmaron de sus nonbres e las otorgaron ante los secretarios e escrivanos
de yuso escriptos, para cada una de las partes la suya, e qualquiera que
paresçier vala, como si anbas a dos paresçiesen; que fueron fechas e otorgadas
en la dicha villa de Tordesillas, el dicho dia e mes e año suso dichos. El
comisario mayor,[18] Don Enrrique, Ruy de Sosa, Don Juan de Sosa, el
Doctor Rodrigo Maldonado, Liçençiatus Arias. Testigos que fueron presentes, que vieron aqui firmar sus nonbres a los dichos procuradores e
enbaxadores e otorgar lo suso dicho, e faser el dicho juramento: el comisario
Pedro de Leon, e el comisario Fernando de Torres, vesinos de la villa de
Valladolid, el comisario Fernando de Gamarre, comisario de Zagra e Cenete,
contino [19] de la casa de los dichos rrey e rreyna, nuestros señores, e Juan
Suares de Sequeira e Ruy Leme e Duarte Pacheco, continos de la casa del
señor Rey de Portugal, para ello llamados. Y yo Fernand Alvares de Toledo,
secretario del rrey e de la rreyna nuestros señores e del su consejo e su
escrivano de camara e notario publico en la su corte e en todos los sus rreynos

---

[17] The treaty was confirmed by Julius II., Jan. 24, 1506, Doc. **11.**
[18] Don Gutierre de Cardenas.
[19] The *continos* were the king's body-guards.

e señorios, fuy presente a todo lo que dicho es en uno con los dichos testigos e con Estevan Vaez, secretario del dicho señor Rey de Portugal, que por abtoridad que los dichos rrey e rreyna nuestros señores le dieron para dar fe deste abto en sus rreynos, que fue asi mismo presente a lo que dicho es; e a ruego e otorgamiento de todos los dichos procuradores e enbaxadores que en mi presençia e suya aqui firmaron sus nonbres, este publico ynstrumento de capitulaçion fise escrivir; el qual va escripto en estas seys fojas de papel de pliego entero, escriptas de anbas partes, con esta en que van los nonbres de los sobre dichos, e mi signo; e en fin de cada plana va señalado de la señal de mi nonbre e de la señal del dicho Estevan Vaez: e porende fise aqui mio signo, que es a tal. En testimonio de verdad, Fernand Alvares. E yo el dicho Estevan Vaez, que por abtoridad que los dichos señores Rey e Reyna de Castilla e de Leon me dieron para faser publico en todos sus rreynos e señorios, juntamente con el dicho Fernand Alvares a ruego e rrequerimiento de los dichos enbaxadores e procuradores a todo presente fuy; e por fe e certidumbre dello aqui de mi publico señal la signe, que tal es.

La qual dicha escriptura de asiento e capitulaçion e concordia suso encorporada, vista e entendida por nos, e por el dicho prinçipe Don Juan nuestro hijo, la aprovamos, loamos, e confirmamos e otorgamos e rratificamos e prometemos de tener e guardar e conplir todo lo suso dicho en ella contenido, e cada una cosa e parte dello, rrealmente e con efeto, çesante todo fraude e cautela, ficçion, e simulaçion, e de no yr ni venir contra ello, ni contra parte dello en tienpo alguno, ni por alguna manera que sea o ser pueda; e por mayor firmeza, nos y el dicho prinçipe Don Juan nuestro hijo juramos a Dios, e a Santa Maria, e a las palabras de los Santos Evangelios do quier que mas largamente son escriptas, e a la señal de la Cruz, en que corporalmente pusimos nuestras manos derechas en presençia de los dichos Ruy de Sosa, e Don Juan de Sosa, e Liçençiado Arias de Almadana, enbaxadores e procuradores del dicho Serenisimo Rey de Portugal nuestro hermano, de lo asi tener e guardar e cunplir e cada una cosa e parte de lo que a nos yncunbe, rrealmente e con efeto, como dicho es, por nos e por nuestros herederos e subçesores, e por los dichos nuestros rreynos e señorios e subditos e naturales dellos, so las penas e obligaçiones, vinculos, e rrenunçiaçiones, en el dicho contrato de capitulaçion e concordia de suso escripto contenidas. Por certificaçion e corroboraçion de lo qual, firmamos en esta nuestra carta nuestros nonbres e la mandamos sellar con nuestro sello de plomo pendiente en filos de seda a colores. Dada en la villa de Arevalo, a doss dias del mes de Jullio, año del nasçimiento de nuestro Señor Jhesu Christo, de mill e quatroçientos e noventa e quatro años.

Yo, EL REY.   Yo, LA REYNA.   Yo, EL PRINÇIPE.

Yo, FERNAND ALVARES de Toledo, secretario del rrey e de la rreyna, nuestros señores, la fise escrevir por su mandado.

. . . doctor.[20]

TRANSLATION.

Don Ferdinand and Doña Isabella, by the grace of God king and queen of Castile, Leon, Aragon, Sicily, Granada, Toledo, Valencia, Galicia, Majorca, Seville, Sardinia, Cordova, Corsica, Murcia, Jaen, Algarve, Algeciras, Gibral-

[20] The editor has been unable to decipher the signature above this word.

tar, and the Canary Islands, count and countess of Barcelona, lord and lady
of Biscay and Molina, duke and duchess of Athens and Neopatras, count and
countess of Roussillon and Cerdagne, marquis and marchioness of Oristano
and Gociano, together with the Prince Don John, our very dear and very
beloved first-born son, heir of our aforesaid kingdoms and lordships. Whereas
by Don Enrique Enriques, our chief steward, Don Gutierre de Cardenas,
chief commissary of Leon, our chief auditor, and Doctor Rodrigo Maldonado,
all members of our council, it was treated, adjusted, and agreed for us and
in our name and by virtue of our power with the most serene Dom John, by
the grace of God, king of Portugal and of the Algarves on this side and
beyond the sea in Africa, lord of Guinea, our very dear and very beloved
brother, and with Ruy de Sousa, lord of Sagres and Berenguel, Dom João de
Sousa, his son, chief inspector of weights and measures of the said Most Serene King our brother, and Ayres de Almada, magistrate of the civil cases in
his court and member of his *desembargo,* all members of the council of the
aforesaid Most Serene King our brother, [and acting] in his name and by
virtue of his power, his ambassadors, who came to us in regard to the controversy over what part belongs to us and what part to the said Most Serene
King our brother, of that which up to this seventh day of the present month
of June, the date of this instrument, is discovered in the ocean sea, in which
said agreement our aforesaid representatives promised among other things
that within a certain term specified in it we should sanction, confirm, swear
to, ratify, and approve the above-mentioned agreement in person: we, wishing to fulfill and fulfilling all that which was thus adjusted, agreed upon, and
authorized in our name in regard to the above-mentioned, ordered the said
instrument of the aforesaid agreement and treaty to be brought before us that
we might see and examine it, the tenor of which, word for word, is as follows:

In the name of God Almighty, Father, Son, and Holy Ghost, three truly
separate and distinct persons and only one divine essence. Be it manifest
and known to all who shall see this public instrument, that at the village of
Tordesillas, on the seventh day of the month of June, in the year of the
nativity of our Lord Jesus Christ 1494, in the presence of us, the secretaries,
clerks, and notaries public subscribed below, there being present the honorable
Don Enrique Enriques, chief steward of the very exalted and very mighty
princes, the lord and lady Don Ferdinand and Doña Isabella, by the grace of
God king and queen of Castile, Leon, Aragon, Sicily, Granada, etc., Don
Gutierre de Cardenas, chief auditor of the said lords, the king and queen, and
Doctor Rodrigo Maldonado, all members of the council of the said lords, the
king and queen of Castile, Leon, Aragon, Sicily, Granada, etc., their qualified
representatives of the one part, and the honorable Ruy de Sousa, lord of
Sagres and Berenguel, Dom Juan de Sousa, his son, chief inspector of
weights and measures of the very exalted and very excellent lord Dom John,
by the grace of God king of Portugal and of the Algarves on this side and
beyond the sea in Africa, lord of Guinea, and Ayres de Almada, magistrate
of civil cases in his court and member of his *desembargo,* all of the council
of the said lord King of Portugal, and his qualified ambassadors and representatives, as was proved by both the said parties by means of the letters of
authorization and procurations from the said lords their constituents, the
tenor of which, word for word, is as follows:

[Here follow the full powers granted by Ferdinand and Isabella to Don Enrique Enriques, Don Gutierre de Cardenas, and Dr. Rodrigo Maldonado on June 5, 1494; and the full powers granted by John II. to Ruy de Sousa, João de Sousa, and Ayres Almada on March 8, 1494.]

[21] Thereupon it was declared by the above-mentioned representatives of the aforesaid King and Queen of Castile, Leon, Aragon, Sicily, Granada, etc., and of the aforesaid King of Portugal and the Algarves, etc.:

[1.] That, whereas a certain controversy exists between the said lords, their constituents, as to what lands, of all those discovered in the ocean sea up to the present day, the date of this treaty, pertain to each one of the said parts respectively; therefore, for the sake of peace and concord, and for the preservation of the relationship and love of the said King of Portugal for the said King and Queen of Castile, Aragon, etc., it being the pleasure of their Highnesses, they, their said representatives, acting in their name and by virtue of their powers herein described, covenanted and agreed that a boundary or straight line be determined and drawn north and south, from pole to pole, on the said ocean sea, from the Arctic to the Antarctic pole. This boundary or line shall be drawn straight, as aforesaid, at a distance of three hundred and seventy leagues west of the Cape Verde Islands, being calculated by degrees, or by any other manner as may be considered the best and readiest, provided the distance shall be no greater than abovesaid. And all lands, both islands and mainlands, found and discovered already, or to be found and discovered hereafter, by the said King of Portugal and by his vessels on this side of the said line and bound determined as above, toward the east, in either north or south latitude, on the eastern side of the said bound, provided the said bound is not crossed, shall belong to, and remain in the possession of, and pertain forever to, the said King of Portugal and his successors. And all other lands, both islands and mainlands, found or to be found hereafter, discovered or to be discovered hereafter, which have been discovered or shall be discovered by the said King and Queen of Castile, Aragon, etc., and by their vessels, on the western side of the said bound, determined as above, after having passed the said bound toward the west, in either its north or south latitude, shall belong to, and remain in the possession of, and pertain forever to, the said King and Queen of Castile, Leon, etc., and to their successors.

[2.] Item, the said representatives promise and affirm by virtue of the powers aforesaid, that from this date no ships shall be despatched—namely as follows: the said King and Queen of Castile, Leon, Aragon, etc., for this part of the bound, and its eastern side, on this side the said bound, which pertains to the said King of Portugal and the Algarves, etc.; nor the said King of Portugal to the other part of the said bound which pertains to the said King and Queen of Castile, Aragon, etc.—for the purpose of discovering and seeking any mainlands or islands, or for the purpose of trade, barter, or conquest of any kind. But should it come to pass that the said ships of the said King and Queen of Castile, Leon, Aragon, etc., on sailing thus on this side of the said bound, should discover any mainlands or islands in the region pertaining, as abovesaid, to the said King of Portugal, such mainlands

[21] From this, the beginning of the treaty proper, as far as to "The said Don Enrique Enriques", on p. 98, the translation is taken from Blair and Robertson, *Philippine Islands*, I. 122-128.

or islands shall pertain to and belong forever to the said King of Portugal
and his heirs, and their Highnesses shall order them to be surrendered to him
immediately. And if the said ships of the said King of Portugal discover
any islands and mainlands in the regions of the said King and Queen of
Castile, Leon, Aragon, etc., all such lands shall belong to and remain forever
in the possession of the said King and Queen of Castile, Leon, Aragon, etc.,
and their heirs, and the said King of Portugal shall cause such lands to be
surrendered immediately.

[3.] Item, in order that the said line or bound of the said division may
be made straight and as nearly as possible the said distance of three hundred
and seventy leagues west of the Cape Verde Islands, as hereinbefore stated,
the said representatives of both the said parties agree and assent that within
the ten months immediately following the date of this treaty their said con-
stituent lords shall despatch two or four caravels, namely, one or two by
each one of them, a greater or less number, as they may mutually consider
necessary. These vessels shall meet at the Grand Canary Island during this
time, and each one of the said parties shall send certain persons·in them, to
wit, pilots, astrologers, sailors, and any others they may deem desirable. But
there must be as many on one side as on the other, and certain of the said
pilots, astrologers, sailors, and others of those sent by the said King and
Queen of Castile, Aragon, etc., and who are experienced, shall embark in
the ships of the said King of Portugal and the Algarves; in like manner
certain of the said persons sent by the said King of Portugal shall embark
in the ship or ships of the said King and Queen of Castile, Aragon, etc.; a
like number in each case, so that they may jointly study and examine to better
advantage the sea, courses, winds, and the degrees of the sun or of north
latitude, and lay out the leagues aforesaid, in order that, in determining
the line and boundary, all sent and empowered by both the said parties in the
said vessels, shall jointly concur. These said vessels shall continue their
course together to the said Cape Verde Islands, from whence they shall lay
a direct course to the west, to the distance of the said three hundred and
seventy degrees, measured as the said persons shall agree, and measured
without prejudice to the said parties. When this point is reached, such
point will constitute the place and mark for measuring degrees of the sun
or of north latitude either by daily runs measured in leagues, or in any other
manner that shall mutually be deemed better. This said line shall be drawn
north and south as aforesaid, from the said Arctic pole to the said Antarctic pole. And when this line has been determined as abovesaid, those
sent by each of the aforesaid parties, to whom each one of the said parties
must delegate his own authority and power, to determine the said mark and
bound, shall draw up a writing concerning it and affix thereto their signatures.
And when determined by the mutual consent of all of them, this line shall
be considered as a perpetual mark and bound, in such wise that the said
parties, or either of them, or their future successors, shall be unable to deny
it, or erase or remove it, at any time or in any manner whatsoever. And
should, perchance, the said line and bound from pole to pole, as aforesaid,
intersect any island or mainland, at the first point of such intersection of
such island or mainland by the said line, some kind of mark or tower shall
be erected, and a succession of similar marks shall be erected in a straight line
from such mark or tower, in a line identical with the above-mentioned bound.
These marks shall separate those portions of such land belonging to each one

of the said parties; and the subjects of the said parties shall not dare, on either side, to enter the territory of the other, by crossing the said mark or bound in such island or mainland.

[4.] Item, inasmuch as the said ships of the said King and Queen of Castile, Leon, Aragon, etc., sailing as before declared, from their kingdoms and seigniories to their said possessions on the other side of the said line, must cross the seas on this side of the line, pertaining to the said King of Portugal, it is therefore concerted and agreed that the said ships of the said King and Queen of Castile, Leon, Aragon, etc., shall, at any time and without any hindrance, sail in either direction, freely, securely, and peacefully, over the said seas of the said King of Portugal, and within the said line. And whenever their Highnesses and their successors wish to do so, and deem it expedient, their said ships may take their courses and routes direct from their kingdoms to any region within their line and bound to which they desire to despatch expeditions of discovery, conquest, and trade. They shall take their courses direct to the desired region and for any purpose desired therein, and shall not leave their course, unless compelled to do so by contrary weather. They shall do this provided that, before crossing the said line, they shall not seize or take possession of anything discovered in his said region by the said King of Portugal; and should their said ships find anything before crossing the said line, as aforesaid, it shall belong to the said King of Portugal, and their Highnesses shall order it surrendered immediately. And since it is possible that the ships and subjects of the said King and Queen of Castile, Leon, etc., or those acting in their name, may discover before the twentieth day of this present month of June, following the date of this treaty, some islands and mainlands within the said line, drawn straight from pole to pole, that is to say, inside the said three hundred and seventy leagues west of the Cape Verde Islands, as aforesaid, it is hereby agreed and determined, in order to remove all doubt, that all such islands and mainlands found and discovered in any manner whatsoever up to the said twentieth day of this said month of June, although found by ships and subjects of the said King and Queen of Castile, Aragon, etc., shall pertain to and remain forever in the possession of the said King of Portugal and the Algarves, and of his successors and kingdoms, provided that they lie within the first two hundred and fifty leagues of the said three hundred and seventy leagues reckoned west of the Cape Verde Islands to the above-mentioned line—in whatsoever part, even to the said poles, of the said two hundred and fifty leagues they may be found, determining a boundary or straight line from pole to pole, where the said two hundred and fifty leagues end. Likewise all the islands and mainlands found and discovered up to the said twentieth day of this present month of June by the ships and subjects of the said King and Queen of Castile, Aragon, etc., or in any other manner, within the other one hundred and twenty leagues that still remain of the said three hundred and seventy leagues where the said bound that is to be drawn from pole to pole, as aforesaid, must be determined, and in whatever part of the said one hundred and twenty leagues, even to the said poles,—they that are found up to the said day shall pertain to and remain forever in the possession of the said King and Queen of Castile, Aragon, etc., and of their successors and kingdoms; just as whatever is or shall be found on the other side of the said three hundred and seventy leagues pertaining to their Highnesses, as aforesaid, is and must be theirs, although the said one hundred and twenty leagues are within the said bound of the said three hundred and seventy leagues pertaining to the said King of Portugal, the Algarves, etc., as aforesaid.

And if, up to the said twentieth day of this said month of June, no lands are discovered by the said ships of their Highnesses within the said one hundred and twenty leagues, and are discovered after the expiration of that time, then they shall pertain to the said King of Portugal as is set forth in the above.

The said Don Enrique Enriques, chief steward, Don Gutierre de Cardenas, chief auditor, and Doctor Rodrigo Maldonado, representatives of the said very exalted and very mighty princes, the lord and lady, the king and queen of Castile, Leon, Aragon, Sicily, Granada, etc., by virtue of their said power, which is incorporated above, and the said Ruy de Sousa, Dom João de Sousa, his son, and Arias de Almadana, representatives and ambassadors of the said very exalted and very excellent prince, the lord king of Portugal and of the Algarves on this side and beyond the sea in Africa, lord of Guinea, by virtue of their said power, which is incorporated above, promised, and affirmed, in the name of their said constituents, [saying] that they and their successors and kingdoms and lordships, forever and ever, would keep, observe, and fulfill, really and effectively, renouncing all fraud, evasion, deceit, falsehood, and pretense, everything set forth in this treaty, and each part and parcel of it; and they desired and authorized that everything set forth in this said agreement and every part and parcel of it be observed, fulfilled, and performed as everything which is set forth in the treaty of peace concluded and ratified between the said lord and lady, the king and queen of Castile, Aragon, etc., and the lord Dom Alfonso, king of Portugal (may he rest in glory) and the said king, the present ruler of Portugal, his son, then prince in the former year of 1479, must be observed, fulfilled, and performed, and under those same penalties, bonds, securities, and obligations, in accordance with and in the manner set forth in the said treaty of peace. Also they bound themselves [by the promise] that neither the said parties nor any of them nor their successors forever should violate or oppose that which is abovesaid and specified, nor any part or parcel of it, directly or indirectly, or in any other manner at any time, or in any manner whatsoever, premeditated or not premeditated, or that may or can be, under the penalties set forth in the said agreement of the said peace; and whether the fine be paid or not paid, or graciously remitted, that this obligation, agreement, and treaty shall continue in force and remain firm, stable, and valid forever and ever. That thus they [22] will keep, observe, perform, and pay everything, the said representatives, acting in the name of their said constituents, pledged the property, movable and real, patrimonial and fiscal, of each of their respective parties, and of their subjects and vassals, possessed and to be possessed. They renounced all laws and rights of which the said parties or either of them might take advantage to violate or oppose the foregoing or any part of it; and for the greater security and stability of the aforesaid, they swore before God and the Blessed Mary and upon the sign of the Cross, on which they placed their right hands, and upon the words of the Holy Gospels, wheresoever they are written at greatest length, and on the consciences of their said constituents, that they, jointly and severally, will keep, observe, and fulfill all the aforesaid and each part and parcel of it, really and effectively, renouncing all fraud, evasion,

---

[22] *I. e.*, the constituents.

deceit, falsehood, and pretense, and that they will not contradict it at any time or in any manner. And under the same oath they swore not to seek absolution or release from it from our most Holy Father or from any other legate or prelate who could give it to them. And even though, *proprio motu*, it should be given to them, they will not make use of it; rather, by this present agreement, they, acting in the said name, entreat our most Holy Father that his Holiness be pleased to confirm and approve this said agreement, according to what is set forth therein; and that he order his bulls in regard to it to be issued to the parties or to whichever of the parties may solicit them, with the tenor of this agreement incorporated therein, and that he lay his censures upon those who shall violate or oppose it at any time whatsoever. Likewise, the said representatives, acting in the said names, bound themselves under the same penalty and oath, that within the one hundred days next following, reckoned from the day of the date of this agreement, the parties would mutually exchange the approbation and ratification of this said agreement, written on parchment, signed with the names of the said lords, their constituents, and sealed with their hanging leaden seals; and that the instrument which the said lords, the king and queen of Castile, Aragon, etc., should have to issue, must be signed, agreed to, and sanctioned by the very noble and most illustrious lord, Prince Don Juan, their son. Of all the foregoing they authorized two copies, both of the same tenor exactly, which they signed with their names and executed before the undersigned secretaries and notaries public, one for each party. And whichever copy is produced, it shall be as valid as if both the copies which were made and executed in the said town of Tordesillas, on the said day, month, and year aforesaid, should be produced. The chief deputy, Don Enrique, Ruy de Sousa, Dom Juan de Sousa, Doctor Rodrigo Maldonado, Licentiate Ayres. Witnesses who were present and who saw the said representatives and ambassadors sign their names here and execute the aforesaid, and take the said oath: The deputy Pedro de Leon and the deputy Fernando de Torres, residents of the town of Valladolid, the deputy Fernando de Gamarra, deputy of Zagra and Cenete, *contino* of the house of the said king and queen, our lords, and João Suares de Sequeira, Ruy Leme, and Duarte Pacheco, *continos* of the house of the said King of Portugal, summoned for that purpose. And I, Fernando Alvarez de Toledo, secretary of the king and queen, our lords, member of their council, and their scrivener of the high court of justice, and notary public in their court and throughout their realms and lordships, witnessed all the aforesaid, together with the said witnesses and with Estevan Vaez, secretary of the said King of Portugal, who by the authority given him by the said king and queen, our lords, to certify to this act in their kingdoms, also witnessed the abovesaid; and at the request and with the authorization of all the said representatives and ambassadors, who in my presence and his here signed their names, I caused this public instrument of agreement to be written. It is written on these six leaves of paper, in entire sheets, written on both sides, together with this leaf, which contains the names of the aforesaid persons and my sign; and the bottom of every page is marked with the notarial mark of my name and that of the said Estevan Vaez. And in witness I here make my sign, which is thus. In testimony of truth: Fernando Alvarez. And I, the said Estevan Vaez (who by the authority given me by the said lords, the king and queen of Castile, and of Leon, to make it public throughout their kingdoms and lordships, together with the said Fernando Alvarez, at the request and summons of the said ambassadors and representatives witnessed everything), in testimony and assurance thereof signed it here with my public sign, which is thus.

The said deed of treaty, agreement, and concord, above incorporated, having been examined and understood by us and by the said Prince Don John, our son, we approve, commend, confirm, execute, and ratify it, and we promise to keep, observe, and fulfill all the abovesaid that is set forth therein, and every part and parcel of it, really and effectively. We renounce all fraud, evasion, falsehood, and pretense, and we shall not violate or oppose it, or any part of it, at any time or in any manner whatsoever. For greater security, we and the said prince Don John, our son, swear before God and Holy Mary, and by the words of the Holy Gospels, wheresoever they are written at greatest length, and upon the sign of the Cross upon which we actually placed our right hands, in the presence of the said Ruy de Sousa, Dom João de Sousa, and Licentiate Ayres de Almada, ambassadors and representatives of the said Most Serene King of Portugal, our brother, thus to keep, observe, and fulfill it, and every part and parcel of it, so far as it is incumbent upon us, really and effectively, as is abovesaid, for ourselves and for our heirs and successors, and for our said kingdoms and lordships, and the subjects and natives of them, under the penalties and obligations, bonds and abjurements set forth in the said contract of agreement and concord above written. In attestation and corroboration whereof, we sign our name to this our letter and order it to be sealed with our leaden seal, hanging by threads of colored silk. Given in the town of Arévalo, on the second day of the month of July, in the year of the nativity of our Lord Jesus Christ, 1494.

I, THE KING.   I, THE QUEEN.   I, THE PRINCE.

I, FERNANDO ALVAREZ de Toledo, secretary of the king and of the queen, our lords, have caused it to be written by their mandate.

. . . doctor.

10.

Compact between Spain and Portugal, signed by the Catholic Sovereigns at Madrid, May 7, 1495.

INTRODUCTION.

The rulers of Spain and Portugal did not put into effect the provision of the treaty of Tordesillas [1] for despatching caravels within ten months in order to determine the line of demarcation. On May 7, 1495, the Spanish monarchs signed an agreement that during the following September commissioners should assemble on the frontier of the two kingdoms to decide upon the method of fixing the line; that upon notification by either party, the other party must cause the said line to be determined in accordance with the method approved by the commissioners; that the departure of the caravels should be postponed, and orders given to place the line on all hydrographical maps made in either kingdom.

The main stipulations of this compact were not carried out. Apparently it was not until 1512 that either monarch planned an expedition to determine the line.[2] The earliest of existing maps on which the line of demarcation appears, is the Cantino map, of 1502. On the Munich-Portuguese map of 1519, and on the Weimar-Spanish (1527) and Ribero (1529) maps, this line does duty also as the prime meridian.[3]

BIBLIOGRAPHY.

Text: MS. The original manuscript of the compact signed by Ferdinand and Isabella at Madrid on May 7, 1495, is in the National Archives at Lisbon, gav. 10, maço 5, no. 4. A manuscript nearly identical but dated April 15, and lacking the royal signatures, which have been cut out, is in the Archives of the Indies, at Seville, Patronato 2-1-1/18, no. 8.

Text: Printed. The text of the manuscript dated April 15 is in Navarrete, *Coleccion de Viages* (1825-1837), tom. II., no. 91, pp. 170-173.

Translation. A translation of the text as printed in Navarrete is in Blair and Robertson, *Philippine Islands* (1903-1909), I. 131-135.

References. See references of Doc. 9.

---

[1] Doc. 9.   [2] *Cf.* Doc. 12, note 5.

[3] All of the above-mentioned maps, and some others on which the demarcation line appears, are included among the *Maps illustrating Early Discovery and Exploration in America, 1502-1530*, reproduced by photography from original manuscripts, and issued, together with text and key maps, under the direction of E. L. Stevenson (1903, 1906).

TEXT.[4]

Don Fernando e Doña Ysabel, por la graçia de Dios rrey e rreyna de Castilla [etc.] : Por quanto en la capitulaçion e asiento[5] que se hizo entre nos y el Serenisimo Rey de Portugal e de los Algarbes de aquende e de allend el mar en Africa, e Señor de Guinea, nuestro muy caro e muy amado hermano, sobre la partiçion del mar oçeano, fue asentado e capitulado entre otras cosas que, desde el dia de la fecha de la dicha capitulaçion fasta diez meses primeros siguientes, ayan de ser en la ysla de la Grand Canaria caravelas nuestras y suyas, con astrologos, pilotos, e marineros, e personas que nos y el acordaremos, tantos de la una parte como de la otra, para yr a fazer e señalar la linea de la partiçion del dicho mar, que ha de ser a trezientas e setenta leguas de las yslas del Cabo Verde a la parte del poniente, por linea derecha del polo Artico al polo Antartico, que es de norte a sul, en que somos concordados en la partiçion del dicho mar por la dicha capitulaçion, segund mas largamente en ella es contenido; e agora nos, considerando como la linea de la dicha partiçion se puede mejor hazer e justificar por las dichas trezientas e setenta leguas, siendo primeramente acordado e asentado por los dichos astrologos, pilotos, e marineros e personas, antes de la yda de las dichas caravelas, la forma e orden que en el demarcar e señalar de la dicha linea se aya de tener, e asi por se escusar debates e diferençias que sobre ello, entre las personas que asi fueren, podrian aconteçer, si despues de ser partidos lo oviesen alla de ordenar; e viendo asimismo que yendo las dichas caravelas e personas antes de se saber ser hallada ysla o tierra en cada una de las dichas partes del dicho mar, a que luego ordenadamente ayan de yr, no aprovecharia; por tanto, para que todo se mejor pueda haser, e con declaraçion e certificaçion de anbas las partes, avemos por bien e por esta presente carta nos plaze, que los dichos astrologos, pilotos, e marineros e personas en que nos acordaremos con el dicho rrey, nuestro hermano, tantos de la una parte como de la otra, e que razonablemente para esto puedan bastar, se ayan de juntar e junten en alguna parte de la frontera destos nuestros rreynos con el dicho rreyno de Portugal, los quales ayan de consultar, acordar, e tomar asiento dentro de todo el mes de Setienbre[6] primero que verna deste año de la fecha desta carta la manera en que la linea de la partiçion del dicho mar se aya de haser por las dichas tresientas e setenta leguas por rrota derecha al poniente de las dichas yslas del Cabo Verde del polo Artico al polo Antartico, que es de norte a sul, como en la dicha capitulaçion es contenido; y aquello en que se concordaren, siendo todos conformes e fuere asentado e senalado por ellos, se aprovara e confirmara por nos y por el dicho rrey, nuestro hermano, por nuestras cartaspatentes; y si antes o[7] despues que fuere tomado el dicho asiento por los dichos astrologos, pilotos, e marineros que asi fueren nonbrados, yendo cada una de las partes por la parte del dicho mar que pueden yr segund lo con-

---

[4] The following text is taken from the original manuscript of the compact signed by Ferdinand and Isabella at Madrid, May 7, 1495, preserved in the National Archives at Lisbon, gav. 10, maço 5, no. 4; from an eighteenth-century copy of this manuscript in the same archives (same pressmark); and from the nearly identical manuscript, dated Apr. 15, preserved in the Archives of the Indies. Since a part of the first of these manuscripts is indecipherable, considerable use has been made of the two last-mentioned texts.

[5] The Treaty of Tordesillas, Doc. **9**.

[6] The draft signed in April reads *Julio*.

[7] The words *antes o* are not in the draft of the compact drawn up in April.

tenido en la dicha capitulaçion, e guardandose en[8] ello lo que en ella se
contiene, fuere hallado e[9] se hallare ysla[10] o tierra que parezca a qualquier
de las partes ser en parte donde se pueda haser la dicha linea segund la forma
dela dicha capitulaçion, e mandando rrequirer la una parte a la otra que
manden señalar la linea suso dicha, seremos nos y el dicho rrey, nuestro
hermano, obligados de mandar haser e señalar la dicha linea, segund la orden
del asiento que fuere tomado por los astrologos, pilotos, e marineros, e personas suso dichas que asi fueren nonbrados dentro de diez meses primeros
contados del dia que qualquier de las partes rrequiriere a la otra ; y en caso
que no sea en el medio dela dicha linea, lo que asi se hallare se hara declaraçion quantas leguas ay dello a la dicha linea, asy de nuestra parte como de
la parte del dicho Serenisimo Rey, nuestro hermano, no dexando por ende
en qualquier ysla o tierra que mas acerca dela dicha linea despues por el
tienpo se hallare haser la dicha declaraçion ; e por se haser lo que dicho es
no se dexara de tener la manera suso dicha, hallandose ysla o tierra debaxo
de la dicha linea, como dicho es, e hasta el dicho tienpo de los dichos diez
meses despues que la una parte rrequiriere a la otra, como dicho es, nos plaze
por esta nuestra carta prorrogar e alargar la yda de las dichas caravelas
e personas, syn enbargo del termino que cerca dello en la dicha capitulaçion
fue asentado e capitulado ; e bien asi nos plase e avremos por bien, para mas
notificaçion e declaraçion de la partiçion del dicho mar que entre nos y el
dicho rrey nuestro hermano por la dicha capitulaçion es fecha, e para que
nuestros subditos e naturales tengan mas ynformaçion por donde de aqui
adelante ayan de navegar e descobrir, e asi los subditos e naturales del dicho
rrey nuestro hermano, de mandar, como de fecho mandaremos, so graves
penas, que en todas las cartas de marear que en nuestros rreynos e señorios
se hisieren de aqui adelante los que ovieren de yr por el dicho mar oçeano,
se ponga la linea de la dicha partiçion, figurando del dicho polo Artico al
dicho polo Antartico, que es de norte a sul, en el conpas delas dichas trezientas
e setenta leguas delas dichas yslas del Cabo Verde por rrota derecha ala
parte del poniente, como dicho es, dela forma que acordaren la medida della
los dichos astrologos e pilotos e marineros que asi se juntaren, siendo todos
conformes ; e queremos e otorgamos que esta presente carta, ni lo en ella
contenido, no perjudique en cosa alguna delas que son contenidas e asentadas
en la dicha capitulaçion, mas que todas e cada una dellas se cunplan e guarden
para todo sienpre en todo e por todo syn falta alguna, asy e tan enteiramente
como en la dicha capitulaçion son asentadas ; por quanto esta carta mandamos
asi faser, solamente para que los dichos astrologos e personas se junten e
dentro del dicho tienpo tomen asiento dela orden e manera en que la dicha
demarcaçion se aya de haser, e para prorrogar e alargar el tienpo dela yda
delas dichas caravelas e personas fasta tanto que sea sabido ser hallada en cada
una delas dichas partes la dicha ysla o tierra a que ayan de yr, e para mandar
poner enlas dichas cartas de marear la linea dela dicha partiçion ;—como todo
mas cunplidamente de suso es contenido. Lo qual todo que dicho es prometemos e seguramos por nuestra fe palabra rreal de cunplir e guardar e
mantener syn arte, ni cautela, ni fingimiento alguno, asy e a tan enteiramente

---

[8] From this point the compact of May 7 is legible except for a few words.
[9] The words *fuere hallado e* are not in the draft made in April.
[10] Between the words *hallare* and *ysla* the draft made in April contains the words
de aqui adelante.

como en ella es contenido. E por firmeza de todo lo que dicho es, mandamos dar esta nuestra carta, firmada de nuestros nonbres e sellada con nuestro sello de plomo, pendiente en filos de seda a colores. Dada en la nuestra villa de Madrid, a siete dias del mes de Mayo, año del nasçimiento de nuestra Senor Jhesu Christo de mill e quatroçientos e noventa e çinco años.

Yo, EL REY.   YO, LA REYNA.

Yo, FERNAND ALVARES de Toledo, secretario del rrey e dela rreyna, nuestros señores, la fes escrevir por su mandado.

Registrada.

TRANSLATION.[11]

Don Ferdinand and Doña Isabella, by the grace of God king and queen of Castile, etc.: Inasmuch as, among other things in the treaty and compact regarding the division of the ocean sea, negotiated between ourselves and the Most Serene King of Portugal and the Algarves on either side of the sea in Africa, and lord of Guinea, our most dear and beloved brother, it was agreed and covenanted that, within the first ten months following the date of this treaty, our caravels and his, accompanied by astrologers, pilots, sailors, and others, agreed upon by ourselves and himself—a like number on either side—should be in the island of the Grand Canary in order to proceed to the determination and drawing of the divisional line of the said sea, which must be three hundred and seventy leagues west of the Cape Verde Islands, in a straight north and south line from the Arctic to the Antarctic pole, as covenanted between us by the said treaty of the division of the said sea, as is more fully set forth therein, and inasmuch as we now consider that the line of the said division at the distance of the said three hundred and seventy leagues can be determined and calculated better if the said astrologers, pilots, sailors, and others come to a definite conclusion and agreement regarding the manner and order of procedure to be observed in the determination and marking of the said line before the sailing of the said caravels, by so doing avoiding disputes and controversies that might arise regarding it among those going, if these had to be arranged after the departure; and inasmuch as it would be quite useless for the said caravels and persons to go before knowing that any island or mainland had been found in each one of the said parts of the said sea, and to which they must proceed immediately and orderly: Now therefore, in order that all this may be done to better advantage, and with the full and free consent of both sides, we agree and by this present letter consent that the said astrologers, pilots, sailors, and others determined upon with the said king, our brother—a like number on either side, and of sufficient number for this matter—must assemble, and they shall assemble, along any part of the frontier of these our kingdoms and the kingdom of Portugal. During the whole month of [September] first following the date of this letter these men shall consult upon, covenant concerning, and determine the manner of making the said divisional line of the said sea at the distance of the said three hundred and seventy leagues west of the said Cape Verde Islands, by means of a straight north and south line from the Arctic to the Antarctic pole, as is set forth in the said treaty. And whatever they determine upon

[11] This translation is reprinted from Blair and Robertson, *Philippine Islands*, I. 131-135. A few changes, indicated by brackets, have been made to bring it into conformity with the text of May 7.

unanimously, and whatever is concluded and marked out by them, shall be approved and confirmed through our letters-patent, by us and by the said king our brother. And if [before or] after the said astrologers, pilots, and sailors, appointed as abovesaid, shall have arrived at a conclusion, each one of the said parties going to that part of the said sea, according to the permission of the said treaty, and thereby observing the contents of said treaty, any island or mainland shall be found, which either of the parties consider to be so situated that the said line can be determined in accordance with the stipulations of the said treaty, and the one party shall cause notification to be given the other party that they shall cause the line abovesaid to be marked out, we and the said king our brother shall be obliged to have the said line determined and marked out in accordance with the method determined upon by the astrologers, pilots, and sailors, and others abovesaid, and appointed as abovesaid, within the period of the first ten months reckoned from the date that either of the parties notified the other. And should it prove that the land thus found is not cut by the said line, a declaration of its distance from the said line shall be given, both on our own part and that of the said most serene king our brother. They shall not, however, neglect to make the said declaration regarding any island or mainland which shall be found afterwards, during the period, nearer the said line. And in doing the aforesaid, they shall not neglect to observe the manner aforesaid, whenever any island or mainland is found in the neighborhood of the said line as aforesaid, and up to the said time of the said ten months after the notification of one party by the other, as aforesaid. It is our pleasure in this our letter to postpone and defer the departure of the said caravels and persons, notwithstanding the limit set and determined in the above-mentioned treaty in regard to it. And we therefore are pleased and consider it advantageous—for the better notification and declaration of the division of the said sea made by the said treaty between ourselves and the said king our brother, and in order that both our subjects and natives and the subjects and natives of the said king our brother may be better informed henceforth as to the regions wherein they may navigate and discover—to order (as in truth we shall order), under severe penalties, that the line of the said division be placed on all hydrographical maps made hereafter in our kingdoms and seigniories by those journeying in the said ocean sea. This line shall be drawn straight from the said Arctic to the said Antarctic pole, north and south, at the distance of the said three hundred and seventy leagues west of the Cape Verde Islands, as aforesaid, being measured as determined unanimously by the said astrologers, pilots, and sailors meeting as abovesaid. And we purpose and stipulate that neither this present letter nor anything contained therein, be prejudicial in any manner to the contents and compacts of the said treaty, but rather that they, all and singular, be observed throughout, *in toto* without any failure, and in the manner and entirety set forth in the said treaty; inasmuch as we have caused the present letter to be made in this manner, simply in order that the said astrologers and persons shall assemble and, within the said time, shall determine the order of procedure and the method to be observed in making the said line of demarcation, and in order to postpone and defer the departure of the said caravels and persons until the said island or mainland whither they must go is known to have been found in each one of the said parts, and in order to command that the line of the said division be placed on the said hydrographical maps, all of which is set forth most fully in the above.   We promise and engage on our kingly faith and word to fulfill and observe all of the foregoing, without any artifice, deceit, or pretense in the manner and in the entirety set down in the above.   And in confirmation of the above, we cause this our letter to be given, signed with our names, and sealed with our leaden seal hanging from threads of colored silk.

[Given in our town of Madrid, the seventh day of the month of May, in the year of the nativity of our Lord Jesus Christ, 1495.

I, THE KING.   I, THE QUEEN.

I, FERNANDO ALVAREZ de Toledo, secretary of the king and of the queen, our lord and lady, have caused it to be written, by their command.

Registered.]

11.

The Bull Ea Quae *(Julius II.).* *January 24, 1506.*

INTRODUCTION.

In 1498 Vasco da Gama reached Calicut by way of the Cape of Good Hope. Two years later, Pedro Alvarez Cabral, hastening to India in command of a Portuguese fleet to follow up Gama's successes, landed, near 16° south, upon the coast of Brazil, of which, nearly three months previously, Pinzon, and, shortly after, Diego de Lepe, had taken formal possession for Castile. The fact that this portion of South America extended beyond the east or Portuguese side of the line of demarcation further complicated the relations of the two countries, whose rivalry now became intense. Expeditions in which Vespucius, detached for a time from Spanish service, sailed under a Portuguese captain (1501-1502, 1503-1504), acquainted the Portuguese with the vast extent of the Brazilian coast, and far to the north, in 1500 and 1501, Gaspare Corte-Real visited lands which the Portuguese located on their side of the line.[1] ~The line, therefore, now had a new value for the Portuguese and it was probably this fact that induced King Emmanuel to ask Pope Julius II. to confirm the treaty of Tordesillas that had established it.[2]

Julius II. was well disposed toward King Emmanuel, who was so zealously laboring for the extension of the faith in Morocco, in Guinea, and notably in India, where the foundations of a colonial empire were beginning to be laid. In the early summer of 1505, a Portuguese embassy of obedience reached Rome, and before its return to Portugal in the following October, had obtained from the pontiff a number of important concessions.[3] In the following spring, the pope bestowed upon the king the consecrated golden rose.[4] A few months after the return of the embassy and before the bestowal

---

[1] As in the Cantino map, compiled from Portuguese data in 1502. This map, which shows the line of demarcation passing west of the land discovered by Corte-Real, is photographically reproduced in the size of the original in E. L. Stevenson, *Maps illustrating Early Discovery and Exploration in America* (1903). Parts of it are reproduced in H. Harrisse, *Les Corte-Real* (1883), portfolio, and in *id., Discovery of North America* (1892), opp. pp. 79 and 111.

[2] F. A. de Varnhagen, *Historia Geral do Brazil* (1854-1857), I. 28.

[3] For a detailed account of this embassy, see the Marquis MacSwiney de Mashanaglass, *Le Portugal et le Saint-Siège*, III. 22-29, and by the same author, "Une Ambassade Portugaise à Rome sous Jules II.", in the *Revue d'Histoire Diplomatique*, 1903, pp. 50-65, and separately printed by Plon, Paris, 1903.

[4] An interesting account of the golden roses sent by the popes to the kings of Portugal in the sixteenth century is given in the former of the volumes cited in the preceding note. For the gift of the golden rose to Alfonso V., see Doc. 1, note 26.

of the rose, in response to a request from King Emmanuel, the pope granted
three bulls, all dated January 24, 1506.[5] Of these bulls, the one here printed
enjoined the Archbishop of Braga and the Bishop of Vizeu to confirm the
treaty of Tordesillas, and cause it to be inviolably observed. The Archbishop
of Braga was the distinguished prelate, Diogo da Souso, who had been
elevated to this dignity only a few months previously, when he had been in
Rome as head of the aforementioned embassy of obedience. The Bishop of
Vizeu was Jorge da Costa, who had been created cardinal of Lisbon in 1476
and who as cardinal protector of Portugal resided in Rome from about that
date till his death in 1508.

BIBLIOGRAPHY.

Text: MS. The original manuscript of the promulgated bull is in the
National Archives at Lisbon, Coll. de Bullas, maço 6, no. 33.

Text: Printed. J. Ramos-Coelho, *Alguns Documentos* (1892), pp. 142-143;
L. A. Rebello da Silva, *Corpo Diplomatico Portuguez* (Acad. Real das
Sciencias, Lisbon, 1862—), I. 91-93.

Reference: Marquis MacSwiney de Mashanaglass, *Le Portugal et le Saint-
Siège* (1898-1904), III. 1-42. Although not directly referring to the
bull of January 24, 1506, this work throws light on the relations existing
between King Emmanuel and the Pope at this date.

TEXT.[6]

Julius, episcopus, servus servorum Dei: Venerabilibus fratribus, archiepiscopo Bracharensi[7] et episcopo Visensi,[8] salutem et apostolicam benedictionem.

Ea que pro bono pacis et quietis inter personas quaslibet, presertim Catholicos reges, per concordiam terminata sunt, ne in redicive contencionis
scrupulum relabantur, sed firma perpetuo et inconcussa permaneant, libenter,
cum a nobis petitur, apostolico munimine roboramus. ⁓ Exhibita siquidem
nobis nuper pro parte carissimi in Christo filii nostri Emanuelis, Portugalie et
Algarbiorum regis illustris, petitio continebat quod olim, postquam per Sedem
Apostolicam clare memorie Johanni, regi Portugalie et Algarbiorum [conces-
sum fuerat][9] quod ipse Johannes et rex Portugalie et Algarbiorum pro tempore
existens, per mare occeanum navegare aut insulas et portus et loca firma infra
dictum mare existencia, perquirere, et inventa sibi retinere liceret, ac omnibus
aliis, sub excommunicationis et aliis penis tunc expressis, ne mare hujusmodi
contra voluntatem prefati regis navigare, aut insulas et loca ibidem repperta

---

[5] These bulls are printed in L. A. Rebello da Silva, *Corpo Diplomatico Portuguez*
(Acad. Real das Sciencias, Lisbon, 1862—), I. 88-93.

[6] The text is from the original manuscript of the promulgated bull, preserved in the
National Archives at Lisbon, Coll. de Bullas, maço 6, no. 33. Dr. Achille Ratti, prefect
of the Vatican Library, has kindly collated it with the Vatican text.

[7] Diogo da Souso, see introduction.

[8] Jorge da Costa, see introduction.

[9] Some such words as " concessum fuerat " are wanted before " quod ipse ". " Johannes
et Rex " should be in the dative.

occupare presumerent, inhibitum fuerat; cum inter prefatum Johannem Regem ex una, et carissimum in Christo filium nostrum Ferdinandum, Aragonum tunc Castelle et Legionis regem illustrem, super certis insulis Lasamillis [10] nuncupatis, per prefatum regem inventas et occupatas," ex alia partibus, lis, controversia, et questionis materia exorte fuissent, partes ipse litibus, controversiis, et questionibus hujusmodi obviare, ac pacem et concordiam inter se pro subditorum suorum commoditate nutrire et vigere desiderantes, ad certas honestas concordiam, conventionem, et compositionem devenerunt, per quam inter cetera voluerunt quod Portugalie et Algarbiorum a certis Castelle vero et Legionis regibus pro tempore existentibus a certis aliis locis usque ad certa alia loca tunc expressa per dictum mare navigare et insulas novas perquirere et capere ac sibi retinere liceret, prout in quodam instrumento publico desuper confecto dicitur plenius contineri."—Quare [12] pro parte prefati Emanuelis Regis nobis fuit humiliter supplicatum, ut concordie, conventioni, et compositioni predictis pro illorum subsistencia firmiori robur apostolice confirmationis adjicere, ac alias in premissis oportune providere de benignitate apostolica dignaremur. Nos igitur, qui inter personas quascumque, presertim regali dignitate fulgentes, pacem et concordiam vigere intensis desideriis affectamus, de premissis certam noticiam non habentes, hujusmodi supplicationibus inclinati, fraternitati vestre per apostolica scripta mandamus, quatinus vos vel alter vestrum, si est ita, concordiam, conventionem, et compositionem predictas, ac prout illas concernunt, omnia et singula in dicto instrumento contenta, et inde secuta quecunque de utriusque regis consensu approbare et confirmare, illamque perpetue firmitatis robur obtinere decernentes, auctoritate nostra curetis, supplentes omnes et singulos defectus, si qui forsan intervenerunt in eisdem. Et nichilominus, si confirmationem et approbationem predictas per vos vigore presencium fieri contigerit, ut prefertur, faciatis dictam concordiam inviolabiliter observari, ac eosdem reges concordia et illius confirmatione et approbatione predictis pacifice gaudere, non permittentes eos inter se, aut per quoscunque alios, desuper indebite molestari, contradictores auctoritate nostra, appellatione postposita, compescendo. Non obstantibus constitutionibus et ordinationibus apostolicis contrariis quibuscunque, aut si eisdem regibus vel [14] quibusvis aliis, communiter vel divisim, ab Apostolica sit Sede indultum, quod interdici, suspendi vel excommunicari non possint, per litteras apostolicas non facientes plenam et expressam ac de verbo ad verbum de indulto hujusmodi mentionem.

Datum Rome apud Sanctum Petrum, anno Incarnationis Dominice millesimo quingentesimo quinto, [15] nono kalendas Februarii, pontificatus nostri anno tercio.

Jo. DE SALDANA. [16]

[10] In the Vatican text, *Lassanullis.* A Portuguese translation of this bull, preserved in the National Archives at Lisbon, reads " certas Ilhas chamadas Antilhas ". *Corp. Dipl. Port.,* I. 92, note. Lasamillis is probably a mistake for " Las Antillas ".

[11] Thus also in the Vatican text.

[12] The treaty of Tordesillas, Doc. **9.**

[13] The Vatican text reads *Quocirca.*

[14] The Vatican text reads *et.*

[15] The Vatican text reads *sexto.*

[16] João de Saldanha seems to have represented Portugal at Rome, whence, Oct. 21, 1504, he wrote to King John that on account of the reports regarding the Indies and Guinea the moment was especially opportune for despatching an embassy of obedience. Rebello da Silva, *Corp. Dipl. Port.,* I. 43-45.

Julius, bishop, servant of the servants of God, to the venerable brothers, the archbishop of Braga and the bishop of Vizeu, health and apostolic benediction.

Those agreements, which have been concluded for the promotion of peace and quiet between any persons whatsoever, and especially between Catholic kings, we gladly confirm by granting our apostolic protection, when this is sought from us, in order that they may not again become matters of contention but remain forever firm and unshaken. A request recently addressed to us on the part of our very dear son in Christ, Emmanuel, the illustrious king of Portugal and of the Algarves, stated that inasmuch as some time ago the permission was granted by the Apostolic See to John, of illustrious memory, king of Portugal and the Algarves, to the effect that the said John and any king of Portugal and of the Algarves for the time being, should be permitted to navigate the ocean sea, or seek out the islands, ports, and mainlands lying within the said sea, and to retain those found for himself, and to all others it was forbidden under penalty of excommunication, and other penalties, then expressed, from presuming to navigate the sea in this way against the will of the aforesaid king, or to occupy the islands and places found there; and inasmuch as between the aforesaid King John, on the one part, and our very dear son in Christ, Ferdinand, at that time the illustrious king of Aragon, Castile, and Leon, on the other part, in regard to certain islands called Las Antillas, which had been discovered and occupied by the aforesaid king, strife, controversy, and occasion for dispute had arisen, the said parties desiring to prevent strifes, controversies, and disputes of this kind, and to foster and strengthen peace and concord between themselves for the benefit of their subjects, came to a certain honorable agreement, convention, and compact, whereby, among other things, they resolved that the kings of Portugal and the Algarves should have the right to navigate the said sea within certain specified limits and seek out and take possession of newly discovered islands and that the kings for the time being of Castile and Leon should have the same right within certain other specified limits, as is said to be more fully set forth in a certain public instrument drawn up in regard to the matter. Wherefore the aforesaid King Emmanuel has humbly besought us to deign to add the authority of the apostolic confirmation to the aforesaid agreement, convention, and compact for the purpose of establishing them more firmly and out of our apostolic good-will to make other fitting provisions in respect to the aforesaid. We, therefore, who strive with intense desire to foster peace and concord between all persons, especially between those whose royal office renders them conspicuous, not having certain knowledge of the aforesaid, but favorably disposed to these petitions, do by these apostolic writings enjoin Your Fraternity that you (or either one of you, if so be) do proceed to approve and confirm by our authority the aforesaid agreement, convention, and compact and everything set forth in the said instrument relating thereto, and all that has followed thereupon with the consent of both kings, decreeing it to possess perpetual authority, and supplying all and singular defects if perchance any should be contained therein. And furthermore if the aforesaid confirmation and approbation are enacted by you, by the authority of these presents, as is aforesaid, you shall cause the said agreement to be inviolably observed, and the said kings to enjoy in peace the aforesaid agreement and the confirmation and approbation thereof, not permitting them without just cause to molest one another, or to be molested by any other on this account, and restraining the disobedient, by our authority, without appeal, all apostolic constitutions and ordinances to the contrary notwithstanding, even if an indult has been granted by the Apostolic See to the said kings or to any others, together or individually, to the effect that they cannot be interdicted or suspended or excommunicated by apostolic letters not making full and express mention, word for word, of the said indult.

Given at Rome, at St. Peter's, on the twenty-fourth day of January, in the year of the incarnation of our Lord, 1505, in the third year of our pontificate.

Jo. DE SALDANA.

12.

The Bull Praecelsae Devotionis (Leo X.). November 3, 1514.

INTRODUCTION.

In March, 1513, Leo X. became pope, and King Emmanuel soon gained his highest favor. A letter from the king to the pope, dated June 6, 1513,[1] set forth the Portuguese successes in India, and especially in Malacca, the great emporium of the spice trade, captured by Albuquerque in 1511. The pope's enthusiastic reception of this news and of the later report of Portuguese victories in Morocco greatly pleased the king, who expressed his appreciation by sending to Rome in the spring of 1514 an embassy of obedience of unequalled splendor.[2] In return the pope showered favors upon the monarch who had so marvellously enlarged the field of missionary enterprise. Like Julius II., Leo X. sent the king the consecrated golden rose, and granted the requests preferred by the Portuguese ambassadors. When the embassy of obedience left Rome, late in May or early in June, Portuguese affairs remained in the hands of the ordinary ambassador, João de Faria, who obtained further concessions from the pope, among which was the bull of June 7, 1514, which gave to the king the patronage of ecclesiastical benefices in Africa and *in all other places beyond the sea,* acquired or to be acquired from the infidels, and subjected them to the spiritual jurisdiction of the Order of Christ.[3] On November 3, a bull was issued which renewed the earlier donations to Portugal, and amplified them in the way in which the bull of September 26, 1493,[4] extended the grants previously made to Castile. The bull of November 3 granted to Portugal the lands and other property acquired from the infidels, not only from capes Bojador and Não to the Indies, but in any region whatsoever, even if then unknown. Thus it appears that Pope Leo X. regarded the demarcation line as confined to one hemisphere, where it served to determine for both powers the route that must be followed to the Indies. For the present bull permitted the Portuguese, following the eastern route, to acquire lands from the infidels, even though these lands were situated more than half-way around the globe. The Portuguese desired

---

[1] Printed in Rebello da Silva, *Corp. Dipl. Port.,* I. 196-199, and in Roscoe, *Leo the Tenth,* vol. I., app., p. xxxiv.

[2] For documents relating to this embassy, see Roscoe, *op. cit.,* appendix; MacSwiney de Mashanaglass, *Le Portugal et le Saint-Siège,* III., appendix; J. Ramos-Coelho, *Alguns Documentos* (1892), pp. 353-356; Rebello da Silva, *op. cit.,* I. 234-243; and Ciutiis, *Ambassade Portuguaise.* See also the description in Goes, *Chronica do Rei D. Manoel,* pt. III., cc. 55-57.

[3] The bull is printed in Rebello da Silva, *Corp. Dipl. Port.,* I. 254-257. In regard to the Order of Christ, see Doc. 2, note 14.

[4] Doc. 8. This bull had revoked the papal grants to Portugal in so far as they might be interpreted as giving her exclusive claim to the Indies.

this bull, it is almost certain, because they harbored doubts as to whether Malacca, or at any rate the coveted Moluccas, which had been visited by them at the end of 1511 or early in 1512, were on their side of the line. As early as 1512 the rumor was current that the Moluccas lay within the Spanish demarcation, and in the autumn of that year the Portuguese ambassador in Spain was much disturbed by King Ferdinand's project of an expedition to seize those islands for the Spanish crown.[5]

BIBLIOGRAPHY.

Text: MS. The original manuscript of the promulgated bull is in the National Archives at Lisbon, Coll. de Bullas, maço 29, no. 6.

Text: Printed. *Bullarum Collectio* (Lisbon, 1707), pp. 8-53; L. A. Rebello da Silva, *Corpo Diplomatico Portuguez* (Acad. Real das Sciencias, Lisbon, 1862—), I. 275-298. A synopsis and extract are in Blair and Robertson, *Philippine Islands* (1903-1909), I. 136-138.

References: Contemporary and early writings. Damião de Goes, *Chronica do Rei D. Manoel* (1749), pt. III., cc. 55-57.

References: Later writings. L. von Pastor, *Geschichte der Päpste*, band IV., abt. I. (1906), pp. 50-53; Marquis MacSwiney de Mashanaglass, *Le Portugal et le Saint-Siège*, I. (1898), 21-28; III. (1904), 85-128; Salvatore de Ciutiis, *Une Ambassade Portugaise à Rome* (1899); W. Roscoe, *Life of Leo the Tenth* (1846), I. 361-364; J. T. Medina, *Juan Diaz de Solis* (1897), tom. I., c. 6, tom. II., docs. 22, 30, 31.

TEXT.[6]

Leo episcopus, servus servorum Dei. Ad perpetuam rei memoriam.

Precelse devotionis et indefessum fervorem, integre fidei puritatem, ingeniique in Sanctam Sedem Apostolicam observantiam, excelsarumque virtutum flagrantiam, quibus charissimus in Christo filius noster, Emmanuel Portugallie et Algarbiorum rex illustris, sese nobis et dicte sedi multipliciter gratum, obsequiosum, et acceptum prebuit, apud archana mentis nostre digne revolventes, presertim cum, magistra rerum experientia teste, perpendimus ac apertis documentis in dies clare conspicimus, quam sedula vigilantia sua Sublimitas et Serenitas suorum predecessorum Portugallie regum gesta sequendo, plerumque in persona, non sine gravissimis laboribus et expensis, nixa sit et continuo ferventius enititur, ut Salvatori nostro ac nomini Christiano infensa Maurorum et aliorum infidelium immanitas nedum a fidelium finibus arceatur quinimo suis flagitiis male perdita, et arctetur funditus et deleatur, et Christiana religio, optata pace freta, votiva in omnibus suscipiat incrementa; hiis considerationibus et plerisque aliis legitimis causis suadentibus, congruum et opere pretium existimamus, ea que a predecessoribus nostris, Romanis pontificibus, ipsius Emanuelis Regis predecessoribus pre-

---

[5] Medina, *Juan Diaz de Solis*, tom. I., c. 6, tom. II., docs. 22, 30, 31.
[6] The text is taken from the original manuscript in the National Archives at Lisbon, Coll. de Bullas, maço 29, no. 6. On the back is the endorsement "Registrata apud me Ja: Sadoletum."

fatis concessa comperimus, nostro etiam munimine confovere ac alia etiam de novo concedere, ut exinde Celsitudo sua, Apostolice Sedi predicte ulteriori munificentia premunita, in prosecutione promissorum non solum ardentius inflametur, sed et liberali ac munifica compensatione accepta ceteros reddat et faciat ad similia promptiores, et ejus erga nos et sedem predictam devotio augeatur, et pro laboribus quos Universali Ecclesie circa Catholice et apostolice fidei exaltationem bene serviendo sustinet condignos honores et gratias reportet.

Dudum siquidem a felicis recordationis Nicolao papa V. et Sixto IV. Romanis pontificibus, predecessoribus nostris, emanarunt diverse littere, tenoris subsequentis.

[Here follow the bulls of June 18, 1452 (a part of which is printed above, Doc. 1, note 37); of January 8, 1455 (Doc. 1); and of June 21, 1481 (Doc. 4), which includes the bulls of January 8, 1455, and of March 13, 1456 (Doc. 2), and the part of the treaty of Alcaçovas relating to Guinea (Doc. 3).]

Nos igitur, qui ejusdem Emmanuelis Regis, fidei augmentum et propagationem jugiter procurantis, commoda et utilitates supremis desideriis affectamus, motu proprio, non ad ipsius Emanuelis Regis vel alicujus alterius pro eo nobis super hoc oblate petitionis instantiam, sed de nostra mera deliberatione et ex certa nostra scientia ac de apostolice potestatis plenitudine, omnes et singulas literas predictas ac omnia et singula in eis contenta et inde secuta quecumque rata et grata habentes, auctoritate apostolica, tenore presentium approbamus et innovamus ac confirmamus, supplentes omnes et singulos defectus, tam juris quam facti, siqui forsan intervenerint in eisdem, ac perpetue firmitatis robur obtinere debere decernimus.

Et pro potiori cautela, omnia et singula in eisdem litteris contenta, ac quecunque alia imperia, regna, principatus, ducatus, provincias, terras, civitates, opida, castra, dominia, insulas, portus, maria, littora, et bona quecunque, mobilia et immobilia, ubicunque consistentia, per eundem Emanuelem Regem et predecessores suos a dictis infidelibus, etiam solitaria quecunque recuperata, detecta, inventa, et acquisita, ac per ipsum Emanuelem Regem et successores suos in posterum recuperanda, acquirenda, detegenda, et invenienda, tam a Capitibus de Bogiador et de Naon usque ad Indos quam etiam ubicunque et in quibuscunque partibus, etiam nostris temporibus forsan ignotis, eisdem auctoritate et tenore de novo concedimus; litterasque supradictas ac omnia et singula in illis contenta ad premissa etiam extendimus et ampliamus, ac in virtute sancte obedientie et indignationis nostre pena quibuscunque fidelibus Christianis, etiam si imperiali regali, et quacunque alia prefulgeant dignitate, ne eundem Emmanuelem Regem et successores suos quomodolibet in premissis impedire, ac eisdem infidelibus auxilium, consilium, vel favorem prestare presumant, auctoritate et tenore premissis inhibemus.

Quocirca venerabilibus fratribus nostris archiepiscopo Ulixbonensi,[1] et Egiptanensi[2] ac Funchalensi[3] episcopis, per apostolica scripta motu simili mandamus quatinus ipsi, vel duo aut unus eorum, per se vel alium seu alios,

---

[1] Martin da Costa, brother of Jorge da Costa. Doc. 11, introduction.
[2] Idanha-Velha, with see at Guarda. In 1514 the bishop was Pedro Vasques.
[3] Funchal is the chief town on the island of Madeira. In 1514 its bishop was Diogo Pinheiro.

presentes litteras ac omnia et singula in eis contenta, ubi et quando expedierit, ac quotiens pro parte Emanuelis Regis et successorum suorum predictorum fuerint super hoc requisiti solemniter publicantes, ac eisdem Emanueli Regi et successoribus in premissis efficacis defensionis presidio assistentes, faciant auctoritate nostra presentes et alias litteras et in eis contenta hujusmodi inviolabiliter observari, non permittentes eos super illis per quoscunque quomodolibet molestari; contradictores per censuram ecclesiasticam, appellatione postposita, compescendo; invocato etiam ad hoc, si opus fuerit, auxilio brachii secularis. Et nihilominus, legitimis super hiis habendis servatis processibus,[10] illos quos censuras et penas per eos pro tempore latas eos[11] incurrisse constiterit, quotiens expedierit, iteratis vicibus, aggravare procurent.

Non obstantibus recolende memorie Bonifacii Pape VIII., similiter predecessoris nostri, qua inter alia cavetur ne quis extra suam civitatem et diocesim, nisi in certis exceptis casibus, et in illis ultra unam dietam a fine sue diocesis ad judicium evocetur, seu ne judices ab Apostolica Sede deputati, extra civitatem et diocesim in quibus deputati fuerint, contra quoscunque procedere, aut alii, vel aliis vices suas committere presumant,[12] et de duabus dietis in concilio generali[13] edita ac aliis apostolicis constitutionibus ac omnibus illis que idem Nicolaus et alii predecessores, qui similes eidem Regi Portugallie fecerunt concessiones, in eorum litteris voluerunt non obstare, contrariis quibuscunque; aut si aliquibus, communiter vel divisim, ab eadem sit sede indultum quod interdici, suspendi, vel excommunicari non possint per litteras apostolicas non facientes plenam et expressam ac de verbo ad verbum de indulto hujusmodi mentionem.

Nulli ergo omnino hominum liceat hanc paginam nostre approbationis, innovationis, confirmationis, suppletionis, decreti, concessionis, extensionis, ampliationis, inhibitionis, et mandati infringere, vel ei ausu temerario contraire. Siquis autem hoc attemptare presumpserit, indignationem Omnipotentis Dei ac beatorum Petri et Pauli apostolorum ejus se noverit incursurum.

Datum Rome apud Sanctum Petrum, anno Incarnationis Dominice millesimo quingentesimo quartodecimo, tertio nonas Novembris, pontificatus nostri anno secundo. JA. SADOLETUS.[14] B. DE COMITIBUS.

TRANSLATION.

Leo, bishop, servant of the servants of God. For an abiding remembrance.

Meditating fittingly in the inmost counsels of our heart upon the unwearied fervor of lofty devotion, the purity of blameless faith, the respect for the Holy Apostolic See, and the ardor of lofty virtues, whereby our very

---

[10] " The steps whereby a controversy is discussed in judgment constitute a process." O. J. Reichel, *Canon Law* (1896), II. 262.

[11] This word, which is in the manuscript, should be omitted to make sense.

[12] See the *Corpus Juris Canonici*, Sexti Decretal. lib. I., tit. III., c. XI. (pt. II., p. 942, in Friedberg's edition).

[13] By the rule of the Fourth Lateran Council, can. 37, no one can be cited by apostolic letters to appear at a place more than two days' journey from his diocese, unless such letters shall have been procured with the assent of the parties, or unless they expressly mention this rule. *Corpus Juris Canonici*, Decretal. Gregor. IX. lib. I., tit. III., c. 28 (pt. II., p. 31, in Friedberg's edition).

[14] Jacopo Sadoleto, the Italian humanist, and Pietro Bembo were the secretaries of Leo X., whose chancery was famous for the brilliancy of its letters.

dear son in Christ, Emmanuel, the illustrious king of Portugal and of the Algarves, has made himself, in manifold ways, pleasing, serviceable, and agreeable to us and to the said see, especially since in the light of experience we consider, and from manifest proofs every day clearly perceive, with what unremitting vigilance his Sublimity and Serenity, following the example of his predecessors, the kings of Portugal, has striven, and ever more zealously strives, for the most part in person and not without the greatest effort and expense, in order that the barbarous hostility of the Moors and of other infidels to our Savior and to the Christian name may not only be warded off from the territories of the faithful, but, perishing in its own iniquity, may be entirely restrained and blotted out, and that the Christian religion may by peaceful means be advanced and promoted in all longed-for ways: persuaded by these considerations and by many other legitimate reasons, we deem it fitting and expedient constantly to guard and protect those concessions which we have learned were granted by our predecessors, the Roman pontiffs, to the aforesaid predecessors of the said King Emmanuel, and also to grant other and new privileges, in order that then his Highness, fortified by the further munificence of the aforesaid Apostolic See, may not only be roused to greater zeal in fulfilling his promises, but having received a liberal and generous reward may induce and cause others more readily to undertake similar work, and that his devotion to us and to the aforesaid see may be increased, and that in return for the labors which he sustains in serving the Church Universal by exalting the Catholic and apostolic faith, he may obtain suitable honors and rewards.

A short while ago, divers letters of the following tenor were issued by our predecessors, Popes Nicholas V. and Sixtus IV., of happy memory.

[Here follow the bulls of June 18, 1452 (a part of which is printed above, Doc. 1, note 37); of January 8, 1455 (Doc. 1); and of June 21, 1481 (Doc. 4), which includes the bulls of January 8, 1455, and of March 13, 1456 (Doc. 2), and the part of the treaty of Alcaçovas relating to Guinea (Doc. 3).]

We, therefore, who passionately strive for the advantage and profit of the said King Emmanuel, since he is continually aiming at the growth and extension of the faith, of our own accord, and not at the instance of the said King Emmanuel or on account of any request offered by any other person in his behalf, but from our mere deliberation and out of our certain knowledge and from the plenitude of apostolic power, approve and renew and confirm by the apostolic authority and by the tenor of these presents, the aforesaid letters, all and singular, regarding their contents, all and singular, and whatever has followed thereupon as established and acceptable, and supplying all and singular defects, both of law and of fact, if any should happen to occur in them; and we decree that they ought to be permanently valid.

And for greater security and by virtue of the authority and in the terms mentioned above, we newly grant everything, all and singular, contained in the aforesaid letters, and all other empires, kingdoms, principalities, duchies, provinces, lands, cities, towns, forts, lordships, islands, harbors, seas, coasts, and all property, real and personal, wherever existing, also all unfrequented places, recovered, discovered, found and acquired from the aforesaid infidels, by the said King Emmanuel and his predecessors, or in future to be re-

covered, acquired, discovered, and found by the said King Emmanuel and
his successors, both from Capes Bojador and Não to the Indies, and in any
place or region whatsoever, even although perchance unknown to us at
present; and we also extend and amplify the aforesaid letters, and their contents, all and singular, to the aforesaid concessions, and in virtue of holy
obedience and under penalty of our wrath, by the authority and in the terms
aforesaid, we inhibit all faithful Christians, even though adorned with imperial, royal, or any other rank, from presuming to hinder in any way the
said King Emmanuel and his successors in respect to the aforesaid concessions, and from furnishing aid, counsel, or favor to the said infidels.

Wherefore by apostolic writings, and of the same accord, we charge our
venerable brothers, the archbishop of Lisbon and the bishops of Idanha-
Velha (Guarda) and Funchal, that they, or two or one of them, by himself,
or through another, or others, solemnly publishing the present letters and all
and singular therein contained, where and when it shall be expedient, and
as often as they shall be required on behalf of King Emmanuel and his successors and, aiding the aforesaid King Emmanuel and his successors with
effectual protection in the aforesaid, do by our authority cause the present
and other letters and the matters contained therein to be inviolably observed
after this manner, not permitting them [*i. e.*, the kings] to be troubled in any
way whatever and by anyone in respect to these matters, restraining the
disobedient by ecclesiastical censure, without permitting appeal, and likewise
if necessary invoking for this purpose the aid of the secular arm. And none
the less, observing the legal process to be followed in these matters, let them
be careful, as often as it shall be expedient, to harass again and again those
who it shall appear have incurred the censures and penalties imposed by them
in accordance with circumstances.

Nor shall the [edict] of Pope Boniface VIII., of celebrated memory,
similarly our predecessor, interfere with these injunctions, in which, among
other things, he forbade that anyone be summoned to trial outside his city
or diocese, except in certain excepted cases, and in those cases not more
than one day's journey from the bounds of his diocese, or that judges, deputed
by the Apostolic See, presume to proceed against anyone outside the city or
diocese in which they shall have been deputed, or that they presume to intrust
their duties to any other person or persons; nor the regulation in regard to
the two days' journey, ordained in the General Council; and other apostolic
constitutions; nor all those constitutions whatsoever to the contrary which
the said Nicholas and others of our predecssors, who made similar concessions to the said King of Portugal, declared to be of no effect in their letters,
even if the said see has granted an indult to any, jointly or singly, that they
may not be interdicted, suspended, or excommunicated by apostolic letters not
making full and express mention, word for word, of such indult.

Let no man whomsoever therefore infringe or with rash boldness contravene this our approval, renewal, confirmation, completion, decree, grant,
extension, amplification, inhibition, and mandate. Should anyone presume to
attempt this, be it known to him that he will incur the wrath of Almighty
God and of the blessed apostles Peter and Paul.

Given at Rome, at St. Peter's, on the third day of November, in the year
of the incarnation of our Lord, 1514, in the second year of our pontificate.

JACOPO SADOLETO. B. DE COMITIBUS.

13.

Treaty between Spain and Portugal, concluded at Vitoria, February 19, 1524. Ratification by the Emperor, February 27, 1524.

INTRODUCTION.

The attainment of India by the Portuguese incited the Spaniards to discover a strait leading westward to the Spice Islands. This was the purpose of Columbus's fourth voyage (1502-1504), and of several other Spanish expeditions, planned or undertaken in the following decade. The King of Portugal kept jealous watch of these enterprises and his protests caused at least one projected expedition of this kind to be postponed.[1]

In 1518 the Portuguese captain Magellan, who had served in the Far East, deeming himself ungratefully treated by King Emmanuel, transferred his allegiance to King Charles of Spain.[2] On the ground that the Spice Islands (Moluccas) lay on the Spanish side of the line of demarcation, he persuaded Charles to employ him to lead an expedition thither by the western route.[3] Despite the King of Spain's assurances that his commanders were charged to respect existing international agreements touching the line of demarcation,[4] Portugal strove to frustrate Magellan's negotiations, and, failing in this, to obstruct the execution of his project.[5]

These attempts failed and in November, 1521, the Spanish expedition, having discovered on the voyage the Ladrones and the Philippine Islands, reached the Moluccas, where the native rulers concluded treaties with the

---

[1] His effectual protest against Pinzon's expedition planned in 1506 is noticed in H. Harrisse, *Discovery of North America* (1892), p. 730. For an account of early attempts to find a western passage to the Spice Islands see J. T. Medina, *Sebastián Caboto* (1908), tom. I., c. 8.

[2] Charles was elected emperor in the following year.

[3] Magellan's instructions, his memorial on the latitude and longitude of the Moluccas, and other related documents are printed in the fourth volume of Navarrete, *Viages*, and summarized in the first volume of Blair and Robertson, *Philippine Islands*. See also *Algs. Docs.*, pp. 423-430. and Medina, *Documentos para la Historia de Chile*, I., II. The belief that the Moluccas lay within the Spanish area was entertained by the Spanish government as early as 1512. Cf. Doc. **12**, introduction and note 5.

[4] See the letter from Charles to King Emmanuel, Feb. 28, 1519, *Algs. Docs.*, pp. 422-423, and Blair and Robertson, *Philippine Islands*, I. 277-279.

[5] Guillemard, *Magellan*, pp. 111-139. Letters to King Emmanuel from the Portuguese ambassador, Sept. 28, 1518, and from the Portuguese factor at Seville, July 18, 1519. are published in the original and in translation in Lord Stanley, *First Voyage* (Hakluyt Soc., no. LII., 1874), pp. xxxv-xlvi, and appendixes 1 and 2. A translation of the former letter is in Guillemard, *op. cit.*, pp. 114-116, and a partial translation of the second letter in the same work, pp. 130-134. The text of the second letter is in *Algs. Docs.*, pp. 431-435.

leaders of the expedition and declared themselves vassals of Spain.[6] In the Moluccas the Spaniards found themselves face to face with the Portuguese, who had discovered the islands ten years before, and manifested their resentment against the intruders by destroying a trading post that the Spaniards were attempting to establish, and by seizing a ship. Portuguese hostility was also displayed in another quarter, when the *Victoria*, the only vessel of the Spanish fleet that completed the voyage round the globe, was obliged, near the end of her course, to put in at the Cape Verde Islands.[7] Here the Portuguese detained several of her crew as prisoners, and the King of Portugal, learning what had occurred, despatched four caravels in vain pursuit of the ship.[8]

Shortly after the return of the *Victoria* to Spain the two courts began negotiations relative to the Moluccas.

Three closely related questions were distinguished: (1) the determination of the line of demarcation in accordance with the treaty of Tordesillas; (2) the possession of the Moluccas; and (3) their ownership. Early in the negotiations the Emperor suggested that in addition to the caravels despatched by each power to make a demarcation, Pope Adrian VI. should send a caravel, and act as umpire.[9] As to possession, both parties claimed it. The Emperor argued that even if the Moluccas had been first seen or discovered by Portuguese ships, yet they had not been taken or possessed, and therefore not *effectually* found by them; while he, on the other hand, was acknowledged by the native rulers as lord of those regions.[10] He admitted, however, that the Portuguese were in possession of Malacca, although many believed that this also lay within the Spanish demarcation. The Portuguese, on the other hand, asserted that they had found the Moluccas, and that therefore, even if they were on the Spanish side of the line of demarcation, Spain should, in accordance with the treaty of Tordesillas, petition the Portuguese for them. The Spanish argued that, on the contrary, such petition should come from the Portuguese.[11]

Among the demands made by Portugal, one was especially displeasing to the Emperor and the Castilian Cortes—that while the questions of possession and ownership remained in dispute, neither party should despatch a trading fleet to the Moluccas. The *Victoria's* cargo had proved of enormous value, and before the end of the year 1522 a second fleet was being hastily

[6] Extracts from these treaties are in Navarrete, *op. cit.*, IV. 295-298.

[7] Guillemard, *op. cit.*, pp. 293 ff.

[8] Andrada, *Chronica del Rey Dom João o III.*, pt. I., c. 17. Santarem, *Quadro Elementar*, II. 32 ff.

[9] *Algs. Docs.*, p. 462.

[10] Blair and Robertson, *op. cit.*, I. 150-153; Herrera, *Historia General*, dec. III., lib. VI., c. 5., and *cf.* Peter Martyr D'Anghera, *De Orbe Novo*, II. 239 (trans. by F. A. MacNutt, 1912).

[11] Blair and Robertson, *op. cit.*, I. 142-158; Navarrete, *op. cit.*, tom. IV., no. 31, pp. 312-320; Herrera, *loc. cit.*

equipped to sail to the Spice Islands from Coruña. In consequence of Portugal's opposition, the Emperor postponed its departure, but in 1523 he promised the Cortes of Castile that it should be despatched as soon as possible and that he would not surrender the " Spicery " or come to any other agreement respecting it that was prejudicial to Castile.[12]

The negotiations ended in the signing of a provisional treaty in the city of Vitoria on February 19, 1524. The principal stipulations were that each party should appoint three astrologers and three pilots to assemble not later than the end of March at the frontier of the two countries to determine the demarcation; and three lawyers to meet at the same time and place to determine the question of possession. If possible the questions were to be decided by the end of May, 1524. Before that time neither party was to despatch a trading expedition to the Moluccas.

The treaty was ratified by the Emperor on February 27, 1524.

Bibliography.

Text: MS. The original ratification signed by the emperor at Vitoria, February 27, 1524, is in the National Archives at Lisbon, gav. 18, maço 6, no. 5. The protocol is in the same archives, gav. 15, maço 10, no. 20, and also in the Archives of the Indies at Seville, Papeles de Maluco de 1519 á 1547, est. 1, caj. 2, leg. 1/15, no. 9.

Text: Printed. The protocol is printed in M. F. de Navarrete, *Coleccion de Viages* (1825-1837), tom. IV., no. 32, pp. 320-326, and in J. T. Medina, *Coleccion de Documentos para la Historia de Chile* (1888-1902), I. 330-337.

Translation. The articles are translated in E. H. Blair and J. A. Robertson, *Philippine Islands* (1903-1909), I. 160-163.

References: Contemporary and early writings. Diplomatic documents: Navarrete, *op. cit.*, IV. 301-305, 312-320, translated in Blair and Robertson, *op. cit.*, I. 139-158; J. Ramos-Coelho, *Alguns Documentos* (1892), pp. 462-463; Viscount de Santarem, *Quadro Elementar* (1842-1876), II. 35 ff. See also A. Rodríguez Villa, *El Emperador Carlos V. y su Corte según las Cartas de Don Martín de Salinas* (1903), *passim*; Fr. d'Andrada, *Chronica do Rey Dom João o III.* (1796), tom. I., cc. 16-18; A. de Herrera, *Historia General de los Hechos de los Castellanos*, dec. III., lib. VI., cc. 3-6 (ed. 1728-1730, II. 178-184); B. Leonardo de Argensola, *Conquista de las Islas Malucas* (1609), lib. I.; *id.*, in *Biblioteca de Escritores Aragoneses*, Sección Literaria, tom. VI. (1891), translated in J. Stevens, *New Collection of Voyages and Travels* (1708-1710), vol. I., pt. 1; Medina, *op. cit.*, toms. I. and II.

References: Later writings. F. H. H. Guillemard, *Life of Ferdinand Magellan* (1890); O. Koelliker, *Die Erste Umseglung der Erde* (1908), gives an extended list of the sources; F. Colin, *Labor Evangélica* (ed. P. Pastells, 1904), II. 600-613, " Discusiones entre España y Portugal acerca del Derecho de Posesión de las Malucas ".

---

[12] *Córtes de los Antiguos Reinos de Leon y de Castilla*, IV. 388 (Real Academia de la Historia, Madrid, 1861, etc.).

TEXT.[13]

Don Carlos, por la gracia de Dios rrei de Romaños e emperador semper augusto, Doña Johana, su madre, e el mesmo Don Carlos, por la mesma gracia rreyes de Castilla, de Leon, de Aragon, de las Dos Seçilias, de Jherusalem, de Navarra, de Granada, de Toledo, de Valencia, de Galizia, de Mallorcas, de Sevilla, de Çerdeña, de Cordova, de Corçega, de Murçia, de Jahen, de los Algarves, de Algezira, de Gibraltar, de las Yslas de Canaria, de las Indias, yslas e tierra firme del mar oçeano, condes de Barçelona, señores de Vizcaya e, de Molina, duques de Athenas e de Neopatria, condes de Ruysellon e de Çerdania, marqueses de Oristan e de Goçiano, archiduques de Austria, duques de Borgoña e de Bravante, condes de Flandes e de Tirol, etc., vimos una escriptura de capitulaçion e asiento hecha en nuestro nombre por Mercurinus de Gratinara,[14] nuestro grand chançiller, e Don Herrnando de Vega,[15] commendador mayor de Castilla, e Don Garçia de Padilla,[16] comendador mayor de Calatrava, y el Doctor Lorenço Galindez de Carvajal,[17] todos del nuestro consejo, e Pero Correa, de Atovia, señor de la villa de Velas, y el Doctor Johan de Faria,[18] embaxadores e del consejo del Serenisimo e Mui Excelente Rei de Portugal,[19] nuestro mui caro e mui amado sobriño e primo, e sus procuradores, su thenor del qual es este que se sigue :

En el nombre de Dios Todo poderoso, Padre y Hijo y Spiritu Sancto. Manifiesto e notorio sea a todos quantos este publico ynstrumento vieren, como en la çibdad de Vitoria a diez e nueve dias del mes de Hebrero, año del nasçimiento de nuestro Salvador Jhesu Christo de mill e quinientos e veinte e quatro años, en presençia de mi, Françisco de los Covos,[20] secretario de sus

[13] The text is taken from the original manuscript of the ratification by the Emperor, dated Feb. 27, 1524, preserved in the National Archives at Lisbon, gav. 18, maço 6, no. 5.

[14] In 1519 Mercurino Arborio de Gattinara, a Piedmontese, formerly employed by the Emperor Maximilian in important negotiations, became grand chancellor of Charles V. and *ex officio* president of the councils. He befriended Las Casas in his controversies with the Council of the Indies and presided over the Cortes of 1523 which petitioned Charles not to surrender the Spice Islands. In 1529, the year before his death, he was created cardinal.

[15] Señor de Grajal, knight-commander in Castile and Leon of the Order of Santiago and president of the Council of the Orders (*i. e.*, of the three oldest orders of knighthood in Spain—Alcántara, Calatrava, and Santiago). He was a member of the Council of the Indies both before and after its reorganization in 1524, and at one time owned land and Indians in the West Indies. In 1515 he was a president of the Cortes. A brief biographical notice of him is in M. Danvila, *Historia de las Comunidades de Castilla*, in the *Memorial Histórico Español* (Real Academia de la Historia, Madrid, 1899), XL. 135.

[16] A member of the early Council of the Indies and of the Cortes of 1518, 1520, and 1523. In 1523 president of the Council of the Orders.

[17] A learned lawyer and historian, member of the Council of the Indies as reorganized in 1524, and of the Cortes of 1520 and 1523; president of the Royal Council of Castile, and appointed by Queen Isabella to prepare a digest of the Castilian law. His *Anales del Rey Don Fernando el Católico* is one of the best authorities for the latter part of that king's reign.

[18] During his embassy at Rome, João de Faria had obtained many favors for Portugal from Leo X. *Cf.* above, Doc. **12**, introduction.

[19] John III., 1521-1537.

[20] In 1517 Cobos, a Spaniard, became secretary to Charles V. and a member of the Council of the Indies. He rose rapidly in favor, and after the death of Gattinara he and Granvelle were Charles's most influential ministers. "All the affairs of Italy, the Indies, and Spain passed under his hand for many years." Gómara, *Annals of the Emperor Charles V.* (ed. R. B. Merriman, 1912), p. 136.

Magestades e su noctario publico, e de los testigos de yuso escripctos, estando
presentes los señores Mercurinus de Gratinara, grand chançiller de sus
Magestades, y Don Hernando de Vega, comendador mayor de Castilla de la
Horden de Sanctiago, e Don Garçia de Padilla, comendador mayor de Calatrava, y el Doctor Lorenço Galindez de Carvajal, todos del consejo de los mui
altos e mui poderosos prínçipes, Don Carlos, por la divina clemençia emperador
semper augusto, rrey de Romaños, y Doña Johana, su madre, e el mesmo
Don Carlos, su hijo, por la graçia de Dios rreyes de Castilla, de Leon, de
Aragon, de las Dos Seçilias, de Jherusalen, etc., sus procuradores bastantes,
de la una parte, e los señores, Pero Correa de Atovia, señor de la villa de Velas,
e el Doctor Johan de Faria, ambos del consejo del muy alto e muy exçelente
señor, el señor, Don Johan, por la graçia de Dios rrey de Portugal, de los
Algarves de aquende y allende el mar en Africa, señor de Guinea y de la
conquista, navegaçion, e comerçio de Ytiopia e Aravia e Persia y de la India.
etc., sus embaxadores e procuradores bastantes, segund ambas las dichas
partes lo mostraron por las cartas, poderes, e procuraçiones delos dichos
señores sus constituyentes, su thenor de las quales *de verbo ad verbum* es
este que se sigue :

[Here follow the full powers granted by the Emperor Charles V. and
Queen Joanna of Castile to Mercurino de Gattinara, Fernando de Vega,
García de Padilla, and Dr. Lorenzo Galíndez de Carvajal, on January 25,
1524; and the full powers granted by John III. of Portugal to Pedro
Corrêa and Dr. João de Faria on January 13, 1524.]

E luego los dichos procuradores de los dichos señores rreyes de Castilla,
de Leon, de Aragon, de las Dos Seçilias, de Jherusalem, etc., e del dicho Señor
Rey de Portugal, de los Algarves, etc., dixeron: Que por quanto entre los
dichos señores sus constituyentes ay dubda sobre la posesion de Maluco y la
propiedad del, pretendiendo cada uno dellos que cae en los limites de su
demarcaçion, la qual se ha de hazer conforme al asiento y capitulaçion [21]
que fue fecha entre los Catolicos rreyes, Don Hernando e Reina Doña Ysabel,
rreyes de Castilla, de Leon, de Aragon, etc., e el muy alto y muy exçelente
señor el Señor Rey Don Johan, rrey de Portugal, de los Algarves, señor de
Guinea, etc., que ayan gloria, por ende ellos e cada uno dellos en los dichos
nombres e por virtud delos dichos poderes de suso encorporados, por bien de
paz e concordia e por conservaçion del debdo e amor que entre los señores
sus constituyentes [ay,] [22] otorgaron, consintieron, e asentaron lo siguiente :

[1.] Primeramente, que para la demarcaçion que se ha de hazer conforme
a la dicha capitulaçion, se nombre[n] por cada una de las partes tres astrologos e tres pilotos e marineros, los quales se ayan de juntar e junten por
todo el mes de Março primero que viene, o antes si ser pudiere, en la rraya
de Castilla y Portugal entre la cibdad de Badajoz e la cibdad de Yelves, para
que por todo el mes de Mayo primero siguiente, deste presente año, haziendo
ante todas cosas, luego commo se juntaren, juramento solene em forma
devida de derecho en poder de dos notarios, uno puesto por la una parte y
el otro por la otra, con abto e testimonio publico, en que juren a Dios e a
Santa Maria e a las palabras de los santtos quatro Evangelios, en que pornan
las maños, que pospuesto todo amor y temor, odio e pasion, ni interese alguno,
y sin tener rrespecto a otra cosa alguna mas de hazer justiçia, miraran el

---

[21] The treaty of Tordesillas, Doc. **9**.   [22] This word is not in the text.

derecho de las partes, determinen conforme a la dicha capitulaçion la dicha demarcaçion.

[2.] Asimismo, que se nombren por cada una de las partes tres letrados, los quales dentro del mesmo termino y lugar, premiso el dicho juramento con las solemnidades e de la manera que de suso se contiene, entiendan en lo de la posesion de Maluco, e lo determinen, rresçibiendo las probanças, escripturas, capitulaçiones, testigos e derechos que antes ellos fueren presentadas, e hagan todo lo que les paresçiere nesçesario para hazer la dicha declaraçion, commo hallaren por justiçia; e que de los dichos tress letrados, el primero nombrado en la comision tenga cargo de juntar a todos los otros diputados de su parte para que con mas cuydado se entienda en la negociaçion.

[3.] Otrosy, que durante el dicho termino fasta en fin del dicho mes de Mayo, primero siguiente, ninguna de las partes no pueda embiar a Maluco, ni contratar ni rescatar, pero si antes del dicho tiempo se determinare en posesion o propiedad, que la parte en cuyo favor se declarare el derecho en cada una de las dichas cosas, pueda embiar y rrescatar; e en caso que se determine lo de la propiedad e demarcaçion, se entienda deçisa e absorvida la quistion de la posesion; y si solamente se determinare lo de la posesion por los dichos dos letrados, sin que lo de la propiedad se pudiese determinar, commo es dicho, que lo que quedare por determinar de la dicha propiedad, e tambien de la posesion del dicho Maluco, quede conforme a la dicha capitulaçion en el estado en que estava antes que se hiziese este asiento; lo qual todo se ha de entender e entienda sin perjuizio del derecho de cada una de las partes en propiedad e posesion conforme a la dicha capitulaçion.

[4.] Pero si a los dichos letrados primero nombrados en las comisiones, antes que se acabe el dicho termino, paresçiere que con alguna prorrogaçion del dicho termino oviese aparençia de se poder acabar e determinar lo asentado, e se les ofresçiere otro camino o modo bueno para que este negoçio se podiese mejor determinar en un cabo o otro, conviene a saber, en posesion o propiedad; en qualquier destos casos los dichos dos letrados puedan prorrogar el tiempo que les paresçiere convenir a la brebe determinaçion dello, e que durante el termino de la dicha prorrogaçion puedan ellos e todos los otros diputados e cada uno dellos en su calidad, entender e conosçer, entiendan e conozcan, commo si fuese dentro del termino prinçipal de su comision; pero quel dicho tiempo se entiende prorrogado con las mismas condiçiones e calidades de suso contenidas.

[5.] Y que todos los abtos que en este caso se ovieren de hazer sean firmados por los dichos dos notarios nombrados por cada una de las partes el suyo, e cada uno escriva los abtos de su parte; y el otro, despues de averlos comprobado e colaçionado, los firme.

[6.] Yten, que cada una de las partes aya de traer rratificaçion e confirmaçion destos capitulos de los dichos señores sus constituyentes, dentro de veinte dias primeros siguientes.

Lo qual todo que dicho es, e cada cosa e parte dello, los dichos Mercurinus de Gratinara, grand chançiller·de sus Magestades, e los dichos Don Fernando de Vega, comendador mayor de Castilla, e Don Garçia de Padilla, comendador mayor de Calatrava, e el Dottor Lorenço Galindez de Carvajal, todos del su consejo, procuradores de los dichos mui altos e muy poderosos Reyna e Rey de Castilla, de Leon, de Aragon, e de Granada, e de las Dos Secilias, de Jherusalem, etc., y por virtud del dicho su poder, que de suso va encorporado, los dichos Pero Correa de Atovia e el Dottor Juan de Faria, procu-

9

radores e embaxadores del dicho muy alto e muy exçelente prinçipe, el Señor
Rey Don Johan de Portugal, e de los Algarves de aquende e allende el mar
en Africa, señor de Guinea, etc., e por virtud del dicho su poder que de suso
va encorporado, prometieron e seguraron en nombre de los dichos sus constituyentes, que ellos e sus subçesores e rreinos e señorios, para siempre
jamas, ternan e guardaran e cumpliran rrealmente e con efecto, a buena
fee e sin mal engaño, cessante todo fraude, cautela, engaño, fiçion, e simulaçion alguna, todo lo que de suso se contiene, e es asentado e concertado, e lo
que por los dichos diputados fuere sentençiado e determinado, e cada cosa
e parte dello, enteramente, segund e commo por ellos fuere hecho e ordenado
e sentençiado e determinado, bien asi e a tan cumplidamente commo si por
los dichos sus constituyentes conformes fuese hecho y determinado e conçertado e commo juizio dado por juezes competentes; e para que asy se
guardara e cumplira, por virtud de los dichos poderes que de suso van
encorporados, obligaron a los dichos sus partes, sus constituyentes, e a sus
bienes muebles e rrayzes e de sus patrimonios e coronas rreales e de sus
subçesores, para siempre jamas, que ellos ni alguno dellos, por si ni por
interposita persona, directe ni indirecte, no yran ni vernan contra ello, ni
contra cosa alguna ni parte dello, en tiempo alguno, ni por alguna manera,
pensada o no pensada, que sea o ser pueda, so las penas en la dicha capitulaçion que de suso se haze minçion contenidas, e, la pena pagada o non pagada
o graçiosamente rremitida, que toda via esta escriptura e asiento e todo lo
que por virtud della fuere hecho e determinado quede y finque firme, estable,
e valedero, para siempre jamas; e rrenunçiaron qualesquier leyes e derechos
de que se puedan aprovechar las dichas partes e cada una dellas para yr o
venir contra lo suso dicho, o contra alguna cosa o parte dello, e por mayor
seguridad e firmeza de lo suso dicho juraron a Dios e a Santa Maria e a la
señal de la Cruz, en que pusieron sus manos derechas, e a las palabras de
los Santtos quatro Evangelios, donde quier que mas largamente son escripctos,
en anima de los dichos sus partes, que ellos e cada uno dellos ternan,
guardaran, e cumpliran todo lo suso dicho e cada una cosa e parte dello,
rrealmente e con efecto, çesante todo engaño, cautela, e simulaçion, e no lo
contradiran en tiempo alguno ni por alguna manera, e so el dicho juramento
juraron de no pedir absoluçion de nuestro muy Santo Padre ni de otro
legado ni perlado que se la pueda dar, y aun que de su proprio mottuo se la
de no usaran della, e asi mesmo los dichos procuradores en el dicho nonbre
se obligaron, so la dicha pena e juramento, que dentro de veinte dias primeros
siguientes, contados desde el dia de la hecha desta capitulaçion, daran la
una parte a la otra e la otra a la otra, aprovaçion e rratificaçion desta dicha
capitulaçion, escriptas en pergamino e firmadas de los nombres de los dichos
señores, sus constituyentes, e selladas con sus sellos de plomo pendientes, de
lo qual todo que dicho es otorgaron dos escripturas de un tenor, la una commo
la otra, las quales firmaron de sus nombres e las otorgaron ante mi, el dicho
secrettario e notario publico de suso escripto, e de los testigos de yuso
escriptos, para cada una de las partes la suya, e qualquier que paresçiere
valga commo si ambas a dos paresçiesen, que fueron fechas e otorgadas en la
dicha çibdad de Vittoria, el dicho dia e mes e año suso dicho. Testigos que
fueron presentes al otorgamiento desta escriptura, e vieron firmar en ella
a todos los dichos señores procuradores, e los vieron jurar corporalmente en
manos de mi, el dicho secretario, Françisco de Valençuela, cavallero de la
horden de Santiago, e Pedro de Salazar, capitan de sus magestades, e

Pedro de Ysasaga, contino[22] de sus magestades, e Go. Casco e Albaro Mexia e Bastian Fernandez, criados del dicho embaxador Pero Correa de Atuvia. Mercurinus, cancelarius, Hernando de Vega, comendador mayor, El comendador mayor,[24] Dottor Carvajal, Pero Correa, Juan de Faria. Por testigo, Françisco de Valençuela. Por testigo, Go. Quasquo. Testigo, Bastian Fernandes, testigo, Alvaro Mexia, por testigo, Pedro de Ysasaga, por el dicho Salazar, Johan de Samaño; e yo, el dicho Francisco de los Covos, secretario de sus Cesarea y Catholicas Magestades, y su escrivaño e notario publico en la su corte e en todos los sus rreynos e señorios de Castilla, presente fuy, en uno con los dichos testigos, al otorgamiento desta dicha escriptura e capitulaçion e juramento della, e de rruego e otorgamiento e pedimiento de los dichos procuradores de ambas las dichas partes, que en mi rregistro ellos e los dichos testigos firmaron sus nombres, esta dicha escriptura fiz escrivir segund que ante mi paso, la qual va escripta en tres hojas de papel con esta en que va my signo, e di a cada una de las dichas personas la suya, por ende en testimonio de verdad fiz aqui este mio signo a tal.

Por ende nos, vista e entendida la dicha escriptura e asiento que de suso va encorporada e cada cosa e parte della, e siendo çiertos e certificados de todo lo en ella contenido, e queriendo guardallo e cumplilla, commo en ella se contiene, loamos, confirmamos, e aprovamos, rratificamos y, en tanto que es nesçesario, de nuevo otorgamos e prometemos [25] guardar la dicha escriptura e asiento que asi por los dichos nuestros procuradores e procuradores [del dicho señor e] muy exçelente rrey nuestro sobrino e primo fue asentado e conçertado en nuestros nombres, e cada cosa e parte dello, rrealmente e con efecto, a buena fee, sin mal engaño, cesante todo fraude e simulaçion, e queremos e somos contentes que se guarde e cumpla segund e commo en ella se contiene, bien asi e a tan cumplidamente commo si por nos fuera fecho, asentado, e capitulado. Dada en Vitoria, a xxvii. dias del mes de Hebrero, año del naçimiento de nuestro Salvador Jhesu Christo de mill y quinientos e veynte y quatro años.

Yo, EL REY.

Yo, FRANCISCO DE LOS COVOS, secretario de sus Cesarea y Catholicas Magestades la fize escrevir por su mandado [notarial sign]. M[ERCURINU]S, Cançiller]. HERNANDO DE VEGA, comendador mayor. Liçentiatus Don GARÇIA. El Doctor CARVAJAL. ANDREUS . . . , chançiller.

TRANSLATION.

Don Charles, by the grace of God king of the Romans and emperor ever august, Doña Joanna, his mother, and the said Don Charles, by the said grace, King and Queen of Castile, Leon, Aragon, the Two Sicilies, Jerusalem, Navarre, Granada, Toledo, Valencia, Galicia, the Majorcas, Seville, Sardinia, Cordova, Corsica, Murcia, Jaen, the Algarves, Algeciras, Gibraltar, the Canary Islands, the Indies, the islands and mainland of the ocean sea, count and countess of Barcelona, lord and lady of Biscay and Molina, duke and

---

[22] See Doc. **9**, note 19.
[24] Don García de Padilla, knight-commander of the Order of Calatrava.
[25] A blot on the manuscript makes two words illegible.

duchess of Athens and Neopatras, count and countess of Roussillon and Cerdagne, marquis and marchioness of Oristano and Gociano, archduke and archduchess of Austria, duke and duchess of Burgundy and Brabant, count and countess of Flanders and Tirol, etc.: We have seen an instrument of agreement and treaty made in our name by Mercurino de Gattinara, our grand chancellor, and Don Hernando de Vega, chief knight-commander of Castile, and Don García de Padilla, chief knight-commander of Calatrava, and Doctor Lorenzo Galindez de Carvajal, all members of our council, and Pero Corrêa d'Atouguia, lord of the town of Bellas, and Doctor João de Faria, ambassadors and members of the council of the most serene and very excellent King of Portugal, our very dear and well-beloved nephew and cousin, and their representatives, the tenor of which is as follows:

In the name of God Almighty, Father, Son, and Holy Ghost. Be it manifest and known to all who shall see this public instrument, that in the city of Vitoria on the nineteenth day of the month of February, in the year of the nativity of our Saviour Jesus Christ, 1524, in the presence of me, Francisco de los Cobos, their majesties' secretary and notary public, and of the undersigned witnesses, there being present the lords Mercurino de Gattinara, grand chancellor of their Majesties, Don Hernando de Vega, chief knight-commander in Castile of the Order of Santiago, Don García de Padilla, chief knight-commander of the Order of Calatrava, and Doctor Lorenzo Galindez de Carvajal, all members of the council of the very exalted and very powerful princes, Don Charles, by the divine clemency, emperor ever august, king of the Romans, and Doña Joanna, his mother, and the said Don Charles, her son, by the grace of God king and queen of Castile, Leon, Aragon, the Two Sicilies, Jerusalem, etc., their qualified representatives, on the one part, and the lords Pero Corrêa d'Atouguia, lord of the town of Bellas, and Doctor João de Faria, both members of the council of the very exalted and very excellent lord, Dom John, by the grace of God king of Portugal, of the Algarves on this side of and beyond the sea in Africa, lord of Guinea and of the conquest, navigation, and commerce of Ethiopia, Arabia, Persia, India, etc., their ambassadors and qualified representatives—as both the said parties proved by the letters, authorizations, and procurations, from the said lords, their constituents, the tenor of which, word for word, is as follows:

[Here follow the full powers granted by the Emperor Charles V. and Queen Joanna of Castile to Mercurino de Gattinara, Fernando de Vega, García de Padilla, and Dr. Lorenzo Galindez de Carvajal, on January 25, 1524; and the full powers granted by John III. of Portugal to Pedro Corrêa and Dr. João de Faria on January 13, 1524.]

And thereupon the said representatives of the said King and Queen of Castile, Leon, Aragon, the Two Sicilies, Jerusalem, etc., and of the said lord King of Portugal, of the Algarves, etc., said: That whereas there is a difference of opinion between the said lords, their constituents, as to the possession and ownership of the Moluccas, each of them claiming that those islands fall within the limits of his demarcation, which must be determined in accordance with the treaty and agreement concluded between the Catholic sovereigns, Don Ferdinand and Queen Doña Isabella, king and queen of Castile, Leon, Aragon, etc., and the very exalted and excellent lord, the lord king Dom John, king of Portugal, of the Algarves, lord of Guinea, etc.

(may they rest in glory)—therefore they, jointly and severally, in the said names, and by virtue of the said powers incorporated above, for the sake of peace and concord, and for the preservation of the relationship and affection which exists between the lords their constituents, authorized, consented to, and agreed to the following:

1. First,[20] there shall be appointed by each one of the parties to this treaty three astrologers and three pilots and sailors for the determination of the demarcation, which must be made according to the terms of the said treaty. These men must assemble, and they shall assemble, by the end of the month of March first following, or before that time if possible, at the boundary line of Castile and Portugal, between the cities of Badajoz and Elvas, in order that by the end of the month of May next following, of this present year, they may determine, in accordance with the terms of the said treaty, the said demarcation—taking a solemn oath as soon as they have assembled, and before attending to anything else, in the form prescribed by law and before two notaries (one for each side) with public declaration and testimony, swearing in the presence of God and the blessed Mary, and upon the words of the four Holy Gospels, upon which they shall place their hands, that, laying aside all love and fear, hate, passion, or any interest, and with regard only to securing justice, they will examine the rights of the two parties involved.

2. Likewise three lawyers shall be appointed by each side, who, within the same period and at the same place, and after having taken the said oath with all the solemn forms and in the manner abovesaid, shall inquire into the possession of Molucca, and receiving the proofs, documents, treaties, witnesses, and rights that shall have been presented before them, shall determine the possession, doing everything that seems necessary for making the said declaration, just as they would do in court. Of the three abovementioned lawyers, he who is named first in the commission shall take charge of assembling all the other deputies of his side, in order that greater care may be exercised in the negotiations.

3. Further, during the said period and up to the end of the said month of May, next following, neither of the parties to this treaty shall despatch expeditions to Molucca for purposes of trade or barter. But if before the end of the said period the question of possession or ownership shall be determined, then the side in whose favor the right of each of the said questions is declared may despatch expeditions and may barter. And in case the question of ownership and demarcation is determined, then that of possession shall be understood to be decided and absorbed. If only the question of possession is determined by the [two] said lawyers, without their being able to determine that of ownership, as aforesaid, then what still remains to be determined of the said ownership, and likewise of the possession of the said Molucca, shall, in accordance with the terms of the treaty, remain in the same condition as before this present compact. All of the above must and shall be investigated without any prejudice to the rights of ownership and possession of either side, in accordance with the said treaty.

4. But if before the conclusion of the said period it shall appear to the lawyers first named in the commissions, as aforesaid, that the settlement

[20] The translation of the six following articles is taken from Blair and Robertson, *Philippine Islands*, I. 160-163.

can, in all probability, be concluded and determined with some further continuation of the time set, as abovesaid, or if another good way or manner of
procedure, by which this matter could be determined better under one head
or another, to wit, that of possession or that of ownership, should offer
itself to them, the two lawyers, as aforesaid, may in either of these cases
prolong, for so long a time as seems convenient to them, the brief determination of the matter. During the period of the said continuation, these lawyers
and all the other deputies, each one in his own capacity, may investigate
and ascertain, and they shall investigate and ascertain, just as if this extension of time were within the principal period named in their commission.
But the said time shall be understood to be continued under the same conditions and obligations as hereinbefore stated.

5. And all the actions taken in this case shall be signed by the two
notaries appointed in his name by each of the parties to this treaty, as aforesaid. Each notary shall write the actions taken by his side; and the other,
after having confirmed and collated them, shall sign them.

6. *Item,* each one of the sides must obtain the ratification and confirmation of these articles from their said constituents, within the twenty days
first ensuing.

All the foregoing, and every part and parcel of it, the said Mercurino de
Gattinara, grand chancellor of their Majesties, the said Don Hernando de
Vega, chief knight-commmander of Castile, Don Garcia de Padilla, chief
knight-commander of Calatrava, and Doctor Lorenzo Galíndez de Carvajal,
all members of their council, and representatives of the said very exalted
and very mighty Queen and King of Castile, Leon, Aragon, Granada, the
Two Sicilies, Jerusalem, etc., and by virtue of their said powers, incorporated
above, [and] the said Pedro Corrêa d'Atouguia and Doctor João de Faria,
representatives and ambassadors of the said very exalted and very excellent
prince, the lord King Dom John of Portugal and of the Algarves on this
side of and beyond the sea in Africa, lord of Guinea, etc., by virtue of their
said powers, incorporated above, promised and affirmed in the name of
their said constituents. [They promised and affirmed] that they and their
successors, and their kingdoms and lordships, forever and ever, shall keep,
observe, fulfill, really and effectively, in good faith and without deception,
renouncing all fraud, mental reservation, deception, fiction, and dissimulation whatsoever, all that is set forth above, and that is agreed to and concluded, and that which shall be decided and determined by the said representatives, and every part and parcel of .it, entirely, according as it shall be
enacted, ordained, adjudged, and determined by them, just as, and as completely as, if it had been enacted, determined, and concluded, by their said
concurring constituents, and rendered as a judgment by competent judges.
In order that the above shall be thus observed and fulfilled, by virtue of the
said powers incorporated above, they pledged the said parties, their constituents, and their goods, movable and real, their patrimonies and royal crowns,
and those of their successors, forever and ever, that neither they nor any of
them, of themselves or through agents, directly or indirectly, shall violate it,
or any part or parcel of it, at any time or in any manner, premeditated or unpremeditated, that may or can be, under the penalties set forth in the said
agreement mentioned above, and that whether the penalty be paid or not paid
or graciously remitted, this instrument and treaty and whatsoever shall be
enacted and determined by virtue thereof, shall nevertheless be and remain

firm, stable, and valid, forever and ever. They renounced all laws and rights of which the said parties or either of them may avail themselves to violate the foregoing, or any part or parcel thereof, and for the greater security and stability of the aforesaid they swore before God and Holy Mary, and upon the sign of the Cross, on which they placed their right hands, and upon the words of the four Holy Gospels, wheresoever they are most largely written, on the consciences of their said constituents, that they, jointly and severally, will keep, observe, and fulfill all the aforesaid, and each part and parcel of it, really and in fact, renouncing all deception, mental reservation, and subterfuge, and they will not gainsay it at any time or in any manner. Under the same oath, they swore not to seek absolution from our most Holy Father, or from any other legate or prelate, who can give it to them, and even though he shall, *proprio motu,* give it them, they will not make use of it. Likewise the said representatives, acting in the said names, bound themselves under the said penalty and oath, that within the twenty days first following, reckoned from the date of this agreement, the parties will mutually exchange the confirmation and ratification of this said agreement, written on parchment, signed with the names of the said lords, their constituents, and sealed with their hanging leaden seals. Of all the foregoing they authorized two copies of the same tenor, both alike, which they signed with their names and executed before me, the said secretary and notary public, whose name is written above, and before the undersigned witnesses—one copy for each party. And whichever copy is produced it shall be as valid as if both should be produced, which were made and executed in the said city of Vitoria, on the day, month, and year aforesaid. Witnesses who were present at the execution of this instrument, and saw all the said representatives sign it, and saw them swear corporally by the hands of me, the said secretary: Francisco de Valenzuela, knight of the Order of Santiago, Pedro de Salazar, captain of their Majesties, Pedro de Ysasaga, *contino* of their Majesties, G[regori]o Casgas, Alvaro Mejia, and Sebastian Fernandez, servants of the said ambassador Pedro Corrèa d'Atouguia. Mercurino, chancellor; Hernando de Vega, chief knight-commander; the chief knight-commander; Doctor Carvajal; Pedro Corrèa; João de Faria. As witness, Francisco de Valenzuela. As witness, G[regori]o Casgas. Witness, Sebastian Fernandez; witness, Alvaro Mejia; as witness, Pedro de Ysasaga; for the said Salazar, Juan de Samano. And I, the said Francisco de los Cobos, secretary of his Imperial Majesty and of their Catholic Majesties, and their scrivener and notary public in their court and in all their kingdoms and lordships of Castile, was present, together with the said witnesses, at the executing of this said instrument and agreement and the oath respecting it, and at the request and petition, and with the authorization, of the said representatives of both the said parties, who with the said witnesses signed their names in my register, I caused this said instrument to be written just as it was executed before me. It is written on three leaves of paper, with this on which is my [notarial] sign, and I gave a copy to each of the said persons. Therefore, in testimony of truth, I made this my sign here, which is thus.

Therefore, having seen and understood the said instrument and treaty, incorporated above, and every part and parcel of it, and being certain and assured of everything set forth therein, and desiring to observe and fulfill it, just as it stands, we commend, confirm, approve, ratify, and, so far as necessary, authorize anew and promise to observe, the said instrument and treaty which thus by our said representatives and the representatives [of the said lord and] very excellent king, our nephew and cousin, was agreed to and concluded in our names, and every part and parcel of it, really and in fact, in good faith, without deception, and renouncing all fraud and subterfuge. And we desire and are content that it shall be observed and fulfilled, just as it stands, in the same manner and as completely as if it had been made, agreed to, and concluded by us. Given in Vitoria on the twenty-seventh day of the month of February, in the year of the nativity of Our Savior Jesus Christ, 1524.

I, THE KING.

I, FRANCISCO DE LOS COBOS, secretary of his Imperial Majesty and of their Catholic Majesties, have caused it to be written by his command. [Notarial sign.]

MERCURINO, chancellor. HERNANDO DE VEGA, chief knight-commander. Licentiate Don GARCIA. Doctor CARVAJAL. ANDRES . . . , chancellor.

14.*

*Draft of an unconcluded treaty between Spain and Portugal.
1526.*

Introduction.

In fulfillment of the terms of the treaty of Vitoria,[1] the " junta of Badajoz "
was held on the Spanish-Portuguese frontier between Badajoz and Elvas
from April 11 to the end of May, 1524, when the Spanish commissioners
voted against its further continuance.[2] The conference was without result.
In the case on possession neither side would act as plaintiff. In the case on
ownership its failure was, indeed, inevitable; for in the then existing state
of knowledge it was impossible to prove the fundamental question of the
length of an equatorial degree, and hence to locate the line of demarcation
or determine the longitude of the Moluccas. The Portuguese commissioners insisted that the 370 leagues should be measured from the eastern
islands of the Cape Verde group, while the Spaniards were determined that
the measurement should begin at the most westerly of these islands. As
measured on the Portuguese and Spanish maps respectively, the distance
from the eastern Cape Verde Islands to the Moluccas differed by 46°. The
Portuguese located the Moluccas 21° west of the demarcation line; the
Spaniards, a greater distance east of that meridian.

The conference having ended, diplomatic negotiations were resumed; and
it was not till the lapse of nearly five years that the dispute was terminated,[3]
in a manner altogether different from that which was at first proposed.
The most important stages in this negotiation, up to 1526, are indicated in
the following draft of a treaty, which was probably drawn up at Seville,[4]
and was not concluded.

Bibliography.

Text: **MS.** The draft is in the Archives of the Indies, Patronato, 1-2-2/16,
no. 3, ramo 12. It has not, it is believed, been printed or translated
hitherto.

References: See references to Doc. **13.**

---

[1] Doc. **13.**
[2] Documents relating to this conference are in Navarrete, *Viages* (1825-1838), IV.;
Blair and Robertson, *Philippine Islands*, I. 165-221; Medina, *Documentos para la Historia de Chile*, II.; id., *El Portugués Esteban Gómez al Servicio de España, 1518-1535*
(1908), pp. 133 ff. For accounts of the conference, see A. de Herrera, *Historia General*,
dec. III., lib. VI., cc. 6-8; and Pastells's edition of Colin, *Labor Evangélica*, II. 606-612.
[3] By the treaty of Saragossa, Docs. **15** and **16.**
[4] Herrera, *op. cit.*, dec. IV., lib. V., c. 10; ed. 1728-1730, II. 93.

En el nonbre de Dios Todo Poderoso, Padre e Hijo e Espiritu Sancto. Magnifiesto e notorio sea a todos quantos este publico imstrumencto vieren, como en [*blank*], a [*blank*] dias del mes de [*blank*], año del nasçimiento de nuestro Señor Jhesu Christo de mill e quinientos e veynte e seis años, en presençia de my, Françisco de los Covos,[6] secretario de sus Magestades e su notario publico, e de los testigos de yuso escritos, estando presentes los señores Mercurinus de Gatinara,[7] grand chançiller de sus Magestades, e Don Fray Garçia de Loaisa,[8] o Bispo de Osma, presidente del Consejo de las Yndias y confesor de su Magestad, e Don Garçia de Padilla,[9] comendador mayor de Calatrava, y el Doctor Lorenço Galindes de Carvajal,[10] todos del Consejo de los muy altos e muy poderosos prinçypes, Don Carlos, por la divina clemençia Enperador semper augusto, rrey de Romanos, e Doña Johana su madre, y el mismo Don Carlos su hijo, por la graçia de Dios rreyes de Castilla, de Leon, de Aragon, de las Dos Seçilias, de Jherusalem, de Navarra, de Granada, etc., sus procuradores bastantes de la una parte, y el señor Liçençiado Asevedo,[11] del Consejo del muy alto e muy exçelente señor, el Señor Don Johan, por la graçia de Dios rrey de Portogal, de los Algarves de aquende y allende el mar en Africa, señor de Guinea, e de la conquista, navegaçion, e comerçio de Ytiopia y Aravia e Persia e de la Yndia, etc., su enbaxador e procurador bastante, segund anbas las dichas partes lo mostraron por las cartas e poderes e procuraçiones de los dichos señores, sus constituyentes, su thenor de las quales, de bervo ad verbo, es este que se sigue:

Los dichos procuradores de los dichos señores Reyes de Castilla, de Leon, de Aragon, de las Dos Seçilias, de Jherusalem, etc., e del dicho señor Rey de Portogal, de los Algarves, etc., dixeron que, por quanto sobre la duda que entre los dichos señores sus constituyentes ay sobre la propiedad e posesion de los Malucos, pretendiendo cada una de las partes que cae en los limites de su demarcaçion, haziendose la demarcaçion, como sea de haser, conforme al asiento y capitulaçion[12] que fue hecha entre los Catolicos Reyes Don Fernando e Reyna Doña Ysabel, etc., y el señor Rey, Don Johan de Portogal, etc., que ayan gloria, por parte del señor Rey de Portogal, estando el Enperador en la çibdad de Segovia[13] el año pasado de mill e quinientos e

[5] The text is taken from a manuscript in the Archives of the Indies, Patronato, 1-2-2/16, no. 3, ramo 12.
[6] See Doc. **13**, note 20.   [7] See Doc. **13**, note 14.
[8] This distinguished prelate, former general of the Dominican Order, and since 1523 the confessor and confidant of Charles V., had great influence at court. Upon the reorganization of the Council of the Indies in 1524, he became its president. Later he was made cardinal, archbishop of Seville, and commissary-general of the Inquisition. A. Touron, *Histoire des Hommes Illustres de l'Ordre de Saint Dominique*, IV. (1747), 93-107.
[9] See Doc. **13**, note 16.   [10] See Doc. **13**, note 17.
[11] One of the Portuguese commissioners at the conference of Badajoz. His powers to conclude a treaty with the Emperor, dated Oct. 18, 1525, are preserved in the Archives of the Indies, Patronato, 1-2-2/16, no. 1. A brief notice of his instructions, Mar. 24, 1525, is in *Algs. Docs.*, pp. 485-486. Many of his letters and papers relative to the Molucca negotiations are in the National Archives at Lisbon. *Cf.* Santarem, *Quadro Elementar*, II. 46 ff.
[12] The treaty of Tordesillas, Doc. **9**.
[13] The Emperor was in Segovia from Sept. 7 to 14, 1525. M. de Foronda y Aguilera, "Estancias y Viages de Carlos V.", *Boletin de la Sociedad Geográfica de Madrid*, tom. XXXVII., no. 7, July, 1895.

veynte e çinco años, fueron movidos y apuntados çiertos medios que son los siguientes:

Los [14] medios que por parte del Rey de Portogal se proponen sobre lo de Maluco, es lo siguiente:

[1.] Que se haga asiento entre su Magestad y el, que por justiçia e por letrados, de una parte e de otra, se vea el derecho de la posesion e propiedad de Maluco, segund forma de las capitulaçiones hechas y de lo que fue asentado que se viese en la rraya, no limitando tienpo, mas prosiguiendo hasta que entre los dichos letrados se tomen conclusion de la manera que les pareçiere derecho, y no siendo conformes se tomen terçeros que lo determinen.

[2.] Yten, que en quanto por los letrados o terçero no se diere sentençia finalmente en la posesion o en la propiedad, que ninguna de las partes enbie a Maluco, ni vengan de Maluco para aca, hasta dar se sentençia final en la propiedad, y, determinandose primero la posesion que la propiedad, aquel por quien la posesion se juzgare pueda enbiar hasta que se determine la dicha propriedad.

[3.] Yten, que bolviendo las naos que agora scan enbiado por parte de su Magestad [15] primero que se determine la dicha posesion o propiedad, que se mande ver la despensa que hizieron, y, si lo que traxeren valiere mas, aquella parte que mas valiere se ponga en deposito y secresto para se entregar a aquel por quien fuere juzgada la posession e propriedad.

[4.] Yten, que este asiento sea jurado por anbas partes y aprovado con todas aquellas solenidades y clausulas que para seguridad de tal caso se rrequiere[n].

A los quales medios, su Magestad, teniendo la voluntad que sienpre tuvo e tiene a la conservaçion del gran devdo y amor que ay entre el y el dicho señor Rey de Portogal, mando rresponder en esta guisa:

Lo [16] que se rresponde por parte del Enperador y Rey nuestro señor a lo que de parte del señor Rey de Portogal, su hermano, nuevamente sea rreplicado sobre lo de Maluco es lo siguiente:

Primeramente, que del amor que el dicho señor Rey tiene, y buena voluntad que muestra, a la conservaçion de la amistad y verdadera unyon de entre su Magestad y el dicho Serenisimo Rey, nunca su Magestad a puesto duda en ello, antes lo ha sienpre tenido por firme, y que rreçiprocamente no deve el dudar que su Magestad no tenga el mysmo amor y voluntad con deseo de sastifazer [sic] a las cosas del dicho Serenisimo Rey, su hermano, quanto la rrason y los negoçios lo sufren y que buenamente se podra haser.

Quantto a lo que el dicho Serenisimo Rey apunta, mostrando descontentamiento de lo que su Magestad dixo, que por olvido, a causa de otras grandes ocupaçiones, no se avia rrespondido al Liçençiado Antonio de Azevedo sobre

[14] Another copy of the following articles, preserved in the Archives of the Indies, Patronato, 1-2-2/16, no. 2, is headed: "Enbio lo su Magestad de Segovia a Toledo", i. e., probably to the Portuguese ambassador, who had been in Toledo while the Cortes was in session there in August. When the Cortes ended the Emperor went to Segovia. P. de Sandoval, *Historia de la Vida del Enperador Carlos V.*, I. (1618), 660, 665.

[15] The Spanish fleet under command of García Jofre Loaysa sailed from Coruña on July 24, 1525. *Cf.* Doc. **15**, note 30.

[16] Another copy of the following reply, preserved in the Archives of the Indies, Patronato, 1-2-2/16, no. 2, is headed as follows: "La respuesta que Su Magestad dió en Segovia al enbaxador sobre los medios."

el dicho negoçio de Maluco antes que la dicha armada partiese, paresçiendo al dicho señor Rey ser cosa grave y que sus cosas no deven ser olvidadas, çierto su Magestad no piensa que el dicho señor Rey tenga por esto justa causa de descontentamiento, pues sabe la calidad y peso de los negoçios tan grandes que entre tanto sean ofreçido a su Magestad, los quales son de tal ynportançia que fuerçan a honbre a olvidar aun sus cosas propias, quanto mas las agenas, y con ellas devria escusarse no solamente aver olvidado lo de Maluco, mas aun se escusaria lo olvidado de otras cosas, muy mas inportantes de sus rreynos hereditarios ; y ansy mismo se deve escusar este olvido, segund en la otra rrespuesta esta dicho, pues consta que por el partir del armada no se hazia mudança en lo que ya estava rrespondido, y no por esto deve pensar el dicho serenisimo rey, que su Magestad no tenga y quiera tener el mismo cuidado de sus cosas que de las propias de su Magestad.

Quanto a los medios que ofreçe—A su Magestad plaze que por letrados y otras personas expertas en la negoçiaçion, tomados por la una parte y la otra, en ygual numero, se vea el derecho de la propiedad e posesion, segund e al thenor e forma de las capitulaçiones [17] hechas y otorgadas entre los rreyes Catolicos y los Serenisimos Reyes de Portogal, no limitando tienpo para ello, mas prosiguiendolo hasta que por las dichas personas se tome conclusyon de la manera que les pareçiere derecho, y que no siendo conformes, se tomen terçeros, que lo determinen, y que se junten en lugar que les pareçiere mas conviniente.

Quanto a lo que el dicho Serenisimo Rey de Portogal pide, que hasta que sea aya dado sentencia final en propiedad o posesion, ninguna de las partes enbie a Maluco, pareçe que es contra justiçia e derecho y no ygual. Pero terna su Magestad por bien que los diputados den sobresto la horden que les pareçiere.

Quanto a lo que pide del secresto de lo que truxeren las naos de su Magestad que agora son ydas, y por que contiene el mismo agravio que el preçedente se rresponde lo mismo que a el esta rrespondido.

Quanto al postrero, que plase a su Magestad que el asiento que sobresto se fiziere sea jurado por anbas partes y aprovado con todas las clausulas e solenidades que para la seguridad del se rrequiere.

A lo demas de la instrucçion del dicho Liçençiado Asevedo rrespondera M[o]ns. de la Chaulx. [18]

A los quales por parte del dicho señor Rey de Portogal fue dado otro memorial del thenor siguiente :

Estos [19] son los capitulos conforme a la rrespuesta de su Magestad para que sea de hazer el asiento para determinaçion de la causa de Maluco en posesyon o propiedad.

[1.] Yten, que por tres letrados, nonbrados de parte de su Magestad y tres por parte del Rey de Portugal, mi señor, y tres astrologos e tres pilotos o marineros expertos, nonbrados por cada una de las partes, se determine la

---

[17] The treaty of Tordesillas, Doc. **9**.

[18] Charles Poupet de la Chaulx (in Spanish, Laxao) had been previously sent as imperial ambassador to Portugal to negotiate the marriage between the Infanta Isabella of Portugal and the Emperor Charles V. Santarem, *Quadro Elementar* (1842, etc.), II. 50, 51.

[19] According to another copy of this document in the Archives of the Indies, Patronato, 1-2-2/16, the Portuguese ambassador gave these articles to his Majesty in Toledo in January 1526.

causa en posesion o propriedad, saber, por los letrados juristas de cada parte
la causa de la posesyon solamente, segund el tenor e forma de las capitulaçiones hechas entre los Catolicos Reyes, Don Fernando e la Reyna Doña Ysabel
y el Rey Don Johan de Portogal, los quales letrados proçederan en la dicha
causa, syn determinaçion o prefiniçion de tienpo, hasta que finalmente sen-
tençiaren e determinaren la dicha causa posesoria, segund hallaren por
derecho, y por que entre los letrados e procuradores de anbas partes se
podrian ofresçer dudas y diferençias sobre qual de las partes seria auttor
o rreo, que por hebitar de luengas y diferençias entre los dichos letrados e
procuradores, y por mas brevemente se poder dar fin a la causa, se proçeda
sin libello y sin toda manera de petiçion mas que los procuradores de cada
una de las partes presenten, y ofrescan ante los letrados que la causa han de
determinar sus capitulos e posiçiones por las quales sean examinados los
testigos de cada una de las partes por las suyas, e se rresçiban todas las mas
provanças de escrituras e instrumentos de que cada una de las partes se
esperare ayudar, y que los testigos juren en presençia de los procuradores
de las partes, e sean examinados e ynterrogados por dos de los letrados, uno
de cada una de las partes que la causa ovieren de determinar, y dadas e
ofreçidas las dichas provanças y testigos sobre las dichas pusyçiones e capitulos, los letrados determinen la dicha causa posesoria por las dichas pusiçiones
y capitulos, y por las provanças escrituras e testigos sobre ellas ofresçidos,
segund les pareçiere justiçia y derecho, e que, siendo determinada y jusgada
la causa posesoria, aquella parte que oviere sentençia por sy y vitoria de la
causa posesoria pueda de la dada de la sentençia mandar sus armadas e
gentes al dicho Maluco y hazer en el sus tratos e mercaderias, y la otra parte,
contra quien fuere dada la sentençia, no podra alla mas enbiar armadas ni
gentes hasta que finalmente se determine sobre la propriedad a qual de las
partes el derecho della pertenesçe.

[2.] Ytem, que, sobre la propriedad e derecho della, los astrologos, pilotos,
o marineros, declarados e nonbrados por cada una de las partes, en el lugar
de la rraya donde fuere acordado se ovieren de juntar, consultaran, acordaran,
e tomaran asiento, sobre la propiedad, conforme a las capitulaçiones hechas
entre el Rey Don Johan de Portogal y el Rey Don Fernando e la Reyna Doña
Ysabel, en la qual causa los dichos astrologos, pilotos, y marineros, otrosy
proçederan hasta lo que neçesario les pareçiere, syn limitaçion de tienpo, mas
prosiguiendo en la dicha causa, segund esta dicho en la causa de la posesion.

[3.] Ytem, que quanto a cada una de las partes enbiar o no sus navios y
gentes al dicho Maluco durante la contienda e juisio de la posesion, quede
a los juezes de la causa, que daran açerca dello la horden y asiento que les
pareçiere de derecho, y que lo que los dichos letrados juezes en ello determinaren y ordenaren se guarde enteramente por cada una de las partes syn
duda ni ynpedimiento que a ello pueda poner, y el mismo modo e manera se
tenga açerca de aver se de secrestar, o no, todo aquello que truxeren los
navios de su Magestad que para el dicho Maluco fueren partidos.

[4.] Ytem, por que, en anbas estas causas de posesion y propriedad, los
diputados y declarados por cada una de las partes con mas acatamiento de
Dios y mas libremente procedan en las dichas causas, que el señor Enperador
y el señor Rey de Portogal fagan juramento solene sobre los Santtos Evangelios, en presençia de los letrados, astrologos, pilotos, o marineros, por ellos
nonbrados para este negoçio, cada uno destos señores delante los suyos, en
presençia de notario e testigo, en que declaren que su yntinçion e verdadera

voluntad es, que ellos, sus letrados, astrologos, pilotos, o marineros hagan
en la determinaçion destas causas, para que son nonbrados por jueses, aquello
que verdaderamente les paresçiere just[icia] e verdad, con toda brevedad,
segund esta declarado, no haviendo rrespeto a ser sus vasallos, ni a otra cosa
alguna que ellos diputados puedan presumir ni rreçelar para dexar de hazer
just[icia] a qual de los que los diputaron les pareçiere que la tiene.

[5.] Yten, que, hecho el dicho juramento por los dichos señores en el modo
suso dicho, los letrados, astrologos, pilotos, o marineros, nonbrados por cada
una de las partes para entender en estas causas, en el lugar de la rraya donde
se ovieren de juntar los unos e los otros se confiesen, y todos juntamente
rreçiban el sacramento, e juraran solenemente sobre el santto sacramento,
que el sacerdote que los hoviere de comulgar terna en sus manos, en presençia
de publico notario, que dello pueda dar fee, que sin themor ni amor ni otra
cosa alguna que los pueda o deva ynpedir, conosçeran de las dichas causas
e dudas contenidas, ansy de la posesion e propriedad y de todo lo demas en
esta capitulaçion contenido, y todas e cada una de las dichas causas y dubdas
que les seran cometidas por los dichos señores, y las determinaran, deçidiran,
y sentençyaran definitiva y finalmente, conforme a derecho y justiçia,
guardando las capitulaçiones, provanças, e testigos, por las partes ofresçidas,
y guardando en la determinaçion de las dichas causas todo lo que les paresçiere derecho y justiçia, de qualquiera de las partes que la toviere, prometi-
endo ansy mismo, so el cargo del dicho juramento, de proçesar las dichas
causas de posesion y propriedad con toda diligençia que posible les fuere,
para con toda brevedad despachar y determinar las dichas causas.

[6.] Yten, que el lugar de la rraya donde los diputados de la una y otra
parte se ayan de ayuntar sea entre las çibdades de Elves y Badajos, donde
ya fueron juntos los diputados que en esta causa los dias pasados entendieron
por ser lugares mas convinientes para ello.

[7.] Yten, que los letrados, astrologos, pilotos, o marineros que en esta
causa han de entender, sean nonbrados hasta tanto, etc.

[8.] Yten, que siendo caso que en qualquiera de las dichas causas de la
posesion o propriedad los letrados en la posesoria fueren diferentes e discordes, o ansy mismo los astrologos, pilotos, o marineros fueren discordes
entre sy, que en tal caso los dichos señores sean obligados a elegir terçero,
o terçeros, tales que sean expertos e sçientes de la causa en que fuere la
discordia entre los diputados, saber, que sy la discordia fuere entre los
letrados juristas, que de la causa posesoria han de conosçer, los terçeros que los
dichos señores tomaren, o terçero, sea otrosy jurista, y, por la misma manera,
sy la discordia o diferençia fuere entre los astrologos, pilotos, o marineros,
que ansy mismo los dichos señores elijan arbitros, o terçeros, astrologos,
pilotos, o marineros, y que aquel terçero, o terçeros, en que se ansy los dichos
señores [blank], vean las dichas causas, e, oydos los procuradores de las
partes, fagan enteramente justiçia ansy como por este asiento y capitulaçion
esta asentado que lo hiziesen los diputados y primero nonbrados, y los dichos
terçeros o terçero en que los dichos señores asentaren y eligieren, tomaran
otrosy el juramento con aquella solenidad que ya esta declarada, confesandose
y comulgundose, y que lo que por los dichos diputados e declarados por cada
uno de los dichos señores, o por la mayor parte dellos, fuere determinado,
asy en la causa posesoria por los letrados juristas como en la propriedad por
los astrologos, pilotos, o marineros, fuere determinado finalmente, y asentado
syendo estos discordes, los quales dichos terçero o terçeros hordenaren e

determinaren y asentaren, juzgando finalmente, los dichos señores, por sy y sus herederos e suçesores, prometen en sus fees rreales, de todo lo tener y guardar e mandar guardar, syn arte e syn cautela alguna, para sienpre jamas, y juraran sobre la señal de la Cruz y por las palabras de los Santtos Evangelios, de todo lo tener, mantener, e guardar y hazer guardar, so obligaçion de todos sus bienes patrimoniales y de la corona de sus reynos, que para ello obligavan, etc.

[9.] Yten, que el primero nonbrado por cada uno de los dichos señores presyda por su parte ansy como en la capitulaçion pasada, que entre estos señores fue hecha hera contenido.

Sobre todo su Magestad mando postreramente dar la rrespuesta siguiente:

Lo que se rresponde por parte del enperador y rey nuestro señor a los capitulos que por parte del señor Rey de Portogal se enbian sobre lo de Maluco es lo siguiente:

Que a su Magestad plase mucho de que al señor Rey de Portogal aya pareçido bien la rrespuesta que dio su Magestad, estando en Segovia,[20] al enbaxador del dicho señor Rey de Portogal sobre los medios que por su parte se movieren a su Magestad en lo de Maluco, y asy para la execuçion dellos mandara luego nonbrar letrados y otras personas expertas en la negoçiaçion, e dalles todas las provisiones nesçesarias, ynserta en ellas la dicha rrespuesta, para que, conforme a ella y a la capitulaçion hecha entre los Catolicos Reyes Don Fernando, e Doña Ysabel, rreyes de Castilla, etc., y el señor Rey Don Johan, rrey de Portogal, etc., entiendan en la determinaçion del dicho negoçio, y tiene por bien por mas conplaser al dicho señor Rey de Portogal de hazer su Magestad a mandar que las dichas personas, nonbradas por su parte, hagan el juramento e solenidad que agora se pide de parte del dicho señor Rey de Portogal, para que en la determinaçion del dicho negoçio proçedan conforme a la dicha rrespuesta, e que, sy entre las dichas personas e diputados de anbas partes no se conçertaren, que sy la diferençia fuere entre los letrados, que el terçero, o terçeros, que se ovieren de nonbrar, sean letrados, y sy la dicha diferençia fuere entre los astrologos e pilotos, que el terçero que se oviere de nonbrar sea de aquella facultad, y que estos entiendan en el dicho negoçio conforme a la rrespuesta que su Magestad dio en Segovia, que de suso va encorporada.

Por ende anbas las dichas partes, por virtud de los dichos poderes que tienen de los dichos señores sus constituyentes, que de suso van encorporados, conformandose con la dicha rrespuesta, dixeron, que seran contentos que, ansy en la diçisyon de la propiedad y posesion como en la horden e forma que en ello se ha de thener, se guarde e cunpla e haga, segund e como se contiene en la dicha rrespuesta, que de suso va encorporada, y en la capitulaçion hecha por el Rey e Reyna Catholicos y el Rey Don Johan de Portogal, y que los diputados rresçiban conjuntamente las petiçiones tales quales se dieren por las partes, y sobrellas proçedan en la causa, sinplemente y de plano, syn estrepitu ni figura de juisio, solamente, la verdad sabida, determinen lo que sea justiçia.

Para lo qual todo que dicho es y cada cosa y parte dello, los dichos Mercurinus de Gatinara, gran chançiller de sus Magestades, y Obispo Don Fray Garçia de Loaysa, y Don Garçia de Padilla, comendador mayor de Calatrava,

[20] See above, note 16.

y el Doctor Lorenço Galindes de Carvajal, todos del su consejo, procuradores
de los dichos muy altos e muy poderosos Reyna e Rey de Castilla, de Leon,
de Aragon, de Granada, e de las Dos Seçilias, de Jherusalem, etc., e por
virtud del dicho su poder que de suso va encorporado, el dicho Liçençiado
Asevedo, procurador y enbaxador del dicho muy alto e muy exçelente prinçipe,
el senor Rey Don Johan de Portogal e de los Algarves de aquende y allende
el mar en Africa, señor de Guinea, etc., e por virtud del dicho su poder, que
de suso va encorporado, prometieron y seguraron en nonbre de los dichos
sus constituyentes, que ellos y sus subçesores e rreynos e señorios, para
syenpre jamas, ternan, guardaran, conpliran, rrealmente e con efetto, a buena
fee, syn mal engaño, çesante todo fraude, cautela, engaño, fiçion e disymula-
çion alguna, lo que de suso se contiene y es asentado e conçertado, y lo que
por los dichos diputados fuere sentençiado e determinado, e cada cosa e parte
dello, enteramente, segund e como por ellos fuere hecho e ordenado y sentençiado e determinado, y cada cosa e parte dello enteramente, segund e
como por ellos fuere hecho y ordenado e sentençiado e determinado y conçertado, e como juisio dado como juezes conpetentes, e para que ansy se
guardara e cunplira, por virtud de los dichos poderes que de suso van
encorporados, obligaron a las dichas sus partes, sus constituyentes, e a sus
bienes muebles e rraises e de sus patrimonias e coronas rreales e de sus
subçesores, para syenpre jamas, que ellos, ni alguno dellos, por sy ni por
ynterposyta persona, directe ni yndirecte, no yran ni vernan contra ello, ni
contra cosa alguna ni parte dello, en tienpo alguno, ni por alguna manera,
pensada o no pensada, que sea o ser pueda, so las penas en la dicha capitulaçion, que de suso se haze minçion, contenidas, y rrenunçiaron qualesquier
leyes y derechos de que se puedan aprovechar las dichas partes, e cada una
dellas, para yr o venir contra lo suso dicho, e contra alguna cosa e parte
dello, e por mayor seguridad e firmesa de lo suso dicho juraron a Dios y a
Sancta Maria y a la señal de la Crus en que pusyeron sus manos derechas
y a las palabras de los Sanctos quatro Evangelios do quiera que mas
largamente son escritos, en anyma de los dichos sus partes, que ellos, y cada
uno dellos, ternan, guardaran, e cunpliran, todo lo suso dicho, e cada una
cosa e parte dello, rrealmente e con efetto, çesante todo engaño, cautela, e
symulaçion, e no lo contradiran en tienpo alguno, ni por alguna manera, e
so el dicho juramento juraron de no pedir asoluçion de nuestro muy Santto
Padre, ni de otro legado ni perlado que gela pueda dar, y aunque de su propio
motuo gela de, no usaran della, e ansy mismo los dichos procuradores en el
dicho nonbre se obligaron, so la dicha pena e juramento, que dentro de
[blank] dias primeros siguientes, contados desde el dia de la fecha desta
capitulaçion, daran la una parte a la otra, y la otra a la otra, aprovaçion e
rratificaçion desta dicha capitulaçion, escritas en pargamino e firmadas de
los nonbres de los dichos señores, sus constituyentes, e selladas con sus sellos
de plomo pendientes, de lo qual todo que dicho es otorgaron dos escrituras
de un tenor, tal la una como la otra, las quales firmaron de sus nonbres e las
otorgaron ante my, el dicho secretario y notario publico de suso escrito, e de
los testigos de yuso escritos, para cada una de las partes la suya, y qualequiera
que paresca, valga como sy anbas e dos pareçiesen, que fueron hechas e
otorgadas in la dicha [blank], el dicho dia et mes e año suso dichos.

Translation.

In the name of God Almighty, Father, Son, and Holy Ghost. Be it manifest and known to all who shall see this public instrument, that in   on the   day of the month of   in the year of the nativity of Our Lord Jesus Christ, 1526, in the presence of me, Francisco de los Cobos, their Majesties' secretary and notary public, and in the presence of the undersigned witnesses, there being present the lords Mercurino de Gattinara, grand chancellor of their Majesties, Don Fray García de Loaysa, bishop of Osma, president of the Council of the Indies and his Majesty's confessor, Don García de Padilla, knight-commander of Calatrava, and Doctor Lorenzo Galíndez de Carvajal, all members of the council of the very exalted and mighty princes, Don Charles, by divine clemency emperor ever august, king of the Romans, and Doña Joanna, his mother, and likewise Don Charles, her son, by the grace of God king and queen of Castile, Leon, Aragon, the Two Sicilies, Jerusalem, Navarre, Granada, etc., their qualified representatives, on the one part, and Licentiate Azevedo, member of the council of the very exalted and very excellent lord, the lord Dom John, by the grace of God king of Portugal, and of the Algarves on this side and beyond the sea in Africa, lord of Guinea and of the conquest, navigation, and commerce of Ethiopia, Arabia, Persia, India, etc., his ambassador and qualified representative, as both the said parties proved by the letters, powers, and procurations of the said lords, their constituents, the tenor of which, word for word, is as follows:

The said representatives of the said lords, king and queen of Castile, Leon, Aragon, the Two Sicilies, Jerusalem, etc., and of the said lord King of Portugal, the Algarves, etc., declared that whereas, in the past year 1525, when the Emperor was in the city of Segovia, certain expedients, which are as follows, were proposed and written down, on the part of the King of Portugal, concerning the question existing between the said lords, their constituents, in regard to the ownership and possession of the Moluccas, each party claiming that they will fall within the limits of his demarcation when the demarcation is made, as it is to be made, in accordance with the treaty and agreement concluded between the Catholic king and queen, Don Ferdinand and Doña Isabella, etc., and the lord King Dom John of Portugal, etc.—may they rest in glory!

The expedients proposed on the part of the King of Portugal in respect to the affair of the Moluccas, are as follows:

1. That a treaty be made between his Majesty [the emperor] and him to the effect that the right to the possession and ownership of the Moluccas shall be investigated by a tribunal and by lawyers of both sides, in accordance with the treaties already concluded and with the agreement that was reached when an investigation was made on the frontier, without the imposition of a time-limit, but continuing the inquiry until a conclusion is reached between the said lawyers in the manner that shall seem to them right; and if they shall not agree, umpires shall be chosen, who shall determine the question.

2. Item, that so long as no final sentence in regard to possession or ownership shall be pronounced by the lawyers or umpire, neither side shall despatch expeditions to the Moluccas or from the Moluccas hither, until the final sentence in regard to ownership be given. If the question of possession be determined before that of ownership, he to whom possession shall be adjudged

10

may despatch expeditions to the Moluccas until the said ownership be determined.

3. Item, that if the ships now despatched on the part of his Majesty return before the said right of possession or ownership be decided, orders shall be given to investigate the expense which they caused. If their cargo be worth more, the surplus shall be placed in deposit and sequestration so that it may be delivered to him to whom possession and ownership shall be adjudged.

4. Item, that this agreement be sworn to by both sides, and approved with all those solemn forms and clauses required in such cases for security.

To these expedients his Majesty, desiring, as he always had and has desired, the preservation of the close relationship and love that exist between him and the said lord King of Portugal, commanded answer to be made in the following manner:

The answer returned on the part of the emperor and king, our lord, to the reply recently made on the part of the lord King of Portugal, his brother, in respect to the affair of the Moluccas is as follows:

First, that his Majesty has never questioned, but rather has always regarded as secure, the love that the said lord king feels and the good-will that he shows for the preservation of the friendship and true union between his Majesty and the said Most Serene King, and reciprocally he [*i. e.*, the King of Portugal] ought not to doubt that his Majesty feels the same love and good-will, together with the desire to adjust satisfactorily the affairs of the said Most Serene King, his brother, so far as reason and negotiations permit, and it can easily be done.

As to what the said Most Serene King writes, showing displeasure at what his Majesty said, namely, that he had not replied to the licentiate, Antonio de Azevedo, about the said negotiation of the Moluccas before the said armada departed, because he had forgotten it on account of other important matters, while it appears to the said lord king that the matter is serious, and that his affairs ought not to be forgotten, certainly his Majesty does not think that this gives the said lord king just cause for displeasure, since he knows the character and gravity of the very important affairs that meanwhile came before his Majesty. These are of such importance that they force a man to forget even his own business, much more another's, and because of them he ought to be excused not only for having forgotten the question of the Moluccas, but even for having forgotten other things much more important to his hereditary kingdoms. Likewise this forgetfulness ought to be excused, as is stated in the other reply, since it appears that the departure of the armada did not affect the reply already made; and the Most Serene King ought not to think on account of this forgetfulness that his Majesty has not and does not desire to have the same solicitude for the former's affairs as for his own.

As to the expedients that he offers, his Majesty is satisfied to have an equal number of lawyers and other persons expert in the negotiation chosen by each side, to investigate the right of ownership and possession according to and in the tenor and form of the treaties made and executed between the Catholic sovereigns and the most serene kings of Portugal. The inquiry shall have no time-limit, but shall be prosecuted until the said persons shall reach a conclusion, in the manner that shall seem to them right. If they do not agree, umpires shall be chosen to decide the question, and these shall meet in the place they deem most convenient.

As to the said Most Serene King of Portugal's request that, until the final sentence regarding ownership or possession shall have been given, neither side shall send expeditions to the Moluccas, this appears contrary to justice and right, and is unfair. But his Majesty will be content to have the deputies regulate this as they shall think best. As to the King of Portugal's request for the sequestration of the cargo which shall be brought by his Majesty's ships that have already sailed, since this contains the same injury as the preceding expedient, the answer is the same as is given to that.

As to the last expedient, his Majesty is satisfied to have the agreement that shall be made in regard to this matter sworn to by both sides, and approved with all the clauses and formalities required for its security.

M. de la Chaulx will answer the rest of the said Licentiate Azevedo's instructions.

Another memorial of the following tenor was given on the part of the said lord King of Portugal to the above.

These are the articles drawn up in accordance with the reply of his Majesty in order that the agreement for determining the cause on possession and ownership of the Moluccas may be made.

1. *Item,* that the cause in respect to possession and ownership shall be determined by three lawyers, named on the part of his Majesty, and by three named on the part of the King of Portugal, my lord, and by three astrologers and three pilots or experienced mariners, named by each side. That is, the cause of possession alone shall be determined by the learned lawyers of each side, in accordance with the tenor and form of the treaties concluded between the Catholic sovereigns, Don Ferdinand and Queen Doña Isabella, and the King Dom John of Portugal. The lawyers shall carry on the said cause without a predetermined time-limit until they shall finally decide and conclude the said possessory cause, in accordance with their just findings. And because doubts and differences might arise between the lawyers and representatives of both sides as to which side should be plaintiff or defendant, in order that delays and controversies between the said lawyers and representatives may be avoided and that the cause may be finished more quickly, the process shall be carried on without written charge and without any kind of petition, except that the representatives of each side shall present and exhibit before the lawyers who have to determine the cause their articles and interrogatories by which the witnesses of each side shall be mutually examined, and all additional written and documentary evidence whereby either side shall hope to be aided shall be admitted. The witnesses shall take the oath in the presence of the representatives of the parties, and they shall be examined and questioned by two of the lawyers, who shall have to determine the cause—one lawyer from each side. After the said evidences and witnesses for the said interrogatories and articles shall have been presented and given, the lawyers shall determine the said possessory cause by means of the said interrogatories and articles, and by means of the written evidence and witnesses presented in respect to them, as shall seem just and right to them. After the possessory cause is determined and adjudged, the side receiving judgment in its favor and victory in the possessory cause, may,

from the time of the giving of the sentence, order its fleets and people to the said Moluccas, and carry on its trade and traffic in them, and the other side, against whom sentence shall have been given, shall not be able to despatch any more fleets or people thither, until the question to which side the right of ownership pertains shall be finally determined.

2. *Item,* that, in regard to ownership and the right thereto, in the place on the frontier where it shall be agreed that the astrologers, pilots, or mariners chosen and nominated by each side are to assemble, they shall deliberate and come to an agreement and understanding in respect to ownership, in accordance with the treaties concluded between King Dom John of Portugal and King Ferdinand and Queen Isabella. Moreover, the said astrologers, pilots, and mariners shall carry on this cause as long as they shall deem it necessary, without time-limit, but shall prosecute the said cause as is said in respect to the cause of possession.

3. *Item,* the question whether during the dispute and trial concerning possession either side shall or shall not send his ships and people to the said Moluccas, shall be left to the judges of the cause, who shall make in regard to it what arrangement and agreement shall seem to them right. What the said learned judges shall decide and ordain in the matter shall be wholly observed by each side without question or hindrance being opposed thereto, and the same procedure shall be followed in deciding whether or not the cargo of his Majesty's ships that shall have departed for the said Moluccas is to be sequestrated.

4. *Item,* in order that in both these causes of possession and ownership, the deputies and witnesses for each party may conduct the said causes with the more reverence to God and more freely, the lord Emperor and the lord King of Portugal shall take solemn oath on the Holy Gospels in the presence of the lawyers, astrologers, pilots, or mariners named by them for this cause— each lord before his men in the presence of a notary and witness. In this oath they shall declare that their intention and true purpose is, that their lawyers, astrologers, pilots, or mariners, in deciding these causes for which they are named as judges, shall do what shall veritably seem to them just and true with all despatch, as is declared, regardless of their vassalage or of any other fact that the said deputies may suspect or fear should deter them from doing justice to whichever of the parties that deputed them shall seem to be in the right.

5. *Item,* that after the said oath has been taken by the said lords in the manner aforesaid, the lawyers, astrologers, pilots, or mariners named by each side to judge these causes, should at the place on the boundary line, where both deputations are to assemble, confess themselves, and all receive the sacrament at the same time. They shall solemnly swear on the holy sacrament—which the priest who shall have to administer it to them will hold in his hands in the presence of the notary public, who may certify thereto—that without fear or favor or any other thing that may or ought to hinder them, they will try the said causes and the unsettled points comprised therein, both of possession and ownership and of everything else contained in this treaty, and all and each of the said causes and unsettled points which shall be intrusted to them by the said lords. They shall determine, decide, and pronounce judgment upon them, definitively and finally, according to right and justice, paying regard to the treaties, evidence, and testimony, presented by the parties, and observing in the decision of the said causes all that appears to

them right and just to whichever side these shall pertain. They shall promise likewise under obligation of the said oath to institute the said causes of possession and ownership with all possible diligence, in order to despatch and determine them as quickly as possible.

6. *Item*, that the place at the boundary line where the deputies of both sides are to assemble shall be between the cities of Elvas and Badajoz, where the deputies who were employed in this cause in past days assembled, because these places are the most convenient for the business.

7. *Item*, that the lawyers, astrologers, pilots, or mariners who are to be employed in this cause shall be named up to the required number.

8. *Item*, that in either of the said causes of possession or ownership—if, in the possessory cause, the lawyers shall differ and disagree, or if, in like manner, [in the cause of ownership] the astrologers, pilots, or mariners shall disagree among themselves, in such case the said lords shall be obliged to choose as umpire or umpires, such men as are experienced and learned in the cause in which the dispute between the deputies shall arise—that is, that if the dispute shall be between the learned jurists who are to try the possessory cause, the umpire or umpires whom the said lords shall select shall likewise be jurists, and, similarly, if the dispute or difference shall be between the astrologers, pilots, or mariners, the said lords shall likewise choose astrologers, pilots, or mariners as arbitrators or umpires. The umpire or umpires whom the said lords thus [agree on] shall investigate the said causes, and having heard the representatives of both sides they shall do entire justice, just as by this agreement and treaty it is arranged that the first named deputies should do. The said umpire or umpires whom the said lords shall agree on and choose will likewise take the oath with the formalities already described, confessing themselves and receiving the sacrament. The decision reached by each of the said persons, or by a majority of the said persons, deputed and named by each of the said lords, both in the possessory cause by the learned jurists and in the cause of ownership by the astrologers, pilots, or mariners, shall be a final decision. After these disagreements are adjusted, which the said umpire or umpires shall regulate, decide, and adjust, giving the final judgment, the said lords shall promise on their royal faith, for themselves and for their heirs and successors, wholly to keep and observe the judgment, and order it to be observed, without any deception or evasion whatsoever, forever and ever ; and on the sign of the Cross and by the words of the Holy Gospels, under pledge of all their patrimonial wealth and that of the crown of their realms, which they pledged therefor, etc., they shall swear wholly to keep, maintain, and observe it, and cause it to be observed.

9. *Item*, that the deputy first named by each of the said lords shall preside over his deputation just as was stipulated in the former treaty made between these lords.

Lastly, his Majesty commanded that the following response be given in regard to the whole matter :

The answer made on behalf of the emperor and king, our lord, to the articles sent on behalf of the lord King of Portugal in respect to the negotiations of the Moluccas is as follows :

His Majesty is greatly pleased that the lord King of Portugal has approved the reply given by his Majesty, while in Segovia, to the ambassador of the said lord King of Portugal, in regard to the expedients which would be offered in behalf of the latter to his Majesty in the negotiations relating to the Moluccas. Therefore in order to execute them, he will immediately command that lawyers and other persons expert in the negotiation be named, and he will give them all the necessary documents, including the said reply, so that, in accordance with the reply and with the treaty made between the Catholic king and queen, Don Ferdinand and Doña Isabella, sovereigns of Castile, etc., and the lord King Dom John, king of Portugal, etc., they may employ themselves in determining the said matter. Moreover in order to please the said lord King of Portugal better, his Majesty deems it good to cause the said persons, named on his behalf, to be commanded to perform the oath and ceremony, now asked for on behalf of the said lord King of Portugal, so that in determining the said matter they may proceed in accordance with the said reply. And if no agreement shall be reached between the said persons and deputies of both parties, if the difference shall be between the lawyers, the umpire or umpires who are to be named shall be lawyers, and if the said difference shall be between the astrologers and pilots, the umpire to be named shall be of that profession, and they shall be employed in the said matter in accordance with the reply that his Majesty gave in Segovia, which is incorporated above.

Therefore, both the said parties by virtue of the said powers, delegated from the said lords, their constituents, and incorporated above, declared, in conformity with the said reply, that they will be satisfied, both in the judgment upon ownership and possession and in the method and order to be followed in it, to have the contents of the said reply, which is incorporated above, and of the treaty made by the Catholic king and queen, and King Dom John of Portugal, observed, fulfilled, and performed; and to have the deputies receive conjointly such petitions as shall be given by the parties and to carry on the cause upon them, simply and openly, without clamor or distortion of judgment, only, the truth being known, they shall determine what may be just.

For all the aforesaid and every part and parcel of it, the said Mercurino de Gattinara, grand chancellor of their Majesties, Bishop Don Fray García de Loaysa, Don García de Padilla, chief knight-commander of Calatrava, and Doctor Lorenzo Galíndez de Carvajal, all members of the council of the said very exalted and very mighty Queen and King of Castile, Leon, Aragon, Granada, and the Two Sicilies, Jerusalem, etc., and their representatives, and by virtue of their said power, incorporated above, and the said Licentiate Asevedo, representative and ambassador of the said very exalted and very excellent prince, lord King Dom John of Portugal and the Algarves on this side and beyond the sea in Africa, lord of Guinea, etc., and by virtue of his said power, incorporated above, promised and asserted in the name of their said constituents, that actually and in fact, in good faith, without deception, and renouncing all fraud, craft, evasion, deception, pretense, and dissimulation whatsoever, they and their successors, and their kingdoms and lordships, forever and ever, will keep, observe, and perform, what is contained, adjusted, and agreed to above, and what shall be decided and determined by the said deputies, and every part and parcel of it, wholly, just as it shall be done, arranged, decided, determined, and concerted by them, and given as a judgment by them as competent judges. In order that it shall be thus observed and performed, by virtue of the said powers incorporated above, they pledged their said parties, their constituents, and their movable and landed property and that of their patrimonial and royal crowns and that of their successors, forever and ever, that neither they nor any of them, by himself or by an agent, directly or indirectly, shall contravene or prevent it, or any part or parcel of it, at any time or in any manner, premeditated or unpremeditated, that may or can be, under the penalties contained in the said above-mentioned treaty, and they renounced all the laws and privileges of which the said parties and each of them may avail themselves in order to contravene or hinder the aforesaid or any part and parcel of it, and for the greater security and stability of the aforesaid, they swore before God and Holy Mary and upon the sign of the Cross, on which they placed their right hands, and upon the words of the four Holy Gospels, wherever they are most largely written, on the consciences of their said constituents, that they and each of them will keep, observe, and perform all the aforesaid, and each part and parcel of it, actually and in fact, renouncing all evasion, deception, and subterfuge, and they will not gainsay it at any time or in any manner, and under the said oath they swore not to seek absolution of our very Holy Father, or of any other legate or prelate, who may be able to give it to them, and even though he shall give it to them of his own motion, they will not use it. Likewise the said representatives bound themselves in the said name, under the said penalty and oath, that within   days next ensuing, reckoned from the date of this treaty, the parties will exchange an approval and ratification of this said treaty, written on parchment, and signed with the names of the said lords, their constituents, and sealed with their hanging leaden seals. Of all the aforesaid they executed two copies of one tenor, both alike. These they signed with their names, and executed them before me the said secretary and notary public above-written and the undersigned witnesses one for each party. And whichever copy shall be produced, it shall be as valid as if both should be produced, which were made and executed in the said   the said day and month and year aforesaid.

15.

Treaty between Spain and Portugal concluded at Saragossa, April 17, 1529. Not ratified.

INTRODUCTION.

Near the beginning of the year 1527, the Emperor Charles V., urgently needing money, entertained the project of selling, or pawning, to the Portuguese crown, his claim to the Moluccas.[1] At about the same time, through the English ambassador in Spain, he attempted to interest Henry VIII. in purchasing the islands.[2] As a condition of entering into the contract, the King of Portugal, John III., required it to be approved and authorized by the Cortes of Castile,[3] to whom the Emperor had given his word that he would not alienate the Moluccas.[4] The Emperor, on the other hand, adduced various reasons to prove that such authorization was unnecessary. It was finally agreed to refer the question of the legal necessity for such approval and authorization to the ten leading lawyers of the Emperor's Royal Council. If the lawyers agreed that the necessity did not exist, the King of Portugal promised to abide by their decision.[5]

Near the beginning of 1528, when the Emperor was on the eve of war with France and England, he despatched Lope Hurtado as ambassador to Portugal, to procure the assistance of that crown against Spain's enemies.[6]

---

[1] Santarem, *Quadro Elementar*, tom. II., p. 55, no. 244.

[2] See Edward Lee's letter of Jan. 20, 1527, calendared in *Letters and Papers of the Reign of Henry VIII.* (ed. Brewer, 1872), vol. IV., pt. II., no. 2813, and Thorne's letter to Lee in R. Hakluyt, *Principal Navigations* (1903), II. 164-181.

[3] Oct.-Dec., 1527. Archives of the Indies, Patronato, 1-2-2/16, no. 9.

[4] Besides his promise to the Cortes of 1523, mentioned above, Doc. **13**, note 12, the Emperor appears to have made a similar promise to the Cortes of 1525. *Cf.* below, art. 11, and Doc. **16**, art. 11.

[5] National Archives at Lisbon, gav. 15, maço 10, no. 21.

[6] A draft of a treaty of defensive alliance between Spain and Portugal, preserved in the Archives of the Indies, Patronato, 1-2-2/16, no. 3, ramo 3, dates from about this time. The articles that refer to the new discoveries follow. In explanation of the third article it may be said that the *Mare Parvum* was situated off the Barbary Coast. See the article by M. Jiménez de la Espada, "España en Berberia", in the *Boletín de la Sociedad Geográfica de Madrid,* tom. IX. (1880).

"3. Item, conventum, concordatum, et conclusum est, pro majori stabilitate, et firmitate, dicte presentis confederationis et ut omnis rupture ipsius atque dissidii tollatur occasio, quod via amicabili arbitrorum juris per eos et eorum quemlibet elligendorum facient decidi et determinari, controversiam sive diferenciam, quam inter se habent de et super Malach, et Mari parvo, cabo de Ager, juxta et secundum quod in capitulationibus et confederationibus alias initis et conclusis inter prefatos felicis memoriae Ferdinandum et Elisabeth, Catholicos et serenissimum Portugalie reges, cautum et conventum fuit. Et ex nunc compromisserunt ac de alto et basso compromissum fecerunt et convenerunt, ac eorum quilibet in spectabiles [*blank for names*] tamque arbitros, juris dantes ipsis

146

Hurtado was also instructed ' to persuade King John to dismiss the French ambassador, Honoré de Caix, who, objectionable on other grounds, apparently desired some concessions from Portugal in the matter of the spice trade.' Hurtado was instructed not to negotiate concerning the Spice Islands—that negotiation was being conducted chiefly through the Portuguese ambassador at the Spanish court—but his correspondence shows that both sovereigns were anxious to settle the long controversy. The Emperor's habitual need of money was intensified by his war with France and by his projected journey to Italy for his coronation, and, in Hurtado's opinion, the King of Portugal's unwillingness to endanger his commerce by engaging in the Spanish war would make him the more ready to satisfy the Emperor in regard to the Spice Islands. Moreover, another Spanish fleet was being fitted out at Coruña.'

---

plenam liberam et omnimodam potestatem laudandi et terminandi predictam controversiam, infra spatium [*blank*] mensium, a die dat' presentium computandorum, promittentes, et eorum quilibet gratum, firmum, et ratum, perpetuo habituros totum id et quicquid per dictos arbitros juris laudatum sentenciatum et diffinitum fuerit. . . .

" 10. Item, conventum, concordatum, et conclusum est, quod prelibate suppetie non prestabuntur ex necessitate hujus conventionis, pacis, atque federis, nisi pro tuitone ac defensione regnorum, provinciarum, statuum, terrarum, civitatuum, villarum, opidorum, et locorum, Castelle, Legionis, Aragonie, Valentie, Navarre, Catalonie, Biscaye, Portugalie, et partium Africe sive Indie.

" 11. Item, conventum, concordatum, et conclusum est, quod per Sanctam Sedem Apostolicam, quondam Regibus Castelle et Legionis, predecessoribus dictorum Catholicorum Regum necnon suis heredibus et successoribus, donate, concesse, et assignate fuerunt insule omnes et terre firme detecte et detegende, reperte et reperiende, versus occidentem et meridiem, et postea, ut discordiarum evitaretur causa et materia, inter prefatos q. Castelle et dictum Portugalie Reges conventum et capitulatum fuit, quod eorum quilibet respective contentus foret insulis et terris detectis et detegendis intra terminos et limites in tractatu et capitulatione super hoc inito et laudato expressos, quod nemo ipsorum regum aggredietur, deteget, aut occupabit, per se, subditos, aut alios aliquid intra limites seu terminos alterius, et, si aliquid occupat vel occupabit per se vel suos intra terminos alterius, hoc sine difficultate et absque processu restituet et restitui faciet quam primum per regem intra cujus terminos seu limites continetur si fuerit ad hoc requisitus, qui vero vasallorum et subditorum predictorum Regum cujuscumque gradus, status, aut conditionis fuerint et quacumque auctoritate poleant secus fecerint vel attentaverint tamquam pacis et federum effractores et violatores eos cohercere et plecti faciet Rex confederatus sub cujus ditione et dominio erunt."

' His instructions are in M. Navarrete, *Col. de Docs. para la Hist. de España* (1842-1895), I. 128 ff. Transcripts of several of Hurtado's letters written from Lisbon to the emperor, are among the Bergenroth manuscripts in the British Museum. They are mostly noticed in *Cal. of St. Pap., Spain*, vol. III., pt. II. See also P. de Gayangos, *Catalogue of Spanish Manuscripts*, II. (1877), pp. 569 ff.

'During a great part of the period between 1518 and 1559, Honoré de Caix represented France at the court of Lisbon. Commission des Archives Diplomatiques, *Recueil des Instructions données aux Ambassadeurs et Ministres de France: III. Portugal*, by Vicomte de Caix de Saint-Aymour (1886), p. xv. Hurtado was to point out that the Hapsburg dominions were a better distributing centre for spices than France and England. Navarrete, *op. cit.*, I. 137, 138. By a treaty of offensive alliance concluded on Apr. 30, 1527, between France and England against the Emperor, it had been provided that spices carried in Portuguese ships into the Channel during the war might not be sold in the Low Countries, *i. e.*, at the spice-market at Antwerp, but only in France and England; and that in case the King of Portugal declared in favor of the Emperor his goods and subjects should be adjudged good prize. Lord Herbert of Cherbury, *The Life and Reign of King Henry VIII.*, in *A Complete History of England* (1706), II. 81.

' A. Rodríguez Villa, *El Emperador Carlos V. y su Corte según las Cartas de Don Martin de Salinas* (1903), p. 417. *Cf.* Doc. **13**, introduction, and Doc. **14**, note 15.

The protest of the Cortes assembled at Madrid in the spring of 1528, was of no avail.[10] At Saragossa, on April 17, 1529, the plenipotentiaries of Spain and Portugal concluded a treaty whose principal provisions were, briefly, as follows:

The Emperor pledged his right in the Moluccas to the King of Portugal for 350,000 ducats, but might redeem his right by returning the money; there should be a line of demarcation from pole to pole, 17° east of the Moluccas, and its position was to be shown on a standard map; Castilians who traded beyond the line might be punished by the Portuguese. Imported spices should be sequestrated, pending investigation, and afterwards assigned to that king from whose lands they were found to have come. Castilians should be punished if they crossed the aforesaid line (except through necessity or ignorance), or if, in the seas navigated by Portugal's India fleet, they sailed further than the direct course to the Strait of Magellan required. If this agreement were proved to have been violated by command of either king, his right should be transferred to the other; the provisions for the punishment of Castilians should not be in force until the Castilians already despatched to the Moluccas should have been notified; astrologers and pilots should be named by both sides to examine the claims of the Emperor and King of Portugal to the Moluccas. If the decision favored Castile it should not be executed until the Emperor returned the 350,000 ducats to Portugal; if it favored Portugal, Castile must return the 350,000 ducats within four years; the King of Portugal was not to build any new fortress in the Moluccas or repair his fortress now there; the King of Portugal and his people should not harm the fleets already despatched by the Emperor to the Moluccas, or hinder their trade; the Emperor should immediately send instructions to his people in the Moluccas to return at once and trade there no more; both kings should swear to fulfill this treaty, and should ask the Pope to confirm it; the Emperor should declare that this treaty was as binding as though approved by the Cortes, and that he cancelled all laws conflicting with it. He was to order his royal council to find out whether it could be made without the approval of the *pueblos*; the treaty of Tordesillas should remain in force save in matters otherwise determined by this treaty; the King of Portugal was to do justice to persons whose goods had been seized in Portugal because they served the Emperor; the Emperor gave the King of Portugal the difference between 350,000 ducats and the actual value of the Moluccas; the party violating this treaty should forfeit to the party that observed it any right derived from it, and a fine of 100,000 ducats. If the Emperor violated it, the sale became unconditional.

Most of these provisions appear, in somewhat altered form, in the definitive treaty concluded five days later.[11]

[10] *Córtes de los Antiguos Reinos de Leon y de Castilla* (Real Academia de la Historia, Madrid, 1861, etc.), IV. 461, 462.
[11] Doc. **16.**

BIBLIOGRAPHY.

Text: MS. The original manuscript, signed by the plenipotentiaries of both crowns, is in the Archives of the Indies at Seville, Patronato, 1-2-2/16, no. 9, ramo 1. This text has not, it is believed, been printed or translated hitherto.

References: Contemporary and early writings. Viscount de Santarem, *Quadro Elementar* (1842-1876), II. 55 ff.; J. Ramos-Coelho, *Alguns Documentos* (Acad. Real das Sciencias of Lisbon, 1892), pp. 487, 492-495; *Calendar of State Papers, Spain*, vol. III. (1877), pt. II., pp. 616-617, 628, 817, 914-915, 996; F. Lopez de Gómara, *Historia General de las Indias*, in B. C. Aribau, *Biblioteca de Autores Españoles: Historiadores Primitivos de Indias*, XXII. (1852) 222; A. de Herrera, *Historia General de los Hechos de los Castellanos* (1728-1730), dec. IV., lib. V., c. 10. On Spanish-Portuguese relations in the Moluccas from 1521 to 1532, see Navarrete, *Coleccion de Viages* (1825-1837), V., parts of which are translated or abstracted in C. R. Markham, *Early Spanish Voyages to the Strait of Magellan* (Hakluyt Soc., 2d ser., no. XXVIII., 1911), and in Blair and Robertson, *Philippine Islands* (1903-1909), II.; B. Leonardo de Argensola, *Conquista de las Islas Malucas* (1609), lib. I., translation in J. Stevens, *A New Collection of Voyages and Travels* (1708, etc.), I.

TEXT.[12]

En el nonbre de Dios Todopoderoso, Padre y Hijo y Spiritu Santo, tres personas y un solo Dios verdadero. Notorio y manifiesto sea a todos quantos este publico ynstrumento vieren, commo en la çibdad de Çaragoça,[13] a diez e syete dias del mes de Abril, año del nasçimiento de nuestro Salvador Jhesu Christo de mill e quinientos y veinte y ñueve años, en presençia de my, Francisco de los Covos,[14] secretario y del consejo del Enperador e Reyna e Rey de Castilla y su escrivano y notario publico en la su corte y en todos los sus reynos e señorios, estando presentes y juntos los señores, el grand chançiller, Mercurino de Gatinara,[15] conde de Gatinara, y el muy reverendo Don Fray Garcia de Loaysa,[16] obispo de Osma, confesor, y anbos del consejo de los muy altos y muy poderosos prinçipes, Don Carlos, por la divina clemençia emperador semper augusto, rrey de Alemania, y Doña Juana, su madre, y el mismo Don Carlos, su hijo, por la gracia de Dios rreyes de Castilla, de Leon, de Aragon, de las Dos Seçilias, de Jherusalem, de Navarra, de Granada, etc., sus procuradores bastantes de la una parte, y el señor Antonio de Azevedo,[17] cutino, del consejo y enbaxador del muy alto e muy poderoso señor Don Juan, por la gracia de Dios rrey de Portugal, de los

[12] The text is from the original manuscript in the Archives of the Indies, Patronato, 1-2-2/16, no. 9, ramo 1.

[13] The Emperor stopped at Saragossa on his way from Toledo to Barcelona, whence he sailed to Italy for his coronation. He left Saragossa on Apr. 17 (M. de Foronda y Aguilera, "Estancias y Viages de Carlos V." in *Boletín de la Sociedad Geográfica de Madrid*, tom. XXXVII., no. 7, July, 1895), or on Apr. 19 (Villa, *op. cit.*, p. 431).

[14] See Doc. **13**, note 20.

[15] The Count of Gattinara was also one of the negotiators of the treaty of Vitoria. See Doc. **13**, note 14.

[16] See Doc. **14**, note 8.   [17] See Doc. **14**, note 11.

Algarves de aquende y allende el mar en Africa, señor de Guinea y de la
conquista, navegaçion, y comerçio de Etiopia y Aravia y Persia y de la India,
etc., su procurador bastante de la otra parte, dixeron que por quanto entre
los dichos muy altos y muy poderosos Catolicos señores, Enperador y Reyes
de Castilla, de Leon, dAragon, de las Dos Seçilias, de Jherusalem, etc., y
el dicho muy alto y muy poderoso señor Don Juan, rrey de Portugal y de los
Algarves, etc., viendo ser asy cunplidero a serviçio de Dios, nuestro Señor,
y al bien de sus rreinos y por conservaçion de la hermandad, debdo, y amor
que entrellos ay, se ha hablado y tratado de tomar, çierto asiento y conçierto
y enpeño y rretro vendendo sobre las yslas de Maluco y otras tierras y mares
de las Indias, que cada uno dellos pretende tener derecho, y para tomar, tratar,
y capitular, hazer y asentar el dicho asiento y conçierto y enpeño de rretro
vendendo entre los dichos sus constituyentes, han dado a ellos sus poderes
cunplidos, firmados de sus nonbres y sellados con sus sellos, segund mas
largamente en los dichos poderes, que anbas las dichas partes mostraron,
firmados de los dichos señores Enperador y Rey de Castilla, y del dicho
señor Rey de Portugal, sellados con sus sellos, commo dicho es, se contiene,
el thenor de los quales, de verbo ad verbum, uno en pos de otro, es este que
se sigue :

[Here follow the full powers granted by the Emperor Charles V. and
Queen Joanna of Castile to the Count of Gattinara and the Bishop of Osma
on April 14, 1529; and the full powers granted by John III. of Portugal
to Antonio d'Azevedo, on October 18, 1528.]

Porende los dichos señores, grand chançiller y obispo de Osma, del consejo
de los dichos muy alto y muy poderoso señor Enperador e Reyes de Castilla,
de Leon, de Aragon, de las Dos Seçilias, de Jherusalem, etc., y sus procuradores, y el dicho señor Antonio Dazevedo, cutino, del consejo del dicho muy
alto y muy poderoso señor Rey de Portugal y de los Algarves, etc., y su
procurador, por virtud de los dichos poderes, que de suso van incorporados,
y usando dellos, asentaron, concordaron, capitularon, y otogaron, en nonbre
de los dichos señores, sus constituyentes, los capitulos que de yuso seran
contenidos, en esta manera :

1. Primeramente,[18] es concordado y asentado quel dicho señor Enperador
y Rey de Castilla da en enpeño y venta de rretro vendendo al dicho señor
Rey de Portugal el derecho que tiene a las yslas de Maluco y a la contrataçion
y comerçio en las otras yslas y tierras a ellas comarcanas, y questan y se
incluyem dentro de la linea que se ha de hechar por la forma y manera que
se yuso sera declarado, por preçio y quantia de trezientos y çinquenta mill
ducados de oro y de peso, dea trezientos y setenta e çinco maravedis[19] da
moneda Castellana, cada ducado, quel dicho señor Rey de Portugal ha de dar
al dicho señor Enperador y Rey de Castilla, pagados en esta manera, los

---

[18] This article corresponds to Doc. **16**, art. 1.

[19] The weight of the *excelente* of Granada, the equivalent of the ducat, was fixed by
law in 1497 at 3.52 grammes of gold $\frac{23}{24}$ fine. Since the gold dollar of the United
States contains about 1.5 grammes of pure gold, the gold in a ducat of 1529 would be
worth about $2.32 in terms of our currency. The *maravedi* was the unit of reckoning
for the whole coinage system. M. J. Bonn. *Spaniens Niedergang während der Preis-
revolution des 16. Jahrhunderts*, pp. 36, 43, in *Münchener Volkswirtschaftliche Studien*
(ed. L. Brentano and W. Lotz, no. 12, 1896) ; and L. Saez. *Demostracion Histórica del
Verdadero Valor de las Monedas* (Real Academia de la Historia, Madrid, 1805).
pp. 236 ff. See also W. G. Sumner, "The Spanish Dollar and the Colonial Shilling",
American Historical Review, III. 607 ff.

dozientos e çinquenta mill ducados dentro de treynta dias primeros siguientes desdel dia queste asiento se otogare, pagados en Castilla o en Lisboa, dondel dicho señor Rey de Portugal mejor los pudiere dar en monedas de oro y de peso, o su justo valor en monedas de plata, y los çientos mill ducados restantes en la feria de Mayo de Medina del Campo [20] deste presente año, al tienpo de los pagamentos della, en la forma e manera suso dicho, que ha de pagar los dichos dozientos y çinquenta mill ducados primeros, los quales todos se daran y pagaran a los dichos tienpos, en contado e fuera de canbio, y los que se ovieren de pagar en Portugal seran en moneda que valga en Castilla los dichos trezientos y setenta y çinco maravedis, cada ducado, a la persona o personas quel dicho señor Enperador y Rey de Castilla para ello nombrare; el qual dicho enpeño y venta de rretrovendendo el dicho señor Enperador y Rey de Castilla haze al dicho señor Rey de Portugal, commo dicho es, con tal pacto y condiçion que cada y quando y en qualquier tienpo quel dicho señor Enperador y Rey de Castilla, o sus herederos o subcesores en los rreynos de Castilla, quisieren quitar, luyr, e rredemi el dicho derecho que asi le enpeña y vende, commo dicho es, bolviendo el preçio que asy rreçibe, lo puedan hazer, y el dicho señor Rey de Portugal sea obligado a lo rreçebir, quedando asy al dicho señor Enperador e Rey de Castilla commo al dicho señor Rey de Portugal y a sus subçesores, su derecho a salvo en el mismo estado y segund y por la manera que primero le tenian, y sin que se les aya hecho ni causado, haga ni cause, perjuizio ni novedad alguna en el, por virtud deste asiento y capitulaçion.

2. Yten,[21] es asentado y concordado que se heche, y desde agora se aya por hechada, una linea simiçirculo de polo a polo, diez y siete grados de los Malucos a oriente, que son dozientas y noventa y siete leguas y media,[22] questa misma linea dizen que pasara por las yslas de Santo Tome de las Velas,[23] questa en este merediano, y a nordeste y subdueste y quarta del este con los Malucos, que asy mismo dizen que dista dellos diez e nueve grados por este rrunbo de nordeste y subdueste, y siendo caso que las dichas yslas de Santo Tome de las Velas esten e disten de Maluco mas o menos, todavia

---

[20] By 1529 the fair of Medina del Campo, long the chief centre in Spain for the exchange of merchandise, had become even more important for the settlement of accounts and the transaction of other financial business. Descriptions of the fair and of the activities of the money changers or bankers are given in M. Colmeiro, *Historia de la Economia Politica en España* (1863), tom. II., c. 74, and C. Espejo and J. Paz, *Las Antiguas Ferias de Medina del Campo* (1912), c. 3.

[21] This article corresponds to Doc. **16**, art. 2.

[22] *Cf.* Doc. **7**, note 19. Magellan and most of the experts at the junta of Badajoz reckoned that a degree of longitude at the equator equalled 17½ Castilian leagues. Actually it equalled about 18¾ Castilian leagues. The methods employed at this period to determine latitude and longitude are described in A. Pigafetta, *Treatise on the Art of Navigation*, printed by A. do Mosto in the *Raccolta Colombiana*, vol. III., pt. V., and, in a translation of an abridged version, in Lord Stanley, *First Voyage round the World* (Hakluyt Soc., no. LII., 1874), pp. 164 ff. See also the works written or edited by J. Bensaude, mentioned in Doc. **9**, note 6.

[23] "Santo Tome de las Velas" appears here as the name of a single group of islands, whereas in the corresponding article of the treaty of Apr. 22 (Doc. **16**), the expression "las islas de las Velas y de Santo Thome" might be taken to indicate two distinct groups. The Islas de las Velas Latinas, said to have been thus named by Magellan because the canoes of the natives carried lateen sails (A. de Herrera, *Descripcion de las Indias*, 1730, p. 56), and commonly known as the Ladrones or Mariannas, are situated in about 12° to 21° N. and 144° to 145° E. If the name Santo Thome really belongs to them, it may be because Magellan discovered them on the day preceding the festival of St. Thomas Aquinas, Mar. 6, 1521.

quede la dicha linea hechada a las dichas dozientas y noventa e siete leguas
y media mas al oriente, que hazen los dichos diez e nueve grados al nordeste
de las sobre dichas yslas de Maluco, y que para saber se por donde la dicha
linea es lançada, se haga luego un padron," en que se hechara la dicha linea
por el modo sobre dicho, y que dara asi asentada para declaraçion del punto
y lugar por donde ella pasa, y este sera firmado del dicho señor Enperador
y Rey de Castilla, y del dicho señor Rey de Portugal, y sellado con sus sellos,
y por el mismo modo, y conforme al dicho padron, se hechara la dicha linea
en todas las cartas de navegaçion por las quales navegaran los subdittos y
naturales de los rreynos del dicho señor Enperador y Rey de Castilla y del
dicho señor Rey de Portugal, y que, para hazer el dicho padron, se nonbren
por los dichos señores rreyes por cada uno dellos tres personas, para que
sobre juramento hagan el dicho padron, y hechen la dicha linea conforme a
lo suso dicho, y asi hecho, los dichos señores Enperador e Rey de Castilla
y el dicho señor Rey de Portugal lo firmen de sus nonbres, y manden sellar
con los sellos de sus armas, y por el se hagan las dichas cartas de marear,
segund dicho es, para que los subdittos y naturales de los dichos señores
rreyes naveguen por ellas, durante el tiempo quel dicho señor Rey de Castilla
no luyere y redimiere el dicho derecho ; pero que rrediniiendo lo e quitandolo,
y acabado este asiento y contrato, y el tal patron y cartas de navegar que asy
se hizieren conforme a lo suso dicho, no pare perjuizio a ninguna de las partes
en su derecho, mas syn enbargo dello quede todo en el mismo estado que
agora esta, y entranto quel dicho patron no se hiziere por qualquier causa
que sea, la dicha linea quede hechada des del otorganiiento deste contrato,
y los que la pasaren incurran en las penas que abaxo seran contenidas, segund
y en la forma y manera que adelante sera declarado.

3. Yten," es asentado y concordado que en todas las yslas y tierras que
entraren dentro de la dicha linea, no puedan las armadas y navios del dicho
señor Enperador y Rey de Castilla, ni de sus subditos, ni de otros por su mandado y consentimiento, o fabor, o ayuda, tratar, ni comerçiar, ni cargar, y que
si algunos subditos del dicho señor Enperador e Rey de Castilla, o otros
algunos, despues deste asiento, fueren tomados dentre de los dichos limites,
rescatando, contratando, comerçiando, o cargando, que puedan ser presos por
los capitanes e gentes del dicho señor rrey, e oydos y castigados, conforme a
justiçia, y que lo mismo puedan hazer contra los que les fuere provado que contrataron, rescataron, comerçiaron, y cargaron dentro de los dichos limites,
despues deste asiento, aunque no sean hallados ni tomados en ellos, y que sy

---

" In 1508 the King of Spain ordered the officials of the Casa de Contratación of
Seville to cause a standard map to be constructed showing the lands and islands of the
Indies discovered hitherto. The revision of the map was entrusted to the aforesaid
officials and to the chief pilot, Navarrete, *Viages*, III. 300. In 1515 and in 1526 pilots
were appointed to revise the map. No copy of the model map is known to exist, but
several extant Spanish charts, dating from 1525-1530, are doubtless derived from it.
H. Harrisse, *Diplomatic History* (1897), pp. 142-151 ; id., *Discovery of North America*
(1892), pp. 258-268, 631-633, *et passim* ; M. de la Puente y Olea, *Los Trabajos Geográficos
de la Casa de Contratación* (1900). The Weimar chart of 1529, executed by the cosmog-
rapher royal, Diego Ribero, was believed by J. G. Kohl to have been compiled in accordance with the terms of the treaty of Saragossa, *Die Beiden Aeltesten General-Karten
von Amerika* (1860), pp. 37, 38. Harrisse, however, dissents from this conclusion, *Discovery of North America*, p. 569. On Ribero's maps, see also E. L. Stevenson, " Early
Spanish Cartography of the New World ", in *Proceedings* of the American Antiquarian
Society, new ser., vol. XIX., pt. III. (1909).

" This article corresponds to Doc. **16**, arts. 4, 5, and 6.

algunos subditos del dicho señor Enperador y Rey de Castilla, o otras personas, traxieren espeçeria o drogueria, de qualquier suerte que fuere, que en quales-quier puertos y partes donde llegaren y vinieren de anbos los dichos señores rreyes, o de qualquier dellos, o de otros que no sean de enemigos, se depositen y esten enbargados por anbos los dichos señores rreyes, hasta que se sepa de cuya demarcaçion fueron tirados y traidas, y sabido y determinado, se entreguen sin ningund detenimiento aquien perteneçieren, o su justo valor, y que para se saber si el lugar y tierra, donde las dichas espeçerias e droguerias fueren traydas, cae dentro de la demarcaçion y limites que, conforme a este contrato, ha de quedar con el dicho señor Enperador y Rey de Castilla, ynbiaran los dichos señores rreyes dos o quatro navios, tantos uno commo otro, en los quales yran personas que entiendan y sepan de aquella arte, tantos de una parte commo de otra, a los dichos lugares y tierras donde dixieren que tiraron y truxieron las dichas espeçerias e droguerias para ver y determinar en cuya demarcaçion caen las dichas tierras donde asy las dichas espeçerias e droguerias se dixere que fueren tiradas, y hallando que las dichas tierras y lugares caen dentro de la demarcaçion del dicho señor Rey de Castilla, y que en ellas ay las dichas espeçerias e droguerias en tanta cantidad que razonablemente las pudiese traer dellos, el dicho señor Rey de Portugal sea obligado a gelas bolver, o su justo valor, estando secrestadas en sus rreynos. E sy fuere hallado y determinado que las hallaron e traxie-ron de tierras de la demarcaçion del dicho Serenissimo Rey de Portugal, no sea obligado a gelas bolver, y que si estovieren secrestadas en los rreinos del dicho señor Enperador y Rey de Castilla, el sea obligado a las bolver y restituyr luego al dicho señor Rey de Portugal, y que por la misma manera se haga, siendo secrestadas en otros qualesquier rreynos e tierras que no sean de los dichos señores rreyes, y que dentro de medio año despues que las dichas espeçerias e droguerias fueren secrestados, commo dicho es, los dichos señores rreyes sean obligados a inbiar los dichos navios y personas para hazer la dicha averiguaçion commo dicho es, y en quanto las dichas espeçerias y droguerias estovieren enbargadas y secrestadas, commo dicho es, el dicho señor Enperador y Rey de Castilla, ni otro por el, ni con su fabor ni consenti-miento, no yran, ni inbiaran, a la dicha tierra, o tierras, donde las dichas espeçerias e droguerias vinieren, y sea obligado a mandar castigar, conforme a justiçia, los que contra lo suso dicho fueren, o pasaren, commo malhechores y quebrantadores de fee y de paz. Pero entienda se que la navegaçion por la mar del Sur ha de quedar y queda libre al dicho señor Enperador y Rey de Castilla y a sus subditos, para poder por alli navegar e contratar, conforme a la capitulaçion hecha entre los reyes Catholicos y el Rey Don Juan de Portugal,[26] que aya gloria, con tanto que no puedan entrar, ni entren, ni pasar, ni pasen, de las mares de la dicha linea a dentro, salvo entrando en ellas con neçesidad de tienpos o de bastimentos, o por ynorançia,[27] no sabiendo la dicha linea, y que en tal caso los navios que asy entraren del dicho señor Enperador y Rey de Castilla, y de sus subditos, dentro de la dicha linea, no caygan en las dichas penas, pero que, hallando dentro de la dicha linea algunas tierras o yslas, no contraten en ellas, sino que las dexen luego y se salgan dellas y de la dicha linea, para que queden libres al dicho señor Rey de Portugal, durante este contrato, segund dicho es, commo sy por sus capitanes

[26] The treaty of Tordesillas, Doc. **9.**
[27] In a letter to Azevedo, dated Jan. 13, 1529, the King of Portugal objected to ex-cepting from punishment those who passed the line in ignorance. Lord Stanley's edition of De Morga, *Philippine Islands* (Hakluyt Soc., no. XXXIX., 1868), app., p. 394.

y gente fuesen descubiertas y halladas, y que siendo caso que asy por hierro
o neçesidad o tienpos contrarios, los tales navios del dicho señor Enperador
e Rey de Castilla o de sus subditos, llegasen a alguna tierra de las que asi
entraren en la dicha linea, y por virtud deste asiento perteneçieren al dicho
señor Rey de Portugal, que sean tratados por los moradores della commo
vasallos de su hermano, y asi commo el dicho señor Enperador y Rey de
Castilla mandaria tratar a los suyos que en esta mañera aportasen a sus
tierras de la Nueva España, o de otras de aquellas partes, lo qual se entienda,
en quanto no constare claramente que los dichos navios y los que en ellos
anduvieren, entraron en los mares y tierras que entran en la dicha linea, con
la dicha ynorançia o neçesidad o tienpo contrario, y que no saliendo fuera,
çesada la dicha neçesidad, caygan en las dichas penas; pero que las naos e
navios del dicho señor Rey de Castilla e de sus subditos, vasallos, y naturales,
puedan navegar y naveguen por los mares del dicho señor Rey de Portugal,
por donde sus armadas van para la Yndia,[28] tan solanmente quanto les fuere
neçesario para tener su derrota derecha por el Estrecho de Magallanes, y
haziendo lo contrario, navegando mas por las dichas mares, yncurriran en
las dichas penas, reservando tanbien en esto la ynorançia, o neçesidad, o
tienpos contrarios, commo esta dicho, y averiguandose y provandose primeramente que por mandado del dicho señor Enperador e Rey de Castilla, o con
su fabor, ayuda, o consentimiento, se contravino a lo suso dicho, en tal caso
de cayga luego del derecho que toviere a ello, y aquel quede aplicado a la
parte que por este contrato estoviere y lo guardare, y este enpeño y retrovendendo quede resoluto, y la venta pura y linpia, commo sy al prinçipio
fuera fecha syn ninguna condiçio. En la qual dicha pena ansymismo ha
de incurrir e incurra el dicho señor Rey de Portugal, averiguandose que por
qualquier manera ha contravenido a lo que por su parte es obligado a guardar
y cunplir.

4. Yten,[29] es asentado y concordado que lo que toca a que, sy algunos
subditos del dicho señor Enperador y Rey de Castilla, o otros algunos, fueren
tomados rescatando, contratando, comerçiando, o cargando, dentro de los
dichos limites, despues deste asiento, sean presos por los capitanes y gentes
del dicho señor Rey de Portugal, y oydos y castigados conforme a justiçia,
y que lo mismo puedan hazer contra los que le fuere provado que contrataron,
rescataron, y comerçiaron, y cargaron, dentro de los dichos limites, despues
este asiento, aunque no se han hallados ni tomados en ellos, y lo demas que
se asienta por este contrato, en quanto toca a no pasar la dicha linea ningunos
subditos del dicho señor Enperador e Rey de Castilla, ni otros algunos por
su mandado, consentimiento, fabor, o ayuda, y las penas que cerca desto se
ponen, aunque esta dicho ariba, despues este asiento, se entienda desdel dia
que fuere notificado a los subditos del dicho señor Enperador y gentes que por
aquellas mares y partes navegan y andan en adelante, y que antes de la
notificaçion no incurran en las dichas penas; pero esto se entienda quanto a
las gentes de las armadas de su Magestad que hasta agora a aquellas partes
son ydas,[30] y que desdel dia de lo otorgamiento deste contrato en adelante,

---

[28] The Atlantic, east of the demarcation line of 1494.
[29] This article corresponds to Doc. **16**, art. 7.
[30] Three Spanish fleets despatched to the Moluccas before 1529 reached the islands—
Magellan's, Loaysa's (*cf.* Doc. **14**, note 15), and Saavedra's. Cortes sent the last from
Mexico, by order of the Emperor, to relieve the Spaniards of Loaysa's fleet, who had
established themselves at Tidore and Gilolo. For accounts of these expeditions, see
Navarrete, *Viages*, V.; Blair and Robertson, *Philippine Islands*, II.; and Markham,
Early Spanish Voyages (Hakluyt Soc., 2d ser., no. XXVIII., 1911).

durante el tienpo del dicho enpeño y rretrovendendo, no pueda inbiar otras algunas de nuevo syn incurrir en las dichas penas.

5. Yten,[31] porque los dichos señores Enperador y Rey de Castilla y Rey de Portugal desean que el derecho de las dichas yslas se determine, es asentado y concertado que para la declaraçion del derecho que cada una dellas pretende tener a las dichas yslas de Maluco y otras, que cada uno dellos pretende estar en sus limites y demarcaçion, se nonbren astrologos, pilotos, o marineros, por cada una de las partes en ygual numero, dentro de un año, o dos, o tres, o mas, conmo el dicho señor Rey de Portugal lo quisiere, que vean el derecho dentre anbas partes en propiedad, conforme a la capitulaçion hecha entre los dichos Reyes Catolicos y el dicho Rey Don Juan de Portugal, y a la respuesta que el dicho señor Enperador y Rey de Castilla dio en Segovia,[32] que es conforme a derecho y a la dicha capitulaçion ; y que no alçen la mano dello despues que lo començaren hasta dar sentençia en fabor de aquel que les pareçiere que tiene el derecho,[33] y en caso que se determine en fabor del dicho señor Enperador y Rey de Castilla, o de sus subçesores, que la sentençia que se diere no se execute, sin que primero buelva rrealmente y con efetto, los dichos trezientos y çinquenta mill ducados, que rreçibe por el dicho enpeño y venta de rretro vendendo, y en caso que la sentençia sea en fabor del dicho señor Rey de Portugal, o de sus subçesores, que el dicho señor Enperador y Rey de Castilla sea obligado a le bolver e rrestituyr los dichos trezientos y çinquenta mill ducados, que asy da el dicho señor Rey de Portugal por el dicho enpeño y venta, dentro de quatro años primeros siguientes despues que se declarare.

6. Otrosy,[34] es concordado y asentado que el dicho señor Rey de Portugal, en las dichas yslas de Maluco, ni en las otras tierras questan dentro de la dicha linea, ni en parte alguna de los terminos que en ella se incluyen, no pueda hazer, ni haga de nuevo fortaleza alguna, ni otro hedefiçio que sea fuerte, y quanto a la fortaleza que esta hecha al presente en una de las dichas yslas[35] de Maluco por el dicho señor Rey de Portugal, que aquella se quede y este, durante el dicho tienpo del enpeño, en el punto y estado que stara dendel dia queste asiento se otorgare y firmare, en un año y medio, sin que se labre, ni edifique, de nuevo en ella, mas de sostenella en el estado en que al dicho tienpo estoviere, dentro del qual dicho tienpo el dicho señor rrey podra mandar notificar a sus capitanes y gente, que tiene en aquellas partes, lo que por este asiento es obligado a tener y guardar çerca desto, y quel dicho señor Rey de Portugal jure y prometa de guardar lo asy.

7. Yten,[36] es asentado que las armadas, que el dicho señor Enperador e Rey de Castilla hasta agora tiene ynbiadas a las dichas partes, sean miradas y bien tratadas y faboreçidas del dicho señor Rey de Portugal y de sus gentes, y no les sea puesto enbaraço ni ynpedimiento en su navegaçion e contrataçion, y que si daño alguno, lo que no se cree, ellas ovieren rreçebido, o reçibieren, de sus capitanes o gentes, o les ovieren tomado alguna cosa, quel dicho señor rrey sea obligado de hemendar y satisfazer y rrestituyr y pagar luego todo aquello en quel dicho señor Enperador y Rey de Castilla e su armada e subditos ovieren sido dagnificados, y de mandar pugnir y castigar a los que lo hizieren, y de proveer que las armadas y gentes del dicho Señor Enperador

---

[31] This article corresponds to Doc. **16**, art. 3. [32] See Doc. **14**, p. 133, and note 16.
[33] This was one of Portugal's demands. The Spaniards had taken advantage of the time-limit of Badajoz.
[34] This article corresponds to Doc. **16**, art. 8. [35] In Ternate.
[36] This article corresponds to Doc. **16**, art. 9.

11

y Rey de Castilla se puedan venir quando quisieren, libremente sin inpedimiento alguno.

8. Iten,[37] es asentado quel dicho señor Emperador y Rey de Castilla mande dar luego sus cartas y provisiones para sus capitanes y gentes que estovieren en las dichas yslas que luego se vengan y no contraten mas en ellas, con que les dexen traer libremente lo que ovieron rrescatado, contratado, y cargado.

9. Yten,[38] es asentado que anbos los dichos señores Enperador e Rey de Castilla e Rey de Portugal, y cada uno dellos, jure solpnemente de guardar y cunplir este asiento y contrato, e todo lo en el contenido, y prometen por el dicho juramento, por sy y por sus subçesores, de nunca en ningund tienpo, venir contra el, en todo ni en parte, por sy ni por otro, en juizio ni fuera del, por ninguna via, forma, modo, ni manera que sea y pensar se pueda, y que, por sy ni por otro, no pediran, en ningund tienpo, rrelaxaçion del dicho juramento, y que puesto que nuestro muy Santo Padre, syn ser pedida [*sic*] por ellos, ni alguno dellos, gelo rrelaxe, que no lo açebtaran, ni usaran, de la tal rrelaxaçion, en ningund tienpo, ni se ayudaran, ni aprovecharan della, por ninguna manera ni via que sea, en juizio ni fuera del.

10. Iten,[39] que, para mayor firmeza e validaçion deste asiento e contrate y de lo en el contenido, anbos los dichos señores Enperador y Rey de Castilla y Rey de Portugal den petiçion y suplicaçion a su Santidad para que lo apruebe e confirme, e mande despachar las bullas de la dicha confirmaçion e aprovaçion, selladas con su sello, inserto en ellas este contrato y asiento de verbo ad verbum, y que se ponga en ellas sentençia de excomunion, asy a las partes prinçipales commo a qualesquier otras personas queste dicho asiento y contrato no guardaren y cunplieren, y contra el fueren, en parte o en todo, por qualquier via, modo, o manera que sea, en la qual sentençia de excomunion declare y mande que yncurran ypso fatto los que contra el dicho contrato fueren, en todo o en parte del, por la manera suso dicha, syn para ello ser rrequiridos ni ser neçesaria otra sentençia de excomunion ni declaraçion della, y que, en caso que por alguna causa o respetto su Santidad no quiera a provar e confirmar este dicho contrato y asiento, o se dexe de confirmar por otra qualquier cabsa, pensada o no pensada, que toda via quede firme y valedero, commo sy no fuese asentado que sea aprovado e confirmado por su Santidad, commo dicho es.

11. Iten,[40] es asentado y conçertado que en las provisiones y cartas que çerca deste asiento y contrato ha de dar y despachar el dicho señor Enperador y Rey de Castilla, se ponga y diga que lo que, segund dicho es, se asienta y generales con consentimiento espreso de los procuradores dellas, y que, para validaçion dello, de su poderio rreal absoluto, de que commo rey e señor natural, no reconoçiente superior en lo tenporal, quiere usar e usa, abroga e deroga, casa y anula la suplicaçion que los procuradores de las çibdades y villas destos rreynos en las cortes que se çelebraron en la çibdad de Toledo el año pasado de quinientos y veinte y çinco le hizieron, çerca de lo tocante a la contrataçion de las dichas yslas y tierras, e la respuesta que a ella dio, capitula y contrata, valga bien, asi commo sy fuese hecho y pasado en cortes

---

[37] This article corresponds to Doc. **16**, art. 10.
[38] This article corresponds to Doc. **16**, art. 16.
[39] This article corresponds to Doc. **16**, art. 17.
[40] This article corresponds to Doc. **16**, art. 11.

y qualquier ley que en las dichas cortes sobre ello se hizo, y todas las otras que a esto puedan ostar."

12. Yten," quel dicho Señor Enperador e Rey de Castilla, por mas seguridad de lo contenido en este asiento y contentamiento del dicho Señor Rey de Portugal, y porque por su parte le ha sydo pedido, mandara que los del su consejo rreal vean sy este asiento y conçierto puede haser sin aprovaçion y otorgamiento de los pueblos del rreyno, y que sy hallaren que se puede hazer sin la dicha aprovaçion e otorgamiento, lo den firmado de sus nonbres ocho o diez dellos.

13. Yten," es asentado y concordado que las capitulaçiones hechas entre los dichos Reyes Catolicos y el dicho Rey Don Juan de Portugal sobre la demarcaçion del mar oçeano se guarden y queden en su fuerça e vigor, salvo en aquellas cosas y casos que por este asiento van de otra manera asentados y declarados, para que aquellas se guarden durante el tienpo deste enpeño e rretrovendendo, commo dicho es, y despues las dichas capitulaçiones enteramente commo en ellas se contiene.

14. Iten," que el dicho Señor Rey de Portugal, porque se escusen las particulares querellas que el dicho Señor Enperador y Rey de Castilla continuamente tiene de sus subditos y de otros de fuera de sus rreinos, que le vinieron a servir, que se quexan que en su Casa de la India " y en su rreyno les tienen enbaraçadas sus haziendas, promete de mandar hazer clara y abierta y breve justiçia, syn tener respetto a enojo que dellos se pueda tener, por aver servido e venido a servir al dicho señor enperador.

15. Iten," es concordado y asentado que puesto quel derecho quel dicho Señor Enperador e Rey de Castilla pretenda tener a lo que por este asiento y contrato da en el dicho enpeño y contrato de rretro vendendo, commo arriba esta dicho, sepa çierto y de çierta sabiduria por çierta ynformaçion de personas que lo saben y entienden, que es de mucho mayor valor y estimaçion y allende de la mitad del justo preçio de los dichos trezientos e çinquenta mill ducados quel dicho Señor Rey de Portugal le da por el dicho enpeño e rretrovendendo que al dicho Señor Enperador e Rey de Castilla le plaze de hazer donaçion al dicho Señor Rey de Portugal y a sus herederos y subçesores y a la corona de sus rreynos, commo de hecho la haze, desde agora para todo sienpre entre vivos de la dicha mas estimaçion e valor de lo que el dicho derecho que asi le enpeña y vende con la dicha condiçion vale allende de la mitad del justo preçio por mucha mayor cantidad y valor que sea, la qual dicha mayor valor y estimaçion allende de la mitad del justo preçio el dicho Señor Enperador e Rey de Castilla renunçia e quita e aparta de sy e de sus subçesores y desmienbra de la corona de sus rreynos para sienpre durante el dicho enpeño y venta de rretrovendendo y lo traspasa todo por virtud desta donaçion y contrato al dicho Señor Rey de Portugal y a sus

---

" The *cuadernos* of the Cortes held at Toledo in 1525 do not include the petition here mentioned. *Córtes de Leon y de Castilla*, IV. 404 ff.

" The provisions of this article are omitted from the ratified treaty. See Doc. **16**, introduction.

" This article corresponds to Doc. **16**, art. 13.

" This article corresponds to Doc. **16**, art. 12.

" The Portuguese House of India (Casa da India) and House of Guinea dealt with the cargoes destined for and received from India. Ch. de Lannoy and H. Vander Linden, *L'Expansion Coloniale: Portugal et Espagne* (1907), p. 83.

" This article corresponds to Doc. **16**, art. 14.

herederos y subçesores y en la corona de sus reinos para siempre jamas rrealmente y con efetto, durante el dicho tienpo.

16. Yten,[47] es asentado y concordado que qualquiera de las dichas partes que contra lo contenido en este asiento y contrato o alguna cosa dello fuere o pasare por qualquier manera, pensada o no pensada, por el mismo caso pierda todo el derecho que toviere a lo suso dicho por qualquiera via, modo, o manera que sea, y asi mismo qualquier otro derecho que toviere por virtud deste contrato durante el dicho enpeño y rretrovendiendo, y que todo luego quede aplicado, junto, e adquerido a la parte que por este contrato estoviere, y lo guardare y no contra viniere, a el y a la corona de sus rreynos averiguandose y provandose primeramente el mandado de la parte que contraviniere, y que provandose y averiguandose primeramente commo dicho es quel dicho Señor Enperador y Rey de Castilla ha contravenido por su parte a lo suso dicho que en tal caso quede luego rresoluto este contrato de enpeño y rretrovendiendo e la venta pura y linpia commo si al prinçipio fuera fecha, sin condiçion alguna, e que porque lo contenido en esta capitulaçion y asiento sea mas firme e valedero e se guarde para sienpre, los dichos señores rreyes se obliguen por sy e por sus subçesores, que qualquier dellos que contra ello fuere, en qualquier manera que sea, pagara a la parte que lo guardare cient mill ducados de pena y en nonbre de pena, e interese en la qual yncurra, tantas vezes quantas contra lo contenido en este asiento y contrato fuere en parte o en todo, averiguando y provandose primeramente, commo dicho es el mandado de la parte que contraviniere, y que la pena llevada o no llevada, todavia el dicho contrato quede firme y valedero para sienpre durante el dicho enpeño y venta de rretrovendiendo, para lo qual obliguen todos sus bienes patrimoniales y fiscales.

Los quales dichos capitulos de suso escripttos, y todas las cosas en ellos y en cada uno dellos contenidos, los dichos señores Grand Chançiller y Obispo de Osma, del consejo y procuradores de los dichos muy altos y muy poderosos señores Enperador e Reyes de Castilla, de Leon, de Aragon, de las Dos Seçilias, de Jherusalem, etc., y el dicho señor Antonio Dazevedo, contino, del consejo y procurador del dicho muy alto e muy poderoso señor Rey de Portugal y de los Algarves, etc., en nonbre de los dichos señores sus constituyentes, por virtud de los dichos poderes a ellos dados e otorgados, que de suso van encorporados, dixieron que se obligaban y obligaron, e prometian y prometieron, y aseguraron, en el dicho nonbre, que los dichos señores, sus constituyentes, y cada uno dellos haran, cunpliran, e guardaran e pagaran, rrealmente y con efetto, çesante todo fraude, dolo, y cautela, todo lo contenido en esta capitulaçion y asiento y conçierto, conviene a saber, cada uno dellos lo que le perteneçe e incumbe e toca de hazer, cunplir, e guardar y pagar, segund y en la forma e manera que en ella se contiene, y que no yran ni vernan contra ello, ni contra cosa alguna ni parte dello, en tienpo alguno ni por alguna manera, por sy ni por otro, direte ni indirete, ni por ninguna via, pensada o no pensada, so las penas en esta capitulaçion contenidas. Dixeron que obligaban e obligaron los bienes de los dichos señores, sus constituyentes, patrimoniales y de las coronas de sus rreynos, y, por mayor firmeza e validaçion de todo lo suso dicho, juraron a Dios y a Santa Maria y a la señal de la Cruz ✠ en que corporalmente tocaron sus manos derechas, en nonbre y en las animas de los dichos señores, sus constituyentes, por virtud

---

[47] This article corresponds to Doc. **16**, art. 15.

de los dichos poderes, que ellos y cada uno dellos ternan, manternan, y
guardaran ynbiolablemente esta dicha capitulaçion y todo lo en ella contenido
y cada cosa y parte dello a buena fee, syn mal engaño, e sin arte ni cabtela
alguna, y prometian e prometieron y se obligaron en el dicho nonbre que los
dichos señores, sus constituyentes, aprovaran e rratificaran, firmaran y
otorgaran de nuevo, esta capitulaçion y todo lo en ella contenido, y cada
cosa y parte dello, y prometeran y [se] obligaran e juraran de la guardar y
cunplir, cada una de las partes por lo que a el incunbe y atañe de hazer, y que
daran y entregaran y haran dar y entregar, cada una dellas a la otra,
aprovaçion y rratificaçion desta dicha capitulaçion y de lo en ella contenido,
jurada y firmada de su nonbre, y sellada con su sello, desdel dia de la fecha
desta capitulaçion en veynte dias luego siguientes, en firmeza de lo qual los
dichos señores procuradores otorgaron dos escriptturas de un thenor, tal la
una commo la otra, y firmaron sus nonbres en el rregistro, y las otorgaron
ante mi, el dicho secretario, Francisco de los Covos, escrivano e notario
publico de suso escripto, y de los testigos de yuso escriptos, para cada una
de las dichas partes la suya, para que qualquiera que parezca, valga commo
sy anbas a dos pareçiesen, que fecha y otorgada en la dicha çibdad de Çaragoça
al dicho dia, mes, y año suso dicho. Testigos que fueron presentes al otorgamiento desta escriptura, e vieron firmar en ella a todos los dichos señores
procuradores, y los vieron jurar corporalmente en manos de mi, el dicho
secretario, Hernando Rodriguez de Sevilla, prothonotario apostolico, y Alvaro
Pexoto, y Hernando Rodriguez, criados del dicho señor enbaxador y procurador del dicho señor Rey de Portugal, y Graviel Calderon, y Alonso de
Ydiaquez, criados de mi, el dicho secretario.

Mercurinus, cancellarius.
Fr. G[arcia], episcopus Oxomen[sis].
Antonio dAzevedo, continho.

Translation.

In the name of God Almighty, Father, Son, and Holy Ghost, three Persons
and only one true God. Be it known and manifest to all who shall see this
public instrument, that in the city of Saragossa, on the seventeenth day of
the month of April, in the year of the nativity of our Savior Jesus Christ,
1529, in the presence of me, Francisco de los Cobos, secretary and member
of the council of the Emperor and Queen and King of Castile, and their
scrivener and notary public in their court and in all their kingdoms and
lordships, there being present and assembled their worships the Grand
Chancellor, Mercurino de Gattinara, count of Gattinara, and the very reverend Don Fray García de Loaysa, bishop of Osma, confessor, both members
of the council of the very exalted and very mighty princes, Don Charles,
by divine clemency emperor ever august, king of Germany, and Doña Joanna,
his mother, and the same Don Charles, her son, by the grace of God king
and queen of Castile, Leon, Aragon, the Two Sicilies, Jerusalem, Navarre,
Granada, etc., their qualified representatives, on the one part, and Señor
Antonio d'Azevedo, *contino,* member of the council and ambassador of the
very exalted and very mighty lord, Dom John, by the grace of God king of
Portugal, of the Algarves on this side and beyond the sea in Africa, lord
of Guinea and of the conquest, navigation, and commerce of Ethiopia,

Arabia, Persia, and India, etc., his qualified representative, on the other part, they declared that, inasmuch as there has been debate and negotiation between the said very exalted and very mighty Catholic lords, the emperor and king and queen of Castile, Leon, Aragon, the Two Sicilies, Jerusalem, etc., and the said very exalted and very mighty lord, Dom John, king of Portugal and of the Algarves, etc., about concluding a certain treaty, agreement, pledge, and *retrovendendo* in respect to the Molucca Islands and other lands and seas of the Indies, to which each of them claims to have the right, seeing that it might be accomplished for the service of God, our Lord, and for the well-being of their kingdoms and for the preservation of the friendship, relationship, and love that exist between them, and in order that they may undertake, negotiate, conclude, make, and adjust the said treaty, agreement, and pledge of *retrovendendo* between their said constituents, these have given them their full powers, signed with their names and sealed with their seals, as is more fully stated in the said powers, which both the said parties showed, signed by the said lord Emperor and King of Castile, and by the said lord King of Portugal, sealed with their seals, as is said, the tenor of which, word for word, one after the other, is as follows:

[Here follow the full powers granted by the Emperor Charles V. and Queen Joanna of Castile to the Count of Gattinara and the Bishop of Osma on April 14, 1529; and the full powers granted by John III. of Portugal to Antonio d'Azevedo, on October 18, 1528.]

Therefore the said lords, the grand chancellor and the bishop of Osma, members of the council of the said very exalted and very mighty lord Emperor and King and Queen of Castile, Leon, Aragon, the Two Sicilies, Jerusalem, etc., and their representatives, and the said Señor Antonio d'Azevedo, *contino*, member of the council of the said very exalted and very mighty lord King of Portugal and of the Algarves, etc., and his representative, by virtue of the said powers, incorporated above and making use of them, adjusted, agreed, concluded, and executed, in the name of the said lords, their constituents, the articles that will be set forth below, as follows:

1. First, it is covenanted and agreed that the said lord Emperor and King of Castile gives to the said lord King of Portugal in pledge and sale of *retrovendendo* the right that the emperor has to the Molucca Islands and to trade and commerce in the other neighboring islands and lands, lying and included within the line that is to be drawn in the method and manner to be set forth below, for the sum and amount of 350,000 ducats of gold, of due weight, each ducat being of 375 *maravedis* of Castilian money. This sum the said lord King of Portugal is to give to the said lord Emperor and King of Castile, paid as follows: within the thirty days next following the day on which this treaty shall be executed, 250,000 ducats, paid in Castile or in Lisbon, where the said lord King of Portugal shall be better able to deliver them, in money of gold, of due weight, or their just value in silver money; and the remaining 100,000 ducats at the May fair of Medina del Campo in this present year, at the time of the payments of the said fair, in the form and manner aforesaid. He is to pay the first said 250,000 ducats, which shall all be delivered and paid at the same time, in cash, and over and above the exchange; and those that should be paid in Portugal will be paid to the person or persons whom the said lord Emperor and King of Castile shall name for that purpose, in money that is worth in Castile the said 375

maravedis per ducat. The said lord Emperor and King of Castile makes the said pledge and sale of *retrovendendo* to the said lord King of Portugal, as aforesaid, with the stipulation and condition that whenever and at whatever time the said lord Emperor and King of Castile, or his heirs or successors in the kingdoms of Castile, shall wish to release, to pay off the pledge, and to redeem the said right which thus he pledges and sells as aforesaid, this may be done by returning the amount which is thus received, and the said lord King of Portugal shall be obliged to receive it. The right of the said lord Emperor and King of Castile, as well as of the said lord King of Portugal, and their successors, shall remain in full force, in the same condition and under the same form as they had it at first, and this right shall not have suffered or undergone, nor shall it suffer or undergo, any prejudice or innovation by virtue of this contract and agreement.

2. *Item*, it is agreed and covenanted that there shall be drawn, and henceforth there shall be considered as drawn, a semicircular line from pole to pole, 17 degrees (which equal 297½ leagues) east of the Moluccas. It is said that this same line will pass through the islands of Santo Thome de las Velas, which are on this meridian northeast by east from the Moluccas. It is likewise said that they are 19° distant from the Moluccas in this northeast and southwest course. In case that the said islands of Santo Thome de las Velas lie, or be situated, a greater or a less distance from the Moluccas, nevertheless the said line shall be drawn the said 297½ leagues farther east, which equal the said 19° to the northeast of the aforesaid Molucca Islands. In order that it may be known where the said line falls, a model map shall at once be made on which the said line shall be drawn in the manner aforesaid, and it will thus be agreed to as a declaration of the point and place through which the line passes. This map shall be signed by the said lord Emperor and King of Castile, and by the said lord King of Portugal, and sealed with their seals. In the same manner, and in accordance with the said model map, the said line shall be drawn on all the navigation charts whereby the subjects and natives of the kingdoms of the said lord Emperor and King of Castile and of the said lord King of Portugal shall navigate. In order to make the said model map, three persons shall be named by each of the said lord kings to make the said map upon oath, and they shall make the said line in conformity to what has been said above. When the map has thus been made, the said lord Emperor and King of Castile and the said lord King of Portugal shall sign it with their names, and shall order it to be sealed with the seals of their arms; and the said marine charts shall be made from it as aforesaid, in order that the subjects and natives of the said lord kings may navigate by them so long as the said lord King of Castile shall not redeem and buy back the said right. But if he redeem and ransom his right, after the completion of this treaty and contract and of such model map and marine charts as shall thus be made in conformity with the aforesaid, no prejudice to the right of either party shall result, but in spite of this everything shall remain in its present state; and so long as for any cause whatever the said model map shall not be made, the said line shall be drawn immediately after the execution of this contract; and those who pass it shall incur the penalties that shall be set forth below, according to and in the form and manner hereafter to be declared.

3. *Item*, it is agreed and covenanted that the fleets and ships of the said lord Emperor and King of Castile, or of his subjects, or of others acting

by his command, consent, favor, or aid, may not trade or traffic or take on cargo in any of the islands or lands that fall within the said line. If after this agreement any subjects of the said lord Emperor and King of Castile, or any other persons, shall be taken within the said limits bartering, trafficking, trading, or taking on cargo, they may be taken prisoners by the captains and people of the said lord king and tried and punished in accordance with justice. They may treat in the same way those who shall be proved to have trafficked, bartered, traded, and taken on cargo within the said limits, after the signing of this treaty, even though they shall not have been found or taken within them. If any subjects of the said lord Emperor and King of Castile, or any other persons, shall bring spices or drugs of any sort whatsoever into any ports or places to which they shall arrive or come, belonging to either of the said lord kings or to others, who may not be enemies, they shall be placed in deposit and under embargo by both the said lord kings, until it shall be known from whose demarcation they were taken and brought ; and when that is known and determined, they, or their true value, shall be delivered without any delay to whomsoever they may belong. To ascertain whether the place and land whence the said spices and drugs shall be brought fall within the demarcation and limits that, in accordance with this contract, should belong to the said lord Emperor and King of Castile, the said lord kings shall send two or four ships—one sending as many as the other—in which persons, skilful and intelligent in that art, as many of one party as of the other, shall go to the said places and lands (whence the aforesaid subjects or others shall say that they obtained and brought the said spices and drugs), in order to see and determine in whose demarcation the said lands fall, where it shall be said that the said spices and drugs were thus obtained. If they find that the said lands and places fall within the demarcation of the said lord King of Castile, and contain such a quantity of the said spices and drugs that they might credibly have been drawn thence, the said lord King of Portugal shall be obliged to restore them or their just value, if they were sequestrated in his realms. If it shall be discovered and determined that they were found in and brought from lands within the demarcation of the said Most Serene King of Portugal, he shall not be obliged to return them, and if they shall have been sequestrated in the kingdoms of the said lord Emperor and King of Castile, he shall be obliged to return and restore them immediately to the said lord King of Portugal. The same procedure shall be followed if they are sequestrated in any kingdoms or lands whatsoever that do not belong to the said lord kings. Within half a year after the said spices and drugs shall have been sequestrated, as aforesaid, the said lord kings shall be obliged to despatch the said ships and persons to make the said investigation, as aforesaid ; and so long as the said spices and drugs shall have been embargoed and sequestrated, as aforesaid, neither the said lord Emperor and King of Castile, nor any other person for him or with his favor or consent, shall go or send to the said land, or lands, from which the said spices and drugs shall come, and he shall be obliged to order those who go or pass contrary to the aforesaid to be punished, in accordance with justice, as malefactors and disturbers of faith and peace. But it shall be understood that navigation through the South Sea should and shall be free to the said lord Emperor and King of Castile and to his subjects, so that they may be able to navigate and trade that way in accordance with the agreement made between the Catholic sovereigns and King

Dom John of Portugal—may he rest in glory—provided that they shall not be able to enter or pass, nor shall they enter or pass, the seas beyond the said line, except on account of foul weather, need of provisions, or through ignorance, because of not knowing the said line. In such cases the ships of the said lord Emperor and King of Castile, and of his subjects, thus entering within the said line, shall not incur the said penalties, but if they find any lands or islands within the said line, they shall not trade in them, but shall immediately leave and depart from them, and from the said line, so that such lands or islands may be undisturbed for the said lord King of Portugal during this contract, as aforesaid, as if they had been discovered and found by his captains and people. If for the sake of anchorage, or on account of necessity or foul weather, the said ships of the said lord Emperor and King of Castile or of his subjects should come to any land lying within the said line, and by virtue of this agreement pertaining to the said lord King of Portugal, they shall be treated by the inhabitants of the land as vassals of his [*i. e.*, the Emperor's] brother, and in the same manner as the said lord Emperor and King of Castile would order the King of Portugal's subjects to be treated, who should in like manner make port in his lands of New Spain, or in other lands in those parts. It shall be understood that they shall incur the said penalties in so far as it is not clearly evident that the said ships and their crews entered the seas and lands situated within the said line on account of the said ignorance, necessity, or foul weather, or unless they depart when the said necessity is over; except that the vessels and ships of the said lord King of Castile, and of his subjects, vassals, and people, may and shall navigate through the seas of the said lord King of Portugal, through which his fleets sail to India, but only so far as shall be necessary in order to hold their direct course through the Straits of Magellan. If they act contrary to this by navigating farther through the said seas, they shall incur the said penalties, with exemption in this case likewise of what is done because of ignorance, necessity, or foul weather, as aforesaid. If it shall first be proved upon investigation, that the aforesaid [agreement] has been violated by command of the said lord Emperor and King of Castile, or with his favor, aid, or consent, he shall in such case immediately lose the right that he might have for such navigation, and that right shall be assigned to the other party, who shall hold and keep it by this contract, and this pledge and *retrovendendo* shall be dissolved, and the sale shall be pure and simple, as though it had been made unconditional at the start. Similarly the said lord King of Portugal must and shall incur the said penalty, if it be found that he has in any way violated what he, on his side, is bound to observe and perform.

4. *Item*, it is agreed and covenanted, with respect to the agreement, that if, after this treaty, any subjects of the said lord Emperor and King of Castile, or any others, shall be caught bartering, trafficking, trading or taking on cargo, within the said limits, they shall be taken by the captains and people of the said lord King of Portugal and tried and punished in accordance with justice, and that the latter may treat in the same way those proved to have trafficked, bartered, traded, and taken on cargo after this treaty within the said limits, even though they have not been found or taken within them, and the rest agreed to by this contract touching the prohibition of crossing the said line by any subjects of the said lord Emperor and King of Castile, or any others by his command, consent, favor, or aid, and the penalties attached thereto:—although the expression " after this treaty " is used above, this

shall be understood to mean, from and after the day when the subjects and people of the said lord Emperor, now in and navigating those seas and regions shall be notified—and that before the notification they shall not incur the said penalties. This, however, shall be understood as referring to the people of his Majesty's fleets hitherto despatched to those parts. From and after the day of the execution of this contract, during the period of the said pledge and *retrovendendo,* he may not despatch any other new expeditions without incurring the said penalties.

5. *Item,* because the said lord Emperor and King of Castile and the lord King of Portugal desire their right to the said islands to be determined, it is agreed and covenanted that in order to determine the right that each of them claims to have to the said Moluccas and other islands, which each asserts are within his limits and demarcation, an equal number of astrologers, pilots, or mariners, shall be named by each side within one, two, three, or more years, as the said lord King of Portugal shall wish, to examine the claim of both parties as to ownership, in accordance with the agreement made between the said Catholic kings and the said King Dom John of Portugal, and with the reply given in Segovia by the said lord Emperor and King of Castile, which accords with right and with the said agreement. After they shall begin the inquiry they shall not relinquish it before pronouncing sentence in favor of him who seems to them to have the right. In case the decision shall be in favor of the said lord Emperor and King of Castile, or of his successors, the sentence pronounced shall not be executed until he shall first actually return the said 350,000 ducats received for the said pledge and sale of *retrovendendo.* In case the sentence shall be in favor of the said lord King of Portugal, or of his successors, the said lord Emperor and King of Castile shall be obliged, within the first four years following the decision, to return and restore to him the said 350,000 ducats, given by the said lord King of Portugal for the said pledge and sale.

6. Moreover, it is covenanted and agreed that the said lord King of Portugal neither may nor shall build *de novo* any fortress, or other edifice that may be fortified, in the said Molucca Islands, or in the other lands within the said line, or in any part of the regions included within the line. As to the present fortress built in one of the said Molucca Islands by the said lord King of Portugal, it shall be left standing during the said period of the pledge in the state and condition in which it shall be in a year and a half from the day when this treaty shall be executed and signed, without any more new work or construction on it than shall keep it in the state in which it shall be at the said time. Within the said period, the said lord king will be able to order his captains and people, whom he has in those parts, to be notified of that which by this treaty he is obliged to keep and observe in this respect; and the said lord King of Portugal shall swear and promise to observe it thus.

7. *Item,* it is agreed that the fleets, which the said lord Emperor and King of Castile has hitherto despatched to the said regions, shall be well regarded, treated, and favored by the said lord King of Portugal and his people. No obstruction or hindrance shall be opposed to their navigation and trade, and if they shall have received, or shall receive, any harm from the King of Portugal's captains or people, which is incredible, or if these latter shall have taken anything from them, the said lord King of Portugal shall be obliged to give satisfaction, restore, make good, and pay immediately

all such damages suffered by the said lord Emperor and King of Castile and his fleet and subjects, and to order the offenders to be punished and chastised and to arrange that the fleets and people of the said lord Emperor and King of Castile may come when they please, freely, without any impediment.

8. *Item,* it is agreed that the said lord Emperor and King of Castile shall order his letters and instructions to be given immediately to his captains and people, who shall be in the said islands, commanding them to return at once, and trade there no more, provided that they be allowed to bring freely what they shall have already bartered, traded, and shipped.

9. *Item,* it is agreed that both the said lord Emperor and King of Castile and the lord King of Portugal, and each of them, shall solemnly swear to observe and fulfill this treaty and contract, and all contained therein, and shall promise by the said oath, for themselves and for their successors, never, at any time, to violate it, in whole or in part, by themselves, or by another, in court or out, in any way, shape, form, or manner that may be, or may be thought of, and that never at any time, by themselves, or by another, will they seek release from the said oath; and even though our Very Holy Father, without being asked by them or either of them, shall release them from it, they will not at any time accept or avail themselves of such release, or help themselves by it, or take advantage of it, in any way or manner whatsoever, in court or out.

10. *Item,* [it is agreed] that in order further to strengthen and validate this treaty and contract and its contents, both the said lord Emperor and King of Castile and the lord King of Portugal shall petition and implore his Holiness to approve and confirm it and order bulls of the said confirmation and approval to be despatched, sealed with his seal, and having this contract and treaty inserted verbatim in them; and that sentence of excommunication shall be imposed in the bulls both against the principal parties and against all other persons who shall not observe and fulfill this said treaty and contract, but shall violate it in part or in whole, in any way, shape, or manner whatsoever. In this sentence of excommunication his Holiness shall declare and ordain that those who shall violate the said contract, in whole or in part, in the manner aforesaid, shall, *ipso facto,* incur excommunication, no other sentence of excommunication, or declaration thereof, being required or necessary for that purpose. If for any cause or consideration his Holiness shall not wish to approve and confirm this said contract and agreement, or if for any other cause whatsoever, premeditated or unpremeditated, it shall not be confirmed, it shall nevertheless be firm and valid as if there had been no agreement that his Holiness should approve and confirm it as aforesaid.

11. *Item,* it is agreed and covenanted that in the instructions and letters that the said lord Emperor and King of Castile is to give and despatch in regard to this treaty and contract, it shall be set down and declared that what is adjusted and concluded and contracted, as aforesaid, shall be as binding as if it had been made and executed in the General Cortes with the express consent of the deputies of that body, and that, in order to validate it, by his absolute royal power, which as king and natural lord, recognizing no superior in temporal affairs, he wishes to exercise and does exercise, he abrogates, repeals, abolishes, and annuls the petition concerning the trade of the said islands and lands made to him by the deputies of the cities and towns of those realms in the Cortes held in the city of Toledo, the past year, 1525; and [he abrogates] the reply that he gave to the petition and any law

made in the said Cortes on this matter, and all other laws that may conflict with this.

12. *Item,* [it is agreed] that for the greater security of the contents of this treaty, and the satisfaction of the said lord King of Portugal, and because the emperor has been asked on [the King of Portugal's] behalf, the said lord Emperor and King of Castile will order the members of his royal council to ascertain whether this agreement and contract can be made without the approval and license of the towns of the realm. If they shall find that it can be made without the said approval and license, eight or ten of them shall give the decision, signed with their names.

13. *Item,* it is agreed and covenanted that the agreements concluded between the said Catholic sovereigns and the said King Dom John of Portugal in regard to the demarcation of the ocean sea shall be observed and shall remain in force and effect, save in those matters and cases which are otherwise settled and determined by this treaty, so that those agreements shall be observed during the period of this pledge and sale of *retrovendendo,* as aforesaid, and afterwards the said agreements shall be observed in their entirety.

14. *Item,* [it is agreed] that the said lord King of Portugal promises to command manifest, sincere, and summary justice to be done, in order to put an end to the individual complaints that the said lord Emperor and King of Castile continually receives from his subjects and others, aliens to his realms, but in his service, who complain that their possessions have been seized by the former's India House of Trade, and in his kingdom, without regard to the annoyance caused them thereby, because they have served the said lord emperor, and have entered his service.

15, *Item,* it is covenanted and agreed, that, although the said lord Emperor and King of Castile has certain definite knowledge through exact information from persons who know and understand the matter, that the right which the said lord Emperor and King of Castile claims to have to that which he gives in the said pledge and contract of *retrovendendo* by this agreement and contract as aforesaid, is of much greater value and worth and more than the half of the just price—the said 350,000 ducats—that the said lord King of Portugal gives to him for the said pledge and *retrovendendo,* the said lord Emperor and King of Castile is pleased to make a gift to the said lord King of Portugal and to his heirs and successors, and to the crown of his kingdoms—as in fact he does make it, henceforth for all time, among the living—of the said excess in value and worth that the said right, which he thus pledges and conditionally sells, is worth above the half of the just price, however much greater the amount and value may be. The said greater value and worth beyond the half of the just price, the said lord Emperor and King of Castile renounces and gives up for himself, and his successors, and separates it from the crown of his kingdoms, forever during the period of the said pledge and sale of *retrovendendo,* and by virtue of this gift and contract he transfers it all to the said lord King of Portugal, and to his heirs and successors, and to the crown of his kingdoms forever, really and effectually, during the said time.

16. *Item,* it is agreed and covenanted that whichever of the said parties shall violate or refute the contents of this treaty and contract, or any part thereof, in any manner, premeditated or unpremeditated, he shall, thereby, lose all the right that, in any way, shape, or manner whatsoever, he shall have

to the aforesaid, and likewise any other right he shall have by virtue of this contract during the said pledge and sale of *retrovendendo*. The whole shall be immediately adjudged and given to, and acquired by the party who shall abide by this contract and observe and not violate it, to him and to the crown of his realms, after the mandate of the party who shall violate it has been first investigated and proved. When it has been proved and found as aforesaid that the said lord Emperor and King of Castile has, on his part, violated the aforesaid, in that case this contract of pledge and *retrovendendo* shall be immediately dissolved, and the sale shall be pure and simple, as if it had been made at the beginning without any condition. In order that the contents of this agreement and treaty may be more binding and valid and in order that it may be observed forever, the said lords kings shall bind themselves, for themselves and their successors, that whichever of them shall violate it, in any manner whatsoever, he will pay to the party who shall abide by it, 100,000 ducats, as a penalty, and under the name of fine and interest. This fine he shall incur as often as he shall violate the contents of this treaty and contract, in part or in whole, after, as has been said, the mandate of the party who shall violate it has been investigated and proved. Whether the fine is exacted or not, the said contract shall remain secure and valid forever, during the said pledge and sale of *retrovendendo*. For this they shall pledge all their patrimonial and fiscal possessions.

In regard to the above-written articles and all the matters contained in them and each of them, the said Grand Chancellor and Bishop of Osma, members of the council and representatives of the said very exalted and very mighty lords, the Emperor and King and Queen of Castile, Leon, Aragon, the Two Sicilies, Jerusalem, etc., and the said Lord Antonio d'Azevedo, *contino*, member of the council, and representative of the said very exalted and very mighty lord King of Portugal and of the Algarves, etc., in the name of the said lords, their constituents, by virtue of the said powers given to them and executed, which are incorporated above, declared that they bound themselves, and they did bind themselves, and promised, and they did promise and affirm, in the said name, that the said lords, their constituents, and each of them, shall do, fulfill, observe, and pay, really and in truth, renouncing all deception, evasion, and mental reservation, everything contained in this treaty, agreement, and bargain—that is, each of them, what pertains to, is incumbent upon, and concerns him to do, fulfill, observe, and pay, according to and in the form and manner contained therein. They will not violate or refute it, or any part or parcel of it, at any time or in any manner, of themselves or through another, directly or indirectly, or in any way, premeditated or unpremeditated, under the penalties contained in this agreement. They said that they pledged, and they did pledge, the possessions of the said lords, their constituents, patrimonial and belonging to the crowns of their realms, and for the greater security and validity of all the aforesaid they swore before God and Holy Mary and upon the sign of the Cross, which they actually touched with their right hands, in the name and on the consciences of the said lords, their constituents, by virtue of the said powers, that they and each of them will inviolably hold, maintain, and observe this said agreement, and everything contained therein, and each part and parcel of it, in good faith, without deception, evasion, or mental reservation whatsoever; and they promised, and they did promise and bind themselves in the said name that the said lords, their constituents, will approve and ratify, and sign and execute anew this agreement and everything contained in it and each part and parcel of it, and they will promise, bind themselves, and swear to observe and fulfill it, each of the parties for that which is incumbent on and appertains to him to do; and each of them will give and deliver, and will cause to be given and delivered to the other party, an approval and ratification of this said agreement and of its contents, sworn to and signed with his name and sealed with his seal, within the twenty days immediately following the date of this agreement. To secure this, the said lord representatives executed two instruments of one tenor, both alike, and signed their names in the register, and executed them before me, the said secretary, Francisco de los Cobos, the scrivener and notary public whose name is above written, and before the undersigned witnesses, each of the said parties having his own instrument, so that, whichever shall be shown, it shall be as binding as though both were shown together. This was made and executed in the said city of Saragossa, on the day, month, and year abovesaid. Witnesses who were present at the execution of this instrument and saw all the said lord deputies sign it and saw them take the corporal oath before me, the said secretary, [were] Fernando Rodriguez de Sevilla, apostolic protonotary, and Alvaro Pexoto and Fernando Rodriguez, servants of the said lord ambassador and representative of the said lord King of Portugal, and Graniel Calderon and Alonso de Ydiaquez, servants of me, the said secretary.

MERCURINO, chancellor.
FRAY GARCÍA, bishop of Osma.
ANTONIO D'AZEVEDO, *contino.*

16.

Treaty between Spain and Portugal concluded at Saragossa, April 22, 1529.   Ratification by Spain, April 23, 1529, and by Portugal, June 20, 1530.

INTRODUCTION.

The treaty concluded at Saragossa on April 17, 1529,[1] by the plenipotentiaries of Spain and Portugal, was not ratified.   Five days later, in the same city, the same plenipotentiaries, with one additional representative of Spain,[2] concluded a second treaty.   This differed from the first in several particulars, most strikingly in the omission of the provisions of the twelfth article—that the Emperor should order his Royal Council to find out whether the treaty could be legally made without the approval of the *pueblos*.   The omission of this article is explained by a document preserved in the National Archives at Lisbon, which contains: (1) the decision reached by lawyers of the Royal Council to the effect that the Emperor and King of Castile might legally enter into the contract in respect to the Moluccas, and that the consent, authorization, and approbation of his towns were not necessary; (2) the Emperor's confirmation and promise to regard the lawyers' decision, and his abrogation of all contrary laws and regulations.   The Emperor's letter is dated April 23, 1529.[3]

---

[1] Doc. **15**.

[2] García de Padilla, who signed the treaty of Vitoria, and was employed in the negotiations of 1526.   See Doc. **13**, note 16, and Doc. **14**.

[3] "Don Carlos, por la divina clemencia etc. enperador semper augusto, rrey de Alemaña, Dona Juana, su madre, y el mismo Don Carlos, su hijo, por la gracia de Dios rreyes de Castilla, de Leon, de Aragon, de las Dos Sicilias, de Jerusalem, de Navarra, de Granada, de Toledo, de Valencia, de Galizia, de Mallorcas, de Sevilla, de Cerdena, de Cordova, de Corcega, de Murcia, de Jaen, de los Algarves, de Algezira, y de Gibraltar, de las Islas de Canaria, de las Indias, Islas, e tierra firme del Mar Oceano, archiduques d'Austria, duques de Borgoña, y de Brabante, condes de Barcelona, Flandes, y Tirol, señores de Viscaya, y de Molina, duques de Atenas, y de Neopatria, condes de Ruysillon, y de Cerdenia, marquezes de Oristan, y de Gociano, etc.

"Hacemos saber a los que esta nuestra carta vieren, que nós mandamos vêr a los del nuestro Real Consejo cierta dubda, sy podriamos concordar e asentar con el Serenissimo, muy Alto, y muy Poderozo Rey de Portugal, nuestro muy caro, y muy amado hermano, sobre las Islas de Maluco, y otras islas, e mares y tierras a ellas comarcanas, y vimos su declaracion, y determinacion en las espaldas d'esta nuestra carta escrita, y dada, y fecha por ellos, y la leimos, y entendimos: la qual aprovamos, confirmamos, e avemos por buena, firme, e valiosa, como en ella es contenido; y esto sin enbargo de qualesquier leyes, derechos, hordenaciones, capitulos de Côrtes, determinaciones, sentencias, glosas, hazañas, y opiniones de dottores, y de qualesquier otras cosas, que en contrario sean, o puedan ser, puesto que sean tales, que por derecho se deva hacer dellas espresa mencion, y derogacion, y abrogamos, y derogamos, e avemos por casadas, e anulladas todas las leyes, e derecho, que en contrario sean, y las leyes, y direchos, que disponen que general renunciacion no vale: Y promettemos por nós, y por nuestros subcesores de nunca yr,

The treaty concluded on April 22, ratified by the Emperor on the following day and by the King of Portugal more than a year later, was disliked in Spain. As late as 1548, the Cortes petitioned the Emperor that the whole realm should redeem the Moluccas in order that Spain might have the benefit of their spice-trade, if only for six years.[4]

By the terms of the treaty of Saragossa, the Philippine Islands fell within the Portuguese demarcation; and when, in 1542-1543, Ruy Lopez de Villalobos led a colonizing expedition thither from New Spain, the Portuguese governor of the Moluccas protested vigorously, demanding his withdrawal on the ground that his occupation of the Philippines violated the aforesaid treaty.[5] In 1568 a fruitless protest was made against Legazpi's colonization;[6] in 1580 Spain's annexation of the Portuguese crown quieted the dispute. Upon the separation of the crowns in 1640, however, as the Portuguese claimed, "the conditions of the Deed of Saragossa gave rise to a new title by which Portugal [might] claim restitution of or equivalent for all that the Spaniards had occupied to the west" of the line fixed by this treaty.[7] The controversy was not ended until 1750, when, by the first and second articles of a Spanish-Portuguese treaty signed at Madrid, it was stipulated that the demarcation lines provided for in the bull of Alexander VI.[8] and

ny venir, ny consentir, ny premitir, que sea ydo, ny venido contra esta determinacion, ny parte alguna della, direte ny indirete en juizio ny fuera del, por causa alguna ny color, que sea, y pueda ser pensada, o no pensada; y para certinidad, e firmeza de todo, mandamos pasar esta nuestra carta firmada de my, el Rey, y sellada con nuestro sello. "Dada en Lerida a veinte tres de Abril, año del nascimiento de Nuestro Salvador Jesus Christo de mil e quinientos e veinte e nueve años. Yo el Rey. Yo Francisco de los Covos, secretario de Sus Cesarea y Catholicas Magestades, la fize screvir por su mandado. Lugar do sello. Herbijna, chanciller. Registrada. Ydiaques. Mercurinus, cancelarius. Fray Garcia, episcopus Oxomensis. El Comendador Mayor. Vuestra Magestade confirma, e ha por bueno el parecer, que los del Consejo dieron sobre la contratacion de Maluco, que está escrità, e firmada dellos en esta otra parte.
"Parecer dos Conselheiros d' Estado sobre a carta acima.—Sacra Catholica Magestad: Los del Consejo Real de Vuestra Magestad dizen, que por justas causas, e consideraciones, que a Vuestra Magestad han dicho, y consultado de palavra con Vuestra Real Persona, son de voto, y parecer que en la capitulacion, e assiento que entre Vuestra Magestad, y el Serenissimo Rey de Portugal se concierta, sobre el empeño de Maluco, que para seguridad d'este empeño, que es con condicion para la poder redemir, y quitar, que nö es necessario que entrevengan procuradores de Cortes, ny de ciddades, ny que sean llamados para lo otorgar. Licentiatus de SANTIAGO. Licentiatus POLANCO. Licentiatus AGUIRRE. Doctor GUEVARA. NUNUS ALVARES. MARTINUS Doctor. El Licenciado MEDINA. FORTUNIUS DERCILLA Doctor." National Archives at Lisbon, gav. 18, maço 3, no. 39.
[4] B. Leonardo de Argensola, *Conquista de las Islas Malucas* (1609), pp. 46, 47. F. López de Gómara, *Annals of the Emperor Charles V.* (ed. R. B. Merriman, 1912), p. 138, and note 4, same page.
[5] *Colección de Documentos Inéditos relativos al Descubrimiento . . . de Ultramar* (Real Academia de la Historia, Madrid), 2d ser., tom. II. (1886), pt. I., pp. 66-94. A. de Morga, *Philippine Islands* (Hakluyt Soc., no. XXXIX., 1868), app. V., pp. 394-396.
[6] J. A. Robertson, "Legazpi and Philippine Colonization", in *Annual Report* of the American Historical Association for the year 1907 (1908), p. 154.
[7] Preamble to the treaty of Madrid, 1750, translated in the *Statement submitted by the United States of Brazil to the President of the United States of America as Arbitrator . . . between Brazil and the Argentine Republic* (1894), III. 5.
[8] Doc. 7.

in the treaties of Tordesillas [*] and Saragossa should be annulled; that Spain should permanently retain the Philippines, "in spite of the conditions contained in the Deed signed at Saragossa on the 22d of April, 1529"; and that the crown of Portugal should not be entitled to recover any part of the price which it paid under the sale effected by the said deed.[19]

BIBLIOGRAPHY.

Text: MS. An original manuscript of the ratification, signed by the King of Portugal at Lisbon, June 20, 1530, is in the National Archives at Lisbon, gav. 18, maço 8, no. 29. One of the original protocols is in the Archives of the Indies at Seville, Patronato, 1-2-2/16, no. 9.

Text: Printed. The Portuguese ratification is printed in J. Ramos-Coelho, *Alguns Documentos* (1892), pp. 495-512, and in G. F. von Martens, *Supplément au Recueil des Traités* (1802-1842), I. 398-421. Navarrete, *Coleccion de Viages* (1825-1837), tom. IV., no. 41, pp. 389-406, prints the protocol, but from a copy instead of from the original manuscript. As an appendix to the treaty of 1750, the treaty of Saragossa is printed in J. Ferreira Borges de Castro, *Collecção dos Tratados de Portugal, desde 1640* (1856-1858), III. 64-82, and elsewhere.

References: See Doc. **15**, Bibliography.

TEXT.[11]

Dom Joham, per graca de Deus rrey de Portugal e dos Algarves daquem e dalem mar em Africa, senhor de Guinee e da comquista, naveguacam, e comercio de Ethiopia, Arabia, Persia, e da Imdia. A quantos esta minha carta de confirmacam, aprovacam, e rretificacam virem, faco saber que antre mym e Dom Carlos, emperador sempre augusto, rrey dAlemanha, de Castela, de Liam, dAraguam, das Duas Cezilias, de Jerusalem, etc., meu muito amado e precado irmaão, avia duvida e debate sobre a propiedade e pose, ou quasy pose, e dereito, naveguacam, e comercio de Maluquo e outras ilhas e mares, por cada huum de nos dizer lhe pertencer e estar em pose de todo o sobredito, e pelo muy coniuncto divido,[12] que anbos temos, e porque amtre nosos vasalos e naturaes se nam podese nunca seguir descontentamento e fose sempre consservado o muito amor, rrezam, e obriguacam que antre nos ha, nos concertamos sobre o que dito he de que se fez por nosos soficientes e abastantes precuradores, pera ello deputados, carta de contrauto, capitolacam, e asento, da qual o teor de verbo a verbo, he o seguinte:

Dom Carlos, por la divina clemencia electo emperador semper augusto, rrey de Alemania, Doña Juana, su madre, y el mismo Dom Carlos, su hiyo,

---

[*] Doc. **9**.

[19] For a sketch of Spanish-Portuguese disputes over the demarcation line subsequent to 1529, see E. G. Bourne, "The Demarcation Line of Pope Alexander VI.", in *Essays in Historical Criticism* (1901), pp. 212-214.

[11] The text is from the original manuscript of the ratification by John III. in the National Archives at Lisbon, gav. 18, maço 8, no. 29.

[12] In 1524 the King of Portugal, who was the Emperor's first cousin, married the Emperor's sister, Catherine, and soon after the Emperor married the Infanta Isabella, sister to John III.

por la gracia de Dios rreies de Castilla, de Leon, de Aragon, de las Dos
Secilias, de Jerusalem, de Navarra, de Granada, de Toledo, de Valencia,
de Galizia, de Sevilla, de Cordova, de Corcega, de Murcia, de Jahen, de los
Algarves, de Algezira, de Gibraltar, de las yslas de Canaria, de las Indias,
yslas e tiera firme del mar Oceano, archiduques de Abstria, duques de
Borgoña y de Bravante, condes de Barcelona, Flandes, e Tirol, señores de
Viscaya e de Molina, duques de Atenas e de Neopatria, condes de Ruisellon
e de Cerdania, marqueses de Oristam e de Gociano, etc., vimos e leimos una
escriptura de capitolacion e asiento de venta com pacto de rretro vendendo
del derecho y posesion, o casy posesion, y action de las yslas de Maluquo,
que em ellas tenemos o podriamos tener, por qualquier via que nos pertenezca
y pertenecer pueda, y en las tierras, yslas, e mares contenidas em la dicha
contratacion e asiento, fecho en nuestro nombre por Mercurio de Gatinara,[13]
conde de Gatinara, gran chamciller de my, el rrey, y por Don Fray Garcia
de Loaysa,[14] obispo de Osma, my confesor, y por Dom Garcia de Padilla,[15]
comendador mayor de Calatrava, todos del nuestro conseyo y nuestros procuradores, y por Amtonyo dAzevedo, couthiño,[16] del conseio y embaxador del
serenisimo, muy alto, e muy poderoso Rey de Portugal, nuestro muy caro
e muy amado hermano, e su procurador, el tenor del qual de verbo ad verbum
es este que se sigue :

En el nonbre de Dios Todopoderoso, Padre e Hijo y Espiritu Santo, tres
Personas y un solo Dios verdadero. Notorio e manifiesto sea, a quantos este
publico ynstrumento de transacion e contrato de venta com pacto de rretro
vendendo vieren, como en la cibdad de Carogoça, que es en el rreino de
Aragon, a veinte e dos dias del mes de Abril, año del nacimiento de nuestro
Salvador Jhesu Christo de mill e quinientos e veinte e nueve años, em
presencia de my, Francisco de los Covos, secretario e del conseio del
emperador, Dom Carlos, e de la rreyna, Doña Juana, su madre, rreina e rrey
de Castilla, y su escriваño y notario publico, y de los testigos de yuso
escriptos, parecieron los señores, Mercurino de Gatinara, comde de Gatinara,
gran chanciler del dicho señor emperador, y el muy rreverendo Dom Fray
Garcia de Loaysa, obispo de Osma, su confesor, y Dom Frey Garcia de
Padilla, comendador maior de la Ordem de Calatrava, todos tres del consejo
de los dichos muy altos e muy poderosos señores principes, Dom Carlos,
por la divina clemencia electo emperador senpre augusto, rrey de Alemania,
y Doña Juana, su madre, y el mismo Don Carlos, su hiyo, por la gracia de
Dios, rreies de Castilla, de Leon, y de Aragon, de las Dos Cezilias, de Jerusalem y de Navarra y de Granada, etc., en nonbre e como procuradores de
los dichos señores, Emperador e Reies de Castilla, de la una parte, y el señor
Antonyo de Azevedo, coutiño, del consejo y embaixador del muy alto y muy
poderoso señor, Dom Juam, por la gracia de Dios rrey de Portugal e dos
Algarves de aquende y de allende el mar em Africa, señor de Guinea y de la
conquista, navegaçion, e comercio de Ethiopia, Arabia, e Persia e de la India,
etc., em nombre y como su procurador, de la otra, segun luego mostraron
por sus soficientes e abastantes procuraciones para este contrato firmadas
por los dichos señores Emperador e Rey de Castilla e Rey de Portugal,
seladas con sus sellos, de las quales dichas procuraciones los treslados, de
verbo ad verbum, son los seguientes :

---

[13] See Doc. 13, note 14, and Docs. 14 and 15.   [14] See Doc. 14, note 8, and Doc. 15.
[15] See Doc. 13, note 16, and Doc. 14.   [16] See Doc. 14, note 11, and Doc. 15.

[Here follow the full powers granted by the sovereigns of Castile to the Count of Gattinara, the Bishop of Osma, and the Chief Knight-Commander of Calatrava on April 15, 1529, and the full powers granted by João III. of Portugal to Antonio d'Azevedo on October 18, 1528.]

Asy presentadas las dichas precuraciones por los dichos señores procuradores, fue dicho que, por quanto antre el dicho señor Emperador e Rey de Castilla, de Leon, de Aragon, de las Dos Secilyas, de Jherusalem, etc., y el dicho señor Rey de Portugual, e de los Algarves, etc., avia dubda sobre la propiedad y posesion y derecho o posesiom, o quasy posesiom, navegacion, e comercio de Maluquo y otras yslas y mares, lo qual cada uno de los dichos señores, Emperador e Rey de Castilla y Rey de Portugual, dize pertenecerle, asy por vertud de las capitolaciones [17] que fueron fechas por los muy altos y muy poderosos y Catholicos princepes Dom Fernando y Doña Ysabel, rreies de Castilla, abuelos del dicho señor emperador y con el rrey Dom Juan el segundo de Portugal, que ayan gloria, acerqua de la demarcacion del mar oceano, como por otras rrezones y derechos que cada uno de los dichos señores emperador e rreis dezia tener e pretendian a las dichas yslas, mares, y tierras ser suias, e estar em posesiom dellas; y que, aviemdo los dichos señores emperador y rreis rrespecto al muy coniuncto deudo e gramde amor que antre ellos ay, lo qual no solamente deve, com mucha rezam, ser conservado, mas, quanto posible fuere, mas acrecentado, y que, por se quitar de dudas e demamdas e debates que antre ellos podria aver, y muchos inconvinientes, que antre sus vasallos y subditos y naturales se podriam seguir, som aguora los dichos señores emperador e rreis y los dichos procuradores em su nombre concordados e concertados sobre las dichas dubdas e debates, en el modo y forma seguiente:

1. Primeramente,[18] dixeron los dichos Gran Chanciler y Obispo de Osma y Comendador Maior de Calatrava, procuradores del dicho señor Emperador e Reis de Castilla, que ellos, em su nonbre, por vertud de la dicha su precuracion, vendian, como luego de fecho vendieron, deste dia pera siempre jamas, al dicho señor Rey de Portugal, pera el y todos sus sobcesores de la corona de sus rreinos, todo el derecho, action, dominio, propiedad, y posesiom, o quasi posesion, y todo el derecho de navegar y contratar y comerciar por qualquier modo que sea, que el dicho señor Emperador e Rey de Castilla dize que tiene y podria tener por qualquier via, modo, o manera que sea, em el dicho Maluquo, ysllas, luguares, tierras y mares, segundo abaxo sera declarado; e esto, con las declaraciones y limitaciones y comdiciones y clausulas abaixo contenidas y declaradas, por precio de trezientos e cimquoenta mil ducados de oro, paguados em monedas corientes en la tierra de oro o de plata, que valguan em Castilla trezientos y satenta y cinquo maravedis, cada ducado, los quales el dicho señor Rey de Portugal dara e pagara al dicho señor Emperador y Rey de Castilla y a las personas que su Magestad pera ello nonbrare, en esta manera: los ciento e cinquoenta mil ducados dellos em Lixbona, demtro de quinze o veinte dias primeros seguientes despues que este contrato, comfirmado por el dicho señor Emperador y Rey de Castilla, fuere llegado a la cidad de Lixboa, o a domde el dicho señor Rey de Portugal estuviere;[19] e trinta mil ducados pagados em Castilla, los vinte

---

[17] The treaty of Tordesillas, Doc. **9**.   [18] *Cf.* Doc. **15**, art. 1, and notes.
[19] An order from the King of Portugal, dated June 1, 1529, directed Hernando Alvarez, his treasurer, to pay to Lope Hurtado de Mendoza, the Castilian ambassador in Portugal, 150,000 *cruzados* toward the amount due for the Moluccas. Two days later the ambassador gave the treasurer a quittance for the sum paid. Santarem, *Quadro Elementar*, II. 67.

mil em Valhadolid, e los dez mil em Sevilla, hasta veinte dias del mes de Maio primero que viene deste año ; y setenta mil ducados em Castilla, paguados en la feria de Maio de Medina del Campo deste dicho anño, a los terminos de los pagamientos della, y los ciem mil ducados restantes, en la feria de Otobre de la dicha villa de Medina del Campo deste dicha anño, a los plazos de los paguamientos della, pagado todo fuera del cambio ; y asy fuere necesario, se daran luego cedulas pera el dicho tiempo ; y, si el dicho señor Emperador y Rey de Castilha quisiere tomar a canbio los dichos cem mil ducados en la dicha feria de Maio deste dicho año, para socorrerse dellos, pagara el dicho señor Rey de Portugal a rrazom de cinquo o seis por ciento de canbio, como su tesorero, Hernand Alvarez, los suele tomar de feria a feria ; la qual dicha venta el dicho señor Emperador y Rey de Castilla haze al dicho señor Rey de Portugal com condiciom que, em qualquiera tiempo que el dicho señor Emperador y Rey de Castilla o sus sobcesores quisieren tornar, y con efecto tornaren, todos los dichos trezientos e cinquoenta mil ducados, y sin dellos faltar cosa alguna, al dicho señor Rey de Portugal o a sus sobcesores, que la dicha vienta quede desfecha, y cada uno de los dichos señores enperador y rreies quede con el derecho e action que agora tienen y pretiendem tener, asy en el derecho de la posesiom, o casy posesiom, como en la propiedad, por qualquier via, modo, y manera que pertenecerles pueda, como se este contrato non fuera hecho, y de la manera que primero lo tenian y pertendian tener, sin que este contrato les haga ni cause per juizo ni ynovacion alguna.

2. Item,[20] es comcordado e asentado entre los dichos procuradores, em nombre de los dichos señores sus constituientes, que, pera se saber las yslas, lugares, tierras, y mares y derecho y actiom dellos que, por este contrato, el dicho señor Emperador e Rey de Castilla asy vende, con la comdiciom que dicha es al dicho señor Rey de Portugal, desde agora pera todo siempre, han por hechada una linia de polo a polo, conviene a saber, del norte al sul, por huum semicirculo que diste de Maluquo al nordeste, tomando la quarta del este, diez y nueve grados, a que conrrespondem diez y sete grados escasos en la equinocial, em que montam dozientas y novienta y sete legoas y media mas a oriente de las islas de Maluquo, dando diez y sete legoas e media por grado equinocial, en el qual mirediano y rrunbo del nordeste y quarta del este, estam situadas las islas de las Velas y de Santo Thome, por donde pasa la sobredicha linia y semicirculo ; y, siendo caso que las dichas yslas estiem y distem de Maluquo mas o menos, todavia, han por bien e sam concordes que la dicha lynia quede lancada a las dichas dozientas y novienta y sete legoas y media mas a oriente, que hacem los dichos diez e nueve grados al nordeste y quarta de leste de las dichas yslas de Maluquo, como dicho es ; y dixeron los dichos procuradores que, pera se saber por donde se ha la dicha linia por lancada, se hagan dos padrones de huu tenor, conformes al padron que esta en la Casa de la Contratacion[21] de las Imdias de Sevilha, por donde navegan las armadas y vasallos y subditos del dicho señor Emperador y Rey de Castilla, y dentro de treinta dias despues de la fecha deste contrato se

[20] *Cf.* Doc. **15**, art. 2, and notes.
[21] *Cf.* Doc. **15**, note 24. The Casa de Contratacion, or India House of Trade at Seville, founded in 1503, supervised all matters connected with maritime affairs. See the article by B. Moses in the *Report* of the Am. Hist. Asso. for 1894, pp. 93-123, and J. Piernas Hurtado, *La Casa de la Contratación de las Indias* (1907), articles published in *La Lectura* and *Ateneo*.

nombre dos personas de cada parte, pera que vean y hagan luego los dichos
padrones, conforme a lo suso dicho, y en ellos sea lançada la dicha linia, por
el modo sobre dicho, y que los dichos senores emperador e rreies los firmen
de sus nonbres y sellen com sus sellos, pera quedar a cada uno el suyo, y
dende em adelante quede la dicha linia por lançada pera declaracion del
punto y lugar por donde ella pasa; y tambien pera declaracion del sitio en
que los dichos vasallos del dicho senor Emperador y Rey de Castilla tienen
situado y asentado a Maluquo, la qual durante el tiempo deste contrato se vea
que esta puesta en el tal sitio, puesto que, en la verdad este em menos o mas
distancia a oriente de lo que en los dichos padrones es sytuado, y para que
en el punto de la situacion em que en los dichos padrones esta situado
Maluquo se continuen los dichos diez y siete grados a oriente, que, por biem
deste contrato el dicho señor Rey de Portugal ha de aver, y que, non se
alhando en la Casa de la Contratacion de Sevilha el dicho padron, las dichas
personas, nombradas por los dichos señores emperador y rreis, dentro de
huum mes hagan los dichos padrones y se firmen y sellen, como dicho es,
y por ellos se haguan cartas de navegar em que se lance la dicha linia en la
manera suso dicha, pera que de aquy adelante naveguen por ellas los dichos
vasallos, naturales, y subditos del dicho señor Emperador y Rey de Castilha,
y para que los naveguantes de una parte y de otra sean ciertos del sitio de
la dicha linia y distancia de las sobredichas dozientas y novienta y sete
leguas y media, que aya entre la dicha linia y Maluquo.

3. Item,[22] es concordado e asentado por los dichos procuradores que em
qualquier tiempo que el dicho señor Rey de Portugal quisiere que se vea el
derecho de la propiedad de Maluco, y las tierras y mares contenidas em este
contrato, y puesto que, al tal tienpo, el dicho señor Emperador y Rey de
Castilla no tenga tornado el dicho precio, ny el dicho contrato sea rresoluto,
se vea en esta manera, conviene a saber, que cada uno de los dichos señores
nombre tres astrologos y tres pilotos o tres marineros, que sean expertos en
la navegacion, los quales se ajuntaran em huum logar de la rraya dentre sus
rreynos, donde fuere acordado que se juntem desdel dia que el dicho señor
Emperador y Rey de Castilha o sus sobcesores fueren rrequerydos por parte
del dicho señor Rey de Portugal, que se nombren hasta quatro meses, y ally
consultaran y acordaran y tomaran asiento de la manera em que ha de hyr
a se ver el derecho de la dicha propiedad, conforme a las dichas capitolaciones e asiento que fue fecho antre los dichos Catholicos rreis, Dom Fernando
y Doña Isabel, y el dicho rrey, Dom Juam el segundo de Portugal; y, siendo
caso que el derecho de la dicha propiedad se juzge al dicho señor Emperador
y Rey de Castilla, no se executara ni usara de la tal sentencia sim que, primero,
el dicho señor Emperador e Rey de Castilla y sus sobcesores tornem rrealmente y com efecto, todos los dichos trezientos e cinquoenta mil ducados
que, por vertude deste contrato, fueron dados; e, juzgandose el derecho de
la propiedad por parte del dicho señor Rey de Portugal, el dicho señor
Emperador e Rey de Castilla y sus sobcesores seran obligados a tornar,
rrealmente e com efecto, los dichos trezientos e cimquoenta mil ducados al
dicho señor Rey de Portugal o a sus sobcesores desdel dia em que la dicha
sentencia fuere dada, hasta quatro annos primeros seguientes.

4. Item,[23] fue concertado e asentado pelos dychos procuradores em
nombre de los dichos señores sus constetuientes, que, siendo caso que em

---

[22] *Cf.* Doc. **15**, art. 5.   [23] *Cf.* Doc. **15**, art. 3.

quanto este comtrato de venta durar y nom fuere desfecho, desdel dia de la fecha del em adelante, vinieren alguunas especiarias o drogarias, de qualquier suerte que seam, a qualesquier puertos o partes de los rreynos e senhorios de cada uno de los dichos señores constetuientes que seam traidas por los vasallos, subditos, y naturales del dicho señor Emperador e Rey de Castilla, o por otras qualesquier personas, puesto que sus subditos y naturales e vasallos non sean, que el dicho señor Emperador e Rey de Castilla em sus reinos e senhorios, y el dicho señor Rey de Portugal en los suios, seam obligados a mandar e hazer e mandem e hagan depositar las dichas especiarias o drogarias em tal manera que el tal deposito quede seguro, sim que aquel a cuya parte viniere sea por el otro pera esto rrequerido, pera que asy estem depositadas em nombre de ambos, em poder de aquella persona o personas em quiem cada uno de los dichos señores em sus tierras e señorios las mamdaren e hizierem depositar; el qual deposito seram los dichos señores obligados a hazer e mamdar hazer por la manera sobredicha, aguora las dichas especerias o droguerias se hallem en poder de aquellos que las traxeren, o en poder de qualquier otra persona o personas, en qualesquier luguares o partes donde fuerem halladas, y los dichos señores emperador y rreies seram obligados de lo mandar asy noteficar desde aguora em sus reinos e señorios para que asy se cumpla, em modo que nom se pueda alegar ignorancia; y viniendo a aportar las dichas especirias o droguerias a qualesquier puertos o tierras que de cada uno de los dichos señores constituientes no fueren, no siendo de enemigos, cada uno dellos por virtud deste contrato podra rrequerir, em nombre de ambos, sin mas mostrar ninguna provisam ni poder de otro a las justicias de los rreinos e senhorios domde las dichas especerias o droguerias vinieren a parar, o fuerem halladas, que las manden depositar e depositen, y em qualquier de las dichas partes donde asy fueren halladas las dichas especearias o droguerias, estaram embargadas e depositadas por ambos hasta se saber de cuya demarcacion fueron sacadas; y para se saber si el lugar e tierras de donde las dichas especearias o droguerias fueron traidas e sacadas caem dentro de la demarcaciom e limites que por este contrato quedan con el dicho señor [Emperador] e Rey de Castilla, e ay em ellas las dichas especearias o droguerias embiaram los dichos señores emperador y rreis dos o quatro navios, tantos el uno como el otro, en los quales yran personas juramentadas que biem lo emtendam, tantos de la una parte, como de la otra, a los dichos luguares e tierras donde dixeren que sacarom y traxerom las dichas especearias o droguerias, pera ver y determinar em cuia demarcacion caen las dichas tierras e luguares de domde asy las dichas especerias o droguerias se dixere que fueron sacadas, e hallamdose que las dichas tierras e luguares caem dentro de la demarcaciom del dicho señor Emperador e Rey de Castilla y que em ellas ay las dichas especerias e droguerias en tanta cantidad que rrazonablemente pudiesen traer las dichas especerias o droguerias, en tal caso, se alcara e quitara el dicho deposito, y se entreguaran libremente al dicho señor Emperador e Rey de Castilla, syn que por ello seam obligados a pagar ningunas costas ny gastos, ny intereses, ny otra alguna cosa; e siendo hallado que fueron sacadas de las tierras e luguares de la demarcaciom del dicho señor Rey de Portugal, asy mesmo sera alcado y quytado el dicho deposito, y se entregaram al dicho señor Rey de Portugal, sim que por ello sea obligado a pagar ningunas costas ni gastos, ny intireses, ny otra alguna cosa de qualquier calidad que sea; y las personas que asy las truxerem seram pugnidos e castigados por el dicho señor empera-

dor, rey de Castilla, o por sus justicias, como quebrantadores de fee y de
paz, conforme a justicia; y los dichos señores Enperador e Rey de Castilla
y el dicho señor Rey de Portugal seram obligados de enbiar los dichos sus
navios e personas tanto que por cada uno dellos al otro fuere rrequerido y,
enquanto asy las dichas especerias o droguerias estuvieren depositadas y
enbargadas en el modo sobredicho, el dicho señor emperador, rey de Castilla,
ny otro por el, ni con su favor ni consentimiento, no iran ni enbiaran a la
dicha tierra o tierras de donde asy las dichas especerias e droguerias fueron
traidas, y todo lo que dicho es en este capitulo acerca del deposito de las
especerias o droguerias, no avra lugar ny se entendera en las especiarias o
droguerias que vinieren a cualesquier partes pera el dicho señor Rey de
Portugal.[24]

5. Item,[24] es concordado y asentado que en todalas yslas, tieras y mares
que fueren de la dicha linea para dentro no puedam las naos, navios, e gentes
del dicho señor Emperador e Rey de Castilla ny de sus subditos, vasallos, e
naturales ny otras algunas personas, puesto que sus subditos ny vasallos
naturales no seam por su mamdado, consentimiento, favor e ajuda, o sin
su mamdado, favor ni aiuda entrar, navegar, tratar ny comerciar ny cargar
cosa alguna que en las dichas yslas, tieras, y mares oviere de qualquier suerte
o manera que sea, y que qualesquier de los sobredichos que de aquy adelante
el contrario de todas las dichas cosas y cada una dellas hiziere, o fuerem con-
prendidos e hallados de dentro de la dicha linea sean presos por qualquier
capitan o capitanes o gentes del dicho señor Rey de Portugal e por los dichos
sus capitanes oydos e castigados e pugnidos como cosarios e quebrantadores
de paz; e, no siendo hallados dentro de la dicha linea por los dichos capitanes
o gentes del dicho señor Rey de Portugal, se vinieren a qualquier puerto,
tiera o senhorio del dicho señor Emperador e Rey de Castilla, que el dicho
señor Emperador e Rey de Castilla e sus justicias donde asy vinieren o
fueren hallados, seam tenidos e obligados de los tomar y prender, entanto que
les fueren presentados autos e pesquisas que les fueren embiados por el dicho
señor Rey de Portugal o por sus justicias por que se muestre ser culpados
en cada una destas cosas sobredichos y los pugnir e castigar enteramente
como malhechores e quebrantadores de fee e de paz.

6. Item,[25] es concordado e asentado por los dichos procuradores que el
dicho señor Emperador e Rey de Castilla no embie por sy ny por otro a las
dichas islas, tierras y mares dentro de la dicha linea ni consientan que alla
vayan de aquy adelante sus naturales e subditos e vasallos o estranjeros,
puesto que sus naturales e vasallos ny subditos no sean ny les de para ello
ajuda ni favor ny se concierte con ellos para ellos alla yr contra la forma e
asiento deste contrato, antes sea obligado de lo defender, estorvar e inpedir
quanto en el fuere, e ynbiando el dicho señor Emperador e Rey de Castilla
por sy o por otro a las dichas yslas, tierras o mares de dentro de la dicha linea,
o consentiendo que alla vaiam sus naturales, vasallos, subditos o extranjeros,
puesto que sus naturales, vasallos ny subditos no sean, dandoles pera ello
ayuda o favor o concertandose com ellos para que alla vayan contra la forma
e asiento deste contrato e sy lo no defendiere y estorvare e inpidiere quanto
en el fuere, que el dicho pacto de rretro vendendo quede luego rresoluto, y
el dicho señor Rey de Portugal no seia mas obligado a rrecibir el dicho precio
ny al rretro vender el derecho e acion que el dicho señor Emperador e Rey

[24] *Cf.* Doc. **15**, art. 3.   [25] *Cf.* Doc. **15**, art. 3.

de Castilha, por qualquier via e manera que sea, podria tener a ello, antes que
aquel por virtud deste contrato tenga vendido e rrenunciado y traspasado
en el dicho señor Rey de Portugal y por el mismo fecho la dicha venta quede
pura e valedera para sienpre jamas, como si al principio fuera fecha sin
condiciom y pacto de rretro vendendo; pero, porque poderia ser que, naveguando los sobredichos por los mares del sur, donde los subditos e naturales
e vasallos del dicho señor Emperador e Rey de Castilha puedem navegar,
les podria sobrevenir tienpo tam forcoso e contrario o necesidad com que
fuesem costreñidos, continuando su camino e naveguacion a pasar la dicha
linea, en tal caso, no incurriran em pena alguna, mas, antes que, aportamdo
e lleguamdo em qualquier de los dichos casos a alguna tierra de las que asy
entraren en la dycha linea, e por vertud deste contrato pertenecieren al dicho
señor Rey de Portugal, que sean tratados por sus subditos e vasalos e moradores della como vasalos de su hermano y asy como el dicho señor Emperador
e Rey de Castilha mandaria tratar a los suyos que desta manera aportasen a
sus tieras de la Nueva España o a otras de aquellas partes, con tanto que,
cesando la dicha necesidad, se salgam lueguo y se buelvan a sus mares del sur;
y, siendo caso que los sobre dichos pasasem por ignorancia la dicha linea,
es concordado e asentado que no incurram por ello em pena alguña, em quanto
no constare claramente que, sabiendo ellos que estavan dentro de la dicha
linea, no se bolvieren e salieren fuera della, como es acordado e asentado em
el caso que entrasem con tiempo forcoso y contrario o de necesidad; porque,
quamdo esto constare, se avra por probado que com malicia pasaran la linea,
y seran pugnidos y avran aquelas penas que han de aver aquellos que entraren
dentro de la linea, como dicho es, y en este contrato es contenido y declarado;
y hallando los sobredichos o descubriendo emquanto dentro de la dicha linea
ansy anduvieren algunas yslas o tierras dentro de la dicha linea, que las tales
yslas o tierras quedem luego libremente e con efecto al dicho señor Rey de
Portugal e a sus sobcesores, como sy por sus capitanes e vasallos descuviertas
e halhadas e poseydas al tal tempo fuesen; y es concordado y asentado por los
dichos procuradores que las naaos e navios del dicho señor Emperador Rey de
Castilla y de sus subditos, vasalos, e naturales puedam yr e navegar por los
mares del dicho señor Rey de Portugal, por donde sus armadas vam para
la Imdia, tanto solamente quanto les fuere necesario para tomar sus derrotas
derechas para el estrecho de Magalhanes; y haziemdo lo contrario de lo
suso dicho, naveguando mas por los dichos mares del dicho señor Rey de
Portugal, de lo que dicho es, yncuriran por el mismo fecho, asy el dicho señor
Emperador e Rey de Castilla, constando que lo hizieron por su mandado,
favor y ajuda o consentimiento, y los que asy navegaren y fueren contra lo
suso dicho en las penas sobredichas, asy e de la manera que de suso em este
contrato es declarado.

7. Item,[26] fue asentado e comcordado que lo que toca a que sy algunos
subditos del dicho señor Emperador e Rey de Castella o otros algunos fueren
tomados e hallados, de aquy adelante, dentro de los dichos limites ariba
declarados, seam presos por qualquier capitan o capitanes o gentes del dicho
señor Rey de Portuguall, y por los dichos sus capitanes, oydos, castigados
y pugnidos como cosarios, violadores e quebrantadores de paz; y que, no
siendo hallados dentro de la dicha linea, y viniendo a qualquier puerto del
dicho señor Emperador e Rey de Castilla, su magestad e sus justicias seam

26 *Cf*. Doc. 15, art. 4.

obligados de los tomar e prender, tanto que les fueren presentados autos e pesquisas que les fueren enbiados por el dicho señor Rey de Portugal e por sus justicias, por los quales se muestre ser culpados en las cosas suso dichas y los pugnir y castigar enteramente, como malhechores y quebrantadores de fee y de paz y lo demas que se asienta por este contrato, em quanto toca a no pasar la dicha linea nimgunos subditos del dicho señor Emperador e Rey de Castilla, ni otros algunos por su mamdado, consentimiento, favor o ayuda ; y las penas que cerca desto se ponen, se entienda desdel dia que fuere note-ficado a los subditos del dicho señor Emperador y gentes que por aquellas mares e partes estam y naveguan, en adelante ; y que, antes de la tal notifi-cacam, no incurram en las dichas penas ; pero esto se entienda quanto a las gentes de las armadas del dicho señor emperador, que, hasta aguora, a aquelas partes son ydas, y que desd el dia del otorgamiento deste contrato em adelante, durante el tempo que la dicha venta no fuere desfecha en la forma suso dicha, no pueda embiar ni embie otras algunas de nuevo, sin incorrir en las dichas penas.

8. Item,[27] fue concordado e asentado por los dichos procuradores que el dicho señor Rey de Portugal no hara por sy ny por otro ny mandara hazer de nuevo fortaleza alguna em Maluco, ny al rrededor del com veinte leguas, ny de Maluco hasta donde por este contrato se ha por lancada la linea ; y es asentado y son concordes todos los dichos procuradores de la una parte y de la otra que este tempo de nuevo se entienda, comviene a saber, desd el tiempo que el dicho señor Rey de Portugal pudiere alla embiar a noteficar que no se haga ninguna fortaleza de nuevo, que sera en la primera armada que fuere del dicho rreino de Portugal para la Imdia, despues deste contrato ser con-firmado e aprobado por los dichos señores sus constituientes, y selado de seus sellos ; y, quanto a la fortaleza que aguora estaa fecha em Maluquo, no se hara mas obra alguna en ella de nuevo, desdel dicho tiempo em adelante, solamente se rreparara e sosterna en el estado em que estuviere al dicho tiempo, si ell dicho señor Rey de Portugal quisiere, el qual jura e prometa de gardalo e comprilo asy.

9. Item,[28] es asentado e concordado que las armadas que el dicho señor Emperador e Rey de Castilha hasta aguora tiene enbiadas a las dichas partes seam miradas y bien tratadas e favorecidas del dicho señor Rey de Portugal y de sus gentes, y no les sea puesto embaraco ni impidimiento en su naveguacion e contratacion, y que si daño alguno, lo que no se cree, ellos ubieren rrecebido o rrecebieren de sus capitanes o gentes, o les ubieren tomado alguna cosa, que el dicho señor Rey de Portugal sea obligado de emmendar e satisfazer e rrestetuir y pagar luego todo aquelo em que el dicho señor Emperador e Rey de Castilla y sus subditos y armadas ubieren sido danificados, e de mamdar pugnir y castigar a los que lo hizieren y de proveer que las armadas y gentes del dicho señor Emperador e Rey de Castilla se puedam venir quando quisieren, libremente sin impidimiento alguno.[29]

10. Item,[30] es asentado que el dicho señor Emperador y Rey de Castilla mamde dar luego sus cartas y provisiones para sus capitanes e gentes que

[27] *Cf.* Doc. **15**, art. 6.   [28] *Cf.* Doc. **15**, art. 7.

[29] A fierce struggle was kept up in the Moluccas for several years between the Portu-guese at Ternate and the Spaniards at Tidore and their respective native allies. See Doc. **15**, bibliography, for references to the history of the two nationalities in the Moluccas from 1521 to 1532.

[30] This article is the same as art. 8 of Doc. **15**.

estuvieren en las dychas yslas que lueguo se vengam y no contraten mas em ellas, com que les dexem traer libremente lo que ubieren rrescatado y contratado y cargado.[31]

11. Item,[32] es asentado e comcordado que en las provisiones e cartas que cerca deste asiento e contrato ha de dar e despachar el dicho señor Emperador e Rey de Castilla, se ponga e digua que lo que, segun dicho es, se asienta, capitula e contrata, valga biem asy como se fuese fecho e pasado em cortes generales com consentimiento expreso de los procuradores dellas; y que, para validacion dello, de su poderio rreal absoluto de que, como rrey e señor natural, no rreconociente superior en lo temporal, quiere usar e usa, abroga e deroga, casa e anula la supplicacion que los procuradores de las cibdades e vyllas destos rreynos en las cortes que se celebraron en la cibdad de Toledo el año pasado, de quinientos e veinte e cinquo, le hizieron cerca de lo tocante a la contrataciom de las dichas yslas e tierras y la rrespuesta que a ello dio y qualquier ley que en las dichas cortes sobre ello se hizo y todas las otras que a esto puedam obstar.

12. Item,[33] es asentado que el dicho señor Rey de Portugal, porque algunos subditos del dicho señor Emperador y Rey de Castilla y otros de fuera de sus rreynos que le vinieron a servir se quexan que em su Casa de la Imdia y em su rreyno le tienem embaracadas sus haziendas, promete de mandar hazer clara e abierta e breve justicia, sin tener rrespecto a henojo que dellos se pueda tener, por aver venido a servir y servido al dicho señor Emperador.

13. Item,[34] fue asentado y concordado por los dichos procuradores em nombre de los dichos sus consteuientes que las capitulaciones hechas entre los dichos Catolicos rreies, Dom Fernando e Doña Ysabel, y el rrey, Dom Juam el segundo, de Portugal, sobre la demarcaciom del mar oceano, quedem firmes e valederas em todo e per todo, como en ellas es contenido e declarado, tirando aquelas cosas em que, por este contrato, em otra manera som concordadas e asentadas; y, siendo caso que el dicho señor Emperador y Rey de Castilla torne el precio que, por este contrato, le es dado, en la manera que dicha es, em modo que la venta quede desfecha, en tal caso, las dichas capitulaciones hechas entre los dichos Catholicos rreyes, Dom Fernamdo e Doña Ysabel, y el dicho rrey, Dom Juam el segundo, de Portugal, quedaran em toda su fuerca e vigor, como si este contrato no fuera fecho, como en ellas es contenido; y seran los dichos señores sus constituientes obligados de las complir e gardar em todo e por todo, como en ellas es asentado.

14. Item,[35] es acordado e asentado por los dichos procuradores que puesto que el derecho e action que el dicho señor Emperador e Rey de Castilla dize que tiene a las dichas tierras, lugares e mares e yslas que ansy por el modo sobredicho vende al dicho señor Rey de Portugal valgua mas de la mitad del justo precio que por ello le da, el dicho señor Emperador e Rey de Castilla sepa cierto e de cierta sabiduria por cierta informacion de personas em ello expertas, que lo muy biem saben y entiendem que es de mucho maior valor y estimacion, alende de la mitad del justo precio que el dicho señor Rey de

[31] The Spaniards in the Moluccas, who had been defending the claims of the Emperor there, first heard of the sale of the islands from the Portuguese in 1532. Navarrete, *Viages*, V. 148, 395.
[32] This article is the same as art. 11 of Doc. **15**.
[33] This article corresponds to Doc. **15**, art. 14.
[34] This article corresponds to Doc. **15**, art. 13. Note that the words " enpeño y retrovendendo " in the corresponding article of the earlier treaty are changed to *venta*.
[35] This article corresponds to Doc. **15**, art. 15.

Portugal da al dicho señor Emperador e Rey de Castilla a plaze hazer dona-
cion, como de hecho la haze, donde el dicho dia para siempre jamas entre bivos
valedera de la dicha maior valia y estimacion que asy vale mas e alemde de la
mitad del justo precio por muy gran mas valia que sea, la qual maior valia
y estimacion, alende de la mitad del justo precio, el dicho señor Emperador e
Rey de Castilla dimitte de sy e de sus subcesores y desmienbra de la corona
de sus rreynos para sienpre, y todo trespasa al dicho señor Rey de Portugal
e a sus subcesores y corona de sus rreynos, rrealmente e com efecto, por el
modo sobredicho, durante el tienpo deste contrato.

15. Item,[16] es concordado y asentado por los dichos procuradores que
qualquier de las partes que contra este contrato o parte del fuere, por sy o
por otro, por qualquier modo, via, o manera, que sea, pensada o no pensada,
que por el mismo hecho pierda el derecho que tiene por qualquier via, modo,
o manera que sea; y todo lueguo quede aplicado, junto, e adquirido a la
otra parte, que por el dicho contrato estuviere y contra el no fuere y a la
corona de sus rreynos, sin para ello el que contra el fuere, sea mas citado,
oydo, ni rrequerido, ny ser necesario sobre ello darse mas otra sentencia por
juez ni juzgador alguno que sea, averigandose y provandose primeramente
el mandado o consentimiento o favor de la parte que contra ello viniere; y
alende desto, el que contra este contrato fuere, por qualquier modo e
manera que sea, em parte o em todo, pague a la otra parte que por el estuviere,
duzientos mil ducados de oro, de pena, y en nombre de pena e intarese, en la
qual pena incuriran tantas vezees quantas contra el fueren, em parte, o em
todo, como dicho es; y la pena llevada o no llevada, todavia este contrato
quedara firme y valedero y estable para siempre jamas em favor de aquel que
por el estuviere, y contra el o parte del no fuere, para lo qual obligaron todos
los bienes patrimoniales e fiscales de los dichos sus constetuientes y de las
coronas de sus rreinos, de todo conplir y mantener asy e tan cumplidamente
como em ellos se contiene.

16. Item,[17] fue asentado e concordado por los dichos procuradores que los
dichos señores sus constetuientes y cada uno dellos, juraram solenemente y
prometeran por el dicho juramiento, que por sy e por sus sucesores nunca
em ninguun tiempo vendram contra este contrato em todo ny em parte, por
sy ny por otro, en juizio ny fuera del, por ninguna via, forma, ny manera
que sea y pensar se pueda, y que nunca em tiempo alguno, por sy ny por otro,
pediran rrelaxacion del dicho juramiento a nuestro muy Sancto Padre, ny a
otro que, pera ello, poder tenga; y, puesto que Su Santidad, o quiem pera
ello poder tuviere, sin le ser pedido, de su propio motu, les rrelaxe el dicho
juramiento, que lo no aceptaran, ny nunca em alguun tiempo usaran de la
dicha rrelaxacion, ny se aiudaran della, ni aprovecharan em ninguna manera
ny via que sea, em juizio, ny fuera del.

17. Item,[18] fue comcordado e asentado por los dichos procuradores que,
para mas corroboraçion y firmeza deste contrato, que este contrato e transacion, com todas sus clausulas, comdiciones, pactos, obligaciones y declaraciones del, asy e por la manera que en el som contenidas, sea juzgado por
sentencia del papa, e confirmado e aprobado por Su Santidad, por bulla
appostolica, com su sello, en la qual bula de sentencia, confirmacion, e aprobacion sera inserto todo este contrato, de verbo ad verbum; y que Su Santidad,

[16] This article corresponds to Doc. **15,** art. 16.
[17] This article corresponds to Doc. **15,** art. 9.
[18] This article corresponds to Doc. **15,** art. 10.

en la dicha sentencia, supla e aya por suplido, de su cierta sciencia, e poderio
absoluto, todo e qualquier defeto e solenidad que de hecho e de derecho
se rrequiera para este contrato ser mas firme e valedero en todo e qualquier
parte dello; y que Su Sanctidad ponga sentencia descomunion, asy en las
partes principales, como em qualesquier otras personas que contra el fueren
y lo no gardaren, em todo o em parte, por qualquier via, modo, e manera que
sea, en la qual sentencia descomunion declarara e mandara que incurram
ipso facto los que contra el dicho contrato fueren, em todo o em parte, sin
para ello se rrequiera ni sea necesaria otra sentencia descomunion ny declara-
ciom della, y que los tales no puedam ser absueltos por Su Sanctidad, ny por
otra persona por su mandado, sin consentimiento de la otra parte a quien
tocare, y sim primero ser para la tal absolucion citada e rrequerida e oyda;
e los dichos procuradores desde agora para entonces, y desde entonces para
agora, em nombre de los dichos sus constetuientes, suplican a Su Sanctidad
que lo quiera asy confirmar e juzgar por sentençia del modo e manera que
em este capitolo esta asentado e declarado, de la qual confirmacion e aprobacion cada una de las partes podra sacar su bulla, la qual los dichos procuradores, em nombre de los dichos sus constituientes peden a Su Sanctidad que
mande dar a cada uno dellos que la expedir quisiere, sim mas la otra parte
para ello se rrequerir para confirmacion e firmeza de su derecho.

Y todo lo sobredicho asy concordado e asentado, como de suso es contenido,
los dichos procuradores, em nombre de los dichos sus constituientes, y por
vertud de las dichas sus procuraciones, dixeron ante mym, el dicho secretario e notario publico, e ante los testigos de yuso escriptos y firmados, que
aprobavan, loavan, y otorgavan pera siempre jamas, asy e tan enteramente,
com todas las clausulas, declaraciones, pactos y convenciones, penas y obligaciones en este contrato contenidas; y promitieron y se obligaron, la una parte
a la otra, la otra a la otra, em nombre de los dichos sus constituientes, estipu-
lantes e aceptantes por solene estipulacion, de asy lo tener e complir y gardar
para siempre jamas, y que los dichos sus constituientes y sus sobcesores y
todos sus vasalhos, subditos, y naturales, ternan y gardaran e compliran,
agora e pera siempre, el dicho contrato e todo lo en el contenido, so las penas
y obligaciones en el declaradas; y que nom yran nim vernam, nym consentiran
ny permitiran que sea ido ny venido contra el, ny parte alguna del, directe
ny indirectemente, em juizio ny fuera del, por ninguna causa, color, ni caso
alguno que sea, o ser pueda, pensada o por pensar; y dixeron los dichos
procuradores em nombre de los dichos senhores sus constituientes que
rrenunciavan, como de hecho rrenunciaran todas las enexaciones y ecepciones
e todos rremedios juridicos, beneficios y concilios ordinarios y extraordinarios,
que a los dichos señores sus constituientes, y a cada uno dellos conpetem, o
podram conpetir e pertenecer por derecho, agora y en qualquier tiempo de
aquy adelante, para anular y rrevocar o quebrantar, en todo o em parte, este
contrato, o para inpedir el efecto del, y ansy mismo rrenunciaran todos los
derechos, leis, costunbres, estilos, hazañas y openiones de doctores, que para
ello les pudiesem aprovechar, em qualquier manera, y especialmente rrenunciaran las leis y derechos que dizem que general rrenunciacion no val, para
lo qual todo asy tener e gardar y conplir obligaron los dichos procuradores
todos los bienes, patrimoniales e fiscales, de los dichos sus constituientes y
de las coronas de sus rreinos; y, por maior firmeza, los dichos procuradores
dixeron que jurarian, como de hecho loguo juraran ante mym, el dicho
secretario y notario suso dicho, e testigos de yuso espritos, a Dios y a Sancta

Maria y a la señal de la Cruz ✠ y a los sanctos Avangelios, que com sus manos derechas tocaran, em nombre y en las animas de los dichos sus constituientes, por virtud de los dichos poderes que especialmente para ello tienem, que ellos, y cada uno dellos, por sy y por sus subcesores, ternam, e gardaran y haran tener y gardar, para siempre jamas, este contrato, como en el es contenido; y que los dichos señores sus constituientes, y cada uno dellos, confirmaran, aprovaran, loaran e rratificaran y otorgaran de nuevo esta capitulacion, y todo lo en ello contenido, y cada cosa, y parte dello, y prometeran y se obligaran y juraran de lo gardar y conplir cada una de las partes, pelo que le toca, incumbe e atañe de hazer e gardar e complir, rrealmente y com efecto, a buena fee, sim mal engaño, y sim arte ni cautela alguna ; y que los dichos sus constituientes ny alguno dellos, no demamdaran, por sy, ny por otras personas, absulucion, rrelaxacion, dispensacion, ny conmutacion del dicho juramiento, a nuestro muy sancto Padre, ni a otra persona alguna que poder tenga para lo dar e conceder ; y, puesto que de propio motu, o en otra qualquier manera, les sea dada, no usaran della, antes, sin enbargo della, ternan, gardaran, y cumpliran, y haran tener y gardar y conplir todo lo contenido en este dicho contrato, com todas las clausulas, obligaciones y penas, y cada cosa, y parte dello, segund en el se contiene, fiel e verdadera, rrealmente e com efecto, y que dara y entregara, cada una de las dichas partes a la otra, la dicha aprobacion e rratificacion deste contrato, jurada e ffirmada de cada huum de los dichos sus constituientes, y sellada com su sello, desd el dia de la fecha del em veinte dias luego seguientes. Em testimonio y firmeza de lo qual, los dichos procuradores otorgaron este contrato en la forma suso dicha, ante mym, el dicho secretario y notario suso dicho, y de los testigos de yuso espritos, y lo firmaron de sus nombres, y pidierom a mym, el dicho secretario y notario, que les diese uno y muchos instrumentos, se les necesario fuesen, sub my publica firma y signo; que fue fecha y otorgada em la dicha cibdad de Caragoca, el dia, mes y anno suso dichos. Testigos que fuerom presentes al otorgamiento deste dicho contrato, y vieron firmar en el a todos los dichos señores procuradores, en el rregistro de mym, el dicho secretario, y los vieron jurar corporalmente em mano de mym, el dicho secretario: Alonso de Valdes, secretario del dicho señor Emperador, y Agustin de Urbina, chancyller de su Magestad, Jeronimo Rancio, criado del dicho señor chanciler, y Conde de Gatynara ; y Hernam Rodriguez y Antonio de Sosa, criados del dicho señor embaixador Antonio de Azevedo, y Alonso de Ydiaquez, criado de mym, el dicho secretario, los quales dichos testigos, asy mismo firmaran sus nombres en el rregistro de mym, el dicho secretario. Mercurinus, cancellarius. Frater Garcia, episcopus Oxomensis. El Comemdador Mayor. Antonio de Azevedo, coutinho. Testigos: Alonso de Valdes, Jeronimo Rancio, Agustin de Urbina, Antonio de Sousa, Fernan Rodriguez, Alonso de Ydiaquez. E yo, el dicho secretario y notario, Francisquo de los Covos, fuy presente, en uno con los dichos testigos, al otorgamiento deste contrato y asiento, y al juramiento en el contenido, que en mis manos hizieron los dichos señores procuradores, y al firmar dellos y de los dichos testigos, en el rregisto que queda en my poder ; e a pedimiento del dicho señor embaxador Antonio de Azevedo, hyze sacar este treslado ; e, por ende, fize aquy mi signo em testimonio de verdad. Francisquo de los Covos.

La qual dicha espritura e asiento, que de suso va incorporado, por nos vista y entendida, y cada cosa y parte dello, y siendo ciertos y certeficados de todo lo en ella contenido, por la presente lo loamos e confirmamos e aprobamos y rreteficamos, y quanto es necesario de nuevo otorgamos, y prometemos de tener y gardar la dicha escriptura y asiento, que asy polos dichos nuestros procuradores, e asy mismo por el dicho embaixador, procurador del dicho serenisimo, muy alto, muy poderoso Rey de Portugal, nuestro ermano, fue asentada e otorgada e concertada em nuestros nombres, y cada cosa e parte dello, de todo lo tener y guardar, rrealmente y com efeto, a buena fee, sim mal emgaño, cesante todo fraude e simulacion, dolo e cautela, e toda otra especie de decebcion y arte; y queremos y somos contentos que se guarde e cumpla, segund y como en ella se contiene, bien asy y tan complidamente, como sy por nos fuera hecha y asentada. E, para validacion e corroboracion e firmeza de la dicha espritura de venta e asiento, derogamos e abrogamos, casamos e anulamos todas las leis e derechos, prematicas, hazañas, y openiones de doctores, que al valor de la dicha espritura de suso emcorporada seam contrarias; especialmente derogamos, casamos, e anulamos quallesquiera peticiones de procuradores del rreyno que en las cortes de Toledo, o en otras qualesquiera que ayamos tenido, no [*sic*] seam fechas sobre que no hagamos este concierto e asiento, ny otro alguno, con el dicho serenisimo rrey, nuestro hermano, puesto que especie de contrato tengan; e asy mismo qualesquiera prematicas, capitolos de cortes, que, sobre las dichas peteciones de procuradores del rreyno, hayamos hecho, porque todas e cada una dellas derogamos, abrogamos, anulamos y casamos, y avemos por ningunas, de nuestro poderio rreal absuluto, no rreconocientes superior en lo temporal; y avemos por buena la dicha spritura de venta, con el dicho pacto de rretro vendendo, y la confirmamos y rreteficamos, desde aguora pera siempre jamas, y la avemos por buena y provechosa a nos y a la corona de nosos rreinos; y queremos que valga como se em cortes, y con consentimiento de los procuradores de las cibdades, villas y pueblos de nuestros rreinos, fuese fecha; la qual asy confirmamos e rreteficamos e aprovamos por causas a nos conocidas y provechosas, y a la corona de nuestros rreinos; y avemos por casadas, anuladas, e abrogadas todas e qualesquiera leies e derechos que en contrario seam; especialmente derogamos, casamos e anulamos las leies que dizen e disponen que general rrenunciacion nom vale. E yo, el rrey, juro a Dios y a Santa Maria, y a las palavras de los Sanctos Avangelios, y a la señal de la Cruz ✠ em que pongo nuestra mano derecha, y prometemos, por nos, y por nuestros subcesores, de nunca yr nem venir, ny consentir, ny permetir que se vaya ny pase contra esta espritura de venta, com pacto de rretro vendemdo, ny parte della, dereite ny inderecite, ny por otra alguna caussa, pensada o no pensada, so color alguna, por nos ny por otro, ny consentiremos ny permiteremos que otra alguna persona o personas vayam contra la dicha espritura e asiento, antes lo defenderemos, y castigaremos e proiberemos quanto a nos posible sea, so cargo del dicho juramiento, del no pediremos rrelaxacion, como por mys procuradores esta otorgado, ny usaremos della, puesto que el papa, o otro que su poder tenga, de su propio motu nos la conceda, puesto que tenga clausulas derogatorias e abrogatorias de todo lo que dicho es, porque todo lo rrenunciamos, y prometemos de no usar dello, so cargo del dicho juramiento, y, para certenidad desta nuestra voluntad y firmeza y validacion de lo suso dicho, mandamos pasar y dar esta nuestra carta de aprobacion, rratificacion, abrogacion y anulacion, firmada por my, el rrey, y sellada con nuestro sello. Dada en la cidad de Lerida, a veinte e tres dias del mes dAbril, año del Señor de mil e quinientos e veinte e nueve años. Yo, El Rey. Yo, Francisquo de los Covos, secretario de Sus Cesarea y Catholicas Magestades, la fize screvir por su mamdado. Mercurinus, cancelarius. Frater Garcia, episcopus Oxomensis. El Comendador Maior.

A qual carta de contrato, capitolacam, e asento de pacto de rretro vendendo, vista por mym, e todas as condicões e clausulas em ella conteudas, de palavra a palavra, bem vistas e entemdidas, a comfirmo, aprovo, e rretefico, e ey por booa e todas as cousas em ella conteudas e cada huũa dellas ; e prometo por minha fee rreal, y juro aos santos Avangelhos, sobre que pus minhas maãos, que as comprirey e gardarey, comvem a saber, aquelas que a mym toca comprir e guardar, por bem, do dito contrato, capitolacam, e asento, asy e tam inteiramente como nela he conteudo e declarado e sem mingoamento alguum, e sob as penas, clausulas, pactos, e condicões que nela se contem. E prometo e juro, por mym e por meus erdeiros e sobcesores, de nunca em nenhuum tempo, nem por modo alguum, por mym, nem por outrem, hiir nem viir contra o dito contrato, capitolacam, e asento, nem contra cousa alguũa das que em elle sam contiudas, antes em todo e por todo as comprirey e guardarey, e farey comprir e gardar, a boa fee, sem arte, cautela, emgano nem malicia alguũa, como dito he. E, por certidam de todo, mamdeey fazer esta carta de comfirmacam, aprovacam e rreteficacam, por mym asinada e aselada do meu selo pendente em chumbo. Dada em a cidade de Lixboa, a vinte dias de Junho. Pero dAlcacova Carneiro a fez. Anno de Noso Senhor Jesuu Cristo de mil e quinhentos e trinta annos.

EL REY.

TRANSLATION.

Dom John, by the grace of God king of Portugal, and of the Algarves on this side and beyond the sea in Africa, lord of Guinea and of the conquest, navigation, and commerce of Ethiopia, Arabia, Persia, and India. Be it known to all who shall see this my deed of confirmation, approval, and ratification, that between me and Don Charles, emperor ever august, king of Germany, Castile, Leon, Aragon, the Two Sicilies, Jerusalem, etc., my very beloved and prudent brother, there was doubt and dispute in respect to the ownership and possession (or quasi-possession), title, navigation, and commerce of the Moluccas and other islands and seas, each of us saying that they belonged to him and that he was in the possession of all the aforesaid ; and because of our very close relationship, and in order that no discontent might ever be felt between our vassals and the natives of our kingdoms, and that the great love, justice, and obligation existing between us might always be preserved, we have concerted in respect to the aforesaid a deed of contract, treaty, and agreement, made by our sufficient and qualified representatives, deputed therefor, the tenor of which, word for word, is as follows :

Don Charles, by the divine clemency elected emperor ever august, king of Germany, Doña Joanna, his mother, and the same Don Charles, her son, by the grace of God king and queen of Castile, Leon, Aragon, the Two Sicilies,

Jerusalem, Navarre, Granada, Toledo, Valencia, Galicia, Seville, Cordova, Corsica, Murcia, Jaen, the Algarves, Algeciras, Gibraltar, the Canary Islands, the Indies, islands and mainland of the ocean sea, archduke and archduchess of Austria, duke and duchess of Burgundy and Brabant, count and countess of Barcelona, Flanders, and Tyrol, lord and lady of Biscay and Molina, duke and duchess of Athens and Neopatras, count and countess of Roussillon and Cerdagne, marquis and marchioness of Oristano and Gociano, etc., we have seen and read a deed of treaty and agreement of sale with compact of *retro-vendendo* of the right and possession, or quasi-possession, and action that we have or may have in the Molucca Islands—in whatever way the right may or can pertain to us—and in the lands, islands, and seas mentioned in the said contract and agreement, made in our name by Mercurino de Gattinara, count of Gattinara, grand chancellor of me, the king, and by Don Fray García de Loaysa, bishop of Osma, my confessor, and by Don García de Padilla, chief knight-commander of Calatrava, all members of our council and our representatives, and by Antonio d'Azevedo, *contino,* member of the council and ambassador of the most serene, very exalted and very mighty King of Portugal, our very dear and greatly beloved brother, and his representative, the tenor of which, word for word, is as follows:

In the name of God Almighty, Father, Son, and Holy Ghost, three Persons, and only one true God. Be it known and manifest to all who shall see this public instrument of adjustment and contract of sale, with compact of *retro-vendendo,* that in the city of Saragossa, which is in the kingdom of Aragon, on the twenty-second day of the month of April, in the year of the nativity of our Savior Jesus Christ, 1529, in the presence of me, Francisco de los Cobos, secretary and member of the council of the emperor, Don Charles, and of the queen, Doña Joanna, his mother, queen and king of Castile, and their scrivener and notary public, and in the presence of the undersigned witnesses, appeared the lords, Mercurino de Gattinara, count of Gattinara, grand chancellor of the said emperor, the very reverend Don Fray García de Loaysa, bishop of Osma, his confessor, and Don Fray García de Padilla, chief knight-commander of the Order of Calatrava, all three members of the council of the said very exalted and very powerful princes, Don Charles, by divine clemency elected emperor ever august, king of Germany, and Doña Joanna, his mother, and the same Don Charles, her son, by the grace of God, king and queen of Castile, Leon, Aragon, the Two Sicilies, Jerusalem, Navarre, Granada, etc., in the name and as representatives of the said lords, emperor and king and queen of Castile, on the one part, and Antonio d'Azevedo, *contino,* member of the council and ambassador of the very exalted and very powerful lord, Dom John, by the grace of God king of Portugal, of the Algarves on this side of and beyond the sea in Africa, lord of Guinea and of the conquest, navigation, and commerce of Ethiopia, Arabia, Persia, and India, etc., in his name, and as his representative on the other part; as they presently proved by their procurations, suitable and sufficient for this contract, signed by the said lords, emperor and king and queen of Castile and the King of Portugal, and sealed with their seals. *Verbatim* transcripts of these said procurations are as follows:

[Here follow the full powers granted by the sovereigns of Castile to the Count of Gattinara, the Bishop of Osma, and the chief Knight-Commander of Calatrava on April 15, 1529, and the full powers granted by John III. of Portugal to Antonio d'Azevedo on October 18, 1528.]

After [22] said authorizations were presented by the said representatives it was declared that, inasmuch as there existed a doubt between the said Emperor and King of Castile, etc., and the said King of Portugal, etc., concerning the ownership, possession, and rights, or possession, or quasi-possession, navigation, and trade of the Moluccas and other islands and seas, which each one of the said lords, the Emperor and King of Castile and the King of Portugal, declares as his, both by virtue of the treaties made by the most exalted, powerful, and Catholic sovereigns, Don Fernando and Doña Isabella, rulers of Castile, grandparents of the said Emperor and the King, Dom John II., of Portugal (may they rest in glory), about the demarcation of the ocean sea, and by virtue of other rights and privileges which each one of the said emperor and monarchs asserts to belong and pertain to said islands, seas, and lands belonging to him of which he is in possession; and inasmuch as the said emperor and monarchs considering the very close relationship and great affection existing between them, and which not only should very rightly be preserved, but as far as possible be increased, and in order to free themselves from the doubts, complaints, and disputes that might arise between them, and the many troubles that might ensue among their vassals and subjects and the natives of their kingdoms, the said emperor and monarchs, and the said attorneys acting in their names, have covenanted and agreed as to the said doubts and disputes in the following form and manner:

1. First, the said Grand Chancellor, the Bishop of Osma, and the Commander-in-chief of Calatrava, attorneys of the said emperor and sovereign of Castile, declared that they, in his name, and by virtue of their said power of attorney, would sell and in fact did sell from this day and for all time, to the said King of Portugal, for him and all the successors to the crown of his kingdoms, all right, action, dominion, ownership, and possession, or quasi-possession, and all rights of navigation, traffic, and trade in any manner whatsoever, that the said Emperor and King of Castile declares that he holds and could hold howsoever and in whatsoever manner in the said Moluccas, the islands, places, lands, and seas, as will be declared hereafter; this, with the declarations, limitations, conditions, and clauses contained and stated hereunder, for the sum of three hundred and fifty thousand ducats of gold, paid in the current money, of gold or silver, each ducat being valued in Castile at three hundred and seventy-five *maravedis*. The said King of Portugal will give and pay this amount to the said Emperor and King of Castile, and to the persons whom his Majesty may appoint, in the following manner: one hundred and fifty thousand ducats to be paid at Lisbon within the first fifteen or twenty days after this contract, confirmed by the said Emperor and King of Castile, shall have arrived at the city of Lisbon, or wherever the said King of Portugal may be; thirty thousand ducats to be paid in Castile—twenty thousand at Valladolid and ten thousand at Seville, by the twentieth day of the month of May of this present year; seventy thousand ducats to be paid in Castile at the May fair of Medina del Campo of this same year, at the terms of the payments of said fair, and the hundred thousand ducats remaining at the October fair at the said town of Medina del Campo, of this same year, at the terms of the payment of the same—all to be paid over and above the rate of exchange. If necessary, notes will

[22] From this point through art. 14 the translation is from Blair and Robertson, *Philippine Islands*, I. 223-238.

13

be given for the said time; and, if said Emperor and King of Castile wishes to take in exchange the said hundred thousand ducats at the said May fair of this said year in order to avail himself of their use, he shall pay the said King of Portugal exchange at the rate of five or six per cent., the rate which his treasurer, Hernand Alvarez, is accustomed to exact from fair to fair. The aforesaid sale is made by the said Emperor and King of Castile to the said King of Portugal on condition that, at whatever time the said Emperor and King of Castile or his successors should wish to return and should return all of the said three hundred and fifty thousand ducats without any shortage to the said King of Portugal or his successors, the said sale becomes null and void and each one of the said sovereigns shall enjoy the right and authority which he now holds and claims to hold, both as regards the right of possession or quasi-possession, and as regards the proprietorship, howsoever and in whatever manner they belong to him, as if this contract were not made, and in the manner in which they first held possession and claimed to hold it, and this contract shall cause no prejudice or innovation.

2. *Item,* it is covenanted and agreed by the said attorneys, in the names of their said constituents, that, in order to ascertain what islands, places, lands, seas, and their rights and jurisdiction, are sold henceforth and forever by the said Emperor and King of Castile, by this contract under the aforesaid condition, to the said King of Portugal, a line must be determined from pole to pole, that is to say, from north to south, by a semicircle extending northeast by east nineteen degrees from Molucca, to which number of degrees correspond almost seventeen degrees on the equinoctial, amounting to two hundred and ninety-seven and one-half leagues east of the islands of Molucca, allowing seventeen and one-half leagues to an equinoctial degree. In this northeast by east meridian and direction are situated the islands of Las Velas and " Santo Thome, through which the said line and semicircle passes. Since these islands are situated and are distant from Molucca the said distance, more or less, the deputies determine and agree that the said line be drawn at the said two hundred and ninety-seven and one-half leagues to the east, the equivalent of the nineteen degrees northeast by east from the said islands of Molucca, as aforesaid. The said deputies declare that, in order to ascertain where the said line should be drawn, two [model] charts of the same tenor shall be made, conformable to the [model] chart in the India House of Trade at Seville, and by which the fleets, vassals, and subjects of the said Emperor and King of Castile navigate. Within thirty days from the date of this contract two persons shall be appointed by each side to examine the aforesaid chart and make the two copies aforesaid conformable to it. In them the said line shall be drawn in the manner aforesaid; and they shall be signed by the said sovereigns and sealed with their seals, so that each one will keep his own chart; and the said line shall remain fixed henceforth at the point and place so designated. This chart shall also designate the spot in which the said vassals of the said Emperor and King of Castile shall situate and locate Molucca, which during the time of this contract shall be regarded as situated in such place, although in truth it is situated more or less distance eastward from the place that is designated in the said charts. The seventeen degrees eastward shall be drawn from the point where Molucca is situated in said charts. For the good of this contract the said King of

---

" The word *of* is omitted from the translation. *Cf.* Doc. **15,** note 23.

Portugal must have said chart, and in case the aforesaid be not found in the House of Trade of Seville, the said persons appointed by the said sovereigns shall make said charts within one month, signed and sealed as aforesaid. Furthermore navigation charts shall be made by them, in which the said line shall be drawn in the manner aforesaid, so that henceforth the said vassals, natives, and subjects of the said Emperor and King of Castile shall navigate by them; and so that the navigators of either part shall be certain of the location of the said line and of the aforesaid distance of the two hundred and ninety-seven and one-half leagues between the said line and Molucca.

3. It is covenanted and agreed by the said deputies that, whenever the said King of Portugal shall wish to prove his right to the proprietorship of Molucca, and the lands and seas specified in this contract, and although at that time the said Emperor and King of Castile shall not have returned the price abovesaid, nor the said contract be cancelled, it shall be done in the following manner, namely, each one of the said sovereigns shall appoint three astrologers and three pilots or three mariners, who are experts in navigation, who shall assemble at a place on the frontier between the kingdoms, where it shall be agreed that they assemble, within four months of the time when the Emperor and King of Castile, or his successors, shall be notified by the said King of Portugal to appoint a day. There they shall consult, covenant, and agree upon the manner of ascertaining the right of said proprietorship conformable to said treaty and contract made between the said Catholic sovereigns, Don Ferdinand and Doña Isabella, and the said king, Dom John II., of Portugal. In case the said Emperor and King of Castile be judged to have the right of said proprietorship, such sentence shall not be executed nor used until the said Emperor and King of Castile, or his successors, shall first have actually returned all the said three hundred and fifty thousand ducats, which by virtue of this contract shall have been given. If the right of proprietorship be conceded to the said King of Portugal, the said Emperor and King of Castile, or his successors, shall be obliged actually to return the said three hundred and fifty thousand ducats to the said King of Portugal, or his successors, within the first four years ensuing after the date of such sentence.

4. *Item,* it was covenanted and agreed by said deputies, in the names of their said constituents, that, since this contract of sale shall be valid and hold good henceforth from date, if any spices or drugs of any sort whatever be brought to any ports or parts of the kingdoms and seigniories of either of the said constituents, in charge of the vassals, subjects, or natives of the kingdoms of the said Emperor and King of Castile, or by any other persons whomsoever who may not be vassals, subjects, or natives of said kingdoms, then the said Emperor and King of Castile in his kingdoms and seigniories, and the said King of Portugal in his, shall be obliged to order and cause, and they shall order and cause, the said spices or drugs to be deposited securely, without him to whose kingdom they have been brought being so notified to do so by the other side; but they shall be deposited in the name of both, in the power of the person or persons whom each one of the said sovereigns shall have ordered to take charge of said deposit in his lands and seigniories. The said sovereigns shall be obliged to order and cause such deposit to be made in the manner abovesaid, whether the said spices or drugs are found in the possession of those who brought them, or in the power of any other person or persons, in whatsoever regions or districts they shall

have been found. The said emperor and kings shall be obliged to give notification to this effect henceforth throughout all their kingdoms and seigniories so that these instructions may be complied with and no one may plead ignorance of them. The said spices or drugs having been taken to any ports or lands that do not belong to either one of the said sovereigns, provided they are not those of enemies, either one of them by virtue of this contract may require, in the name of both, and without showing any further provision or power of the other to the justice of the kingdoms and seigniories where said drugs or spices happen to be, or to have been found, and they may order them to be deposited, and they shall be deposited. In whatsoever ports said drugs or spices are thus found they will be under embargo and deposited by both until it is known from whose demarcation they were taken. In order to ascertain if the places and lands from which the said spices or drugs are taken and brought fall within the demarcation and limits which by this contract remain to the said King of Castile, and if they contain the said spices or drugs, the said emperor and kings shall despatch two or four ships, an equal number being sent by both. In these an equal number of persons from both sides, sworn to fulfill their obligation, shall sail to those places and lands whence the said spices or drugs were said to have been taken and brought, in order to ascertain and determine within whose demarcation are situated the said lands and places whence the said spices or drugs are said to have been brought. Should it be found that said places and lands are within the demarcation of the said Emperor and King of Castile, that the said spices and drugs exist there in such quantity that they could reasonably be carried away, then the said deposit shall be given up and freely delivered to the said Emperor and King of Castile without his being obliged to pay any costs, expenses, interests, or any other thing. If, on the other hand, it be discovered that said drugs or spices were taken from the districts and lands belonging to the said King of Portugal, the said deposit shall be ceded and delivered in like manner to the said King of Portugal without his being obliged to pay any costs, expenses, interests, nor anything whatsoever. The persons who thus imported said drugs or spices shall be penalized and punished by the said Emperor and King of Castile or by his justices, as violators of peace and faith, according to law. Each one of the aforesaid, the emperor and king of Castile and the king of Portugal, shall be obliged to send as many ships and persons as may be required by the other. As soon as the said spices or drugs shall be deposited and placed under embargo in the manner aforesaid, neither the said Emperor and King of Castile, nor his agents, nor anyone with his favor or consent, shall go or send to the said land or lands whence were taken the said drugs or spices in this manner. All that is set forth in this section about the deposit of the spices or drugs shall not be understood to refer to the spices or drugs which may come to any places whatsoever for the said King of Portugal.

5. *Item*, it is covenanted and agreed that, in all the islands, lands, and seas within the said line, the vessels and people of the said Emperor and King of Castile, or of his subjects, vassals, or natives of his kingdom, or any others (although these latter be not his subjects, vassals, or natives of his kingdoms), shall not, with or without his command, consent, favor, and aid, enter, navigate, barter, traffic, or take on board anything whatsoever that may be in said islands, lands, or seas. Whosoever shall henceforth violate any of the aforesaid provisions, or who shall be found within said line,

shall be seized by any captain, captains, or people of the said King of Portugal, and shall be tried, chastised, and punished by the said captains as privateers and violators of the peace. Should they not be found inside of said line by the said captains or people of the said King of Portugal and should come to any port, land, or seigniory whatsoever of the said Emperor and King of Castile, the said Emperor and King of Castile, by his justices in that place, shall be obliged and bound to take and hold them. In the meantime the warrants and examinations proving their guilt in each of the aforesaid things shall be sent by the said King of Portugal, or by his justices, and they shall be punished and chastised exactly as evil-doers and violators of the peace and faith.

6. *Item,* it is covenanted and agreed by said deputies that the said Emperor and King of Castile shall not personally, or through an agent, send the natives of his kingdoms, his vassals, subjects, or aliens (and although these latter be not natives of his kingdoms, or his vassals or subjects), to the said islands, lands, and seas within said line, nor shall he consent nor give them aid or favor or permit them to go there contrary to the form and determination of this contract. Rather he shall be obliged to forbid, suppress, and prevent it as much as possible. Should the said Emperor and King of Castile, personally or through an agent, send natives of his kingdoms, or his vassals, subjects, or aliens (although these latter be not natives of his kingdoms, or his vassals or subjects), to the said islands, lands, or seas within the said line, or consent to such a thing, giving them aid or favor or permitting them to go contrary to the form and determination of this contract; and should he not forbid, suppress, or prevent it as much as possible, the said agreement of *retrovendendo* becomes null and void; and the said King of Portugal shall no longer be obliged to receive the said sum, nor to sell back the rights and dominion which the said Emperor and King of Castile might have therein, in any manner whatsoever, but which he has sold, renounced, and delivered to the said King of Portugal by virtue of this contract, and by this very act the said sale shall remain complete and valid forever, as if at first it were made without condition and agreement to sell back. However, since it may happen that, when the aforesaid subjects, natives, or vassals of the said Emperor and King of Castile, navigating as aforesaid in the southern seas, should meet with winds so tempestuous or contrary that they would be constrained by necessity to continue their course and navigation within the said line, they shall in such case incur no penalty whatever. On the contrary, when, in such circumstances, they shall come to and anchor at any land included within the said line, pertaining by virtue of this contract to the said King of Portugal, they shall be treated by his subjects, vassals, and inhabitants of said land as the vassals of his brother, as in the same manner the Emperor and King of Castile would command the Portuguese subjects to be treated who should in like manner arrive at ports in his lands of New Spain or in any other of his ports. It is understood, however, that when such necessity ceases they shall immediately set sail and return to their part of the southern seas. Should the aforesaid subjects cross said line through ignorance, it is herein covenanted and agreed that they shall incur on that account no penalty whatsoever, and as long as it is not fully evident that they know themselves to be within the said line, they shall not turn about and go outside of it as is covenanted and agreed in case of entering on account of tempestuous and contrary winds or necessity. But, when such a fact is

quite evident, if it shall be proved that they have entered the line maliciously, they shall be punished and dealt with as those who shall enter the line as aforesaid and as is set forth in this contract. Should the aforesaid discover any islands or lands while navigating within the said line, such islands or lands shall belong freely and actually to the said King of Portugal and his successors, as if they were discovered, found, and taken possession of by his own captains and vassals at such time. It is covenanted and agreed by said deputies that the ships and vessels of the said Emperor and King of Castile and those of his subjects, vassals, and the natives of his kingdoms may navigate and pass through the seas of the said King of Portugal, whence his fleets sail for India, only as much as may be necessary to take a due course toward the Strait of Magellan. And if they violate the abovesaid and sail farther over the said seas of the said King of Portugal than is mentioned above, both the said Emperor and King of Castile, if it is proved that they did it by his order, countenance, aid, or consent, and those sailing in this manner and violating the abovesaid, shall incur the above penalties in the completeness set forth above in this contract.

7. *Item,* it was covenanted and agreed that if any of the subjects of the said Emperor and King of Castile or any others shall henceforth be seized and found within the said limits above declared, they shall be imprisoned by any captain, captains, or subjects whatsoever of the said King of Portugal and shall be tried, chastised, and punished as privateers, violators, and disturbers of the peace by the said captains. Should they not be discovered within the said line, and should afterwards come to any port whatever of the said Emperor and King of Castile, his Majesty and his justices shall be obliged to seize and imprison them until the warrants and testimonies sent by the said King of Portugal, or his justices, shall have been presented. If proved guilty of the aforesaid offenses they shall be punished and chastised to the limit as evil-doers and violators of the faith and peace, and of everything else set forth in this contract in regard to the crossing of said line by any subjects of the said Emperor and King of Castile, or any others by his command, consent, favor, or aid. It is understood that these penalties shall apply from the day when the subjects and people of the said emperor now in and navigating those seas and regions shall be notified. Before such notification they shall not incur said penalties. It is to be understood, however, that the aforesaid refers to the people of the fleets of the said emperor which have until now gone to those parts, and that no others be sent without incurring said penalties from the day of the signing of this contract, and henceforth during the time that the said sale be not cancelled in the aforesaid manner.

8. *Item,* it was covenanted and agreed by the said deputies that the said King of Portugal shall not build nor order built for himself, or any other, any new fortress whatever in Molucca, nor within twenty leagues of it, nor any nearer Molucca than the line which is to be drawn according to this contract. It is covenanted unanimously by the said deputies of both sides that this provision shall take effect, namely, from the time that the said King of Portugal can send there a notification to make no new fortress whatever, that is to say, in the first fleet which shall sail for India from the said kingdom of Portugal after this contract shall have been confirmed and approved by the said constituents and sealed with their seals. There shall be no new work whatsoever undertaken on the fortress which is already built at Molucca.

from the said time henceforth; it shall only be repaired and kept in the same condition in which it may be at the aforesaid time, if the said King of Portugal so desires; to the above he shall swear and promise full compliance.

9. *Item,* it was covenanted and agreed that the fleets which heretofore have been despatched to those regions by the said Emperor and King of Castile be well treated in every way by the said King of Portugal and his people; and that no embargo or obstacle to their navigation or traffic be imposed upon them. If there should be any damage, which is not looked for however, which they shall have received or shall receive from his captains or people, or shall anything have been seized from them, the said King of Portugal shall be obliged to give satisfaction, restore, make good and pay immediately all such damages suffered by the said Emperor and King of Castile and his subjects and fleets; he shall order the offenders to be punished and chastised, and he shall allow the fleets and people of the said Emperor and King of Castile to come and go as they please, freely, without any obstacle whatever.

10. *Item,* it is covenanted that the said Emperor and King of Castile command letters and instructions to be given immediately to his captains and subjects who are in the said islands that they do no more trading henceforth and return at once, provided that they be allowed to bring freely whatever goods they shall have already bartered, traded, and taken on board.

11. *Item,* it is covenanted and agreed that in the instructions and letters relating to this covenant and contract, which are to be given and despatched by the said Emperor and King of Castile, it shall declare that this statement, instruction, and contract as above made is as binding as though it were made and passed in the General Cortes," with the express consent of the deputies " thereof; and to make it valid by his royal and absolute power, which, as king and natural lord, recognizing no temporal superior, he may exercise and shall exercise, abrogate, abolish, repeal, and annul the supplication made by the deputies of the cities and towns of these kingdoms at the cortes held in the city of Toledo in the past year, [one thousand] five hundred and twenty-five, concerning the trade of the said islands and lands, the reply given to it, and any law that was made on this subject in the said cortes or in any others that may conflict with this.

12. *Item,* it is hereby covenanted that the said King of Portugal promises to command manifest, sincere, and summary justice to be executed, because certain subjects of the said Emperor and King of Castile and other aliens of his kingdoms who entered his service complain that their possessions have been seized by the former's India House of Trade " and in his kingdoms, without any regard to the annoyance caused them thereby, because they have entered the service and did serve the said emperor.

13. *Item,* it was covenanted and agreed by the said deputies in the names of their said constituents that the treaties negotiated between the said Catholic sovereigns, Don Ferdinand and Doña Isabella and the King Dom John II., of Portugal, in regard to the demarcation of the ocean sea, shall remain valid and binding *in toto* and in every particular, as is therein contained and declared, excepting those things which are otherwise covenanted and agreed upon in this contract. In case the said Emperor and King of Castile returns

" The editor has ventured to alter the translation in respect to this word.
" The translation has been slightly altered.

the sum which, according to this contract, is to be given in the manner aforesaid, thus cancelling the sale, the said treaties negotiated between the said
Catholic sovereigns, Don Ferdinand and Doña Isabella and the said king Dom
John II., of Portugal, shall remain in full force and power as if this contract
were not made; and the said constituents shall be obliged to comply with it
in every respect, as is therein agreed.

14. *Item*, it is covenanted and agreed by the said deputies that although
the rights and dominion which the said Emperor and King of Castile claims
to possess in the said lands, districts, seas, and islands, and which he sells
to the said King of Portugal in the manner abovesaid are worth more than
[the] half of the just price given, and the said Emperor and King of Castile
has certain definite knowledge, through exact information, of persons who
are experts on the subject, and who have investigated and ascertained definitely, that said rights are of much greater value and worth, more than
[the] half of the just price that the said King of Portugal gives to the said
Emperor and King of Castile, he is pleased to make him a gift of it, as he
does in fact, which from the said day henceforth shall be valid among the
living, of the said excess in value above the half of the just price, however
great that excess may be. This excess in value above the half of the just
price the said Emperor and King of Castile relinquishes for himself and
his successors, and disunites the same from the royal crown of his kingdoms
forever, and delivers it entire to the said King of Portugal, to him and to his
successors and crown of his kingdoms, really and effectually, in the aforesaid manner and during the time of this contract.

15. *Item*, it is covenanted and agreed by the said representatives that whichever of the parties shall violate this contract, or part of it, of himself or
through another, in any way, shape, or manner, premeditated or unpremeditated, he shall, *ipso facto,* lose the right that he holds in any way, shape, or
manner whatsoever. The whole shall be immediately adjudged, given to,
and acquired by the other party, who shall abide by the said contract and
not violate it, and to and by the crown of his realms. He who shall violate
it shall not be cited, heard, or notified further; nor shall it be necessary that
any further sentence be given in respect to that matter, by any judge or
judicator whatsoever, provided that the command, consent, or support of
the party who shall violate it shall have been first investigated and proved.
Furthermore, he who shall violate this contract in any form or manner
whatsoever, in part or in whole, shall pay to the other party, who shall
abide by it, 200,000 ducats of gold, as a penalty and under the name of fine
and interest. This fine they shall incur as often as they shall violate the treaty
in part or in whole, as has been said; and whether this fine be exacted or not,
the contract will, nevertheless, remain secure, valid, and stable forever and
ever, to the advantage of him who shall abide by it, and to the disadvantage
of the party who shall violate it. To this end they have pledged all the possessions, patrimonial and fiscal, of their said constituents, and of the crowns of
their realms, to fulfill and maintain all in the same manner and as completely as is set forth therein.

16. *Item*, it was covenanted and agreed by the said representatives that
the said lords, their constituents, and each one of them, shall solemnly swear
and shall promise on the said oath, that neither they nor their successors
will ever, at any time, violate this contract, in whole or in part, of themselves
or through another, in court or without, in any way, shape, or manner what-

soever, or that may be thought of ; and that never, at any time, of themselves or through another, will they seek release from the said oath from our Very Holy Father, or from any other who may have power to release them. And although his Holiness, or whoever shall have power to release them, shall, without being asked, but *proprio motu,* release them from the said oath, they will not accept it, or ever, at any time, make use of the said release, or help themselves by it, or avail themselves of it, in any manner or way whatsoever, in court or out.

17. *Item,* it was covenanted and agreed by the said representatives, that, for the further corroboration and strengthening of this contract, this contract and adjustment, with all the clauses, conditions, compacts, obligations, and declarations thereof, as and in the manner in which they are set forth therein, be adjudged by sentence of the Pope, and confirmed and approved by his Holiness, by an apostolic bull, with his seal, in which bull of sentence, confirmation, and approval, all this contract will be inserted *verbatim*; and that, in the said sentence, his Holiness supply and consider as supplied, of his certain knowledge and absolute power, all or any defect or formality, which may be required, in fact or in law, to render this contract more secure and valid, in all and every part of it ; and that his Holiness impose sentence of excommunication both upon the principal parties and upon all other persons who shall violate it, and shall not observe it, in whole or in part, in any way, shape, or manner whatsoever. In this sentence of excommunication, he shall declare and ordain that those who shall violate the said contract, in whole or in part, shall incur excommunication *ipso facto,* without any other sentence of excommunication, or declaration thereof, being necessary or required for that purpose ; and that those who violate it cannot be absolved by his Holiness, or by any other person acting by his command, without the consent of the other party concerned, and without his being first cited, notified, and heard in regard to the said absolution. The said representatives, henceforth and forever, and forever and henceforth, acting in the name of their said constituents, entreat his Holiness that he will thus consent to confirm and adjudicate the contract in the form and manner agreed upon and stated in this article. Of this confirmation and approval each one of the parties will be able to obtain a copy of the bull, which the said representatives, acting in the name of their said constituents, shall solicit from his Holiness ; and the latter shall order it to be given to either one of them who shall choose to ask for it, without the other party's requiring it for the preservation and strengthening of his right.

And all the foregoing having thus been covenanted and agreed, as is set forth above, the said representatives, acting in the name of their said constituents, and by virtue of their said powers of attorney, declared before me, the said secretary and notary public, and before the undersigned witnesses, that they approved, commended, and authorized this contract forever and ever, as it is and in its entirety, with all the clauses, declarations, compacts and conventions, penalties, and obligations set forth in it ; and they promised and bound themselves reciprocally, in the name of their said constituents, stipulating and accepting as a formal stipulation, that they will keep, fulfill, and observe it in this manner forever ; and that their said constituents and their successors, and all their vassals, subjects, and natives of their kingdoms, shall keep, observe, and fulfill, now and forever, the said contract and all that is set forth therein, under the penalties and obligations stated therein ;

and that they will not violate it, or consent or permit that it, or any part of it, be violated, directly or indirectly, in court or out, for any cause, pretext, or contingency, which may or can be, premeditated or unpremeditated. The said representatives declared in the name of the said lords, their constituents, that they renounced, as in fact they did renounce, all releases, exceptions, and all juridical remedies, benefits, and ordinary and extraordinary councils which are or may be due or rightfully pertain to the said lords, their constituents, and to each one of them, now and at any future time, to annul, revoke, and break this contract, wholly or in part, or to obstruct the effect of it, and in like manner they renounced all the rights, laws, customs, uses, decisions, and opinions of doctors of the law, which could protect them in any manner; and they renounced specifically the laws and rights which declare that a general renunciation is invalid; and as guarantee that they would keep, observe, and fulfill all this, the said representatives pledged all the patrimonial and fiscal possessions belonging to their said constituents and to the crowns of their realms. For greater security, the said representatives declared that they swore, as in fact they did swear forthwith, before me, the said secretary and notary aforesaid, and the undersigned witnesses, in the presence of God and of Holy Mary and upon the sign of the Cross ✠, and upon the Holy Gospels, which they touched with their right hands, in the name and on the consciences of their said constituents, by virtue of the said powers which they had especially for this purpose, that they, jointly and severally, themselves and their successors, will keep and observe this contract and will cause it to be kept and observed forever and ever, as is set forth therein; and that the said lords, their constituents, and each one of them, will confirm, approve, commend, ratify, and authorize anew this agreement and all that is set forth therein, and each part and parcel of it, and that they will promise, bind themselves, and swear to observe and fulfill it, each one of the parties [promising] to do, observe and fulfill, really and in effect, in good faith and without any deception, evasion, or mental reservation whatsoever, that which concerns, is incumbent upon, and appertains to him; and that neither their said constituents nor any of them will ask for himself or for others, absolution, release, dispensation, or commutation of the said oath, from our Very Holy Father, or from any other person who may have power to give and grant it; and even though he gives it to them *proprio motu* or in any other way whatsoever, they will not make use of it, but rather, in spite of this, they will keep, observe, and fulfill, and will cause to be kept, observed, and fulfilled, all that is set forth in this said contract, with all the clauses, obligations, penalties, and every part and parcel thereof, as they stand, faithfully and truly, really and effectively, and that each one of the said parties will give and deliver to the other the said approval and ratification of this contract, sworn to, and signed by each one of their said constituents, and sealed with his seal, within the term of the first twenty days following the day when it is dated. In testimony and assurance of this, the said representatives authorized this contract in the foregoing form, before me, the aforesaid secretary and notary, and the undersigned witnesses; and they signed it with their names and they requested me, the said secretary and notary, to give them one, and, if they should need them, many instruments written under my public signature and sign. This was made and authorized in the said city of Saragossa on the day, month, and year abovesaid. Witnesses who were present at the authorization of this said contract, and saw it signed by all the said representatives in the register made by me, the said secretary, and saw them take oath in person, by the hand of me, the said secretary: Alonso de Valdés, secretary of the said lord emperor; Augustin de Urbina, chancellor of his Majesty; Geronimo Ranzo, servant of the said lord Chancellor and Count of Gattinara; Fernando Rodriguez and Antonio de Sosa, servants of the said lord ambassador, Antonio d'Azevedo; Alonso de Idiaquez, servant of me, the said secretary. The said witnesses likewise will sign their names in the register made by me the said secretary: Mercurinus, chancellor. Fray García, bishop of Osma. The Chief Knight-Commander. Antonio de Acevedo, *contiño*. Witnesses: Alonso de Valdés, Hieronimo Ranzo, Agustin de Urbina, Antonio de Sousa, Fernando Rodriguez, Alonso de Idiaquez. I, the said secretary and notary, Francisco de los Cobos, was present, together with the said witnesses, at the authorization of this contract and treaty, and at the oath set forth therein, which the said representatives made by my hands, and at the signing of it by them, and by the said witnesses, in the register which remains in my possession; and at the instance of the said ambassador, Antonio d'Azevedo, I have caused this transcript to be made, and for that reason I have made this my sign here, in testimony of the truth, Francisco de los Cobos.

Spanish ratification.

The said instrument and treaty, incorporated above, and every part and parcel of it, having been seen and understood by us, we, being certain and assured of all its contents, commend, confirm, approve, and ratify it, by these presents, and so far as is necessary we execute it anew, and we promise to keep and observe the said instrument and treaty, which thus by our said representatives, and likewise by the said ambassador, representative of the said most serene, very exalted, and very mighty King of Portugal, our brother, was agreed to, authorized, and concerted in our names, and every part and parcel of it, to keep and observe it all, really and in truth, in good faith, without deceit, renouncing all fraud and subterfuge, imposition and mental reservation, and every other form of deception and evasion; and we desire and are content that it shall be observed and fulfilled just as is set forth therein, in the same manner as, and as completely, as if it had been made and adjusted by us. And for the validation, corroboration, and security of the said instrument of sale and treaty, we abolish and abrogate, repeal and annul, all the laws and rights, rescripts, decisions, and opinions of doctors of the law that may be opposed to the validity of the said instrument incorporated above. In particular, we abolish, repeal, and annul any petitions from deputies of the realm that, in the Cortes of Toledo, or in any other cortes whatsoever held by us, they may have presented against our concluding this or any other agreement and treaty with the said Most Serene King, our brother, although they may regard the petition as a kind of contract; and likewise whatever rescripts and articles of the Cortes we may have made, in respect to the said petitions of the deputies of the realm, we, of our absolute royal power, recognizing no superior in temporal affairs, abolish, abrogate, annul, and repeal all and each of them, and deem them as nothing, and we consider as good the said deed of sale, with the said compact of *retrovendendo*, and we confirm and ratify it, from now on forever and ever. And we regard

it as good and profitable for us and for the crown of our realms; and we
desire that it shall be valid, as if it had been made in the Cortes and with
the consent of the deputies of the cities, villages, and towns of our realms.
We thus confirm, ratify, and approve it, for reasons known and profitable to
us and to the crown of our realms; and we consider as repealed, annulled,
and abrogated all and whatsoever ordinances and laws may be contrary to
it. In particular we abolish, repeal, and annul the laws that state and direct
that a general renunciation is not valid. And I, the King, swear before God
and Holy Mary and on the words of the Holy Gospels and on the sign of the
Cross ✠ on which I place my right hand, and we promise for ourselves and
for our successors never to violate or permit to be violated by ourselves or
by another this deed of sale with compact of *retrovendendo,* or any part of
it, directly or indirectly, for any other cause, premeditated or unpremeditated,
under any pretext; nor shall we consent or permit any other person or persons
to violate the said deed and treaty, but rather we will forbid, punish, and
prohibit it, as much as we can, under obligation of the said oath. We will
not ask to be released from the oath as it was executed by my representatives,
nor will we make use of the release although the Pope, or other person who
shall have his power, shall grant it to us *proprio motu,* and although it shall
have clauses abolishing and abrogating all that is said; for we renounce it all
and promise not to make use of it, under obligation of the said oath. And
to secure this our will, and to establish and validate the aforesaid, we order
this our letter of approval, ratification, abrogation, and annulment, signed
by me, the King, and sealed with our seal, to be drawn up and delivered.
Given in the city of Lerida, on the twenty-third day of the month of April,
in the year of the Lord, 1529. I, the King. I, Francisco de los Cobos, secretary of his Imperial Majesty and of their Catholic Majesties, caused it to
be written by his command. Mercurino, chancellor. Fray Garcia, bishop of
Osma. The Chief Knight-Commander.

Portuguese ratification.

This instrument of contract, agreement, and compact of *retrovendendo,*
having been seen by me, and all the conditions and clauses contained therein,
having been, word for word, seen and well understood, I confirm, approve,
and ratify it, and I approve of all and every part of its contents; and I promise
on my royal faith and I swear on the Holy Gospels, on which I place my hands,
that I will fulfill and will observe as good the contents of the said contract,
treaty, and agreement (*i. e.,* such parts of it as it pertains to me to fulfill
and observe), as, and as entirely, as is contained and declared in it, and
without any diminution, and under the penalties, clauses, compacts, and
conditions contained therein; and I promise and swear, for me and for my
heirs and successors, never, at any time, or in any way, of myself, or through
another, to contravene or violate the said contract, agreement, and treaty,
or any of its contents, but rather, I will fulfill and observe them wholly and
completely, and I will cause them to be fulfilled and observed in good faith,
without any evasion, mental reservation, deception, or malice, as is aforesaid;
and to secure this I command this instrument of confirmation, approval, and
ratification to be made, signed by me and sealed with my hanging leaden
seal. Given in the city of Lisbon on the 20th day of June. Pero d'Alcaçova
Carneiro made it. In the year of our Lord Jesus Christ, 1530.

THE KING.

17.

Articles concluded between France and Portugal at Lyons, July 14, 1536.

INTRODUCTION.

As early as 1512 King Ferdinand of Spain complained that the King of Portugal sheltered in his ports French vessels lying in wait for the Spanish ships from the West Indies.[1] A few years later the French corsairs became a terrible plague to both Spanish and Portuguese mariners, who in turn made reprisals on French shipping.[2] When the Emperor and Francis I. renewed war in 1536, they both desired the friendship of Portugal, situated near the pathway of their ocean commerce. Portugal, fearing the overgrown power of the Emperor, needing the good-will of the French in order that her spice-fleet might sail safely to Flanders,[3] and hoping that the French king

---

[1] C. Fernández Duro, *Armada Española* (1895-1903), tom. I., app. 14, pp. 420, 421. Later complaints, which throw light on the meaning of the articles of Lyons, are printed in *Cal. St. Pap., Spain, 1538-1542*, vol. VI., pt. I., p. 294, and in T. Buckingham Smith, *Coleccion de Varios Documentos para la Historia de la Florida* (1857), I. 116, translated in J. P. Baxter, *Memoir of Jacques Cartier* (1906), p. 359.

"I see . . . . no chance for the present of the Portuguese consenting to join their fleet to that of the Emperor, and should the war with France break out . . . . I fear these people will do everything they can to keep neutral, though on the other hand, should the Emperor put some pressure upon them they will hardly dare to decide for the French.

"If a vessel from France happens to meet with bad weather at sea she makes for the coasts of this kingdom, shelters and takes in provisions. The same thing they do as if they were the friends and confederates of Portugal in the lands and territories which this king has on the other side, such as the Terceiras and the island of Madeira, and there prowl about for Spanish vessels returning from the Indies. Should it be known and published that these Portuguese are the friends and allies of the Emperor, the French would not venture on such expeditions." *Cal. St. Pap., Spain, loc. cit.*

In 1541 in a "Statement of what was agreed upon in the Council of the Indies in regard to the fleet to be fitted out to resist that of the French which is said to have set out for the Indies" . . . ., the following passage occurs: "The most important thing to provide for at present, it seems, is that your Majesty ask the Most Serene King of Portugal not to allow the French ships to take shelter in any of the ports of his kingdom or in the Azores; and that if they should enter port they be treated as enemies of your Majesty and his enemies too, since it is well known that for no other purpose can they sail in that sea than to do injury to your Majesty and his Highness; and that with reference to this matter there should, on your Majesty's part, be shown the king of Portugal all the urgency the case demands." J. P. Baxter, *loc. cit.*

[2] For accounts of the French corsairs in the early years of the sixteenth century, see Ch. de La Roncière, *La Marine Française*, III. (1906) 243 ff.; Fernández Duro, *op. cit.*, tom. I., c. 15; Guénin, *Ango et ses Pilotes*; Paul Gaffarel, "Jean Ango" in the *Bulletin* of the Société Normande de Géographie, tom. XI. (1889); G. Marcel, *Les Corsaires Français au XVIe Siècle dans les Antilles* (1902).

[3] *Cal. St. Pap., Spain, 1536-1538*, p. 318. *Cf.* Doc. **15**, introduction, note 8.

would prohibit his subjects from going to Brazil and other Portuguese colonies, inclined toward France.[4]

The negotiations conducted by the Portuguese ambassador in France[5] were advanced by the French admiral, Chabot, a pensionary of Portugal.[6] In Portugal negotiations were probably entrusted to the French ambassador, Honoré de Caix,[7] an agent especially obnoxious to the Emperor.[8]

On July 14, 1536, at Lyons, the temporary residence of the French court,[9] a treaty between France and Portugal was concluded. It provided for the protection of the neutral commerce of Portugal—a neutrality which, according to the Portuguese, the French had violated during the first war between Francis I. and the Emperor[10]—and it permitted the French to bring prizes—and these, for the most part, would be Spanish ships—into the harbors of the King of Portugal. Now, the regions east of the Antilles especially frequented by the French corsairs in wait for the Spanish treasure-ships, were the Azores, Madeira, and the coasts of Portugal. By this treaty the harbors of all these were opened to the French as places from which to pounce upon the enemy or to which to bring the prizes they had made.

The Emperor soon observed the ill effects of this treaty. In February, 1537, he instructed his ambassador to Portugal to represent to John III. the many injuries that the French were inflicting upon the Emperor in all parts of the world, " the principal cause of such damages and injuries at sea being that French vessels are allowed to enter and take shelter in the ports of Portugal ". The ambassador was to request the king to order that no French vessels of any description be allowed to enter the ports of the Azores, or take shelter there.[11]

For some years France remained on amicable terms with Portugal. In 1536, Francis I. charged his officers to punish violators of the treaty and restore what they had taken from the Portuguese; in 1537 and 1538, he ordered members of the Parliament of Normandy to punish infractors of the treaty.[12] In 1537, 1538, and 1539, he forbade his subjects to sail to

---

[4] *Relations des Ambassadeurs Vénitiens* (ed. M. N. Tommaseo), I. (1838) 88, 89, in *Coll. de Docs. Inédits sur l'Histoire de France.*

[5] Luiz de Sousa, *Annaes de El Rei Dom João Terceiro* (pub. by A. Herculano, 1844), pp. 400, 401.

[6] La Roncière, *op. cit.,* III. 291, 292. The Venetian ambassador (*cf.* note 4), writing in 1535 about the Franco-Portuguese negotiations, described the situation succinctly: " L'amiral traite pour la France, l'ambassadeur de Portugal pour son roi; mais les riches présents que celui-ci donne à l'amiral traînent l'affaire en longueur." The Admiral arrived at Lyons on June 2, 1536. *Cal. St. Pap., Spain,* 1536-1538, p. 136.

[7] Two days after the signing of the treaty, Francis I. ordered 1350 livres to be paid to Honoré. *Cat. des Actes de François Ier* (1887, etc.), III. 228.

[8] *Cal. St. Pap., Spain,* 1536-1538, p. 318, and *cf.* Doc. **15**, introduction.

[9] F. Decrue, *Anne, Duc de Montmorency, à la Cour de François Ier* (1885), p. 255.

[10] Guénin, *op. cit.,* p. 192.

[11] *Cal. St. Pap., Spain,* 1536-1538, pp. 314, 315. For Portugal's answer, see *ibid.,* pp. 317, 318, 334, 335. *Cf.* also *ibid.,* p. 374; and above, note 1.

[12] Santarem, *Quadro Elementar,* III. 257-260; Guénin, *op. cit.,* 204.

Brazil, or Guinea, or the lands discovered by the Portuguese.[13] In 1540, however, upon the discovery of Admiral Chabot's dealings with the Portuguese ambassador, this embargo was removed, and the French seamen at once prepared to invade again those regions.[14]

BIBLIOGRAPHY.

Text: MS. A copy of the treaty that was signed by Francis I. and Bayard at Lyons, July 14, 1536, is in the National Archives at Lisbon, Corpo Chronologico, parte 1ª, maço 57, doc. 65.

Text: Printed. The text has never, it is believed, been printed. An abstract, in Portuguese, is in Viscount de Santarem, *Quadro Elementar* (1842-1876), III. 254-256, and a French translation of this abstract is in E. Guénin, *Ango et ses Pilotes* (1901), pp. 201, 202.

References. Guénin, *op. cit.*, pp. 156, 157, 166, 167; Santarem, *op. cit.*, III. lxxxviii ff.

TEXT.[15]

Pera continuar a amizade, aliança, e confederação dantre o Rey Christianisimo e el Rey de Portugal, e pera bem e proveito dos ditos senhores reis e de seus sugeitos seram gardados os artigos que se seguem.

[1.] Primeiramente, que os ditos portos e avras dos ditos princepes fiquaram e seram livres [16] e comuuns a seus sugeitos, e seram suas pesoas, navios, beens, e mercadarias rrecebidas em seguridade, e lhe seram dados mantimentos e tudo o que lhe for necesario, pagaudo rrezoadamente a tudo aquilo que for por seus sugeitos respeitivamente tomado e comprado.

[2.] Item, pera entretimento e liberdade do dito comerçio entre os sugeitos dos ditos senhores reis, os embaixadores do Rey Christianisimo que estam com o senhor Rey de Portugal, depois de feita por elas inquisiçam e tomado as copias [*blank in original*] daram certeficaçam, asinadas de suas mãos e aseladas de seus selos, aos Portugueses, como os navios e mercadarias declaradas na dita certeficaçam pertencem aos ditos Portugueses ou a outros que nam sejam imigos do dito Christianisimo Rey.

[3.] E pera que as ditas certefycações posam ser mais seguramente feitas, o dito senhor Rey de Portugal fara defesas, sob confiscaçam dos corpos e avras, a todos de qualquer estado ou condiçam que sejam, que nam careguem nos ditos seus portos e avras alguma mercadaria que pertença aos Espanhoes e a outros quaes quer sugeitos do emperador, debaixo do nome dos Portugueses e como a eles pertençem.

Sob semelhantes penas sera defeso pelo dito senhor Rey de Portugal a seus sugeitos, que nam metam nem careguem alguuma mercadaria em navios

---

[13] The decree of Dec. 22, 1538, is printed in Guénin, *Ango et ses Pilotes*, pp. 203-205; see also La Roncière, *La Marine Française*, III. 292. This decree was referred to by the Portuguese ambassador to England, when he was urging Elizabeth to prohibit her subjects from sailing to Guinea. *Cal. St. Pap., Foreign, Elizabeth*, 1562, p. 54.

[14] La Roncière, *op. cit.*, III. 297.

[15] The text is from a copy, written on paper, preserved in the Archivo Nacional at Lisbon, Corpo Chronologico, parte 1ª, maço 57, doc. 65.

[16] The words *e seram livres* are repeated in the text.

dEspanhoes e outros imigos do Rey Christianisimo se nam tiver certeficaçam de seus enbaixadores.

[4.] E se for achado alguuma mercadaria que pertença aos imigos del Rey Christianisimo em navios de Portugueses sem a dita certeficacam, tudo sera de boa presa, asy o navio como a mercadaria, ora pertença aos Portugueses ora aos imigos do dito Christianisimo Rey.

[5.] Igualmente, sera de boa presa a mercadaria que pertencer aos Portugueses que for achada nos navyos dos Espanhões e outros imigos do dito Rey Christianisimo, se nam for certeficada per seus enbaixadores pela maneira sobredita.

Que aqueles que tomaren navios e mercadaryas de Portugueses tendo a dita certeficaçam dos embaixadores do dito Christianisimo Rey, tomando os embaixadores do dito Christianisimo Rey verificaçam do caso feyta pelos Portugueses, sejam punidos pela justiça do dito senhor Rey de Portugal como quebrantadores de paz, segundo o caso rrequer.

E se os ditos rroubadores nam forem tomados pelos navios e gentes do dito Rey de Portugal, e levarem seus navios ou mercadarias rroubadas ao senhorio do Christianisimo Rey, o dito senhor Rey lhe mandara fazer a puniçam e justiça, como dito he.

[6.] E igualmente sera feito aos Portugueses que tomarem navios e mercadaria que pertençer aos sugeitos do Christianisimo Rey.

[7.] E por tirar os enganos que poderiam ser feitos por alguuns piratas e rroubadores dos navios e mercadarias Portuguesas, não obstante as certeficações dos ditos embaixadores, escondendoas ou queymandoas ou lance-andoas no mar, podera o dito senhor Rey de Portugal cometer e deputar alguumas pesoas nos portos e avras do dito senhor Rey Christianisimo, e fazer secrestar os ditos navios e mercadaria per autoridade de justiça, onde seram achados, ate que seja conhecido e verificado se levavam certeficaçam expedida pelos ditos embaixadores, os quaes lhe daram pelo treslado de seus rregistos tudo aquilo que se achar que nisso fose feyto.

[8.] E iguaes certeficaçoes acima ditas seram dadas e expedidas pelo embaixador do dito Christianysimo Rey que estaa com el Rey de Ingraterra aos mercadores Portugueses que quiserem caregar na dita terra.

[9.] E por nam impedir o dito comercio entre os ditos Franceses e Portugueses, os portos e avras del Rey de Portugal seram franquos e livres de todas as presas dantre os Franceses e seus inigos nem poderam fazer presas huuns sobre os outros nos ditos portos e avras.

[10.] Mas as presas que forem feitas fora das ditas avras em plano e alto mar por os Franceses sobre seus imigos nam seram impedidas pelo dito senhor Rey de Portugal nem por seus navios nem pelos de seus sugeitos, posto que depois as ditas presas, navios, gentes, e mercadarias fosem levadas aos portos e avras do dito senhor Rey de Portugal, onde poderam fazer e despor delas como dautras presas feytas sobre imigos.

[11.] Hos quaes artiguos e defesas neles nomeadas seram feytas e publicadas nos portos e avras dos ditos senhores Reys, por tal que nenhuum posa pretender causa de inorancia.

E por tal que as ditas publicaçoẽs e defesas sejam rrespeitivamente feitas em França e em Portugal em iguaes tempos, seram declarados os dias em que se faram as ditas publicaçoẽs.

Sera contente o dito senhor Rey Christianisimo de emviar a Flandres huuma pesoa pera fazer e expedir aos Portugueses taes e semelhantes certeficaçoes como asyma he feyto mençam, que se fara em Portugal e Inglaterra, avendo o dito senhor Rey de Portugal salvo conduto suficiente pera a dita pesoa e o tera pera o dito efeito na dita terra de Frandes as suas custas e despesas.

Sera asy mesmo contente o dito Senhor Rey Christianisymo que os juizes ja ordenados sobre o feyto dos rroubos procedam segundo as comisões ja expedidas no lugar e dentro daquele tempo que sera ordenado. Feyta em Lyam a xiiii dias de Julho de 1536.

FRANCISQUO.[17]   BAYARD.[18]

TRANSLATION.[19]

For the continuance of the friendship, alliance, and confederation between the Most Christian King and the King of Portugal, and for the good and advantage of the said lord kings and of their subjects the following articles shall be kept:

1. First, that the said ports and roadsteads of the said princes shall remain and be free and common to their subjects, and their persons, ships, goods, and merchandise shall be received in safety, and they shall be provided with provisions and everything they may require, everything respectively taken and bought by their subjects to be paid for at a reasonable rate.

2. Item, for the fostering and freedom of the said commerce between the subjects of the said lord kings, the ambassadors of the Most Christian King to the lord King of Portugal, after making inquiry and taking the copies [*blank in original*], shall give a certificate signed by their hands and sealed with their seals to the Portuguese, that the ships and merchandise specified in the said certificate belong to the said Portuguese, or to others not enemies of the said Most Christian King.

3. And in order that the said certificates may be given with greater security, the said lord King of Portugal shall make prohibition to all men, of whatever sort or condition they may be, under penalty of confiscation of their persons and goods, forbidding them to lade in his said ports or roadsteads any merchandise belonging to Spaniards, or any other subjects of the Emperor, under the name of Portuguese or seeming to be their property.

The said lord King of Portugal shall prohibit his subjects, under the like penalty, from shipping or embarking merchandise in ships belonging to Spaniards, or other enemies of the Most Christian King, without the certificate of his ambassadors.

4. And should any merchandise belonging to enemies of the Most Christian King be found in Portuguese ships without the said certificate, all shall be lawful prize, both ship and merchandise, whether belonging to the Portuguese, or to the enemies of the said Most Christian King.

5. Likewise, merchandise belonging to the Portuguese which shall be found in Spanish ships, or those of other enemies of the said Most Christian King, uncertified by his ambassadors in the manner aforesaid, shall be lawful prize.

[17] The Portuguese form of the name François.
[18] Gilbert Bayard, seigneur de Lafont, one of the *secrétaires des finances*. *Cf.* Doc. 18, note 4.
[19] The translation is by Miss Amalia Alberti.

Those who shall seize ships or merchandise belonging to the Portuguese having the said certificate of the ambassadors of the said Most Christian King, the said ambassadors having verified the case brought by the Portuguese, justice shall be done upon them by the lord King of Portugal as breakers of the peace, as the case may require.

And should the said robbers not be taken by the ships and forces of the said King of Portugal, and should they bring such stolen ships or merchandise into the dominions of the said Most Christian King, the said lord king shall order them to be brought to justice and punished as aforesaid.

6. And the like shall be done to such Portuguese as shall seize ships or merchandise belonging to the subjects of the Most Christian King.

7. And to avoid the frauds which might be practised by any pirates and robbers of Portuguese ships and merchandise, in spite of the certificates of the said ambassadors, by concealing, burning, or throwing them into the sea, the said lord King of Portugal may commission and depute certain persons in the ports and roadsteads of the said Most Christian King, and cause the said ships and merchandise to be sequestrated by authority of justice, wherever they may be found, until it can be known and ascertained whether they carried certificates granted by the said ambassadors, who shall supply a copy from their registers of everything to be found that has been done in connection therewith.

8. And similar certificates to the abovesaid shall be given and granted by the ambassador of the said Most Christian King to the King of England to Portuguese merchants wishing to embark merchandise in that country.

9. And that the said commerce between the said French and Portuguese may not be impeded, the ports and roadsteads of the King of Portugal shall be closed to and free from all prizes taken from the French by their enemies, nor shall they take prizes from each other in the said ports and roadsteads.

10. But prizes taken outside the said roadsteads, on the high seas, by the French from their enemies shall not be impeded by the said lord King of Portugal nor by his ships, nor by those of his subjects, though the said prizes, ships, men, and merchandise be afterwards brought into the ports and roadsteads of the said lord King of Portugal, where they may do with them and dispose of them as other prizes captured from their enemies.

11. The said articles, and prohibitions therein mentioned, shall be made and proclaimed in the ports and roadsteads of the said lord kings so that no man may be able to plead ignorance.

And in order that the said proclamations and prohibitions may be made respectively in France and Portugal at the same time, dates shall be appointed for the said proclamations.

The said Most Christian King shall be obliged to send some person to Flanders to issue such similar certificates to the Portuguese as those to be issued in Portugal and England, as aforesaid, the said lord King of Portugal having sufficient safe conduct for such person; and he will maintain him for that purpose in the said land of Flanders, at his own cost and expense.

The said Most Christian King shall likewise be obliged to have the judges already appointed in the case of thefts proceed in accordance with the commissions already issued, in the place and within the time which shall be appointed.

Given at Lyons the 14th day of July, 1536.

FRANCIS.   BAYARD.

18.

Treaty concluded between France and Spain, at Crépy-en-Laonnois, September 18, 1544;[1] separate article relating to the Indies, signed by the plenipotentiaries of France on the same day.

INTRODUCTION.

Among the articles considered by the Emperor at the end of November, 1537, in connection with the instructions to his ministers, Cobos and Granvelle, for treating with Montmorency, the grand master of France, the following was included: "Whether some article ought not to be introduced concerning the Indies, to prevent King Francis from undertaking anything in that quarter?"[2] In the truce of Nice (June 18, 1538), which was the fruit of these negotiations, no reference to the Indies, however, appears to have been made.[3]

In July, 1542, the King of France, Francis I., irritated by the Emperor's action in respect to the Milanese, broke the truce of Nice by declaring war against him. Francis had as allies the Turks and some of the minor European powers; the Emperor formed an alliance with Henry VIII. of England. Both the last-named allies invaded France, and the Emperor terrified Paris by his successful siege of Saint-Dizier (July 5–August 25) and his subsequent march toward the capital. While the siege of Saint-Dizier was in progress, Francis made overtures of peace. From August 29, there were frequent conferences, at which France was represented by the Admiral d'Annebaut, Gilbert Bayard, secretary of state, and Erraut de Chemans, keeper of the seals, whose place was soon taken by Charles de Neuilly, master of requests. The Emperor's representatives were his chancellor, Nicolas Perrenot, sieur de Granvelle, Ferrante Gonzaga, viceroy of Sicily, Antoine Perrenot, bishop of Arras, and Alonso de Idiaquez, one of the Emperor's secretaries.[4] At Crépy-

---

[1] This is the date and place as given in the treaty. Some have maintained that it was concluded a day or two earlier at Soissons, or that it was signed as late as Sept. 19. *Cf. Cal. St. Pap., Spain*, 1544, vol. VII., pp. xxvii, 348; Gachard, *Trois Années,* p. 62; Paillard, *L'Invasion Allemande*, pp. 391 ff., 412 ff. The text of the treaty of peace is printed in F. Leonard, *Recueil des Traites* (1693), II. 430 ff., and in J. Dumont, *Corps Diplomatique* (1726-1731), tom. IV., pt. II., pp. 279 ff.

[2] *Cal. St. Pap., Spain*, 1536-1538, p. 407. "Sy se tractara y articulara alguna cosa tocante a las Indias, a fin que el dicho Rey de Francia no emprenda de aqui adelante algo en perjuyzio de Su Magestad." British Museum Add. MSS., 28590, f. 27.

[3] The text of the truce is in Leonard, *op. cit.*, II. 407 ff. For its effect on depredations by the French in the West Indies, see La Roncière, *La Marine Française*, III. 296.

[4] Gachard, *Trois Années*, pp. 54 ff.; Paillard, *L'Invasion Allemande*, pp. 366 ff.

en-Laonnois, on September 18, a treaty of peace was signed, which provided, among other things, for a marriage between the Duc d'Orléans and either a daughter or a niece of the Emperor, with either Flanders and Burgundy, or the Milanese, as dower. A secret treaty included the stipulation that France should aid the Emperor in repressing heresy.[5] On September 18, the French commissioners also signed the separate article relating to the Indies, which is printed below. To understand this article it is to be recalled that the incursions of the French into the western seas had caused immeasurable annoyance to Spain.[6] It was bad enough when the French confined themselves to attacking Spanish treasure-ships and settlements in the West Indies; they became even more obnoxious when they attempted to explore and colonize. Jacques Cartier's third voyage had greatly disturbed the Emperor.[7] The Council of the Indies sent a spy to France to ascertain the equipment and destination of Cartier's fleet. The Emperor despatched a caravel to the region of Newfoundland,[8] and vainly tried to persuade the King of Portugal to join him in preventing the French from settling in those regions.[9]

The article respecting the Indies provided that France would leave the Emperor and Portugal in peaceable possession of the West and East Indies, and would not attempt any discoveries or other enterprises therein; but it reserved to the subjects of France the right to go to these Indies, for trade only. Probably the French were the more ready to make this concession because of their disappointment in the "gold and diamonds" of Canada that Cartier had brought back.[10] However that may be, the article signed by them, and apparently accepted by the Emperor and Prince Philip,[11] was displeasing to the Council of the Indies, the council of state summoned at Valladolid by Prince Philip,[12] and the Royal Council of Castile; although, on the other hand, Fr. Garcia de Loaysa,[13] president of the Council of the Indies,

[5] Paillard, *op. cit.,* p. 414.

[6] For instances of depredations committed by the French in the West Indies prior to 1544. see E. Ducéré, *Histoire Maritime de Bayonne: Les Corsaires* (1895), app. II., pp. 345 ff.; Fernández Duro, *Armada Española* (1895-1903), tom. I., app. 14; La Roncière, *op. cit.,* III. 249 ff.; G. Marcel, *Les Corsaires Français au XVIe Siècle dans les Antilles* (1902).

[7] As is shown by the documents printed in T. Buckingham Smith, *Coleccion de Varios Documentos,* pp. 103-116, and in translation in J. P. Baxter, *Memoir of Jacques Cartier,* pp. 347-359; and in the letter from the Emperor in Häpke, "Der Erste Kolonisationsversuch in Kanada (1541-1543)", in *Hansische Geschichtsblätter,* 1911, Heft 2, pp. 450-451.

[8] J. T. Medina, *Una Expedición Española a la Tierra de los Bacallaos en 1541* (1896).

[9] T. Buckingham Smith, *op. cit.,* pp. 112-114; J. P. Baxter, *Memoir of Jacques Cartier,* pp. 354-356.

[10] La Roncière, *La Marine Française,* III. 326.

[11] A copy of a ratification of the article by Prince Philip is in the Archives of the Indies, Patronato, 2-5-1/26, ramo 1.

[12] Prince Philip's letter to the Emperor, Dec. 14, 1544, *Cal. St. Pap., Spain,* 1544. vol. VII., pp. 479-480.

[13] See Doc. 14, note 8.

believed that "the clause should be accepted with some modifications, and that trade should be permitted "."[14] The objection of the councils was based on the opinion that the contemplated permission to trade would make trouble, because the French would not trade in accordance with regulations. The Council of the Indies urged that in this, as in former treaties, matters pertaining to the Indies should not be mentioned at all. If, however, the French were permitted to trade, they should be held to the laws prohibiting the removal of gold and silver from territory subject to Castile, even in exchange for merchandise, and their homeward-bound ships should be obliged to touch at Cadiz or San Lucar.[15] The King of Portugal also objected to the article, declaring that the French went in armed ships not only for the purpose of trading, but in order to rob with more security.[16] Doubtless on account of the strong opposition, the article, as would appear, was never duly ratified ; and in 1545, in accordance with the Emperor's demand, Francis I. forbade his subjects to go to the oversea possessions of Spain.[17]

BIBLIOGRAPHY.

Text: **MS.** The original of the article relating to the Indies, printed below. it is believed for the first time, is in the Archives of the Ministry of Foreign Affairs in Paris, Mémoires et Documents, Espagne, vol. 306, f. 196.

[14] *Cal. St. Pap., Spain*, 1544, vol. VII., pp. 495-496.
[15] The opinions of the councils are given in a document in the Archives of the Indies, Patronato, 2-5-1/26, ramo 1. The opinion of the Council of the Indies is as follows: " Paresce al Consejo que por algunos inconvinientes que se seguiran de la contractaçion de los Françeses en las Indias, fuera mas servyçio de Su Magestad, que en estas pazes no se tractara en las cosas de las Indias mas que en las pazes y capitulaciones hasta qui hechas, y que se guardara en esto lo que siempre se ha hecho, que los Franceses no fueran a contratar a las Indias, como nunca havian ydo, sin hazer sobresto nuevo asiento, y que esto quedara con la costumbre muy usada, que ha havido desde el tiempo del descubrimiento y publicacion de las Indias, de no passar a ellas Franceses. Pero sy los negocios vinieron a terminos que se sospechava, que aunque con estos reynos hoviera paz, el Rey de Francia y sus subditos molestaran e hizieran daño a las Indias, y que para assentar bien las cosas dellas, no se pudo, o no se puede, dexar de conçeder este capitulo que se ha visto en consejo, en tal caso, por lo que conviene la paz a las Indias, paresçe que se puede sufrir lo tractado en el capitulo con tanto que entienda el Rey de Françia que sus subditos que fueren a contratar a las Indias, han de guardar en todo las leyes y prematicas que ellos mismos y los Ingleses y Portugueses y vassallos de qualquier reyno estraño guardan en estos reynos de Castilla y de Leon, de cuya corona son las Indias, quando vienen a contratar en ellos ; en las quales entre otras cosas se dispone que ningunos mercaderes ny otras personas, estrangeros ny naturales, no puedan sacar de los reynos de Castilla oro ny plata, en pasta ny en moneda ny vellon, aunque lo ayan habido en precio y pago de las mercaderias que a ellos traen, por que si en retorno de sus mercaderias hoviesen de sacar oro o plata, era enriqueçer el reyno de Françia y enpobreçer estos reynos, y sy con esto se pudiese tractar que los navios Françeses a la buelta de las Indias fuesen obligados a tocar en Caliz o en Sanlucar, y manifestar lo que traen ally, escusar seyan algunos inconvinientes que se temen desta contractaçion y ellos no rodeavan mucho en su viage."
[16] Santarem, *Quadro Elementar*, III. 308-309.
[17] La Roncière, *op. cit.*, III. 302, 303.

Translation. A Spanish translation (manuscript) is in the Archives of the
Indies in Seville, Patronato, 2-5-1/26, ramo 1.

References: Contemporary and early writings. Letter from Prince Philip
of Spain to the Emperor, Dec. 14, 1544, in *Calendar of State Papers,
Spain*, 1544, pp. 495-496; T. Buckingham Smith, *Coleccion de Varios
Documentos para la Historia de la Florida*, I. (1857) 103-116, with
translation in J. P. Baxter, *Memoir of Jacques Cartier* (1906), collateral
documents, nos. 13-17, pp. 347-359; Viscount de Santarem, *Quadro
Elementar* (1843-1876), III. 306-309, with translation (not wholly trustworthy) in E. Guénin, *Ango et ses Pilotes* (1901), pp. 232-233.

References: Later writings. Ch. de La Roncière, *Histoire de la Marine
Française*, III. (1906) 293-305, 315-326; R. Häpke, " Der Erste Kolonisationsversuch in Kanada (1541-1543)", in *Hansische Geschichtsblätter*,
1911, Heft 2.   Accounts of the negotiations leading to the treaty of
Crépy, but not referring to the article respecting the Indies, are in
L. P. Gachard, *Trois Années de l'Histoire de Charles-Quint, 1543-1546*
(1865); Ch. Paillard, *L'Invasion Allemande en 1544* (ed. Hérelle, 1884),
pp. 366 ff.; A. Rozet and J.-F. Lembey, *L'Invasion de la France et le
Siège de Saint-Dizier par Charles-Quint en 1544* (1910), ch. 12.

TEXT.[14]

L'article suyvant a este accorde par nous, Claude, sieur d'Annibault, chevalier de l'ordre du Roy Tres Chrestien, mareschal et admyral de France, lieutenant general dudict sieur roy en ses armées en l'absence et soubz l'auctorité de
Messieurs les Daulphin et Duc d'Orleans, Maistre Charles de Nully, conseiller
et maistre des requestes ordinaire de l'hostel dudict sieur roy, et Gilbert
Bayard, sieur de la Fons, aussi conseiller et secretaire d'estat dicelluy sieur
roy et de ses finances, et contrerolleur general de ses guerres, procureurs
et ambassadeurs du Roy Tres Chrestien, en passant le traicté de paix entre
l'Empereur et ledict sieur roy avec tres illustre sieur Don Fernando de
Gonzague, chevalier de l'ordre de la Toison d'Or, prince de Melphete, duc
de Ariano, visroy de Sicille, et lieutenant general de l'armée de l'Empereur,
et Messieur Nicolas Perrenot, chevalier, sieur de Grantvelle, commandeur
de Calamer en l'ordre d'Alcantara, premier conseiller d'estat et garde des
sceaulx de sa Majesté Impériale, procureurs et ambassadeurs dudict sieur
Empereur, au lieu de [*blank*], le XVIII° jour de Septembre, l'an mil cinq
cens quarante quatre.

Et pource que de la part dudict sieur Empereur a esté remonstré que
aucuns subgectz dudict sieur Roy Tres Chrestien s'avancent de armer navires
et bateaulx soubz ombre d'aller descouvrir aux Indes, nonobstant que Sadicte
Majesté Impériale maintient que a luy et au Roy de Portugal, son beaufrère,
appartiennent a bon et juste tiltre selon la division de traictez dentre eulx,
toutes les terres des Yndes, tant en isles que de terre ferme, descouvertes et
a descouvrir, tant par eulx que par le moyen des feurent roys et reynes de
Castille et de Portugal, sans que autre y puisse emprendre, como qu'il soit

---

[14] The following text is taken from the original manuscript, preserved in the archives
of the Ministry of Foreign Affairs in Paris, Mémoires et Documents, Espagne, vol. 306,
f. 196. The editor is indebted to Mr. H. P. Biggar for knowledge of this document.

soubz ceste coulleur de descouvrement se font plusieurs roberies et pilleryes en mer, a esté accordé par ledict sieur Roy Tres Chrestien que doresnavant luy et ses successeurs, roys de France, et ses subgectz, laisseront paisibles lesdicts sieurs Empereur et Roy de Portugal en tout ce qui concerne lesdictes Yndes, descouvertes et a descouvrir, sans directement ou indirectement y faire emprises quelconques, en quelque lieu ou endroict que ce soit, reservant seullement que les subgectz de France pourront aller marchandement en icelles Yndes, descouvertes et qui se descouvriront par lesdicts sieurs Empereur et Roy de Portugal, et que en cas que soubz coulleur de ceste navigacion ilz font aucune violances, soit esdictes Yndes en allant ou retournant, quilz soient chastiez selon et où ilz seront trouvez coulpables.

D'ANNIBAULT.   DE NULLY.   G. BAYARD.

19.

Articles concluded between Spain and Portugal in 1552.

INTRODUCTION.

Near the close of the year 1551, when France and Spain were on the eve of war and Spain was reorganizing the defense of her commerce,[1] the Emperor Charles V., acting through Lope Hurtado de Mendoza, his ambassador at the Portuguese court,[2] endeavored to arrange with the King of Portugal a union of armaments for securing Spanish and Portuguese shipping against the French corsairs.[3] The Emperor had long identified his interest in protecting ocean commerce with that of Portugal;[4] but Portugal had preferred a French to an imperial alliance.[5] The recent capture by the French of richly laden vessels, bound from Lisbon to Flanders,[6] had, however, impressed upon Portugal the necessity of better guarding her ships. Moreover, as was urged, the proposed union of armaments need cause no breach between Portugal and France, since " the corsairs were not a fleet in the pay of the French King but robbers " whom Portugal had a right to punish.[7]

[1] Fernández Duro, *Armada Española*, tom. I., app. 14, p. 438, " Prior y Cónsules de la Universidad al Emperador ", and pp. 440, 441; Navarrete, *Coleccion de Documentos Inéditos para la Historia de España* (1842-1895), L. 265 ff., " Copia del asiento de D. Alvaro de Bazan sobre el armada, Valladolid 14 de Febrero 1550"; *Ordenanzas Reales para la Casa de la Contratacion de Sevilla* (1604), ff. 49-53; *Cal. St. Pap., Spain*, 1550-1552, pp. 27, 364 ff.

[2] *Cf.* Doc. **15**, introduction. Lope Hurtado de Mendoza was first appointed to the Portuguese court in 1527. A few years later he was withdrawn and was reappointed in 1543. Santarem, *Quadro Elementar*, II. 84.

[3] Papers concerning this negotiation are in the Archives at Simancas, Secretaría de Estado, leg. 375.

[4] Thus, in 1531, the Emperor had intervened in favor of the King of Portugal in the latter's dispute with France over the issue of French letters of marque against the Portuguese. E. Guénin, *Ango et ses Pilotes* (1901), ch. 6. The Emperor's instructions on foreign policy sent to Prince Philip in 1548 included an injunction " to keep a good understanding with Portugal, especially in what relates to the Indies, and their defence ". P. de Sandoval, *Historia de la Vida y Hechos del Emperador Carlos V.*, II. (1614) 650; or *Papiers d'État du Cardinal de Granvelle*, III. (1842) 296 (ed. by Ch. Weiss, in *Coll. de Docs. Inédits sur l'Histoire de France*). *Cf.* also in Prince Philip's letter to the Emperor, Sept. 28, 1544, the passage beginning " Your Majesty knows already that I wrote to the King of Portugal requesting him to send his fleet to the Azores, in order to escort the vessels returning from the Indies ". *Cal. St. Pap., Spain*, VII. (1899), 375.

[5] *Cf.* Doc. **17**, introduction.

[6] Ch. Piot, " La Diplomatie concernant les Affaires Maritimes des Pays-Bas vers le Milieu du XVIᵉ Siècle jusqu' à la Trêve de Vaucelles ", in *Bulletin de l'Académie Royale des Sciences*, 2d ser., tom. XL. (Brussels, 1875), p. 847, note 2.

[7] " Paresce que para buscar los corsarios, unos por una parte y otros por otra, se devria conformar, syn embargo del respecto que el señor Rey de Portugal quiere tener a no romper por el presente con Francia, pues que estos corsarios no son armada que anda a sueldo del rey, syno ladrones, que andan a robar a toda ropa, como paresce por el daño que Portugueses han recibido dellos, y justamente el señor Rey de Portugal los puede mandar buscar y seguir para castigallos." Archives of Simancas, Secretaría de Estado, leg. 375, f. 120.

In the convention that was concluded, Portugal agreed to provide a coast-guard, to send vessels to protect the region of the Azores, and to order ships bound for the African islands and mainland and Brazil to sail at fixed seasons, armed and with an armed convoy. Ships bound for the Antilles might accompany these fleets. Spain agreed to guard the straits of Gibraltar and Galicia, and to share with Portugal the defense of the Azores and Cape St. Vincent.

BIBLIOGRAPHY.

Text: MS. No signed manuscript of the articles has been found. A manuscript account of the contents of the articles is in the Archives at Simancas, Secretaria de Estado, leg. 375, f. 102. It corresponds almost precisely to the printed account mentioned below, except that it omits particulars as to the stations of the Portuguese coast-guard.

Text: Printed. An account of the articles is in Fr. d'Andrada, *Chronica do Rey Dom João o III.* (1796), pt. IV., c. 91, pp. 369-372.

References: Contemporary and early writings. For notices relative to the corsairs and the Spanish and Portuguese fleets about 1552, see C. Fernández Duro, *Armada Española* (1895-1903), tom. I., app. 14, pp. 438 ff.; Viscount de Santarem, *Quadro Elementar* (1842-1876), III. 330 ff.

References: Later writings. For diplomatic relations between Portugal and France, see Viscount de Santarem, *op. cit.*, III. xcvi ff. For accounts of the Spanish treasure fleets, see C. Fernández Duro, *La Mar Descrita por los Mareados—Mas Disquisiciones* (1877), " Disquisicion Novena : Galeones y Flotas de Indias " ; and *Naval Tracts of Sir William Monson* (ed. by M. Oppenheim for the Navy Record Society, 1902), vol. II., app. B, " The Spanish Treasure Fleets of the Sixteenth Century ".

TEXT.[1]

El Rey nosso senhor[2] e o Emperador Carlos Quinto, vendo as perdas e danos que seus vassalos recebião dos continuos roubos e insultos dos cossayros, que em todos os tempos e lugares andavaõ sempre vigiando o mar para este effeito, como erão princepes Cristianissimos e zelosissimos do bem de seus reynos, assentaraõ antre sy este anno de 1552, mandarem sair suas armadas ao mar para guarda e defensaõ das suas costas e segurança do comercio de seus vassallos ; e o concerto foy que Sua Alteza mandaria armar vinte navios latinos de vinte e cinco até trinta tonelladas cada hum,[3] que andassem sempre ha vista da terra para guarda da sua costa, de que os tres aviaõ d'estar em Cascaes,[4] coatro na Atougia,[5] coatro em Caminha, [6] coatro em Lagos,[7] dous

---

[1] The text is from Andrada, *Chronica do Rey Dom João o III.*, pt. IV., c. 91, pp. 369-372.
[2] John III., king of Portugal from 1521 to 1557.
[3] For an account of the various kinds of Portuguese ships at this period, see H. Lopes de Mendonça, " Estudos sobre Navios Portuguezes nos Seculos XV. e XVI.", in *Centenario do Descobrimento da America: Memorias da Commissão Portugueza* (Acad. Real. das Sciencias, Lisbon, 1892).
[4] A town 14 miles west of Lisbon.
[5] Near Cape Carvoeiro.
[6] At the mouth of the Minho river, which separates Portugal from Spain.
[7] About twenty miles east of Cape St. Vincent.

em Villa nova," e tres em Cizimbra ou Sinis," qual milhor parecesse, que
erão os lugares a que os navios armados custumavaõ vir, e que tambem os
navios Portugueses e Castelhanos aviaõ de vir demandar forçadamente; e
mandaria mais coatro náos ou galeões para correrem a costa deste reyno mais
ao mar, e ajuntarião a sy cada vez que cumprisse os vinte navios acima
declarados; e afóra estas armadas se ordenaria outra para a costa do reyno
do Algarve de coatro navios de remo, hum navio grosso e tres caravellas,
que tambem ajuntariaõ a sy, cada vez que fosse necessario, os outros navios
latinos que aviaõ de andar continuamente na costa do mesmo reyno, os quais
navios todos mandaria Sua Alteza que no verão e inverno andassem sempre
no mar sem se recolherem a porto algum, senaõ com necessidade, tirando
os de remo, que se recolheriaõ no inverno; e para as Ilhas " se mandariaõ
cada anno, no mes de Abril, dez navios armados, tres náos ou galeoens e
sete caravellas.   Mandaria Sua Alteza que os navios que ouvessem de navegar
para Arguim, Cabo Verde, tratos de Guiné, costa da Malagueta, Mina, Ilha
de São Tomé, e Brasil, fossem e viessem em tres mouções, huma em Janeyro,
outra em Março, em companhia das náos da India, e outra em Setembro; e
que alem dos navios armados de Sua Alteza, que aviaõ de ir naquellas mouções,
se ordenaria que todos os outros navios, ou os mais delles, fossem tambem
armados, e de se navegar por aquellas mouções parecia que se podia esperar
segurança para os que navegassem para aquellas partes, e para as Antilhas,
que tambem se podiaõ aproveitar dellas, e alem disso seria cousa de muyto
proveyto para ajudar a guardar as Ilhas dos Açores, aonde todas aquellas
frotas aviaõ de ir demandar.   O Emperador da sua parte parecia que devia
de mandar guardar o estreyto, conforme has novas que tivesse dos Turcos
e Franceses," porque quanto importava a guarda do estreyto, se conhecia
entaõ claramente do trabalho que dava a toda Christandade estar pejado o
canal de Frandes.   Parecia que devia o Emperador mandar cada anno, no
mes d'Abril, has Ilhas os dez navios redondos," que então se dizia que para
lá se armavaõ em Sevilha, e que deviaõ de ir bem armados, por quanto
importava a segurança daquella paragem, onde se dizia que aviaõ de ir
armadas grossas; e por boa rezão parecia que naõ deixaria de ser assy, porque
em ninhuma outra parte podiaõ ellas fazer tanto proveito para sy, com dano
de todas as outras partes a que pretendessem fazello; e que esta armada
devia andar nas Ilhas até o fim do mes d'Agosto, e ametade della devia andar
todo o anno ao mar do cabo de Saõ Vicente, que era a paragem onde vinhaõ
demandar os navios que vinhaõ das Antilhas e do Perú, e que na costa de
Galiza devia o Emperador de trazer coatro ou cinco navios armados, para
favor daquella costa, e segurança das náos, que de todas aquellas navegaçoes
com alguns tempos contrarios hião demandar os seus portos; e que as navegaçoes dos Castelhanos, Framengos, e Portugueses destas partes para Frandes
fossem cos navios todos juntos, e em duas monções, huma em Abril, e outra
em Setembro; e as navegações de Frandes para estas partes fossem em

---

" Villa Nova de Portinão, east of Lagos.
" Cezimbra is situated on a bay 11 miles W.S.W. of Setubal.
" The Azores.
" In the early part of the year 1552, the Turks, whose sea-power was then at its
height, were preparing to aid the French in maritime operations against the Emperor.
Négociations de la France dans le Levant (1848-1860), II. 175, 177, *et passim* (pub. by
E. Charrière in *Coll. de Docs. Inédits sur l'Histoire de France*).
" For descriptions of the various kinds of Spanish ships of this period, consult
C. Fernández Duro, *Disquisiciones Náuticas* (1876-1881), general index, tom. VI.

outras duas monções, huma em Janeyro, e outra em Junho; e que para se bem
effeituar o que acima fica dito, devia mandar o Emperador dar ordem para
que as urcas, que então estavão reteudas em Frandes, e por este respeito outros
muytos navios de Castella e Portugal, viessem logo na milhor ordem que
ser pudesse; e viessem cada anno aos tempos acima declarados, porque de
navegarem todos juntos e nas moucões acima ditas se seguiria segurança
naõ sómente das mercadorias que elles levassem e trouxessem, mas ainda
das dos outros que navegassem dentro daquelles lemites de hunas partes
para outras; e alem destes proveitos, se seguiriaõ outros muytos grandes aos
estados do Emperador e d'el Rey nosso senhor; e que mandaria Sua Alteza
que os navios das suas armadas e dos seus vassallos dessem favor e ajuda
aos do Emperador, e o Emperador mandaria que os das suas armadas fizessem
o mesmo aos de Sua Alteza, o que se entenderia sómente sendo necessario
para defensaõ de huns e dos outros. O que tudo se aprovou pollo Emperador
e por Sua Alteza, e ficou antre ambos assentado de se cumprir inteyramente.

TRANSLATION.[20]

Our lord, the king, and the Emperor Charles V., in view of the loss and
injury which their vassals were suffering from the continual robberies and
insults of the corsairs, who at all times, and in all places, kept constant watch
at sea for that purpose, and since they were most Christian princes and most
zealous for the good of their kingdoms, agreed together in this year of 1552,
to send their fleets out to sea for the protection and defense of their coasts,
and the security of the commerce of their vassals. The agreement was that
his Highness was to have twenty lateen-rigged vessels equipped, of from
twenty-five to thirty tons each, which were to cruise continually in sight of
land, in order to guard the coast: of which three were to be stationed at
Cascaes, four in the Atouguia, four at Caminha, four at Lagos, two at
Villanova, and three at Cezimbra or Sinis, as should be thought best—these
being the places whither the armed vessels were wont to resort, and to
which the Portuguese and Castilian vessels were forced to put in. He [*i. e.*,
his Highness] was also to send four more ships or galleons to cruise along the
coast of this kingdom, further out to sea, and join with the twenty ships aforesaid whenever it should be advisable. Besides these fleets, another fleet was
also to be prepared for the coast of the kingdom of the Algarve, consisting
of four oared vessels, one large ship, and three caravels, which were also to
unite, whenever it should be necessary, with the other lateen-rigged vessels.
that were to cruise constantly along the coast of that kingdom. His Highness
was to order all those ships to remain constantly at sea, summer and winter,
without putting into any port, unless in case of necessity, excepting the oared
vessels, which were to go in during the winter. Ten armed ships, three
ships or galleons, and seven caravels were to be sent to the Islands every
year in the month of April. His Highness was to order the ships bound for
Arguin, Cape Verde, trade of Guinea, coast of Malagueta, Elmina, Island
of St. Thomas, and Brazil, to come and go during the three monsoons,
[namely], the one in January, the one in March (in company with the ships
from India), and the one in September. Besides the armed ships of his

[20] The translation is by Miss Amalia Alberti.

Highness, which were to sail during those monsoons, orders were to be given that all the other ships, or most of them, were also to be armed ; and by sailing during those monsoons, it was thought that the vessels journeying to those regions might hope for security, as well as those bound for the Antilles, which might also take advantage of the monsoons. In addition to this, it would be of great advantage in helping to guard the islands of the Azores, where all these fleets had to put in. It was thought best for the Emperor, on his side, to order the guarding of the Straits, in accordance with the news that he might have of the Turks and French, the importance of such guarding of the Straits being then clearly apparent from the trouble caused to the whole of Christendom by the channel of Flanders being blocked. It was thought best for the Emperor to send to the Islands, every year, in the month of April, the ten square-rigged ships which, it was said, were to be equipped for that purpose in Seville ; and that they should be well armed, because of the importance of the safety of that region, whither it was reported that great fleets [of the corsairs] were about to sail. There was good reason to believe that such would not fail to be the case, for in no other region could they gain so much profit for themselves or do so much damage to all other parts, as indeed was their intent. [It was thought best] for this fleet to remain off the Islands until the end of the month of August, and that half of it should cruise at sea during the whole year off Cape St. Vincent, since that is the region through which the ships from the Antilles and Peru must pass ; that the Emperor should keep four or five armed ships off the coast of Galicia, for the protection of that coast, and the security of the ships from all the aforesaid routes, which might be driven into its ports by bad weather ; that the voyages of the Castilian, Flemish, and Portuguese from these parts to Flanders should be made by their ships all together, during the two monsoons, [namely], the one in April, and the other in September, and the voyages from Flanders to those parts during the two other monsoons, [namely], the one in January, and the other in June ; that for the good accomplishment of what is set forth above, the Emperor should order the armed fly-boats then retained in Flanders, and for the same reason, many other Castilian and Portuguese ships, to come at once, in the best way possible, and to come every year at the seasons above named, for by voyaging all together during the monsoons, as aforesaid, they would ensure the safety not only of the merchandise which they brought and carried themselves, but also that of others journeying within those limits from one place to another. Besides these benefits, others, many and great, would ensue to the states of the Emperor and of our lord, the king. [It was thought best] for his Highness to order the ships of his fleets, and those of his vassals, to favor and assist those of the Emperor, and for the Emperor to do the like for those of his Highness, this to be understood only in case of necessity for the defense of each other. All of the abovesaid was approved by the Emperor and by his Highness, and the faithful observance thereof was agreed between them.

20.

Truce between France and Spain, concluded at Vaucelles, February 5, 1556; separate article relating to the Indies and Savoy.

The war begun in 1552 between the Emperor Charles V. and Henry II. of France involved several other European powers and also spread to America. The corsairs of Guipúzcoa did much damage to the French fisheries of Newfoundland, Spanish troops were landed on the island, and many ships were captured in the ports and neighboring seas.[1] In Porto Rico and Cuba the French committed depredations; in 1555, Havana was taken and pillaged by the French Protestant, Jacques de Sores.[2]

Through the marriage of his son Philip with Queen Mary, Charles V. hoped to gain England as an ally against France, but the English would not be drawn into a Spanish quarrel. Their interest lay in bringing about a cessation of hostilities and Queen Mary undertook the rôle of mediator. The Pope also desired peace and appointed Cardinal Pole to negotiate it; but Pole had little success.[3] Towards the close of 1555, however, conditions were favorable to a truce. Charles V. had already begun abdicating his various dignities, and wished to transfer to his son a realm at peace. He was also alarmed by the alliance between the King of France and the newly-elected pope, Paul IV. Henry II., on the other hand, feared lest his union with the Pope might drive England into an alliance with Spain. Moreover, both realms were impoverished.[4] Near the end of the year the French commissioners, Admiral Coligny and Sébastien de l'Aubespine, and the Imperial commissioners, Charles de Lalaing and Simon Renard, who were already conferring at the abbey of Vaucelles, near Cambray, were empowered to

---

[1] " Informacion hecha en la villa de San Sebastian, el año de 1555, para acreditar las acciones marineras de los capitanes armadores de Guipúzcoa durante la guerra con Francia ", printed by C. Fernández Duro, *Disquisiciones Náuticas*, VI.: " Arca de Noé " (1881), pp. 355-378; and by E. Ducéré, *Histoire Maritime de Bayonne: Les Corsaires*, pp. 333-344.

[2] Ducéré, *op. cit.*, pp. 347, 348; La Roncière, *La Marine Française*, III. 579-584.

[3] For Pole's part in the negotiations, see P. Friedmann, *Les Dépêches de Giovanni Michiel, Ambassadeur de Venise en Angleterre de 1554 à 1557* (1869), pp. xxxv ff.; and Martin Haile, *Life of Reginald Pole* (1910), espec. chs. 20-22, and 23 to p. 480.

[4] *Papiers d'État du Cardinal de Granvelle*, IV., 556, 557; Romier, *Les Origines Politiques*, I. 488 ff.

conclude a peace or truce.' In addition, Charles de Tisnacq, Philibert de Bruxelles, and Gian Battista Schizzo were appointed to act for the Emperor and Philip. The five years' truce, signed on February 5, 1556, as a result of their deliberations, included the separate article, printed below, relating to the Duke of Savoy, the Emperor's ally, and to the Indies. By this article it was agreed that during the truce the subjects of the King of France should not sail to or trade in the Spanish Indies without special license from King Philip. Against those that acted to the contrary, force might be used without impairing the validity of the truce. This renunciation of trade in the Indies was obtained with great difficulty from the French, who claimed that the trade had been permitted them.' In later treaties with France, *e. g.*, in those of 1559 and 1598, Spain was unable to obtain a similar renunciation, and as late as the middle of the seventeenth century she harked back to this truce as a reason why the French should keep away from Spanish America.' The Spanish contention was of course weak since it rested on an article of a truce that was valid for only a short period.

BIBLIOGRAPHY.

Text: MS. A copy of the separate article on the Indies and Savoy, certified by Josse de Courtewille, secretary of state to Philip II., is in the Archives Nationales at Paris, K. 1643 (D. 6).

Text of the separate article: Printed. F. Léonard, *Recueil des Traites de Paix* (1693), II. 506-507; J. Dumont, *Corps Diplomatique* (1726-1731), tom. IV., pt. III., p. 84; G. Ribier, *Lettres et Mémoires d'Estat* (1666), II. 629-631 (verbal variations from Leonard).

References: Contemporary and early writings. *Papiers d'État du Cardinal de Granvelle* (1841-1852), IV. 541 (ed. by Ch. Weiss, in *Collection de Documents Inédits sur l'Histoire de France*); C. Fernández Duro, *Armada Española* (1895-1903), I. 451.

References: Later writings. Ch. de La Roncière, *Histoire de la Marine Française*, III. (1906) 583, 584. The history of the negotiations preliminary to the truce is given in F. Decrue, *Anne, Duc de Montmorency, sous les Rois Henri II., François II., et Charles IX.* (1889), ch. 8; A. Segre, " La Questione Sabauda e gli Avvenimenti Politici e Militari che prepararono la Tregua di Vaucelles ", in *Memorie della Reale Accad. delle Scienze di Torino*, 2d ser., LV. (1905) 383-451; L. Romier, *Les*

' The powers given to Coligny and l'Aubespine on Dec. 25, 1555, to conclude a peace or truce are printed in J. Du Bouchet, *Preuves de l'Histoire de l'Illustre Maison de Coligny* (1662), pp. 475, 476; Henry II.'s instructions to Coligny, Jan. 25, 1556, are printed in part in J. Delaborde, *Gaspard de Coligny* (1879), I. 606-607.

' Renard wrote to King Philip: " Quant à l'article concernant les Indes, ilz l'ont avec grande difficulté accordé, disans que par cy-devant la navigation marchande leur a esté permise, comme vostre majesté verra." *Papiers d'État du Cardinal de Granvelle*, IV. 541.

' Thomas Le Fèvre du Grand Hamel, *Discours Sommaire de la Navigation* (Rouen, 1650), p. 97.

Origines Politiques des Guerres de Religion (1913, etc.), tom. I., liv. IV.; G. Duruy, *De pactis anno 1556 apud Valcellas Indutiis* (1883). These writers do not, however, refer to negotiations respecting the Indies.

TEXT.[1]

Commil soit que aujourdhuy, date de cestes, ait este traicte tresve marchande et communicative entre messres Charles, conte de Lalaing, baron de Scornetz, chevalier de lordre du thoison dor, lieutenant et capitaine general, et grand bailly de Haynnau, Simon Renard, Charles Tisnacq, Phillibert de Bruxelles, et Jehan Baptista Schicio, senateur et regent de Milan, conseilliers et procureurs de lempereur, et de treshault, tres excellent, et tres puissant prince, Don Philippe, roy dangleterre, de Naples, etc., et messres Gaspar de Coligny, sieur de Chastillon, admiral de France, gouverneur et capitaine general tant en lisle de France quen Picardie, et Sebastien de Laubespine, abbe de Bassefontaine et de Sainct Martin en Ponthoise, conseillier et maistre des requestes du Roy tres Chrestien de France. Iceulx commis dudit seigneur Roy tres Chrestien ont en vertu de leur povoir oultre le contenu en ladite tresve accorde et promis que ledit seigneur Roy de France payera ou fera payer, reallement et de fait, durant ladite tresve et chacune annee dicelle, aux termes cy apres speciffiez, au sieur Duc de Savoye,[2] ou ses procureurs ou entremecteurs ayans quictance de luy, la valeur du revenu annuel du plat pays et deppendans de la ville de Ivree,[10] tel que sera estime et liquide par commis quy seront pour ce nommez et choisiz. Et se fera ledit paiement en la ville de Lyon par marchant particulier quy sera advise, assavoir la moictie au dernier jour de Juillet prochainement venant, et lautre moictie au dernier jour de Janvier suyvant, et consequamment de termes en termes. Dont ledit seigneur donnera mandemens et lettres en forme requise pour seurete et payement de la somme. Et joyra ledit seigneur duc ses pays, subjectz, et serviteurs du benefice de ladite tresve, tout ainsi que les subjectz et pays desdits sieurs Empereur et roys. Et rentreront lesdits subjectz en la joyssance de leurs biens, droictz, et actions, comme lesdits subjectz et serviteurs de leursdites majestez. Et audit sieur duc ne sera mis empeschements en ce quil tient et possede, et se treuvera tenir et posseder, au temps de la date des presentes. Aussy a este expressement convenu et capitule, que jaçoit ladite tresve soit marchande et communicative, sy est ce les subjectz dudit seigneur Roy de France ou aultres par leur adveu ne pourront naviguer, trafficquer, ou negocier aux Indes appertenant audit sieur Roy dangleterre, sans son expres conge et licence. Autrement, faisans le contraire, sera licite user contre eulx dhostilite, demeurant toutte ffois ladite tresve en sa force et vigeur.

[1] The following text is from a copy, certified by Philip II.'s secretary, preserved in the Archives Nationales at Paris, K. 1643 (D. 6).

[2] Emmanuel Philibert, who succeeded to the dukedom in 1553. The question of restoring to the Emperor's ally, the Duke of Savoy, the territories taken from him by France, had been the chief obstacle to an earlier conclusion of the negotiations. The truce was finally arranged on a basis of *uti possidetis*. The duke, bitterly disappointed, rejected the yearly stipend promised him by this article. A. Segre, " La Questione Sabauda ", in *Memorie della Reale Accad. delle Scienze di Torino*, 2d ser., tom. LV. On the importance of the question of Savoy in these negotiations, see also Romier, *Les Origines Politiques*, tom. I., liv. IV., ch. 1.

[10] Ivrea, a town 27 miles N.N.E. of Turin, taken from Savoy by France in 1553.

Moyennant aussy que soubz ceste umbre riens neste face ou commecte au prejudice des subjectz dudit seigneur Roy tres Chrestien quy se treuveront voiaiger par mer, ailleurs a leurs commoditez, et ou bon leur sembleroit, comme du passe. Le marquis Albert de Brandenburg est comprins de la part dudit seigneur Roy tres Chrestien en la presente tresve. Mais pour son esgard a este declaire, que nonobstant la comprehension faicte de luy par ledit seigneur roy, lon entend quelle ne puisse avoir lieu en ce que concerne lempire, sinon apres que ledit marquis qui est au ban dudit lempire se sera reconcilie et remis comme devant ; et sera bon content que la justice et chambre imperialle y pourvoye commil appertiendra par droict et raison. A la charge aussy que cependant dune part ny dautre ne se donnera faveur ny ayde audit marquis, directement ou indirectement, pour emprendre contre les estatz, pays, et royaulmes de leurs Majestez, ny en quelque lieu que ce soit. Oultre la comprehension generalle, en laquelle la Royne Leonore sera inseree en la tresve, sy bon luy semble, aians les depputez de Sa Majeste Imperiale, et du Roy dengleterre son filz fait instance des arreraiges de son dot, et voulu entrer en la vigeur et contenu aux traictez qui font mention de ladite dame, Les depputez dudit seigneur Roy tres Chrestien ont respondu nen avoir aucune charge, et remis le tout a Sa Majeste royalle pour en adviser, ainsy que de raison. Aussy aiant les depputez dudit seigneur Roy tres Chrestien fait semblable instance pour Madame la Duchesse de Parme, ceulx de sadite Majeste Imperiale et dudit seigneur roy son filz ont remis le tout a leurs Majestez, Comme nen aiant aucune charge esperant quelles y auront tel regard que de raison. Tous lesquelz articles et chacun diceulx auront et sortiront effect comme sy distinctement ilz estoient comprins en ladite tresve generalle. En signe dequoy lesdits deputez ont promis et jure lobservation et ratiffication diceulx comme de ladite tresve. Et iceulx signez de leurs seingz. Au lieu de Vaulcelles, le cincqizesme jour de Febvr', lan quinze cens cinc-quante cincq." Ainsy signe, C. de Lalaing, Renard, de Tisnacq, P. de Bruxelles, Giovanni Battista Sichzo, de Coulligny, et S. de Laubespine.

Collationne avecq la lettre originale, escripte en parchemin et signee comme dessus par moy.

COURTEVVILLE."

" The year is reckoned from March 25.

" Comparison of signatures shows that this is Josse (or Joseph) de Courtewille, clerk of the Order of the Golden Fleece and commander in the Order of Calatrava. Philip II. took him to Spain to serve as secretary of state for the affairs of the Low Countries. He died in 1572.

21.*

Treaty between France and Spain, concluded at Cateau-Cambrésis, April 3, 1559. Oral agreement concerning the Indies.

INTRODUCTION.

The truce of Vaucelles was soon broken. Within a year, Henry II. renewed the papal alliance and began hostilities against Spain. In the ensuing war both sides won notable victories, which offset each other. In October, 1558, after preliminary conferences, the kings empowered plenipotentiaries to negotiate the peace, which both monarchs ardently desired.[1] Philip's resources were nearly exhausted. Henry hoped that the return of the Constable Montmorency, who had been held as prisoner, would check the growing power of the Guises. Both sovereigns wished to begin a domestic campaign against Protestantism.[2] In a castle of the Bishop of Cambray, a treaty between France and Spain was signed on April 3, 1559. A treaty between France and England, the ally of Spain, was signed on the day preceding.[3]

The treaty of Cateau-Cambrésis, supplemented in 1598 by the treaty of Vervins, was " the fundamental charter of Europe up to the treaty of Westphalia ". Contemporaries considered it disgraceful to France, which surrendered two hundred towns to Savoy and Spain, and abandoned her pretensions to Italy. Among other things the treaty stipulated the marriage of Philip II. and the daughter of the King of France.

In the course of the negotiations the right of the French to go to the Spanish Indies was discussed repeatedly and at length.[4]

[1] The powers are printed in *Traicté de Paix fait à Chasteau-Cambresis* (1637), pp. 160-165. The French plenipotentiaries were: the Cardinal of Lorraine, the Constable Montmorency, the Marshal Saint-André, Jean de Morvilliers, bishop of Orleans, Claude de l'Aubespine, secretary of state, and later, his brother, Sébastien de l'Aubespine, bishop of Limoges. Spain was represented by the Duke of Alva, William, prince of Orange, Ruy Gomez de Silva, count of Melito, Antoine Perrenot de Granvelle, bishop of Arras, and President Viglius. Bishop Thirlby, the Earl of Arundel, and Nicholas Wotton represented England. The Duke of Savoy and the King of Navarre also sent plenipotentiaries. From the middle of October, 1558, till nearly the end of the following January, negotiations were conducted at Cercamp; afterwards, at Cateau-Cambrésis.

[2] For the causes that made Philip desire peace, see L. P. Gachard, *Relations des Ambassadeurs Vénitiens sur Charles-Quint et Philippe II.* (1855), pp. 314, 315.

[3] The text of the French-Spanish treaty is in F. Leonard, *Recueil des Traitez* (1693), II. 535 ff.; and J. Dumont, *Corps Diplomatique* (1726-1731), tom. V., pt. I., pp. 34 ff.; the text of the French-English treaty is in P. Forbes, *Full View of Public Transactions in the Reign of Q. Elizabeth* (1740-1741), I. 68-81.

[4] *Papiers d'Etat du Cardinal de Granvelle*, V. 285, 286, 546, 564; *Négociations relatives au Règne de François II.*, p. 279; Archives of Simancas, Secretaría de Estado, leg. 518, f. 88.

Philip thought the question of great importance. During the truce, in violation of the separate article,[5] and during the war just passed, the Spanish
islands had been the prey of French corsairs. Villegagnon's colony in Brazil
seemed a new danger to Spain as well as to Portugal.[6] In 1557 the Venetian
ambassador in Spain ascribed the recent rupture between that country and
France partly to the sending of French ships to the Indies " to occupy some
place and obstruct the navigation ".[7] The Council of the Indies advised Philip
to arrange in the negotiations for the punishment of French corsairs and for
the surrender of French pretensions to the Indies.

The Spanish commissioners based their claim to a monopoly of the western
navigation on the bulls of Pope Alexander VI. and Julius II. and on the fact
that Spain alone had borne the labor and expense of discovery. They urged
that Villegagnon should be recalled.[8] The French deputies, arguing that the
sea was common, and making a distinction used by the English merchants
during the Anglo-Portuguese negotiations of 1555, would not agree to exclude
Frenchmen from places discovered by them and not actually subject to the
kings of Portugal or Castile ; but they would consent either that the French
keep away from lands actually possessed by the aforesaid sovereigns, or,
as an alternative, that, as in earlier treaties, the Indies should not be mentioned,
and if Frenchmen were found doing what they should not they might be
chastised. Philip did not approve of the former alternative. The Indies
were, therefore, not mentioned in the treaty, but an oral agreement was
made, apparently to the effect that west of the prime meridian and south of
the Tropic of Cancer might should make right, and violence done by either
party to the other should not be regarded as in contravention of treaties.
Beyond these " lines of amity " treaties should lose their force. Ships captured there were considered good prize.[9] At a later period the Spaniards and

[5] Doc. **20.** Ch. de La Roncière, *La Marine Française*, III. (1906) 584.
[6] *Papiers d'État du Cardinal de Granvelle*, IV. 659.
[7] E. Albèri, *Relazioni degli Ambasciatori Veneti*, sér. I., tom. III. (1853). p. 304.
[8] Letter from the French deputies to the King of France, dated Mar. 13, 1559.
Archives of the Ministry of Foreign Affairs, Correspondance Politique, Espagne, vol.
IX., ff. 168-170.
[9] On Mar. 13, 1559, the Spanish plenipotentiaries at Cateau-Cambrésis wrote to King
Philip as follows : . . . . "Oultres ce, nous avons longuement debatu pour exclure les
Franchois de la navigation des Indes : mais nous ne les avons sceu attraire a ce quilz
voulussent exclure leurs subjectz de la ditte navigation, ny que lon leur donnast mettes ou
limites : du moins quil ne leur fut permis daller aux lieux que si bien ilz sont descouvertz,
toutesfois nobeissent ny au royaulme de Castille ny a celluy de Portugal. Bien consenti-
roient ilz quilz nallassent aux terres possedées par Vôtre Majesté et par le Roy de Portugal, ou que lon demeurast aux termes des traictez passez, quest quil ne sen fist mention, et
que si lon les trouve faisant chose quilz ne doibvent que lon les chastye : alleghans les
argumens ordinaires que la mer soit commune, et nous au contraire nous servant du
fondement de la bulle du pape Alexandre et du pape Julle second, de la sommation que
se fit aux princes Cretiens pour scavoir ceulx que vouldriont contribuer aux frais du
descouvrement, la demarcation que sen fit, et que ce nestoit raison que aultres vinssent
joyr des travaulx et fraiz faictz par aultruy pour descouvrir les dittes Indes. Et que
nous leur voulions bien declarer que silz y venoient, encoires quil fut en paix, que lon

French differed as to the situation of the prime meridian. The former placed it in the Azores; the latter in Ferro, the westernmost of the Canaries.[10] In 1634 Louis XIII. ordered French cartographers to place the prime meridian on their globes and charts at the island of Ferro.[11]

It may be noted that the "lines of amity" recognized by the Spaniards roughly corresponded to what may be described as the Portuguese demarcation line of the bull of 1455, Doc. **1**—the meridian of Cape Non[12]—and the Spanish demarcation line of the bull of May 4, 1493, Doc. **7**.[13]

---

procureroit de les jecter au fond, sans que par ce nous entendissions que lon peust alleguer davoir contrevenu ausdits traictez en ce quilz traictent de la communication et conversation des subjectz de lung sur les pays de laultre. Et finablement, après longue dispute, nous nous sumes arrestéz a ce que nous ferions coucher ung article sur ce point, lequel nous pourrions veoir et regarder si sur icelluy nous scaurions accorder. En quoy nous avons enchargé au docteur portugais qui est icy apres lavoir informé de ce quest passé dy besoigner ceste nuict et demain le matin." . . . Archivo General de Simancas, Secretaria de Estado, tom. 518, f. 88.

The following extract from a letter, apparently written by a member of the Council of the Indies, probably dates from or about the year 1565. It is in the Archives Nationales at Paris, K. 1504, No. 19a (Fonds de Simancas). "Illustre Señor. Quando Su Mag[esta]d en Flandes tomo el ultimo assiento de las pazes con el Rey de Françia, embio a mandar a este consejo le advirtiese si en lo que tocaba a las Yndias avia que tratar cosas que tocasen a su servicio, y el consejo rrespondio que ordinariamente andavan françeses cosarios por la mar aguardando a los navios que venian de las Yndias por hazer alguna presa, o rrobo en ellos, y que estos se debrian castigar como rrobadores, cosarios, y ynquietadores de la paz y amistad de los rreyes. Y asi mesmo que debria asentarse con el Rey de Françia, que se apartase de qualquier pretension que tuviese en tierra de las Yndias, pues Su Mag[esta]d las tenia y poseya con tan justos titulos.

"Y enquanto al primer capitulo se allanaron, y satisfizieron bien, pero enquanto a lo segundo rrespondieron que no tocarian en las tierras que Su Mag[esta]d poseya en las Yndias, pero que en las tierras que Su Mag[esta]d no poseya ni navegar por la mar no se las devia estorvar, ni se consentirian pribar de la mar y cielo.

"Esto es lo que me acuerdo que entonçes se trato y rrespondio en sustançia, pero yo hacer buscar la diçha consulta y rrespuesta y vista advertire a v. m. si en ella oviere otra cosa de alguna ymportançia que se me olbide."

Henry IV., writing on Sept. 20, 1604, to Maximilien de Béthune, remarked apropos of the treaty recently concluded between Spain and England (Doc. **27**): "Je croy qu'ils en useront de part et d'autre, comme ont faict mes sujets et les Espagnols depuis la paix de l'an mil cinq cens cinquante-neuf, que les François ont continué les dicts voyages, jaçoit qu'il n'en soit fait mention par la dicte paix; mais comme les Espagnols les rencontrans par delà la ligne les ont traittez en ennemis, les dicts François leur ont rendu la pareille et pour cela l'on n'a entendu que la dicte paix fut violée." (Le Roi à Béthune, 20 Sept., 1604. Bibl. Nat. 500 Colbert, 348: 590. Printed in P. Laffleur de Kermaingant, *L'Ambassade de France en Angleterre sous Henri IV.: Mission de Christophe de Harlay (1602-1605)* (1895), I. 193, note 1.) See also the letters written by the Queen Regent of France to the King of England in 1610 and 1611, quoted in D. Asseline, *Antiquités de Dieppe*, II. 149 ff., and in E. Guénin, *Ango et ses Pilotes* (1901), p. 269 ff. In a document of the year 1588 (Santarem, *Quadro Elementar*, III. 510, 511) the tropic of Cancer is mentioned in connection with the prime meridian—the two constituting the "lines of amity".

[10] There is an interesting memoir by Richelieu on this question in the Ministry of Foreign Affairs in Paris, Mémoires et Documents, France, 792.

[11] F. A. Isambert *et al.*, *Recueil Général des Anciennes Lois Françaises* (1822-1827), XVI. 409-411.

[12] See Doc. **1**, note 40.

[13] For instances of the use of the demarcation line of the treaty of Tordesillas as the prime meridian, see Doc. **10**, introduction.

BIBLIOGRAPHY.

Text. No statement of the wording of the oral agreement has been found.

References: Contemporary and early writings. *Papiers d'État du Cardinal de Granvelle* (1841-1852), V. 169 ff. (ed. by Ch. Weiss, in *Coll. de Docs. Inédits sur l'Histoire de France*); *Négociations relatives au Règne de François II., tirées du Portefeuille de Sébastien de l'Aubespine, Évêque de Limoges* (ed. by L. Paris in the same collection, 1841), p. 271 ff. Under the title *Traicté de Paix fait á Chasteau-Cambresis* a collection of letters from the French deputies was printed in 1637. This contains nothing about the Indies, but some omitted passages relating to the Indies are preserved in manuscript form in the Ministry of Foreign Affairs, Correspondance Politique, Espagne, vol. IX., ff. 168-170.

References: Later writings. The history of the treaty, but without reference to the question of the Indies, is in F. Decrue, *Anne, Duc de Montmorency, sous les Rois Henri II., François II., et Charles IX.* (1889), ch. 10; A. de Ruble, *Le Traité de Cateau-Cambrésis* (1889).

22.

Treaty between the King of Spain and the Catholic Princes of France, concluded at Joinville on January 16, 1585.[1]

INTRODUCTION.

On June 10, 1584, the Duke of Anjou, brother of Henry III., died, and Henry of Navarre, chief of the Huguenot party, became heir to the French crown. In anticipation of this event, the Duke of Guise, who secretly aspired to the throne, his brother, the duke of Mayenne, and other Catholic nobles, had already proclaimed the old and simple Cardinal of Bourbon as heir presumptive, and revived the Holy League of 1576 to oppose the succession of the King of Navarre. The Duke of Guise had long been in the pay of Philip II. That monarch was now at odds with the ruling family of France because of their dealings with his rebellious subjects in the Netherlands and their befriending of Dom Antonio, prior of Crato, a claimant of the crown of Portugal, which Philip had recently annexed to Spain. Thus a common hostility to the Valois and Protestants brought Philip and the Guises into alliance. Negotiations already begun through the Spanish agents, Juan Moreo and Juan Bautista de Tassis, were continued from the last days of December, 1584, to January 16, 1585, at the château of the Duke of Guise at Joinville on the Marne. On the latter date, a treaty of offensive and defensive alliance was signed by Tassis and Moreo on behalf of Philip II., by the Sieur de Mainville on behalf of the Cardinal of Bourbon, and by the dukes of Guise and Mayenne in their own names and those of their brother, the Cardinal of Guise, and their cousins, the dukes of Aumale and Elbœuf. The treaty was ratified by Philip,[2] and renewed at Rheims by the Duke of Guise on September 2, 1585.[3] Its chief provisions were as follows: the Cardinal of Bourbon should be declared presumptive heir to the throne of France, from which all heretical princes or countenancers of heresy should be excluded, and, if necessary, opposed with arms; the Cardinal of Bourbon should, on his accession, confirm the treaty of Cateau-Cambrésis;[4] in France, only Catholic forms of worship should be permitted, no places should be left in

---

[1] The main text of the treaty is dated Dec. 31, 1584; one of the separate articles, Jan. 1, 1585; the other, Jan. 16, 1585. J. B. de Tassis, one of the negotiators, states with regard to the treaty: "confectum est foedus decima sexta die Januarii, octuagesimi quinti, etiamsi instrumentum Calendis ipsis asserat confectum." *Commentariorum Libri Octo*, p. 446.

[2] *Ibid.*, p. 461; Rübsam, *Johann Baptista von Taxis*, pp. 75, 76.

[3] See below, p. 225.

[4] *Cf.* Doc. 21.

the hands of heretics, those who would not return to the Catholic Church should be exterminated, and the decrees of the Council of Trent should be observed; alliances with the Turks and voyages of the French to the Indies and Azores should cease; the King of Spain should pay the contracting princes 50,000 crowns monthly, for the expenses of the war, and advance other sums, as specified; Cambray and the places in the Netherlands yielded by the heretics to the French should be restored to Spain, and every effort made to prevent the French from trading with or helping the heretics in the Netherlands; all French Catholics might enter the League, but the contracting parties to the treaty might not *separately* admit a foreign Catholic prince, or treat with any prince, including the King of France, to the League's prejudice, or make the treaty public. The dukes of Mercœur and Nevers being absent, a space should be left for them to sign the treaty; the King of Spain, the Cardinal of Bourbon, and the dukes of Mercœur and Nevers should ratify the treaty before the end of the following March. In two important separate articles,[5] the dukes of Guise and Mayenne promised that, on the outbreak of war, they would endeavor to have Dom Antonio delivered up to the King of Spain, on condition that nothing be attempted against his person; and the Cardinal of Bourbon promised that every effort should be made to put all the lands of the King of Navarre situated outside France into possession of the King of Spain.

There were obvious reasons why Philip and the Catholic Leaguers should desire to stop the voyages of the French to the Indies, and to the Azores where the Indian fleets regularly put in. Within the last two and a half years, the Queen-Mother, Catherine de' Medici, to whom Dom Antonio had promised Brazil, had used the naval power of France in an attempt to preserve his authority in the Azores. The French captains who undertook the western voyages and chafed under the commercial restrictions imposed by Spain[6] were mostly Protestants.[7] The far-sighted Huguenot statesmen, Coligny and Duplessis-Mornay, had both planned a French invasion of Philip's western dominions in order to stop at its source the " golden Indian stream " that flowed through the Spanish king's coffers into the hands of the soldiers, agents, and rebels who fought with him against Protestantism. The plan of Duplessis-Mornay, which had been submitted to the King of France a few months before, included an attack upon the treasure fleet; an occupation of the Isthmus of Panama which would give the French command of both oceans and a short route to the Moluccas; and the diverting of the East Indian trade into the hands of the French by employing the route to Suez and

---

[5] Printed in de Tassis, *Commentariorum Libri Octo*, pp. 456-460.

[6] *Cf.* " Plaintes sur les obstacles apportés au commerce maritime des Rouennais par les Espagnols ", Aug. 20, 1584, in E. de Fréville, *Mémoire sur le Commerce Maritime de Rouen* (1857), II. 503-505.

[7] La Roncière, *La Marine Française*, IV. (1910) 31.

thence to the Mediterranean through the territory of their Turkish allies,[8] who had recently proposed to establish at Antwerp, under the Duke of Anjou, a staple for all their European trade in Asiatic commodities, which should be conveyed across France from Marseilles to Bordeaux.[9]

The League was never able to give effect to the article in the treaty of Joinville concerning the Indies. After the death of Henry III., Philip offered in vain to allow the French to trade there on condition that the League should recognize him as protector of France, and agree to the marriage of his daughter (niece of Henry III.) with a French prince, who should become King of France after the death of the Cardinal of Bourbon.[10]

BIBLIOGRAPHY.

Text: MS. No original manuscript of this treaty has been found. Two copies of the French text are in the Bibliothèque Nationale, Fonds Français, 3363, f. 9, and 3974, f. 67. These are similar and in the same hand. The former is printed in part below.

Text: Printed. The French text of the treaty, without the additional articles, is printed in F. Leonard, *Recueil des Traites de Paix* (1693), II. 636-642, and J. Dumont, *Corps Diplomatique* (1726-1731), tom. V., pt. I., pp. 441-443. The Latin text, including the two separate articles, is in *Joannis Baptistae de Tassis Commentariorum de Tumultibus Belgicis sui Temporis Libri Octo*, in C. P. Hoynck van Papendrecht, *Analecta Belgica* (1743), tom. II., pt. II., pp. 446-460.

References: Contemporary and early writings. J. B. de Tassis, *Commentariorum Libri Octo* (etc., as above), tom. II., pt. II., pp. 442-446, 461.

References: Later writings. J. Rübsam, *Johann Baptista von Taxis* (1889), Kap. 3; E. Saulnier, *Le Rôle Politique du Cardinal de Bourbon (Charles X.), 1523-1590* (1912), in *Bibliothèque de l'École des Hautes Études*, fasc. 193.

TEXT.[11]

Traicté faict avec le Roy d'Espagne l'an 1585 par Messieurs les Cardinal de Bourbon et Ducz de Guise et du Mayne en Janvier, 1585, a Janville. Le dict traicté depuis fut renouvellé par le dict sieur Duc de Guise le deuxiesme Septembre, mil V⁰ quatre vingtz cinq, a Reims.[12]

[8] *Mémoires et Correspondance de Duplessis-Mornay* (1824-1825), II. 580 ff., and see La Roncière, *op. cit.*, IV. 201-205.

[9] J.-A. de Thou, *Histoire Universelle* (1734), VIII. 646.

[10] "Que le commerce de la marchandise sera ouvert aux François pour aller aux terres de Perou et autres terres nouvellement conquises par Sa Majesté, et se pourront associer avec les Espagnols ou Portugais, ou naviger à part si bon leur semble." P. V. Palma Cayet, *Chronologie Novenaire*, in Michaud and Poujoulat, *Nouvelle Collection des Mémoires* (1836-1839), 1ʳᵉ sér., tom. XII., pt. I., p. 190. See also J. Nouaillac, *Villeroy* (1909), pp. 170 ff.

[11] The text is taken from a copy in the Bibliothèque Nationale, Fonds Français, 3363, f. 9.

[12] In margin in MS.: "Escript en pappier de la main de . . . , secretaire de Monsieur dumaine." This note is in a hand different from that of the text but like that in which the names of the signatories and the notes at the end of the text are written.

Au nom de Dieu le Createur. A tous ceux qui ces presentes lettres verront, soit notoire comme ainsy soict qu'il ny aict en ce monde rien que oblige daventaige, ny en quoy les rois, princes, et tous Chrestiens soient plus tenuz, qu'a ce qui est du service de Dieu, tuition, deffence, et conservation de sa saincte loy; et que les seectes et heresies de long temps dispersees par la Chrestienté ayent pris tel accroissement que grande partie dicelle sen trouve gastee et infectee, voires sy avant qu'en plusieurs contrees grandes et notables lon est venu jusques a la, que de banir la religion catolique, appostolicque, et Romaine, en faisant tout l'effort possible pour l'extirper et ruyner de fond en comble, et que les chefz et ministres des dictes sectes et heresie ne veillent, jour et nuict, par tous les subtilz couvertz et publicqz moiens quilz peuvent, que a corrompre et gaster de mesme ce quelle a encores, graces a Dieu, dentier et net, et que au lieu qu'entre les princes Chrestiens, les sectaires et hereticques debvroient estre traictez et tenuz comme communs ennemiz; ce neantmoings du costé de la France et d'aulcuns Francoys ilz ayent esté tellement supportez, favorisez, et entretenuz au Pais Bas, qu'ilz nauroient peu estre chastiez, puniz, et reduictz, comme il appartient par tres hault, tres excellent, et tres puissant prince, le Roy Catolicque, leur souverain. Ce que les soubzscritz catolicques de la dicte France disent avoir esté faict en icelle seullement par le mauvais conseil et persuasion de certaines personnes, plus soigneux de leur proffict particullier que de lhonneur de Dieu, du service de leur roy, et du bien de leur patrie; et qu'en cecy lon y continue encores a present plus que jamais par negotiations, promesses, exortations, pour les rendre tousjours plus obstinez et endurciz en leurs pernitieuses intentions, mesmes que au dedans de la France les catolicques se plaignent de veoir limpunité du blaspheme, quilz appellent liberté de conscience, permise entreux, et daultre part, les villes, les forteresses, leurs maisons, et leurs familles, voires les peuples entiers, estre livrez et habandonnez au bon plaisir et domination des hereticques. En quoy, oultre ce que lestat de la dicte France se dissippe par ce moien, encores sont ce aultant d'arcenacqs et magasins dressez pour les hereticques affin d'endommager plus aysement les catolicques, et sestant faict plusieurs et diverses plainctes sur ce particulier a tres hault, tres excellent, et tres puissant prince, le Roy Tres Chrestien, leur souverain, tant aux assemblees des estatz generaulx et particulliers que par les tres humbles requestes, supplications, et remonstrances faictes par plusieurs princes et aultres gens de quallite, lesquelles n'auroient peu obtenir aucune consideration par les artifices de personnes trop soigneuses de leur proffict, comme dit est, et sur le poinct du plus grand denger, que depuis la mort de feu tres excellent prince, monsieur le Duc dAlençon, le prince du sang, qui de tout temps et encores a present est chef des hereticques, se pretendant attribuer le premier degré en la succession de la couronne de France, a par nouveau serment juré et confirmé la protection des dicts hereticques, non obstant ce peril si present,[19] luy ont esté accordées nouvelles investitures pour plusieurs annees des villes quil possede, contre toutte raison, comme si de propos delibere, lon le voulloict conduire ainsy ennemy de la foy quil est a la succession de ceste couronne de France, advenant le deceds sans hoirs masles du Roy Tres Crestien, qui seroict preparer de longue main lentiere ruyne de leglise de Dieu. Et combien quil soict en sa divine main de donner enffens audict sieur Roy Treschrestien, quant il luy plaira, si estre quil n'est moings possible quil puisse deceder sans iceux, et pour lors il seroict trop tard de penser aux remedes des certains dangers que le present estat des affaires menassent, non seullement a la

[19] Leonard, *Recueil des Traitez*, II. 637, reads *pressant*.

France, mais generallement a toutte la Chrestienté, dont lon sapperceoit maintenant a veue doeil. Pour ces cau[s]es, nous, Phillippes, par la grace de Dieu deuxiesme de ce nom, roy de Castille, de Leon, dAragon, Portugal, de Navarre, de Naples, de Seecille, de Jhierusalem, de Majorque, de Sardaigne, des Isles, Indes, et terre ferme de la mer occeane, archiduc d'Autreiche, duc de Bourgongne, de Lottier, de Braban, de Lambourg, de Luxembourg, Gueldres, et de Milan, conte de Hasbourg, de Flandres, d'Artois, de Bourgongne, palatin de Haynault, de Holande, et de Zelande, de Namur, et de Zutphun, prince de Zvanem, marquis du Sainct Empire, seigneur de Frise, de Sallins, de Malignes, des citez, villes, et pais dutrecq, doverissel, et de Groayningin, et dominateur en Asie et Affricque, desirans en tant qu'a nous est subvenir au grand et pressant d'enger de la religion catolicque, et nous, Charles, Cardinal de Bourbon, premier prince du sang de France, legat du Sainct Siege appostolicque au conté d'Avignon, primat de Normandie, archevesque de Rohan, etc., considerans lestroicte obligation que nous avons premierement a Dieu et apres a ce royaume, comme premier prince du sang et legitime heritier de la couronne de France, de prevenir et nous opposer au danger de la religion et a levidante et prochaine ruine de la couronne ; Lois, cardinal de Guise, archevesque et duc de Reims, premier pair de France ; Henry de Lorraine, duc de Guise et de Chevreuse, souverain de Chasteauregnault et des terres d'oultre et decza la Meuse qui en deppendent, prince de Joinville, comte deu, baron de Lamberg, Orgon, et Esgallieres, pair et grand maistre de France, gouverneur et lieutenant general pour le Roy Tres Chrestien en ses pais de Champaigne et Brie ; Charles de Lorraine, duc de Maynne, pair et grand chambellan de France, gouverneur et lieutenant general pour Sa Majesté Tres Chrestienne en ses pais et duché de Bourgongne ; Charles de Lorraine, duc d'Aumalle, pair et grand veneur de France ; Charles de Lorraine, duc delbeuf, aussy pair de France, resentans le debvoir qui nous oblige a la religion catolicque, estans princes Chrestiens et ne pouvans deffaillir aux pais de nostre naissance, comme membres principaulx dicelluy, en ung besoing si grand et remerquable et ou il est question de lhonneur de Dieu, de la conservation de son eglise et salut de son peuple, apres que noz susdictes supplications et remonstrances, tant de fois reyterees, nont peu rien obtenir ; tous unanimement, poussez d'entier zelle de sa gloire et honneur, et invocans pour la bonne issue de ceste entreprise l'intercession de la sacree Vierge mere et de tous les sainctz, avons par ensemble traicté, conclud, et arreste, traictons, conchuons, et arrestons par ces presentes confederation, union, et ligue, offencive et deffencive, perpetuelle et a tousjours, pour nous et noz hoirs, pour la seulle tuition, deffence, et conservation de la religion catolicque, apostolicque, et Romaine, restauration dicelle, et pour lentiere extirpation de touttes sectes et heresies de la France et des Pais Bas, et ce aux charges et conditions qui sensuyvent :

. . . .

Renoncera[14] le dict sieur Cardinal de Bourbon ou ses successeurs, comme font aussy lesdicts princes catolicques, entierement aux ligues et confedera-

---

[14] The Latin text in de Tassis, *Commentariorum Libri Octo*, pp. 450, 451, is as follows : " Renuntiabunt prorsus dictus D. Cardinalis aut ejus successor atque etiam principes foederati amicitiis foederibusque initis atque contractis cum Turca, neque posthac poterunt cum eo ejusque successoribus inire alia foedera aut commercia in praejudicium vel tantillum religionis Christianae, quod similiter se facturum spondet Rex Catholicus. Cessabunt statim omnia latrocinia, pyratica, maritimaeque rapinae, omnesque aliae navigationes illicitae, Indiam Insulasque versus sub ea comprehensas quae sunt dominii Regis Catholici, quae navigationes posthac non sunt permittendae."

tions que la couronne de France a de present avec le Turc, et ne pourront doresnavant en dresser daultres, ou avoir avec icelluy Turc ou ses successeurs aucune corespondance qui puisse tant soict peu prejudicier a la Chrestienté, non plus que ne fera Sa Majesté Catolicque.

Cesseront incontinant touttes pirateries, escumeries de mer, et touttes aultres navigations illicites vers les Indes et Isles comprises soubz icelle apartenans a Sa Majeste Catolicque, sans quelles puissent estre permises de la en avant.

. . . .

Ce traicte fut faict, clos, conclud, et arresté, au chasteau de Joinville, au nom et de la part de Sa Majesté Catolicque, par le sieur Jehan Baptiste de Tassis, chevallier et commandeur de Bien venida, de lordre de Monseigneur Sainct Jacques, conseiller du conseil de guerre et vedor general du camp et armee de Sadicte Majeste Catolicque au Pais Bas, a ce speciallement commis et depute par icelle et assisté de frere Jehan Moreo, chevallier et commandeur dalfosses de lordre de St. Jehan de Jhierusalem, y envoyé a cest effect de par Sadicte Majesté Catolicque, Francoys de Roncherolles, sieur de Mayneville et Hengueville, premier baron de Normandie, conseiller nay en la cour de parlement dudict pais, cappitaine de cinquante hommes darmes soubz la charge de Monsieur le Conte de Soissons, a ce commis et deputte speciallement par le dict sieur Cardinal de Bourbon. Les susdicts Ducz de Guise et de Mayenne, en propres personnes et au nom et de la part desdicts sieurs Cardinal de Guise, Ducz daumalle et delbeuf, le dernier jour de decembre, lan 1584.

> Jo. Ba[u]t[is]ta de Tassis.
> Francois de Rocherolles.
> Henry de Lorraine.
> Charles de Lorraine, duc de Maine.

| Cest escript est de la main de Monsieur de Guise. | tant en nostre nom que nous faisans fortz de Messieurs les Cardinal de Guise et Ducz daumalle et delbeuf. | Nota. Ilz ont laisse espace entre la signature de Monsieur daumalle et la leur pour y mectre 2 signatures, et encores place au bas diceux pour y en mectre 4 ou 5. |

23.

League between France, England, and the United Netherlands against Spain. Accession of the United Netherlands, concluded at the Hague, October 31, 1596.

INTRODUCTION.

In January, 1595, Henry IV., king of Navarre and France, formally declared war against Spain. He appealed to Queen Elizabeth for help, but she responded with demands for the cession of Calais. After Calais had fallen to the Spaniards, Henry sent an embassy to the queen, in April, 1596, to conclude an offensive and defensive alliance, which the United Provinces and other Protestant powers should be invited to join, against the common enemy. Elizabeth appeared reluctant to aid Henry further. She had already spent large sums in support of armies in France and Flanders, was now burdened with the rebellion fostered by Spain in Ireland and with preparations for a naval expedition against Cadiz, and on the eve of the negotiations, she learned of the death of Hawkins and Drake off the coast of America. Nevertheless she yielded to the threat that the King of France, if unaided, would conclude a separate peace with Spain; and the conferences, which had been conducted chiefly by the Duke of Bouillon and the Sieur de Sancy on the part of France and Lord Burghley on the part of England, terminated in the signing at Greenwich of two treaties, one public and the other secret.[1] The public treaty, dated May 14/24, stipulated in articles 1 to 7 that earlier treaties should be confirmed; an offensive and defensive league should be formed against Spain, which all interested princes and states should be invited to join; an army should be raised as soon as possible from the combined forces of the allies to invade the Spanish dominions; neither sovereign was to treat for peace or truce with the King of Spain or his officers without

---

[1] For an account of the negotiations, see the "Discours de la Negotiation de Messieurs de Bouillon et de Sancy en Angleterre, 1596", in G. Du Vair, *Oeuvres* (1625); De Thou, *Histoire Universelle*, tom. XII., liv. 116, pp. 647-661; A. Poirson, *Histoire du Règne de Henri IV.* (1862-1867), tom. II., ch. 7; Motley, *United Netherlands*, III. 450-460; L. A. Prévost-Paradol, *Élisabeth et Henri IV., 1595-1598* (1855); J. B. Black, *Elizabeth and Henry IV.* (1914), pp. 103 ff. Du Vair, a negotiator of the public treaty, says nothing of the private treaty, for which see P. Laffleur de Kermaingant, *L'Ambassade de France: Mission de Jean de Thumery* (1886), pp. 44 ff., or Motley, *loc. cit.* The public treaty is printed in F. Leonard, *Recueil des Traites* (1693), II. 652-655; Dumont, *Corps Diplomatique*, tom. V., pt. I., pp. 525-527. The secret treaty is printed in part in Kermaingant, *op. cit., pièces justificatives*, pp. 256-258.

the other's consent; the truce in Brittany should be extended to England, when renewed; no general truce was to be made with places held by the enemy except with the queen's consent, and particular truces were not to be continued more than two months without consent of both sovereigns.   Articles 8 to 19 provided chiefly that the queen should send 4000 infantry to serve against the Spaniards, but not more than fifty miles from Boulogne; that she should advance their pay for six months; and that if the queen's dominions were invaded and she should ask aid of the French king he should send 4000 infantry to England to serve at her expense not more than fifty miles inland. Articles 20 to 23 stipulated that each sovereign might buy munitions of war and provisions from the other, if mutually convenient; that there should be reciprocal protection of merchants and freedom in trading; and that the King of France and his successors should not permit any subject of the queen to be molested on account of his religion.   Two days later a secret treaty was signed, annulling certain stipulations of the public alliance by providing that the queen should send only 2000 men to France, and advance their pay for only four months, and that she need not spend anything for the invading army of the allies, in spite of the article to the contrary inserted in the public treaty " for the reputation of the league ".

These treaties having been duly confirmed by both sovereigns, negotiations with the States General were conducted at the Hague by the Duke of Bouillon, Buzanval, the regular French ambassador there, and George Gilpin, English councillor in the Council of State of the United Provinces.   The public treaty allured the Dutch to the alliance, in which, for the first time in international affairs, they ranked on an equality with other sovereign powers. The terms of their accession to the league, signed on October 21/31, 1596, were the same as articles 1 to 7 and 20 to 23 of the Franco-English treaty of May 14/24, summarized above.

Before the conclusion of this alliance, as well as after it, the Dutch co-operated with England against the maritime power of Spain.   By the contract concluded between Elizabeth and the States General at the end of 1577,[2] and again in the treaty concluded between the same in 1585,[3] it had been agreed that the Dutch should send ships of war to resist the enemy's fleet in co-operation with English ships under the English admiral.   In June, 1596, the Dutch had gone beyond their treaty obligations in sending a squadron under Admiral Duyvenvoord to join the English in the expedition against Cadiz,[4] the staple town for all the American and Eastern trade.   To save the outward-bound American fleet from falling into the hands of the allies,

---

[2] Printed in Dumont, *op. cit.*, tom. V., pt. I., p. 315.
[3] Printed in Dumont, *ibid.*, pp. 454, 455.
[4] For the Cadiz expedition, see *Cal. St. Pap., Dom.*, 1595-1597, especially pp. 231-235, 255-258, 271-273, 290; Oppenheim's edition of Monson, *Naval Tracts*, I. 344-395, II. 1-20; J. S. Corbett, *Successors of Drake* (1900), ch. 3.

the Spaniards had burned all the ships and cargo, losing, it was estimated, 12,000,000 ducats, and "completely dislocating the American trade". In 1597, after the Dutch had bound themselves by the triple alliance to offensive action, they contributed another squadron, also under Duyvenvoord, which accompanied Essex on the unfortunate Islands voyage,[5] projected for the purpose of destroying the Adelantado's fleet, intercepting the homeward-bound American fleet, and occupying the Azores.

The triple alliance was of short duration, for Henry, in spite of his promise and contrary to the wishes of his allies, made peace with Philip at Vervins, on May 2, 1598.[6] In these negotiations, as in the Franco-Spanish negotiations at Cateau-Cambrésis,[7] the question of the Indian trade was discussed; but Henry did not succeed in obtaining any further concessions from Spain.[8]

BIBLIOGRAPHY.

Text: **MS.** The original of the ratification by the States General is in the London Public Record Office, T. R., Diplomatic Documents, no. 1175. It is in bad condition, but the parts which are illegible can be supplied from a good copy in B. M., Add. MSS., 19876.

Text: **Printed.** J. Dumont, *Corps Diplomatique* (1726-1731), tom. V., pt. I., pp. 531-537 (Dutch and French translation); P. Bor, *Nederlandsche Oorlogen* (1679-1684), IV. 262-265.

Translation. *A General Collection of Treatys* (1732), II. 97-102.

References: Contemporary and early writings. J. A. de Thou, *Histoire Universelle* (1734), tom. XII., liv. 116, pp. 663-671; P. Bor, *Nederlandsche Oorlogen* (1679-1684), vol. IV., bk. XXXIII., pp. 257-267.

References: Later writings. R. Fruin, *Tien Jaren uit den Tachtigjarigen Oorlog, 1588-1598* (5th ed., 1899), ch. 16; J. L. Motley, *United Netherlands* (1904), III. 450-465; *Naval Tracts of Sir William Monson*, I. 362 ff., II. 1-20, "The Cadiz Voyage", II. 21-83, "The Islands Voyage", ed. by M. Oppenheim in *Publications* of the Navy Records Society, XXII., XXIII. (1902); P. J. Blok, *Geschiedenis van het Nederlandsche Volk* (2d ed., 1912-1915), II. 294 ff., or, in English translation, *History of the People of the Netherlands* (1898-1912), vol. III., ch. 8.

[5] For the Islands voyage, see *Cal. St. Pap., Dom.*, 1595-1597, pp. 437-438, instructions, pp. 439-441, *et passim*; Oppenheim's edition of Monson, *Naval Tracts*, II. 21-83; Corbett, *op. cit.*, chs. 7, 8.

[6] The text is in Dumont, *op. cit.*, tom. V., pt. I., pp. 561-573.

[7] Doc. 21.

[8] [Anno 1600.] "Il [le Roy] me parla particulièrement de quelque plainte qu'on faisoit des recherches contre ceux qui avoient pris quelques Espagnols aus Indes, et me dict que ne devions pas favoriser lesdits Espagnols; et puisqu'ils ne vouloient pas permettre que l'on traictast aux Indes, Brésil, et autres lieux au delà de la ligne, et qu'au traicté de paix dernier il n'y avoit peu rien gaigner, qu'il n'entendoit pas qu'on fist recherche aucune de ce qui avoit esté exécuté par nos gens ausdits lieux; et puisqu'ils prenoient nos vaisseaux quand ils les y trouvoient, qu'ainsi on leur debvoit rendre la pareille." *Mémoires de Claude Groulart*, in Michaud and Poujoulat, *Nouvelle Collection des Mémoires*, 1re sér., tom. XI., p. 585.

TEXT.[*]

Comme ainsi soit que pour resister aux entreprinses et desseins ambitieux du Roy d'Espaigne contre tous les princes et potentats de la Chrestienté, le Treschrestien Roy de France et la Serenissime Royne d'Angleterre ayent conclud, accordé, et juré entre eulx une ligue offensive et defensive, pour la conservation de leurs personnes, royaumes, pays et subjects, contre les invasions dudit Roy d'Espaigne, leur ennemy commun, ses royaulmes, estats, pays, et subjects, et qu'a ceste occasion leursdites majestez ayent advisé et resolu d'associer en ceste confederation leurs treschers et bons amys, Messieurs les Estatz Generaulx des Provinces Unies du Pays Bas, comme ceulx qui ont aultant ou plus d'interest que nuls aultres princes, ou estatz souverains, et pour cest effect commis et envoyé leurs deputez pardevers eulx. A ces causes, nous, Henry de la Tour, duc de Bouillon, viconte de Turenne, mareschal de France, assisté du Seigneur de Buzanval, gentilhomme ordinaire de la chambre dudit Sieur Roy, et son ambassadeur ordinaire esdites Provinces Unies des Pays Bas, et nous, Georges Gilpin, conseiller introduit de la part de ladite Serenissime Royne d'Angleterre au Conseil d'Estat desdites Provinces Unies, authorisez de la part de leursdites Majestez par lettres de creance qui seront inserées a la fin du present traicté, d'une part, et nous les Estatz Generaulx desdites Provinces Unies du Pays Bas d'aultrepart, avons faict et faisons entre nous esdits noms les accords, traicté, et conventions qui ensuivent; cest ascavoir, nous, Duc de Bouillon, assisté dudit Sieur de Buzanval, et en vertu du pouvoir a nous donné par ledit Sieur Roy, qui sera aussi inseré a la fin de ce present traicté, et nous, George Gilpin, authorisé comme dessus, avons receu et associe, recevons et associons par ce present traicté, pour et au nom dudit sieur Roy Treschristien et de ladite Serenissime Royne d'Angleterre et leurs successeurs ausdits royaulmes, iceulx Estatz Generaulx desdites Provinces Unies du Paysbas, ascavoir de Gueldres avecq Zutphen, Hollande avecq Westfrize, Zelande, Utrecht, Frize, Overyssel, Groeningen et Ommelanden, avecq tous les membres, villes, et habitans d'icelles, et les nobles, villes, et forteresses du Pays de Brabant et Flandres, qui sont a present unis avecq lesdits Estatz Generaulx, et les Pays de Drenthe, ensemble les provinces, nobles, membres, et villes de Brabant, Luxembourg, Flandres, Artois, Haynault, et aultres provinces dudit Paysbas, qui se joindront et reuniront au corps desdits Estatz Generaulx dedans deux ans, a compter du jour et date des presentes, en ladite ligue offensive et defensive contre ledit Roy d'Espaigne, leur ennemi commun, ses royaumes, estats, pays, et subjects, avecq toutes leurs Souverainetez, droicts, privileges, et franchises, et ce aux clauses et conditions dudit traitté faict entre lesdits sieur Roy et Royne, duquel la teneur ensuit:

.   .   .   .

[2.] Erit confoederatio haec offensiva et defensiva inter dictos regem et reginam eorumque regna, status, dominia, etc., contra Regem Hispaniarum et regna et dominia ejus.

[3.] Ad hoc foedus a praefatis principibus contrahentibus invitabuntur et intrare in idem poterunt omnes alii principes et status, quorum interest

[*] This text is taken from the original manuscript of the ratification by the States General except where that is illegible, when a copy in the British Museum, Add. MSS., 19876, has been used.

sibimet ipsis praecavere ab ambitiosis machinationibus et invasionibus quas Rex Hispaniarum molitur contra omnes vicinos suos, et ad hunc effectum mittentur nuncii seu legati a praefatis rege et regina ad tot principes et status, quot dicti confoederati censuri sunt idoneos ad eos permovendos ut intrent in eandem confoederationem.

[4.] Quanto citius commode fieri poterit et negotia praefatorum regis et reginae id permittent, conscribetur unus exercitus de communibus copiis, tam praefatorum regis quam reginae ac aliorum principum et statuum qui intraturi sunt in hanc confoederationem, ad invadendum Regem Hispaniarum et dominia quaecunque sua.

. . . .

Laquelle ligue, nous, lesditz Estatz Generaulx desdites Provinces Unies du Pays bas cy dessus nommez, apres avoir indurement sur icelle deliberé en nostre assemblée avecq le hault et tresillustre seigneur, Maurice, né prince d'Oranges, comte de Nassau, marcquis de la Vere et Vlissingues, gouverneur et capitaine general de Gueldres avecq Zutphen, Hollande avecq Westfrize, Zelande, Utrecht, Overyssel, et des villes et forteresses de Brabant et Flandres, admiral general, ensemble avecq le Conseil d'Estat desdites Provinces Unies, et trouvé icelle ligue et confederation estre treshonnorable, utile, et necessaire pour la conservation desdites Provinces contre l'ambition dudit Roy d'Espagne, avons icelle ditte ligue avecq tous et chacuns les articles et conventions y contenues, accepté, et acceptons par ces presentes, moyennant lesquelles leursdites Majestés, leurs successeurs ausdits royaulmes, et lesdits Estatz Generaulx desdites Provinces Unies seront et demeureront respectivement tenuz et obligez a l'entretenement et observation de tous et chascun les points et articles contenuz audit traitte de ligue, promettans nous, Duc de Bouillon, assisté dudit Sieur de Buzanval, et en vertu de nostre dit pouvoir, de fournir et delivrer dedans six mois prochainement venants, ou plustost si faire se peult, ausdits Estats Generaulx lettres de ratification dudit traitte contenu cy dessus, dudit sieur Roy Treschrestien, pour luy et ses successeurs, en bonne et deue forme ; comme pareillement nous, Georges Gilpin, authorisé comme dessus, avons promis et promettons de procurer que ladite Serenissime Royne d'Angleterre leur fournisse et delivre ses lettres de ratification, aussi en bonne et deue forme et dedans ledit temps de six mois, ou plustost si faire se peut, pendant lequel temps sera neantmoins ledit traitte executé et accompli par lesdits sieur roy, royne, et lesdits Estats Generaulx, en tous et chascuns ses poincts et articles, selon la forme et teneur, pour la conservation de leursdits royaulmes, pays, et estats, ensemble des estats, pays, et subjects de tous roys et royaulmes, princes, electeurs du Sainct Empire, seigneuries, et republiques qui entreront et seront receus en icelle ligue.

[Here follow the Duke of Bouillon's credentials from the King of France, dated August 16, 1596; George Gilpin's credentials from the Queen of England, dated September 11, 1596, and the powers granted by the King of France to the Duke of Bouillon, " assisted by Buzanval ", dated July 9, 1596.]

En foy dequoy, nous, lesdits Duc de Bouillon, de Buzanval, et ledit Georges Gilpin, authorisez ainsique dessus, avons signé le present traitté de nos mains et a icelluy apposé le seel de nos armes, et nous, lesdits Estatz Generaulx desdites Provinces Unies du Paysbas, avons faict appendre a icelluy le grand seel desdits Estatz et signer par nostre greffier. Faict a la Haye en Holland l'an de grace mil cincq cens quatre vingt seize, le trentuniesme et dernier jour du mois d'Octobre.

Henry de la Tour, Paul de Choart Buzanval, Geo. Gilpin.

Par ordonnance desditz Seigneurs Estatz Generaulx.

C. Aerssenz.

Translation of Articles.

2. This league between the said king and queen, their kingdoms, states, dominions, etc., shall be offensive and defensive against the King of Spain and his kingdoms and dominions.

3. All other princes and states whose interest it is to take precautions with them against the ambitious plans and attacks that the King of Spain is preparing against all his neighbors, shall be invited by the aforesaid contracting princes to join this league, and shall be able to enter into it. To bring this about, envoys or ambassadors shall be sent by the aforesaid king and queen to as many princes and states as the said allies shall think fit, in order to persuade them to enter the said league.

4. As quickly as can be conveniently done, and as the affairs of the aforesaid king and queen allow, one army shall be formed from the combined forces, both of the aforesaid king and queen and of the other princes and states that shall enter this league, in order to attack the King of Spain and all his dominions.

24.*

* *Cession of the Netherlands by Philip II. of Spain to his daughter, Isabella-Clara-Eugenia, on condition of her marriage with the Archduke Albert. Madrid, May 6, 1598.*

INTRODUCTION.

On May 6, 1598, Philip II., the dying king of Spain, signed two acts, a public and a private, conditionally ceding to his daughter Isabella, in anticipation of her marriage to the Archduke Albert of Austria, the old Burgundian dominions—the seventeen provinces of the Netherlands, and the counties of Burgundy and Charolais. The public act—part of which is printed below—regulated the mode of succession to the principality; provided that in default of descendants from the "Archdukes" the territory should revert to the Spanish crown; that the principality should not be infeoffed or alienated without the consent of Spain; that a female ruler should marry the King of Spain, his son, or some one acceptable to the king, and that marriages of children of rulers should also be acceptable to the king; that future rulers must take an oath to hold to the Catholic faith; and that neither the rulers nor their subjects should trade in the East or West Indies. The private act [1] stipulated that Spain should, at its discretion, keep Antwerp, Ghent, and some other strong places in the southern provinces, regulating and paying for their defense; and that the archdukes and their successors should persecute heretics and retain none but Catholics in their household or service.

By thus establishing a quasi-independent government in the Netherlands, Philip II. had hoped to induce the rebellious northern provinces to reunite with the southern.[2] In August, 1598, the government at Brussels wrote to the States General at the Hague, urging them to reunion.[3] Toward the end of 1598, the new King of Spain, Philip III., attempted to coerce the Dutch by closing to them the very profitable trade with Spain and Portugal; and about the same time the archdukes also prohibited commerce with the rebels.[4] But the Dutch would be neither persuaded nor coerced into submission. In March, 1599, they responded to the overtures of the Brussels government by pointing out the disadvantageous character of the terms of Philip's cession,

---

[1] The private act is in Brants, *Ordonnances des Pays-bas, Règne d'Albert et Isabelle*, I. 12-13, and in Navarrete, *Col. de Docs. para la Hist. de España*, XLII. 222-225.
[2] L. P. Gachard, *Documents Inédits concernant l'Histoire de la Belgique* (1833-1835), I. 378.
[3] Gachard, *Actes des États Généraux de 1600*, pp. xxxiii ff.
[4] Gachard, *ibid.*, pp. lxxii-lxxiv.

and in particular of the article that shut out the Netherlanders from the American and East Indian trade.[5] To the commercial restrictions they replied by prohibiting all trade with Spain and the Belgian provinces;[6] by equipping a fleet to act against the Spanish armada, the treasure-ships, and the coasts of Spain and America; and by organizing that direct trade with the East Indies and America which was soon to give them the pre-eminence in wealth that Spain and Portugal were unable to retain.[7]

BIBLIOGRAPHY.

Text: MS. A contemporary copy is in the Register of the States of Hainaut, in the State Archives at Mons, États de Hainaut: Inaugurations et Serments des Princes, Obsèques, 1549-1717, no. 660, I., p. 53.
Text: Printed. French. V. Brants, *Recueil des Ordonnances des Pays-Bas, Règne d'Albert et Isabelle, 1597-1621* (1909), I. 7-12. This text, from the Register at Mons, differs considerably from that in J. Dumont, *Corps Diplomatique* (1726-1731), tom. V., pt. I., pp. 573-575, and in E. van Meteren, *Histoire des Pays-Bas* (1618), liv. XX., pp. 425, 426. **Spanish.** M. F. de Navarrete, *Coleccion de Documentos Inéditos para la Historia de España* (1842-1895), XLII. 218-222.
References: Contemporary and early writings. Meteren, *op. cit.*, liv. XX., p. 428; P. Bor, *Nederlandsche Oorlogen* (1679-1684), vol. IV., bk. XXXVI., *passim.*
References: Later writings. L. P. Gachard, *Actes des Etats Généraux de 1600* (1849), introduction; A. Levae, *Recherches Historiques sur le Commerce des Belges aux Indes* (1842), pp. 5-8; R. Fruin, *Tien Jaren uit den Tachtigjarigen Oorlog, 1588-1598* (5th ed., 1899), ch. 19; G. Turba, "Beiträge zur Geschichte der Habsburger: Aus den Letzten Jahren des Spanischen Königs Philipp II.", in *Archiv für Oesterreichische Geschichte*, Bd. LXXXVI. (1899), pp. 367 ff.; H. Pirenne, *Histoire de Belgique* (1900, etc.), IV. 215-222.

TEXT.[8]

Philippe, etc. A tous présens et à venir qui ces lettres verront ou lire oyront. Comme nous ayons trouvé convenir tant au bien de la Chrestienté en général qu'au particulier de noz pays d'embas, de ne dilayer plus longuement le mariage de nostre très chère et très amée bonne fille aisnée, l'infante Isabel Clara Eugenia, et qu'estans à ce meu, tant à cause de la conservation de nostre maison que d'aultres bon respectz, comme aussy pour l'affection particulière que portons à nostre très cher et très amé bon frère, nepveu, et cousin,

---

[5] The document in which the Dutch criticize the terms of the cession is printed in Bor, *Nederlandsche Oorlogen*, IV. 542.
[6] Gachard, *op. cit.*, p. xxxvii.
[7] Gachard, *ibid.*, pp. lxxiv, lxxv.
[8] This text is from the contemporary copy in the Register of the States of Hainaut, in the State Archives at Mons, États de Hainaut, Inaugurations et Serments des Princes, Obsèques, 1549-1717, no. 660, I., p. 53.

l'archiducq Albert, pour nous lieutenant gouverneur et capitaine général de noz pays d'embas et de Bourgoigne, ayons jecté l'oeil sur sa personne, faisant choix de luy pour futur mary de nostre susdite fille aisnée, le tout tant par consentement et gré de nostre Sainct Père le Pape qui en a accordé les dispensations requises, comme aussy à la communication en tenue avecq très hault, très excellent, et très puissant prince, nostre très chier et très amé bon frère, nepveu, et cousin Rodulphe, le second du nom, empereur des Romains, ensemble à nostre très chère et très amée bonne soeur, l'impératrice, sa mère, quoy considéré et afin que nostre susdicte fille soit pourveue des moyens qu'est raisonnable pour ses grandes qualitez et mérites, mesmes pour de nostre costel faire démonstration de l'amour singulier que tousjours avons porté et portons à nosdicts pays d'embas et de Bourgoigne, ayons prins résolution de, à l'advancement dudict mariage, faire à nostredicte fille donation d'iceulx noz pays et avecq tout ce qu'en dépend, en la manière que sera dict et spéciffié cy dessoubz, le tout moyennant et à l'intervention, volonté et consentement de nostre très cher et très amé bon filz, le prince Philippe, nostre seul filz et unicque héritier, suivant l'advertence que par nous et icelluy prince nostre filz en a esté donné aux principaulx seigneurs chevaliers de nostre ordre, consaulx, et estatz de nosdicts pays d'embas soy tenans en nostre obéissance, ensemble à ceux de nostre pays et conté de Bourgoigne, qui ont déclairé et tesmoigné par leur responce la joye et contentement qu'ilz avoient receu de telle nostre bénigne résolution qu'ils coignoissent et confessent estre pour le bien et repos de nosdicts pays d'embas, et que s'est le vray chemin pour parvenir à une bonne et solide paix, et se délivrer d'une si ennuyeuse guerre, de laquelle ils ont esté travaillez par si longue espace d'années, laquelle tranquillité et repos leur avons tousjours désiré, et considérant ce que à tous est notoire, que le plus grand heur que peult advenir à ung pays est de se trouver régy et gouverné à la veue et par la présence de son prince et seigneur naturel, Dieu est tesmoing des paines et soing qu'avons eu souvent de ne l'avoir ainsy peu faire personellement par dela, comme en vérité l'avons grandement désiré si les aultres grands et importans affaires de noz royaulmes d'Espaigne ne nous eussent obligez à tenir ferme et continuelle résidence en iceulx, sans nous esloigner comme semblablement ils nous obligent à présent, et combien que l'eaige de nostredict filz le prince semble plus à propos que poinct le nostre pour voyager, touttesfois ayant esté le bon plaisir de Dieu de nous donner tant d'aultres royaulmes et pays pour le bon gouvernement desquels ne manqueront jamais affaires de très grand emport, pour lesquels sera aussy requise sa présence par deca, avons trouvé convenable de prendre ceste résolution, afin de ne laisser nosdicts pays d'embas es mesmes inconvéniens que du passé, y joinct la raison qu'il y a de faire partaige à nostredicte fille l'infante selon ses mérites et la grandeur de sa naissance, attendu aussy en particulier que après ledict prince, nostre filz (a qui Dieu conserve par longues années avecq la prospérité qu'il sera servy luy donner), nostredicte fille aisnée est la première et plus prochaine, et que, moyennant le vouloir de nostredict filz, elle peult dès maintenant estre admise, nous avons choisy tel moyen, soubz espoir que par icelluy pourront nosdicts pays d'embas retourner à leur ancienne fleur, repos, et prospérité qu'ilz ont eu du passé. Sçavoir faisons que désirans à présent mectre en effet audict endroict ce que tant meurement y avons résolu, et attendu le consentement volontaire que nostredict filz le prince y a si libéralement donné et presté de sa part, mesmes après avoir cognu la submission avecq laquelle se sont nosdicts pays conformé à ceste nostre bonne intention, nous avons résolu de céder et transporter à la susdicte nostre fille l'infante en advancement dudict mariage tous nosdicts pays d'embas et de Bourgoigne, par la forme et manière et aulx pactz et conditions cy embas expressées et mentionnées.

. . . .

[8.] Item, à condition et non aultrement que nostre dicte fille l'infante et son mary ny aucuns de ses successeurs ausquelz seront devoluz lesdicts pays ne tiendront en aucune manière, commerce, trafficq, ou contractation aux Indes Orientales ou Occidentales, ne aussy envoyeront aucune sorte de batteaux, à quelque tiltre, couleur, ou prétexte que ce soit, auxdicts endroictz, à paine que lesdicts pays seront dévoluz au cas de ladicte contravention, et au cas qu'aucuns de leurs subjects s'acheminassent vers lesdictes Indes contre ladicte deffence, que les seigneurs desdicts pays les auront à chastoyer de paine de confiscation de biens et d'aultres griesves, mesmes de la mort.

. . . .

Et afin que de tout ce que dessus il conste ouvertement et soit chose ferme et stable, perpétuellement et à tousjours, nous avons signé ces mesmes présentes de nostre nom et y faict mectre nostre grand seel, veuillant et ordonnant que enregistration et intérinement en soit faict, en tous et chacun de noz consaulx et chambres des comptes où il appartiendra.

Donné en nostre ville de Madrid, royaulme de Castille, le sixiesme jour du mois de May en l'an de grasce XV^c nonante huict, et de nos règnes, assavoir de Naples et de Hierusalem le XLVe, de Castille, d'Arragon, Sicille, et des aultres, le XLIIIe, et de Portugal le XIXe.

N. D. v[idi]t.

PHILIPPE.
Par le Roy.
A. DE LALOO.

25.

Treaty between England and the United Netherlands concluded at Westminster, August 6/16, 1598. Ratification by the States General, September 20, 1598.

INTRODUCTION.

For some months before and after the conclusion of the treaty of Vervins,[1] it appeared doubtful whether Elizabeth would make peace with Spain or would continue the war and the Dutch alliance. She urged the Dutch to conclude peace with Spain, pressed them to reimburse her for the sums she had spent in their behalf, failed to come to an agreement with the Dutch envoys who were in England from March to May, 1598, but in June despatched Sir Francis Vere to the Hague to propose negotiations for a treaty. Thereupon another embassy, which included the Advocate Olden-barnevelt and Admiral Duyvenvoord, was sent to London. Elizabeth's councillors were divided. A Burgundian party, led by the Cecils, did not lack arguments for peace.[2] The English could not endure to see the Dutch growing rich and powerful through the employment of their ships in the West India trade, and through their traffic with Spain and Portugal, from which the English were debarred.[3] Peace with Spain would diminish the danger from rebellious Ireland. It was said that the war had become less profitable since Spain had learned to defend her American possessions.[4]

On the other hand, the war party, which included Essex and other supporters of the Dutch alliance, argued that Spain's peace proposals were deceitful, as in 1588; that the States could not make peace since this would re-establish Spanish sovereignty and Catholicism in the United Provinces; that England could not honorably or safely make a separate peace, since Spain would demand the cautionary towns held by English garrisons in the

---

[1] May 2, 1598. See Doc. 23, last paragraph of introduction.

[2] J. S. Corbett, *Successors of Drake* (1900), p. 233, remarks that after the treaty of Vervins, which secured the retirement of Spain from the Channel and the re-establishment of England's naval position in the Narrow Seas, "It cannot be wondered at if in the eyes of Burghley, who could never rise to an appreciation that the real struggle with Spain was for the new world, there was very little left to fight about", and, p. 316, "That the struggle with Spain was really a vital contest for the commercial and colonial supremacy of the world [Sir Robert Cecil] never seems to have grasped".

[3] Deventer, *Gedenkstukken*, II. 262; *Letters written by John Chamberlain during the Reign of Queen Elizabeth*, ed. by S. Williams for the Camden Society, LXXIX. (1861) 11-13; *cf.* Motley, *United Netherlands*, III. 524, 525.

[4] Camden, *History of England*, II. 606.

Netherlands;[a] that England and the Netherlands would together hold the empire of the seas,[6] which would fall to Spain if the Netherlands should submit to their former sovereign; that offensive warfare in America would still be found profitable and might open up American commerce to Europeans, who desired nothing more than this;[7] that the peacemakers were ready to renounce the trade to the Indies.[8] The party of Essex won the day. The difficult question of repaying the queen's loan was finally settled, and an offensive and defensive treaty of alliance was concluded at Westminster on August 6/16. Its principal provisions were as follows: that the Anglo-Dutch treaty of alliance of 1585 should be confirmed, with the exception of certain articles; that the queen should be represented in the Dutch Council of State by one councillor instead of two; that the States should repay the queen's advances in large installments and should bear the charge of the English garrisons in the cautionary towns; that the States should furnish military and naval aid to England against Spain; and, in particular, should co-operate in offensive warfare undertaken by England against the Azores and the Indies.[9] This last stipulation looked towards a continuation of the policy of the two preceding years, when the English and Dutch squadrons acted together in the expeditions sent against Cadiz and other Spanish ports, and the Azores;[10] and it was followed by the attempt made in 1601-1602 to unite these squadrons against Spain and the treasure-fleet.[11]

BIBLIOGRAPHY.

Text: MS. The original of the ratification by the United Provinces is in the London Public Record Office, T. R., Diplomatic Documents, no. 1174.

Text: Printed. French. T. Rymer, *Foedera* (1704-1735), XVI. 340-343; J. Dumont, *Corps Diplomatique* (1726-1731), tom. V., pt. I., pp. 589-591. **Dutch.** Dumont, *ibid.*, pp. 584-589; P. Bor, *Nederlandsche Oorlogen* (1679-1684), IV. 475-478.

Translation. *Cal. St. Pap., Venice*, 1592-1603, pp. 356-360.

References: Contemporary and early writings. M. L. van Deventer, *Gedenkstukken van J. van Oldenbarnevelt* (1860-1865), II. 175 ff.; Historical MSS. Commission, *Calendar of MSS. of Marquis of Salisbury*

---

[a] These arguments are used in the *Apologie*, written by the Earl of Essex in 1598 and published in 1603.

[6] Deventer, *op. cit.*, II. 265.   [7] Camden, *op. cit.*, II. 607.

[8] Essex, *Apologie*: "Trade into the Indies our zealous peacemakers will not stand for, lest the enemy offended will grant no peace at all."

[9] The offer to join with the queen in sending a fleet against the Azores, the Indies, or other dominions of the King of Spain, was made by the States' envoys, British Museum, Cotton MSS., Galba, D. XII., ff. 176 (183), 216 (223), 226 (233); Bor, *Nederlandsche Oorlogen*, IV. 479.

[10] See Doc. 23, introduction.

[11] Corbett, *op. cit.*, pp. 362, 365 ff.; *Naval Tracts of Sir William Monson*, II. "Sir Richard Leveson and Sir William Monson to the Coast of Spain" (ed. by M. Oppenheim in *Publications* of the Navy Records Society, XXIII. 1902).

at Hatfield House (1883, etc.), VIII. 84, 128, 250, 388, 533-538, *et passim*; W. Camden, *History of England during the Life of Elizabeth,* trans. in [J. Hughes], *A Complete History of England* (1706), II. 606-610; P. Bor, *op. cit.,* IV. 475 ff.; E. van Meteren, *Histoire des Pays-Bas* (1618), p. 429.

References: Later writings. J. L. Motley, *United Netherlands* (1904), III. 524 ff., 550-562; R. Fruin, *Tien Jaren uit den Tachtigjarigen Oorlog, 1588-1598* (5th ed., 1899), ch. 20, pp. 363 ff.

TEXT.[13]

Les Estats Generaux des Provinces Unies des Pays Bas, a tous ceulx qui ces presentes lettres verront ou orront, salut.

. . . .

8. Cas advenant que l'ennemy commun ou ses adherens envoye armee navale pour assaillir, durant ladite guerre, le royaulme d'Angleterre, où les isles appartenantes,—vizt. de Vicht, Sorlingues, Guernezey et Gerzey, et que Sa Majesté appreste et mette en ordre sa flotte pour luy faire teste, lesditz Sieurs Estatz furniront pour le service de Sa Majesté et a sa requisition, trente, ou, si faire se poeult, quarante navires de guerre bien equippees, dont le [*sic*] moytie sera de deux cents et l'aultre moietie entre cent et deux centz tonneaux, pour estre employees soubz le commandement du general chieff ou admiral de Sa Majesté, en conformite et ensuyvant les conditions dudit traicte de l'an mil cincq cents quattre vintz et cincque, en tous pointz, et mesmes concernant les conquestes a faire sur l'ennemy.

9. Et semblablement, l'ennemy venant assaillir et faire descente sur le royaume d'Angleterre ou l'isle de Vicht, lesditz Sieurs Estatz furniront (le requerant Sa Majesté) un nombre de cincq mille hommes de pied, et cincq centz chevaux, a estre employez soubz le commandement du general de Sa Majesté, ou bien a l'election et choix de Sadite Majesté, les gages et soulde de tel nombre, sur le pied des gages arresté aux traictez de l'an mil cincq centz quattre vintz et cinque, ledit payement a commencer dez le jour que l'ennemy aura faict descente, et de continuer jusques à ce qu'il en soit entierement desfaict, repoulsé ou chassé.

10. Si Sa Majesté trouvera bon, selon les occurrences des affaires, d'entreprendre offensivement durant ladite guerre, sur l'ennemy·commun par armée consistant au moins de cinquante ou soixante navires de guerre, se faisant telle entreprinse par mer sur les pays d'Espaigne, Portugal, Isles, ou Indes, lesditz Sieurs Estatz joindront a la flotte de Sa Majesté a leur despens un pareil nombre de vaisseaux de guerre, et de semblable qualité qu'est contenu en l'article precedent; ou si tant sera que Sa Majesté se resouldra dedans ledit temps de jecter une bonne armée au moins de dix mille hommes de pied et de deux mille chevaux es Pays de Flandres ou Brabant, avec train et provisions d'artillerie et munitions, pour faire la guerre à l'ennemy susdit; se tiendront lesditz Sieurs Estatz obleigez d'y furnir a rate de la moytie des

---

[13] The text is taken from the original manuscript of the ratification by the United Provinces, preserved in the Public Record Office, T. R., Diplomatic Documents, no. 1174, except where that is illegible when the text in Rymer, *Foedera,* XVI. 340-343, printed from the same manuscript, has been used.

trouppes et forces de Sa Majesté avecq artilleries et munitions proportionnables, usant des conquestes selon la proportion comme dessus.

. . . .

Faict, accorde, conclu et soubzsigné par les seigneurs du Conseil de Sa Majesté d'une part, et par lesditz deputez de Messieurs les Estatz Généraux des Provinces-Unies d'aultre part, a Westminster, le seiziesme jour du mois d'Aoust, l'an de nostre Seigneur mil cincq cens nonante huict.

Estoit signé:

Tho. Egerton, C. S.	J. v. Duvenvoirde.
Essex.	Jehan van Oldenbarnevelt.
Notingham.	Jehan van Warck.
G. Hunsdon.	Jehan van Hottinga.
R. North.	And. d'Hessels.
T. Buckehurst.	Noel de Caron.
W. Knollys.	
Ro[bert] Cecyll.	
Fortescu.	

et cachette du cachet d'armes desditz seigneurs du conseil de Sa Majesté, et des susditz deputez des Seigneurs Estatz Généraulx respectivement.

Nous ayans agréables tous et chacun les pointz et articles contenuz et déclairez au dit traicté, avons icelle traicté ratifie, approuve, et confirme, ratifions, approuvons, et confirmons par ces presentes, promettans . . . eans en bonne foy de l'accomplir et satisfaire tous et chacun ses pointz, pour aultant qu'il nous touche, [sans] contrevenir directement ou indirectement en quelque sorte ou manière ce soit.

En tesmoing de quoy avons faict appendre à ces presentes nostre grand sel et signer par nostre greffier à la Haye en Hollande le vingtiesme de septembre, l'an mil cincq cens quatre vingtz dix huict.

J. Hottinga.

Par ordonnance desdicts seigneurs Estatz Generaulx.

Aerssens.

26.

Agreement signed by the King of France at Villers Cotterêts on July 19, 1603, and by the King of England and Scotland at Hampton Court on July 30/August 9, 1603.

INTRODUCTION.

Upon the accession of James I. to the English throne, March 24/April 3, 1603, the King of France and the States General of the United Provinces feared that James's pacific tendencies would lead him to conclude a peace with the King of Spain to whom, in spite of the treaty of Vervins,[1] Henry IV. had remained opposed. On June 17, 1603, the Marquis of Rosny (later the Duke of Sully) arrived in London as ambassador extraordinary from France, with instructions[2] to persuade James to enter into a secret agreement to aid the United Provinces; to find out what he would do in regard to an offensive and defensive alliance against Spain; and to urge him to continue Elizabeth's policy of sending naval expeditions to the coasts of Spain and Portugal and toward the Indies. In the additional and secret instructions which, according to Rosny, were also given him, was a clause to the following effect: " Que la France, l'Angleterre, le Dannemarc, la Suede et les Pays-Bas à frais communs, et neantmoins proportionnez aux puissances d'un chacun, essayassent de se saisir des Indes ou à tout le moins des isles qui sont sur le chemin des flottes d'Espagne, afin d'en empescher le traject, et ce, par le moyen de trois armées navales de huict mille hommes chacune, lesquelles se rafraischiroient de huict en huict mois, afin de remplacer ce qui seroit devenu defectueux en icelles."[3] Sully probably invented these " secret instructions ", but in any event they are of some interest, especially when compared with the suggestion made by the Dutch embassy to James, in a harangue delivered on May 27, 1603—that if the various states opposed to Spain should form a general league against that power, they would soon bring the Spaniards to reason; otherwise, England and her allies, as masters of the sea, would deprive them of the East and West Indies.[4]

To an unusual extent Rosny negotiated directly with the king himself, and in about a fortnight after his arrival obtained James's oral consent to a written

---

[1] Doc. **23**, last paragraph of introduction.

[2] Two sets of instructions are in Sully's *Mémoires* in Michaud and Poujoulat, *Mémoires*, 2ᵉ sér., tom. II., ch. 115. See Ch. Pfister's article in the *Revue Historique*, IV. 296 ff., for an examination of the authenticity of the " secret instructions ".

[3] *Mémoires, ed. cit.,* tom. II., p. 441.

[4] E. van Meteren, *Histoire des Pay-Bos* (1618), liv. XXV., p. 531.

agreement providing that the Franco-Scottish and Franco-English alliances should be renewed and strengthened by means of a defensive league in which allies of both kings should be comprised; that the two kings should procure reasonable conditions of peace for the United Provinces, their chief ally, and, pending this, should secretly assist them with money and men; that if, on account of this assistance, either king were attacked by Spain, the other should send an army to his aid; that if both were attacked or decided to make war on Spain, they should aim at the complete independence of the seventeen provinces of the Low Countries; that the King of France should send an army to the Low Countries and so dispose other troops and his Mediterranean fleet as to divert the attention of Spain; that the King of England should provide two great fleets to attack the Indies and the Spanish coasts, and an army for operations on land; and that neither king was to make peace, diminish his forces or cease from hostilities without consent of the other. The draft drawn up by Sully and agreeed to by James I. was signed by Henry IV. on July 19, 1603, and by James at Hampton Court on July 30/August 9, of the same year. But when in August, 1604, James concluded a peace with Spain,[5] the English government regarded this earlier agreement with France as a dead letter.[6]

BIBLIOGRAPHY.

Text: MS. The original of the agreement signed by Henry IV. on July 19, 1603, is in the London Public Record Office, State Papers Foreign, Treaties, no. 50.

Text: Printed. The agreement signed by James I. on July 30/August 9, 1603, is printed in F. Leonard, *Recueil des Traitez de Paix* (1693), V. 1-3; J. Dumont, *Corps Diplomatique* (1726-1731), tom. V., pt. II., pp. 30, 31; J. A. de Abreu y Bertodano, *Coleccion de los Tratados de España: Reynado del Rey D. Phelipe III.* (1740), I. 164-169.

Translation. *A General Collection of Treatys* (1732), II., 128-131.

References: Contemporary and early writings. Duc de Sully (Maximilien de Béthune), *Mémoires* in Michaud and Poujoulat, *Nouvelle Collection des Mémoires* (1836-1839), 2ᵉ sér., tom. II., cc. 114-122, and in other editions; P. Laffleur de Kermaingant, *L'Ambassade de France en Angleterre sous Henri IV.: Mission de Christophe de Harlay, 1602-1605* (1895), *pièces justificatives*, pp. 110-121 (letters from Henry IV. to Beaumont); *Calendar of State Papers, Venice*, 1603-1607, nos. 64, 81, 86, 87, 90, 91, 93, 98, 107, 118, 127, 139, 141, 147, 161, 162, 259, 739 (p. 518), *et passim*.

References: Later writings. Laffleur de Kermaingant, *op. cit.*, ch. 2, pp. 110-119; S. R. Gardiner, *History of England, 1603-1642* (1894-1896), I. 106, 107; L. von Ranke, *History of England* (1875), I. 388, 389. In the *Revue Historique*, tom. LV. (1894), pp. 70 ff., 291 ff., Ch. Pfister examines critically Sully's account of his English embassy.

[5] Doc. **27.**
[6] Kermaingant, *L'Ambassade de France*, I. 244; Gardiner, *History of England, 1603-1642*, I. 217, 218.

TEXT.[1]

Articles traittez et accordez avec le Roy d'Angleterre et d'Escosse[2] par le Sieur Marquis de Rosny, grand maître de l'artillerie et grand voyer de France, ambassadeur et envoyé par Sa Majesté vers ledit roy.

. . . .

8.[3] Davantage a esté accordé, que si les deux roys estoient ensemblement attaqués par l'Espagne ou qu'ilz fussent contraints par raison d'estat et pour la seureté, repos, et utilité de leurs personnes, royaumes, et subjects, d'ouvrir communement la guerre, que un chascun d'eux la fera de son costé, non point à demy mais selon qu'il convient à la dignité et grandeur de telz princes, et avec moyens suffisans pour en faire esperer l'entiere delivrance des dix-sept Provinces des Pays-Bas.

9. A sçavoir de la part du roy avec une armee de quinze ou vingt mil hommes, qu'il jettera vers lesdits Païs bas, et tiendra les provinces de Guyenne, Languedoc, Provence, Dauphiné, Bresse, et Bourgogne, munyes d'un suffisant nombre de gens armez, ensemble d'une suffisante quantité de galeres en equipage de guerre dans la mer de Levant, afin de tenir non seulement ses costes en seureté, mais donner juste jalousie au Roy d'Espagne, et par consequent occuper et divertir partie de ses forces.

10. Et de la part du dit Roy d'Angleterre la guerre se fera avec deux grandes flottes dignes de faire de bons exploits vers les Indes et costes d'Espagne; et une armee de terre, laquelle ne pourra estre moindre que de six mil hommes, le tout levé et soudoyé à ses fraiz et despens, sans que durant tout ce temps de guerre commune ledit Roy d'Angleterre puisse presser Sa Majesté de ce qu'il luy pourra lors debvoir de reste.

. . . .

Faict a Villiers Costerets le dixneufiesme jour du moys de Juilet, 1603.

HENRY.
DE NEUFVILLE.

---

[1] The text is from the original manuscript of the agreement signed by Henry IV. on July 19, 1603, preserved in the P. R. O., State Papers Foreign, Treaties, no. 50.
[2] See Doc. **27**, end of text, after note 19.
[3] The articles are not numbered but the text is paragraphed.

27.

Treaty between Spain and Great Britain concluded at London, August 18/28, 1604. Ratification by the King of Spain, June 5/15, 1605. [Ratification by the King of Great Britain, August 19/29, 1604.]

INTRODUCTION.

James I. of England, a lover of peace and favorably disposed toward Spain, regarded the Anglo-Spanish war of Elizabeth's reign as a personal quarrel between sovereigns, which had been ended by Elizabeth's death and his accession.[1] In accordance with this theory, on June 23/July 3, 1603, he issued a proclamation that Spanish ships and goods taken by his subjects after April 24/May 4, 1603, should be restored to their owners.[2] On May 19/29, 1604, he empowered his leading councillors, Thomas Sackville (earl of Dorset), Charles Howard (earl of Nottingham), Charles Blount (earl of Devonshire), Henry Howard (earl of Northampton), and Lord Robert Cecil, to treat for peace with the deputies of Spain, Juan de Velasco (constable of Castile), the Spanish ambassador in London, Juan de Tassis (count of Villa Mediana), and Alessandro Rovida (senator of Milan), and with the deputies of the archdukes, Charles, prince-count of Arenberg, President Richardot, and the Audiencer Verreycken. In the negotiations, which began at the residence of the Spanish ambassador on May 20/30 and lasted six weeks, controversy centred about two questions—Anglo-Dutch relations, and the rights of English traders in Spain, Flanders, and the East and West Indies. The English commissioners refused to renounce trade with the Dutch, or, for the present, to hand over the cautionary towns to Spain; but they agreed that English subjects should not transport Dutch merchandise to the King of Spain's dominions or to the archdukes' provinces, or Spanish merchandise to the United Provinces, or use Dutch ships in the Spanish trade. They also consented to several somewhat ambiguous articles, offensive to the Dutch, which Cecil declared would be rendered harmless by England's friendly interpretation.[3] In regard to trade with Spain it was provided that imports from Britain and Ireland into the Spanish dominions, and exports from the Spanish dominions into Britain and Ireland, should be exempt from the recently imposed 30 per cent. tax; and that English traders in the Spanish

---

[1] The king's speech to his first Parliament. *Journals of the House of Commons,* I. 142.
[2] Rymer, *Foedera,* XVI., 516, 517. *Cf.* below, art. 2.
[3] Winwood, *Memorials,* II. 27, 28.

dominions should not be molested " for the cause of conscience ", " so as they give not scandal unto others " (art. 21). Concerning trade to the East and West Indies, an arrangement but no real agreement was reached. The instructions[1] of the English commissioners in this matter, identical with those for the abortive Anglo-Spanish negotiations at Boulogne, four years

[1] Instructions to English commissioners, May 22/June 1, 1604. . . . " Lastly, it is likely they will forbid us trade into the Indias, wherein you must by all arguments you can maintaine that it is very disconsonant with trewe amitie to forbid their freinds those common liberties. Yea, though the whole Indias were as meerely subject to their sover-aignetie as Spaine it selfe is, especiallie when in former treaties there have been con-trarie clauses, which have given freedome of trade into all their domynions. And yet because it shall appeare that wee will not be found unreasonable, you shall let them knowe that, to avoyde all inconveniences that may peradventure happen in places so remote, when the subjects of other princes shall fall in companie one with another, where their lawes and discipline cannot be so well executed, wee are contented to prohibite all repaire of our subjects to any places where they are planted, but onely to seeke their traffique by their owne discoveries in other places, whereof there are so infinite dymensions of vast and great territories as themselves have no kind of interest, but do trade with divers great kings of those countryes but as forrayners and strangers, from which to barre ourselves by accord, seeing it is not in his power to do it by force, no not to any pettie prince, were both an unkindnesse and an indignitie to be offered." P. R. O., State Papers Foreign, Spain, bundle 10. Also B. M., Cotton MSS., Vesp. C. XIII., f. 61. With these it is of interest to compare the following instructions for the negotiations at Bourbourg in 1587 : " 15. It is likely allso, that some speciall article will be required to forbyd all trafick of our people into the Indias, both of the west belonging to the crowne of Castill and to the Est allso, now in the K. of Spaynes possession by reason of Portingall. To this it may be allso sayde, that we shall be content to observe such orders as were in any force in the tyme of the Emperor Charles being possessed of the West Indias. And as for the Est Indias, wee are content to covenannt to observe allso all such orderes as were att any tyme accorded and used in the tyme of the King Sebastian. And if these generall answeres shall not content them, then ye shall require of them, what other speciall article they wolde reasonably desyre, for that ye are not warranted otherwise to yeelde to them. But yet our meaning is ye shall as of yourselves reason with them, as it may appeere that ther is no reason to barre our subjects to use trade of merchandise in the Indias, where the Frenche are daily suffred so to doo, so as the same be with the goodwill of the inhabitants of the countryes, and only for lawfull trade of marchandise. And likewise it is no reason by a large naming of the Indias, to barre our marchantes to trade in any places dis-covered or to be discovered by our own people, being places where neyther in the tyme of the Emperor Charles, nor of the King that now is, any Spanyard, Portingale, or any other Christian people have had any habitation, residence or resorte. And to those provisions mentioned (as of yourself) to be annexed to the generall prohibitions, if they will condescend ye may saye, ye will send to knowe our opinion, what we lyke therof, and what other conditions we will require to be excepted out of the generall prohibition for our subjects to sayle into the Indias.

" In the argument therof ye may aledge that the cheefe reasons why the Emperor Charles and the King of Portingale in their tymes did seeke to prohibite all others than their own subjectes to trade into those Indias discovered by their people, was in recompence of the charges sustayned by the discoverers that the proffitt of the riches discovered might recompence the first discoverers and their heires. A matter agreable to good reason, but not so to be extended as by the large titles and nomination of the Indias (wherof ther is no certain limitation) all parts of the worlde in the West or in the East, that were not or should not be discovered by the subjects of the said Emperor. or by the kinges of Portingale should still so remayne undiscovered and not to be by any other Christians with their laboure sought out and discovered and brought to the knowl-edge of God, and of Christ the Saviour of the Worlde, for that were against all Christian charitie, and against all humain reason, and directly againste that generall proposition in the holy Scripture : Coelum coeli Domino, terram dedit filiis hominum." P. R. O., State Papers Foreign, Flanders, 1585-1587, I. Also in B. M., Cotton MSS., Vesp. C. VIII., and *ibid.*, Galba D. II. f. 318 b, a draft in Burghley's hand.

before,[4] sanctioned only one concession—that Englishmen should be prohibited from going to any places in the Indies where the Spaniards were actually " planted ". This was in accordance with a principle formulated by the French and English long before[5] and recently embodied in the charter granted to the English East India Company on December 31, 1600.[6] It was rejected by the Spaniards, who insisted that the English should be excluded from every part of the Indies, either expressly or by clear implication; or else, that the King of England should declare in writing that his subjects would trade in the Indies at their own peril. These demands the English refused. Cecil and Northampton alleged that an express prohibition to trade would wrong James's honor since Spain had not put it in the treaties made with France and other princes; and that a denial of reciprocal freedom of intercourse was contrary to the law of nations. The Senator of Milan answered " that though ordinary societies by law should be equal, yet that they might be limited by conventions, and that the same ought not to be found strange in this case, because the said Indias was a new world ". After much debate it was resolved that in the article for general intercourse the following words should be inserted : " In quibus ante bellum fuit commercium juxta et secundum usum et observantiam antiquorum foederum." This left the matter " to the liberty of interpretation of former treaties and the observance and use thereof ".[8] Now, from the time of Hawkins, the English, and Cecil in particular, had interpreted the clauses for mutual intercourse in the old Anglo-Spanish and Anglo-Burgundian treaties as permitting them to trade in the Indies,[9] and the government continued to hold to this interpretation.[10] Soon after the conclusion of the treaty Cecil wrote to the English

[4] The instructions are in P. R. O., State Papers Foreign, France, bundle 44.

[5] *Cal. St. Pap. Foreign*, 1561-1562, p. 72; and *cf.* J. Williamson, *Maritime Enterprise, 1485-1558* (1913), pp. 288 ff.

[7] The charter is in S. Purchas, *Hakluytus Posthumus or Purchas His Pilgrimes* (Maclehose ed., 1905-1907), II. 366-391.

[8] Journal of the negotiations. See below, bibliography.

[9] *The Hawkins' Voyages* (ed. C. R. Markham for the Hakluyt Soc., LVII. (1878) 30-34, 38) ; W. Camden, *History of England during the Life of Elizabeth*, in [J. Hughes], *A Complete History of England* (1706), II. 410; *cf. Cal. St. Pap., Spain*, 1558-1567, 593.

[10] *Cf.* the instructions for the negotiations at Bourbourg printed above, note 4. In " Reasons for the trade to the East and West Indians ", compiled by Robert Cotton for Northampton's use in the negotiations of 1604 (Brit. Mus., Cotton MSS., Vesp. C. XIII., ff. 47-50), the " former leagues " of 1489, 1507, 1515, 1520, 1529, and 1543, are adduced. The last four were concluded between Henry VIII. and Charles of Spain. Philip II. had refused to confirm the treaties with England. The article of mutual intercourse in the last two treaties mentioned above refers back to the article in the treaty of Apr. 11, 1520, which is as follows: " Item, conventum, concordatum, et conclusum est quod omnes et singuli subditi regnorum et dominiorum dictorum principum eorumdemque actores, factores, negotiorum gestores, attornati, servitores, et ministri, cum rebus, navibus, bonis, et mercibus suis quibuscumque, ad omnia et singula terras, patrias, dominia, civitates, oppida, villas, castra, portus, jurisdictiones, et districtus utriusque principum praedictorum accedere, navigare per terram, mare, vel aquas dulces, venire, morari, et perhendinare, ibique omnium mercium genera, cum quibuscumque mercatoribus cujuscumque nationis, emere, vendere, permutare, et cum eisdem vel

ambassador in France: "If it be well observed how the [ninth] article is couched, you shall rather find it a pregnant affirmative for us than against us; for, sir, where it is written that we shall trade in all his dominions, that comprehends the Indies; if you will say, *secundum tractatus antiquos*, no treaty excluded it "." The Spaniards, on the other hand, resolutely affirmed that the terms of the peace excluded the English from the Indies.[12] However, as was remarked in the instructions cited above, they were not able to bar out the English by force; and the latter not only continued their trade in the East, but, in spite of Spanish opposition,[13] proceeded to colonize Virginia under a charter which allotted to the grantees a portion of America " not actually possessed by any Christian prince or people ".[14]

The treaty was not signed until August 18/28, after the arrival in London of the Constable of Castile, who had been detained in Flanders. It was confirmed by King James on the following day, and ratified by the King of Spain on June 15, 1605.

BIBLIOGRAPHY.

Text: MS. The original manuscript of the ratification by the King of Spain, June 15, 1605, is in the London Public Record Office, Museum, Case G. The ratification by the archdukes is in the Public Record Office, T. R., Diplomatic Documents, no. 1176; and the enrolled treaty is in the same depository, Treaty Roll, no. 216.

Text: Printed. T. Rymer, *Foedera* (1704-1735), XVI. 585-596, 617-629; J. Dumont, *Corps Diplomatique* (1726-1731), tom. V., pt. II., pp. 32-36, and, more completely, pp. 625-631; J. A. de Abreu y Bertodano, *Coleccion de los Tratados de España: Reynado de Phelipe III.* (1740), I. 243-286; separate articles defining art. XXI. are in R. Winwood, *Memorials of Affairs of State in the Reigns of Elizabeth and James I.* (1725), II. 29; concerning German merchandise, in Abreu, *loc. cit.* Several early edi-

---

aliis bonis, navibus, rebus, et mercibus suis ad alia regna, loca, portus, et ad quemcumque vel quaecumque locum vel loca voluerint recedere, et omne genus commercii invicem exercere libere et licite valeant, juxta et secundum vim, formam, et effectum tractatus intercursus mercium de data vicesimi quarti diei mensis Februarii, anno domini millesimo quadringentesimo nonagesimo quinto, et articulorum subsequentium, durante provisione praesenti." Rymer, *Foedera*, XIII. 715, 716. The treaty of Feb. 24, 1495/6, is the well-known *Intercursus Magnus. Ibid.*, XII. 578-591.

[11] P. R. O., State Papers Foreign, Spain, bundle 10. *Cf.* the answer of James I. to the Venetian ambassador, Nov. 2, 1604. *Cal. St. Pap., Venice*, 1603-1607, pp. 189-190; and Cecil's letter to Winwood, "For the matter of the Peace which is lately concluded, it was a very good judgment of Barnevelt, when he said, that *Litera occidit, spiritus autem vivificat*; for so treaties are commonly carried between great princes, where many things are left to interpretation for saving reputation to those that will make no quarrell for things done, though they never give consent thereunto by their treaty." Winwood, *op. cit.*, II. 27.

[12] Grotius, *Annals* (1665), p. 920; and *cf.* Doc. **29**, introduction and note 5.

[13] See the letters from Zuñiga to the King of Spain and from the King of Spain to Zuñiga in A. Brown, *Genesis of the United States* (1890), I. 45, 46, 88-91, 97-99, 102-104, etc.

[14] The expression occurs in the preamble of the charter. The charter is printed in Brown, *op. cit.*, I. 52 ff.

tions and translations of the text are listed in the British Museum Catalogue, under " England: Treaties ". This appears to have been the first English treaty printed by royal authority.

Translations. *Articles of Peace . . . 1604* (ed. R. Barker, 1605) ; *A General Collection of Treatys* (1732), II. 131-146; British Museum, Harleian MSS., 35.

References: Contemporary and early writings. A journal of the negotiations by Sir Thomas Edmondes is in the London Public Record Office, Treaty Papers, 64; copies of the journal are in the British Museum, Harleian MSS., 35, and Add. MSS., 14033 ; several copies are mentioned in the *Reports* of the Commission on Historical Manuscripts, and one is printed in part in the appendix to the *Eighth Report*, pt. I., pp. 95-98 ; *Calendar of State Papers, Venice*, 1603-1607, *passim* ; Winwood, *op. cit.*, II. 1 ff. ; *Works of Sir Walter Ralegh* (1829), VIII. 299-316, " A Discourse touching a War with Spain, and of the Protecting of the Netherlands " ; E. van Meteren, *Histoire des Pays-Bas* (1618), pp. 547-550.

References: Later writings. S. R. Gardiner, *History of England, 1603-1642* (1894-1896), I. 206-217, 342; P. Laffleur de Kermaingant, *L'Ambassade de France en Angleterre sous Henri IV.: Mission de Christophe de Harlay, 1602-1605* (1895), ch. 3 ; L. Willaert, " Négociations Politico-Religieuses entre l'Angleterre et les Pays-Bas Catholiques (1598-1625)", II. " Intervention des Souverains Anglais en Faveur du Protestantisme aux Pays-Bas ", in *Revue d'Histoire Ecclésiastique*, July, 1907, pp. 514 ff.

TEXT.[15]

Philippus Tertius, Dei gratia rex Castellae, Legionis, Aragonum, Utriusque Siciliae, Hierusalem, Portugaliae, Navarrae, Granatae, Toleti, Valentiae, Galleciae, Majoricarum, Hispalis, Sardiniae, Cordubae, Corsicae, Murtiae, Giennis, Algarbii, Gibraltaris, Insularum Canariae, necnon Indiarum Orientalium et Occidentalium, insularum ac terraefirmae maris Occeani ; archidux Austriae, dux Burgundiae et Mediolani, comes Abspurgi, Barchinoniae, Cantabriae, et Molinae Dominus, etc.: omnibus et singulis ad quos praesentes literae pervenerint, salutem. Cum tractatus quidam firmae amicitiae et pacis perpetuae ac commertii inter commissarios et deputatos nostros et serenissimorum principum Alberti et Isabellae Clarae Eugeniae, archiducum Austriae, ducum Burgundiae, et Jacobi, Magnae Britanniae, etc., regis, fratrum et consanguineorum nostrorum charissimorum, Londini, vigesimo octavo die Augusti, stillo novo, anno Domini millesimo sexcentesimo quarto, concordatum et conclusum fuerit, cujus tenor sequitur : Noverint omnes et singuli quod post diuturnum et saevissimum bellorum incendium, quo Christianae provintiae per multos annos insigni jactura conflagrarunt, Deus, in cujus manu omnia posita sunt, ex alto respiciens et sui populi (cui ut pacem afferret et relinqueret, proprium sanguinem effundere non dubitavit) calamitates miseratus, potentissimorum Christiani imperii principum stabili conjunctione, saevientem ignem potenter restinxit, et diem pacis, diem tranquillitatis, hujusque magis optatam quam speratam, misericorditer attulit. Devolutis enim, per ipsius Dei maximi gratiam, ad extirpanda discordiarum semina, Angliae

---

[15] The following text is printed from the original manuscript of the ratification in the Public Record Office, Museum, Case G.

et Hiberniae regnis ad Serenissimum Jacobum Scotiae regem, sublatisque
ideo illis dissensionum causis quae bella inter antecessores serenissimorum
principum, Philippi III., Hispaniarum regis, et Alberti ac Isabellae Clarae
Eugeniae, Austriae archiducum, ducum Burgundiae et Serenissimi Jacobi
regis Angliae tamdiu aluerunt, animadverterunt dicti omnes principes (Deo
corda illorum illuminante) nihil superesse cur odiis, quae nunquam inter
ipsos extiterunt, certarent, vel armis, a quibus majores ipsorum semper
abstinuerunt, contenderent, et ab antiquissimo ac supra hominum memoriam
custodito foedere discederent, arctissimaque necessitudinis, quae praedicto
serenissimo Regi Angliae cum serenissimis Austriaca et Burgundica familiis
intercedit, vincula disrumperent, ac veterem amicitiam, novis semper ac indies
cumulatis amoris ac benevolentiae officiis excultam, violarent.　Propterea,
audito de successione dicti Serenissimi Scotiae Regis ad regna Angliae et
Hiberniae, missisque ex parte Serenissimi Regis Hispaniarum, Domino
Joanne Taxio, comite Villaemedianae et, ex parte dictorum Serenissimorum
Archiducum, Domino Carolo, principe comite Arembergii, qui de regni successione, nomine serenissimorum principum, respective, gratularentur dicto
Serenissimo Regi Angliae, eaque legatione humanissime suscepta, legatisque
amantissime receptis, certiores redditi fuerunt dicti Serenissimi Rex Hispaniarum et Archiduces a suis legatis de propensa Serenissimi Regis Angliae
voluntate, nedum ad observanda antiqua foedera, sed alia (si opus foret)
arctiora et firmiora ineunda.　Quare nihil ab ipsis praetermittendum esse
putarunt, quo posset communis Reipublicae Christianae tranquillitas pro-
moveri, et populorum sibi commissorum utilitati prospici ; et ut quamprimum
et sedulo opus tam pium conficeretur, commissarios suos ac procuratores
generales ac speciales constituerunt, cum amplissima facultate ad ineunda
cum ipso serenissimo Rege Angliae ac stabilienda foedera, renovandaque
jamdiu intermissa commercia, pacemque ac amicitiam perpetuo duraturam
inter ipsos principes, confirmandam.

Quapropter, nos, Johannes Velaschius, Castellae et Legionis comestabilis,
dux civitatis Friensis, comes Hari, dominus villarum Villalpandi et Pedratiae
de la Sierra, dominus domus Velaschiae et Septem Infantium de Lara,
cubicularius major Serenissimi Philippi III., Hispaniarum, etc., regis, ac suus
in pertinentibus ad statum ac bellum consiliarius, ac preses Italiae, procurator
et commissarius specialis a R[egia] C[atholica] M[ajestate] constitutus, ad
praedicta et infrascripta omnia stabilienda et peragenda, cum amplissima
facultate (ut patet in mandato regis, facto in Valladolid primo Octobris, anno
1603, manu propria dicti Catholici regis subscripto, et suo sigillo regio munito,
de verbo ad verbum inferius registrando) ; et nobiscum, Joannes Taxius,
comes Villaemedianae, a cubiculo regis et cursorum in regnis et dominiis
Regis Catholici generalis praefectus, et a Regia Catholica Majestate ad
tractatum pacis nominatus ; et Alexander Rovidius, collegii Mediolanensis
jurisconsultus et Mediolanensis provintiae senator, a nobis nomine S[uae]
R[egiae] C[atholicae] M[ajesta]tis nominatus, et a nobis pariter, dum
properantes in Angliam, superveniente valitudine, in Belgio distineremur,
virtute facultatis regiae nobis concessae ad ipsam pacem, interea, cum eadem
facultate et auctoritate quae nobis tributa fuerat, tractandam—una cum dicto
Comite Villaemedianae—substitutus (ut patet mandato facto Bergis Sancti
Winoci, decimo quinto Maii, 1604, inferius de verbo ad verbum registrando)
omnes commissarii ex parte dicti Serenissimi Regis Hispaniarum ; Carolus,

princeps comes Arembergii, eques Ordinis Aurei Velleris, a consiliis rerum
status, admiralius generalis; Joannes Richardotus, eques, Secreti Consilii
preses et a rerum status consiliis; Ludovicus Verreycken, eques, primarius
secretarius et audientiarius, serenissimorum principum Archiducum legati et
deputati (ut patet mandato facto Bruxellis, die duodecimo mensis Aprilis,
1604, inferius quoque registrando) ; Thomas, comes de Dorset, baro de Buc-
hurst, thesaurarius magnus Angliae; Carolus, comes Nottingham, baro
Howard de Effingham, capitalis justitiarius et justitiarius itinerans omnium
forestarum citra Trentam, magnus admiralius Angliae et praefectus generalis
classium et marium regnorum Angliae, Franciae, et Hiberniae, ac insularum
et dominiorum eorundem; Carolus, comes Devoniae, baro de Mountjoy,
locumtenens pro serenissimo Rege Angliae, etc., in regno suo Hiberniae,
munitionum bellicarum praefectus, gubernator oppidi, insulae, et castri Portis-
mout,—praenobilis Ordinis Garterii milites; Henricus, comes Northamp-
toniae, dominus Howard de Marnehil, custos et admiralius Quinque Portuum
maritimorum ; et Robertus, dominus Cecil, baro de Esingden, primarius dicti
Serenissimi Regis secretarius, magister curiae Wardorum et Liberationum,—
consiliarii e Secretioribus Consiliis Serenissimi Regis Angliae deputati et
commissarii pro dicto Serenissimo Rege Angliae (ut patet mandato facto in
palatio Suae Majestatis Westmonasterii, sub die nono Maii, stillo veteri, anno
Domini 1604, inferius registrando).

Praemissis prius diligenti rerum omnium examine ac discusione, factisque
pluribus sessionibus et conferentiis, ac post diuturnam disceptationem ad
Omnipotentis Dei gloriam, totius Christiani orbis beneficium, subditorumque
dictorum serenissimorum principum utilitatem et quietem, fuit per nos conclusum, stabilitum, ac concordatum prout infra :

1.[16] Primo, conclusum, stabilitum, et accordatum fuit et est, ut ab hodie
in antea, sit bona, sincera, vera, firma, ac perfecta amicitia et confoederatio
ac pax perpetuo duratura, quae inviolabiliter observetur, inter Serenissimum
Regem Hispaniarum et Serenissimos Archiduces Austriae, duces Burgundiae,
etc., Serenissimum Regem Angliae eorumque haeredes et successores quoscumque, eorumque regna, patrias, dominia, terras, populos, homines ligeos,
ac subditos quoscumque, praesentes et futuros, cujuscumque conditionis,
dignitatis, et gradus existant, tam per terram quam per mare et aquas dulces ;
ita ut praedicti vassalli ac subditi sibi invicem favere, et mutuis prosequi
officiis ac honesta affectione invicem se tractare habeant.

2. Cessetque imposterum omnis hostilitas ac inimicitia, offensionibus omnibus, injuriis, ac damnis quae (durante bellorum incendio) partes quoquomodo
percepissent, sublatis ac oblivioni traditis; ita ut imposterum nihil alter ab
altero, occasione quorumcumque damnorum, offensionum, captionum, aut
spoliorum pretendere possit, sed omnium abolitio sit et censeatur facta, ab
hodie in antea ; omnisque actio extincta habeatur, salvo et praeterquam
respectu captionum [17] factarum a die vicesimo quarto Aprilis, 1603,[18] citra
(quia de illis debebit reddi ratio) ; abstinebuntque in futurum ab omni praeda,
captione, offensione, ac spolio, in quibuscumque regnis, dominiis, locis, ac
ditionibus alterutrius ubivis sitis, tam in terra quam in mari et aquis dulcibus.
Nec per suos vassallos, incolas, vel subditos, aliquid ex praedictis fieri con-

---

[16] The articles are paragraphed but not numbered.
[17] Thus, in the enrollment. The ratification reads *cautionum*, which is, of course,
wrong.
[18] *Cf.* above, introduction and note 2.

sentient ; omnemque praedam, spolium, ac captionem, ac damnum quod inde
fiat vel dabitur, restitui facient.

 . . . .

9. Item conventum ac stabilitum fuit et est, quod inter dictum Serenissimum
Regem Hispaniae ac dictum Serenissimum Regem Angliae ac cujuslibet
eorum vassallos, incolas, et subditos, tam per terram quam per mare et aquas
dulces, in omnibus et singulis regnis, dominiis, ac insulis, aliisque terris,
civitatibus, oppidis, portubus, ac districtibus dictorum regnorum et dominiorum, sit [et] esse debeat commertium liberum in quibus ante bellum fuit
commercium, juxta et secundum usum et observantiam antiquorum foederum
et tractatuum ante bellum. Ita ut, absque aliquo salvo conductu, aliaque
licentia, generali vel speciali, tam per terram quam per mare et aquas dulces,
subditi et vassalli unius et alterius regis possint et valeant ad regna et
dominia praedicta, eorumque omnium civitates, oppida, portus, littora, sinus,
ac districtus, accedere, intrare, navigare, et quoscunque portus subire, in
quibus ante bellum fuit commercium, et juxta et secundum usum et observantiam antiquorum foederum et tractatuum ante bellum, cum plaustris,
equis, sarcinulis, navigiis, tam onustis quam onerandis, merces importare,
emere, vendere in eisdem quantum voluerint commeatum, resque ad victum
et profectionem necessarias justo pretio sibi assumere, restaurandis navigiis
et vehiculis propriis vel conductis aut commodatis operam dare, illinc cum
mercibus bonis ac rebus quibuscunque (solutis juxta locorum statuta teloniis
ac vectigalibus praesentibus) tantum eadem libertate recedere, indeque ad
patrias proprias vel alienas quomodocumque velint et sine impedimento
recedere.

 . . . .

Et in omnium et singulorum fidem manu nostra propria subscripsimus.
Londini, die vigessimo octavo Augusti stilo novo, et die decimo octavo
ejusdem mensis stilo veteri, anno Domini millesimo sexcentesimo quarto.
Joan de Velasco, condestable, El Conde de Villa Mediana, Alex[ander]
Rovidius, Charles P. Co. D'Arenberg, Praeses Richardotus, L. Verreycken,
T. Dorset, Nottingham, Densier [*sic*], H. Northampton, Ro. Cecil.

 . . . .

Dat. Vallisoleti, decimo quinto die mensis Junii, anno Domini millesimo
sexcentesimo quinto.

PHILIPPUS.

Notandum[19] praefatum Serenissimum Principem Jacobum, Magnae Britanniae, etc. regem, in ipso tractatu capitulorum praedictorum atque adeo
in instrumento suo ratificationis eorundem, procuratoribus Domini mei
Clementissimi Philippi, ejus nominis tertii, Hispaniarum, etc. regis, tradito,
titulo usum esse Regis Angliae Scotiaeque, quem ex illo tempore in stilum
Magnae Britanniae mutavit. Dominus Rex mandavit mihi.

ANDREAS A PRADA.

TRANSLATION.

Philip III., by the grace of God king of Castile, Leon, Aragon, the Two
Sicilies, Jerusalem, Portugal, Navarre, Granada, Toledo, Valencia, Galicia,
the Majorcas, Seville, Sardinia, Cordova, Corsica, Murcia, Guinea, Algarve,

---

[19] What follows is written in another hand, evidently that of the secretary, who signs it.

Gibraltar, the Canary Islands, also of the East and West Indies, and the islands and mainlands of the ocean sea, archduke of Austria, duke of Burgundy and Milan, count of Hapsburg, Barcelona, and Biscay, and lord of Molina, etc. To all and singular to whom the present letters shall come, greeting. Whereas our commissioners and deputies and those of the most serene princes, Albert and Isabella Clara Eugenia, archdukes of Austria, dukes of Burgundy, etc., and of James, king of Great Britain, etc., our dearest brothers and kinsmen, agreed and concluded at London on August 28, n. s., A. D. 1604, a treaty of firm friendship and perpetual peace, and of commerce, whose tenor follows: Be it known to all and singular that after the long and very fierce fires of the wars that for many years have devastated Christendom, at great cost, God, in whose hands all things are, beholding from on high and pitying the calamities of his people (for whom, in order that he might bring them peace and leave it with them, he did not hesitate to shed his own blood) effectually extinguished the raging fire by a stable union of the most powerful princes of Christendom, and mercifully brought a day of peace and tranquillity—a thing wished rather than hoped for. For when, by the grace of Almighty God, and to extirpate the seeds of discord, the kingdoms of England and Ireland had devolved on James, the most serene king of Scotland, and those causes of dissension had on that account been removed which so long had nourished the wars between the predecessors of the most serene princes, Philip III., king of the Spains, and Albert and Isabella Clara Eugenia, archdukes of Austria, dukes of Burgundy, and the Most Serene James, king of England, etc., all the said princes considered (God illuminating their hearts) that there was no longer any reason why they should contend in hate, which never existed between them, or fight with arms, from which their ancestors had always abstained, or why they should withdraw from the very ancient alliance, observed beyond the memory of man, or should sever the very close bonds of friendship that existed between the aforesaid Most Serene King of England and the most serene families of Austria and Burgundy, or violate the ancient friendship, daily cultivated with new and additional offices of love and good-will. Therefore, notice being received of the succession of the said Most Serene King of Scotland to the kingdoms of England and Ireland, and the lord Juan Tassis, count of Villa Mediana, having been sent on the part of the Most Serene King of the Spains, and the lord Charles, prince-count of Arenberg, on the part of the said most serene archdukes, to congratulate, respectively, in the name of their most serene princes, the said Most Serene King of England on his succession to the throne, and those embassies having been most kindly accepted and the ambassadors most lovingly received, the said Most Serene King of the Spains and the archdukes were informed by their ambassadors that the Most Serene King of England was inclined not only to observe the ancient treaties, but, if necessary, to enter into others that should be closer and more binding. Wherefore they thought they should neglect no means of promoting the common tranquillity of Christendom and the interests of the people committed to their charge; and to accomplish so pious a work with all speed and diligence, they appointed general and special commissioners and procurators, with the fullest powers, to enter into and conclude treaties with the said Most Serene King of England, to renew long-interrupted commerce, and to confirm a perpetual peace and amity among the said princes.

Wherefore we, Juan de Velasco, constable of Castile and Leon, duke of the city of Frias, count of Haro, lord of the towns of Villalpando and Pedraza-de-la-Sierra, lord of the house of Velasco and of the Seven Lords of Lara, grand chamberlain of the Most Serene Philip III., king of the Spains, and his councillor in affairs of state and war, president of Italy, appointed by his royal Catholic Majesty procurator and special commissioner, with the fullest power to decide and complete all matters mentioned above and below (as appears in the royal commission executed in Valladolid October 1, 1603, signed personally by the said Catholic king and sealed with the royal seal and to be registered word for word below) ; and with us, Juan Tassis, count of Villa Mediana, gentleman of the king's chamber and postmaster general in the kingdoms and dominions of the Catholic king, and named by his Royal Catholic Majesty to treat for peace; and Alessandro Rovida, professor of law in the college of Milan and senator of the province of Milan, nominated by us in the name of his Royal Catholic Majesty and, while we on our way to England were detained in Flanders by illness, substituted by us by virtue of the royal commission granted to us for this peace, in order that he might treat meanwhile, together with the said count of Villa Mediana, with the same power and authority that had been given to us (as appears in the commission executed at Bergues-St. Winoc, May 15, 1604, to be registered word for word below)—all commissioners on the part of the said Most Serene King of the Spains ; Charles, prince-count of Arenberg, knight of the Order of the Golden Fleece, councillor of state, and admiral general; Jean Richardot, knight, president of the privy council and councillor of state; and Louis Verreycken, knight, principal secretary and audiencer—ambassadors and deputies of the most serene princes, the archdukes (as appears by a commission executed at Brussels April 12, 1604, also to be registered below) ; Thomas, earl of Dorset, baron of Buckhurst, high treasurer of England ; Charles, earl of Nottingham, baron Howard of Effingham, chief justice and justice in eyre of all forests on this side Trent, high admiral of England and captain general of the navies and seas of England, France, Ireland, and the islands and dominions thereof ; Charles, earl of Devonshire, baron of Mount-joy, lieutenant in the kingdom of Ireland for the Most Serene King of England, etc., master of the ordnance, governor of the town, island, and castle of Portsmouth—knights of the most honorable Order of the Garter ; Henry, earl of Northampton, Lord Howard of Marnhull, warden and admiral of the Cinque Ports; and Robert, lord Cecil, baron of Essingden, principal secretary of the said Most Serene King, master of the Court of Wards and Liveries—all lords of the Privy Council of the Most Serene King of England—deputies and commissioners for the said Most Serene King of England (as appears in the commission executed in his Majesty's palace at Westminster on May 9, o. s., A. D. 1604, to be registered below).

After diligent preliminary examination and discussion of the whole affair, after many sessions and conferences had been held, and after long-continued debate, it was agreed, settled, and concluded by us, for the glory of Almighty God, the benefit of all Christendom, and the advantage and quiet of the subjects of the said most serene princes, as below :

1. First, it was and is agreed, settled, and concluded that from this day forward there shall be a good, sincere, true, firm, and perfect amity, league, and peace, to endure forever, and inviolably to be observed, both by land and sea and fresh waters, betwixt the Most Serene King of the Spains and the

Most Serene Archdukes of Austria, Dukes of Burgundy, etc., and the Most
Serene King of England, and all their heirs and successors whomsoever, and
all their kingdoms, countries, dominions, lands, peoples, vassals, and subjects,
present and future, of whatsoever condition, dignity, or rank they may be;
so that the aforesaid vassals and subjects shall each favor the other, shall
act one toward the other with mutual courtesies, and shall treat one another
with sincere affection.

2. And that from henceforth all hostility and enmity shall cease, and all
offenses, injuries, or damages which either part (during the period while
war was waging) has sustained in any manner shall be offered and consigned
to oblivion, so that hereafter neither party may make any claim against the
other, because of any damages, offenses, depredations, or spoils, but that,
from this day henceforth, all such claims shall be abolished and shall be
considered as closed; and all actions [for the same] shall be considered as
extinguished, except in regard to such depredations as are committed after
April 24, 1603 (because of these a reckoning ought to be made); and each
party shall hereafter abstain from all booty, depredation, offenses, and spoils,
both by sea and land and fresh waters, in any of the kingdoms, dominions,
places, or jurisdictions of the other, wherever they may be situated. Neither
shall they [*i. e.*, the aforesaid princes] consent that any of the aforesaid be
done by their vassals, the inhabitants of their kingdoms, or their subjects;
and they shall cause restitution to be made of all booty, spoils, depredations,
and damages which shall hereafter be committed.

. . . .

9. *Item,* it was and is agreed and settled that there shall be and ought to
be free commerce between the said Most Serene King of Spain and the said
Most Serene King of England, and the vassals, inhabitants of their kingdoms,
and subjects of each of them, both by land and by sea and fresh waters, in
all and singular their kingdoms, dominions, islands, other lands, cities, towns,
ports, and straits of the said kingdoms and dominions, where commerce
existed before the war, agreeably and according to the use and observance
of the ancient alliances and treaties before the war: so that, without any safe
conduct, or other special or general license, the subjects and vassals of both
kings may, and shall have the power, both by land and by sea and fresh
waters, to approach, enter, and sail to the aforesaid kingdoms and dominions,
and to the cities, towns, ports, shores, bays, and straits of all of them; to
enter any ports in which there was commerce before the war, agreeably and
according to the use and observance of the ancient alliances and treaties before
the war, with wagons, horses, packs, and boats, laden and to be laden, to
bring in merchandise and, in these places, to buy and sell as much as they
wish, and to procure for themselves, for a just price, supplies and commodities
necessary for their sustenance and voyage, and attend to the necessary
repair of boats and vehicles, whether their own, hired, or borrowed. They
will be equally free to depart thence with their merchandise, goods, and all
other commodities, on payment of the tolls and duties then in force, according to the ordinances of the places; and they may go thence to their own or
other countries, as they please, without hindrance.

. . . .

And in pledge of all and singular we have subscribed our names with our
own hand. London, August 18/28, A. D. 1604. Juan de Velasco, constable,

the Count of Villa Mediana, Alessandro Rovida, Charles, prince-count of Arenberg, President Richardot, L. Verreycken, T. Dorset, Nottingham, Devonshire, H. Northampton, Robert Cecil . . .

Given at Valladolid, June 15, A. D. 1605.

PHILIP.

It is to be noted that the aforesaid Most Serene Prince James, king of Great Britain, etc., in the treaty of the aforesaid articles itself, and hence in his instrument of ratification of them delivered to the representatives of my Most Clement lord Philip, king of the Spains, etc., third of his name, made use of the title, King of England and Scotland, which afterwards he changed to the style of Great Britain. The lord king has commanded me.

ANDRÉS DE PRADA.

28.

Truce between Spain and the United Netherlands, concluded at Antwerp, April 9, 1609. Ratification by Spain, July 7, 1609. [Ratification by the States General, April 11, 1609.]

INTRODUCTION.

By separately concluding the treaty of Vervins with Spain,[1] Henry IV. of France had seemingly abandoned both his allies, England and the United Provinces, although, contrary to the treaty, he actually continued a limited aid to the Dutch;[2] by signing the treaty of London[3] the King of England had weakened the Dutch still further in their struggle with Spain. This defection of their allies, Spinola's military successes, and especially the proposals of Henry IV. to assume sovereignty over the Provinces, alarmed the great Advocate of Holland, Oldenbarnevelt, who with his followers dominated the States General, and inclined them to listen to the overtures for peace which in 1606 and early in 1607 came from the archdukes, the rulers of the southern provinces. On the other hand, a party led by Prince Maurice and Count William Lewis of Nassau, and including among its most ardent adherents those who had an interest in the East India and American trade, desired the continuance of the war. The merchants knew that Spain would demand the renunciation of the distant traffic as the price of peace, and even were the trade permitted it would be less profitable under conditions of peace than when conducted in armed vessels.

The hope of expelling the Dutch from the forbidden regions was believed by many to be the principal motive that induced Spain to treat.[4] Within a few years Dutch trade beyond the oceans had attained great proportions. When peace negotiations began, the powerful East India Company, chartered in 1602, had seriously undermined the power of the Portuguese in the East; with Guinea, Brazil, Guiana, Punta del Rey, Cuba, and Hispaniola,

---

[1] Doc. **23**, last paragraph of introduction.
[2] An excellent account of Franco-Dutch relations at this period is in Nouaillac, *Villeroy*, pp. 373 ff., and ch. 5.
[3] Doc. **27**.
[4] Jeannin asserted that it was the principal motive, *Négociations* (ed. Petitot), III. 291, and cf. ll. 95, 96, 199; Prince Maurice said the same, Bentivoglio, *Relazione* (1644), p. 111, *Relations* (1652), p. 106; Grotius says that the Spaniards declared that it was the main reason, *Annales*, lib. XVII.

the Dutch were also prosecuting an active trade.[5] In consequence of their
losses the Portuguese were earnestly petitioning Philip to end the war;[6]
and among the influences that inclined the Spanish government toward peace
were reports of the project of a Dutch West India Company " that should
with a strong fleet carry, at once, both war and merchandise into America ",
and drive the enemy thence. William Usselinx had been advocating the
formation of this company for several years, and in 1606 his plan was
approved by the States General and a draft charter submitted to the cities.[7]

In the peace parleyings held early in 1607, the United Provinces demanded
the recognition of their independence as an indispensable preliminary step.
To this demand the archdukes yielded by declaring in somewhat equivocal
terms that they would treat with them for a peace or long truce " in the
quality of and as holding them for free provinces and states over which they
had no pretensions ".[8] The archdukes, in their turn, asked for an eight
months' armistice, which the United Provinces conceded, but on condition
that Spain should confirm the armistice as well as the recognition of their
independence.

It was not until October, 1607, that this recognition was received from
Spain,[9] and meanwhile negotiations were at a standstill. During this interim,
however, representatives of those neighboring princes upon whom the Provinces had formerly leaned were gathering at the Hague to watch or, if
possible, to direct the negotiations. France was represented by Jeannin,
president of the Parlement of Burgundy, by Buzanval,[10] the regular resident
at the Hague, and by De Russy; England, by Sir Ralph Winwood, who, in
accordance with treaty provisions, had sat in the States General as Councillor of State, and by Sir Richard Spenser.[11] Denmark and several of the
Protestant princes of Germany also sent envoys. A possible danger to the
Dutch lay in the interest felt by Henry and Jeannin in the project of forming

[5] Meteren, *Histoire des Pays-Bas*, p. 629. On the relations of the Dutch with America
at this time, see reports by J. F. Jameson and G. L. Burr in U. S. Commission on
Boundary between Venezuela and British Guiana, *Report and Papers* (1897), I. 37 ff.,
99 ff.; and articles by G. Edmundson in the *Eng. Hist. Rev.*, XVIII. (1903) 642 ff., XXI.
(1906) 229 ff. For further bibliographical indications respecting Dutch colonial trade,
see C. de Lannoy and H. Vander Linden, *L'Expansion Coloniale: Néerlande et Danemark* (1911), and, in addition, F. Rachfahl, " Die Holländische See- und Handels-
macht ". etc., in *Lenz-Festschrift* (1910), pp. 39-88.

[6] Grotius, *op. cit.*, lib. XV.

[7] *Ibid.*, English translation (1665), p. 864; Jameson, *Willem Usselinx*, pp. 31-32, in
Papers of the Am. Hist. Assoc., II.; G. M. Asher, *Bibliographical and Historical Essay
on New-Netherland* (1854-1867), p. 46.

[8] This formula was embodied in the preamble of the truce.

[9] The declaration, armistice, and confirmation are printed in Jeannin, *Négociations*,
and thence in Dumont, *Corps Diplomatique*, tom. V., pt. II., pp. 83, 84. The Spanish
ratification offered to the States in July, 1607, was not accepted by them.

[10] Buzanval died in the autumn of 1607.

[11] The instructions of the English commissioners are in Winwood, *Memorials*, II.
329-335.

French companies for trading in the East and West Indies; and in their belief that if Dutch merchants failed to obtain the India " navigation ", they might be attracted to France.[12] On the other hand, these statesmen realized how important the India trade was to the Dutch, and how much damage it had enabled and would enable them to inflict upon Spain, the common enemy."

The States having accepted the Spanish confirmation, deputies were appointed by the principal parties to the negotiations. The archdukes' delegates, who were also empowered to treat in the name of the King of Spain, were the Marquis Spinola, Secretary Don Juan de Mancicidor, President Richardot, the Audiencer Verreycken, and Father Neyen. The States were represented by Count William Lewis of Nassau and Walraven van Brederode, delegates at large, and by one delegate from each of the seven provinces, among whom Oldenbarnevelt played the leading rôle. On February 1, 1608, the archdukes' ambassadors reached the Hague, and a few days later conferences began at the Binnenhof. The main points of dispute were the recognition of the independence of the United Provinces, the restitution of places held by them in Brabant and Flanders, toleration of the public exercise of the Roman Catholic religion in the United Provinces, and the India trade.

The debate on the India trade began on February 13, continued through many sessions, and was marked by great vehemence. Both sides regarded the question as vital. The Dutch believed the trade necessary to their existence. It drew money to them from other nations; maintained sailors and armed vessels without expense to the state; sapped Spain's strength; made them superior to her in sea-power; and caused the republic to be desired as a friend by other nations. By renouncing it they would betray the native princes who had aided them, and having once abandoned these they could never reinstate themselves. The Dutch had a right to the traffic, for in many parts where they traded the King of Spain exercised no authority, or was hated by the natives, or was unable to defend himself. To withdraw from a traffic which was allowed them by the laws of nature and of nations would prejudice their status as a sovereign power, and the principle of the freedom of the seas. Finally, the archdukes and Spain had agreed to treat on the basis of *uti possidetis,* and the Dutch were in possession of the India trade. They suspected that the negotiations had been begun for the purpose of weakening them by obtaining their withdrawal from the navigation, after which Spain would try to reduce them again to her authority. If the Dutch would relinquish the trade, the archdukes offered to give up their title of sovereigns over all the Netherlands and to abstain from using the seal of the seventeen

[12] Jeannin, ed. Petitot, II. 135-136, 204, 258, 322-323, III. 262, 280-284. See La Roncière, *La Marine Française* (1899, etc.), IV. 268 ff.; P. Laffleur de Kermaingant, *L'Ambassade de France en Angleterre: Mission de Christophe de Harlay* (1895), I. 288-293.
[13] Jeannin, *ed. cit.*, II. 136, 534. III. 290 ff., 296 ff., 305.

provinces; and Philip would reopen the trade with Spain." On the other hand, if Spain conceded the India trade to the States it might cause other rulers to demand the same liberty for their subjects, or to take it without demanding it; and the Dutch might undersell the Portuguese or oblige the king to give up the tribute that he levied on the Portuguese trade."

At the end of February the States brought forward three alternative means of accommodation: " peace, with free trade to those parts of the Indies not actually possessed by Spain; peace in Europe, and a truce in the Indies for a term of years with permission to trade during that period; trade to the Indies "at their peril" after the example of the French and English. The Catholic deputies totally rejected the first and third propositions but would submit the second to Spain if it were acceptably modified. They rejected a draft to the effect that whatever might happen in the Indies during or after the truce, peace should not fail to be perpetual as far south as the tropic of Cancer," for they wished to confine the dispute to the East Indies, and feared that by referring to the tropics, which encircled the earth, the West Indies would seem to be comprised. They wished the States to declare expressly that they would abstain from going to the West Indies, and that in the East Indies they would not visit the places held by the Portuguese." The States, who meanwhile had tried to frighten their opponents by showing a renewed interest in the West India Company," finally drafted an acceptable article, stipulating that during nine years after the conclusion of the truce they might trade anywhere in the Indies except in places held by the King of Spain where they might go only with the consent of the governors or in case of necessity. Before the termination of the nine years, an attempt should be made to come to a lasting agreement." The West Indies were not specifically mentioned."

In April this draft was despatched to the King of Spain for his consideration, and negotiations flagged; in August it was known that Spain insisted on the prompt withdrawal of the States from both the East and the West Indies and complete toleration for the public exercise of the Catholic religion in the Provinces as indispensable conditions of her recognition of the independence of the States." It was certain that peace was unattainable and negotiations were broken off.

" For the debates on the India trade, see especially Deventer, *Gedenkstukken*, III. 178 ff., Meteren, *Histoire des Pays-Bas*, pp. 626 ff.; and Jeannin, *ed. cit.*, III. 198 ff., 236, 239 ff., 251, 252, 287, etc.
" Jeannin, *ed. cit.*, III. 251-252.
" Rodríguez Villa, *Ambrosio Spinola*, p. 217; Deventer, *op. cit.*, III. 188-189; Jeannin, *ed. cit.*, III. 287; Grotius, *op. cit.*, lib. XVII.
" Jeannin, *ed. cit.*, III. 311; Deventer, *op. cit.*, III. 196.
" Deventer, *op. cit.*, III. 198; Jeannin, *op. cit.*, III. 315.
" Jameson, *op. cit.*, p. 35; Jeannin, *ed. cit.*, III. 289; Grotius, *loc. cit.*
" Meteren, *ed. cit.*, p. 633 b; Grotius, *loc. cit.*; Jeannin, *op. cit.*, III. 373, 374.
" Jeannin, *ed. cit.*, III. 326.   " Meteren, *ed. cit.*, p. 650 b; Jeannin, *ed. cit.*, IV. 86.

This result could scarcely have been displeasing to Jeannin, who preferred a truce to a peace, since the former would leave the Dutch more dependent on France and suspicious of Spain. In concert with the English ambassadors, and in spite of the bitter opposition of Prince Maurice and the Zeelanders, he persuaded the States to revive negotiations in behalf of a truce, and to employ the French and English ambassadors as intermediaries.

In February, 1609, the French and English ambassadors opened their conference with the deputies of the archdukes at Antwerp. The principal point of difficulty was the India trade. The Catholic deputies would not have the word Indies in the treaty, lest other governments should demand the same concession, and thought it sufficient to proclaim the truce general. Henry IV. saw an advantage in omitting the term Indies, since if it were used the King of Spain would make a distinction between the East and West Indies, excluding the Dutch from the latter. The French statesmen were inclined to minimize the value that this trade would have for the Dutch when carried on in accordance with agreement and not *par hostilité.*[23] Yet Jeannin labored for the end desired by the States, not because France wished to strengthen the States unduly, but because she was unwilling to restore Spain to her former strength, or to play into the hands of the English, who were believed to desire the trade for themselves.[24] After much discussion it was agreed that the second article should declare a general truce without mention of the Indies. The fourth article contained a concession of the India trade, veiled by circumlocutions:—traffic was permitted in Spain's European lands and in any other of her possessions where her allies were permitted to trade; *outside these limits* (*i. e.*, in the Indies) subjects of the States could not traffic without express permission from the king in places held by Spain; but in places not thus held they might trade upon permission of the natives, without hindrance from the king or his officers. In order to make the meaning of this fourth article unmistakable, Jeannin further insisted on inserting the fifth article, which declared that owing to the time that must elapse before news of the truce could reach the forces and ships " outside the stated limits " the truce would not begin there until a year from the date on which the treaty was signed. This the Catholic deputies conceded with great reluctance.[25] The agreement that Spain would not hinder the subjects of the States in their trade with other princes and peoples " outside the limits " was also strengthened by a special and secret treaty, to be considered as forming part of the principal treaty, in which the name Indies was again avoided. The name,

[23] Jeannin, *ed. cit.*, V. 214, 233, 234, 237.
[24] *Ibid.*, pp. 235-238, 321. Henry was also jealous of the settlement of the English in Virginia. On March 28, 1609, Villeroy wrote to Jeannin that they had heard " que le roi d'Angleterre a dessein de s'accroitre et établir en ces pays-là, et que dès à présent il a envoyé des colonies entières pour fortifier les siens en un lieu qu'ils nomment la Virginia: de quoi notre Roi n'est sans martel qui aiguise son appétit en ces affaires." *Ibid.*, V. 321-322.
[25] *Ibid.*, p. 242.

however, appeared in an act signed by the French and English ambassadors, which certified that the archdukes' deputies had agreed that just as the Dutch should not traffic in places held by the King of Spain in the Indies without his permission, so subjects of the King of Spain should not traffic in places held by the States in the Indies without their permission; and secondly, that the States' deputies had declared that if their native allies in the Indies were molested, they would aid them, and that such action should not be a violation of the truce.

Other principal points of dispute were adjusted as follows: the independence of the States was acknowledged; the exercise of the Catholic religion in the Provinces was not conceded; the States were left in enjoyment of the places that they occupied in Brabant and Flanders; and they kept a tax on vessels passing through the Scheldt to Antwerp.

Toward the middle of March, after the success of the negotiations had become assured, Jeannin acquainted the States General with what had passed in the conferences at Antwerp, and with the articles as agreed to by the deputies of the archdukes, persuaded them suitably to recognize the services of Prince Maurice and of his house,[26] and promised that if Spain disturbed the India commerce the kings of France and England would deem it a rupture of the truce.[27] Toward the end of the month, the deputies of the States General, who with one exception[28] were the same as those of the preceding year, met with the deputies of the kings and of the archdukes at Antwerp, and on the ninth of April the treaty and the additional acts were signed in that city. They were ratified a few days later by the States General at Bergen-op-Zoom, and by the archdukes, and after an interval of three months by the King of Spain, who added that he hoped that during the truce the States would treat the Catholics well.[29]

BIBLIOGRAPHY.

Text: **MS.** The original manuscript of the ratification by the King of Spain is in the Rijksarchief at the Hague, Secrete Casse, Spaignen en de Ertzhertogen, casse B, loquet A, no. 24.

Text: **Printed. French.** Authorized editions were issued by Velpius in Brussels and by Jacobsz in the Hague in 1609. They do not include the secret treaty and the ambassadors' certificates, which are published together with the text in P. Jeannin, *Négociations* (1st ed., 1656; in Petitot, *Collection des Mémoires*, toms. XI-XV., 1821-1822, V. 365-383), and thence in J. Dumont, *Corps Diplomatique* (1726-1731), tom. V., pt. II., pp. 99-102, and in J. A. de Abreu y Bertodano, *Coleccion de los Tratados de España: Reynado de Phelipe III.* (1740), I. 458-489. A

---

[26] *Ibid.*, pp. 292-303, 305, 310, 311.
[27] Grotius, *op. cit.*, lib. XVIII.; Jeannin, *op. cit.*, V. 302.
[28] Cornelius Renessen was substituted for Nicholas Berk, deputy for Utrecht.
[29] See below, p. 267.

recent edition of the text with some cognate documents is in V. Brants, *Recueil des Ordonnances des Pays-Bas, Règne d'Albert et Isabelle, 1597-1621*, tom. I. (1909), pp. 402-411. **Dutch.** *Groot Placaet-Boeck van de Staten Generael* (1658-1796), I. cols. 55-72.

References: Contemporary and early writings. P. Jeannin, *Négociations*, 1st ed., 1656; in Petitot, *Collection des Mémoires*, toms. XI.-XV., and other editions; M. L. van Deventer, *Gedenkstukken van J. van Oldenbarnevelt* (1860-1865), III. 71-312—a diary of the negotiations for the truce from Feb. 1, 1608, to Mar. 4, 1609, is on pp. 168-239; R. Winwood, *Memorials of Affairs of State in the Reigns of Elizabeth and James I.* (1725), II. 298-492, III. 1-17; A. Rodríguez Villa, *Ambrosio Spinola* (1904), pp. 150-255, 627-651, 667, 704, 705; *Recueil des Lettres Missives de Henri IV.*, tom. VII. (1858), *passim* (ed. by M. Berger de Xivrey in *Collection de Documents Inédits sur l'Histoire de France*); *Lettres d'Henry IV. et de Messieurs de Villeroy et de Puisieux à Mr. Antoine Le Fevre de la Boderie, 1606-1611* (1733), 2 vols., *passim*; *Resolutien* of the States of Holland (1772-1798), vols. for the years 1607-1609, *passim*; Cardinal G. Bentivoglio, "Relatione del Trattato della Tregua di Fiandra", in *Opere . . . cio è Relatione di Fiandra*, etc. (1644), pp. 99-130, also in *Collezione de' Classici Italiani* (1802-1850), CLXXXIV. 255-339; English translation, entitled *Historical Relations of the United Provinces and of Flanders* (1652), pp. 95-127; E. van Meteren, *Histoire des Pays-Bas* (1618), livs. XXVIII.-XXX.; Hugo Grotius, *Annales et Historiae de Rebus Belgicis* (1657, etc.), libs. XV.-XVIII., English translation (1665), pp. 858-974; Dominicus Baudius, *Induciarum Belli Belgici Libri Tres* (1st ed., 1613, 3d ed., 1629); *Calendar of State Papers, Venice*, 1603-1607, *passim*, and *id.*, 1607-1610, *passim*; *Kroniek van Historisch Genootschap te Utrecht*, Jaarg. 28, 1872 (1873), pp. 226-239, 242-283, 363-375; G. Groen van Prinsterer, *Archives de la Maison d'Orange-Nassau* (1835, etc.), 2ᵉ sér., II. 369 ff.

References: Later writings. J. L. Motley, *The United Netherlands* (1904), vol. IV., cc. 46-52; P. J. Blok, *Geschiedenis van het Nederlandsche Volk* (2d ed., 1912, etc.), II. 346-362, abridged English translation, *History of the People of the Netherlands* (1898-1912), III. 304-314, German translation, *Geschichte der Niederlande* (1902, etc.), III. 623-655, in Heeren und Ukert, *Geschichte der Europäischen Staaten* (1829, etc.) ; J. F. Jameson, *Willem Usselinx*, pp. 22-46, in *Papers* of the American Historical Association, II. (1887); M. Philippson, *Heinrich IV. und Philipp III.* (1870-1876), III. 67-252; J. Nouaillac, *Villeroy* (1909), pp. 461-477; J. P. Arend *et al.*, *Algemeene Geschiedenis des Vaderlands* (1840, etc.), III. (2), 244-344.

TEXT.[30]

Comme ainsi soit que les Serenissimes Archiducqz. Albert et Isabella Clara Eugenia, etc., ayent dez le vingt-quatriesme d'Apvril, seize cens et sept, fait une trefve et cessation d'armes pour huict mois avec Illustres Seigneurs les Estatz Generaulx des Provinces Unies des Pays Bas, en qualité et comme

[30] From the original manuscript of the Spanish ratification in the Rijksarchief at the Hague, Secrete Casse, Spaignen en de Ertzhertogen, casse B, loquet A, no. 24.

les tenans pour Estatz, Provinces, et Pays libres, sur lesquelz ilz ne pre-
tendoyent rien, laquelle trefve debvoit estre ratiffiee avec pareille declaration
par la Majesté du Roy Catholicque, en ce qui le povoit toucher et lesdites
ratiffications et declarations delivrees ausdits sieurs Estatz trois mois apres
icelle trefve, comm'il s'est fait par lettres patentes du dix-huictiesme de
Septembre audit an, et oultre ce donne procuration specialle ausdits sieurs
Archiducqz du dixiesme de janvier, seize cens huict, pour tant en son nom
comme au leur, faire tout ce qu'ilz jugeroyent convenable pour parvenir a
une bonne paix, ou trefve a longues annees, en suyte de la quelle procuration,
lesdits sieurs Archiducqz auroient aussi, par leurs lettres de commission du
xxvii du mesme mois, nommé et deputé commissaires pour en conferer et
traicter esdits noms et qualitez, et a cest' occasion consenty et accorde que
ladite trefve fut prolongee et continuee par diverses fois, mesme le xxe de
May jusques a la fin de la dite annee, XVI^c huict, mais apres s'estre assemblez
plusieurs fois avec les deputez desdits sieurs Estatz, qui avoient aussi procuration et commission d'eulx, datee du ve de febvrier audit an, ilz n'auroient
peu demeurer d'accord de la dite paix, pour plusieurs grandes difficultez
survenues entr' eulx, au moyen de quoy les sieurs ambassadeurs des Roys
Treschrestien et de la Grande Bretaigne, des Princes Electeurs Palatin et
de Brandenbourg, Marquiz d'Ansbach, et Landtgrave de Hessen, envoyez
sur le lieu de la part desdits sieurs roys et princes pour ayder a l'advancement
d'ung si bon oeuvre, voyans qu'ilz estoient prestz de se separer et rompre tout
traité, auroient proposé une trefve a longues annees, a certaines conditions
contenues en ung escript, donné de leur part aux ungz et aux aultres, avec
priere et exhortation de s'y vouloir conformer. Sur lequel escript plusieurs
aultres difficultez estans derechef survenues, en fin ce jourd'huy neufiesme
du mois d'Apvril, mil six cens et neuf, se sont assemblez Messire Ambrosio
Spinola marquiz de Benaffro, chevalier de l'Ordre de la Thoison d'Or, du
conseil d'estat et de guerre de sa dite Majeste Catholicque, mestre de camp,
general de ses armees, etc., Messire Jehan Richardot, chevalier, sieur de
Barly, du conseil d'estat, chief president du conseil privé de leurs Altezes,
etc., Jehan de Mancicidor, du conseil de guerre et secretaire de sa dite
Majesté Catholicque, reverend pere frere Jehan Neyen, commissaire general
de l'Ordre de St.-François es Pays-Bas, et Messire Loys Verreyken, chevalier, audiencier et premier secretaire de leurs dites Altezes, en vertu des
lectres de procuration desdits sieurs Archiducqz, pour traitter, tant en leurs
noms qu'au nom dudit sieur Roy Catholicque, la teneur de laquelle procuration
est cy apres inseree, avec celle dudit sieur Roy, d'une part, et Messire
Guillaume Loys, conte de Nassau, Catzenellebogen, Vianden, Dietz, etc.,
sieur de Bilsteyn, gouverneur et capitaine general de Frize, ville de Groeningen et Ommelanden, Drente, etc., Messire Walrave, sieur de Brederode,
Vianen, viconte d'Utrecht, sieur d'Ameyden, Cloutingen, etc., les sieurs
Cornille de Gendt, sieur de Loenen et Meynerswyck, viconte et juge de
l'empire, et de la ville de Nyemegen, Messire Jehan d'Oldenbarnevelt, chevalier, sieur de Tempel, Rodenrys, etc., advocat et garde du grand seel, chartres,
et registres de Hollande et Westfrize, Messire Jacques de Malderee, chevalier,
sieur des Heyes, premier et representant la noblesse aux Estatz et conseil de
la conté de Zelande, les sieurs Gerard de Renesse, sieur van der Aa, de
Streeffkercken, Nyeuwlekkerlandt, etc., Gellius Hillama, docteur es droitz,
conseillier ordinaire du conseil de Frize, Jehan Sloeth, sieur de Salick,
drossard du pays de Vollenhoo et chastellain de la seigneurie de Cunder, et

Abel Coenders de Helpen, sieur en Faen et Cantes, au nom desdits sieurs Estatz, aussi en vertu de leurs lettres de procuration et commission, cy apres semblablement inseree, d'autre, lesquelz avec l'intervention et par l'advis de Messire Pierre Jeannin, chevalier, baron de Chagny et Montjeu, conseillier du Roy Tres-chrestien en son Conseil d'Estat et son ambassadeur extra-ordinaire vers lesdits sieurs Estatz, et Messire Elye de la Place, chevalier, sieur de Russy, viconte de Machault, aussi conseillier audit Conseil d'Estat, gentilhomme ordinaire de la chambre dudit sieur roy, bailly et capitaine de Vitry le François, et son ambassadeur ordinaire resident pres lesdits sieurs Estatz, Messire Richard Spencer, chevalier, gentilhomme ordinaire de la Chambre Privee du Roy de la Grande Bretaigne et son ambassadeur extra-ordinaire vers lesdits sieurs Estatz, et Messire Rodolphe Winwood, chevalier, ambassadeur ordinaire, et conseillier dudit sieur Roy au Conseil d'Estat des Provinces Unies, sont demeurez d'accord en la forme et maniere que s'ensuyt :

1. Premierement, lesdits sieurs Archiducqz declarent tant en leurs noms que dudit sieur Roy, qu'ilz sont contens de traicter avec lesdits sieurs Estatz Generaulx des Provinces Unies en qualité et comme les tenans pour pays, provinces, et estatz libres, sur lesquelz ilz ne pretendent rien, et de faire avec eulx, es noms et qualitez susdites, comme ilz font par ces presentes, une trefve, aux conditions cy apres escrites et declarees.

2. Asscavoir, que ladite trefve sera bonne, ferme, loyalle, et inviolable, et pour le temps de douze ans, durant lesquelz il y aura cessation de tous actes d'hostilité, de quelque façon qu'ilz soyent, entre lesdits sieurs roy, archiducqz, et Estats Generaulx, tant par mer, aultres eaues, que par terre, en tous leurs royaulmes, pays, terres, et seigneuries, et pour tous leurs subjects et habitans, de quelque qualité et condition qu'ilz soyent, sans exception de lieux ny de personnes.

3. Chacun demeurera saisy et jouyra effectuellement des pays, villes, places, terres, et seigneuries, qu'il tient et possede a present, sans y estre trouble ny inquieté, de quelque façon que ce soit, durant ladite trefve ; en quoy on entend comprendre les bourgs, villages, hameaux, et plat pays qui en dependent.

4. Les subjectz et habitans es pays desdits sieurs roy archiducqz, et Estatz, auront toute bonne correspondence et amitie par ensemble, durant ladite trefve, sans se resentir des offences et dommaiges, qu'ilz ont receu par le passé. Pourront aussi frequenter et sejourner es pays l'ung de l'aultre, et y exercer leur trafficq et commerce en toute seureté, tant par mer, aultres eaues, que par terre. Ce que toutesfois ledit sieur roy entend estre restrainct et limité aux royaulmes, pays, terres, et seigneuries, qu'il tient et possede en l'Europe et aultres lieux et mers ou les subjectz des roys et princes qui sont ses amis et alliez ont ledit trafficq de gré a gré. Et pour le reguard des lieux, villes, portz, et havres qu'il tient hors les limites susdits, que lesdits Sieurs Estatz et leurs subjectz, n'y puissent exercer aulcun trafficq, sans la permission expresse dudit sieur roy.

Bien pourront ilz faire le dit trafficq, si bon leur semble, es pays de tous aultres princes, potentatz, et peuples, qui le leur vouldront permettre, mesme hors lesdits limites, sans que ledit sieur roy, ses officiers, et subjectz, qui dependent de luy, donnent aulcun empeschement a ceste occasion ausdits princes, potentatz, et peuples, qui le leur ont permis ou permettront, ny pareillement a eulx ou aux particuliers, avec lesquelz ils ont fait et feront ledit trafficq.

5. Et pour ce qu'il est besoing d'un assez long temps pour advertir ceulx qui sont hors lesdits limites avec forces et navires de se desister de tous actes d'hostilité, a esté accordé que la trefve n'y commencera que d'aujourd'huy en ung an. Bien entendu que si l'advis de ladite trefve y peult estre plustost, que deslors l'hostilité y cessera, mais si apres le dit temps d'un an quelque hostilité y estoit commise, le dommage en sera reparé sans remise.

. . . .

Ainsi faict et conclu en la ville et cité d'Anvers, ledit neufiesme jour d'Apvril, mil six cens et neuf, et signé par les seigneurs ambassadeurs des Roys Tres Chrestien et de la Grande Bretaigne, comme mediateurs, et les deputez des seigneurs archiducqz et estatz, etc.

Su Magestad haviendo visto lo contenido en esta scritura de tregua y capitulacion que le hassido embiada por sus muy charos y amados hermanos, los Serenissimos Archiduques Alberto y Isabel Clara Eugenia, cerca de la tregua otorgada en nombre de su Magestad, por su poder y en el de sus Altezas, por si mismos, con los Estados Generales de las Provincias Unidas de los Payses Baxos, haviendolo bien y maduramente considerado declara que loá, aprueva, confirma y ratifica la dicha tregua en quanto la cossa le puede tocar y manda que se guarde y cumpla enteramente por su parte lo contenido en la dicha scritura y capitulacion por todo el tyempo que la dicha tregua durare y assi lo certifica y, sperando que durante la tregua han de hazer los dichos Estados de las Provincias Unidas buen tratamyento a los Cattolicos que entre ellos residen, promete y assegura. En fee y palabra real de guardar lo y cumplirlo puntualmente y no hazer cossa en contrario. En testimonio de lo qual su Magestad ha firmado la presente y hechola sellar con su sello. Segovia a siete de Jullio de mill y seyscientos y nueve años.

YO, EL REY.
Por mano del rey nuestro señor.
ENDRES DEPRADA.

Secret Treaty.[31]

Comme ainsi soit que par l'article quatrième du traité de la trefve fait ce mesme jour entre la Majesté du Roy Catholique, les Serenissimes Archiducs d'Autriche d'une part, et les sieurs Estats Generaux des Provinces-Unies, d'autre, le commerce accordé ausdits sieurs les Estats et à leurs sujets, ait esté restreint et limité aux royaumes, pays, terres, et seigneuries que ledit sieur roy tient en l'Europe et ailleurs, esquels il est permis aux sujets des roys et princes qui sont ses amis et alliez d'exercer ledit commerce de gré à gré; et outre ce, ledit sieur roy ait declaré qu'il n'entendoit donner aucun empesche-ment au trafic et commerce que lesdits sieurs les Estats et leurs sujets pourront avoir cy-après en quelque pays et lieu que ce soit, tant par mer que par terre, avec les potentats, peuples, et particuliers qui le leur voudront permettre, ny pareillement à ceux qui feront ledit trafic avec eux, ce que toutesfois n'a esté couché par escrit audit traité. Or est-il, que ce mesme jour, neufvième

[31] The text of the secret treaty could not be found in the Rijksarchief at the Hague. It is printed here from Jeannin, *Négociations* (ed. 1656), pp. 638-639. From the same source it is printed in *British Guiana Boundary, Arbitration with the United States of Venezuela: Appendix to the Counter-case on behalf of Her Britannic Majesty*, Foreign Office print (1898), pp. 323-324, where it is accompanied by an English translation.

Avril mil six cents neuf, qui est celuy auquel ladite trefve a esté accordée, les
sieurs Marquis Spinola, President Richardot, Mancicidor, frere Jean de
Neyen, et Verreiken, au nom et comme deputez tant dudit sieur Roy que
Archiducs, en vertu du mesme pouvoir à eux donné et sous la mesme promesse
de faire ratifier en bonne et deuë forme ce present escrit avec le traité
general et dans le mesme temps, ont promis et prometent au nom dudit
sieur Roy et de ses successeurs pour le temps que ladite trefve doit durer,
que Sa Majesté ne donnera aucun empeschement, soit par mer ou par terre,
ausdits sieurs les Estats ny à leurs sujets, au trafic qu'ils pourront faire cy-
après és païs de tous princes, potentats, et peuples, qui le leur voudront
permettre, en quelque lieu que ce soit, mesme hors les limites cy-dessus
designés, et par tout ailleurs, ny pareillement à ceux qui feront ledit trafic
avec eux, et d'effectuer tout ce que dessus de bonne foy, en sorte que ledit
trafic leur soit libre et assuré, consentans mesme afin, que le present escrit
soit plus autentique, qu'il soit tenu comme inseré au traité principal, et faisant
partie d'iceluy.   Ce que lesdits sieurs Deputez les Estats ont accepté.   Fait à
Anvers les an et jour susdits.   Signé, AMBROISIO SPINOLA, le President
RICHARDOT, MANCICIDOR, Frere JEAN DE NEIYEN, et VVERREIKEN.

*Certificate of the French and English ambassadors concerning the "limits",
and commerce with the Indies.*[32]

Nous soubzsignez ambassadeurs des Roys Treschrestien et de la Grande
Bretaigne certiffions a tous quil apartiendra, que par l'article troisiesme du
traité faict ce jourd'huy entre les deputes des sieurs Archiducz et Estatz
Generaux des Provinces Unies, on a entendu d'une part et d'autre, et nous
l'avons ainsi compris, que tout ce que les dits sieurs Estatz tiennent en
Brabant et en Flandre aussi bien que autre provinces dont ils jouissent leur
doibt demourer en tous droictz de superiorité, mesme le marquisat de Bergue
sur le Zoom, les baronnyes de Breda, Graves, ect ce qui y est joint et uny
avec tous les bourgs, villages, hameaux, et territoire en dependant.   Certiffions aussi les deputez des dits sieurs archiducz avoir consenty et acordé tout
ainsi que les dits Estatz et leurs subjetz ne pourront trafficquer aux portz,
lieux et places tenues par le Roy Catholicque aux Indes, s'il ne le permet,
quil ne sera loisible non plus a ses subjetz de trafficquer aux portz, lieux, et
places que tiennent les dits sieurs Estatz en dites Indes, si ce n'est avec leur
permission.   Et outre ce que les deputez des dits Estatz ont declaré plusieurs
fois en notre presence [et] des deputez des dits Archiducz, si on entreprend
sur leurs amis et alliez en dits pays quilz entendent les secourir et assister, sans
qu'on puisse pretendre la trefve estre enfreinte et violee a cest occasion.
    Faict a Anvers le neufiésme jour d'Avril mil six cens et neuf.
    P. JEANNIN, ELIJE DE LA PLACE, RUSSI, RI. SPENCER, RODOLPHE
WINWOOD.

His Majesty having examined the contents of this instrument of truce
and agreement, which has been sent him by his very dear and beloved brother
and sister, the Most Serene Archdukes of Austria, Albert and Isabella Clara

----

[32] From the original manuscript in the Rijksarchief.   An English translation is in
the app. to the *British Counter-case* (referred to in note 31), p. 324.

Eugenia, in regard to the truce executed with the States General of the Low Countries in the name of His Majesty by his authority, and in the name of their Highnesses by their own authority, and having considered it well and maturely, declares that he commends, approves, confirms, and ratifies the said truce, in so far as the matter can pertain to him; and he orders that the contents of the said instrument and agreement be completely observed and executed on his part for the whole time during which the said truce is to last. Accordingly, he affirms it, and, in the hope that during the truce the said States of the United Provinces will show good treatment to the Catholics who live among them, he gives his promise and assurance, on his royal faith and word, to observe and execute it faithfully, and not to violate it in any way. In testimony of which, His Majesty has signed the present and has had it sealed with his seal. Segovia, July 7, 1609.

I, THE KING.

By the hand of the King our lord.

ANDRÉS DE PRADA.

29.

Treaty of Guaranty between the United Netherlands, France, and Great Britain, concluded at the Hague, June 7/17, 1609. Ratification by the States General, July 6/16, 1609. [Ratification by France July 16, and by Great Britain July 10/20, 1609.]

INTRODUCTION.

Among the matters treated of at the Hague during the summer of 1607 were alliances between France and the United Netherlands, and England and the United Netherlands, to guarantee the observance of the peace then being negotiated between the States General of the United Provinces and Spain.[1] The Dutch greatly desired these alliances; and the French, and ultimately the English, were ready to become their confederates if safeguarded against a consequent embroilment with Spain.

By the defensive alliance concluded on January 23, 1608,[2] the King of France promised to help the States to obtain a satisfactory peace with Spain, to protect them against its infringement, and, if necessary for this purpose, to send them 10,000 infantry for as long as required. In return the States agreed, if the king were attacked, to supply him with 5000 infantry or with ships of war, equipped and manned, and of not less than 200 or 300 tons burden. Neither party, after having received aid from the other, should make a treaty with an aggressor without the other's consent. The similar treaty between England and the United Provinces, signed June 16/26, 1608, provided that in case of violation of the peace, the King of England should aid the States with 20 well-equipped ships of from 300 to 600 tons, and with 6000 infantry and 400 cavalry, yearly. If any of England's dominions were attacked, the States should send the king an equal naval force, and assist him yearly with 4000 infantry and 300 cavalry.[3] This Anglo-Dutch alliance was obnoxious to the King of Spain,[4] who, during the negotiations, remonstrated against England's occupation of Virginia, perhaps in order to impress

---

[1] See Doc. **28**, introduction.
[2] The ratification by the States on Jan. 25, 1608, is printed in Jeannin, *Négociations*, ed. cit., III. 148-157, and thence in Dumont, *Corps Diplomatique* V. (2), 89-91.
[3] The ratification by the States, June 17/27, 1608, and by the King of Great Britain, July 20/30, 1608, are in T. Rymer, *Foedera* (1704-1735), XVI. 667-673; the protocol is in L. van Aitzema, *Saken van Staet en Oorlogh* (1669-1672), I. 13, 14, and thence in Dumont, *op. cit.*, V. (2), 94, 95.
[4] Winwood, *Memorials*, II. 403, 404, 408, 413 ff.

the Dutch as well as the English with the reality of his intention to retain a monopoly of the Indies.[5]

When the peace conferences at the Hague failed, and were followed by negotiations for a long truce, the Dutch wished the former guaranties to be extended to the observance of the truce, and, in particular, to the concession of trade in the Indies. On account of some obscurity in the article granting this trade, caused by the determination of the Spaniards to avoid naming the Indies, the English king and council hesitated to give the desired guaranty. They finally consented however, because of the agreement of the archduke's deputies to declare to the deputies of the States, in the presence of the French and English ambassadors, that the article gave the Dutch liberty to trade to the Indies, which, during the truce, the King of Spain did not intend to impede.[6]

[5] A. Brown, *Genesis of the United States* (1890), I. 88 ff., *Cal. St. Pap., Venice*, 1607-1610, p. 102.

[6] Winwood, *op. cit.*, II. 481-483, 489-491, III. 2. The text of the certificate of the Archduke's declaration was incorporated in the instructions of Oct. 28, 1645, for the States' representatives at Münster. It is as follows:

"16. Nous ambassadeurs des Roys Tres-Chrestien et de la Grande Bretagne, et nous deputés de Messieurs les Estats Generaux des Provinces Unies des Pays Bas. certiffions par ces presentes, qu'estans ce jour d'huy dernier du mois de Mars 1609, assemblés en cette ville d'Anvers, avec les sieurs deputés du Roy Catholique et des Serenissimes Archiducs Albert et Isabella, grand differant se seroit meu pour les commerces des Indes, que les deputés desdits Sieurs Archiducs vouloient bien consentir de gré à gré au nom dudit Sieur Roy, és mots et termes contenues és articles quatre et cinquiéme de la trefve, qu'ils disoyent n'estre suffisans pour exponer ledit commerce en ce que mention expresse n'y fut faite des Indes, dont ils s'abstenoient d'user pour certains respects, qui ne sont d'aucun prejudice auxdits Sieurs les Estats, mais regardent seulement le contentement particulier dudit Sieur Roy, qui entend les en laisser joüir par effect, en toute liberté pendant la trefve, sans y donner aucun empeschement soit à leurs subjects et à ceux qui trafiqueront avec eux, ou aux princes et peuples qui leur permettront ledit traficq en leur pays; ce que toutesfois nous deputés desdits Sieurs les Estats, ne voulions accepter, requerans que les Indes fussent nommement exprimés, et l'article couché si intelligiblement, qu'il n'y eust aucune ambiguité ny pretexte pour y faire difficulté à l'advenir. Ayans lesdits deputés, tant les archiducs que des Estats, priez nous ambassadeurs des Roys Tres-Chrestien et de la Grande Bretagne qui estions presens à leur dispute, de vouloir ayder à composer ce different, comme avions fait ceux advenus és autres articles du traitté, à quoy nous serions volontiers employé essayans de persuader aux deputés des archiducs de faire l'expression dont ils estoient requis, puisqu'en la subsistance de la chose ils estoient d'accord et affirmoyent avec grands serments, que ledit Sieur Roy d'Espagne avoit accordé iceluy commerce de bonne foy, et en intention de n'y jamais contrevenir, remonstrans d'autre part aux deputés des Estats qu'ils avoyent aussi subject de se contenter de l'expression contenuë auxdits articles quatre et cinquiéme comme estans suffisans, sans qu'il soit besoin d'y adjouster ce qu'ils desirent de plus: mais les uns et les autres perseverans en leur opinion, en sorte que ledit traitté sembloit devoir estre rompu à cét occasion; enfin nous deputés desdits Sieurs Estats aurions declaré estre contens d'accepter lesdits articles pourveu que lesdits Sieurs Roy Tres-Chrestien et de la Grande Bretagne, ci-devant priés de la part des Estats de se vouloir rendre guarands de l'observation de la trefve avec asseurance de leur secours en cas d'infraction, consentent de s'obliger specialement pour l'observation dudit commerce comme promis et accordé par lesdits articles aussi valablement, que si le mot des Indes y estoit exprimé, ce que les deputés des archiducs auroient derechef declaré estre veritable; et que ledit Sieur Roy entendoit garder de bonne foy ce qu'ils promettoient en son nom, et nous ambassadeurs susdis promis et consenti à cét occasion de faire iceluy traitté de guarantie en la [forme] susdite pour estre bien informés que leurs Majestés auront agreable, tout ce que ferons, pour parvenir

The joint treaty of guaranty, signed by the representatives of France, England, and the United Netherlands on June 7/17, 1609, confirmed the treaties of guaranty signed separately by each king in the preceding year, as mentioned above; it specified that the aid promised by the earlier treaties should be supplied, if, during the truce, the Dutch should be troubled by the Spaniards or Flemish in the Indian trade, or if Indian princes should be molested for permitting the Dutch to traffic within their territories. Any question as to the infringement of the truce should be decided by the two kings together with the States. During the truce the States should not make any treaty with the King of Spain or the archdukes without the kings' consent; nor the kings with any prince to the prejudice of the States or of their liberty.

BIBLIOGRAPHY.

Text: MS. The original agreement is in the London Public Record Office, State Papers Foreign, Treaties, no. 294; the original manuscript of the ratification by the States General is in the same depository, T. R., Diplomatic Documents, no. 1179.

Text: Printed. P. Jeannin, *Négociations* (in Petitot, *Collection des Mémoires,* tom. XI.-XV., 1821-1822), V. 485-488; L. van Aitzema, *Saken van Staet en Oorlogh* (1669-1672), I. 16; F. Leonard, *Recueil des Traites de Paix* (1693), V. 14-16; J. Dumont, *Corps Diplomatique* (1726-1731), tom. V., pt. II., p. 110.

References: Contemporary and early writings. R. Winwood, *Memorials of Affairs of State in the Reigns of Elizabeth and James I.* (1725), II. 369 ff., 481-483, 488-492, III. 1-3, 5, 17, 65; P. Jeannin, *Négociations, ed. cit.,* III. 218, 219, 234, V. 171, 212-215, 245-318, *passim,* 404, 443, 468; *Cal. St. Pap., Venice,* 1607-1610, pp. 96, 102, 260, *et passim.*

TEXT.[7]

Les Estatz Generaulx des Pays Bas Unis a tous ceulx qui ces presentes lettres verront, salut. Comme, en vertu des pouvoirs respectivement donnez par les Treshaults, Tresexcellents, et Trespuissants Roys, Treschrestien, etc.,

à la conclusion de ladite trefve, dont les deputés des Estats se sont contentés, et ont par effect arresté de conclure le traitté d'icelle trève, ce qu'ils n'eussent autrement fait, ayans ensemblement nous ambassadeurs susdits et deputés des Estats, dressé et signé le present acte, que certifions et affirmons à tous qu'ils appartiendra estre veritable sur nostre foy et honneur.

"Fait à Anvers les an et jours susdit. Estoit signé, P. Joannijn, Elye de la Place, Russi, Ri: Spencer, Rodolphe Winwood, Guilleaume Louis Comte de Nassau, W. de Brederode, Cornelis van Gent, Johan van Oldenbarnevelt, R. Malderée, G. V. Renesse, G. Hillama, Johan Sloeth, Ab. Coenders." L. van Aitzema, *Verhael van de Nederlandsche Vrede-handelingh* in *Saken van Staet en Oorlogh,* III. 53, and VI. (2), 206. The text and the English translation are in *British Guiana Boundary, Arbitration with the United States of Venezuela: The* [British] *Counter Case* (Foreign Office, 1898), app., pt. 2, pp. 328, 329.

[7] The following text is printed from the original manuscript of the ratification, P. R. O., T. R., Diplomatic Docs., no. 1179.

et de la Grande Bretaigne, etc., et nous, a noz communs deputez, ilz ayent, le dixseptiesme jour de Juing dernier passé, conclu et arresté entre eulx, aulx noms de leursdites Majestez et des nostres, le traicté dont la teneur ensuit :

Comme ainsi soit que les Roys Treschrestien et de la Grande Bretaigne se soyent employez dès long temps avecq grand soing et affection pour faire cesser la guerre des Pays Bas par une paix perpetuelle, et pour n'y avoir peu parvenir ayent depuis proposé une trefve á longues annees, dont le succes eust esté aussi peu heureulx, si, pour oster toute defiance aulx Estatz Generaulx des Pays Bas Uniz, leurs Majestez ne leur eussent offert de s'obliger á l'observation d'icelle trefve, et de leur donner assistence et secours au cas qu'elle fust enfreinte et violee, mesmes s'ilz estoient troublez et empeschez au commerce des Indes, que les deputez des Archiducqz leur accordoient de gré á gré par ladite trefve au nom du Roy Catholicque, sans neantmoins l'exprimer nommeement, ainsi que lesdits sieurs Estatz le demandoient pour leur plus grande seureté, eulx faisans á cest occasion reffus de l'accepter, si ladite promesse de garentie, faicte de bouche par les ambassadeurs desdits sieurs Roys en presence mesme des deputez desdits sieurs Archiducqz, ne les y eust induict, de l'accomplissement de laquelle promesse lesdits sieurs Roys ayants esté priez, requis, et sommez, et y voullans satisfaire de bonne foy, ce jour d'huy dixseptiesme jour de Juing, mil six cens et neuf, se sont assemblez Messire Pierre Jeannin, chevalier, baron de Chagny et Montjeu, conseiller dudit sieur Roy Treschrestien en son Conseil d'Estat, et son ambassadeur extraordinaire vers lesdits Sieurs Estatz, et Messire Elye de la Place, chevalier, sieur de Russy, viconte de Machault, aussi conseiller audit Conseil d'Estat, gentilhomme ordinaire de la chambre dudit sieur Roy et son ambassadeur ordinaire resident pres lesdits sieurs Estatz, au nom et comme ayants charge de Treshault, Trespuissant, et Tresexcellent prince Henry quatriesme, par la grace de Dieu roy de France et de Navarre, messire Richard Spencer, chevalier, gentilhomme ordinaire de la chambre privée dudit sieur Roy de la Grande Bretaigne et son ambassadeur extraordinaire vers lesdits sieurs Estatz, et messire Rodolphe Winwood, chevalier, ambassadeur ordinaire et conseiller dudit sieur roy au Conseil d'Estat des Provinces-Unies, aussi au nom et comme ayants charge de Treshault, Trespuissant, et Tresexcellent prince Jacques, par la grace de Dieu roy de la Grande Bretaigne, etc.; et les sieurs Cornille de Gent, sieur de Loenen et Meynerswyck, viconte et juge de l'Empire et de la ville de Nymmegen, messire Johan d'Oldenbarnevelt, chevalier, sieur de Tempel, Rodenrys, et advocat et garde du grand seel, chartres, et registres de Hollande et Westfrize, messire Jacques de Malderee, chevalier, sieur des Heyes, et premier et representant la noblesse aulx Estatz et Conseil de la conté de Zelande, les sieurs Gerard de Renesse, sieur vander Aa, de Streeffkercken, Nyeuleckerlant, etc., Ernestus d'Aylua de Heerwey et grietman d'Oostdongerdeel, Johan Sloeth, sieur de Sallick, drossard du pays de Vollenhoe et chastellain de la seigneurie de Cunder, et Abel Coenders de Helpen, sieur en Faen et Cantes, au nom des Haults, puissants, et illustres sieurs, les Estatz Generaulx des Pays Bas Uniz, lesquelz, en vertu de leurs pouvoirs, et avec promesse de faire ratifier respectivement le contenu en ces presentes auxdits sieurs roys et Estatz dans deux mois prochains, ont consenty et accordé ce que s'ensuit :

Asscavoir, que les traictéz faictz separement avec lesdits Sieurs Estatz Generaulx par ledit sieur Roy de France, le xxiii° de Janvier seize cens et huict, et par ledit sieur Roy de la Grande Bretaigne le xxvi° Juing au mesme an, pour l'observation de la paix, qu'on pretendoit lors faire, ensemble les conventions, promesses, et obligations reciprocques y contenues pour la deffence et conservation mutuelle de leurs royaulmes, pays, terres et seigneuries, seront entretenues et gardees pour le temps que ladite trefve doibt durer, tout ainsi que si elles estoient repetees et inserees de mot à aultre au present traicte.

Et auront lieu lesdites obligations et assistence de secours, non seulement en cas d'infraction de trefve es limites specifiez par le quatriesme article du traicte de celle trefve, mais aussi si lesdits sieurs Estatz ou leurs subjectz sont troublez et empesschez pendant ledit temps au commerce des Indes, de la part desdits sieurs Roy Catholicque ou Archiducqz, leurs officiers et subjectz ; et sera aussi entendu ledit trouble et empeschement, tant s'il est faict aulx subjectz desdits sieurs Estatz qu'à ceulx qui ont faict ou feront ledit commerce avec eulx, ou bien si les princes et peuples qui leur auront donne la permission d'exercer ledit trafficq en leur pays estoient a cest occasion molestez, eulx ou leurs subjectz, pourveu toutesfois que, pour obliger lesdits sieurs roys a donner ce secours, le jugement desdits empeschemiens soit faict par advis commun d'eulx et desdits sieurs Estatz. A quoy ilz promettent apporter la diligence et sinceritié requise pour faire reparer le dommage aulx interessez, et repoulser la violence dont on auroit usé contr' eulx. Pourront toutesfois lesdits sieurs Estatz, s'il y a de la longeur en ladite deliberation, pourveoir a la seurete de leurs affaires et subjects, comme ilz trouveront convenir.

En recognoissance de laquelle garentie, et du secours que lesdits Estatz ont desja receu desdits sieurs Roys, ils leur promettent de ne faire aulcun traicte durant icelle trefve avec lesdits sieurs Roy Catholicque ou Archiducqs, sans leur advis et consentement, et pareillement lesdits sieurs Roys de ne faire aulcun traicte avec quelque prince ou potentat que ce soit, au prejudice de celuy-cy et de leur liberte, de la conservation de laquelle et de leurs Estatz ilz auront soing comme de leurs bons amys et alliez. Ainsy faict, accorde, conclu, signé, et cachetté par lesdits sieurs ambassadeurs et deputez.

A la Haye, l'an et jour susdits. Et estoit signé, P. Jeannin, Elye de la Place-Russy, Ri. Spencer, Rodolphe Winwood, Cornelis van Gent, Johan van Oldenbarnevelt, J. de Malderee, G. v. Renesse. Ernestus Aylua, Johan Sloeth. Ab. Coenders, et cachette des armes desdits sieurs ambassadeurs et deputez respectivement.

Nous ayants ledit traicte aggreable en tous et chacuns ses poinctz et articles, avons iceulx en general et en particulier acceptez, approuvez, ratifiiez. et confirmez, acceptons, approuvons, ratiffions, et confirmons, et le tout promettons [de garder], entretenir, et observer inviolablement sans jamais [aller] ou venir au contraire, directement ou indirectement, en quelque sorte et maniere que ce soit, soubz l'obligation et hypotecque de tous les biens et revenuz desdits Provinces Unies en general et en particulier, presens et advenir.

En tesmoing de quoy nous avons faict sceller ces presentes de nostre grand seel, et signer par nostre greffier. A la Haye, ce seizièsme jour de juillet, l'an seize cens et neuff.

Fr. Hanghema.

Par ordonnance desdits Sieurs Estatz Generaulx.

Aerssens.

1609.

30.

Treaty of alliance between Denmark and the United Netherlands, concluded at the Hague, May 14, 1621. Ratification by the States General, August 9, 1621. [Ratifications not exchanged.]

INTRODUCTION.

Christian IV. of Denmark included among his ambitious aims the development of Danish commerce, not only within European waters, but beyond the seas. In 1616 he founded an East India Company after the Dutch pattern,[1] and two years later negotiated with the Dutch for privileges in the East India trade. The Dutch commissioners employed in these negotiations deprecated any attempt on the part of the Danes to undermine the Dutch company or to make common cause with Spaniards or Portuguese against them; they refused to infringe the monopoly of Eastern commerce granted by the States General to their own company, or to allow Dutch seamen to serve on foreign ships. On the other hand, they consented to the Danes' undertaking explorations in unoccupied lands in the East and agreed to order the Dutch in those regions to treat them as friends. They attempted to divert the attention of the Danes from the East by referring to the West Indies, and even went so far as to hand them a project for a Danish West India Company.[2]

A few months later Dr. Jonas Charisius, Danish ambassador at the Hague, was instructed to establish friendship and union between the Danish and Dutch East India companies, and to recruit in the Netherlands ships' officers for the voyages to Guinea, the West Indies, and Terra Australis.[3]

The need of mutual political support seemed for a time to outweigh commercial rivalry. At the close of 1620, when the twelve years' truce with Spain[4] was about to expire and the Catholics were winning victories in the Palatinate and Bohemia, the States General joined the German Protestant Union in urging King Christian, who although a Lutheran had shown a leaning toward Spain, to help the Protestant cause. The king and Rigsraad were compliant. Christian was anxious to separate the Dutch from their allies,

[1] Ch. de Lannoy and H. Vander Linden, *L'Expansion Coloniale: Néerlande et Danemark* (1911), pp. 402 ff.
[2] Arend *et al., Algemeene Geschiedenis,* III. (3), 31, 35-39, 587.
[3] G. W. Kernkamp, *Verslag van een Onderzoek in Zweden, Noorwegen, en Denemarken naar Archivalia* (1903), pp. 207-208. In the minds of most men at this time, the term *Terra Australis* referred, not to Australia but to a southern continent which was supposed to bound the Indian Ocean on the south.
[4] Doc. **28.**

Sweden and the Hanse towns, and to win their aid in procuring his son's succession to the archbishopric of Bremen.[5] In February, 1621, he sent the Danish chancellor, Jacob Ulfeldt, to the Hague to negotiate an alliance.[6] This was concluded on May 14, following, but in general and provisional terms that left the most important points undecided. The eighth and final article of the treaty, which stipulated for the further consideration of undetermined matters, including the question of navigation and trade in the East and West Indies, is given below. In spite of objections from the ambassadors of some of the Hanse towns, the treaty was ratified by the States General on August 9, 1621. The ratification, given to the Dutch commissioners appointed for the Bremen conference,[7] was, however, never exchanged, since the King of Denmark failed to ratify the instrument.[8]

BIBLIOGRAPHY.

Text: MS. An original manuscript of the protocol is in the Ryksarchief at the Hague, Secrete Casse, Denemarcken, casse C, loquet O, no. 4.

Text: Printed. The ratification by the States General is printed in L. van Aitzema, *Saken van Staet en Oorlogh* (1669-1672), I. 41-42; and thence in J. Dumont, *Corps Diplomatique* (1726-1731), tom. V., pt. II., pp. 399-402. A text of the treaty will doubtless be included in the work now being edited by L. Laursen at the expense of the Carlsbergfond—*Traités du Danemark et de la Norvège: Danmark-Norges Traktater, 1523-1750* (1907, etc.), III. 411 ff.

Translation: A French translation of the Dutch ratification is in Dumont, *loc. cit.*

References: Contemporary and early writings. *Letters from and to Sir Dudley Carleton, Knt., during his Embassy in Holland from January, 1615/6 to December, 1620* (2d ed., 1775), pp. 244, 250, 253, 311; *Resolutien* of the States of Holland for the years 1618, 1621, and 1622, *passim*; G. W. Kernkamp, *Verslag van een Onderzoek in Zweden, Noorwegen, en Denemarken naar Archivalia* (1903), pp. 207, 208, 240, 241, 276, 324.

References: Later writings. J. P. Arend *et al., Algemeene Geschiedenis des Vaderlands* (1840, etc.), III. (3), 31, 35-39, 586-609, 648-658; Niels Slange, *Geschichte Christian des Vierten, Königs in Dännemark* (ed. J. H. Schlegel, 1757-1771), III. 87 ff., 92 ff., 124, 165-172; F. C. Dahlmann, cont. by D. Schäfer, *Geschichte von Dänemark* (1840, etc.), V. 392, in Heeren and Ukert, *Geschichte der Europäischen Staaten*; P. J. Blok, *Geschiedenis van het Nederlandsche Volk* (2d ed., 1912, etc.), II. 511, or, German trans., *Geschichte der Niederlande* (1902, etc.), IV. 284, 285, in Heeren and Ukert's above-mentioned series.

---

[5] Arend *et al., loc. cit.,* pp. 589 ff.

[6] Ulfeldt's proposals to the States General and the answer of the latter are printed in the *Kronijk van het Historisch Genootschap te Utrecht,* Jaarg. 22 (1866), pp. 481-488, and are summarized in the *Resolutien* of the States of Holland, Mar. 9-Apr. 8, 1621, pp. 20, 21, 24, 25, and *cf.* pp. 27, 28.

[7] Doc. **31,** introduction.

[8] Arend *et al., loc. cit.,* p. 657; manuscript instructions for the conference at Bremen, *cf.* Doc. **31,** note 2.

Text.[*]

Aldewijle de durchluchtigste ende grottmachtige koning ende heere, heere Christian der Vierte, tott Dennemarcken ende Norwegen, der Wenden ende Gotten koning, hertogh tott Schleswich, Holstein, Stormarn, ende der Ditmarschen, grave tott Oldenburch ende Delmenhorst, etc., ende die Hoge Mogende Heeren Staten General der Vereinigden Nederlanden, van langen tijden herwaertz in goede, uprechte, ende nhabuijrliche frundtschap ende correspondentz geleefft ende gestaen hebben, soe hebben beijder deelen nu een tijtt lang herwaerts (considererende de constitutie ende gelegentheitt van de tegenwoirdige tijden ende saecken van geheele Christenh[eit] ende insonderh[eit] vant interesse, soe de eene ahn des anderen status conserva- tionem, welstandt, ende prosperiteit is hebbende) noch naerder bij sich bedacht ende overwogen, om hun nauwer tsaemen the doen, ende the ver- binden, begerende uth rechten zele ende Christlichen vornemen ende ijver, tott het welvarren vant gantze gemeene evangelische wesen, ende beijder deelen eigene staten, the contracteren ende verdragen, over eene sincere ende mutuele frundtschap, alliance, ende verbondt, tott conservatie ende defensie van heure respective staten ende underdanen, in voegen, datt hochst ende hochg[emel]te deelen, beijder sijdts, unlangs nae rijpe ende ernstige delib- eratie hebben gegeven last ende commissie, the weeten, hochstg[emel]te sijne Kon[incklijcke] Ma[jestei]t ahn den edlen gestrengen Heere Jacob van Uleveldt zu Urop, derselven rijcks cantzler ende rhatt, oich amptman tott Nijborch, in krafft sijner overgeleverden credentz brieff in dato den xi. Februarij lestleden ther eenre, ende die Hoge Mogende Heeren Staten Generael der Vereinigde Nederlanden, die edle, gestrenge, ernveste, wijse, sehr discrete heeren, Gysbert van Boetzeler, heere then Boetzeler, erffschenck dess furstendombs Cleve, amptman ende dijckgrave tuschen Maes ende Wael, Jacob van Wassenaer ende Duvenvoirde, heere van Updam, Heinsbroeck, Spierdijck, Suijtwijck, lieutenant admirael van Hollandt ende Westfrieslandt, Hugo Muys van Holij, ridder, baillieu ende dijckgrave des Landts van Stryen, Reinier Pauw, oudt burgerm[eeste]r ende raedt der stadt van Amsterdam, Jacob Magnus, ridder, heere van Berg-Ambacht, Melissant, etc., Arent van Zuijlen van Nievelt, heere tott Gerestein ende Teckop, Marck van Licklama tott Nieholtt, grietman over Stellingwerff Oostende, Boldewijn Sloot, rent- meister generael van domeinen des landes van Vollenhoe ende der heer- lich[eit] Cuijnder, ende Gosen Schaffer, tott Uthhuijsen ende de Mehden Hoveling, raedt der stadt Groningen, derselven gedeputeerde, ende alle mede gecommitteerden in haere Ho: Mog: vergaederinge, ther andere sijden, then einde deselve solden moegen confereren, communiceren, ende delibereren over die openinge ende middelen, dienende om voort the setten ende int werck the stellen dit heijlsaem goedt werck, ende te brengen tott een goede conclusie, tott welcken eijnde dan die welg[emel]te gesandte ende gedeputeerden ahn wedersijden, om hun in alles getrouwelick the quijten, then lesten over een gekoemen sijnde, geconcludeert ende gearresteert hebben, up hett welbe- hagen, verbeteringe, modificatie, ende aggreatie van Hochstg[emel]te Sijne Kon[incklijcke] Ma[jestei]tt ende Heeren Staten Generael, dese nhafolg- ende poincten ende articulen:

. . . .

[*] The text is taken from the original manuscript in the Rijksarchief at the Hague, Secrete Casse, Denemarcken, casse C, loquet O, no. 4.

8. Ende sal dit tractaet ofte verbondt behorlich geconfirmeert ende geaggreert worden deur sijne hochstg[emelt]e Ma[jestei]tt ende de Ho[oge] Mog[enden] Heeren Staten Generael voorn[oemt] in den tijtt van drije maenden, ofte soo veele eer als 't selve sal konnen geschieden. Ende sullen beyde deelen, mitt den eersten, up tijtt ende plaetze soe ende daert sijne hochstg[emelt]e Ma[jestei]tt believen sall, mitt een ander in naerder communicatie ende handel treden, umme the weeten mitt watt macht ende middelen de partijen malcanderen sullen moeten assisteren, soo wanneer d'een ofte d'ander mitt openbaren oirloch in sijne rijcken ofte landen angevochten worden ; ende up de forma, maniere, ende quantiteit vandien, als mede vanden tijtt up dewelcke deselve beginnen ende aenfangen sall loop the nehmen, gelijck oick vande restitutie vandien, oft deselve behoiren sall the geschieden, ende hoe verre. Ende alsoe inde conferentie vermaen is gedaen van eenige havenen, daer men niet gewoon en solde sijn the handelen, sal in de voorg[ehade] bijeenkompste mede getracteert worden, umme deselve then wedersijden uth the drucken, ende daeraf voirts the moegen verdragen, sulcx als then meesten besten van beijde de partijen bevonden sal worden te behoiren, sullende oick mede in de voorn[oemde] bijeenkompste naerder communicatie ende handel vallen over de navigatien ende trafficquen inde Oost- ende West-Indien, daervan de welg[emel]te heere gesandte[10] mede meldinge hefft gedaen. Up welcken allen, getracht sal worden bij beijde deelen behoirlicke satisfactie ende contentement elckanderen the geven, ist doenlick.

Aldus gedaen, geslooten, geaccordeert, ende bij uns undergeschreven geteijckent in des Gravenhage up den xiiii Maij in den jaere XVI^c een en twintich.

Jacob Ulffeldt.
J. van Wassenaer ende
    Duvenvoirde.
Reinier Pauw.
A. van Zuyllen van Nyevelt.
Boldewyn Sloet.

Gisbert van Witt zu Boetzelar.
J. Muys van Holy.
J. Magnus.
Marck van Lyclama.
G. Schaffer.

Translation.

Since the most serene and very powerful king and lord, Lord Christian the Fourth, king of Denmark and Norway, of the Vandals and Goths, duke of Schleswig, Holstein, Stormarn, and Ditmarsh, count of Oldenburg and Delmenhorst, etc., and the High and Mighty lords, the States General of the United Netherlands, have for a long time lived and stood in good, sincere, and neighborly friendship and correspondence ; and since both parties, for now a long time (considering the constitution and opportunity of the present times and affairs of all Christendom, and particularly the interest that each state has in the conservation, well being, and prosperity of the other) have taken into closer consideration and have resolved, in order to bring and bind them closer together (desiring it out of righteous zeal and Christian intention and diligence, for the welfare of all the Evangelical Community, and the states of both parties) to contract and agree concerning a sincere and mutual friendship, alliance, and league for the conservation and defense of their respective states and subjects, therefore the aforesaid parties, on both sides, have, lately, after ripe and earnest deliberation, given charge and com-

[10] Jacob Ulfeldt.

mission—to wit, his aforesaid royal majesty to the noble and austere lord Jacob van Ulfeldt of Urup, chancellor and councillor of the said kingdom and bailiff of Nyborg, by virtue of his letter of credence, dated February 11 last, on the one part, and their High and Mighty Lords, the States General of the United Netherlands, to the noble, austere, honorable, wise, and discreet lords, Gysbert van Boetzelaer, lord of Boetzelaer, hereditary cupbearer of the principality of Cleves, bailiff and dike-grave between Maas and Waal, Jacob van Wassenaer and Duvenvoorde, lord of Obdam, Heinsbroeck, Spierdijck, and Zuidwijk, lieutenant admiral of Holland and West Friesland, Hugo Muys van Holy, knight, bailiff and dike-grave of the country of Stryen, Reinier Pauw, ex-burgomaster and councillor of the city of Amsterdam, Jacob Magnus, knight, lord of Berg-Ambacht, Melissant, etc., Arent de Zuylen van Nievelt, lord of Gerestein and Teckop, Marcus van Lycklama of Nijeholt, lord of Stellingwerf Oostende, Boldewijn Sloet, receiver general of the domains of the country of Vollenhoven and of the lordship of Cuynder, and Goozen Schaffer, of Uithuizen and Meeden, councillor of the city of Groningen, their deputies and also deputies in the assembly of their High Mightinesses, on the other part—in order that they might confer, communicate, and deliberate, respecting the overtures and means serving to advance and execute so salutary a work, and bring it to a good conclusion. For which purpose, the said ambassador and deputies on both sides, in order to acquit themselves faithfully in all things, having finally reached an agreement, have concluded and agreed, subject to the pleasure, correction, modification, and approval of his aforesaid royal majesty and the lords States General, on the following points and articles:

. . . .

8. This treaty or alliance shall be duly confirmed and ratified by his Majesty, aforesaid, and by their High Mightinesses, the lords States General, aforesaid, in three months, or as much sooner as is possible. Both parties shall enter into further conversation and conference, at the first opportunity, at a time and place pleasing to his said Majesty, in order to determine with what forces and means they shall be obliged to help each other, whenever either is attacked with open war in his realms or lands; and to determine the form, manner, and quantity of the forces, and when they shall begin to be sent; and also in respect to their restitution, whether it should be made, and to what extent. And since reference has been made in the conference to some harbors where it has not been customary to trade, this matter shall also be treated of in the intended conference, in order that both sides may express their opinions about it, and come to such agreement as shall be found most acceptable to both parties. Another subject of discussion in the aforesaid conference shall be navigation and trade in the East and West Indies, which the said ambassador has also mentioned. In respect to all the above, both parties shall endeavor to give one another due satisfaction and contentment, if possible.

Thus done, concluded, agreed, and signed by us the underwritten at the Hague, on May 14, 1621.

JACOB ULFFELDT.	GISBERT VAN WITT ZU BOETZELAR.
J. VAN WASSENAER ENDE	J. MUYS VAN HOLY.
DUVENVOIRDE.	J. MAGNUS.
REINIER PAUW.	MARCK VAN LYCLAMA.
A. VAN ZUYLLEN VAN NYEVELT.	G. SCHAFFER.
BOLDEWYN SLOET.	

31.

Recess signed by the Commissioners of Denmark and the United Netherlands at Bremen, September 30/October 10, 1621.

INTRODUCTION.

The conference stipulated by the eighth article of the treaty of the Hague [1] was held at Bremen in August and September, 1621, between the Danish commissioners, Jacob Ulfeldt and Holger Rosenkrantz, and the Dutch commissioners, led by Reinier Pauw of Holland. The principal subjects of discussion were (1) reciprocal financial aid, and (2) trade relations in Europe and in both Indies.

The instructions [2] to be followed by the Dutch commissioners, in case the Danes introduced the question of the Indian trade, distinguished between the East and West Indies. With reference to the East Indies, the commissioners were to declare that neutral lands were open to Danish traders, but that places fortified by the Dutch East India Company, or districts in which the company had treaty rights, were closed to the Danes, as to all others. With reference to the West Indies, the commissioners were to urge that the King of Denmark and his subjects might, like anyone else, take shares in the recently formed Dutch West India Company, and thus participate in directing its policy. The article finally agreed to—which differed somewhat from the

---

[1] Doc. **30**.

[2] The instructions are preserved in the Ryksarchief at the Hague and have the same pressmark as the text. The paragraph concerning the West Indies is as follows:

"Ende wat aengaet de handelinge oft traficque op West-Indien, alsoo Hare Ho: Mo: goetgevonden hebben deselve te begrijpen in eene generale compaignie, die volgende het octroy daertoe verleent, hier te lande werdt opgerecht, in welcke generale compaignie een yeder vrijstaet soodanige capitalen ende sommen van penningen te participeren als hem goetduncken sal, soo ist hoochstgedachte Sijne Ma[jestei]t ende desselffs onder-saten oock vrij ende open daerinne soo veel te herederen, als deselve geraden sullen mogen vinden. Sullende Sijne Ma[jesteit] ende desselffs ondersaten oock behoorlijck erkent ende geaccommodeert werden inde kennisse, directie, ende 't beleyt der saecken, sulcx ende in conformité als 't voorsz. octroy daarvan is medebrengende oft anders-sints soo men in tijden ende wijlen opt selve stuck metten anderen naerder sal connen overeencomen ende verdragen."

Translation: "And as to that which concerns commerce or trade to the West Indies since their High Mightinesses have consented to comprehend the same in a general company, which, in accordance with the charter granted thereto, has been erected in this country, in which general Company each free state shall hold as much capital and money as it shall think good—so his abovementioned Majesty and his subjects are also free to invest as much therein as they shall find convenient. His Majesty and subjects would also be suitably recognized and received into the knowledge, direction, and man-agement of affairs, like and according as the aforesaid charter requires, or otherwise as at the time it shall be possible mutually to agree and contract."

Dutch instructions—implied the right of the Danes to acquire possessions in
the neutral land of *both* the Indies, and prohibited subjects of one power from
trading in the Indian possessions of the other, and from aiding the enemies
of the other in those regions. In regard to the West Indies the Danes were
inclined to question the good faith of the Dutch, probably because the States
General had promised in the forty-fifth article of the Dutch West India
Company's charter that they would in no way diminish the privileges of the
company by any treaty with any neighboring power.[3]

Although the articles on financial help and European trade presented great
difficulties, all the commissioners signed three articles, on September 30/
October 10, and referred them to their principals for ratification. Prince
Maurice advocated their acceptance, but Amsterdam and Hoorn refused
to confirm them; nor were they ratified by Denmark.[4]

BIBLIOGRAPHY.

Text: **MS.** An original manuscript is in the Ryksarchief at the Hague,
Secrete Casse, Denemarcken, casse C, loquet O, no. 4, and another manuscript, in the Rigsarkiv at Copenhagen, is mentioned in G. W. Kernkamp,
*Verslag van een Onderzoek in Zweden, Noorwegen, en Denemarken
naar Archivalia* (1903), p. 324.

Text: **Printed.** L. van Aitzema, *Saken van Staet en Oorlogh* (1669-1672),
I. 42-44. The text will doubtless be included in L. Laursen, *Traités du
Danemark et de la Norvège: Danmark-Norges Traktater, 1523-1750*
(1907, etc.).

References: See Doc. **30**, references.

TEXT.[5]

Nademael, van wegen den durchluchtichsten ende grootmachtichsten
coninck ende heere, heere Christian den Vierden, zu Danemarcken, Norwegen, der Wenden, unnd Gotten coninck, hertogen zu Schlieswich, Holsten,
Stormarn, unnd Diettmarschen, grave zu Oldenburch unnd Delmenhorst, etc.,
als oock van wegen de Hooge ende Mogende Heeren Staten-Generael der
Vereenichde Nederlanden, wij, Jacob van Ulfelt zu Urup ende Holger
Rosencrants zu Rosenholm, ende wij, Reynier Pauw, Marck van Lijclama zu
Nieholt, Sweer van Haersolte zu Harst, unnd Goosen Schaffer zu Wutthusen,
unnd mede respective gecommitteerde unnd gesanten, om het tractaet van
vrintschap ende alliantie van den 14en May lestleden, tusschen Hoochgemelte
Hare Co[nincklycke] Ma[jesteit] ende Hare Ho[oge] Mo[gentheden], op

[3] Arend *et al., Algemeene Geschiedenis,* III. (3), 656. The text of the charter is
printed in the *Groot Placaet-Boeck,* vol. I., cols. 565-578, and thence, with an English
translation, in A. J. F. van Laer, *Van Rensselaer Bowier Manuscripts,* pp. 86-115.

[4] Arend *et al., op. cit.,* pp. 657, 658; *Resolutien* of the States of Holland for 1622, pp.
24, 90, 185, etc.

[5] The text is from the original manuscript in the Ryksarchief at the Hague, Secrete
Casse, Denemarcken, casse C, loquet O, no. 4.

aggreatie, modificatie, ende verbeteringe beyder deelen in den Hage doenmael
gesloten, wijder in etlijcke doenmaels noch niet affgehandelde poincten ende
artickelen te readsumieren ende voltrecken, nu hier tot Bremen versamelt
geweest sijn; daerbenevens over d'selve artickelen nyet alleen een geruyme
tijt conferentie geholden hebben, dan ooch aen onsen aldergenedichsten
coninck ende Hare Hooch Mogentheden onse besoigneerde gelangen laten,
ende haere voor ditmael eyntelicke resolutie daerop ontfangen ende ingeno-
men, is evenwel over die beyde artickelen van handel ende wandel ende
van de mutuele gelthulpe eenige differentie verbleven, van wegen Haare
Ma[jesteit], wij, gesanten ende gecommitteerde, persisterende bij d'artickelen
soo d'selve hiernae ingestelt zijn, tot aenneminge van de welcke wij, gesanten
van Hare Ho[oge] Mo[gendheden], ons niet wijder hebben vermocht in te
laten als ons gerescribeert was daerbij dan wij oock persisterende veroor-
saeckt zijn desen te laten berusten tot naerder erweginge van onse Heeren
principalen. . . .

· · · · · · · · ·

Hebben derhalven Hare Co[nincklycken] Ma[jestei]ts wij, gecommitteerden ende gesanten, die articulen soo alhier gereassumeert unnde tractiert,—
soo wel die beyde van handel ende wandell daer 't poinct van verbodene
havenen niet inbegrepen, ende van die mutuele gelthulpe, de welcke noch
eeniger maten different verbleven, alsoock die artickel van vertrouwlijcke
vruntschap, bij de navigatien unnd negotiatien op beyde Indiën, etc., over de
welcke geen verschil en valt—soo ende dergestalt schriftelijck vervatet ende
Hare Ho[ogen] Mo[gendheden] gesanten overgegeven, als Hare Co[ninck-
lycke] Ma[jesteit] de selvige, neffens alle andere in voriger unnd jegen-
woordiger tractation accordeerden artickelen, eyntelijck te aggrieren,
genadichst gesinnet; jedoch dat de artickel van gelthulpe als die maer
temporeel ende te veranderen, in een besonder instrument gestelt ende
geaggrieert werden.

Ende luyden die artickelen van woorde te woorde alsoo:

· · · · · · · · ·

2. Sall oock goede vertrouwliche vruntschap unnd correspondentz seyn
unnd blijven tusschen beyder deelen, landen, unnd ondersaten, bij alle navigatien, negotiatien, ende traffijcken, te lande ende te water, met schepen ende
goederen, op alle rijcken, landen, eylanden, unnd plaetsen in Oost- unnd West-
Indien, Africa, Guinea, Terra Australis,[*] unnd alle solche uuytlandische
faerten; yedoch dat eenes yederen gerechticheyt aen die landen, eylanden,
unnd plaetsen, die hij, off durch forten tot sijne defentie, in heeft unnd holdet,
off deur eenige derzelver landen, koningen, princen, ofte oversten, speciale
contracten unnd verbundteniszen, die commerszien, defentien, unnd derge-
lijcken aengaende, erlanget, unnd possideert hier mitt, in allen gants niet
benomen unnd praejudicieert werde; anders sall alle wege dat eenedeel
dem anderen allen vrundtschap unnd beforderunge bij alle occasien die sich
op solche navigatien unnd trafijcken voorvallen mochte erzeygen unnd
beweysen; ende jo geene dem anderen in eenige wegen als sie in hen off zu
rugge reysen, off oock in de selve landen, daer zij ein ander antreffen muegen,
geene wederwillen, ongelegentheyt off verhinderingen toe, voegen; doch
dat oock geen deel des anderen, opentlijcke aen de selve oorden, vijanden,
eenige behulffp off thoevoer, heimlijck off opentlijck, sick te doen onderstahn,

· See Doc. **30**, note 3.

die desen opgerechten verbont tegen sijn mochte; unnd als het sick thoe droege dat eynes ofte andere deels, schepen unnd luyden, durch sturm, onweder, ofte andere noot, in eenige der selven van den anderen deel bereyts occupieerden unnd possideerden landen, havenen, unnd revieren, ingedrungen werden mochten, alsdan sullen sie eynander alle goede freuntschap unnd bevorderingh erzeygen unnd beweysen, unndt haer nootdruftich refraichissement te erlangen, unnd wat van nooten sein werd te repareren, vergunnen. Doch dat hier onder niet gemenet wert dat aen sulcke oorden eenige ladinge, handelinge, unnd traffijcken toegelaten sijn sullen.

. . . .

Van desen recessen sijn twee exemplaren, d'een in de Duytsche ende d'ander in de Nederlantsche spraecke, gemaeckt ende geschreven, de welcke in de woorden wel verschillen, maer voor soo veel in den sin, substantie, en meninge over een comen, soo nae men sulcx heeft connen doen, hier naer respective onderteeckent zijn in Bremen, den 30^{en} September, stylo vetery, ende den 10^{en} October, stylo novo, XVI^C, een ende twintich.

JACOB ULFFELDT.   REINIER PAUW.   S. VAN HAERSOLTE.
HOLGER ROSZENKRANTZ.   M. V. LYCLAMA.   G. SCHAFFER.

TRANSLATION.

Whereas, in the name of the most serene and very powerful king and lord, Lord Christian the Fourth, king of Denmark, Norway, the Vandals and Goths, duke of Schleswig, Holstein, Stormarn, and Ditmarsh, count of Oldenburg and Delmenhorst, etc., and likewise in the name of the High and Mighty lords, the States General of the United Netherlands, we, Jacob van Ulfeldt of Urup and Holger Rosenkrantz of Rosenholm, and we, Reinier Pauw, Markus van Lyclama of Nyeholt, Zweder van Haersolte of Haerst, and Goozen Schaffer of Uithuizen, their respective deputies and envoys, have now assembled here in Bremen to consider the treaty of friendship and alliance of May 14 last, concluded at the Hague between His Royal Majesty and Their High Mightinesses, aforesaid, upon the agreement and with the modifications and amendment of both parties; and further to frame and complete some points and articles which were left unsettled; and [whereas we] have not only conferred for a long while about these articles, but have sent our results to our most gracious king, and to Their High Mightinesses, and have received their resolution thereupon, nevertheless some differences remained in respect to the articles about trade and about mutual financial help; for we, ambassadors and deputies of His Majesty, insisted on the articles as they are given below, and we, ambassadors of Their High Mightinesses, unable to go beyond our instructions in accepting these, insisted that they be left for the further consideration of our principals. . . .

. . . .

We, therefore, commissioners and envoys of His Royal Majesty, have drawn up and negotiated these articles—both of trade, omitting the matter of prohibited harbors, and of mutual financial help, in regard to which some differences persisted, and likewise the article of confidential friendship, respecting navigation and trade to both the Indies, about which there is no disagreement—and we have delivered them in writing, together with all

the other articles agreed to in the earlier and present negotiations, to the
ambassadors of Their High Mightinesses, in the form that His Majesty was
finally graciously disposed to agree to, except that the article about financial
help, as more temporary and subject to alteration, is given and agreed to in
a separate instrument.

The articles, word for word, are as follows:

. . . .

2. A good and trustworthy friendship and correspondence shall also be and
remain between the countries and subjects of both parties in all navigation,
trade, and traffic, by land and water, with ships and goods, to all realms, lands,
islands, and places in the East and West Indies, Africa, Guinea, Terra Australis, and all such foreign voyages. But the right of each power in the
lands, islands, and places that it either possesses and holds by forts for its
defense, or else obtains and possesses through any kings, princes, or rulers
of those lands, by special agreements and treaties concerning commerce,
defense, and the like, is hereby in nowise detracted from or prejudiced. But
each party shall in every way show and testify to the other all friendship and
assistance on all occasions that may arise in such navigation and trade, and
neither shall inflict upon the other any injury, vexation, or hindrance, in any
way, be it in journeying to or fro or in the said lands where they may encounter one another. And neither party shall venture, secretly or openly, to render
to the public enemies of the other in those regions any aid or supplies that
might be contrary to this established alliance. And if it should happen that
ships and men of one or the other party be forced by storm, tempest, or
other necessity into lands, havens, and districts already occupied and possessed by the other party, then they shall show and testify all good friendship
and assistance to one another and allow them [aliens] to obtain needed
refreshment and whatever is necessary for repairs. But it is not meant by
this that any lading, trade, or traffic shall be permitted in those regions.

. . . .

Two copies of these recesses, made and written, one in the German
language, the other in the Dutch, which differ in wording but are as nearly
as possible alike in substance and meaning, are both signed at Bremen on
September 30, o. s., October 10, n. s., 1621.

JACOB ULFFELDT.   REINIER PAUW.   S. VAN HAERSOLTE.
HOLGER ROSZENKRANTZ.   M. V. LYCLAMA.   G. SCHAFFER.

32.

Treaty between the United Netherlands and France, concluded at Compiègne, June 10, 1624. Ratification by the King of France, September 4, 1624. [Ratification by the States General, July 12, 1624.]

INTRODUCTION.

At the beginning of the year 1621, when the twelve years' truce between the United Provinces and Spain[1] was drawing to a close, the States General attempted to renew their alliances with France and England that terminated with the truce.[2] The French court, however, deeply offended by the treatment accorded to Oldenbarnevelt, remained unfriendly, until, early in 1624, a change of ministers in France brought in a new foreign policy, expressive of Richelieu's aims.[3] Profiting by this turn of affairs, the States General sent an embassy to negotiate a league. The ambassadors were instructed to ask for aid, preferably financial, for the war against Spain, and to propose the formation of a French West India Company, which should co-operate with the Dutch West India Company in winning booty and conquests from Spain in the seas west of the Cape of Good Hope and on the American coasts.[4] The Dutch desired this co-operation as a protection against the " powerful force . . . put to sea . . . by Spain . . . for the purpose of crushing [their] company in its infancy ", and also as a means of forestalling the international difficulties likely to follow from the erection of rival West India companies in France and England.[5] Conferences began at Compiègne on April 22.[6] The French commissioners wished to reduce the articles to writing quickly; the Dutch desired further instructions from the Hague. At the fourth meeting, the French produced written articles stipulating, among other things, that the Dutch should join the French in voyages to the East as well as to the West Indies. This proposal was unacceptable to the States General, the more so, as the alliance of the Dutch and English East India companies[7] had led to continual dissensions, culminating in the " massacre " of Amboyna in February, 1623. Since no definitive agreement respecting the East and West India commerce could be reached, the treaty merely stipulated that these

---

[1] Doc. **28**.   [2] *Cf.* Doc. **29**, introduction.
[3] *Cal. St. Pap., Venice*, 1623-1625, XVIII., pp. 139 (no. 179), 248 (no. 307).
[4] Arend *et al., op. cit.*, III. (4), 25.   [5] Brodhead, *Documents*, I. 29.
[6] Arend *et al., loc. cit.*, p. 26.
[7] The text of this treaty is given in English in *A General Collection of Treatys* (1732), II. 188-196.

navigations should form the subject of later negotiations by the French ambassador at the Hague. The treaty further provided that a loan should be made by the king to the States General, to be repaid after the conclusion of a Dutch-Spanish peace or truce, which should be made only with the advice of the king ; that if the king should need money or go to war, the States should aid him with half the amount of his loan to them, or with men and ships ; that within six months the States should guarantee the western part of the Mediterranean [8] against the depredations of the corsairs of Algiers and Tunis, and restore French ships and goods taken by the pirates in those waters and found in Dutch ports ; and that commissioners of the Admiralty, who should have no interest in the war-ships or prizes they adjudged, should decide French claims within three months. A special article permitted the exercise of the Catholic religion to Frenchmen in the house of the French ambassador in the Netherlands.

The treaty was concluded on June 10. It is curious that Richelieu says in his *Mémoires* that it was concluded on July 20, and that the Dutch agreed thereby " que non-seulement ils ne donneront point d'empêchement, mais toute assistance, à nos marchands trafiquans aux Indes orientales et occidentales ; leur laisseront le choix des côtes pour y trafiquer en toute sûreté et liberté, et les associeront avec eux en leurs navigations èsdits pays ".[9] Doubtless Richelieu is also responsible for the same false account of the treaty given in the *Mercure François*.[10]

On December 9, when the French ambassador, d'Espesses, presented his letters of credence at the Hague, he recommended the pretensions of the East India Company of Dieppe ; [11] but neither the desire of the French to share Dutch trade in the East, nor the desire of the Dutch to organize with the French against Spain on the western seas, was carried into effect.

BIBLIOGRAPHY.

Text: MS. The original manuscript of the protocol and the ratification by the King of France are in the Ryksarchief at the Hague, Secrete Casse, casse A, loquet S, nos. 36 and 37. No original manuscript of the treaty was found by the editor in the Paris archives, but several copies are in the archives of the Ministry of Foreign Affairs in Paris, Correspondance Politique, Hollande, vol. IX., ff. 270-352.

Text: Printed. The protocol and the French and Dutch ratifications are in L. van Aitzema, *Saken van Staet en Oorlogh* (1669-1672), I. 284-287,

[8] Aitzema (*op. cit.*, I. 288) interprets " la mer du ponent " thus.
[9] Michaud and Poujoulat, *Nouvelle Collection*, 2° sér., tom. VII., p. 297.
[10] Tom. X. (1625), pp. 492-495. I. Disraeli, *Life and Reign of Charles I.* (1851), I. viii, says that Richelieu supplied accounts of state documents, including treaties, to the *Mercure François*.
[11] Aitzema, *op. cit.*, I. 357. An account of the French East India companies is given in P. Bonnassieux, *Les Grandes Compagnies de Commerce* (1892), pp. 254 ff.

and in J. Dumont, *Corps Diplomatique* (1726-1731), tom. V., pt. II., pp. 461-463. The protocol is in F. Leonard, *Recueil des Traitez de Paix* (1693), V. 25-28. The text in Aitzema and in A. van Wicquefort, *L'Histoire des Provinces Unies* (1719), II. 624-627, omits the words *et occidentales* from the fifth article.

Translation: Dutch. Aitzema, *op. cit.*, I. 287-290.

References: Contemporary and early writings. Aitzema, *op. cit.*, I. 284, 351-355; J. R. Brodhead, *Documents relative to the Colonial History of New York* (1853-1883), I. 29-33; *Calendar of State Papers, Venice*, 1623-1625, pp. 139 (no. 179), 219 (no. 274), 248 (no. 307), 299 (no. 375), 314 (no. 394); *Resolutien* of the States of Holland for the year 1624, pp. 9, 10, 16, 20, 62, 65, 73, 74, 78, 79; Cardinal de Richelieu, *Mémoires*, liv. XV. (1624) in Michaud and Poujoulat, *Nouvelle Collection des Mémoires* (1836-1839), 2° sér., tom. VII., pp. 295-297.

References: Later writings. J. P. Arend *et al.*, *Algemeene Geschiedenis des Vaderlands* (1840, etc.), III. (4), 23-31, 63; P. J. Blok, *History of the People of the Netherlands* (1898-1912), IV. 11-13; *Calendar of State Papers, Venice*, 1623-1625, preface, pp. xlvi, xlvii; G. W. Vreede, *Inleiding tot eene Geschiedenis der Nederlandsche Diplomatie* (1856, etc.), II. (2), 50 ff.

TEXT.[12]

Louis, par la grace de Dieu roy de France et de Navarre, a tous ceulx qui ces presentes lettres verront, salut. Les commissaires par nous depputez et ceulx de noz tres chers et grandz amis, les Sieurs les Estatz Generaulx des Provinces Unyes des Pays-Bas, ayans, en vertu des pouvoirs a eulx respectivement donnez, resolu et arresté en nostre nom et des dictz Sieurs les Estatz Generaulx, a Compiegne, le dixiesme jour de juin aussy dernier, le traicté et articles d'alliance et confederation qui ensuivent:

Comme ainsy soit que tres hault, tres puissant, et tres excellent Prince Louis XIII°, par la grace de Dieu roy treschrestien de France et de Navarre, ayant cy devant esté prié et requis par ses tres chers et bons amys, allies, et confederez, Messieurs les Estatz Generaulx des Provinces Unyes du Pays-Bas, de les vouloir assister sur ce qu'ilz auroient faict representer a Sa Majesté par leurs ambassadeurs l'estat de leurs affaires avec les consequences tres dangereuses qui en peuvent arriver au prejudice du general de la Chrestienté et de ceulx mesmes qui penseroient en profiter, Sa dite Majesté desirant tesmoigner aus dictz Sieurs les Estatz, ses tres chers et bons amys, la souvenance qu'elle veult avoir de la bonne volonté que le feu Roy Henry le grand, son tres honnoré seigneur et pere (que Dieu absolve), leur a souvent faict paroistre pour leur bien, repos, et advantaige, et continuer la sienne a son imitation, attendant que Sa dite Majesté puisse par effect asseurer la tranquilité publicque et particulierement celle des Pays-Bas, tres importante a la manutention de la paix universelle de la Chrestienté, tousjours desirée et affectionnée par Sa dite Majesté comme doibt faire ung roy tres-chrestien, tel que Dieu la constitué, Sa dite Majesté a nommé, choisy, et depputé Monsieur le duc de Lesdiguieres, pair et connestable de France, et les Sieurs Marquis

---

[12] The text is from the original manuscript of the French ratification in the Ryksarchief at the Hague.

de la Vieuville, chevalier des ordres de Sa Majesté, conseiller en son conseil d'estat, mareschal de ses campes et armées, l'un de ses lieutenans-generaulx au gouvernement de Champaigne, et surintendant de ses finances, et de Bullion, conseiller en ses dictz conseils d'estat et finances, pour avec les Sieurs Henry d'Essen, conseiller de Gueldres et Zutphen, etc., Nicolas de Bouchorst, sieur de Noortwijck, etc., Adrian Pauw, chevalier, sieur de Heemstede, etc., et Gedeon de Boetzeler et d'Asperen, seigneur et baron de Languerack et du Saint Empire, au nom et en qualité d'ambassadeurs extraordinaires de Messieurs les Estatz Generaulx des Provinces Unyes du Pays-Bas, adviser et traicter des moiens plus convenables a cest effect, lesquelz reciproquement, en vertu des pouvoirs a eulx donnez, dont coppie sera inserée en fin des presentes, ont, apres plusieurs conferances, convenu et arresté les articles qui ensuivent :

.   .   .   .

5. Quant au trafficq des Indes Orientales et Occidentales, en sera traicté sur les lieux par l'ambassadeur de Sa Majesté selon et suivant les memoires et instructions qui luy seront baillez a cest effect.

.   .   .   .

Lesquelz articles et traictez pour les susdictes trois annees, sy tant la guerre dure, seront ratiffiez bien et deuement par lesdictz sieurs les Estatz Generaulx dans deux mois du jour et datte des presentes, et iceulx avec la ratification presentez a Sa Majesté par leur ambassadeur ordinaire resident prez icelle, pour estre pareillement lesdictz articles et traictez ratiffiez par Sadite Majesté quinze jours aprés, et delivrez ausdictz sieurs les Estatz.

[Here follow the full powers granted by the King of France to his commissioners on April 18, 1624; and those issued by the States General of the United Provinces to their commissioners on March 18, 1624.]

En foy de quoy nous, susdits commissaires et ambassadeurs soubz signez, avons esdits noms signé ces presentes de nos seing ordinaire et a icelles faict apposer le cachet de noz armes. A Compiegne ce jourdhuy dixiesme juing, mil six cent vingtquatre. Escrit signé Lesdiguieres, La Vieuville, Bullion, H. van Essen, Nicolaes de Bouchorst, Adrian Pauw, et G. de Boetzeler et d'Asperen.

[Here follows the separate article concerning religion referred to above, p. 286.]

Lequel susdit traicté et articles ayans esté approuvez, confirmez, et ratiffiez par les dictz Sieurs les Estatz a La Haye, le xii⁰ juillet en suivant, Nous, apres avoir faict veoir le tout en nostre conseil pour satisfaire a ce qui est requis de nostre part sur ce subject, avons iceluy agreable en tous et chacuns les poinctz et articles qui y sont contenuz et declarez, et iceulx en general et en particulier, tant pour nous que pour noz heritiers, successeurs, royaumes, pays, terres, seigneuries, et subjectz, acceptez, approuvez, ratiffiez, et confirmez, acceptons, approuvons, ratiffions, et confirmons, et le tous promettons en foy et parolle de roy et soubz l'obligation et hipotecque de tous et chacuns noz biens presens et a venir, garder observer, et entretenir inviolablement sans aller n'y venir jamais au contraire directement ou indirectement, en quelque sorte ou maniere que ce soit. Car tel est nostre plaisir. En tesmoing dequoy nous avons signé ces presentes de nostre propre main et a icelles faict mettre et apposer nostre seel.

Donné a St. Germain en Laye le iiii⁰ jour de Septembre, l'an de grace mil six cens vingt quatre et de nostre reigne le quinziesme.

Louis.
Par le Roy.
Potier.

33.

Treaty of offensive and defensive alliance between the United Netherlands and Great Britain concluded at Southampton, September 7/17, 1625. Ratification by the States General, December 14, 1625. [Ratification by the King of Great Britain, December 20/30, 1625.]

INTRODUCTION.

On account of James I.'s bias toward Spain and his eagerness to marry his son to the Spanish infanta, the Dutch, after the expiration of the truce of Antwerp,[1] were unable to form an alliance with England until 1624, when all hopes of the Spanish match had vanished. Even then, although the Dutch ambassadors offered James the opportunity of joining in an enterprise of the Dutch West India Company, and promised him all the fortresses or places that the united fleets might conquer,[2] James was unwilling to pledge himself to declare war on Spain. The Anglo-Dutch alliance, concluded on June 5/15, 1624, was defensive merely.[3]

After the death of James, March 27/April 6, 1625, the chief object of Charles's foreign policy was to restore to his brother-in-law, Frederick, elector palatine and king of Bohemia, the electorship, and both the Palatinates, which had been occupied by the forces of Spain and of the German Catholic League. Hence Charles aimed at alliances and war on the Continent. The House of Commons, however, preferred a naval war against Spain.[4] In the opinion of Buckingham and Charles, the naval operations should be conducted in accordance with the old Elizabethan methods, but more openly.

As in 1596, the English government sought aid from the States.[5] In a convention signed at the Hague on August 2, 1625, the Dutch agreed to add twenty ships to the English fleet of eighty-two vessels.[6] Not till October did the united force sail, and it failed ingloriously to accomplish its purpose of taking Cadiz and intercepting the plate fleet.[7] Meanwhile (July-September),

[1] Doc. **28.**
[2] Arend *et al., Algemeene Geschiedenis*, III. (3), 749 ff. *Cf.* also the States' proposal to France in 1624, Doc. **32**, introduction.
[3] The text is in Dumont, *Corps Diplomatique*, tom. V., pt. II., pp. 458-461.
[4] *Debates in the House of Commons in 1625* (ed. S. R. Gardiner for the Camden Soc., new ser., vol. VI., 1873), p. iii.
[5] *Cf.* Doc. **23.**
[6] The treaty is in Dumont, *op. cit.*, p. 478.
[7] See *The Voyage to Cadiz in 1625*, a journal by John Glanville, ed. Rev. A. B. Grosart for the Camden Soc., new ser., vol. XXXII. (1883).

a Dutch embassy led by the celebrated Francis van Aerssen, lord of Sommels-dijk, was negotiating with Buckingham and other English commissioners an alliance that should be closer and more comprehensive than that of 1624. The States' representatives displayed great skill. Desiring a league with England they wished to avoid offending France,[8] with whom the States had lately signed a treaty.[9] By carefully adjusting their relations to each of these powers, they hoped to guard their own independence. They even went so far as to suggest to the French ambassador that a large French fleet should capture the treasure-ships, so that England might not obtain the exclusive advantage of the existing equipment.[10]

Since both powers desired an alliance they came to terms with comparative ease. The treaty, concluded at Southampton on September 7/17, provided for an offensive and defensive league " for the purpose of attacking the King of Spain in open war in all his realms . . . in all places, on this side and beyond the line, by land and sea ". The league was to continue so long as the King of Spain should make war upon the United Provinces or so long as he and his allies should occupy the electoral dignity or estates of the Palatinate, or for at least fifteen years. During this period the confederates were not to treat separately for peace. Interested powers should be received into the alliance. The confederates should equip one or more fleets to invade the enemy's ports and destroy his commerce in Europe and the two Indies. Other articles dealt with the operations, composition, command, and mutual relations of the fleets; the division of prizes; rights of ships of either power in the ports of the other; contraband, here first defined by treaty, and trade with Spain and its dominions. Letters of marque and reprisal against the subjects of either confederate were annulled. Articles 27-33 and 35-38 related to land forces and operations; article 34 permitted the King of England to buy ships, arms, etc., in the United Provinces. The treaty was ratified by the States General on December 14, 1625, and by Charles I. on December 20/30.[11]

The treaty entirely failed to adjust satisfactorily the maritime relations of the signatory powers. The Dutch complained bitterly that it debarred them from a lucrative trade with Spain and that their ships and goods continued to be arrested and seized by the English.[12]

Among the interests endangered by England's interference with Dutch shipping was the American trade of the Dutch West India Company, includ-

[8] *Cal. St. Pap., Venice,* 1625-1626, vol. XIX., p. 161.

[9] Doc. **32**.

[10] Arend *et al., op. cit.,* III. (4), 102.

[11] Aitzema, *Saken van Staet,* I. 473.

[12] P. R. O., Treaty Papers, Holland (1625-1627), no. 43: "Summary of what the ambassadors of the States General proposed to the Privy Council", Dec. 9/19, 1625, and " Remonstrance to the Privy Council by Ambassadors of the States General ", July 21/31, 1626. *Cf.* also the " Remonstrance " of the Dutch ambassador, Jan. 20/30, 1626, printed in *Documents illustrating the Impeachment of the Duke of Buckingham in 1626,* ed. S. R. Gardiner for the Camden Soc., new ser., vol. XLV. (1889), pp. 47-53.

ing that with New Netherland. This plantation was regarded by the English as an intrusion into their domain. In 1622, the English government, acting through its representative at the Hague, required of the States that the colony should not be advanced further and that certain ships destined thereto should be stayed.[13] In 1624 it ordered the detention of a Dutch ship, then riding in Plymouth harbor and bound to New Netherland.[14] To prevent such interference the Dutch West India Company " made humble suite unto his Majestie, that their shipps employed thether [*i. e.*, to the west coast of Africa and the coasts of America], either in trade of marchandize, or on warrfare for the weakening of the common ennemy, might quietly pass on their intended voyages, both outward, and homeward bound, without anie molestation, stay, or hinderance, by his Majesties owne shipps, or those of his subjects, employed with letters of marque, to the southward or elsewhere ". Whereupon, on September 5, 1627, Charles I. ordered that " the said West India Companie, their captaines, masters, marriners, shipps, and prizes by them taken, or to be taken hereafter, upon the said enemy ; and all their goods and other things, whatsoever to them belonging ; shall have free ingrees, egress, and regresse into and out of all his Majesties ports, havens, roads, and creekes, as by the articles of the treaty, made at Southampton, the 7th of September, 1625, more at large appeareth ". Articles 15, 16, 17, 18, 19, 23, and 24 follow, together with an injunction to all his Majesty's officers and subjects to observe them.[15]

In contravention of this order, as the Dutch Company alleged, one of their ships from New Netherland was detained in an English harbor in 1632, upon the ground that its rich cargo of beaver skins was bought within British territory.[15a] The struggle between English and Dutch for control of the region north of Virginia grew more and more serious. For a time however the relations of their respective colonies planted on those shores were rendered more friendly by the conclusion of this treaty of Southampton. It was among the causes that led the governor and council at Manhattan, in March, 1627, to write a friendly letter to the authorities at Plymouth, suggesting the establishment of mutual trade, and it was one of the reasons that induced Bradford to accept that proposal,[16] although a monopoly of the trade from 40° to 48° had been granted to the Council of New England.

By signing the treaty of Madrid,[17] Charles flagrantly violated the treaty of Southampton.

[13] J. R. Brodhead, *Documents relative to the Colonial History of the State of New York* (1853-1883), III. 6-8.
[14] *Acts of the Privy Council of England, Colonial,* I. 82 ; Brodhead, *op. cit.,* III. 12.
[15] *Acts of the Privy Council, Colonial,* I. 119 ; Brodhead, *op. cit.,* III. 12, 13.
[15a] Brodhead, *op. cit.,* I. 45 ff. ; G. L. Beer, *Origins of the British Colonial System, 1578-1660* (1908), p. 178.
[16] *Bradford's History of Plymouth Plantation* (ed. W. T. Davis, 1908), pp. 223-227, in J. F. Jameson, *Original Narratives of Early American History.*
[17] Doc. **35.**

BIBLIOGRAPHY.

Text: MS. Original manuscripts of the protocol and ratification are in the London Public Record Office, State Papers Foreign, Treaties, no. 296.

Text: Printed. L. van Aitzema, *Saken van Staet en Oorlogh* (1669-1672), I. 469-473; J. Dumont, *Corps Diplomatique* (1726-1731), tom. V., pt. II., pp. 478-481; *State Papers collected by Edward, Earl of Clarendon* (1767-1786), I. 27-33.

Translations: English. *A General Collection of Treatys* (1732), II. 248-258. **Dutch.** Aitzema, *op. cit.,* I. 473-476.

References: Contemporary and early writings. *Verbaal van de Ambassade van Aerssen, Joachimi, en Burmania naar England, 1625,* in *Werken uitgegeven door het Historisch Genootschap te Utrecht,* nieuwe reeks, no. 10 (1867); L. van Aitzema, *op. cit.,* I. 468 ff.; *Resolutien* of the States of Holland for the year 1625, pp. 50, 52, 56, 61, 63, 64, 140, 143, 158-159, *et passim; Calendar of State Papers, Venice,* 1625-1626, vol. XIX., pp. 68 (no. 93), 161 (no. 235), 165 (no. 244), 175 (no. 260), 194 (no. 282), 203 (no. 296), 225 (no. 333).

References: Later writings. J. P. Arend *et al., Algemeene Geschiedenis des Vaderlands* (1840, etc.), III. (4), 90-108; G. Edmundson, *Anglo-Dutch Rivalry during the First Half of the Seventeenth Century* (1911), ch. 4; S. R. Gardiner, *History of England, 1603-1642* (1894-1896), VI. 6; P. J. Blok, *History of the People of the Netherlands* (1898-1912), IV. 22-24; G. W. Vreede, *Inleiding tot eene Geschiedenis der Nederlandsche Diplomatie* (1856-1865), II. (2), 77 ff.

TEXT.[18]

Les Estats Generaulx des Provinces Unies du Pais Bas, a tous ceux qui ces presentes verront, salut. Comme ainsy soit que le septiesme jour de Septembre, l'an present XVI^c vingt cinq, un traité d'alliance de ligue offensive et defensive ayt este faict et accorde a South Hampton entre les seigneurs commissaires du Serenissime Roy de la Grande Bretaigne au nom dudit roy et ses royaumes et les ambassadeurs par nous envoyez a sadite Majeste en nostre nom et de nostre Republicque, dont la teneur s'ensuit:

Comme ainsy soit que pour d'un commun effort rompre le progres des injustes usurpations du Roy d'Espaigne, et ses ambitieuses entreprises, par lesquelles il trouble journellement le repos et estats des roys et princes de l'Europe, et particulierement celuy des Provinces Unies des Pays Bas, Treshault Tres excellent et Trespuissant Prince Charles, par la grace de Dieu Roy de la Grande Bretaigne, France, et Irlande, defenseur de la foy, etc., auroit esté instamment requis de la part de Hauts et Puissants Seigneurs les Estats Generaux desdites Provinces Unies des Pays Bas, par le moyen de Messires François d'Aerssen, chevalier, sieur de Sommelsdyck de la Plate, Albert Joachimi aussi chevallier, sieur a Oostende et Oedekenskerck, et Rienck de Burmania a Fervert, grietman de Ferweradeel, ambassadeurs vers saditte Majesté de la part desdits Seigneurs Estats, d'entrer avec eux en une confederation plus estroicte, et en ligue offensive et defensive contre

[18] The text is from the original manuscript of the Dutch ratification in P. R. O., Treaties. 296.

ledit Roy d'Espaigne et ses adherens, sadite Majesté de la Grande Bretaigne, etc. en continuation de l'affection et soing que les roys et reynes ses predecesseurs, et notamment le feu roy de glorieuse memoire, son treshonoré seigneur et pere, ont tousjours eu de la conservation et subsistence desdites Provinces, contre ledit Roy d'Espaigne, et ennemis de leur liberté, comme aussi des assistences et grands secours qui leur ont esté donnés de temps en temps, tant par la dame Reyne Elisabeth, que par ledit Seigneur Roy, pere de Sa Majesté; pour ces causes, et pour le passioné desir qu'a sadite Majeste à l'entier restablissement de son trescher frere Frederic, serenissime prince electeur Palatin du Rhin, en ses estats, possessions, et dignitez hereditaires, dont il á esté injustement depossedé par ledit Roy d'Espaigne, et ses adherens, Sa Majeste ayant nommé et constitué les Seigneurs Jacques, baron Ley, son grand thesorier d'Angleterre, George, duc de Buckingam,[19] son grand admiral d'Angleterre, Guilliaume, comte de Pembrock,[20] chambellan de son hostel, Jacques, comte de Carlile,[21] Henry, comte d'Hollande,[22] Edouard, baron Conwey,[23] premier secretaire d'Estat, Fulke, baron Brooke,[24] Robert Naunton, chevalier maistre des Gardenobles,[25] Albert Mourton nagueres chevalier[26] et l'autre des premiers Secretaires, et Richard Weston chevalier, chancelier de son Exchequier, ou six d'iceux, tous et un chacun d'eux Conseillers en son Conseil d'Estat et privé, et iceux garnis de pouvoir suffisant dont copie sera inserée à la fin de ce present traitté, pour avec lesdits sieurs ambassadeurs desdits Seigneurs Estats, munis aussi de pouvoir suffisant, dont copie sera pareillement inserée après celle desdits seigneurs commissaires de sadite Majeste, traitter, convenir, et conclure, d'une ligue offensive ou defensive entre sadite Majesté et lesdits Seigneurs Estats, contre ledit Roy d'Espaigne et ses adherens: lesquels commissaires de sadite Majesté, et ambassadeurs desdits Seigneurs Estats, apres plusieurs assemblées et deliberations tenues sur ce suject, ont convenu, conclu, et arresté les poincts et articles qui s'ensuivent:

1. Premierement, il y aura alliance de ligue offensive et defensive entre sadite Majesté d'une part, et lesdits Seigneurs Estats d'autre part, afin d'assaillir le Roy d'Espaigne a guerre ouverte, en tous ses royaumes, terres, subjects, et droicts, en tous lieux, deçà et delà la ligne,[27] par mer et par terre.

2. Laquelle dicte alliance durera si longuement que le Roy d'Espaigne continuera de pretendre par guerre, voyes de faict, et autres ambitieuses menées, sur la liberté et droicts desdites Provinces Unies, et que la dignité electorale, terres, et autres estats patrimoniaux du Palatinat, demeureront occupez par luy, ou par ses adherens; au moins pour le terme de quinze ans.

3. Et ne pourront sadite Majesté de la Grande Bretaigne, etc., ny lesdits Seigneurs Estats, traitter avec ledit Roy d'Espaigne, ny ses adherens, dans ledit terme de quinze ans prochain venants, a commencer du jour de la presente convention, de paix, trefve, suspension d'armes,[28] ny entrer en aucune autre

[19] George Villiers.   [20] William Herbert, lord chamberlain.   [21] James Hay.
[22] Henry Rich.   [23] Edward Conway.   [24] Fulke Greville, first Lord Brooke.
[25] Master of the Court of Wards.
[26] Sir Albertus Morton died the day before the conclusion of the treaty.
[27] The equator.
[28] For the measures taken by England to enforce both the prohibition of trade with Spain and also article 20 of this treaty, dealing with contraband, see *Documents relating to Law and Custom of the Sea,* ed. by R. G. Marsden for the Navy Records Society, I. (1915) 404, 405.

negociation tendante à pareille fin, directement ou indirectement, ny aussi quitter ou renoncer à la presente alliance, que de l'advis, et consentement commun. Et seront sadite Majesté et lesdits Seigneurs Estats, tenuz se declarer sur la continuation de la presente alliance, un an auparavant que lesdits quinze ans viendront a expirer.

4. Seront receus en cette alliance tous les roys, princes, republiques, villes, et communautez, interessez en cette cause, qui le desireront, à condition equitable; lesquels seront requis solennellement par deputation expresse de ce faire, par sadite Majesté, et lesdits Seigneurs Estats, separement, ou ensemblement, dans trois mois apres la conclusion du present traitté, et plustost [si] faire se peut."

5. Il y aura bonne et sincere correspondence pour la defense mutuelle des royaumes, estats, et subjects, l'un de l'autre, entre sadite Majesté et lesdits Seigneurs Estats, qui demeureront respectivement tenus de procurer a leur possible, le bien, seureté et advantage l'un de l'autre comme aussi d'advancer le dommage, affoiblissement et ruine dudit Roy d'Espaigne, leur ennemy commun.

6. Lequel commun ennemy, sadite Majesté et lesdits Seigneurs Estats seront obligez d'attacquer de toute leur puissance, par mer et par terre, et feront à cette fin tous les ans equipper et entretenir, une, deux, ou plusieurs flottes, au moyen desquelles ils le feront envahir et infester par descente d'armée en terre ferme, ou par autres aggressions, en tous ses ports, et isles, avec tant de vigueur, que la communication de la mer, le commerce parmy l'Europe, le negoce des deux Indes, et principalement le retour annuel de ses flottes, luy en puisse demeurer couppé et retranché.

7. Et afin d'entreprendre tel desseing avec ordre, et une despense reiglée et partagée, sans la laisser toute a la charge de sadite Majesté ou desdits Seigneurs Estats seuls, il a esté dict et convenu, que sadite Majesté de la Grande Bretaigne, etc., tiendra un bon nombre de vaisseaux equippez, et armez en guerre, aux costes et isles d'Espaigne, pour en tenir d'ordinaire bouchées les entrées des rivieres de Lisbone, de St. Lucar, et la Baye de Cadiz, autant que faire se pourra; comme seront pareillement lesdits Seigneurs Estats tenus de leur part, de faire aux costes de Flandres, pour en tenir les ports fermez, et la mer libre de pirateries, a leur possible.

8. Mais si en outre il est trouvé bon, pour faire une plus gaillarde impression, et occuper plus sensiblement ledit Roy d'Espaigne en ses propres royaulmes et estats, de mettre une grande flotte en mer, avec un desseing reiglé et concerté entre sadite Majesté et lesdits Seigneurs Estats, en tel cas lesdits Seigneurs Estats seront tenus de contribuer une quatriesme partie du nombre des vaisseaux que sadite Majesté a cette fin fera armer, et jetter en mer, montez et munitionnez, pour pareil temps, [et] proportionnez à la mesme grandeur et port de ceux de sa Majesté.

9. Sa Majesté aura le commandement sur toute telle flotte, par son Admiral, ou Vice Admiral, subsecutivement, toutes fois il a esté convenu et accordé que l'Admiral et Vice Admiral qui commanderont la flotte desdits Seigneurs Estats, quand ils seront conjoincts avec celle de sadite Majesté pourront

---

" By the treaty of the Hague Nov. 29/Dec. 9, 1625, Denmark was brought into an alliance with England and the States " for the preservation of the liberty, rights, and constitutions of the empire ", and it was provided that the rulers of France, Sweden, Venice, Savoy, the Electoral Princes, and others should be invited to join the league. Aitzema, *op. cit.,* I. 480-481 ; Dumont, *op. cit.,* tom. V., pt. II., pp. 482-483.

arborer une seconde baniere, assister avec quelques vieux capitaines, et avoir voix à toutes les tenues et deliberations du conseil de guerre, et que les commandemens qui se feront sur ladite flotte desdits Seigneurs Estats par l'Admiral ou Vice Admiral de sadite Majeste se feront mediatement, et par l'entremise de l'Admiral ou Vice Admiral desdits Seigneurs Estats, lesquels dits Admiral ou Vice Admiral desdits Seigneurs Estats, auront aussi toute justice sur leurs officiers, soldats, et mariniers, quand ils auront dispute entre eux. Mais s'il arrivoit quelque dispute ou controverse entre quelques uns de la flotte de sadite Majesté et de celle desdits Seigneurs Estats, le different sera examiné et decidé selon les loix, et ordonnances, par l'Admiral ou Vice Admiral de sadite Majesté au conseil de guerre.

10. Aux exploits de guerre qui se feront pour forcer quelques havres, monter des rivieres, assaillir les navires ennemis, ou aux aultres actions de pareil danger, et nature, il sera gardé cest ordre: qu'il ne sera employé plus grand nombre des navires desdits Seigneurs Estats que proportionné à celuy de sadite Majesté, selon la quantité du secours, si, d'un commun consentement des chefs, de part et d'aultre, il n'est aultrement resolu.

11. Si l'une ou l'autre flotte venoit en mer à avoir besoing d'aide, et assistence de vivres, munitions, voiles, ou autres appareaux, les Admiraux les en feront secourrir, s'il y a moyen, a prix raisonnable, où a la charge d'en faire rendre autant au retour des flottes a l'option de ceux qui l'auront demandé.

12. Si ces flottes, ainsi conjointes, et armées, font quelque prinse sur les ennemis communs, en mer ou par terre, d'hommes, de navires, d'or, d'argent, de marchandises, et d'aultres meubles, sera incontinent fait un estat et registre de toutes telles prinses, en presence et par le moyen des officiers des deux flottes ensemble, de bonne foy, et sans en rien cacher, ou destourner: lesquels seront par apres equitablement partagez, a proportion du nombre et du port des vaisseaux que sadite Majesté et lesdits Seigneurs Estats auront reellement et de faict fourny, pour parformer leur flotte commune, nonobstant qu'il pourroit arriver, que lors de la prinse, nul des navires de sa Majesté, ou vice versa, desdits Seigneurs Estats, s'y seroit rencontré, pourveu que telles prinses ayent esté faictes par une partie des vaisseaux de [20] la flotte commune.

13. Mais sy sadite Majesté de la Grande Bretaigne, etc., trouvoit bon de faire embarquer à ses despens une bonne armée, et la descendre quelque part à terre au pays de l'ennemy, afin d'y faire invasion, et occuper quelque ville, ou assiette forte à y loger sadite armée en seureté et lieu commode pour advantager ses desseings, il est accordé, que les occupations qui de cette sorte se feront en terre ferme, appartiendront, et demeureront purement et simplement à sadite Majesté, nonobstant que la flotte desdits Seigneurs Estats y pourroit avoir assisté et aydé.

14. Bien entendu toutes fois, que si a telle descente et execution, les subjects desdits Seigneurs Estats entreviennent qu'ils auront aussi leur part aux butins et meubles proportionnée de leur nombre à celuy des subjects de sadite Majesté, a laquelle seule demeureront tous les acquests immeubles, des isles, villes et terres.

15. Ceux qui auront commission de sadite Majeste de la Grande Bretaigne, ou desdits Seigneurs Estats, pourront en vertu de cette alliance, poursuivre,

---

[20] The manuscript of the ratification has *et* instead of *de*. The latter reading, which is that of the protocol and of the treaty as printed by Aitzema, is doubtless correct.

combattre, prendre, et emmener par tout leurs ennemis, en quelques endroicts qu'ilz viennent a les rencontrer, mesmes aux rades, emboucheures de rivieres, et aux ports de mer, de part et d'autre : a la charge que ceux qui auront esté prins aux rades, emboucheures et auxdits ports, ne pourront estre emmenez, devant que d'en payer les droicts, devoirs, et coustumes, a ceux qu'il appartiendra : lesquels ports et rades de sadite Majesté et desdits Seigneurs Estats seront ouverts et libres aux navires de guerre et marchands, de part et d'aultre, qui y pourront entrer, demeurer, sortir, et rader, sans nul empeschement. Se reigleront neantmoins iceux navires selon les loix, droicts, et coustumes des lieux.

16. Si par tempeste, poursuite de pirates, ou par quelque autre contrainte et meschef, aucuns navires marchands prennent port dans le pays de l'obeissance de sadite Majesté ou desdits Seigneurs Estats, iceux s'en pourront retirer librement à leur volonté, sans pource estre tenus de descendre, trocquer, ou vendre leurs marchandises, ny d'en payer aucuns droits.

17. Les capitaines commandans les navires de guerre de sadite Majesté, ou desdits Seigneurs Estats, et envoyez en mer avec des commissions privées de leurs souverains, n'estans point compris au corps de ladite flotte commune, pourront pareillement en toute seureté mener aux ports et rades de sadite Majesté et desdits Seigneurs Estats, leurs prinses, faictes sur les ennemis communs, et les en retirer par apres franchement à leur plaisir, pour les conduire au lieu qu'ilz doibvent par leur commission, sans estre tenus de notifier leursdits prinses aux officiers du lieu, ou leur en payer aucuns droicts, mais à la charge toutes fois de monstrer leurs commissions, s'ils en sont requis par iceux.

18. Si durant la presente confederation aucuns navires, par tempeste, ou autre mesadventure, viennent a s'eschoüer, ou se perdre, sur les costes de sadite Majesté de la Grande Bretaigne, etc., ou sur celles desdits Seigneurs Estats, tels navires ou leurs debris pourront estre reclamez et repetez dans l'an, par ceux ausquels ilz appartiendront de droict, ou en ayans cause et procuration d'eux, et leur seront rendus, sans autre forme de proces, payans selon les droicts et coustumes des lieux.

19. Si sur telle ou pareille occurrence, il arrivoit dispute entre les subjects de part et d'autre, les officiers des lieux seront obligez de leur faire et administrer bonne et courte justice, sans trainer, et entretenir les parties en longueur, par aucune formalité de proces.

20. Toutes marchandises de contrebande, comme sont munitions de bouche et de guerre, navires, armes, voiles, cordages, or, argent, cuivre, fer, plomb, et semblables, de quelque part qu'on les voudra porter en Espaigne, et aux autres terres de l'obeissance dudit Roy d'Espaigne, et de ses adherens, seront de bonne prinse, avec les navires et hommes qui les porteront.

21. Sadite Majesté fera instance envers les autres roys, princes, estats, villes, et communautez neutres, de faire defense à leurs subjects de traffiquer, tant que la presente guerre durera, aux royaulmes et autres possessions dudit Roy d'Espaigne, et de ses adherens, afin de ne leur laisser encourir, a leur escient, aucun dommage.

22. Ce que ne venant à s'obtenir de leur gré, il est convenu, que les navires qui se trouveront a la mer, suspects de prendre leur route devers l'Espaigne, les Isles, où autres estats dudit Roy d'Espaigne, et de ses adherens, seront obligez d'ammener, pour estre recognus et visitez, sans pour ce les pouvoir retarder ou endommager.

23. Le negoce, ou commerce, sera cependant ouvert et permis par tout ailleurs, aux royaulmes, villes, terres et pays des alliez, et des princes, et amiz neutres, sans interruption, ny destourbier.

24. Pareillement pourront sadite Majesté et lesdits Seigneurs Estats se faire fournir aux pays l'un de l'autre, de toutes sortes de munitions, d'armes, cordages, voiles, et victuailles, pour le necessaire equipage de leurs flottes, sans pour l'achept, ou transport, estre tenus payer d'avantage que ceux du pays auquel ces emploites auront esté faites.

25. Sa Majesté traittera lesdits Seigneurs Estats en amis et voisins alliez avec elle d'une alliance si estroicte, en ce qui concerne la traitte d'artillerie et balles ou boulets a canon, leur permettant d'achepter et transporter hors de ses royaumes et dominions, telle proportion d'artillerie et boulets pour l'usage de la flotte commune, que l'on pourra departir commodement, a tel prix et aux mesmes conditions que les autres alliez de sa Majesté ou ses propres subjects ont accoustumé de l'avoir.

26. Et avenant que par cy apres, sadite Majesté et lesdits Seigneurs Estats separement, ou ensemblement, viendroient à descouvrir de nouveaux moyens, et expediens propres pour endommager plus puissamment ledit [31] Roy d'Espaigne, par mer, que ceux desquels il est convenu en ce traitté, et demandoient d'adjuster leurs entreprises avec commune deliberation et advis, il est accordé qu'ils en communiqueront et concerteront par leurs ambassadeurs, quand bon leur semblera, ou par deputation, et envoy expres s'il est trouvé utile et à propos.

.   .   .   .

39.[32] Toutes lettres de represailles, marque, arrests et autres semblables, qui ont esté cy devant octroyées et decernées contre les subjects de l'un [33] ou l'autre des confederez, pour quelque cause que ce soit, n'auront lieu de part et d'aultre, ains sont des maintenant, et demeureront nulles et de nul effect, et pour l'advenir n'en seront aucunes octroyées, mais justice sera rendue et administrée, ainsy que de droit appartiendra.

40. Par la presente alliance, ny par aucunes paroles y contenues, generales, où speciales, n'est pas compris ou entendu, qu'il y ait aucune innovation, interruption, ou changement en la liberté de la navigation, et commerce, es royaumes, estats, et pays de sa Majesté, desdits Seigneurs Estats, et autres roys, princes, villes, amis, alliez et neutres, ny aussi aux loix et coustumes des admirautez, payemens de daces, imposts, subsides, devoirs, de part et d'aultre, ny aux droicts appellez coustomes en Angleterre: Ains à esté convenu [34] et accordé, que ladite liberté, droits, daces, imposts, loix, coustumes et payemens susdits demeureront en leur pleine, et entière force, et vertu, comme ils estoyent le jour precedent de la conclusion du present traitté.

Lesquelles conventions, pactions et articles cy dessus contenus, et chascun diceux ont este traictez, stipulez, accordez, et passez, entre lesdits Seigneurs Commissaires de sadite Majesté, et lesdits Sieurs ambassadeurs desdits

---

[31] The manuscript reads *lesdits*.

[32] The following provision was modified by King Charles's " protest ", made at Titchfield on Sept. 9/19, in which he declared that unless, within eighteen months, the States did justice in regard to the Amboyna massacre, he would be free to issue letters of reprisal to his subjects or to use his own forces to avenge them. Aitzema, *op. cit.,* I. 476-477.

[33] The ratification reads *une* ; the protocol, *un*.

[34] The protocol and Aitzema's text read *expressement convenu*.

Seigneurs Estats Generaulx, soubs le bon plaisir de sadite Majeste et desdits Seigneurs Estats Generaux, promettans de bonne foy, et s'obligeans en vertu de leurs commissions respectivement, qui seront inserées à la fin du present traitté que dans trois mois prochainement venans, ou plustost, si faire se peult, ilz feront fournir, scavoir les Seigneurs Commissaires de sadite Majesté aux Sieurs Ambassadeurs desdits Seigneurs Estats, et lesdits Sieurs Ambassadeurs desdits Seigneurs Estats aux Seigneurs Commissaires de sadite Majesté, la declaration speciale de la volonté de leurs Souverains sur iceluy traitté, ou lettres de ratification en forme suffisante et vallable.

En foy et tesmoingnage de toutes lesquelles pactions, conventions, et articles, lesdits Seigneurs Commissaires et Sieurs Ambassadeurs, ont signé ce present traicté, et a iceluy apposé le seel de leurs armes. Faict en la ville de South Hampton ce septiesme jour de Septembre l'an mil six cents vingt cinq, stile d'Angleterre.

[Here follow the powers granted by Charles I. to his commissioners, August 25, 1625, and by the States General to their commissioners on June 12, 1625.]

Estoit signé Jaques Ley, G. Buckingam, Pembrock, Carlile, Hollande, E. Conwey, Rich. Weston, Francoy d'Aerssen, Alb. Joachimi, et R. v. Burmania. Plus bas au dessoubs des signatures estoit cachette des cachets des armes respectivement desdits Seigneurs commissaires et ambassadeurs.

Nous ayants ledit traitte agreable en tous et chacuns ses points, avons iceux points en general et en particulier acceptez, approuvez, ratifiez, et confirmez, les acceptons, approuvons, ratifions et confirmons par ces presentes, promettans les garder, entretenir, et observer inviolablement, sans aller ne venir au contraire, directement ou indirectement, en quelque sorte et maniere que-ce soit, soubs l'obligation et hypotheque de tous les biens et revenus desdites Provinces Unies en general et en particulier, presens et advenir. En tesmoing de quoy nous avons faict seeler ces presentes de nostre grand seel, parapher et signer par nostre greffier a la Haye le xiiiime de Decembre l'an XVI^c vingt cinq.

T. VARUER v[idi]t.
Par ordonnance desdits Seigneurs Estats Generaux.
J. VAN GOCH.

34.

Treaty between Great Britain and France signed at Susa and London, April 14/24, 1629. Ratification by the King of France, July 4, 1629. [Ratification by the King of Great Britain, June 11, 1629.]

Introduction.

The failure of Charles I. of England to fulfill the conditions of the contract of marriage between him and the sister of Louis XIII. of France, resulted in friction between the two courts. Further irritation was caused by the refusal of France to enter the league signed at the Hague against the House of Austria;[1] and, in 1626, by her conclusion of a treaty with Spain.[2] The growing ill-will was heightened by commercial disputes[3] arising from England's seizure, following provisions of the treaty of Southampton,[4] of French ships and merchandise employed in the Spanish trade; by retaliatory arrests of English ships and goods on the part of France; by England's interference in behalf of the Huguenots of Rochelle, and by her jealousy of Richelieu's endeavors to strengthen French sea-power.

On March 20, 1627, France and Spain concluded an alliance which provided for an attack upon England by their combined fleets.[5] Nine days later, Buckingham was empowered to grant letters of reprisal against the French; a month later to grant letters of marque as well.[6] In June, an English fleet sailed to relieve Rochelle.

The war thus begun offered England an opportunity to drive the French from Canada and Acadia and occupy them herself. For this purpose, in 1628, David Kirke and his brothers, having obtained letters of marque and a royal commission, captured and destroyed French vessels in the gulf and

[1] *Cf.* Doc. **33**, note 29. Gardiner, *History of England, 1603-1642*, VI. 37-44.

[2] Dumont, *Corps Diplomatique*, tom. V., pt. II., pp. 487 ff. On this treaty of Monzon, see E. Rott, *Histoire de la Représentation Diplomatique de la France auprès des Cantons Suisses* (1900, etc.), tom. IV., pt. I., pp. 47 ff.

[3] These were the principal causes according to a manuscript entitled " The causes of the war with France " (P. R. O., Treaty Papers, France, no. 10).

[4] Doc. **33**, arts. 20-22.

[5] *Mémoires du Cardinal de Richelieu*, in Michaud and Poujoulat, *Nouvelle Collection des Mémoires*, 2ᵉ sér., tom. VII., p. 446; *Mémoires de Messire François Duval, Marquis de Fontenay-Mareuil*, same collection, 2ᵉ sér., tom. V., p. 185.

[6] Rymer, *Foedera*, XVIII. 861, 887. *Cf.* also *ibid.*, p. 1052. According to R. G. Marsden, the distinction between letters of marque and letters of reprisal seems not recognized until after the peace with Spain in 1630. *Law and Custom of the Sea*, I. (Navy Records Society, 1915), pp. xxvi, xxvii. See also pp. 406, 407 for notes on the letters of marque and reprisal issued during this war.

app. B (p. 2[?]4 [?]) for evidence [?] settlen[?]
made, *not* in 1628, *but* in 1629.)

river of St. Lawrence, including the first fleet sent out by the Company of
New France with supplies for Quebec; took the forts of Port Royal, St. John,
and Pentagoet (Penobscot);[7] devastated the settlements at Miscou and
Cape Tourmente; but demanded in vain the surrender of Quebec. During
the same summer, Sir William Alexander, patentee of Nova Scotia, planted
a colony at Port Royal[8] and in the following winter he joined the Kirkes in
forming the Scottish and English Company, which was given a monopoly
of trade in the gulf and river of St. Lawrence, with power to seize French
vessels and goods and " displant " the French in that region. In the spring
of 1629 the company sent out two fleets, one of which carried Lord Ochiltree
and his colony to Cape Breton, while the other, under command of David
Kirke, proceeded up the St. Lawrence. A detachment of the latter fleet
having appeared before Quebec on July 19, Champlain surrendered that place
to the English on the following day,[9] being unaware that three months previously peace had been concluded between England and France.

Peace had been brought about by the mediation of the enemies of Spain—
Venice, the United Provinces, and Denmark—as well as by the complete
failure of the English to relieve Rochelle, which made the continuance of
hostilities useless. The negotiations, mainly conducted through Contarini and
Zorzi, ambassadors of Venice at the respective courts of England and France,
dealt chiefly with the Huguenots, Queen Henrietta Maria's household, and
the restitution of a French vessel taken by the English in the neutral waters of
the Texel.[10] Negotiations resulted negatively in the postponement both of the
settlement of the commercial questions, and of the formation of an anti-
Hapsburg league, desired by Richelieu; and in the virtual abandonment of the
Huguenots by Charles. The treaty provided that the Anglo-French marriage
articles should be confirmed; that the question of the queen's household
should be left for later adjustment; that prizes made before the peace should
be retained, but, if made later, restored; and that there should be an exchange
of ambassadors.

On April 14/24, 1629, both kings signed the treaty, which is named from the
place where Louis signed it, Susa, a principal fortress of Savoy, which had
been recently taken by France in the course of the Mantuan war, and was
held as a pledge for the performance of a treaty, lately concluded there
between France and Savoy.[11]

[7] *Report on Canadian Archives, 1894* (ed. Brymner), p. ix. Champlain refers to the
loss of Pentagoet, C.-H. Laverdière, *Oeuvres de Champlain* (1870), VI. 295.
[8] C. Rogers, *Memorials of the Earls of Stirling* (1877), I. 103, 104.
[9] H. P. Biggar, *Early Trading Companies of New France* (1901), pp. 143-145;
H. Kirke, *The First English Conquest of Canada* (2d ed., 1908). For the terms of capitulation, see Laverdière, *op. cit.*, VI. 240-243, or E. Hazard, *Historical Collections* (1792-
1794), I. 285-287, or *Cal. St. Pap., Colonial*, 1574-1660, pp. 98, 99.
[10] Dorchester to Wake, Jan. 12/22, 1628/9, P. R. O., Treaty Papers, Savoy, no. 15.
[11] E. Lavisse, *Histoire de France* (1900-1910), tom. VI., pt. II., pp. 270-271; *cf.* Doc.
35, introduction.

BIBLIOGRAPHY.

Text: **MS.** The original manuscript of the protocol is in the archives of the French Ministry of Foreign Affairs, Correspondance Politique, Angleterre, vol. 43, ff. 247 ff.; the original manuscript of the articles signed by Charles I. on April 14/24, is in the same volume, ff. 49 ff. The original manuscript of the final ratification by Louis XIII., July 4. 1629, is in the Public Record Office, Treaties, no. 53. The final ratification, signed by Charles at Westminster, June 11, 1629, is in the bureau of the archives of the French Ministry of Foreign Affairs.

Text: **Printed.** T. Rymer, *Foedera* (1704-1735), XIX. 87-88; F. Leonard, *Recueil des Traitez de Paix* (1693), V. 35-37; J. Dumont, *Corps Diplomatique* (1726-1731), tom. V., pt. II., pp. 580-582; *Mercure François*, XV. (1631) 147-149.

Translation: *A General Collection of Treatys* (1732), II. 266-267.

References: **Contemporary and early writings.** *Mémoires du Cardinal de Richelieu*, in Michaud and Poujoulat, *Nouvelle Collection des Mémoires pour Servir à l'Histoire de France* (1836-1839), 2ⁿ sér., tom. VIII., pp. 10-12; *Lettres, Instructions Diplomatiques, et Papiers d'État du Cardinal de Richelieu* (1853-1877), III. 27, 225-230 (ed. Vicomte d'Avenel for the *Collection de Documents Inédits sur l'Histoire de France*); L. von Ranke, *A History of England, principally in the Seventeenth Century* (1875), V. 438-444; *The Court and Times of Charles the First* (1848), I. 391-394, II. 5, 6, 7, 11, 13, 14, etc.; *Calendar of State Papers, Domestic,* 1628-1629, pp. 345, 351, 352, 356, etc.; *Calendar of State Papers, Venice,* 1626-1628, vol. XX., 1628-1629, vol. XXI., *passim*. References to materials for the history of this treaty in so far as it relates to America are included in the bibliography of Doc. **36.**

References: **Later writings.** S. R. Gardiner, *History of England, 1603-1642* (1894-1896), vol. VI., cc. 56, 59, and pp. 345-347, 365-376, VII. 97-101; L. von Ranke, *op. cit.,* II. 3-7, V. 436-438. For the events connected with New France, see Doc. **36**, References. G. P. Insh, Scottish Colo..

Schemes, 1620-1686, app. 3.

TEXT.[12]

Louis par la grace de Dieu Roy de France et de Navarre, A tous ceux qui ces presentes lettres verront, salut. Les differendz qui estoient survenuz entre nous et nostre trescher et tresamé bon frere, beaufrere, cousin, et ancien allié, le Roy de la Grande Bretagne, et nos royaumes et subjectz, ayans esté composez et terminez par ce traicté de paix conclud et aresté dés le vingtquatriesme du mois d'Avril dernier, et ayans pourveu par iceluy à tous ce qui estoit necessaire pour le restablissement de l'ancienne amitié qui estoit entre nos couronnes, et du commerce et trafic public de nosdits subjectz, en quoy nous avons grande occasion de nous loüer de l'entremise de nos amis communs et bons alliez, et particulierement de la Serenissime Republicque de Venize, que à contribué par ses ambassadeurs tout ce qui se pouvoit attendre d'elle en ung si bon et loüable dessein, nous ne voulons rien obmettre de ce qui est à faire de nostre part pour tesmoigner à nostredit bon frere et beaufrere

---

[12] The text is from the original manuscript of the ratification by the King of France, preserved in the P. R. O., State Papers Foreign, Treaties, no. 53.

la ferme resolution que nous avons de faire accomplir entierement touttes les choses promises et accordées par ledit traicté. A ces causes nous avons aggrée, confirmé, et ratifié, aggréons, confirmons et ratifions par ces presentes signées de nostre main ces articles dudit traicté ainsy quilz sont y dessoubz transcritz.

Articles de paix entre les deux Couronnes.

1.[13] Premierement. Les deux Roys demeureront d'accord de renouveler les anciennes alliances entre les deux couronnes, et les garder inviolablement avec ouverture du commerce seur et libre. Et pour le regard dudit commerce, s'il y â quelque chose à adjouster ou diminuer se fera de part et d'autre de gré à gré, ainsy qu'il sera jugé à propos.

2. Et d'autant qu'il seroit difficille de faire les restitutions de part et d'autre des diverses prises qui ont esté faictes durant la guerre, les deux couronnes sont demeurées d'accord qu'il ne s'en fera aucune et ne s'accordera aucune reprezaille par mer ou autre façon quelconque pour ce qui s'est passé entre les deux roys et leurs subjects durant cette derniere guerre.

3. Quant à ce qui regarde les articles et contractz de mariage de la Royne de la Grande Bretagne, ilz seront confirmez de bonne foy, et sur ce qui concerne la maison de la Royne, s'il y â quelque chose à adjouster ou diminuer se fera de part et d'autre de gré à gré ainsy qu'il sera jugé plus à propos pour le service de ladite Royne.

4. Touttes les anciennes alliances tant de l'une que de l'autre couronne demeureront en leur vigueur sans que pour ce present traicté il y ayt aucune alteration.

5. Les deux roys par ce present traicté estans reunis en l'affection et intelligence en laquelle ilz estoient auparavant, s'employeront respectivement à donner assistance à leurs alliez et amis selon que la constitution des affaires et l'advantage du bien[14] public le requirront et le pourront permettre. Le tout a dessein de procurer ung entier repos à la Chrestienté pour le bien de laquelle les ambassadeurs des deux couronnes seront chargez de propositions et d'ouvertures.

6. Touttes cesdites[15] choses estans restablies et acceptées de costé et d'autre, ambassadeurs extraordinaires, personnes de qualité, seront envoyéz reciproquement avec ratification de ce present accord, lesquelz porteront aussy la dénomination des ambassadeurs ordinaires pour resider à l'un et à l'autre cour, affin de rafirmir cette bonne union, et empescher touttes les occasions qui la pourront troubler.

7. Et d'autant qu'il y â beaucoup de vaisseaux encores en mer avec lettres de marque et pouvoir de combattre les ennemis, qui ne pourront[16] pas si tost entendre cette paix ny recevoir ordre de s'abstenir[17] de toute hostilité, il sera accordé par cét article que tout ce qui se passera l'espace de deux mois prochains apres cét accord fait, ne désrogera, ny empeschera cettedite paix,

[13] The articles are numbered in the English ratification, but not in that signed by the King of France.
[14] The word *bien* is not in the English ratification.
[15] *Lesquelles* takes the place of *cesdites* in the English ratification.
[16] *Pourroyent* in the English ratification.   [17] *Abstenir* in the English ratification.

ny la bonne volonté de ces deux couronnes, a la charge touttes fois que [18] ce qui sera pris dans l'espace de deux mois depuis la signature du traicté sera restitué de part et d'autre."[19]

Faict et aresté à Suze le vingtneufiesme Avril mil six cens vingtneuf. Promettans en foy et parolle de Roy tant pour nous que pour nos heritiers et successeurs roys de garder et entretenir de poinct en poinct le contenu ausdits articles, sans y contrevenir ny souffrir qu'il y soit contrevenu en aucune sorte et maniere que ce soit; car tel est nostre plaisir. En tesmoing de quoy nous avons faict mettre nostre seel à cesdits presentes.

Donné au camp de Bezouches le quatriesme jour de Juillet l'an de Grace mil six cens vingtneuf et de nostre régne le vingtiésme.

Louis.
Par le Roy.
Bouthillier.

[18] The English ratification reads *tout ce*.

[19] The English ratification contains the following additional article: " 8. Les deux Roys signeront les presents articles dans le 14/24 du mois d'Avril, les quels seront consignes en mesme temps par leur commandement es mains des Seigneurs Ambassadeurs de Venize residens pres de leurs personnes pour les delivrer reciproquement auxdits deux roys a jour prefix incontinent que chacun d'eux aura sceu l'un de l'autre quilz ont lesdits articles entre les mains : et du jour de la signature tous actes d'hostilite tant par mer que par terre cesseront et les proclamations necessaires a cest effect seront faites en un mesme jour dans les deux royaumes."

35.

*Treaty of peace and commerce between Spain and Great Britain,
concluded at Madrid, November 5/15, 1630. Ratification by
the King of Spain, December 17, 1630. [Ratification by the
King of England, same date.]*

INTRODUCTION.

When the Duke of Mantua died, in December, 1627, Spain and France gave
their support to different claimants to the succession. The brief Franco-
Spanish alliance [1] was consequently dissolved, and the two kingdoms came
into conflict in northern Italy. In view of the coming struggle, Spain desired
to make peace with England. Hence Savoy, Spain's ally, sent the Abbé
Scaglia as mediator to the English and Spanish courts, and in the spring of
1629 the Spanish government despatched Rubens to England to arrange
a suspension of arms and an exchange of ambassadors. [2] The painter's able
diplomacy paved the way for a treaty favorable to Spain. Indeed, Charles I.,
whose quarrel with Parliament left him without money to continue hostilities, was not in a position to drive a good bargain. He agreed to conclude
peace with Spain in the form of the treaty of 1604, [3] on condition that Spain
should restore to his brother-in-law, the Elector Palatine, the places held by
Spanish garrisons in the Palatinate; [4] and he despatched Sir Francis Cottington, a leader of the pro-Spanish party, to negotiate the treaty at Madrid.

Cottington was instructed that he might conclude an article respecting
trade with the Indies in the general terms used in the treaty of 1604, [5] but
that he must not permit British subjects to be more restricted in that trade
than the subjects of any other nation. [6] Extracts from the truce of Antwerp [7]
and from the guaranty treaty of the Hague [8] " wherein particular mention
is made of the Indies", were sent him for his guidance, with the reminder
that " that which a Prince undertakes for others is always to be understood
he intends for his own subjects ". [9]

On November 15, 1630, more than nine months after Cottington's arrival
in Madrid, he, Olivares, and the Spanish commissioners, the Count of Oñate
and the Marquis of Flores Davila, signed a treaty of thirty-one articles, which

[1] Doc. **34**, introduction.
[2] *Correspondance de Rubens* (ed. Rooses and Ruelens), V. 24-25, 34-35.
[3] Doc. **27**. [4] *Correspondance de Rubens, ed. cit.,* V. 77, 109. [5] Doc. **27**, text, art. 9.
[6] Letters to Cottington, June 29, July 9, 1630, in P. R. O., State Papers Foreign, Spain,
no. 34. [7] Doc. **28**. [8] Doc. **29**. [9] Letter to Cottington, July 9, 1630, *loc. cit.*

was nearly identical with that of 1604. Articles 7 and 8 of the earlier treaty, which concerned the cautionary towns in the United Provinces, were, however, omitted; and a few articles were modified. The modifications in article 2 (corresponding to article 2 of the earlier treaty) and in article 7 (corresponding to article 9 of the earlier treaty) need alone be noticed here.

The second article provides that all actions on account of past depredations shall be extinguished by the treaty, but that restitution shall be made for depredations committed after the publication of peace, or after the lapse of certain specified periods, sufficient to permit of notification of the peace in different parts of the world. The Spaniards desired that the beginning of the periods after which restitution should be made should antedate the treaty, as was the case in the treaty of 1604. But Cottington pointed out that the time there assigned was that of Queen Elizabeth's death, after which no commissions were issued and the crowns were at amity, while in the present war hostilities were in continuance. The Spaniards thereupon proposed that the day might be a month after the date of the publication of the peace,[10] and when the English government, to whom the matter was referred, fixed the time as fifteen days after the peace for the district within the Narrow Seas, three months for the district between the Narrow Seas and the Islands, and a year for beyond the equator, the Spaniards refused to allow more than nine months for the last-named region.[11]

It is of interest to note that in framing this article the English clearly departed from the principle that treaties lost their force in the distant latitudes " beyond the lines of peace ".[12] By this article both parties explicitly agreed to restore prizes even though these were made south of the equator.

The ninth article of the old treaty, avoiding the name of the Indies, provided that the English should trade where they did " ante bellum ". The draft of a corresponding article sent by Cottington to England for consideration provided that the English should trade where they did before 1575. This alteration Charles would not accept, " because the king his father, though the time was left more at large and indefinite than in nominating a precise year of '75, yet in the opinion of the world did suffer in his reputation as if he had excluded himself and his subjects from trade [*i. e.,* to the Indies] more than other princes and their subjects were ". Moreover, it was argued, if the date were allowed, the rights of the English in the East Indies might be impaired because of an article in the treaty of 1571 between Queen Elizabeth and King Sebastian of Portugal, which provided " ne quis navigationem

[10] Letter from Cottington, Aug. 24, 1630, P. R. O., State Papers Foreign, Spain, no. 35.
[11] Letter from Dorchester to Cottington, Sept. 27, 1630, *ibid.*; and " A note of the alterations in the signed treatie ", P. R. O., Treaty Papers, Spain, no. 65.
[12] *Cf.* above, pp. 220, 221.

institueret in maria et terras conquestus Portugalliae ".[13] In the draft returned to Cottington therefore, the words *ante bellum* were restored. The Spaniards insisted on adding phrases to indicate clearly that Elizabeth's war, not Charles's, was intended, and King Philip himself took great pains to assist in altering the provision so as to make its meaning unmistakable. The Spanish commissioners protested that they did not intend even to question the English navigation to the East Indies, or to impeach it by this article. Cottington felt sure that if Charles would " admit of negative articles ", not to trade in certain specified harbors possessed by the Portuguese, or not to sail into specified bays, the Spaniards would " capitulate a free navigation into those seas [of the East Indies], and not only into those seas but (on those conditions) to the coast of America also, particularly allowing the plantations of Virginia and others ". This they had promised him, but he was far from advising Charles " to think of such restrictions, for certainly a little more time will open the navigation into all parts, so long as there are no negative capitulations or articles to hinder it ". He added that the Spaniards were " fearful of incroachments upon the coast of the West Indies and of the English sailing into those seas, which they would gladly remedy or at least limit, if they could ".[14] Peace was proclaimed on December 5/15, and the treaty was ratified by both kings on December 7/17, 1630.[15]

On January 12, 1631, representatives of the two crowns concluded at Madrid a secret league against the Dutch, providing that war should be made against them, by land and sea, until they were reduced to obedience to Spain.[16]

In 1632 and 1634 the States General were warned by their agents that the Spanish ambassador in England was trying to foment an Anglo-Dutch quarrel about the colony of New Netherland.[17]

BIBLIOGRAPHY.

Text: MS. The original manuscript of the ratification by the King of Spain is in the Public Record Office, State Papers Foreign, Treaties, no. 465.

Text: Printed. T. Rymer, *Foedera* (1704-1735), XIX. 219-227; J. Dumont, *Corps Diplomatique* (1726-1731), tom. V., pt. II., pp. 619-623; J. A. de

---

[13] Letter from Dorchester to Cottington, Sept. 27, 1630, P. R. O., State Papers Foreign, Spain, no. 35. From the references to the Anglo-Portuguese treaty of 1571 in Dorchester's and Cottington's letters, cited above, it would seem that this treaty was actually signed. For a contrary opinion, *cf.* V. M. Shillington and A. B. W. Chapman, *Commercial Relations of England and Portugal* (1907), p. 143.

[14] Letter from Cottington, Nov. 17, 1630, P. R. O., State Papers Foreign, Spain, no. 35; Treaty Papers, Spain, no. 65.

[15] Sainsbury, *Papers illustrative of the Life of Sir Peter Paul Rubens*, p. 154, n. 107; *Cal. St. Pap., Dom.*, 1629-1631, p. 402; Rymer, *Foedera*, XIX. 226-227; Dumont, *Corps Diplomatique*, tom. V., pt. II., p. 623.

[16] The text is printed in *State Papers collected by Edward, Earl of Clarendon* (1767-1786), I. 49, 50.

[17] J. R. Brodhead, *Documents relative to the Colonial History of the State of New York* (1853, etc.), I. 45, 72.

Abreu y Bertodano, *Coleccion de los Tratados de España: Reynado de Phelipe IV.* (1744-1751), II. 204-232.
Translations: English. *A General Collection of Treatys* (1732), II. 275-292. **Spanish.** Abreu, *loc. cit.*
References: Contemporary and early writings. *Codex Diplomaticus Rubenianus: Correspondance de Rubens et Documents Épistolaires concernant sa Vie et ses Oeuvres* (ed. Max Rooses and Ch. Ruelens, 1887-1909), IV., V., *passim.* This great collection includes most of the documents published in the three following works: W. N. Sainsbury, *Original Unpublished Papers illustrative of the Life of Sir Peter Paul Rubens, as an Artist and a Diplomatist* (1859), pp. 68 ff., 129-155; Cruzada Villaamil, *Rubens Diplomático Español: Sus Viajes á España y Noticia de sus Cuadros, segun los Inventarios de las Casas Reales de Austria y de Borbon* (1874); L. P. Gachard, *Histoire Politique et Diplomatique de Pierre-Paul Rubens* (1877), appendixes V.-XXIII.
References: Later writings. L. P. Gachard, *op. cit.,* pp. 38-195; S. R. Gardiner, *History of England, 1603-1642* (1894-1896), VI. 160-164, 185, 331-334, 371-376, VII. 101-108, 169-177; L. von Ranke, *History of England* (1875), vol. II., ch. I.; Martin A. S. Hume, *The Court of Philip IV.* (1907), pp. 214-225.

TEXT.[18]

Philippus, Dei gratia Hispaniarum, Utriusque Siciliae, Hierusalem, Indiarum, etc., rex, archidux Austriae, dux Burgundiae, Mediolani, etc., comes Habspurgi, Tirolis, etc.   Cum tractatus quidam firmae amicitiae et pacis perpetuae ac commertii inter commissarios et deputatos nostros et Serenissimi Caroli, Angliae regis, commissarium, deputatum, et extraordinarium legatum, utriusque regis nomine, Matriti, decimoquinto die mensis Novembris proximè praeteriti, anni Domini millesimi sexcentesimi trigesimi, fuerit concordatus et conclusus, cujus tenor sequitur:

Omnibus et singulis notum sit ac manifestum, quod post diutina ac cruenta bella, quibus Hispaniarum et Angliae regna jam olim invicem agitabantur, accito tandem Summi Dei (qui pacis est Auctor) immensa providentia ad coronae Anglicanae successionem, Serenissimo Jacobo, Scotiae rege, cui, et Hispaniarum Regibus, tutae et sincerae pacis conjunctio semper intercesserat; cum eodem supremi Numinis ductu ageretur de constituenda quoque cum Angliae regno eadem firma pace et concordia, ea demum, vigesima octava die mensis Augusti, anno Domini millesimo sexcentesimo quarto, foeliciter inita fuit, ac postmodum à Serenissimis Philippo Tertio, Hispaniarum, et praelibato Jacobo, Magnae Britaniae, regibus, subscripta ac promulgata;[19] necnon mutuis inter utrumque regem intercedentibus amicitiae officiis, fraternaeque benevolentiae pignoribus, longa annorum serie, sanctè, aequè, ac utiliter observata.   Quamvis vero rerum et temporum vicissitudo, et acris illa contentio qua humani generis hostis eidem indefesse studet officere, tum vero varii casus et accidentia, quibus potentiora regna et imperia plerumque sunt obnoxia, nonnullis dissidiis occasionem praebuere, quae mox in apertum

---

[18] The following text is from the original manuscript of the Spanish ratification, P. R. O., Treaties, no. 465.
[19] Doc. 27.

bellum et mutuas utrinque hostilitates evaserunt, Omnipotens ille Deus, in cujus manibus corda principum sunt posita, Serenissimorum Philippi Quarti, Hispaniarum regis Catholici, et Caroli, regis Magnae Britaniae, animis nequaquam voluit excidere antiquam illam amicitiam qua regiae istae coronae tanquam firmissimo nexu, hactenus obstringebantur aut indefessum studium, quo regii eorum progenitores Christiano sanguini parcere, et subjectos sibi populos almae pacis tranquillitate beare quaesiverunt, quo et praeviis apud utrunque regem, nomine Caroli Emmanuelis, ducis Sabaudiae, à D. Alexandro Caesar Scaglia, abbate de Staffarda, Sussa, et Mulegio, ejus intimo consiliario et legato, aliisque ministris eundem in finem adhibitis amicabilibus officiis, factum est, ut pacis non ita pridem injecta mentio, non lubenti solum animo excepta, sed etiam regii legati qui de ea sancienda agerent, utrinque missi fuerint: à Serenissimo quidem Magnae Britaniae Rege ad aulam Hispanicam, D. Franciscus Cottingtonus, eques baronetus, Caroli Regis intimus consiliarius et regii in Anglia scaccarii cancellarius, in Angliam vero ab Hispaniarum Rege Catholico, D. Carlus Coloma, ejusdem ab intimis consiliis, et supremus prefectus arcis et territorii Cameracensis: explorata igitur utriusque regis pia et innatae regiae generositati et magnanimitati consentanea ad pacem propensione, instituta fuit Matriti desuper tractatio, et ad eam pro parte Serenissimi Hispaniarum Regis Catholici specialiter fuerunt deputati D. Gaspar de Guzman, comes Olivarensis, dux de Sanlucar majori nuncupata, ejus summus cubicularius et equitii regii praefectus, magnus Indiarum cancellarius, etc., D. Inicus Velez de Guevara, comes de Ognate, etc., et Petrus de Cuniga, marchio de Flores Davila, etc., omnes ab intimis Serenissimi Regis consiliis sub commissione et mandato tenoris subsequentis. . . .

[Here follow the powers given by the King of Spain to his above-named deputies, at Madrid, May 31, 1630; and the powers given by the King of Great Britain to Cottington at Westminster, October 20/30, 1629.]

Quiquidem utriusque regis comissarii et deputati, facto aliquoties congressu, praeviaque solerti tantae rei discussione et matura adhibita deliberatione, Deo piis coeptis favente, ad majorem ejus gloriam, orbis Christiani beneficium, utriusque vero regis subditorum commodum et tranquillitatem, subsequentes pacis perpetuo duraturae articulos concordarunt et stabilierunt:

1. Primo, conclusum, stabilitum, et concordatum fuit et est, ut ab hodie in antea sit bona, sincera, vera, firma, et perfecta amicitia, et confederatio, ac pax perpetuô duratura, quae inviolabiliter observetur inter Serenissimum Regem Hispaniarum et Serenissimum Magnae Britaniae Regem, eorumque haeredes ac successores quoscumque eorumque regna, patrias, dominia, terras, populos, homines, ligios, ac subditos, quoscunque, praesentes et futuros, cujuscunque conditionis, dignitatis, et gradus existant, tam per terram quam per mare et aquas dulces, ita ut praedicti vasalli et subditi sibi invicem favere, et mutuis prosequi officiis ac honesta affectione invicem se tractare habeant.

2. Cessetque in posterum omnis hostilitas ac inimicitia, offensionibus omnibus, injuriis, et damnis quae durante bello partes quoquomodo percepissent, sublatis et oblivioni traditis, ita ut in posterum nihil alter ab altero occasione quorumcunque damnorum, offensionum, captionum, aut spoliorum praetendere possit; sed omnium abolitio sit, et censeatur facta ab hodie in antea, omnisque actio extincta habeatur, salva et praeter quam respectu captionum

factarum intra districtum maris arctioris [20] spatio quindecim dierum, et intra arctioris maris Insularumque [21] tractus spatio trium mensium; atque ultra lineam [22] spatio novem mensium integro elapso à die publicatae pacis, sive statim à significatione pacis infra dictos limites et loca sufficienter, facta per declarationes, aut diplomata authentica respective monstranda, quia de illis debebit reddi ratio fierique restitutio. Abstinebuntque in futurum ab omni praeda, captione, offensione, et spolio in quibuscunque regnis, dominiis, locis, et ditionibus alterutrius ubivis sitis, tam in terra quam in mari et aquis dulcibus, nec per suos vassallos, incolas, vel subditos aliquid ex praedictis fieri consentient, omnemque praedam, spolium, ac captionem, aut damnum quod inde fiet vel dabitur restitui facient.

. . . .

7. Item, conventum et stabilitum fuit et est, quod inter Serenissimum Regem Hispaniarum et Serenissimum Regem Angliae ac cujuslibet eorum vassallos, incolas, et subditos, tam per terram quam per mare et aquas dulces, in omnibus et singulis regnis, dominiis, et insulis, aliisque terris, civitatibus, oppidis, villis, portubus, ac districtibus dictorum regnorum et dominiorum sit et esse debeat commercium liberum, in quibus inter dicta regna fuit commercium ante bellum inter Philippum Secundum Hispaniarum regem, et Elisabeth Angliae Reginam, prout stabilitum fuit in tractatu pacis [23] anni millesimi sexcentesimi quarti articulo nono; juxta et secundum usum et observantiam antiquorum foederum, et tractatuum supradictum tempus antecedentium; ita ut absque aliquo salvoconductu, aliaque licentia generali, vel speciali, tam per terram quam per mare et aquas dulces, subditi et vasalli unius et alterius regis possint et valeant ad omnia praedicta eorumque omnium civitates, oppida, portus, littora, sinus, et districtus accedere, intrare, navigare, et quoscunque portus subire, in quibus ante supradictum tempus fuit mutuum commercium, et juxta et secundum usum et observantiam antiquorum foederum et tractatuum praedictorum, cum plaustris, equis, sarcinulis, navigiis, tam onustis quam onerandis, merces importare, emere, vendere in iisdem quantum voluerint, commeatum resque ad victum et profectionem necessarias justo pretio sibi assumere, restaurandis navigiis, et vehiculis propriis, vel conductis aut commodatis operam dare; illinc cum mercibus, bonis, ac rebus quibuscumque, solutis juxta locorum statuta teloniis et vectigalibus praesentibus tantum, eadem libertate recedere, indeque ad patrias proprias, vel alienas, quomodocunque velint, et sine impedimento exire.

. . . .

31. . . . Quae omnia supra contenta a nobis praenominatis utriusque regis deputatis, legatis, et commissariis, dictarum commissionum vigore nostrorumque regum nomine concordata, stabilita, et conclusa fuerunt. In quorum omnium et singulorum fidem manu propria subscripsimus, decimoquinto die

---

[20] The interpretation of the expression " Narrow Seas ", where the English kings claimed " sovereignty ", was extended by the English, after the early years of the seventeenth century, to include not only the channel between England and France, but also the sea between England and the Netherlands. See G. Edmundson, *Anglo-Dutch Rivalry during the First Half of the Seventeenth Century* (1911), app. B.

[21] The ocean islands then under the rule of Spain—the Cape Verde, Azores, etc.

[22] The equator. " In the late agreement betwixt the kings of Great Britain and Spain [anno 1630, art. 2] the Equinoctial Line is the Bound appointed in the Sea." J. Selden, *Mare Clausum: the Right and Dominion of the Sea* (1663), p. 138.

[23] Doc. 27.

Novembris, anno Domini millesimo sexcentesimo trigesimo. Don Gaspar de Guzman. El Conde de Oñate. El Marques de Flores. Franciscus Cottingtonus.

Nos, igitur, omnia et singula dicti tractatus capitula suprascripta per nostros, et Serenissimi Magnae Britaniae Regis commissarios, legatos et deputatos praedictos, conventa, concordata, et conclusa, et omnia et singula super inde in eisdem contenta et specificata, rata, firma, et grata habentes, ea omnia et singula pro nobis, haeredibus et successoribus nostris, quatenus ad nos, haeredes, successores, vel subditos nostros, concernunt, aut concernere poterunt, acceptamus, approbamus, et rattificamus, ac inviolabiliter, firme, et fideliter tenebimus, observabimus, et adimplebimus ; et cum effectu faciemus (ut in dictis capitulis continetur) etiam per subditos nostros ac regnorum nostrorum incolas teneri, observari, et adimpleri ; nec eis directe nec indirectè per nos contraveniemus, nec per subditos nostros et regnorum nostrorum incolas contravenire directè nec per indirectum consentiemus, et ita in bona fide et in verbo regio promettimus. In quorum omnium praemissorum fidem et testimonium, his praesentibus literis manu nostra subscriptis, et per infrascriptum secretarium nostrum referendatis, sigillum nostrum apponi fecimus. Datum Matriti, decima septima die mensis Decembris, anno Domini millesimo sexcentesimo trigesimo.

PHILIPPUS.
ANDREAS DE ROCAS.

TRANSLATION.

Philip, by the grace of God king of the Spains, the Two Sicilies, Jerusalem, the Indies, etc., archduke of Austria, duke of Burgundy, Milan, etc., count of Hapsburg, Tyrol, etc.—Whereas, between our commissioners and deputies and the commissioner, deputy, and ambassador extraordinary of the Most Serene Charles, king of England, and in the name of both kings, there was agreed and concluded at Madrid on November 15, last, A. D. 1630, a certain treaty of firm friendship and perpetual peace, and of commerce, the tenor of which follows :

Be it known and manifest to all and singular that when, after the long and bloody wars whereby the kingdoms of the Spains and England were some time ago mutually troubled, at length, by the boundless providence of the supreme God, the author of peace, the Most Serene James, king of Scotland, who had always been united to the kings of the Spains in a firm and sincere peace, was called to the succession of the English crown ; and when, by the same guidance of the supreme deity, negotiations were begun for establishing the same firm peace and concord with the kingdom of England as well, this was at last happily concluded on August 28, A. D. 1604, and afterwards ratified and proclaimed by the Most Serene Philip III., king of the Spains, and the aforesaid James, king of Great Britain; and by mutual friendly services and pledges of fraternal good-will between the two kings, it was for a long series of years sacredly, justly, and advantageously observed. And although the vicissitude of things and times and that cruel obstinacy whereby the enemy of the human race incessantly labors to do it harm, as well as the various occurrences and accidents to which the mightiest kingdoms and empires are commonly subject, gave occasion for some dissensions, which later developed into open war and mutual hostilities on both sides, yet the Omnipotent God, in whose hands the hearts of princes lie, did not wish the Most Serene Philip IV., Catholic king of the Spains, and the Most Serene Charles, king of Great Britain, to forget that ancient friendship whereby those royal crowns were hitherto joined as with the stoutest band, or the tireless zeal whereby their royal progenitors sought to spare Christian blood and bless the peoples subject to them with the tranquillity of bountiful peace. By whom and by the preliminary friendly offices rendered to both kings for this purpose in the name of Charles Emmanuel, duke of Savoy, by Alessandro Cesare Scaglia, abbot of Stafforda, Susa, and Mulegio, his privy councillor and ambassador, and by other ministers, it was brought about that not only was the proposal of peace, made a little while before, willingly adopted, but royal ambassadors were likewise sent from both sides to treat for its establishment. Sir Francis Cottington, knight baronet, member of the privy council of King Charles and chancellor of the royal exchequer, was sent to the court of Spain on behalf of the Most Serene King of Great Britain; and Don Carlos Coloma, member of his council of state, and governor of the fortress and territory of Cambray, was sent to England by the Catholic king of the Spains. When therefore the pious inclination of both kings to peace, so consistent with their inherent royal generosity and magnanimity, was known, negotiations for it were instituted at Madrid. To these negotiations, the Most Serene Catholic King of the Spains specially deputed Don Gaspar de Guzman, count of Olivares, duke of San Lucar la Mayor, principal chamberlain and master of the royal stable, grand chancellor of the Indies, etc., Don Iñigo Velez de Guevara, count of Oñate, etc., and Don Pedro de Zuñiga, marquis of Flores Davila, etc., all members of the Council of State of the said most serene king, and empowered by a commission and command of the following tenor:

[Here follow the powers given by the King of Spain to his above-named deputies, at Madrid, May 31, 1630; and the powers given by the King of Great Britain to Cottington at Westminster, October 20/30, 1629.]

These commissioners and deputies of both kings, after holding several conferences and engaging in skillful preliminary discussion and mature deliberation upon so important a matter, God favoring their pious undertakings, for His greater glory, the benefit of Christendom, and the advantage and quiet of the subjects of both kings, have agreed upon and settled the following articles of perpetual peace:

1. First, it was and is concluded, settled, and accorded, that from this day forth, there shall be a good, sincere, true, firm, and perfect amity, league, and perpetual peace, which shall be inviolably observed and kept, both by land and by sea and fresh waters, between the Most Serene King of the Spains and the Most Serene King of Great Britain, and all their heirs and successors, and all their kingdoms, countries, dominions, lands, peoples, vassals, liegemen, and subjects, now being or which hereafter shall be, of whatever condition, rank, or degree they may be, so that the aforesaid vassals and subjects must henceforth favor each other mutually, and render each other mutual services, and treat each other, mutually, with sincere good-will.

2. And that from henceforth all hostility and enmity shall cease, and all the offenses, injuries, and damages, which the parties have in any way

sustained, shall be put aside and forgotten; so that in future neither party may have any claims against the other, on account of any damages, offenses, captures, or spoils; but they shall all be annulled, and considered as annulled, from this day forth; and all actions [for the same] shall be regarded as extinguished, saying and except for captures made within the strait of the Narrow Seas after the space of fifteen days, and between the Narrow Seas and the Islands after the space of three months, and beyond the Line after the space of nine months fully ended, to be reckoned from the publication of the peace, or immediately after notice of the peace is sufficiently given within the said limits and places by declarations or by authentic documents which should be respectively shown, because an accounting must be made concerning these and restitution made. And hereafter each party shall abstain from all depredations, captures, offenses, and spoils, both by land and by sea and fresh waters in all the kingdoms, dominions, places, and jurisdictions of the other, wherever situated; nor shall they consent that any of the aforesaid wrongs shall be committed by their vassals, inhabitants of their kingdoms, or subjects, and they shall cause restitution to be made of all booty, spoils, and captures, or for damages proceeding or resulting therefrom.

7. *Item*, it was and is agreed and settled that between the Most Serene King of the Spains and the Most Serene King of England and the vassals, inhabitants of their kingdoms, and subjects of each of them, there shall and ought to be free commerce, both by land and by sea and fresh waters, in all and singular their kingdoms, dominions, and islands, and other lands, cities, towns, villages, harbors, and straits of the said kingdoms and dominions, where there was commerce between the said kingdoms before the war between Philip II., king of the Spains, and Elizabeth, queen of England, according as it was settled in the treaty of peace of the year 1604, in the ninth article, agreeably and according to the use and observance of the ancient alliances and treaties made before the said time. So that, without any safe-conduct, or other general or special license, the subjects and vassals of both kings may, and shall have the power, both by land and by sea and fresh waters, to approach, enter, and sail to all the aforesaid [kingdoms and dominions], and to the cities, towns, ports, shores, bays, and straits of all of them; to enter all ports in which there was mutual commerce before the aforesaid time; and agreeably and according to the use and observance of the ancient alliances and treaties aforesaid, with wagons, horses, packs, and boats, laden and to be laden, to bring in merchandise and, in these places, to buy and sell as much as they wish, and to procure for themselves, for a just price, supplies and commodities necessary for their sustenance and voyage, and attend to the necessary repair of boats and vehicles, whether their own, hired, or borrowed. They will be equally free to depart thence with their merchandise, goods, and all other commodities, on payment of the tolls and duties then in force, according to the ordinances of the places; and they may go thence to their own or other countries, as they please, without hindrance.

31. . . . . All the matters contained above have been agreed upon, settled and concluded by us, the aforesaid deputies, ambassadors, and commissioners of both kings, by virtue of the said commissions and in the name of our kings. In pledge of all and singular of them, we have subscribed them with our own

hands, on November 15, A. D. 1630.   Don Gaspar de Guzman.   The Count of Oñate.   The Marquis of Flores.   Francis Cottington.

The above-written articles of the said treaty, all and singular, having been covenanted, agreed upon, and concluded by our aforesaid commissioners, ambassadors, and deputies, and those of the Most Serene King of Great Britain—and all and singular contained and specified therein being considered by us, on that account, as fixed, settled, and acceptable—we, therefore, accept, approve, and ratify them, and will inviolably, firmly, and faithfully hold, observe, and fulfill them, all and singular, for us, our heirs and successors, in so far as they concern or can concern us, our heirs, successors, or subjects; and we will, in fact (as is set forth in the said articles), likewise cause them to be kept, observed, and fulfilled by our subjects and the inhabitants of our kingdoms; nor will we contravene them directly or indirectly ourselves, or consent that they be contravened by our subjects or by the inhabitants of our kingdoms, directly or indirectly; and thus we promise in good faith and on our royal word.   In faith and testimony of all the aforesaid we have caused our seal to be affixed to these present letters, subscribed by our hand and countersigned by our secretary, whose name is written below.   Given at Madrid, December 17, A. D. 1630.

PHILIP.
ANDRÉS DE ROCAS.

36.

Treaty concluded between Great Britain and France at St. Germain-en-Laye, March 19/29, 1632. [Ratified by the King of Great Britain, April 13/23, 1632.]

INTRODUCTION.

The treaty of Susa[1] was of a very general character, providing for little more than peace and the exchange of ambassadors extraordinary. On June 22/July 2, 1629, such ambassadors—Charles de l'Aubespine, marquis de Châteauneuf, and Sir Thomas Edmondes—crossed the channel on their respective ways to the courts of England and France. Châteauneuf was instructed[2] to inquire into the discriminations made against French merchants engaged in the English trade, to investigate the arrest and search of French ships going to Spain, and to find out means of establishing a " general settlement " for the liberty[3] and security of commerce. He was to discover Charles's plans for assisting the Elector Palatine and the other Protestant German princes, whom Richelieu expressed a desire to aid, and to encourage Charles, if still hostile to Spain, to use his ships in attacking its coasts, and in intercepting the fleets from the Indies, " Le seul moyen qui peut plus ruiner et incommoder les Espagnols, comme l'ont fait les Hollandois ".[4] He was also to treat respecting the queen's household. Probably the most important object of his mission was to try to prevent an accommodation between France and Spain.

Edmondes was instructed[5] to get certain legal proceedings relating to the seizure of English merchants' goods stopped and the sentences annulled, and to persuade Louis to make peace with the Huguenots as a preliminary to ratifying the treaty of Susa.

Negotiations dragged, for the English were disinclined to make a general commercial regulation with France so long as their war with Spain—and hence the opportunity of seizing French merchant-ships—continued.[6] In

---

[1] Doc. **34.**

[2] The instructions are in the archives of the French Ministry of Foreign Affairs, Correspondance Politique, Angleterre, Supplément, vol. I. (1326-1674), ff. 264 ff.

[3] That is, freedom from discriminations by one government against the subjects of the other—made, for example, in respect to import and export duties.

[4] Probably the reference is particularly to Piet Hein's recent exploit in capturing the entire West India treasure-fleet.

[5] The instructions are in the P. R. O., State Papers Foreign, France, vol. 84, ff. 133 ff.

[6] Letters from Châteauneuf, Oct. 21 and Dec. 8, 1629, Jan. 20, 1630, in the archives of the French Ministry of Foreign Affairs, Correspondance Politique, Angleterre, vol. 43, ff. 332, 357, vol. 44, ff. 1, 10. The last is printed in Doughty, *Report for 1912*, pp. 35-36.

the course of a few months new grievances, mostly of the nature of captures made after the peace, were reported to both governments. The most important were: that the French had taken three English ships of very great value on the coasts of Barbary and Guinea and had brought two of them to Dieppe;[7] that they had attacked the English at St. Christopher's;[8] and that the English had seized Quebec, together with the peltries and other merchandise found there belonging to the United Company, the predecessor of the Company of New France.[9] Toward the end of the year, the English government also learned that Captain Daniel, commander of a fleet of the Company of New France, had surprised Lord Ochiltree and his colonists at Cape Breton and had brought some of them as prisoners to Dieppe.[10]

Before the arrival of this last report, Châteauneuf, at the instigation of Champlain, had begun to press for the restitution of Canada, Acadia, and the furs and goods seized at Quebec. Negotiations respecting the return of these, and other captures made by both powers since the treaty of Susa, continued during two and a half years, under the conduct of various agents. Early in 1630, Châteauneuf was succeeded at London by Fontenay-Mareuil, ambassador ordinary, and about the same time Edmondes withdrew from Paris, leaving the business in the hands of the residents, De Vic and Augier, until the arrival of the ambassador ordinary, Isaac Wake, in the spring of 1631.

By the time Châteauneuf left England, he had drafted a treaty of commerce and had obtained from Charles a promise to restore all prizes made since the war, including the places, goods, and ships taken in Canada, and in particular the fort of Quebec.[11] Châteauneuf found Charles compliant, for the king's attempt to rule without Parliament had left him in extreme financial need, but the ambassador had much more difficulty with the privy councillors, most of whom, he asserted, were interested in " the navigations, plantations, and letters of marque ":[12] and were " partners and sharers in the captures that are made ".[13]

Negotiations stuck on the question of the restitution of Port Royal. The English argued that before their arrival the coasts of Port Royal and Cape

---

[7] King Charles to Edmondes, Sept. 17/27, 1629; letters from Edmondes, Sept. 23/ Oct. 3, Oct. 3/13, 1629, and later—all in P. R. O., State Papers Foreign, France, vols. 84, 85.

[8] Dorchester to Edmondes, Sept. 17/27, 1629, King Charles to Edmondes, same date; letter from Edmondes, Oct. 16/26, 1629—all in P. R. O., State Papers Foreign, France, vol. 84, f. 300, vol. 85, ff. 49 ff.; *Cal. St. Pap., Colonial,* 1574-1660, p. 103.

[9] Doc. **34**, introduction.

[10] *Cal. St. Pap., Colonial,* 1574-1660, p. 104, and cf. Doc. **34**, introduction.

[11] Answer of the commissioners, Feb. 1/11, 1630, Laverdière, *Oeuvres de Champlain,* VI., *pièces justificatives,* no. viii; *Cal. St. Pap., Colonial,* 1574-1660, p. 107.

[12] Letter from Châteauneuf, Oct. 18, 1629, French Ministry of Foreign Affairs, Correspondance Politique, Angleterre, vol. 43, f. 307; the same to Richelieu, Nov. 18, 1629, Doughty, *op. cit.,* pp. 27-29.

[13] Châteauneuf to Richelieu, Jan. 20, 1630, Doughty, *op. cit.,* p. 33.

Breton had been abandoned by the French and that therefore they had a right to occupy them.[14] Châteauneuf on the other hand declared that the English should withdraw from Port Royal in order that all things might be restored to the state in which they had been before the outbreak of hostilities.[15] Meanwhile Edmondes was pressing for payment of the remainder of Queen Henrietta Maria's dowry. But since the French were well aware that the retention of this money and of the valuable prize ships at Dieppe gave them an important advantage in bargaining,[16] they desired to wait until Charles should cede Port Royal, using the cost of the Franco-Spanish war in Italy as a pretext for postponing the settlement.[17] The King of England also asked for a delay in order that he might advise with Sir William Alexander, patentee of Nova Scotia, and with the Scottish Privy Council in regard to the surrender of Port Royal.[18]

The absorption of the rulers of France in the conduct of the war in Italy appears to have been another cause of the delay in the negotiations.[19] Naturally Alexander was reluctant to lose his vast domain, and he seems to have attempted to bribe Châteauneuf, but without success.[20] He also recommended the Convention of the Scottish Estates to petition Charles to retain Nova Scotia.[21] Meanwhile the English government learned from its agents in France that the French were making extraordinary naval preparations, intended for the recovery of Canada by force.[22] Under the circumstances Charles felt obliged to yield. He softened the blow to Alexander by raising him to the dignity of viscount and appointing him to a salaried office.[23] Dorchester declared that " Port Royal was too poor a business to interrupt that royal friendship [which] is drawn to so near a point of conclusion betwixt the two crowns ".[24] Charles was determined, however, that the remainder

[14] Châteauneuf to Bouthillier, Feb. 20, 1630, Doughty, *op. cit.*, p. 37. The Convention of the Scottish Estates also urged that Port Royal "had never beene repossessed nor claimed by the French, since they were first removed from the same ", *i. e.*, by Argall, and that therefore nothing had been taken from them. Rogers, *Memorials*, I. 126.

[15] Dorchester to Wake, Apr. 15, 1630, P. R. O., State Papers Foreign, France, vol. 86, f. 251 ; *Cal. St. Pap., Colonial*, 1574-1660, p. 113.

[16] Letter from Edmondes, Jan. 6/16, 1629/30, P. R. O., State Papers Foreign, France, vol. 86, f. 3.

[17] Châteauneuf to Richelieu, Dec. 8, 1629, Ministry of Foreign Affairs, vol. 43, f. 357.

[18] Dorchester to Wake, Apr. 15/25, 1630, State Papers Foreign, France, vol. 86, f. 251 ; *Cal. St. Pap., Colonial*, 1574-1660, p. 113 ; letter from Augier and De Vic, Nov. 18/28, 1630, P. R. O., State Papers Foreign, France, vol. 87, fol. 420 ; from the same, Dec. 7/17, 1630, *ibid.*, f. 487 ; "articles . . . 1631 ", Doughty, *op. cit.*, p. 40; letter from Montagu, May 23, 1631, *ibid.*, p. 42. For Charles's extraordinary dealings with the Scots in this matter, see Rogers, *op. cit.*, ch. 5.

[19] Laverdière, *op. cit.*, VI. 313.

[20] Rogers, *op. cit.*, I. 121-122.

[21] *Ibid.*, pp. 124-127 ; *Cal. St. Pap., Colonial*, 1574-1660, pp. 119-120.

[22] Letter from Edmondes, Jan. 6/16, 1629/30, from De Vic, Mar. 28/Apr. 7, 1630, P. R. O., State Papers Foreign, France, vol. 86, ff. 3, 159.

[23] Rogers, *op. cit.*, I. 127.

[24] Letter, Whitehall, Dec. 18/28, 1630, P. R. O., State Papers Foreign, France, vol. 87, f. 526.

of the queen's dowry should be paid when or before Canada and Acadia were ceded. Since the French would not have the dowry mentioned in the treaty, it was arranged that the merchant Philip Burlamachi should be sent to Paris to receive the money or securities and at the same time deliver the orders for the surrender of New France.[25]

After Burlamachi's arrival in Paris, at the end of August, 1631, more time was consumed over the tedious dispute between the United Company and the Scottish and English Company regarding the furs seized at Quebec. Again the controversy ended in favor of the French.[26] At last, on March 19/29, 1632, the English ambassador and the French commissioners signed two treaties at St. Germain-en-Laye. One provided for the revocation of all letters of marque and reprisal issued by either signatory power against the subjects of the other, and laid down rules for the search of merchant-vessels by warships, and the treatment of prizes made at sea.[27] The other treaty, printed below, provided for the restoration to the King of France of all places occupied by the English in " New France, Acadia, and Canada "; for the withdrawal of the English therefrom; for a large payment to Guillaume De Caen, representing the United Company, for merchandise found at Quebec; for the return of various prize ships, or a money equivalent for ships and goods. Charles confirmed both treaties on April 13/23. In the following summer Quebec was restored to the United Company, and Port Royal to the Company of New France.[28]

BIBLIOGRAPHY.

Text: MS. The original of the protocol is in the archives of the Ministry of Foreign Affairs at Paris, Correspondance Politique, Angleterre, vol. 45, ff. 94-98. The joint confirmation of this treaty and of the treaty of commerce, dated April 13, 1632, is entered on the Treaty Rolls, in the London Public Record Office. It does not include the articles themselves.

Text: Printed. The articles are in T. Rymer, *Foedera* (1704-1735), XIX. 361-363; N. Denys, *Description Geographique et Historique des Costes de l'Amerique Septentrionale* (1672), pp. 238-267; id., *Description and Natural History of the Coasts of North America (Acadia)* (trans. and ed. by W. F. Ganong, Champlain Soc., 1908), pp. 508-513; F. Leonard, *Recueil des Traitez de Paix* (1693), V.; J. Dumont, *Corps Diplomatique* (1726-1731), tom. VI., pt. I., pp. 31-33; *Mémoires des Commissaires du Roi et de Ceux des Sa Majesté Britannique sur les Possessions et les Droits respectifs des Deux Couronnes en Amérique* (1755-1757), II. 5-10; *Collection de Manuscrits relatifs à la Nouvelle France édités sous*

[25] Fontenay to Richelieu, June 5, 1631, Doughty, *op. cit.*, pp. 45-46; King Charles to Wake, June 12, 1631, *Report on Canadian Archives*, 1884 (ed. Brymner), pp. lx-lxi.
[26] Biggar, *Trading Companies*, pp. 162-163.
[27] Dumont, *Corps Dipl.*, tom. VI., pt. I., p. 33.
[28] Biggar, *op. cit.*, pp. 164-165.

les Auspices de la Législature de Québec (1883-1885), I. 86-94; *Mercure François*, XVIII. (1633) 40-52. The confirmation of the articles is in T. Rymer, *op. cit.*, XIX. 368.

Translations: *A General Collection of Treatys* (1732), II. 305-309; N. Denys, *op. cit.* (ed. Ganong), pp. 229-239.

References: Contemporary and early writings. *Calendar of State Papers, Colonial,* [America and West Indies], 1574-1660, pp. 96-108, 111-115, 117-120, 128-132, 134, 139, 142, 143, 145, 151, 152; *Acts of the Privy Council, Colonial* (1908-1912), I. 136-149, 155-156, 170-171, 180-184; C. H. Laverdière, *Oeuvres de Champlain* (1870), tom. VI., pp. 294 ff., and *pièces justificatives*, nos. i-xxviii; *Report of the Work of the Archives Branch for the Year 1912* (ed. A. G. Doughty, 1913), pp. 24-53; *Report on Canadian Archives, 1883* (ed. Brymner, 1884), pp. 120 ff.; *ibid., 1884,* note D, pp. lx-lxii; *ibid., 1894,* pp. viii-x; *Lettres, Instructions Diplomatiques, et Papiers d'État du Cardinal de Richelieu* (ed. Vicomte d'Avenel, 1853-1877), III. 420, *et passim,* IV. 143, 202, 203, especially letters to Châteauneuf, *passim,* instructions to Fontenay, III. 518 ff., letter to the Treasurer of England, III. 671-673, in *Collection de Documents Inédits sur l'Histoire de France*; C. Rogers, *Memorials of the Earl of Stirling and of the House of Alexander* (1877), vol. I., chs. 3, 4, 5, *passim;* T. Rymer, *op. cit.*, XIX. 303-304; E. Hazard, *Historical Collections* (1792-1794), I. 314, 315.

References: Later writings. H. P. Biggar, *Early Trading Companies of New France* (1901), chs. 8, 9; E. M. Faillon, *Histoire de la Colonie Française en Canada* (1865-1866), I. 244-261; W. Kingsford, *History of Canada* (1887-1898), vol. I., chs. 9, 10; F.-X. Garneau, *Histoire du Canada* (5th ed., by H. Garneau, 1913), tom. I., liv. I., ch. 3; C. Rogers, *op. cit.*, chs. 3-5.

TEXT.[29]

Articles arrestez entre les Sieurs de Bulion conseiller du Roy très chrestien en ses conseilz d'Estat et privé, et Bouthillier, aussi conseiller de sa Majesté [30] en sesdits conseilz et secretaire de ses commandemens, commissaires deputtez par sadite Majesté, et le sieur Isaac Wake, chevalier, et ambassadeur du Roy de la Grande Bretagne, deputté dudit sieur roy pour la restitution des choses qui ont esté prises depuis le traitte de paix fait entre les deux couronnes le xxiiii° jour d'avril mil six cens vingt neuf.

De la part de sa Majesté de la Grande Bretagne le Sieur Isaac Wake, chevalier, et son ambassadeur pres du Roy tres chrestien, en vertu du pouvoir qu'il a, lequel sera inseré en fin des presentes, a promis et promet pour et au nom de sadite Majesté de rendre et restituer a sa Majesté tres chrestienne tous les lieux occupez en la Nouvelle France, la Cadie, et Canada, par les subjectz de sa Majesté de la Grande Bretagne; iceux faire retirer desdits lieux, et pour cet effect ledit sieur ambassadeur delivrera lors de la passation et signature des presentes aux commissaires du Roy Tres chrestien en bonne forme, le pouvoir qu'il a de sa Majesté de la Grande Bretagne pour la restitu-

[29] The text is taken from the original manuscript of the articles, preserved in the archives of the French Ministry of Foreign Affairs, Correspondance Politique, Angleterre, vol. 45, ff. 94-98.
[30] Written throughout the manuscript *sa Ma^te*.

tion desdits lieux, ensemble les commandemens[31] de sadite Majesté a tous ceux qui commandent dans le Port Royal, Fort de Quebec, et Cap Breton, pour estre lesdits places et fort rendus et remis es mains de ceux qu'il plaira a sa Majesté tres chrestienne ordonner, huit jours apres que lesdits commandemens auront este notiffiez a ceux qui commandent ou commanderont esdits lieux : ledit temps de huit jours leur estant donné pour retirer cependant hors desdits lieux, places, et fort, leurs armes, bagages, marchandises, or, argent, ustenciles, et generalement tout ce qui leur appartient : ausquelz, et a tous ceux qui sont esdits lieux, est donné le terme de trois sepmaines apres lesdits huit jours expirez, pour durant icelles, ou plustost si faire se peult, rentrer en leurs navires avec leurs armes, munitions, bagages, or, argent, ustenciles, marchandises, pelleteries, et generalement tout ce qui leur appartient, pour dela se retirer en Angleterre sans sejourner davantage esdits païs.

Et comme il est necessaire que les Anglois envoyent esdits lieux pour reprendre leurs gens, et les ramener en Angleterre, il est accordé que le General de Caen[32] payera les frais necessaires pour l'équipage d'un navire de deux cens, ou deux cens cinquante tonneaux de port que les Anglois envoyeront esdits lieux, assavoir le loüage du navire d'aller et retour, victuailles des gens, tant de marine pour la conduite du navire, que de ceux qui sont a terre, lesquelz on doibt ramener, salaire d'iceux, et generalement tout ce qui est necessaire pour l'équipage d'un navire dudit port, pour un tel voyage, selon les usances et coustumes d'Angleterre.

Et de plus, que pour les marchandises loyales et marchandes qui pourront rester es mains des Anglois non trocquées, qu'il leur donnera satisfaction esdits lieux, selon qu'elles auront cousté en Angleterre, avec trente pour cent de proffict, en consideration des risques de la mer, et port d'icelles payez par eux.[33]

Procedant par les subjetz de sa Majesté de la Grande Bretagne a la restitution desdites places, elles seront restituées en mesme estat qu'elles estoient lors de la prinse, sans aucune demolition des choses existantes lors de la dite prinse.

Les armes et munitions contenues en la deposition du Sieur de Champlain,[34] ensemble les marchandises et ustenciles qui furent trouvées a Quebec lors de la prinse, seront renduës, ou en espece, ou en valeur, selon que le porte la deposition dudit Sieur de Champlain, et sera le contenu en icelle, ensemble tout ce qui est justiffié par la dite deposition avoir esté trouvé audit lieu, lors de la prinse, rendu et delaissé audit fort entre les mains des françois : Et si quelque chose manque du nombre de chacune espece, sera satisfait et payé par

---

[31] Orders for restitution and withdrawal are printed in Doughty, *op. cit.*, pp. 46-51 ; Laverdière, *op. cit.*, VI., *pièces justificatives*, no. xxvi. p. 26. See also *Cal. St. Pap., Colonial*, 1574-1660, pp. 143, 151.

[32] Guillaume De Caen, general of the fleet of New France. In 1621 he and his nephew, Éméric De Caen, were granted a monopoly of trade in the St. Lawrence. In the following year, their company joined the earlier one of Champlain to form the United Company, which enjoyed the trade of the river until the summer of 1633. Biggar, *op. cit.*, pp. 115-120.

[33] D. Kirke and the other Adventurers to Canada thought this allowance of 30 per cent. unreasonably small. They complained that, in general, the treaty sacrificed their interests. Laverdière, *op. cit.*, VI., *pièces justificatives*, no. xxviii, pp. 27-31.

[34] The deposition is printed in Laverdière, *op. cit.*, VI., *pièces justificatives*, no. xxvii, pp. 26, 27.

le Sieur Philippe Burlamachy, a qui par sa Majesté tres-chrestienne sera
ordonné, hors mis les cousteaux, castors, et provenu des debtes enlevez par
les Anglois, dequoy on a convenu cy-dessoubz et satisfaction a esté donnée
audit General de Caen, pour et au nom de tous ceux qui y pourroient avoir
interest.

De plus, ledit Sieur Burlamachy, de la part de sa Majesté de la Grande
Bretagne, pour et au nom de sadite Majesté, à la requeste et commandement
dudit Sieur Ambassadeur, selon l'ordre qu'il a receu d'elle, et encore en son
propre et privé nom, a promis et promet de payer audit General de Caen, dans
deux mois du jour de la signature et datte des presentes, pour toutes et
chacunes lesdites pelleteries, cousteaux, debtes deues par les sauvages audit
General de Caen, et autres marchandises a luy appartenantes trouvées dans
ledit fort de Quebec en l'an 1629, la somme de quatre vingtz deux mil sept
cens livres tournois.

Plus luy faire rendre et restituer en Angleterre la barque nommée l'Helene,[35]
agretz, canons, munitions et appartenances, selon le memoire qui en a esté
justifié pardevant les seigneurs du Conseil d'Angleterre.

Seront de plus restituées audit General de Caen dans l'habitation de
Quebec toutes les barriques de gallettes, barils de pois, prunes, raisins, farines,
et autres marchandises et victuailles de traicte, qui estoient dans ladite barque
lors de la prinse d'icelle en l'an 1629, ensemble les marchandises a luy appar-
tenans, qui ont esté deschargées et laissées l'année derniere a Quebec, en la
riviere de Sainct Laurens, pais de la Nouvelle France.

Et en outre promet ledit Sieur Burlamachy audit nom que dessus, payer ou
faire payer dans Paris, a qui par sa Majesté tres-chrestienne sera ordonné,
la somme de soixante mil six cens deux livres tournois dans ledit temps, pour
les navires le Gabriel de Sct. Gilles, Sᵗᵉ Anne du Havre de Grace, la Trinité
des Sables d'Ollonne, le Sᶜᵗ Laurens de Sᶜᵗ Malo, et le Cap du Ciel de Calais,
canons, munitions, agretz, cordages, victuailles, et marchandises, et generalement toutes choses comprinses es inventaire et estimations desdits navires
faites par les juges de l'admirauté en Angleterre, pareillement pour la barque
d'advis, envoyée par les associez du Cappitaine Bontemps, avec les canons,
munitions, agretz, apparaux, marchandises, et victuailles, la somme que l'on
trouvera que ladite barque et marchandises, agretz, canons, et munitions
auront esté vendus ou evaluez par ordre des juges de l'admirauté d'Angleterre: et le mesme pour le vaisseau donné par ledit Bontemps aux Anglois,
repassez en Angleterre selon l'evaluation qui en aura esté faite—comme
dessus.

Comme aussy de la part de sa Majesté Treschrestienne, suivant le pouvoir
qu'elle en a donné aux Sieurs de Bullion, conseiller du Roy en ses conseilz
d'Estat et privé, et Bouthillier, aussi conseiller du Roy en sesdits conseilz
et secretaire de ses commandemens, dont coppie sera inseree a la fin des
presentes—il est promis et accordé que les Sieurs Lumagne ou Vanelly
donneront caution et assurance au nom de sadite Majesté et en leur propre
et privé nom,[36] des ce jourdhui datte des presentes de payer dans l'espace

---

[35] The patache of Éméric De Caen, captured by Thomas Kirke on his way back to
Tadoussac after the taking of Quebec. Laverdière, *op. cit.*, VI. 251 ff.; *pièces justificatives*, no. xxviii, pp. 28-29.

[36] The following words—*dans le terme de dix jours apres la signature et*—have been
struck out. The word *presentement*, written above them, is also struck out. Marks
indicate that the words *des ce jourdhui*, entered in the margin, should be inserted here.

de deux mois, a compter du jour de ladite datte, audit ambassadeur, ou a qui il ordonnera, en la ville de Paris, la somme de soixante quatre mil deux cens quarante six livres quatre solz trois deniers tournois pour les marchandises du vaisseau le Jaques; et la somme de soixante neuf mil huict cens nonante six livres neuf sols deux deniers tournois pour les marchandises du vaisseau la Benediction,[37] le tout au taux du roy; et que dans quinze jours[38] lesdits deux navires le Jaques, et la Benediction, estans maintenant au port et havre de Dieppe, avec leurs cordages, canons, munitions, agretz, apparaux, et victuailles, qui furent trouvez à leur arrivée audit Dieppe, seront restituez audit sieur ambassadeur d'Angleterre, ou a qui il ordonnera; et si quelque chose de cela vient a manquer luy sera payé en argent comptant.

Et pour le regard du navire la Bride ou Espouze, les sommes ausquelles se trouveront monter ce qui a esté vendu a Calais, tant des vins, et autres marchandises, que du corps du navire, canons, munitions, agretz, apparaux, et victuailles d'iceluy, seront payez, ensemble les sommes ausquelles se trouveront monter le reste de la charge dudit navire, trouvée dans iceluy lors qu'il fut prins, lesquelles seront payées sur le pied de la derniere vente faite audit Calais, pour le payement dequoy lesdits Sieurs Lumagne ou Vanelly passeront caution pour le payer à Paris audit sieur ambassadeur, ou a qui il ordonnera dans le terme susdit.

A esté accordé que sur les sommes qui doibvent estre restituées par les François et Anglois seront desduitz les droitz d'entrée: ensemble ce qui aura esté baillé pour la garde des marchandises et reparation desdits navires, et particulierement douze cens livres pour ce qui touche les droitz d'entree des marchandises dudit General de Caen, et douze cens livres qu'il doibt payer pour les vivres fournis aux François a leur retour en Angleterre et France en 1629.

De plus a esté convenu de part et d'autre, que si lors de la prinse desdits vaisseaux, le Jaques, la Benediction, le Gabriel de Sᵉᵗ Gilles, Sᵗᵉ Anne du Havre de Grace, La Trinité des Sables d'Olonne, le Sᵉᵗ Laurens de Sᵉᵗ Malo, le Cap du Ciel de Calais, a este prinse aucune chose contenue es inventaires et qui neantmoings n'aura este comprise es proces verbaux des ventes ou estimations; comme aussi si lors de la prinse desdits vaisseaux il a este soubztrait ou enlevé quelque chose non comprise es inventaires faitz, tant en France qu'en Angleterre, par les officiers de la marine, et officiers de l'admirauté, il sera loisible aux interessez desdits navires de se pourveoir par les voies ordinaires de la justice, contre ceux qu'ilz pourront prouver estre coulpables de ce delict, pour iceux estre contraintz par corps a la restitution de ce qui sera prouvé avoir esté enlevé par eux. Et qu'a ce faire ilz seront

---

[37] One of the two valuable prizes which, with 900 negroes, were brought by Capt. Bontemps to Dieppe. In April(?), 1630, Sir Nicholas Crisp and his partners, who had sent this ship to trade to "the river of Senegal, in Guinea", and who estimated their loss by her capture at more than £20,000, petitioned the Privy Council for relief upon such French goods as were then under sequestration, or for letters of reprisal; soon after the government gave the merchants a charter, with a monopoly of the trade from Capes Blanco to Good Hope. *Cal. St. Pap., Colonial*, 1574-1660, p. 114. Ch. de La Roncière, *Histoire de la Marine Française* (1899, etc.), IV. 700; W. R. Scott, *Joint-Stock Companies* (1910-1912), II. 14. The Adventurers to Canada complained that in the proceeding about this ship the French valuation of the captured goods was accepted, and the English rejected. Laverdière, *op. cit.*, VI., *pièces justificatives,* no. xxviii, p. 31. The other prize, the *James,* was valued, with its cargo, at £24,000. *Cal. St. P., Domestic,* 1629-1631, pp. 39, 133, 466, *et passim.*

[38] The words *quinze jours* appear to have been written in after the rest of the document.

contraintz solidairement, le soluable pour l'insoluable, sans toutesfois que lesdits interessez puissent pour raison de ce pretendre aucune reparation de leurs griefs par represailles ou lettres de marque, soit par mer, ou par terre.

Pour l'execution de ce que dessus, toutes lettres et arrestz necessaires seront expediez de part et d'autre, et fournis dans quinze jours.[39]

[Here follow the full powers given by Louis XIII. of France to the Sieurs Bullion and Bouthillier, on January 25, 1632, and by Charles I. of England to Sir Isaac Wake, on June 9/19, 1631.]

. . . .

En foy dequoy nous commissaires et ambassadeur susdits, en vertu de nos pouvoirs avons signé les presentes articles a Sainct Germain en Laye [40] le 29 jour de Mars mil six cens trente deux

BULLION, BOUTHILLIER, ISAACUS WAKUS.

[39] The words *quinze jours* have been written in after the rest of the manuscript and the words following them—*ensemble les obligations necessaires desdits Sieurs Lumagne ou Vanelly et Burlamachy pour parvenir a lacomplissement de ce que dessus*—have been struck out.

[40] The word *Paris* has been struck out.

37.

Treaty of alliance between Portugal and France concluded at Paris, June 1, 1641.

INTRODUCTION.

In December, 1640, the Portuguese people, encouraged by a rebellion then proceeding in Catalonia, revolted against the government of Philip IV. of Spain and acclaimed the Duke of Braganza as king of Portugal, under the name of John IV. The unequal political union of the two kingdoms in the person of the Spanish monarch had been well-nigh ruinous to the Portuguese. While they complained of such wrongs as illegal taxation and the appointment of unfit officials, they seem to have resented even more bitterly the destruction of their naval power, commerce, and world-wide colonial empire.[1] Their vast commerce, formerly protected by their traditional policy of peace and by their strong navy, had been ruined by their union with a warlike country whose enemies, Holland, England, and France, had usurped Portugal's trade and stripped her of her mostly undefended colonies in the Orient, on the coast of Africa, and in Brazil. Spain's indifference to the welfare of Portugal appeared, as the Portuguese thought, in the terms of the truce of Antwerp of 1609. The truce was limited to regions north of the Line, and left the southern latitudes, the seat of the principal Portuguese colonies, open to attack.[2] The Spanish government also showed its indifference by forbidding the Portuguese access to the Spanish Indies, while it permitted Castilians to enjoy the colonies of Portugal.[3]

In spite of the fact that Holland, England, and France had robbed Portugal of colonies, it was to these countries, as enemies of Spain, that the new king John IV. naturally turned for aid. Early in 1641 he despatched ambassadors to Paris, London, and the Hague, as well as to Copenhagen and Stockholm. Support from France, at war with Spain since 1635, was already pledged. Richelieu, indeed, had fomented the rebellion and worked for its success.[4] He warmly welcomed the Portuguese ambassadors, Francisco de Mello and

---

[1] The "manifesto" of Feb., 1641, which sets forth the Portuguese grievances, is in Abreu y Bertodano, *Coleccion de los Tratados de España: Reynado de Phelipe IV.*, III. 422-477. For the commercial grievances, see pp. 440-449, or Fernández Duro, *Armada Española* (1895-1903), IV. 273-277.

[2] The "manifesto" mentioned in the foregoing note refers to this grievance. For the truce, see above, Doc. **28.**

[3] G. Scelle, *La Traite Négrière aux Indes de Castille* (1906), I. 413, 474.

[4] Commission des Archives Diplomatiques, *Recueil des Instructions: Portugal*, pp. xviii ff.

Dr. Antonio Coelho de Carvalho, upon their arrival in Paris toward the end of March,[5] since he believed that an alliance between Portugal, France, and Holland would mean the ruin of Spain.[6] The ambassadors' principal proposals[7] were, briefly, as follows: that an offensive league should be formed against Spain, to include the friends of both crowns and in particular the United Netherlands; that France should aid the rebellious Catalans; that, in April, France should send twenty warships to the coasts of Portugal to join the Portuguese and Dutch ships in destroying the Castilian fleet at Cadiz, in seizing the principal ports, and in capturing the West India silver fleet—an enterprise which, according to the ambassador, would, if carried out, end the war; that a similar joint naval expedition should be made each year so long as the war lasted; that none of the allies should withdraw from the league without the consent of the others, or make a separate peace with Spain; that France should aid Portugal with cavalry and officers and by permitting the export of arms and ammunition; and that there should be reciprocal freedom of commerce between the two crowns. Richelieu drew up a *projet*[8] embodying most of these demands, but with some modifications, such as, that the supreme command of the naval forces should be given to the Admiral of France and that the French contingent should not join the fleet of Portugal till June. A serious stumbling block was the desire of the Portuguese to bind the King of France not to make peace with Spain without them. To this Richelieu would not agree, under the pretext that it would hinder a general peace. Finally, "pour contenter leur imagination", he framed a separate and secret article whereby the King of France conditionally promised to endeavor, in concluding a treaty with Spain, to retain the liberty of assisting the King of Portugal "in his just pretensions". On the other hand, this article bound Portugal to make no treaty with Spain except with the consent of France and her allies.[9] Since Portugal's existence seemed to depend on alliance with France her envoys felt constrained to accept this article. The treaty was signed on June 1.

A French squadron of thirty-two ships, under command of the Marquis de Brezé (who in the preceding year had sunk several of the West Indian galleons), arrived at Lisbon on August 6, 1641, to co-operate with the naval forces of the Portuguese and Dutch. The combined fleets sailed from Lisbon about a month later, but accomplished little of importance.[10]

---

[6] Santarem, *Quadro Elementar*, IV. (1). 27.
[6] *Lettres de Richelieu* (ed. Avenel), VI. 771-772, and note.
[7] For the ambassadors' public and private instructions, see Santarem, *op. cit.*, IV. (1), 5-13, 16-21.
[8] Printed in Bittard des Portes, "Une Alliance entre la France et le Portugal" in *Revue d'Histoire Diplomatique*, XII. 198, 199.
[9] *Lettres de Richelieu* (ed. Avenel), VII. 859, 860.
[10] Santarem, *op. cit.*, IV. (1), pp. 42-45; C. Fernández Duro, *op. cit.*, IV. 262 ff., 269 ff.

BIBLIOGRAPHY.

Text: MS. A copy of the protocol is in the Bibliothèque Nationale in
Paris, Cinq Cents de Colbert, vol. 305, p. 257. This is the manuscript
of the treaty referred to by the Viscount de Santarem, *Quadro Elementar*
(1842-1876), tom. IV., pt. I., p. 35, note 30. We are informed that
another copy of the protocol is in the National Archives of Portugal,
at Lisbon. According to the Viscount de Santarem the secret article
of this treaty exists in the manuscript memoirs of the embassies of Luiz
Pereira de Castro, p. 13 (MSS. da Corôa). No original manuscripts of
this treaty have been found.

Text: Printed. J. F. Borges de Castro, *Collecção dos Tratados de Portugal desde 1640* (1856-1858), I. 16-23 ; F. Leonard, *Recueil des Traites
de Paix* (1693), IV. ; J. Dumont, *Corps Diplomatique* (1726-1731),
tom. VI., pt. I., p. 214 ; J. A. de Abreu y Bertodano, *Coleccion de los
Tratados de España: Reynado de Phelipe IV*. (1744-1751), III. 570-575 ;
Revue d'Histoire Diplomatique, vol. XII. (1898), pp. 204-207.

Translations: Portuguese. Borges de Castro, *loc. cit.* **Spanish.** Abreu y
Bertodano, *loc. cit.*

References: Contemporary and early writings. *Lettres, Instructions Diplomatiques, et Papiers d'État du Cardinal de Richelieu* (ed. Vicomte
d'Avenel, 1853-1877), VI. 768, 772, 773, 794, 795, 799, and notes, VII.
283, 288, 857-864, 1048, VIII. 369, 370, in *Collection de Documents
Inédits sur l'Histoire de France* ; Santarem, *op. cit.,* tom. IV., pt. I.,
pp. 5-38 ; R. Bittard des Portes, " Une Alliance entre la France et le
Portugal au XVIIᵉ Siècle ", in *Revue d'Histoire Diplomatique,* vol. XII.
(1898), pp. 196-212, *passim.*

References: Later writings. R. Bittard des Portes, *op. cit.* ; Commission
des Archives Diplomatiques, *Recueil des Instructions données aux Ambassadeurs et Ministres de France depuis les Traités de Westphalie
jusqu'à la Revolution Française* (1884—), III. *Portugal* (ed. Vicomte
de Caix de Saint-Aymour), pp. xvi-xxxi ; Viscount de Santarem, *loc. cit.,*
pp. clxxxix-cciv ; J. B. G. de Raxis de Flassan, *Histoire Générale de la
Diplomatie Française* (1811), III. 60-65 ; H. Schäfer, *Geschichte von
Portugal* (1836-1854), IV. 508-511, in Heeren and Ukert, *Geschichte
der Europäischen Staaten* ; L. A. Rebello da Silva, *Historia de Portugal
nos Seculos XVII. e XVIII*. (1860-1871), IV. 282-298 ; E. Lavisse,
Histoire de France (1900-1910), tom. VI., pt. II., pp. 350-352 ; J. Knight,
*La Diplomatie Française et l'Indépendance du Portugal au XVIIᵉ
Siècle* [1640-1668], (Positions, École des Chartes, 1902), pp. 57-68.

TEXT.[1]

Le roi, sçachant l'amittié et bonne intelligence qui a esté entre les rois
ses predecesseurs et les antiens rois de Portugal, desquels le Roi D. Jean IV.,
á present regnant, a esté recongneu unanimement par tous les Portugais pour
legitime successeur, duquel sa Majesté a esté bien aise de voir icy les ambassadeurs qu'il a envoiés vers elle pour renouveller cette antienne amitié, et

[1] The text is from a copy in the Bibliothèque Nationale at Paris, Cinq Cents de Colbert, vol. 305, p. 257.

l'assurer par une alliance entre elle et ledit roy, surquoy les commissaires de sa Majesté aiant plain pouvoir d'elle sont convenus avec lesdits Sieurs Ambassadeurs, aiant aussi plain pouvoir dudit Roi de Portugal, des articles suivans :

1.[12] Il y aura doresnavant paix et alliance perpetuelle entre les Roys de France et de Portugal et leurs roiaumes, provinces, mers, ports, et havres.

. . . .

3. Messieurs les États Generaux des Provinces Unies des Pais Bas seront admis en ceste alliance, aux conditions qui seront convenues avec eux.

4. Pendant la présente guerre que le roy a contre le Roi de Castille[13] laquelle il continura puissament le Roy de Portugal agira de son costé continuellement contre ledit roy, et l'attaquera de sa puissance tant par terre que par mer.

5. Pour en faciliter le moien sa Majesté demeure d'accord de joindre a la fin de Juin vingt de ses vaisseaux bien armes, et equipés en guerre a vingt gallions du Roy de Portugal que ses ambassadeurs asseurent et promettent au nom du dit Roy leur Maistre qu'ils seront trouves, et mesme davantage armés, et bien equippés en guerre et tous prestz à faire voille, dont les moindres seront de trois cens tonneaux,[14] affin que lesdites deux flottes fortifiees de 20 vaisseaux que les dits Estats Generaux doivent donner de secours au dit Roy Don Jean allant attaquer la flotte des Castillans venant des Indes, ou entreprendre dans les Estats du dit Roi de Castille par des descentes dans ses terres, ce qui sera estimé plus à propos, bien entendu que lesdits vaisseaux, tant de Portugal que desdits Sieurs les Estats Generaux, defereront a ladmiral de France le comandement et tous les autres honneurs qui luy sont deús, et qu'en cas que la flotte dudit Roy de Castille vint à estre prinse, elle sera partagee egalement entre les confederes.

6. Si les années suivantes les deux rois et lesdits Sieurs Estats jugent quil soit a propos de continuer une pareille entreprise on le fera par avis commun.

7. Il y aura libre trafic et commerce entre les subjets, roiaumes, et etats des deux roix, comme du temps des anciens Rois de Portugal, en sorte que leurs subjets pourront negocier et traffiquer en toute seuretté les uns avec les autres comme amis et allies, sans qu'il leur soit donné aucun empeschement, ains toute sorte de protection et soulagement pour leur trafficq mesme, sy besoin est, leur sera accordé de part et d'autre des privileges et libertes plus grandes que par le passé.

. . . .

9. Les susdits articles ont esté signés au nom du Roy par Monsr Seguier, chevalier et chancellier de France, Monsr Bouthiller, commandeur, grand-

---

[12] The articles are not numbered in the manuscript.
[13] In recognition of the separation of the Portuguese from the Spanish crown, Philip IV., in this and the following treaty, is styled " Roy de Castille ", instead of " Roy d'Espagne ". The reason for this change is explained by D. Antonio de Sousa de Macedo in his *Lusitania Liberata* (1645), pp. 6, 7, as follows: " Sed quia verè toti Hispaniae citeriori dominabantur ; postquam verò Portugalliae Regnum occuparunt, jam non Hispaniae appellabantur Reges, sed, Hispaniarum, videlicet citerioris et ulterioris ; . . . passimque apud alios Hispaniarum Rex nuncupabatur, atque hodiè, postquam eum è Portugalliâ jus dejecit, excusabiliter à populo nominabitur Rex Hispaniae, nempè citerioris ; quamvis propriùs à scientibus Regis Castellae titulo cognoscatur."
[14] The Portuguese contingent actually consisted of only seventeen ships, of which only ten were of 300 tons or over. Santarem, *op. cit.*, IV. (1), pp. 45, 46, note 45.

tresorier des Ordres du Roy et sur-intendant des finances de France ; Mons'
Bouthiller de Chavigny, aussy commandeur, grand-trésorier des Ordres de
sa Majesté, secrettaire destat et de ses commandements ; et au nom dudit
Roy de Portugal par Don Francisco de Mello, du conseil dudit Roi et son
grandveneur, et Don Antonio Coelho de Carvalho, aussy du conseil du dit
Roy et du conseil de son parlement supreme, ses ambassadeurs pres sa
Majesté tres-Chrestienne, et seront ratifiez respectivement par sa Ma[jes]tè
et par ledit Roy de Portugal, dans le terme de quatre mois. Fait à Paris le
1 Juin, 1641.

Signé, S<small>EGUIER</small>, B<small>OUTHILLER</small>, B<small>OUTHILLER</small>.

Separate article.

Bien qu'il ne soit point parlé dans le traitté public passé cejourdhuy
entre [les Sieurs Commissaires du Roy Trés Chrestienne et les ambassadeurs
du Roy de Portugal] [15] de ce qu'il se poura faire en faveur du Roy de Portugal
au cas que le Roi et ses conféderes viennent a conclure la paix avec la maison
d'Autriche, le roy toutesfois par sa generositté a bien voulu assurer le Roy
de Portugal, son bon frère, que lorsqu'il viendra a la conclusion d'un traitté
de paix, il fera son possible pour se reserver la liberté de l'assister tousjours
en ses justes prétentions, pourveu que les allies de Saditte Majesté consentent
d'entrer avec elle en une pareille obligation, bien entendu qu'en tel cas le
Roy de Portugal s'obligera a ne faire aucun traitté avec le Roy de Castille
sans le consentement de Sa dite Majesté et de ses allies.

Le susdit article secret sera signé au nom du Roy par [Monsieur le Cardinal
Duc de Richelieu] [15] et au nom du Roy de Portugal par [Don Francisco de
Mello] [15] et sera respectivement ratiffié par Sa Majesté et ledit Roy de Portu-
gal dans le terme de quatre mois. Fait à Paris le 1 jour de Juin, 1641.

Signé, S<small>EGUIER</small>, B<small>OUTHILLER</small>, B<small>OUTHILLER</small>.

[15] The bracketed words are from a copy in the National Archives at Lisbon.

38.

Treaty of truce and commerce between Portugal and the United Netherlands, concluded at the Hague, June 12, 1641. Ratification by the King of Portugal, November 18, 1641. [Ratification by the States General, February 20, 1642.]

INTRODUCTION.

Early in 1641, John IV., having accepted the crown of Portugal upon its severance from that of Spain, and needing support from Spain's enemies,[1] sought alliance with the United Netherlands. The States General were well disposed toward the new king, and, in accordance with suggestions from Richelieu, had already resolved to despatch an envoy to Portugal and to equip a fleet to act with that of France in favor of Portugal and against Spain.[2] Nevertheless there were obstacles to an alliance. During the twenty years of hostilities between the United Netherlands and Spain, following the expiration of the truce of Antwerp,[3] the two great trading companies of the Dutch had endeavored to supplant the Portuguese in their colonial possessions and trade, which were, for the most part, insufficiently defended by the Spanish government. In the Far East, by the end of January, 1641, the Dutch East India Company had expelled the Portuguese from part of Ceylon and from Malacca. In Brazil, the Dutch West India Company had gained control of the captaincies from Maranhão to Sergipe del Rey; and in Africa, the same company, with a view to securing the supply of slaves needed for the Brazilian sugar plantations, had dislodged the Portuguese from the forts of Cape Coast Castle and St. George of the Mine (1637) and from the island of Arguin (1638).[4]

The Portuguese ambassador, Tristão de Mendoça, having been detained in England, did not deliver his credentials to the States General until April 12. His proposals[5] were as follows:

1. A ten years' truce should be concluded between Portugal and the States General in the East and West Indies and wherever the King of Portugal should be recognized.

---

[1] *Cf.* Doc. **37**, introduction.
[2] Arend, *Algemeene Geschiedenis*, III. (5), 300; Aitzema, *Saken van Staet*, II. 753 ff.
[3] Doc. **28**.
[4] J. G. Doorman, " Die Niederländisch-West-Indische Compagnie an der Goldküste" in *Tijdschrift voor Indische Taal-, Land- en Volkenkunde*, XL. (1898) 443, 444; De Lannoy and Vander Linden, *L'Expansion Coloniale: Néerlande et Danemark*, p. 97.
[5] Arend, *op. cit.*, III. (5), 307.

2. The States General should aid Portugal with twenty big ships and ten frigates. Spanish prizes should be divided according to the number of ships used by each party—Dutch, Portuguese, or French—in the attack.

3. Conquests made by the West India Company in Brazil should be restored to Portugal for reasonable compensation, or for permission to the company to appropriate conquests which should be made by the united forces in the Indies of Castile.

4. Navigation and trade between both allies should be open and free and the king should impose no higher customs upon Dutch goods than did his predecessors.

5. The ambassador should take from the United Netherlands a certain number of officers, engineers, etc., at the expense of the Portuguese crown.

These proposals were not pleasing to the great companies. The West India Company was unwilling to restore Brazil to Portugal or to grant Portugal the benefit of a truce. The East India Company considered that if a truce were to be proclaimed, it must only be after a delay. Next to the continuance of the war the companies preferred a peace. A truce was the least desired alternative. The States of Holland, influenced by the remonstrances of the East India Company, proposed a truce in Europe only, until information should be received as to conditions in the East. The inland provinces, the Prince of Orange and the Council of State, being more concerned about the European land campaign, acknowledged that the interests of the trading companies must be considered, but were anxious to conclude an alliance as speedily as possible. They argued that the Portuguese, if refused aid by the Dutch, would seek help from France and England, and that these powers would then be induced " to mix in the Indian trade ".

Holland and Zeeland desired that the Portuguese ambassador should accept, with certain modifications, the articles drawn up by the trading companies for securing their interests; and to this the States General agreed.[6]

News of the conclusion of a treaty between Portugal and France expedited the negotiations at the Hague; for the Dutch did not wish Portugal to consider the French more friendly than themselves.[7] On June 12 the treaty was signed.

The first article stipulated a ten years' truce on both sides of the Line, to go into effect immediately after the conclusion of the treaty in Europe and outside the limits of the East and West India companies. Articles 2-7, which refer to the East India Company, provided, among other things, that within the limits of this company the truce should begin one year after the Portuguese ratification reached the Hague, or whenever notification of the truce was received. East Indian rulers, friends of the States General, or of the company, should be included in the truce. Subjects of either party might

⁶ *Ibid.*, III. (5), 311.   ⁷ *Ibid.*, III. (5), 312.

sail to, trade in, and possess lands in the East Indies, as at the time of the publication of the truce, without being molested by subjects of the other power. Articles 8-23, which were identical with those concluded between the Dutch West India Company and the Portuguese ambassador,[8] provided, in essentials, as follows: Within the limits of the company the truce should have effect for ten years; but the Portuguese ambassador promised that within a specified period the King of Portugal would send one or more plenipotentiaries to treat for peace. During the truce the Dutch and Portuguese should aid each other, and places and persons in Brazil favoring Castile should be regarded as common enemies; subjects of both parties should remain in possession of their goods; the company should not import Brazilian products into Portugal; nor the Portuguese import them into the United Netherlands. In Brazil the Portuguese should not trade in or frequent the dominions of the Dutch, or *vice versa*. The Portuguese in sailing to, or trading in Brazil, were not to use the ships of any foreign nation except the Dutch; neither Portuguese nor Dutch should send any ships, negroes, or merchandise to the Castilian Indies or to other places which had sided with the Castilians. The Portuguese and Dutch possessions on the coasts of Africa need not be delimited; these coasts were to be open to both nations on condition that each should trade only near the towns or forts of the other. The remaining articles stipulated, mainly, that conquests subsequently made in the Castilian West Indies should be divided or enjoyed by common consent; that all inhabitants of either nation might visit and traffic in any kind of merchandise in the territories of either power situated in Europe, or elsewhere north of the Line, without paying greater duties than the inhabitants of the country visited, and with the privileges enjoyed before Portugal was subjected to Castile; that Christian subjects of the United Provinces in Portuguese territories on either side of the Line should enjoy liberty of conscience in their houses and free exercise of their religion on their ships; that a Portuguese-Dutch fleet should be employed on the coasts of Portugal and Spain against the common enemy, and prizes divided *pro rata*; that the King of Portugal might enroll officers and engineers in the Provinces; that the houses of Dutch merchants in Portuguese territories in Europe should not be forcibly entered, or their letters or accounts examined; and that each power might appoint consuls to the ports of the other in Europe.

On the day after the conclusion of the truce, the States General proclaimed an immediate suspension of arms in accordance with its provisions, *i. e.*, outside the limits of the two India companies.[9] The ratification by Portugal, dated November 18, 1641, did not reach the United Provinces till the following February, when the Dutch ratification of the truce, although opposed by

---

[8] Aitzema, *op. cit.*, II. 755 ff.
[9] *Groot Placaet-Boeck van de Staten Generael* (1658-1796), vol. I., cols. 127-128; *Mercure François*, XXIV. (1647) 259.

Holland and Zeeland, was sanctioned by the States General.[10] The delay in ratification had given the Dutch companies an opportunity to continue their conquests at the expense of the Portuguese. In pursuance of suggestions received from the West India Company, Dutch forces took possession of Saint Paul de Loanda, the chief town in Angola, of the island of St. Thomas, off the African coast, and of the captaincy of Maranhão in Brazil.[11] In vain did Portuguese ambassadors reiterate their demands for the restitution of these places,[12] but what Portuguese diplomacy failed to achieve, native uprisings, backed to some extent by the Portuguese government, brought to pass. Before the end of 1648, the Dutch had lost to the Portuguese their abovementioned conquests in Africa, and all they had held in Brazil except the Recife (Pernambuco) and three forts.[13] In 1654 these also capitulated to the Portuguese. Thus Portuguese independence, at first welcomed by the Dutch as a blow struck at Spain, soon proved an important cause of the decline and ultimate ruin of the fortunes of the Dutch West India Company.

BIBLIOGRAPHY.

Text: MS. Original manuscripts of the protocol and of two ratifications by the King of Portugal, one in Latin and the other in Portuguese, are in the Rijksarchief at the Hague, Secrete Casse, casse B, loquet R. An original manuscript of the protocol is mentioned by J. F. Borges de Castro, *Collecção dos Tratados de Portugal desde 1640* (1856-1858), I. 24, as in the Torre do Tombo.

Text: Printed. De Castro, *op. cit.*, I. 24-49; J. Dumont, *Corps Diplomatique* (1726-1731), tom. VI., pt. I., pp. 215-218; J. A. de Abreu y Bertodano, *Coleccion de los Tratados de España: Reynado de Phelipe IV.* (1744-1751), III. 581-598; J. Le Clerc, *Négociations Secrètes de Munster et d'Osnaburg* (1725-1726), IV. 520-530.

Translations: French. J. Le Clerc, *Négociations Secrètes, loc. cit.* **Dutch.** *Groot Placaet-Boeck van de Staten Generael* (1658-1796), I., cols. 118-126; L. van Aitzema, *Saken van Staet en Oorlogh* (1669-1672), II. 756-760, VI. (2), *Vrede-handeling*, pp. 149-152. **Portuguese.** De Castro, *loc. cit.*; C. Calvo, *Recueil Complet des Traités* (1862-1866), I. 54-66. **Spanish.** Abreu y Bertodano, *loc. cit.*

References: Contemporary and early writings. Don Luiz de Menezes, conde da Ericeira, *Historia de Portugal Restaurado* (1st ed., 1679-1698; 3d ed., 1751, tom. I., pt. I., liv. III.); L. van Aitzema, *op. cit.*, II. 753-759, 831, 832, 865, 866, 892, 922, 923.

References: Later writings. J. P. Arend *et al.*, *Algemeene Geschiedenis des Vaderlands* (1840, etc.), III. (5), 299-213; P. M. Netscher, *Les Hollandais au Brésil* (1853), pp. 122 ff.; L. A. Rebello da Silva, *Historia de Portugal nos Seculos XVII. e XVIII.* (1860-1871), IV. 284, 304-310;

[10] Netscher, *Les Hollandais au Brésil*, p. 124; Aitzema, *op. cit.*, II. 831, 832.
[11] Netscher, *op. cit.*, pp. 119 ff.   [12] Aitzema, *op. cit.*, II. 832 ff., 892, 922, 923.
[13] Netscher, *op. cit.*, pp. 157-159.

H. Schäfer, *Geschichte von Portugal* (1836-1854), IV. 517-522, in Heeren and Ukert, *Geschichte der Europäischen Staaten*. For the history of Portuguese-Dutch relations in the colonies about the year 1641, see Ch. de Lannoy and H. Vander Linden, *Histoire de l'Expansion Coloniale: Portugal et Espagne* (1907), pp. 74-77; and *id., Histoire de l'Expansion Coloniale: Néerlande et Danemark* (1911), pp. 95 ff., 100 ff., 121 ff.

TEXT.[14]

Joannes, Dei gratia rex Portugaliae et Algarbiorum citra ultraque mare in Africa, dominus Guineae, atque expugnationis, navigationis, et commercii Aethiopiae, Arabiae, Persiae, et Indiae, etc. Notum facimus omnibus prae-
as patentes, approbationis, ratihabitionis, et confirmationis
is, quoniam die duodecima elapsi mensis Junii, praesentis
ntesimi quadragesimi primi, Hagae-Comitis in Hollandia,
n, cessationisque omnis hostilitatis actus, ut et navigationis
, initus, et conclusus fuerit decennio, pariterque succursus
Tristam de Mendoça Furtado, consiliarium, legatum, et
um destinatum ab una parte, et, ab altera, magnificos
Huyghens, J.[15] Van Brouchoiven, Cats, Gs. van Vos-
teede, J. van Veltdriel, Van Haersolte, Vigbole Aldringa,
atos Potentissimorum Ordinum Generalium Unitarum
i, vigore eorundem procurationis, cujus tractatus tenor
hic inscribitur :

um et cessationis omnis hostilitatis actus, ut et naviga-
pariterque succursus, inter Serenissimum ac Praepo-
annem, ejus nominis Quartum, Lusitaniae, Algarbiae
arte maris Africae Regem, dominum in Guinea, atque
ionis et commercii in Aethiopia, Arabia, Persia, ac India,
os Ordines Generales Unitarum Provinciarum ab altera
conclusus per Dominum Tristão de Mendoça Furtado,
ium Serenissimae Majestatis, et Dominos Rutgerum
Jacobum à Brouchoven, ex-consulem urbis Lugduni
Cats, equitem, consiliarium, pensionarium Hollandiae
ilis, Casparem a Vosbergen, equitem, dominum de
Reede, dominum de Renswoude et Thiens, dominum
annem Veltdriel, consulem urbis Doccum, Assuerum
i ac Echde, satrapam Zallandiae, Wigboldum Aldringa,
roninganae, toparcham Sybaldebueri, respectivè depu-
-memoratorum Dominorum Statuum Generalium ex
Iollandiae, Zelandiae, Ultrajecti, Frisiae, Trans Isula-
ningae atque Omlandiae, commissarios eorumdem
i Generalium, nempe inter memoratum dominum
rescripti regii, certarumque litterarum Serenissimae
de dato Lisbon xxi° Januarii jampridem elapsi, et
ommissarios, vigore eorundem procurationis, quorum
copiae, eorundemque translata respectivè hic infra inserentur.

[14] From the original manuscript of the Portuguese ratification preserved at the Rijksarchief at the Hague, Secrete Casse, casse B, loquet R.
[15] In manuscript, P.

Holland and Zeeland, was sanctioned by the States General.[10] The delay in ratification had given the Dutch companies an opportunity to continue their conquests at the expense of the Portuguese. In pursuance of suggestions received from the West India Company, Dutch forces took possession of Saint Paul de Loanda, the chief town in Angola, of the island of St. Thomas, off the African coast, and of the captaincy of Maranhão in Brazil.[11] In vain did Portuguese ambassadors reiterate their demands for the restitution of these places,[12] but what Portuguese diplomacy failed to achieve, native uprisings, backed to some extent by the Portuguese government, brought to pass. Before the end of 1648, the Dutch had lost to the Portuguese their abovementioned conquests in Africa, and all they had h⌐ the Recife (Pernambuco) and three forts.[13] In 1654 th to the Portuguese. Thus Portuguese independence, at the Dutch as a blow struck at Spain, soon proved an im⌐ decline and ultimate ruin of the fortunes of the Dutch W

BIBLIOGRAPHY.

Text: MS. Original manuscripts of the protocol and by the King of Portugal, one in Latin and the othe in the Rijksarchief at the Hague, Secrete Casse, An original manuscript of the protocol is mentio de Castro, *Collecção dos Tratados de Portugal desc* I. 24, as in the Torre do Tombo.

Text: Printed. De Castro, *op. cit.*, I. 24-49; J. Dumont (1726-1731), tom. VI., pt. I., pp. 215-218; J. A. de *Coleccion de los Tratados de España: Reynado d* 1751), III. 581-598; J. Le Clerc, *Négociations Se d'Osnaburg* (1725-1726), IV. 520-530.

Translations: French. J. Le Clerc, *Négociations Secr Groot Placaet-Boeck van de Staten Generael* (165 126; L. van Aitzema, *Saken van Staet en Oorl* 756-760, VI. (2), *Vrede-handeling*, pp. 149-152.] tro, *loc. cit.*; C. Calvo, *Recueil Complet des Traités* **Spanish.** Abreu y Bertodano, *loc. cit.*

References: Contemporary and early writings. D conde da Ericeira, *Historia de Portugal Restaurao* 3d ed., 1751, tom. I., pt. I., liv. III.) ; L. van Aitzen 831, 832, 865, 866, 892, 922, 923.

References: Later writings. J. P. Arend *et al.*, *Alger Vaderlands* (1840, etc.), III. (5), 299-213; P. ℕ *landais au Brésil* (1853), pp. 122 ff.; L. A. Rebell *Portugal nos Seculos XVII. e XVIII.* (1860-18'

---

[10] Netscher, *Les Hollandais au Brésil*, p. 124; Aitzema, *op. cit.*, II. 831, 832.
[11] Netscher, *op. cit.*, pp. 119 ff.   [12] Aitzema, *op. cit.*, II. 832 ff., 892, 922, 923.
[13] Netscher, *op. cit.*, pp. 157-159.

H. Schäfer, *Geschichte von Portugal* (1836-1854), IV. 517-522, in
Heeren and Ukert, *Geschichte der Europäischen Staaten.* For the history of Portuguese-Dutch relations in the colonies about the year 1641,
see Ch. de Lannoy and H. Vander Linden, *Histoire de l'Expansion
Coloniale: Portugal et Espagne* (1907), pp. 74-77; and *id., Histoire de
l'Expansion Coloniale: Néerlande et Danemark* (1911), pp. 95 ff., 100 ff.,
121 ff.

TEXT.[14]

Joannes, Dei gratia rex Portugaliae et Algarbiorum citra ultraque mare
in Africa, dominus Guineae, atque expugnationis, navigationis, et commercii
Aethiopiae, Arabiae, Persiae, et Indiae, etc. Notum facimus omnibus praesentes nostras litteras patentes, approbationis, ratihabitionis, et confirmationis
visuris et inspecturis, quoniam die duodecima elapsi mensis Junii, praesentis
anni millesimi sexcentesimi quadragesimi primi, Hagae-Comitis in Hollandia,
tractatus induciarum, cessationisque omnis hostilitatis actus, ut et navigationis
et commercii, factus, initus, et conclusus fuerit decennio, pariterque succursus
pro tempore, inter Tristam de Mendoça Furtado, consiliarium, legatum, et
procuratorem nostrum destinatum ab una parte, et, ab altera, magnificos
et illustres Rutgher Huyghens, J.[16] Van Brouchoiven, Cats, Gs. van Vosberghen, Joan van Reede, J. van Veltdriel, Van Haersolte, Vigbole Aldringa,
commissarios deputatos Potentissimorum Ordinum Generalium Unitarum
Provinciarum Belgii, vigore eorundem procurationis, cujus tractatus tenor
de verbo ad verbum hic inscribitur:

Tractatus induciarum et cessationis omnis hostilitatis actus, ut et navigationis ac commercii pariterque succursus, inter Serenissimum ac Praepo-
tentem Dominum Joannem, ejus nominis Quartum, Lusitaniae, Algarbiae
ab hac atque altera parte maris Africae Regem, dominum in Guinea, atque
acquisitionis, navigationis et commercii in Aethiopia, Arabia, Persia, ac India,
etc. ab una, et Dominos Ordines Generales Unitarum Provinciarum ab altera
parte factus, initus et conclusus per Dominum Tristão de Mendoça Furtado,
legatum ac consiliarium Serenissimae Majestatis, et Dominos Rutgerum
Huygens, equitem, Jacobum à Brouchoven, ex-consulem urbis Lugduni
Batavorum, Jacobum Cats, equitem, consiliarium, pensionarium Hollandiae
et Frisiae Occidentalis, Casparem a Vosbergen, equitem, dominum de
Isselaer, Joannem a Reede, dominum de Renswoude et Thiens, dominum
de Woudenberch, Joannem Veltdriel, consulem urbis Doccum, Assuerum
ab Haersolte, Haerstii ac Echde, satrapam Zallandiae, Wigboldum Aldringa,
senatorem civitatis Groninganae, toparcham Sybaldebueri, respectivè deputatos in consessu alte-memoratorum Dominorum Statuum Generalium ex
Provinciis Geldriae, Hollandiae, Zelandiae, Ultrajecti, Frisiae, Trans Isula-
niae, ac Urbis Groningae atque Omlandiae, commissarios eorumdem
Dominorum Ordinum Generalium, nempe inter memoratum dominum
legatum, vigore certi rescripti regii, certarumque litterarum Serenissimae
Majestatis, utrumque de dato Lisbon xxi° Januarii jampridem elapsi, et
memoratos dominos commissarios, vigore eorundem procurationis, quorum
copiae, eorundemque translata respectivè hic infra inserentur.

---

[14] From the original manuscript of the Portuguese ratification preserved at the
Rijksarchief at the Hague, Secrete Casse, casse B, loquet R.
[16] In manuscript, P.

Experientia docuit quod Don Philippus Secundus, Castellae Rex, vi et
potentia armorum quondam invaserit coronam Lusitaniae, et consequenter
privaverit Serenissimum Praepotentemque Regem Don Joannem (olim
Ducem de Bragança) indubitabili suo successionis jure et justitia in alte-
memoratam coronam Lusitaniae, tanquam legitimum et proximum haeredem
Serenissimae Dominae D. Catarinae, ac continuarunt successores praedicti
Regis Castellae, multis contiguis annis, in violenta occupatione alte-memo-
ratae coronae Lusitaniae, infringentes foedera et pacta amicitiae, confi-
dentiae, et commercii, quae Domini Reges coronae Lusitaniae continue cum
aliis principibus ac nationibus in Europa sancte coluerant, deorbantes bonos
subditos et vassallos ejusdem coronae eorum juribus, legibus, et consuetudinibus, insuperque eos onerantes injustitia, intolerabilibus vexationibus, et
diversis aliis speciebus tyrannidis, injungentes illis excessiva onera, quae
Reges Castellae simulac cum patrimonio regiae coronae Lusitaniae dilapi-
darunt et consumpserunt evitabilibus bellis. Quibus praedicti boni subditi
et vassalli ejus coronae ita stimulati atque iracundia mactati, tandem, haud
levi habita patientia, magno cum animo, ausu, et circumspectione, injustum
illud ac intolerabile jugum Regis Castellae excusserunt, ac semetipsos
libertati restituerunt, demumque, communi applausu, saepius alte-memoratum
Joannem Quartum regem elegerunt, proclamarunt, eique homagium ac jus
jurandum fidelitatis praestiterunt. Praepotentes Domini Ordines Generales,
quoque passive pro comperto habentes intolerabilem tyrannidem et perdura
onera praefati Castellae Regis, pariterque ejusdem nefarium institutum ad
consequendam monarchiam multo saeculo jam super universa Europa
jactatam, in commodum boni publici dijudicarunt expedire laudabili ac
honesto jam alte-memorati Regis Joannis Quarti proposito succurrere, cumque
eodem inire et consummare praesens hoc pactum et tractatum; nec non
praetermittere varias et diversas commoditates, quas alias pro proprio par-
ticulari commodo atque utilitate, nacto hoc rerum statu, tam citra quam ultra
lineam possent usu capere et percipere, maluntque eorum loco, ut reviviscat
vetus illa amicitia, amor reciprocus, ac commercium, quae inter Dominos
Reges coronae Lusitaniae ac Belgas ultro citroque antiquitus floruerunt.

1. Primo, conclusum est verum, firmum, sincerum, ac inviolabile induciarum pactum cessationisque omnis hostilitatis actus inter alte-memoratum Regem et Ordines Generales, tam mari aliisque aquis quam terra,
intuitu omnium subditorum atque incolarum Unitarum Provinciarum,
cujuscumque conditionis illi fuerint, citra exceptionem locorum personarumve, ut et pariter intuitu omnium subditorum atque incolarum regionum
alte-memorati regis, cujuscunque conditionis fuerint, citra exceptionem
locorum personarumve quae partes Serenissimae Majestatis adversus Regem
Castellae tuentur, aut inposterum tueri reperientur, idque omnibus in locis
et maribus ab utraque parte lineae juxta conditiones et restrictiones hic
infra respective explicatas, tempore decennii. Quod induciarum pactum
cessationisque omnis hostilitatis actus in Europae plagis, ac alicunde sitis,
extra limites respective privilegiorum, societatibus Indiarum Orientalium
atque Occidentalium ante hac nomine hujus status respective concessorum,
statim facta substrictione hujus tractatus, ordietur.

.   .   .   .

8. Saepius dictae induciae ac cessatio omnis hostilitatis actus effectum
sortiantur tempore decennii in locis et maribus pertinentibus sub districtu
privilegii a Dominis Ordinibus Generalibus Societati Indiae Occidentalis

harum Provinciarum concessi, a dato cum ratihabitio super hoc tractatu
nomine Regis Lusitaniae hic loci fuerit oblata, et publica manifestatio praedictarum induciarum cessationisque omnis hostilitatis actus porro alicubi
praenominatorum locorum ac marium respective pervenerit, a quo tempore
utraque pars in istiusmodi locis et maribus respective sese cohibeat ab omni
hostilitatis actu. Ita tamen, ut intra [16] octo menses, postquam praedicta
ratihabitio hic loci fuerit allata, conveniendum sit cum corona Lusitaniae
de pace in saepius dictis locis et maribus, pertinentibus sub districtu privilegii
Societatis Indiae Occidentalis harum Provinciarum, ad quae Dominus Tristão
de Mendoça Furtado, legatus et consiliarius Regiae Majestatis Lusitaniae,
hisce pollicetur, ut intra praedictos octo menses post praefatam ratihabi-
tionem Regiae Serenissimae Majestatis hic loci oblatam, quoque obveniant
necessarium mandatum, ordo, ac instructio pariterque persona aut personae
autoritate regia munitae, ad tractandum de praedicta pace; attamen, si in
eventum contra omnem expectationem pacis conditio non iniretur, ut, eo
non obstante saepiusdictae [17] induciae cessatioque omnis hostilitatis actus,
tempore decennii, modo praemisso [18] et juxta articulos infra explicatos, plenum
effectum sortiantur.[19]

9. Societas Indiae Occidentalis harum Provinciarum, ut et subditi ac
incolae ejusdem terrarum acquisitarum, nec non omnes illi inde dependentes,
cujuscunque nationis, conditionis, aut religionis sint, gaudeant et fruantur
in singulis terris et locis Regis Lusitaniae, ac ad eandem coronam spectantibus,
in Europa sitis, hujusmodi commercio, exemptionibus, libertatibus, et juribus,
quibus reliqui subditi hujus status, vigore hujus tractatus, gaudebunt et
fruentur. Hac tamen conditione, ne Societas Indiae Occidentalis harum
Provinciarum, ut et subditi ac incolae in ejusdem terris acquisitis, sicut pariter
omnes reliqui ab illa dependentes conentur ex Brasilia transferre ad regnum
Lusitaniae saccharum, lignum Brasilicum ac alias merces in Brasilia existentes et provenientes; sicut pariter nec Lusitanica natio, ut et subditi ac
incolae in ejusdem terris acquisitis, nec minus ab ea dependentes, conabuntur
ex Brasilia transferre intra has Provincias et regiones saccharum, li[g]num
Brasilicum, aliasque merces in Brasilia existentes et provenientes.[20]

10. Natio Belgica ut et Lusitanica, durantibus induciis et cessatione omnis
hostilitatis actus, sibi invicem succurrent atque opem ferent, pro virili, cum
occasio et status rerum illud postulaverit.

11. Omnia fortalitia, urbes, naves et particulares personae, sive sint
Lusitani aut alii, in Brasilia vel aliorsum sita et reperti, qui partes Regis
Castellae fovent, aut postmodum in eorum potestatem redigentur, non
aliter respicientur ac reputabuntur quam communes hostes, quos adoriri,
prosequi, ac vincere cuilibet parti licitum sit, nullo habito respectu limitum.
Hoc attento, si qua alterutra pars ejusmodi loca aut fortalitia occuparet, illi
quoque cedat jurisdictionis et latorum camporum ambitus et reliqua emolu-
menta antiquitus his annexa, non obstante talia loca et fortalitia (ut supradictum est) in alterius limitum districtum sortiantur.

[16] In MS. *ultra.* [17] In MS. *saepius induciae dictae.* [18] In MS. *permisso.*
[19] A treaty of peace was not concluded until Aug. 6, 1661. Borges de Castro, *Collecção dos Tratados,* I. 260-293.
[20] In 1638 the Dutch West India Company threw open the Brazilian trade, except in
regard to slaves, munitions of war, and dye-wood, and permitted those Portuguese resident in Brazil to export their products into Holland. Netscher, *op. cit.,* pp. 93, 94.
The regulation is printed in E. Luzac, *Hollands Rijkdom* (1780-1783), II. 260-265.

12. Quilibet utriusque partis subditorum relinquetur ac remanebit in bonis suis uti illa tempore manifestationis induciarum et cessationis omnis hostilitatis actus tum deprehendentur, et lati campi inter utriusque partis extrema fortalitia siti (qui necessario inde intelligendi sunt pro acquisitis ac eorum dominio vindicatis) utrinque divisi exstabunt, sub his comprehendendo gentes et nationes sub iisdem sortientes; quibus finibus modo praemisso positis et statutis, Lusitanicae nationi ab illa, et subditis harum Provinciarum ab hac parte, constabit, quae loca, commoditates, et ambitus latorum camporum, quilibet pro suis agnoscat et tueatur.

13. Quod vero attinet particularium proprietates ac possessiones, quae sub praedicta divisione ad unam vel alteram partem pertinebunt, de his forsitan nonnulla loca exstabunt derelicta et populata, alia vero culta ac gente instructa. At vero quod spectat loca, quorum incolae et proprietarii sese ad hanc vel alteram partem recepisse deprehendentur, exinde nulla omnino restitutio fiet, neque illorum mobilium ibidem relictorum et repertorum, sed quilibet eo contentus vivat oportet, quod ex derelictis locis secum asportavit et abstulit.

14. Attamen in dictis locis et terris, quae suis proprietariis, aut aliis possessoribus eorum nomine et parte remanserunt, illis utrinque cognita causa, jus suum et possessio asservabitur, visis prius eorum necessariis documentis et probationibus.

15. Super quibus utriusque partis regimen in suo cujusque districtu respective disponat, pro ut videbitur convenire, non concesso, ut alius quispiam his sese immisceat.

16. Commercia ad utriusque partis ditiones, tractus, et ambitus locorum in Brasilia,[21] quaelibet sibi ipsis relinquantur, exclusis omnibus aliis, nec ipsis Lusitanis fas esto hujus status, neve subditis hujus status Lusitanorum ditiones, tractus, et ambitus locorum frequentare, nisi communi voluntate et consensu postmodum aliud visum fuerit convenire.

17. Ne permissum sit Lusitanis in Brasiliam navigare, commercari, aut mercaturam exercere cum navibus alienae nationis, aut cum ipsissimis nationibus extraneis, sed indigentes aliquibus extraneis navibus ad navigationem, mercaturam, et commercium in Brasiliam tenebuntur illi tales conducere, aut emere a subditis harum Provinciarum,[22] quo casu emptionis vel conductionis, nullae minores naves in Brasiliam aptentur ac impendantur quam centum et triginta onerum, aut ducentorum et sexaginta vasorum, munitae ad minimum sedecim tormentis (alias Gotelingem) vibrantibus singulatim quinque aut sex libras ferri respective, munitioneque belli provisae secundum proportionem, et quando majores naves a Lusitanis in Brasiliam conducentur atque ementur, ac deinceps applicabuntur, ut supra, tum illae

---

[21] The English were alarmed at the retention by the Dutch of direct trade with Brazil, while they themselves were obliged to "fetch the compass". V. M. Shillington and A. B. Wallis Chapman, *The Commercial Relations of England and Portugal*, p. 181.

[22] Upon learning of the foregoing clause, the English regarded it as so prejudicial to their own merchants that they suspended the negotiations then in progress for a treaty between England and Portugal. See *Cal. St. Pap., Dom.*, 1641-1643, pp. 37, 40, 47, 49; and especially the letter from Philip Burlamachi to Sommelsdyck in G. Groen van Prinsterer, *Archives*, 2d sér., III. 481, 482. When the treaty was finally concluded, on Jan. 29, 1642, it was provided (art. 16) that within two years both parties should appoint and send commissioners or ambassadors to treat and agree "concerning freighting of the ships of the subjects of the Most Renowned King of Great Britain by the Portugals, for their commerce and navigation into Brazil". *British and Foreign State Papers*, vol. I., pt. I., p. 478.

secundum proportionem onerum tanto plus muniantur et provideantur, et hoc omne sub poena amissionis et confiscationis praedictarum navium una cum earum requisitis, quae alias, ut antea, cedant commodo Societatis Indiae Occidentalis, harum Provinciarum, aut vero eorum, qui ab ea dependent vel appendent, si qua illae ab his forte deprehenderentur et caperentur.

18. Neque Lusitanis neque incolis harum Provinciarum liceat ullam navium, nigrorum, mercium, aliorumve necessariorum vecturam praestare Indiis Castellanorum aliisque locis ab eorumdem parte stantibus sub poena amittendae navis et bonorum, pariterque personae quae in ibi reperientur ut hostes apprehendentur et tractabuntur.[23]

19. Illud, quidquid tam Lusitani quam subditi harum Provinciarum in oris Africae possident, nulla indiget limitum divisione, cum inter utrumque diversae gentes et nationes sortiantur, quae finium limites statuunt et dividunt.

20. Quod vero attinet negotiationem et frequentationem earundem orarum, Insulae S. Thomae, aliarumque insularum, hisce comprehensarum, ea utriique libera sit; hac tamen conditione, si eadem navigatio et commercium, sive illud sit auri, nigrorum, aliarumque mercium, quomodolibet illa nuncupanda veniunt, fiat, et destinata sint in vel circa urbes et fortalitia quae forte alteruter occupat et possidet, ut inde pendantur eadem vectigalia et jura quibus consueverunt incolae Lusitani ac eorundem locorum liberi homines exsolvere, et viceversa.[24]

21. Et quia Ordines Generales sua dominia et terras in Brasilia aliisque locis propria virtute acquisiverint eo tempore quo eorum subditi atque incolae ad huc exstarent vassalli et subjecti Regis Castellae et hujus status hostes, cujusmodi naturae et sortis illi fuerunt qui modo ibidem ad obsequium Regis Lusitaniae redierunt, amicosque et foederatos huic statui sese dederunt, ex

[23] The King of Spain also forbade his subjects to trade with the Portuguese. Throughout the decade the Spanish Indies suffered from the interruption of the slave-trade. In 1642 two British merchants offered to supply them with negroes, but the proposal was rejected. G. Scelle, *La Traite Négrière*, I. 482 ff.
[24] In regard to the African trade the Portuguese agreed with the English, by the treaty of Jan. 29, 1642, as follows (Art. 13): "And because the commerce and free coming of the subjects of the King of Great Britain to the coasts and parts of Africa, the island of St. Thomas and other islands comprehended under them, could not yet be agreed on by reason of the defect of the powers sent by the Most Renowned King of Portugal to his ambassadors, that by this debate this present treaty of peace and amity between both kings and their subjects be not delayed, it is on both parts concluded on, that in the lands, places, castles, ports, and coasts of Africa. Guinea, Binc, etc., the island of St. Thomas and other islands comprehended under them, wherein it shall appear that the subjects of Great Britain have dwelt for trade of merchandise, or have had trade or commerce there in the time of the Kings of Castile, or hitherto, there shall be no alteration or change, neither shall they have any trouble or injury done them by the Portugals for that cause. And if any customs be to be demanded from the subjects of the King of Great Britain, on any cause, in the castles, islands, and places aforesaid, they shall not be greater or more grievous than those which shall be demanded from other nations in league with the King of Portugal; and the subjects of the King of Portugal wanting foreign ships for their navigation and commerce to the coasts and islands aforesaid, may freely, at their own pleasure, hire the ships of the subjects of the King of Great Britain: and that commissioners and ambassadors shall be named by both kings, who shall treat and conclude concerning the commerce and free coming to the coasts, islands, and places aforesaid, which hath been demanded by the commissioners of the King of Great Britain, for the subjects of their king; being persuaded, out of the confidence of the ancient amity which hath been between the predecessors of the same kings, that the most renowned King of Portugal will grant to no nation more ample rights, immunities, and privileges, than he will grant unto the subjects of the King of Great Britain." *British and Foreign State Papers, loc. cit.*, pp. 477, 478.

quo in futurum utrinque durabile foedus et sincera confidentia patet, simul ac alter alteri inposterum justa praestandae justitiae administratione rite tenebitur.

22. Ita vero comparatum est, ut cum, mutatione quae in multifariis proprietatibus et possessionibus mobilium atque immobilium bonorum extitit (solummodo per calamitatem molesti belli), diversi modi subditi sub et post initium ad obsequium hujus status harum Provinciarum devenerint, quorum pars ad incitas redacta, pars diffusa sunt; ac cum plurimi Belgae ibidem per emptionem dominiorum, vulgo nuncupatorum *ingenhos*, aliorumque bonorum immobilium, sedem fixerint, ratio status rerum inibi acquisitarum nullo modo ferre potest, ut ulla bona, jure postliminii vel quasi, repetantur aut revertantur, neque ut subditi Dominorum Ordinum Generalium a Lusitanis, neque Lusitani ab subditis harum Provinciarum ulla debita aliave onera exigant, multominus ut talia consequantur, conveniat executionis via uti, sed quilibet salvus remanebit, uti possidet tempore dictae manifestationis.

23. Subditi atque incolae ditionum altememorati Regis Joannis Quarti et Dominorum Ordinum respective, durantibus decennii induciis et cessatione omnis hostilitatis actus, mutua confidentia amicitiam colent sine ulla recordatione offensionum et damnorum, quae olim perpessi sunt.

24. Et si forte postmodum, unanimi ac mutuo consensu, sedes belli in India Occidentali Castilianorum transferretur, atque incenso bello ibidem quidquam ad detrimentum communis hostis acquiriretur, tum illud distribuendo, permutando, et fruendo amice et communi consensu, ut praemissum est, conveniendum erit, sicut pariter durantibus saepe memoratis induciis et cessatione omnis hostilitatis actus, permissum esto utriusque partis communi consensu atque applausu praedictos articulos, aut partem eorum immutare.

25. Et liberum esto utriusque partis subditos, cujuscunque nationis, conditionis, qualitatis, et religionis, nullis exceptis (sive illi in alterutrius ditione nati sint, sive inibi habitasse dicantur) frequentare, navigare, et commercari qualibet mercium et mercaturae sorte in regnis, provinciis, territoriis, et insulis respective in Europa atque aliorsum ab hac lineae parte sitis.[29] Nec fas esto neutrius subditos mercandi gratia confluentes in alterius terris, sitis ut supra, in mercibus asportandis, aut vero exportandis magis aggravare gabellis, impositionibus, aliisve juribus, quam ipsissimos incolas et subditos earundem terrarum, sed gaudeant pariter respective hujusmodi indultis et privilegiis, quibus antehac illi usi sunt, priusquam Lusitania Castilianis fuerit subacta.

26. Subditi ac incolae harum Provinciarum qui Christiani sunt, in omnibus locis, urbibus, et territoriis etiamque provinciis ac insulis regni Lusitaniae aut ab eo appendentibus et dependentibus, sive illud sit ab utraque parte lineae, tam in Europa quam extra, ubi frequentandi locus datur, utentur et fruentur libertate conscientiae in domubus suis privatis, ac intra naves libera religionis exercitio; si vero legatus aut alius publicus hujus status minister in Lusitaniam forte mitteretur, tum illi respective utentur et fruentur in aedibus suis et domiciliis hujusmodi libertate ac religionis exercitio, sicuti in hoc statu praesenti domino legato Lusitaniae permittitur.

[29] This provision did not affect Brazil, where all the captaincies lay to the south of the equator; nor did it alter the commercial status of New Netherland, since in 1638 the Amsterdam Chamber had opened the trade of that colony to "all inhabitants of the United Provinces and of friendly countries". J. B. Brodhead, *History of the State of New York*, I. 288.

27. Domini Ordines Generales, non expectata Serenissimae Majestatis ratihabitione ad hunc tractatum, proprio suo sumptu adsistent regi ac coronae Lusitaniae sub idoneo archithalasso, aliisque necessariis suis officiariis, quindecim navibus bellicis et quinque scaphis majoribus, bene munitis ac instructis, provisis de victu, etiamque tormentis ac aliis munitionibus belli.[26]

28. Ad hanc classem altememoratus Rex comparabit aut conducet Serenissimae Majestatis, propriis sumptibus, et sub ejusdem proprio directorio, similem numerum quindecim navium bellicarum et quinque scapharum majorum, aeque bene munitarum, instructarum nautis et militibus, etiam provisarum de victu, tormentis, et aliis belli munitionibus, ut conjunctim una cum navibus et scaphis majoribus harum Provinciarum impendantur ad littora atque oras Lusitaniae et Hispaniae respective, ad detrimentum Regis Castellae communis hostis.

29. Rex Lusitaniae propriis suis expensis instruat decem aut plures galeones in Lusitania, easque adjungat supradictae classi, ut conjunctim impendantur adversus Castellae Regem ejusque subditos.

. . . .

31. Praedarum aliorumque emolumentorum virtute praedictae classis et galeonum acquisitorum, erit partitio et distributio pro rata, juxta numerum corporum navium, idque ad praeveniendum ac evitandum disputandi diversitatem, quae alias ex divisione praedarum aliorumque bonorum, aut horum occasione ob certos respectus resultaret.

. . . .

35. Hic tractatus confirmabitur et ratihabebitur per Regem Lusitaniae et Dominos Ordines Generales respective in solita atque optima forma, uti par est, infra tres [27] menses, incipientes a dato hujus, et praestabitur idem ab utraque parte candide ac sincere, et deinceps, quando Serenissimae Majestatis ratihabitio hic Hagae intra praedictum tempus fuerit oblata, tum eadem cum altememoratorum Dominorum Ordinum Generalium ratihabitione mutabitur et transsumetur.

[Here follow the full powers granted by the King of Portugal to his ambassador on January 6, 1641, and by the States General to their ambassadors on June 9, 1641 ; also a letter from the King of Portugal to the States General, dated January 6, 1641.]

Et nos, legatus ac commissarii praedicti, hunc tractatum propriis nostris manibus subsignavimus, eundemque nostris signetis munivimus.

Actum Hagae Comitis die duodecima Junii, anno millesimo sexcentesimo quadragesimo primo. Tristão de Mendoça Furtado. Ruthger Huÿghens. J. van Brouchoven. Cats. J.[28] Van Vosberghen. Joan van Reede. J. Van Veltdriel. J.[28] van Haersolte. Wigbo[l]t Aldringa.

Proinde nos, praefatum tractatum induciarum, cessationisque omnis hostilitatis actus pariterque succursus pro tempore, acceptum ferentes, eundem

---

[26] The Dutch fleet, under Admiral Gijsels, reached Lisbon in the autumn of 1641 and returned to the Provinces in January of the following year, having failed to intercept the West Indian fleet or to gain any glory from a combat with a Spanish squadron near Cape St. Vincent. On account of the ill-feeling that soon arose between the Dutch and Portuguese, the fleet was not sent again to Lisbon. Arend, *op. cit.*, III. (5), 313, 334, 372, 373 ; Aitzema, *op. cit.*, II. 831 ; C. Fernández Duro, *Armada Española*, IV. 269-273.

[27] In MS. *ter.*   [28] *Sic.*

acceptavimus, approbavimus, ratihabuimus, et confirmavimus, sicut eundem
acceptamus, approbamus, ratihabemus, et confirmamus per praesentes litteras,
spondentes nos omnia inviolabiliter observaturos, servaturos, et impleturos;
neve admissuros ut ullo modo quomodolibet id accidat, aut accidere poterit,
per directum vel indirectum, huic fiat contradictio aut contrarium, sub
hypotheca atque obligatione omnium bonarum et proventuum, generalium et
specialium, praesentium et futurorum, nostrorum regnorum, statuum, et
regiae coronae, tantumodo declarantis quod ad certiorem ac promptiorem
executionem illius quod in articulo 26 continetur circa exercitionem religionis,
quae a subditis et incolis dictarum Provinciarum Unitarum profitetur, cum
sit materia quae sub regia jurisdictione saeculari, qua utimur, non compre-
hendetur, recursum faciemus ad Sanctissimum Patrem Urbanum papam
Octavum, ut cum approbatione et consensu ejusdem stabiliatur et confirmetur;
et interea subditi et incolae dictarum Provinciarum Unitarum in omnibus
regnis, statibus, et dominiis nostris, tanta fruentur benevolentia et favore, ut
ex dicta causa conscientiae et religionis omnimodo non molestentur, vel
inquietentur, ubi scandalum non dederint. Ad quorum firmitatem et stabili-
tatem praesentes litteras aparari jussimus, nostra propria manu inscriptas,
et majori sigillo regii nostri stemmatis roboratas. Datae fuerunt Olisippone
die duodecima (*sic*) octava Novembris. Joannes Suarez de Brito fecit, anno
nativitatis Dominicae millesimo sexcentesimo quadragesimo primo. Et
ego, Franciscus de Lucena, Sacrae Regiae Magestatis a consiliis atque status
secretarius inscribere feci.

EL REY.

TRANSLATION.

John, by the grace of God king of Portugal and of the Algarves on this
side and beyond the sea in Africa, lord of Guinea, and of the conquest, navigation, and commerce of Ethiopia, Arabia, Persia, and India, etc. Be it
known to all who shall see and inspect our present letters patent of approval,
ratification, and confirmation, that on the twelfth day of the past month of
June, of the present year, 1641, at the Hague in Holland, a treaty of truce
and suspension of all hostilities, as well as of navigation and commerce, for
ten years, and likewise of aid for that time, was made, entered into, and concluded between Tristão de Mendoça Furtado, our councillor, ambassador, and
representative appointed on the one side, and, on the other side, the distinguished and illustrious Rutger Huyghens, J. van Brouchoven, [J.] Cats,
Gaspar van Vosbergen, Johan van Reede, J. van Veltdriel, van Haersolte, and
Wigbold Aldringa, deputy commissioners of the High and Mighty States
General of the United Provinces of the Netherlands, by virtue of their
powers. The tenor of this treaty, word for word, is as follows:

Treaty of truce and suspension of all hostilities, as well as of navigation,
commerce, and likewise of aid, between the Most Serene and Very Powerful
Dom John, the fourth of his name, king of Portugal, of the Algarve on this
side of the sea and beyond the sea in Africa, lord of Guinea and of the conquests, navigation, and commerce in Ethiopia, Arabia, Persia, and India,
etc., on the one part, and the Lords States General of the United Provinces
on the other part, made, entered into, and concluded by Dom Tristão de
Mendoça Furtado, ambassador and councillor of his Most Serene Majesty,

and by the lords Rutger Huyghens, knight, Jacob van Broekhoven, ex-burgomaster of the city of Leyden, Jacob Cats, knight, councillor-pensionary [Raadpensionaris] of Holland and West Friesland, Gaspar van Vosbergen, knight, lord of Issellaer, Johan van Reede, lord of Renswoude and Thiens, lord of Woudenberg, Johan Veltdriel, burgomaster of the city of Dokkum, Zweder van Haersolte, lord of Haerst and Echde, governor of Salland, Wigbold Aldringa, deputy from the state of Groningen, administrator of Sijbrandaburen, respectively deputies in the assembly of the aforesaid Lords the States General of the provinces of Gelderland, Holland, Zeeland, Utrecht, Friesland, Overyssel, and of the city of Groningen and of the Ommeland, commissioners of the said Lords the States General, [which treaty] was concluded between the aforesaid lord ambassador, by virtue of a certain royal rescript, and of certain letters-patent of his Most Serene Majesty, both dated in Lisbon on the 21 of January last past, and the aforesaid lords commissioners, by virtue of their powers, copies of which and their translations are, respectively, hereinafter inserted.

It is well known that formerly Don Philip Second, king of Castile, forcibly and by might of arms usurped the crown of Portugal and thereby deprived the Most Serene and Very Powerful King Dom John (formerly Duke of Braganza), of his undoubted right and just claim to succeed to the said crown of Portugal as lawful and next heir of the Most Serene Lady Dona Catharine. The successors of the aforesaid King of Castile, moreover, continued for many consecutive years in forcible occupation of the aforesaid crown of Portugal, breaking the treaties and agreements of amity, trust, and commerce, which the lord kings of the crown of Portugal had always religiously observed with the other princes and nations in Europe; depriving the good subjects and vassals of this crown of their rights, laws, and customs, besides oppressing them with injustice, intolerable annoyances, and tyranny of various kinds, and imposing excessive taxes upon them, which, together with the patrimony of the royal crown of Portugal, the kings of Castile squandered and consumed in avoidable wars. Having been thus tormented and wrathfully immolated, and having exercised no little patience, the aforesaid good subjects and vassals of this crown at length with great courage, enterprise, and foresight, shook off that unjust and intolerable yoke of the King of Castile, and restored themselves to freedom; and finally, by general consent, they chose and proclaimed king the aforesaid John IV., and rendered him homage and took the oath of fealty. Their High Mightinesses, the Lords States General, having also known by experience the intolerable tyranny and great oppression of the aforesaid King of Castile, and likewise his abominable purpose to attain to that monarchy which for many years he has boasted to have over all Europe, have deemed it in accordance with the public good to aid the praiseworthy and honorable purpose of the aforesaid King John IV., and to enter into and conclude with him the present agreement and treaty, and to overlook many and divers opportunities which, in the present state of affairs, they might otherwise seize and turn to their own particular profit and use, both on this side of and beyond the line, and in place of these they prefer that the old amity, reciprocal friendship, and trade, which of old flourished mutually between the kings of the crown of Portugal and the Netherlands shall be revived.

1. First, there is concluded between the aforesaid king and the States General for the space of ten years a true, firm, sincere, and inviolable truce

and suspension of all acts of hostility, both by sea and other waters and by land, in respect to all the subjects and inhabitants of the United Provinces, of whatever condition they may be, without exception of places or persons ; likewise in respect to all the subjects and inhabitants of the territories of the aforesaid king, of whatever condition they may be, without exception of any places or persons, who now uphold, or in future shall be found to uphold, the party of his Most Serene Sacred Majesty against the King of Castile ; and this [truce shall be observed] in all the places and seas on both sides of the line, in conformity with the conditions and restrictions hereafter respectively set forth. This compact of truce and suspension of all hostilities shall go into effect immediately after the conclusion of this treaty, in the countries of Europe, and in those lying elsewhere, outside the limits of the charters previously granted in the name of this state to the East India and West India companies, respectively.

·   ·   ·   ·   ·   ·   ·   ·   ·   ·   ·   ·

8. In the lands and seas pertaining to the district of the charter granted by the Lords States General to the West India Company of these Provinces, the aforementioned truce and suspension of all hostilities shall have effect for a period of ten years from the date when the ratification of this treaty, in the name of the King of Portugal, shall be brought to this place, and the public notification of the aforesaid truce and suspension of all hostilities shall moreover have arrived at any of the aforementioned places and seas respectively. From that time both parties shall abstain from all acts of hostility in the said places and seas respectively ; provided that within eight months after the aforesaid ratification shall have been presented in this place, an agreement shall be made with the crown of Portugal concerning peace in the aforementioned places and seas comprehended within the district of the charter of the West India Company of these Provinces. To this end Dom Tristão de Mendoça Furtado, ambassador and councillor of His Royal Majesty of Portugal, promises by these presents, that within the aforesaid eight months after the aforesaid ratification of his Most Serene Royal Majesty has been presented here, the necessary power, order, and instruction shall come to treat of the aforesaid peace as well as a person or persons empowered by royal authority ; and that if, contrary to all expectation, peace is not concluded, the aforesaid truce and suspension of all hostilities shall nevertheless have their full effect for the space of ten years, in the manner aforesaid and according to the articles set forth below.

9. The West India Company of these Provinces, as well as the subjects and inhabitants of its acquired lands, likewise all of its dependents, of whatever nation, condition, or religion they may be, shall have and enjoy in all the lands and places of the King of Portugal, and in those pertaining to that crown, situated in Europe, the same [rights of] commerce, exemptions, liberties, and rights, that the rest of the subjects of this state shall have and enjoy, by virtue of this treaty ; under this condition, however, that the West India Company of these Provinces, as well as the subjects and inhabitants in its acquired lands, likewise all the rest of its dependents, shall not attempt to bring from Brazil to the kingdom of Portugal, sugar, brazil-wood, or other commodities existing in and coming from Brazil ; nor, similarly, shall the Portuguese nation, or the subjects and inhabitants of its acquired lands, or its dependents, attempt to bring from Brazil to these Provinces

and regions, sugar, brazil-wood or other commodities existing in or coming from Brazil.

10. During the truce and suspension of all hostilities the Dutch and Portuguese nations shall mutually aid and assist each other, according to their ability, when occasion and the state of affairs shall demand it.

11. All the fortresses, cities, ships, and individuals, whether Portuguese or of other nationality, situated and found in Brazil or elsewhere, that favor the party of the King of Castile, or that shall, in future, be brought under its control, shall be held and reputed not otherwise than as common enemies, whom each party shall be permitted to attack, pursue, and overcome, without regard to limits. [This shall be] with this understanding, that if either of the two parties shall occupy any of the said places or fortresses, that party shall likewise acquire all the extent of the jurisdiction and open territory of that place or fortress, and the emoluments anciently annexed to it, notwithstanding that such places and fortresses (as is aforesaid) are within the district of the limits of the other party.

12. All the subjects of both parties shall be left and shall remain in possession of their own goods just as they have them at the time of the notification of the truce and suspension of all hostilities; and the open districts lying between the furthest fortified places of each party (which therefore are necessarily to be understood as acquired and subject to their dominion), together with the tribes and nations dwelling in them, shall be divided between the two parties. These limits having been fixed and determined, in the aforesaid manner, the Portuguese nation, on the one hand, and the subjects of these Provinces, on the other hand, shall agree what places, commodities, and extent of the open country, each shall acknowledge and defend as his own.

13. As to that which relates to the goods and possessions of individual persons which by the aforesaid division shall pertain to one or the other party, some of these places will, perhaps, be abandoned and despoiled, and others cultivated and peopled. But as to the places whose inhabitants and proprietors shall be found to have passed to one or the other side, no restitution at all shall be made thereafter, nor shall any restitution be made of the movable property left and found there, but each one shall have to content himself with that which he has carried off and taken away from the abandoned places.

14. Nevertheless in the said places and lands which have remained to their proprietors, or to other possessors holding in their name and on their behalf, their right and possession shall be preserved to both parties when the case has been investigated, and after the necessary documents and proofs have been examined.

15. In respect to these, the government of both parties, shall, respectively, dispose in their own districts, as shall seem most fitting, and neither party shall be permitted to interfere with the other.

16. Each party shall have exclusive trade to its dominions, districts, and regions in Brazil; nor shall the Portuguese be permitted to frequent the dominions of this state, nor shall the subjects of this state frequent the dominions of the Portuguese, unless hereafter, by common agreement and consent, some other provision should be found convenient.

17. The Portuguese shall not be permitted to sail to Brazil or trade or traffic in that province, with ships of a foreign nation or with foreign nations themselves, but if they need any foreign ships for navigating, trading

and trafficking to Brazil, they shall be obliged to hire or buy them from the subjects of these Provinces. In this case (of buying or hiring) no smaller ships shall be equipped and employed to Brazil, than those of 130 lasts or 260 tons, protected by at least sixteen cannon (otherwise called *Gotelingen* [pedereros]), each shooting iron balls of 5 or 6 pounds, respectively, and provided with munitions of war in proportion. And if greater ships shall be hired or bought by the Portuguese for Brazil, and afterwards employed as above, they shall be defended and provided with more, in proportion to their lasts. All this shall be done under penalty of the loss and confiscation of the aforesaid ships together with their armament, which if different from the above, shall go to the use of the West India Company of these Provinces, or of its dependents, if they should happen to surprise or seize any of them.

18. Neither the Portuguese nor the inhabitants of these Provinces shall be permitted to take any ships, negroes, merchandise, or other necessities, to the Indies of the Castilians, or to other places which side with them, under penalty of losing the ship and goods. Likewise, the persons found on board shall be seized and treated as enemies.

19. All that which the Portuguese and the subjects of these Provinces possess on the coasts of Africa needs no delimitation, since there are various peoples and nations between them who determine and form the limits.

20. As to what pertains to the navigation and frequenting of the said coasts and of the island of St. Thomas and other islands comprehended with them, it shall be free to both nations; but on this condition, that the said navigation and commerce, whether of gold, negroes, or other commodities, by whatever name they are called, shall be made and [the goods] directed to or near to the towns and forts which either nation happens to occupy and possess, in order that the same tolls and customs may be paid there as the Portuguese residents and the free men of these places are accustomed to pay; and vice versa.

21. And inasmuch as the States General have acquired by their own valor their dominions and lands in Brazil and other places, at a time when the subjects and inhabitants of these places were still vassals and subjects of the King of Castile and enemies of this state, which was the nature and condition of those who now, in the same place, have returned to the obedience of the King of Portugal, and have associated themselves to this State as friends and allies, whereby in the future a way will be open for a durable alliance and sincere correspondence on both sides, and at the same time each will henceforth be solemnly bound to treat the other with equitably administered justice:

22. Therefore, it has been agreed that since, through the alteration that has taken place in many properties and possessions of both movable and immovable goods (occasioned only by the misfortunes of this grievous war), various subjects, at and after its beginning, have passed to the obedience of this state of these Provinces, of whom a part were reduced to extremity and a part were dispersed; and since a great number of Dutchmen, by purchase of estates, commonly called *ingenhos*, and of other immovable goods, have fixed their residence there, a regard for the [actual] status of property there acquired will nowise permit that any goods should be demanded back or restored under right or quasi-right of postliminy; nor that the subjects of the Lords States General should exact from the Portuguese, nor the Portuguese from the subjects of these provinces, any debts or other charges, much less may it be proper for them to press for such things by means of judicial

prosecution; but each shall remain secure in the possession of that which he has at the time of the said notification.

23. During the ten years' truce and suspension of all hostilities, the subjects and inhabitants of the dominions of the aforesaid King John IV. and those of the Lords States General, respectively, will cultivate friendship, with mutual confidence, forgetting the offenses and damages which they have formerly suffered.

24. And if, in future, by mutual common consent, the seat of war shall be transferred to the West Indies of the Castilians, and, after the outbreak of the war there, any conquests shall be made to the detriment of the common enemy, in that case, it shall be agreed to distribute, exchange, and enjoy them amicably, and with common consent, as is aforesaid; as, likewise, during the abovementioned truce and suspension of hostilities, it shall be permitted, with the common consent and approval of both parties, to alter the aforesaid articles or a part of them.

25. The subjects of both parties, of whatever nation, condition, quality, or religion they may be, without any exception (whether said to have been born in or to have dwelt in the jurisdiction of either of the two), may freely visit, sail to, and trade with any kind of wares and merchandise in, the kingdoms, provinces, lands, and islands respectively, situated in Europe or elsewhere on this side of the line. It shall not be permitted that the subjects of either power who, for the sake of trading, resort to the lands of the other, situated as aforesaid, be burdened, in importing or exporting merchandise, with greater excise duties, imposts, or other taxes than the inhabitants and subjects of the said lands; but they shall, respectively, equally enjoy such favors and privileges, as they previously exercised, before Portugal was subjected to the Castilians.

26. The subjects and inhabitants of these Provinces, who are Christians, in all the places, cities, and territories, as well as in the provinces and islands, of the kingdom of Portugal, or in its dependencies, whether on this or on the other side of the Line, both in Europe and outside it, wherever they are permitted to go, shall have and enjoy liberty of conscience in their private houses, and free exercise of religion on board their ships; and if any ambassador or other public minister of this state shall happen to be sent to Portugal, they shall, in such case, respectively have and enjoy, in their houses and domiciles, such liberty and exercise of religion as is permitted in this state to the present lord ambassador of Portugal.

27. The Lords States General, without waiting for his Most Serene Majesty's ratification to this treaty, will, at their own expense, assist the king and crown of Portugal with fifteen ships of war and five frigates, under a suitable admiral and the other necessary officers, well armed and equipped, and provided with victuals, cannon, and other munitions of war.

28. For this fleet the aforesaid king will buy or hire at his Most Serene Majesty's own expense, and under his own command, the same number of fifteen ships of war and five frigates, equally well armed and equipped with sailors and soldiers, and provided with victuals, cannon, and other munitions of war, so that jointly with the ships and frigates of these Provinces they may be employed upon the coasts and shores of Portugal and Spain respectively, to the injury of the King of Castile, the common enemy.

29. The King of Portugal shall, at his own expense, equip in Portugal ten or more galleons, and shall add them to the aforesaid fleet in order that they may be employed jointly against the King of Castile and his subjects.

31. The prizes and other perquisites taken by the aforesaid fleet and galleons shall be divided and distributed *pro rata,* according to the number of the hulks of the ships, in order to prevent and avoid various disputes which otherwise, for various reasons, might result from the division of the prizes and other goods, or because of them.

. . . .

35. This treaty shall be confirmed and ratified by the King of Portugal and the Lords States General respectively, in the accustomed and best form, as is fit, within three months beginning from the date of this treaty. The treaty shall be fulfilled by each party candidly and sincerely ; and when the ratification of his Most Serene Majesty shall, within the aforesaid time, have been presented here at the Hague, the same shall be exchanged with, and taken over for, the ratification of the aforesaid Lords States General.

[Here follow the full powers granted by the King of Portugal to his ambassador on January 6, 1641, and by the States General to their ambassadors on June 9, 1641 ; also a letter from the King of Portugal to the States General, dated January 6, 1641.]

And we, the ambassador and commissioners aforesaid, have signed this treaty with our own hands, and sealed it with our own seals.

Done at the Hague on the twelfth day of June, in the year 1641.

Tristão de Mendoça Furtado. Rutger Huygens. J. van Brouchoven. Cats. J. van Vosbergen. Johan van Reede. J. van Veltdriel. J. van Haersolte. Wigbolt Aldringa.

Therefore we, declaring accepted the aforesaid treaty of truce and suspension of all hostilities, and likewise of temporary aid, have accepted, approved, ratified, and confirmed the same, as we now accept, approve, ratify, and confirm it by these present letters, solemnly promising that we will inviolably observe, guard, and fulfill everything ; and will not permit in any way whatever that may or might happen, that it shall be contravened or opposed directly or indirectly, under pledge and obligation of all goods and issues, general and special, present and future, of our kingdoms, states, and royal crown, only declaring that for the more certain and prompt execution of that which is set forth in article 26 concerning the exercise of religion, which is promised for the subjects and inhabitants of the said United Provinces, since this is a matter which is not comprehended under the royal secular jurisdiction that we enjoy, we shall have recourse to the most Holy Father, Pope Urban VIII., in order that it may be established and confirmed with his approval and consent; and meanwhile the subjects and inhabitants of the said United Provinces, in all our kingdoms, states, and dominions, shall enjoy such good-will and favor that they shall not be troubled or disturbed at all for the said cause of conscience and religion, where they occasion no scandal. For the confirmation and establishment whereof, we have ordered the present letters to be prepared, and they have been inscribed by our hand, and confirmed by the greater seal of our royal house. Given at Lisbon, on the eighteenth of November, in the year of the Lord's nativity 1641. Made by João Suarez de Brito. And I, Francisco de Lucena, member of his Sacred Royal Majesty's councils, and secretary of state, have caused them to be inscribed.

THE KING.

39.

Agreement concluded between the Governor of Massachusetts and the Commissioner of the Governor of Acadia, at Boston, October 8, 1644. Ratification by the Commissioners of the United Colonies, September 2, 1645. [Ratification by D'Aulnay, September 28, 1646.]

INTRODUCTION.

The treaty of St. Germain,[1] which restored Canada and Acadia to France, did not define the boundaries of those regions. The French government, however, appears to have ordered the newly appointed governor of Acadia, the Commandeur De Razilly, to clear the coast of the English as far as Pemaquid.[2] In accordance with this alleged order, in 1633, one of De Razilly's lieutenants, La Tour, "displanted" the English from their "trading house" at Machias;[3] and in 1635 De Razilly's other lieutenant, D'Aulnay, seized the fortified trading post at Penobscot[4] (Pentagoet), which in 1630, two years after it was captured from the French by Kirke,[5] had been taken over by the Plymouth colonists.[6]

The Plymouth colony, planning to recover Penobscot by force of arms, desired help from Massachusetts.[7] Though at first inclined to co-operate, Massachusetts ultimately refused. Governor Winthrop was anxious to avoid difficulties with the French government, partly, no doubt, lest these should lead to interference by England in the management of New England's relations with the adjacent settlements of the French and Dutch. Such interference had, indeed, been recently threatened.[8] But although Winthrop

[1] Doc. **36**.
[2] Mass. Hist. Soc., *Collections*, 3d ser., VII. 94; *Winthrop's Journal* (ed. Hosmer), I. 157, 201.
[3] *Winthrop's Journal* (ed. cit.), I. 113: Bradford, *History of Plymouth Plantation* (ed. Mass. Hist. Soc., II. 133, and note; ed. Davis, p. 284).
[4] Bradford, *op. cit.* (ed. Mass. Hist. Soc., II. 206, 207; ed. Davis, p. 318) ; Winthrop, *ed. cit.*, I. 157.
[5] *Report on Canadian Archives*, 1894 (ed. Brymner), p. ix; N. Denys, *Description and Natural History of the Coasts of North America* (ed. W. F. Ganong, for the Champlain Soc., 1908), p. 98.
[6] Bradford, *op. cit.* (ed. Mass. Hist. Soc., II. 80-87; ed. Davis, pp. 254-259).
[7] Bradford, *op. cit.* (ed. Mass. Hist. Soc., II. 211-214, and notes; ed. Davis, pp. 320-321) ; Winthrop, *ed. cit.*, I. 159.
[8] By the "Commission for Regulating Plantations", 1634, the commissioners were empowered to make laws and ordinances concerning the demeanor of the colonies "towards foreign princes and their people". Bradford, *op. cit.* (ed. Mass. Hist. Soc., II. 184; ed. Davis, p. 416).

would not openly attack D'Aulnay, now settled at Penobscot, he regarded him as a dangerous neighbor and was inclined to favor La Tour, with whom the Boston merchants traded.' After the death of De Razilly in 1635, strife had broken out between his two lieutenants. La Tour, whose tenure of land and office in Acadia antedated D'Aulnay's, maintained that the latter had dispossessed him; moreover they were rivals in the fur trade.[10] In vain did the King of France try to end the contention by dividing Acadia between them, giving D'Aulnay jurisdiction over the coast of the Etchemins from the St. John River toward the Virginias.[11] Between 1641 and 1643 La Tour made three attempts to form an alliance with Massachusetts Bay, stipulating liberty of commerce and assistance against D'Aulnay. The Massachusetts magistrates were willing to accept the former but not the latter provision. Yet in 1643 Winthrop went so far as to permit La Tour to hire any ships that were in Boston harbor; and several of these, together with a number of the Massachusetts colonists, were employed by La Tour in an attack on D'Aulnay. Alarmed at the probable consequences of participation in this attack, the Massachusetts authorities issued an order forbidding their people " to use any act of hostility otherwise than in their own defence, towards French or Dutch, till the next general court ". In May, 1644, they wrote to D'Aulnay, enclosing a copy of this order, assuring him that the offending colonists had acted without any commission from them but offering to make due satisfaction, and complaining of D'Aulnay's actions in taking Penobscot. in refusing trade at Port Royal, in threatening to make prize of their vessels sailing beyond Penobscot to trade with La Tour, and in issuing commissions to his captains to take their vessels and goods. They desired D'Aulnay to answer promptly, in order that they might know whether he was disposed to peace or war; asked him to call in his commissions without delay; and refused to prevent their merchants from trading with La Tour, or from defending themselves in case they should be assaulted during their trade.[12] If it should appear that D'Aulnay was bent on war, the commissioners of the United Colonies authorized the General Court of Massachusetts to buy La Tour's fort at St. John, or, if he would not part with it, to secure it so that it might not fall into D'Aulnay's hands.[13] D'Aulnay, meanwhile, had safeguarded his own position by appealing to the government of France. from which he obtained royal letters or decrees deposing La Tour, ordering

---

' Winthrop, *ed. cit.*, II. 88, *et passim.*

[10] Garneau, *Histoire du Canada*, I. 189, and notes; N. Denys, *ed. cit.*, introduction, pp. 4, 5.

[11] The royal letter is in *Mémoires des Commissaires du Roi* (1755-1757), II. 495, 496; *Memorials of the English and French Commissaries concerning the limits of Nova Scotia* (1755), 711, 712.

[12] For the relations between the government of Massachusetts and La Tour and D'Aulnay from 1641 to 1644, see Winthrop, *op. cit.*, under those years; also Mass. Hist. Soc., *Collections*, 3d ser., VII. (1838), 92 ff.

[13] *Records of the Colony of New Plymouth*, IX. 25.

his return to France, and appointing D'Aulnay governor and lieutenant-general on the coast of Acadia." In the autumn of 1644, D'Aulnay's envoy, M. Marie, journeyed to Boston, showed Governor Endicott a commission from the King of France in which La Tour was condemned as a rebel; complained of the assistance given to La Tour; and proffered peace and amity. Massachusetts colony, however, had not the power to conclude an alliance independently, since in May, 1643, it had agreed to the articles of the New England Confederation, whereby all matters pertaining to war, peace, and leagues, were entrusted to the commissioners of the Confederacy." On condition of ratification by the Confederation the magistrates signed an agreement with M. Marie on October 8, stipulating that the English of Massachusetts, and the French under D'Aulnay in Acadia, should keep peace with each other; should have mutual liberty of trade; and should make no reprisals, until satisfaction had been asked and refused—provided, that the English colony should not be bound to prohibit their merchants from trading with any persons whatsoever. The fact that this last provision left the people of Massachusetts free to trade with La Tour indicated a diplomatic victory for their side. Ratification of the treaty was delayed, for relations between the colony and La Tour led at once to further differences with D'Aulnay. It was not until several more conferences had been held that the latter signed the agreement, on September 28, 1646." The commissioners of the United Colonies had previously ratified it on September 2, 1645, on condition that it should be ratified by D'Aulnay.

BIBLIOGRAPHY.

Text: **MS.** No original manuscript of the actual agreement has been found. A Latin draft of the ratification by the Commissioners for the United Colonies, beginning " Conventione et articulis suprascriptis ", and agreeing with the printed version *verbatim,* is preserved in the Massachusetts State Archives, CCXL. 79. Manuscript volumes of the Acts of the Commissioners of the United Colonies of New England, containing the English text printed below, are in the same archives, as well as in the state archives at Hartford.

Text: **Printed. Latin.** T. Hutchinson, *Collection of Original Papers relative to the History of the Colony of Massachusetts-Bay* (1769), pp. 146, 147; another edition of the same, *The Hutchinson Papers,* in the *Publications* of the Prince Society (1865), I. 164-167; E. Hazard, *Historical Collections* (1792-1794), I. 536-537. **English.** *Records of the Colony of New Plymouth in New England* (ed. N. B. Shurtleff and D. Pulsifer, 1855-1861), IX. *Acts of the Commissioners of the United Colonies of*

" See Garneau, *op. cit.,* I. 190, note 24, for authorities.
" Art. 9. The articles are in *Records of the Colony of New Plymouth,* IX. 3-8; Winthrop, *ed. cit.,* II. 100-105.
" *Records of Massachusetts Bay,* III. 44, 45, 76-78; Winthrop. *ed. cit.,* II. 285.

New England, I. 59-60; *The Hutchinson Papers* in the *Publications* of the Prince Society (1865), I. 164, 165; Hazard, *op. cit.*, II. 53-54. Slightly different English versions are in *Winthrop's Journal: "History of New England"* (ed. J. K. Hosmer, 1908), II. 203, in J. F. Jameson, *Original Narratives of Early American History*; W. Hubbard, *A General History of New England* (1815), p. 488.

References: **Contemporary and early writings.** *Winthrop's Journal*, *ed. cit.*, I. 113, 146, 157, 163, 201, II. 43, 85, 88, 105-116, 127-132, 136-137, 151, 178, 180-183, 197, 201-205, 225-226, 247-248, 255, 269-271, 276, 284-286; " Papers relative to D'Aulney and La Tour " in the *Collections* of the Massachusetts Historical Society, 3d ser., VII. (1838) 90 ff.; T. Hutchinson, *op. cit.*, pp. 113-134; *Records of the Colony of New Plymouth, ed. cit.*, IX. 24, 25, 56-59. The papers, etc., referred to under the last two titles are also in Hazard, *op. cit.*, I. 497-516, II. 21, 22, 50-53; *Records of the Governor and Company of the Massachusetts Bay* (ed. N. B. Shurtleff, 1853-1854), II. 157-159, III. 44, 45, 76-78; W. Hubbard, *op. cit.*, ch. 54.

References: **Later writings.** J. Winsor, *Memorial History of Boston*, (1880-1881), I. 282-295; B. Murdoch, *History of Nova-Scotia* (1865-1867), vol. I., chs. 12-13; C. Moreau, *Histoire de l'Acadie Française* (1873), ch. 15; F. Parkman, *The Old Régime in Canada* (1894), chs. 1, 2; F.-X. Garneau, *Histoire du Canada* (5th ed., by H. Garneau, 1913), vol. I., liv. III., ch. 2; H. S. Burrage, *Beginnings of Colonial Maine* (1914), ch. 15.

Latin Text.[17]

Conventio inter Johannem Endecott, gubernatorem Massachusets in Nova Anglia, et reliquos magistratus ibidem, et Dominum Marie, delegatum Domini Aulnay, militis, gubernatoris et deputatus Serenissimi Regis Galliae in Acadia, provincia Novae Franciae, facta et firmata apud Boston in Massachusets praedictum, 8 die mensis 8,[18] 1644.

Dominus Gubernator et reliqui magistratus promittunt Domino Marie praedicto, quod illi et omnes Angli infra jurisdictionem Massachusets in Nova Anglia firmam pacem colent et servabunt cum Domino D'Aulnay, gubernatore, etc., et omnibus Gallis sub potestate ejus in Acadia, etc. Et Dominus Marie promittit pro Domino D'Aulnay, quod ille et homines ejus firmam pacem servabunt, etiam cum gubernatore et magistratibus praedictis, et omnibus inhabitantibus in jurisdictione Massachusets praedicto. Et quod bene licebit omnibus hominibus, tam Gallis quam Anglis, mutua commercia exercere inter se; ita ut, si aliqua occasio offensionis acciderit, neuter eorum attentabit aliquid hostili modo contra alterum, nisi manifestatio et querela de injuria prius facta, ac satisfactione secundum aequitatem non praestita. Proviso semper, quod Dominus gubernator et magistratus praedicti non teneantur cohibere mercatores suos commercia exercere cum navibus suis cum quibuscunque hominibus, sive Gallis sive aliis, ubicunque locorum degentibus. Proviso etiam, quod plena ratificatio et conclusio hujus conventionis ad proximum conventum delegatorum Confaederatarum Coloniarum

---

[17] The Latin text is taken from T. Hutchinson, *Collection of Original Papers*, pp. 146, 147. [18] October.

Novae Angliae deferatur, pro continuatione vel abrogatione ejusdem, et interim firma et inviolata manebit.

Conventione et articulis suprascriptis a delegatis Confaederatarum Coloniarum Novae Angliae praelectis et matura consideratione eorum habitis, cum in animis eorum semper fuerit, ut pax firma et perpetua inter omnes Anglos et propinquos eorum universos instaurata maneret: Ita ut unusquisque communem omnium intentionem incultae hujus regionis in usum humani generis (qua ratione universa terra a Deo primò Adami filiis donata fuit) subigendae prosequatur, nec non ut barbaras has gentes, bonis moribus prius instructas, ad veri Dei et Domini nostri Jesu Christi congnitionem (Divino favente Numine) tandem perducamus, aequum et necessarium illis videtur ut conventio et articuli praedicta (omnibus confaederatis Coloniis praedictis in illis unà comprehensis) confirmare debeant. Sed cum plurimae quaestiones et injuriae ex utraque parte et alligatae et objectae sint, delegati easdem, opportuno tempore et loco exaudire et secundum justitiae normam componi, et interea pace a confederatis Novae Angliae coloniis plene et firmiter, secundum conventionem praedictam, conservari volunt; ea lege, ut Dominus D'Aulnay eandem, chirographo suo signatam, confirmare etiam et observare velit. In quorum fidem et testimonium, delegati praedicti chirographa sua praesentibus apposuerunt.

Datum Boston in Nova Anglia tertio die Septembris, Anno Domini 1645.

Jo. WINTHROP, Praeses.

GEO. FENWICKE.   HERBERT PELHAM.   THO. PRINCE.
EDW. HOPKINS.   THEOPH. EATON.   JOHN BROWNE.
            STEPHEN GOODYEARE.

ENGLISH TEXT.[19]

An agreement between John Endicott, governor of the Massachusets in New England, and the rest of the majestrats there, and Monsr: Marie, commissioner for Monsr: De Aulney, knight, governor and leiftennant of his heighnesse the King of France in Accady, a province of New France, made and confirmed at Boston in the Massachusets aforesaid, the eight day of the eight month 1644.

The governor and majestrates do promise to Monsr: Marie aforesaid that they and all the English within the jurisdiction of the Massachusets in New England shall observe and keepe firme peace with Monsr: De Aulney governor etc. and all the French under his goverment in Accady and also Monsr: Marie promiseth for Monsr: de Aulney that hee and all his people shall keepe firme peace alsoe with the governor and majestrates aforesaid, and all the inhabitants of the said jurisdiccion of the Massachusetts, and that it shalbe lawfull for all their people, aswell French as English, to trade eich with other, so as if any occasion of offence shall happen, neither of them shall attempt any thing against the other in a hostile way, except complaint and manefestacion of the injurie be first made, and satisfaccion according to equitie bee not given; provided alwayes that the governor and majestrates

[19] The English text is taken from *Records of the Colony of New Plymouth*, IX. 59-60.

aforesaid bee not bound to restrayne their merchantes from tradeing with the ships with what people soever, whether French or others, in what place soever inhabiting.   Provided also that the full ratifycacion and conclusion of this agreement be referred to the next meeteing of the commissioners of the united colonies of New England for the continuance or abrogation thereof, and in the meane[time] to remayne firme and inviolable.

The commissioners for the united colonies of New England, haveing perused and considered the agreement and articles above written, and being desireous that a firme and generall peace might be mayntayned betweene the English and all their neighbours, that every one might pursue the common intention of subduing this wildernes for the use of man in that way for which the earth was first given to the sonnes of Adam, and for bringing these barbarous people first to civilitie (and so by divine assistance) to the knowledg of the true God and our Lord Jesus Christ, it seemes fitt and necessary unto them, that the agreement and articles afore specifyed (comprehending therein all the said united colonies) should be confirmed.   But whereas there are certaine questions and injuries on both parts alledged and charged, the commissioners are willing that in due tyme and place the same shalbe duly heard and composed according to justice, and that peace in the meane tyme be fully and firmely kept by the English colonies according to the late agreement.   Provided that Monsr. De Aulney under his owne hand doe confirme and observe the same.

These foregoing conclusions were subscribed by the commissioners for the severall jurisdiccions this second of September 1645.

JOHN WINTHROP, Pres[nt].   GEO. FENWICK.
HERBERT PELHAM.   EDWA. HOPKINS.
THO. PRENCE.   THEOPH. EATON.
JOHN BROWNE.   STEPHEN GOODYEARE.

40.

Treaty between Spain and the United Netherlands, concluded at Münster on January 30, 1648. Ratification by Spain, March 1, 1648. [Ratification by the States General, April 18, 1648.]

INTRODUCTION.

During the twenty years following the expiration of the truce of Antwerp[1] in 1621, the most important of the many negotiations that took place for a peace or truce between the United Provinces and Spain, were those of the years 1632 and 1633.[2] These negotiations failed, chiefly because of the impossibility of coming to an agreement on colonial matters, particularly those in which the Dutch West India Company was involved. In 1632 this company possessed the Recife of Pernambuco in Brazil, which it had captured from the Portuguese, then under the rule of Spain. It looked forward to a rapid extension of its authority and trade in this region, and to profits from raids undertaken thence against the Spanish treasure-fleets, the West Indian Islands, and Central America, and from supplying Brazilian sugar plantations with Guinea and Angola slaves.[3] The company therefore opposed the plan that the States General should exchange Pernambuco for Breda and a large sum of money. Having acquired a great fleet, equipped for war, it was opposed to any peace or truce[4] with Spain that should extend beyond the Line; unless, indeed, Spain should permit the Dutch to trade in both Indies. The Dutch commissioners supported the contentions of the company.[5] Since the King of Spain persisted in requiring the restitution of Pernambuco, and in refusing the company's demands, the negotiations ended fruitlessly.

Besides the Dutch West India Company, another advocate of the continuance of the Spanish-Dutch war was Richelieu, cautiously moving towards the open breach with Spain which he effected in 1635. In that year, after

---

[1] Doc. 28.

[2] For the history of these negotiations the most important source is *Actes des États Généraux de 1632* (1853, 1866), edited by L. P. Gachard, in the *Collection de Documents sur les Anciennes Assemblées Nationales de la Belgique*. Among modern works, M. G. de Boer's *Die Friedensunterhandlungen zwischen Spanien und den Niederlanden in den Jahren 1632 und 1633* (1898), and A. Waddington's *La République des Provinces-Unies, La France, et les Pays-Bas Espagnols de 1630 à 1650* (1895-1897), I. 181 ff., are of especial value.

[3] P. M. Netscher, *Les Hollandais au Brésil*, pp. 52 ff.

[4] The remonstrance of the company against a peace with Spain is in J. R. Brodhead, *Documents relative to the Colonial History of New York*, I. 62-68.

[5] Aitzema, *Saken van Staet*, II. 22.

353

entering into an alliance with the United Provinces, France began to play her ultimately successful part in the Thirty Years' War. Hopelessly worsted by France and her allies, the Hapsburgs were prepared to make large concessions. A preliminary treaty, signed at Hamburg on December 25, 1641,[*] provided for the assembling of a great peace congress at the two Westphalian towns of Münster and Osnabrück. The plenipotentiaries of France and her allies, including the United Provinces, were to meet the deputies of the Emperor and Spain at the former place. The Spanish-Dutch negotiations of 1646-1648, which thus formed part of the proceedings of the famous congress of Westphalia, were carried on under widely different circumstances from those of 1632-1633, mentioned above. In 1646-1648 Spain was exhausted by her efforts against rebels in Portugal, Catalonia, and Naples, as well as against external foes. Moreover, the chief obstacle to peace had been removed by her loss of Brazil and the other Portuguese colonies. The Dutch East and West India companies, however, were still inclined to war, as appears from the " Considerations " which they presented to the States General in 1645, when instructions were being prepared for the Dutch envoys.[*] The East India Company deemed it advantageous to continue the war with the Castilians, since in any case the company was obliged to be always armed and on its guard; but in the event of a peace or truce they hoped that their High Mightinesses would take care that the Castilians should not extend their navigation beyond its present limits. Above all the Castilians must be excluded from the Portuguese Indies, lest under pretext of recovering them they should appear there with a great force. The "considerations " presented by the Dutch West India Company were as follows: (1) That, in case of union between the two companies, which was strongly desired by the West India Company, it would be more profitable for the united companies to continue the war in both the East and West Indies, the coast of Africa, Brazil, the South Sea, and other quarters south of the Tropic of Cancer or beyond the Equinoctial Line, than to conclude any peace or truce with the King of Spain; (2) that, in case the union should not be effected, if their High Mightinesses would grant renewal of the West India Company's charter for twenty-five years, and requisite subsidies, peace or truce would be serviceable to them if also accepted by the East India Company; (3) that, in case of a general peace or truce, the company should be assured of its observance by Spain, so that they might diminish their garrisons, powerful ships, etc., without danger, and be maintained in exercising the privileges of their charter; (4) that in such peace or truce should be included all potentates and peoples with whom their High Mightinesses or the West India Company were in friendship and alliance, within the

[*] Dumont, *Corps Diplomatique*, VI. (1), 231-233.
[*] Aitzema, *Vrede-handeling*, in *Saken van Staet*, VI. (2), 186, 187.

limits of their charter; (5) that the company should be allowed to promote their trade in all places within the aforesaid limits where the King of Spain had no castles, jurisdiction, or territory, with whatever merchandise, wares, slaves, etc., they should see fit; (6) that the subjects of Spain should not be permitted to navigate or trade in any harbors or places where the West India Company had any castles, forts, and territory or warehouses, unless similar privileges were granted to the said company in all districts and places under the dominion of the said King of Spain; (7) that each should continue to possess and enjoy such cities, castles, strongholds, trading places and lands, as, at the conclusion of this treaty, should belong to each.

In so far as the "considerations" put forward by the two companies suggested stipulations to be made in regard to the Indies in case of a peace or truce, they were incorporated (together with an additional provision that officers and servants of the said companies should be unmolested in the countries of the King of Spain in Europe) in two articles, which were included in a draft of the instructions prepared for the Dutch envoys to Münster. But on October 14, 1645, a fortnight before the date of the completed instructions, these two articles were stricken from the draft.[1] The only articles dealing with the East and West Indies and left standing in the instructions—nos. 10, 11 (second part), 13, 14, 15, and 16—were comparatively insignificant. Article 10 consisted of the "certificate" signed by the French and English ambassadors on April 9, 1609.[2] The second part of article 11 stated that outside these limits (*i. e.*, outside Europe or wherever else the king's friends were permitted to trade) the States and their subjects should not trade in the lands of the King of Spain without his express permission; but they should be allowed to trade in the territories of all other princes and peoples who would permit them, even outside the aforesaid limits, without the said king or his officers or subjects molesting the said princes or peoples or the Dutch themselves. (This provision was the same as that of the truce of 1609, article 4.) Article 12 merely stated that "the preceding article consists of two parts: the first is left as it is", thus abrogating the second part. Article 13 provided that the navigation and traffic to each of the Indies should be maintained. Article 14 declared that in the limits of the East India Company's charter the truce should not begin under a year after the date of its conclusion; nor in the limits of the West India Company's charter until six months after its conclusion; but that if notification of the truce should be made sooner within the aforesaid limits, all hostilities must cease; and if, after the lapse of a year or six months, respectively, any act of hostility should be committed in the said limits, the loss should be repaired without delay. The fifteenth article asserted that on March 31, 1609, the ambassadors of France and England made a declaration concerning

[1] *Ibid.*, pp. 205, 206.   [2] Printed above, Doc. **28**, p. 268.

the matters referred to in articles 13 and 14. This declaration, printed above,[10] constituted the sixteenth article. Concerning the rest of the 116 articles of the instructions, it need only be observed that they called for the conclusion of a truce of at least twelve years, during which each party should keep its own possessions; for full recognition of the independence of the United Provinces; and for the maintenance of a close correspondence with the French plenipotentiaries at Münster, in accordance with the Franco-Dutch treaty of 1644.

Armed with these instructions, which it had taken two years to frame, the eight Dutch envoys arrived in Münster on January 11, 1646—Barthold van Gent, lord of Meinerswijk, from Gelderland; Johan, lord of Mathenesse, and Adriaan Pauw, lord of Heemstede, from Holland; Johan de Knuyt, from Zeeland; Godard van Reede, lord of Nederhorst, from Utrecht; Frans van Donia, from Friesland; Willem van Ripperda, lord of Hengeloo, from Overyssel; Adriaan Clant, from Groningen. They had been preceded in time at Münster by the Spanish commissioners—Don Gaspar de Bracamonte, count of Peñaranda, councillor of the king, Joseph de Bergaigne, archbishop of Cambrai, who died in October, 1647, and Antoine Brun. Among the Dutch, Pauw and Knuyt were the ablest; among the Spaniards, Brun.[11]

After the coming of the States' plenipotentiaries, negotiations opened promptly, but they were soon halted by the dissatisfaction of the Dutch with the Spaniards' full powers. The Dutch insisted that before negotiations could proceed, new powers, conforming to a draft prepared by them, must be obtained from Spain. Meanwhile two alarming reports reached Pauw and his colleagues, (1) that a marriage between the King of France and the Spanish Infanta was arranged and that the latter would receive the Netherlands as dowry; (2) that the King of Spain had placed the whole peace negotiations in the hands of his sister, the queen regent of France. Toward the end of February, Pauw and Knuyt journeyed with these tidings to the Hague. Returning to Münster early in May, they would not resume negotiations until the Spanish envoys promised to deliver to them, before the first of July, full powers such as they desired. At about the same time, envoys of both parties signed an agreement concerning the manner of holding conferences, providing that all the writings that had to be made for the treaty should be in the French and Dutch languages, which should be regarded as equally authentic.[12]

On May 17 the Dutch accepted the proposal, made by the Spaniards on January 28,[13] for a truce modelled on that of 1609, and in turn proposed 71 articles, based on their instructions, as the conditions for renewing the

---

[10] Doc. **29**, note 6.

[11] For characterization of the Dutch and Spanish envoys, see Waddington, *République des Provinces-Unies*, II. 167 ff.

[12] Aitzema, *op. cit.*, VI. (2), 232.   [13] *Ibid.*, VI. (2), 220, 221.

truce.[14] Since the principal articles relating to the Indies had been stricken from the instructions, the 71 articles failed to provide for settling the India question. The few references to the Indies contained in these 71 articles were as follows: article 5 carried out the directions of article 13 of the instructions by stating that it was understood that the navigation and trade of the East and West Indies were held and maintained, and that in the future articles would be drawn up concerning this; and article 6 was the same as article 14 of the instructions. Since the Spanish envoys accepted nearly all of the 71 articles, the Dutch plenipotentiaries desired to end the negotiations by coming to an agreement in regard to the India trade, and wrote repeatedly to the Hague for instructions thereon.[15] Before these were received, about the first of July, amended " full powers " arrived at Münster from Spain. The seventy provisional articles were then signed [16] by all of the Spanish plenipotentiaries and by three of the Dutch—van Meinerswijk, Heemstede, and Pauw. Nederhorst, and later Ripperda, who favored France, would not sign. Towards the end of the month some of the Dutch deputies. having returned to the Hague, reported to the States General the seventy provisional articles, and requested further instructions on certain unsettled points, including the matter of the East and West Indies.[17]

On September 18, it was decided to substitute a peace for a truce. While Holland strongly favored this change, Zeeland, foreseeing that a peace would further damage the already declining fortunes of the East and West India companies,[18] opposed it, but finally yielded. By means of some amendments the 70 articles were then converted into a treaty of peace, and a few new articles were added. Among other changes resolved upon was the striking out of the fifth of the seventy articles, and the substituting of two articles (5 and 6), based upon the two articles that had been stricken out of the drafted instructions, as mentioned above.[19]

In these substituted articles the principal novelties were: (1) that among the places in the East and West Indies which the King of Spain and the Lords States should, respectively, continue to hold, on the ground of previous possession, were to be especially included places taken by the Portuguese from the States, and places which, hereafter, without infringement of the present treaty, the States " might come to conquer and possess "; (2) reciprocal freedom of trade between the Dutch West India Company and the subjects of Spain in the places possessed by either within the limits of the Dutch West India Company.

[14] *Ibid.,* VI. (2), 234-239.
[15] *Ibid.,* VI. (2), 239-244, 245, 246.
[16] By the combining of two articles the number had been reduced from 71 to 70.
[17] Aitzema, *op. cit.,* VI. (2), 249, 250.
[18] A "Report on the affairs of the West India Company", January, 1648, is printed in J. R. Brodhead, *op. cit.,* I. 216-248.
[19] Aitzema, *op. cit.,* VI. (2), 264.

In case the latter stipulation were rejected an alternative provision was to be proposed, *viz.*, that Spaniards and Dutch should refrain from sailing to and trading in the ports or places occupied by either party with forts, warehouses, or castles.[20] On December 13, 1646, the Dutch plenipotentiaries delivered to the Spaniards, at Münster, the "amendments and additions to be made in the seventy provisional articles . . . with six fresh articles, both signed and in the French language".[21] The Spaniards strongly objected to the new articles relating to the Indies. They declared that "the King could not agree to the trade in the West Indies; that was quite an innovation and unknown in the treaties of truce, and since the trade in the Indies was not permitted any foreign nations by any treaty, and moreover the subjects of England, Denmark, the Portuguese, so long as these were under the dominion of the King, France before the war, the Aragonese, the Neapolitans, and even the inhabitants of the Spanish Netherlands, were not allowed any trade in the West Indies, therefore our State could not enjoy what was refused the subjects of the King".[22]

They consented that the States General "be permitted to recover all that the Portuguese shall have occupied of theirs in Brazil", but with the proviso that the King of Spain should retain "his rights over all that he had there at the beginning of the Portuguese rebellion". Brun went so far as to suggest that after the peace the Spaniards would gladly make an alliance with the Dutch "to share Brazil, and perhaps more".

To meet the objections of the Spaniards, who threatened to break off negotiations, the two articles concerning the Indies (nos. 5 and 6) were modified. Article 5 was altered from the form of the revised instructions by adding to the expression "places taken by the Portuguese from these States", the phrase "since the year 1641". Article 6 may be regarded as the second "alternative" provision of the Dutch instructions, modified by the conditional concession from the Spaniards in respect to the territory occupied by the Dutch in Brazil, and by the addition of a few phrases. The introduction of the phrase "and all others" was very disadvantageous to the West India Company; for whereas the second alternative had provided that subjects of either party should keep away from places occupied by the other party with forts, warehouses, or castles, the article as adopted stipulated that they should also refrain from visiting all other places.

The modified articles 5 and 6 were agreed to on December 27.[23] The 73 articles signed by the Spaniards, together with an article declaring that,

---

[20] Aitzema, *op. cit.*, VI. (2), 266.

[21] The Dutch version was given to the Spaniards on Dec. 14, *British Counter-Case*, pp. 333, 334.

[22] This and the following quotations are from the translation printed in the *British Counter-Case*, pp. 336-339, from the official report of the Dutch embassy, preserved in the Rijksarchief at the Hague, St. Gen., 25, 225, vol. III. *Cf.* also Le Clerc, *Négociations*, III. 393, and Aitzema, *op. cit.*, VI. (2), 269 ff.

[23] *British Counter-Case*, pp. 341, 342.

in accordance with the treaty concluded with France in March, 1644, these articles should not have the force of a real treaty unless France were satisfied, were signed by seven of the Dutch plenipotentiaries on January 8, 1647.[24] On the ground that the signing was an act unfriendly to the French, as well as on account of the introduction of the words " and all others ", Nederhorst refused to affix his name.[25]

When the 73 articles were referred back to the States General, and by them to the Provinces, they were variously received. Several provinces disliked certain provisions. Zeeland objected to the additions to article 6.[26] Holland, which tried to show that these additions favored Dutch commerce, was urgent for a speedy peace, and in April announced that unless France were more conciliatory the Dutch must conclude a separate treaty. For some months thereafter the Dutch tried to mediate between the French and Spaniards. One of the chief obstacles was Portugal, which France, always desiring the abasement of Spain, was determined to aid.[27] Despite the wish of France, Spain would not tolerate any recognition of the Portuguese rebels in the treaties; moreover, she insisted that France should surrender Lorraine. On July 29, 1647, a futile treaty of reciprocal guarantee was concluded betwen the States General and France.[28] The party in the United Provinces that desired peace with Spain, even without France, successfully continued their activities. Zeeland was won over by a promise of aid for the West India Company; and all difficulties with Spain were finally adjusted. The Dutch gave France a fixed period within which to come to terms with Spain respecting Lorraine.[29] No agreement having been reached, on January 30, 1648, despite the Franco-Dutch treaty of 1644, the Dutch concluded a separate peace with Spain.[30] As before, Nederhorst refused to sign. France protested,[31] and several provinces opposed a ratification, but were gradually won over, with the exception of Zeeland.[32] The Spanish ratification, dated March 1, 1648, having arrived at Münster, the treaty was ratified on April 18[33] by a resolution of the States General. On May 15 ratifications were exchanged. When June 5 was fixed as the date for proclaiming the peace, Zeeland yielded. She would publish it, not with rejoicing, but with fasting and prayer.[34] For her it meant the end of profitable privateering,[35] and the

[24] Aitzema, *op. cit.*, VI. (2), 273.   [25] *Ibid.*, VI. (2), 294.   [26] *Ibid.*, VI. (2), 297 ff.
[27] Le Clerc, *Négociations Secrètes*, IV. 375.   [28] Aitzema, *op. cit.*, VI. (2), 326-327.
[29] *Coleccion de Documentos Inéditos*, LXXXIV. 87.
[30] A special article respecting navigation and commerce was signed at Münster on Feb. 4, 1648. Aitzema, *op. cit.*, VI. (2), 354-355.
[31] Aitzema, *op. cit.*, VI. (2), 355 ff.   [32] *Ibid.*, VI. (2), 364 ff.
[33] The ratification is printed in the *Groot Placaet-Boeck*, vol. I., cols. 103-106, and in Dumont, *Corps Diplomatique*, VI. (1), 438.
[34] Aitzema, *op. cit.*, VI. (2), 383 ff.; Waddington, *op. cit.*, II. 231.
[35] Asher, *Bibliographical Essay*, p. 62. On April 7, 1648, the Directors of the West India Company wrote to Stuyvesant in regard to the sale of two ships, " The low price leads us to surmise that these ships were pretty well worn out and by your Honor

rapid dissolution of the West India Company, now debarred from continuing those hostilities against Spain for which it was primarily created.

From the standpoint of this volume the chief interest of the treaty of Münster lies in the fact that therein, for the first time, Spain conceded to another nation, in clear and explicit terms, and in a public treaty, the right to sail to, trade, and acquire territory in the West Indies.

BIBLIOGRAPHY.

Text: MS. The original manuscript of the Spanish ratification is preserved in the exhibition room of the Rijksarchief at the Hague.
Text: Printed. French. J. A. de Abreu y Bertodano, *Coleccion de los Tratados de España: Reynado del Rey D. Phelipe IV.* (1744-1751), V. 309-360; J. Dumont, *Corps Diplomatique* (1726-1731), tom. VI., pt. I., pp. 429-441; J. J. Schmauss, *Corpus Juris Gentium Academicum* (1730), I. 614-629. **Dutch.** *Groot Placaet-Boeck van de Staten Generael* (1658-1796), vol. I., cols. 79-110; L. van Aitzema, *Saken van Staet en Oorlogh* (1669-1672), III. 259-268; *id., Verhael van de Nederlandsche Vrede-handeling, ibid.,* VI. (2), 386-398.
Translations: English. *A General Collection of Treatys* (1732), II. 335-367; the same in C. Jenkinson, *Collection of all the Treaties between Great Britain and Other Powers* (1785), I. 10-40; *Venezuela-British Guiana Boundary Arbitration: the Case of the United States of Venezuela* (1898), III. 4-21. **Spanish.** Abreu y Bertodano, *loc. cit.*
References: Contemporary and early writings. L. van Aitzema, *Saken van Staet en Oorlogh* (1669-1672), II. 884 ff., 959, 967 ff., 975 ff.; III. 42 ff., 103 ff., 205 ff., 241 ff.; *id., Verhael van de Nederlandsche Vrede-handeling* (1671), pp. 198 ff., in *Saken van Staet en Oorlogh,* deel VI. (2), and separately; Navarrete, *Coleccion de Documentos Inéditos para la Historia de España* (1842-1895), LXXXII.-LXXXIV. (diplomatic correspondence of the Spanish plenipotentiaries at Münster from 1643 to 1648); N. Clément, *Mémoires et Négociations Secrètes de la Cour de France, touchant la Paix de Munster* (1710), 4 vols:, Clément's collection is included in [J. Le Clerc], *Négociations Secrètes touchant la Paix de Munster et d'Osnaburg* (1725-1726), 4 vols.; *Lettres du Cardinal Mazarin* (ed. M. A. Chéruel, 1872-1906), II., *passim,* in the *Collection de Documents Inédits sur l'Histoire de France; British Guiana Boundary, Arbitration with the United States of Venezuela, Appendix to the* [British] *Counter-Case* (Foreign Office print, 1898), pt. II., " Special appendix to illustrate Chapter V. of the Counter-Case: the Treaty of Munster " (documents with translations) ; States of Holland, *Resolutien* for the years 1646-1648, *passim;* A. Contarini, *Relazione del Congresso di Münster* (1864), pt. II.; F. Ogier, *Journal du Congrès de Munster* (ed. A. Boppe, 1893; G. Groen van Prinsterer, *Archives de la*

---

considered unfit to be used in the service of the Company. We could not, under the circumstances, expect to employ them with great advantage to us, for we can now seek our fortune only against the treacherous Portuguese, since the peace with Spain has been arranged and signed ". B. Fernow, *Documents relating to the History of the Early Colonial Settlements on Long Island* (1883), p. 84.

Maison d'Orange-Nassau (1835, etc.), 2d ser., IV. 148 ff., *passim*;
A. van Wicquefort, *Histoire des Provinces-Unies des Païs-Bas* (1861-1874), I. 76 ff.
References: Later writings. J. Basnage, *Annales des Provinces-Unies*
(1726), I. 3-111; G. H. Bougeant, *Histoire du Traité de Westphalie*
(1751), 6 vols.; J. P. Arend, *et al., Algemeene Geschiedenis des Vaderlands* (1840, etc.), III. (5), 460-805, *passim*; Comte de Garden, *Histoire
Générale des Traités de Paix* (1848-1851), I., section 3, espec. 165 ff.;
A. Waddington, *La République des Provinces-Unies, La France, et les
Pays-Bas Espagnols de 1630 à 1650* (Annales de l'Université de Lyon,
1895-1897), II. 155-250; United States Commission on Boundary between Venezuela and British Guiana, *Report and Papers* (1896-1897),
I. 71-96, " Report as to the meaning of articles V. and VI. of the Treaty
of Münster ", by G. L. Burr, reprinted in *The Counter-Case of the
United States of Venezuela* (1898), II. 1-16; *British Guiana Boundary:
Arbitration with the United States of Venezuela, The* [British] *Counter-
Case* (1898), pp. 46-51; P. J. Blok, *History of the People of the Nether-
lands* (1898-1912), IV., ch. VI.; G. M. Asher, *A Bibliographical and
Historical Essay on the Dutch Books and Pamphlets relating to New
Netherland* (1854-1867), pp. 58 ff.

TEXT.[16]

Don Philippe Quatriesme, par la grace de Dieu roy de Castille, de Leon, de
Arragon, dés Deux Siciles, de Jerusalem, de Portugal, de Navarre, de
Granada, de Toledo, de Valençia, de Galliçia, de Mallorca, de Menorca, de
Sevilla, de Cerdeña, de Cordova, de Corçega, de Mursia, de Jaen, de los
Algarves, de Algesira, de Gibraltar, dés Isles de Canarie, dés Indes Orientales
et Occidentales, isles et terreferme de l'Occean, archiduc d'Austriche, sieur
de Bourgogne, de Brabant, de Milan, comte de Habspurg, de Flandres,
Tyrol, Barçelone, seigneur de Viscaya et Molina, etc., A tous ceux qui ces
presentes lettres verront, salut. Comme ainsy soit, que pour delivrer les
Provinces du Pais Bas de la guerre de laquelle par un si long espace d'années
elles ont esté affligées, les descharger dés miseres et calamités d'icelle, les
remettre en repos, splendeur, et prosperité, comme aussy pour assoupir les
guerres espandues en autres pais, et mers lointaines,

Nous depuis longtemps avons desiré de venir á une bonne paix avec les
Seigneurs Estats Generaux dés Provinces Unies libres du Pais Bas, au
soulagement de touts ceux qui del'un et de l'autre costé sentent les calamités
dela susditte guerre, et que de commun concert ayt esté choisie la ville de
Münster en Westphale pour l'assemblée et traitté de paix; si ont les affaires
audit lieu eu succes si favorable, que nos ambassadeurs extraordinaires et
plenipotentiaires en vertu de nos pouvoirs ont faict et conclu avec les ambassadeurs extraordinaires et plenipotentiaires désdits Seigneurs Estats le traitté
de paix çy inseré de mot á mot :

Au nom et à la gloire de Dieu, soit notoire à touts, qu'apres le long cours
des sanglantes guerres qui ont affligé par tant d'années les peuples, subjects,

---

[16] From the original manuscript of the Spanish ratification in the exhibition room
of the Rijksarchief at the Hague.

royaumes, et pais de l'obeissance des Seigneurs Roy des Espagnes et Estats Generaux des Provinces Unies du Pais-Bas, eux Seigneurs Roy et Estats, touchez de compassion Chrestienne, et desirants mettre fin aux calamitez publiques et arrester les deplorables suittes, inconvenients, dommages, et dangers, que la continuation ulterieure des dites guerres des Pais-bas pourroit tirer apres soy, mesme par une extension en autres estats, pais, terres, et mers plus reculées, et àfin d'en changer les sinistres effects en ceux tres agreables d'une bonne et sincere pacification de part et d'autre, et aux doux fruicts d'un entier et ferme repos, pour le soulagement des dits peuples et estats de leur obeissance, et pour le restablissement des dommages passez, au bien commun, non seulement des Pais-bas, mais de toutte la Chrestienté, conviants et priants les autres princes et potentats d'icelle de se laisser fleschir par la grace divine, à la mesme compassion et aversion des malheurs, ruines, et disordres, que ce pesant fleau de la guerre a faict si longuement et durement ressentir ; pour parvenir a une si bonne fin et à un but tant desirable, ont iceux Seigneurs Roy des Espagnes, Don Philippe Quatriesme, et Estats Generaux desdites Provinces Unies du Pais-bas, commis et deputé, c'est à sçavoir ledit Seigneur Roy, Don Gaspar de Braccamonte et de Guzman, comte de Peñaranda, seigneur de Aldeaseca de la Frontera, chevalier de l'Ordre de Alcantara, administrateur perpetuel de la comanderie de Daymiel del'Ordre de Calatrava, gentilhomme de la chambre de sa Majesté, de son conseil et chambre, ambassadeur extraordinaire vers sa Majesté Imperiale, et premier plenipotenciaire pour le traicté de la paix generale ; et Messire Anthoine Brun, chevalier, conseiller de sa Majesté Catolique en son conseil d'Estat et Supreme pour les affaires des Pais-bas et de Bourgogne, prés de sa personne, et son plenipotentiaire aux traictés de la paix generale ; et lesdicts Seigneurs Estats Generaux des Provinces Unies du Pais-bas, le Sieur Bartolt de Gent, sieur de Loenen et de Meinderswyck, senechal et dyck grave de Bommel, Tieler, et Bommelerwaerden, deputé de la noblesse de Geldre à l'assemblée des Seigneurs Estats Generaux ; le Sieur Jean de Mathenesse, sieur de Mathenesse, Riviere, Opmeer, Souteveen, etc., deputé au conseil ordinaire de Hollande et Westfrise, et à l'assemblée des Seigneurs Estats Generaux, de la part des nobles de ladite province, conseiller, et heemrade de Schieland ; Messire Adriaen Pauw, chevalier, sieur de Heemstede, Hogers-milde, etc., premier president, conseiller, et maistre des comptes de Hollande et Westfrise, et de par[t] de ladite province deputé à l'assemblée des Seigneurs Estats Generaux ; Messire Jean de Knuyt, chevalier, sieur de vieux et nouveau Vosmar, premier et representant la noblesse aux Estats et conseil de la comté de Zeelande, et de l'admiraulté d'icelle, premier conseiller de Son Altesse Monsieur le Prince d'Orange, deputé ordinaire à l'assemblée des Seigneurs Estats Generaux ; le Sieur Godart de Reede, sieur de Neder-horst, Vredelant, Cortehoef, Overmeer, Horstwaert, etc., president à l'assem-blée des nobles de la province d'Utrecht, et deputé de leur part à l'assemblée des Seigneurs Estats Generaux ; le sieur François de Donia, sieur de Hinnema en Hielsum, deputé à l'assemblée des Seigneurs Estats Generaux de la part de la Province de Frise ; le Sieur Guillaume Ripperda, sieur de Hengeloe, Boxberghen, Boculoe, et Russenborg, etc., deputé de la noblesse de la Province d'Overyssel à l'assemblée des Seigneurs Estats Generaux ; le Sieur Adriaen Clant de Stedum, sieur de Nittersum et deputé ordinaire de la province de la ville de Groningue et Ommelandes, à l'assemblée des Seigneurs Estats Generaux ; tous ambassadeurs extraordinaires en Allemagne et plenipotenciaires desdits Seigneurs Estats Generaux, aux traittés de la paix generale, touts garnis de pouvoirs suffisants, qui seront inserez à la fin des presentes: lesquels assembléz en la ville de Munster en Westphale, de commun concert destinée au traicté general de paix de la Crestienté, en vertu de leurs dits pouvoirs pour, et au nom desdits Seigneurs Roy et Estats, ont faict, conclu, et accordé les articles qui s'ensuivent.

1.er Premierement, declare ledit Seigneur Roy et recognoist que lesdits Seigneurs Estats Generaux des Païs-bas Unis, et les provinces d'iceux respectivement, avec touts leurs païs associez, villes, et terres y appartenants, sont libres et souverains estats, provinces, et païs, sur lesquels ni sur leurs païs, villes, et terres associées, comme dessus, luy dit Seigneur Roy ne pretend rien, et que presentement, ou cy apres, pour soy-mesme, ses hoirs, et successeurs, il ne pretendra jamais rien; et qu'en suitte de ce il est content de traicter avecq lesdits Seigneurs Estats, comme il faict par le present, une paix perpetuelle, aux conditions ci apres escrites et declarées.

2. A sçavoir, que ladite paix sera bonne, ferme, fidelle, et inviolable, et qu'en suitte cesseront et seront delaissez touts actes d'hostilité, de quelque façon qu'ilz soient, entre lesdits Seigneurs Roy et Estats Generaux, tant par mer, autres eaux, que par terre, en touts leurs royaumes, païs, terres, et seigneuries, et pour touts leurs subjects et habitants, de quelque qualité ou condition qu'ilz soient, sans exception de lieux ni de personnes.

3. Chascun demeurera saisi, et jouira effectivement des païs, villes, places, terres, et seigneuries, qu'il tient et possede à present, sans y estre troublée, ni inquieté, directement ni indirectement, de quelque façon que ce soit. . . .

. . . .

5. La navigation et trafique des Indes Orientales et Occidentales sera maintenue, selon et en conformité des octroys[m] sur ce donnés, ou à donner cy apres; pour seurté de quoy servira le present traicté, et la ratification d'iceluy, qui de part et d'autre en sera procurée: et seront compris soubs ledit traitté touts potentats, nations, et peuples, avec lesquels les dits Seigneurs Estats, ou ceux de la Societé des Indes Orientales et Occidentales en leur nom, entre les limites de leurs dicts octroys sont en amitié et alliance; et un chacun, sçavoir les susdits Seigneurs Roy et Estats respectivement demeureront en possession et jouiront de telles seigneuries, villes, chasteaux, forteresses, commerce et païs ès Indes Orientales et Occidentales, comme aussi au Brasil et sur les costes d'Asie, Afrique, et Amerique respectivement, que lesdits Seigneurs Roy et Estats respectivement tiennent et possedent; en ce compris specialement les lieux et places que les Portugais depuis l'an mille six cens quarante et un ont pris et occupé sur les dits Seigneurs Estats;[n] compris aussi les lieux et places, qu'iceux Seigneurs Estats ci apres sans infraction

---

[l] *Cf.* this and the following article with articles 1 and 2 of the truce of 1609 (Doc. 28).

[m] The charter of the East India Company, 1602, is printed in the *Groot Placaet-Boeck*, vol. I., cols. 530-538. The charter of the West India Company, of June 3, 1621, is printed in the same volume, cols. 565-578, and thence, together with an English translation, in A. J. F. van Laer, *Van Rensselaer Bowier Manuscripts*, pp. 86-115.

[n] ". . . compris aussi les lieux . . . viendront à conquerir et posseder". Whether this clause gave the Dutch the right to acquire unconquered territory from the native tribes, as well as to recapture it from the Portuguese, was a debated point in the Venezuela-British Guiana boundary controversy. The arguments for one interpretation are given by Professor G. L. Burr in his "Report as to the Meaning of Articles V. and VI. of the Treaty of Münster"; and for the other, in the *British Counter Case*, ch. 5.

du present traicté viendront à conquerir et posseder. Et les Directeurs de
la Societé des Indes, tant Orientales que Occidentales, des Provinces Unies,
comme aussi les ministres, officiers, hauts et bas, soldats, et matelots, estants
en service actuel del'une, ou del'autre desdites compagnies, ou aiants esté
en leur service, comme aussi ceux, qui hors leur service respectivement,
tant en ces païs, qu'au district desdites deux compagnies continuent encor,
ou pourront ci aprés estre employés, seront et demeureront libres, et sans
estre molestez, en touts les païs estants soubs l'obeissance dudit Seigneur
Roy en l'Europe, pourront voyager, trafiquer, et frequenter, comme touts
autres habitants, des pais desdits Seigneurs Estats. En outtre a esté condi-
tionné et stipulé, que les Espagnolz retiendront leur navigation en telle
maniere, qu'ilz la tiennent pour le present ès Indes Orientales,[46] sans se
pouvoir estendre plus avant; comme aussi les habitants de ces Pais-bas
s'abstiendront de la frequentation des places, que les Castellans ont ès Indes
Orientales.

6. Et quant aux Indes Occidentales, les subjects et habitants des royaumes,
provinces, et terres desdits Seigneurs Roy et Estats respectivement, s'abstiendront de naviger et trafiquer en touts les havres, lieux et places garnies
de forts, loges ou chasteaux, et touttes autres possedées par l'une ou l'autre
partie; sçavoir, que les subjects dudit Seigneur Roy ne navigeront et trafiqueront en celles tenues par lesdits Seigneurs Estats, ni les subjects desdits
Seigneurs Estats en celles tenues par ledit Seigneur Roy; et entre les places
tenues par lesdicts Seigneurs Estats, seront comprises les places que les
Portugais depuis l'an mille six cens et quarante un ont occupées dans le
Brasil sur les dits Seigneurs Estats, comme aussi touttes autres places qu'ilz
possedent à present, tandis qu'elles demeureront aux dits Portugais; sans
que le precedent article puisse deroger au contenu du present.

7. Et pour ce qu'il est besoin d'un assez long temps pour advertir ceux
qui sont hors les dites limites avec forces et navires, à se desister de touts
actes d'hostilité; a esté accordé, qu'entre les limites de l'octroy ci devant
donné à la societé des Indes Orientales du Pais bas, ou à donner par continuation, la paix ne commencera pas plus tost qu'un an apres la date de la
conclusion du present traitté. Et quant aux limites del'octroy, ci devant
donné par les Estats Generaux, ou à donner par continuation à la Societé des
Indes Occidentales, qu'aux dits lieux la paix ne commencera pas plus tost
que six mois après la date que dessus. Bien entendu, que si l'advis de ladite
paix sera de la part du public de part et d'autre parvenu plus tost entre les
dits limites respectivement, que dès l'heure del'advis l'hostilité cessera auxdits
lieux; mais si apres le terme d'un an et de six mois respectivement dans les
limites des octroys susdits se faict aucun acte d'hostilité, les dommages en
seront repares sans delay.

. . . .

16. Les villes Anseatiques, avecq touts leurs citoiens, habitants, et païs,
jouiront quant au faict de la navigation et trafique en Espagne, royaumes,
et estats d'Espagne, de touts et mesmes droicts, franchises, immunités, et
privileges, lesquels par le present traicté sont accordés, ou s'accorderont ci
après, pour et au regard des subjects et habitants des Provinces Unies des
Païs-bas. Et reciproquement les dits subjects et habitants des Provinces
Unies jouiront de touts et mesmes droicts, franchises, immunités, privileges,

[46] In the East Indies Spain retained the Philippines. *Cf.* Doc. **16**, introduction.

et capitulations, soit pour l'establissement des consuls dans les villes capitales, ou maritimes d'Espagne, et ailleurs, ou il sera besoin, comme aussi pour les marchands, facteurs, maistres de navires, mariniers, ou autrement, et en la mesme sorte, que les dites villes Anseatiques en general, ou en particulier, ont obtenu et pratiqué ci devant, ou obtiendront et pratiqueront ci apres, pour la seurté, bien, et avantage de la navigation et trafique de leur villes, marchands, facteurs, commis, et autres, qui en dependent.

72. En ce present traicté de paix seront compris ceux qui devant l'eschange de l'agreation ou ratification, ou trois mois après, seront nommés de part et d'autre, dans lequel terme ledit Seigneur Roy nommera ceux qu'il jugera convenir. De la part desdits Seigneurs Estats sont nomméz le Prince Lant Grave de Hessen Cassel, avec ses païs, villes et estats, le Comte d'Oostfrise, la ville d'Emden, le Comté et Païs d'Oostfrise, les Villes Anseatiques, et particulierement Lubec. Bremen, Hamborgh; et reservent les dits Seigneurs Estats de nommer dans le susdit terme tels autres qu'ilz trouveront convenir.

77. Sera le present traicté ratifié et approuvé par les dits Seigneurs Roy et Estats, et les lettres de ratification seront delivrées de l'un à l'autre, en bonne et deüe forme, dans le terme de deux mois; et si ladite ratification arrive auparavant, cesseront dèslors touts actes d'hostilité entre les parties, sans attendre l'expiration dudit terme. Bien entendu, qu'apres la conclusion et signature du present traicté l'hostilité des deux costéz ne cessera, qu'au preallable la ratification dudit Seigneur Roy d'Espagne ne soit delivrée en deüe substance et forme, et changée contre celle desdits Seigneurs Estats des Provinces Unies.

78. Si bien que cependant les affaires des deux costez demeureront en mesme estat et constitution, que lors de la conclusion du present traicté ils seront trouvéz; et ce jusques à tant que la susdite ratification reciproque sera changée et delivrée.

79. Sera ledit traicté publié par tout ou il appartiendra, incontinent apres que les ratifications de part et d'autre, seront changées et delivrées, et cesseront dès alors touts actes d'hostilité.

[Here follow the powers of the Spanish and of the Dutch plenipotentiaries.]

En foy de tout ce que dessus nous ambassadeurs extraordinaires et plenipotenciaires des dits Seigneur Roy des Espagnes et Estats Generaux des Provinces Unies, en vertu de noz pouvoirs respectifs, avons signé le present traicté et cachette du cachet de nos armes. Faict à Munster en Westphale, le trentiesme Janvier mil six cent quarante huict.

(L. S.) El Conde de Peñaranda.   (L. S.) Bartolt de Gent.
(L. S.) A. Brun.   (L. S.) Johan van Matenes.
                                     (L. S.) Adriaen Pauw.
                                     (L. S.) I. de Knuÿt.
                                     (L. S.) G. Van Reede.
                                     (L. S.) F. V. Donia.
                                     (L. S.) Wilhelm Ripperda.
                                     (L. S.) Adr. Clant.

Lequel traitté, çy escrit et inseré, comme dessus, nous ayant esté representé par nosdits ambassadeurs extraordinaires et plenipotenciaires, apres l'avoir tout veu et meurement examiné de mot á mot en nostre conseil, nous, pour nous, nos hoirs, et successeurs, comme aussy pour les vassaux, subjects, et habitants de tous nos royaumes, pais, et seigneuries, tant dedans que hors l'Europe, sans aucun excepter, iceluy traitté, et tout le contenu d'iceluy, et chacun point en particulier, en tous ses membres, avons receu, pour bon, ferme, et vallable, l'avons agrée, approuvé, et ratifié, le recevons, aggréons, appreuvons, et ratifions par cette presente; promettants en foy et parolle de Roy et Prince, pour nous, nos successeurs, roys, princes, et heritiers, sincerement et en bonne foy, de l'ensuivre, observer, et accomplir, inviolablement et punctuellement, selon la forme et teneur, le faire ensuivre, observer, et accomplir tout ainsy comme si nous l'avions traitté en nostre propre personne, sans rien faire ny laisser faire en aucune maniere ny souffrir d'estre fait au contraire, directement ny indirectement, en quelque façon que ce puisse estre; et si contravention estoit faite, ou vinst á se faire en aucune maniere, la faire reparer sans aucune difficulté, ny remise, punir, et faire punir les contraventeurs en toute vigueur, sans graçe ny pardon, obligeants á l'effect que dessus touts et chacun de nos royaumes, païs, et seigneuries, comme aussy touts nos autres biens, presents et à venir, aussy nos heritiers et successeurs, ensemblement tous nos vassaux, subjects, et habitants de tous nos royaumes, païs, et seigneuries, en quelque lieu, que tant dedans que hors l'Europe ils se puissent treuver sans rien excepter, et pour la validité de cette obligation, nous renonçons à toutes loix, coustumes, et toutes autres choses à ce contraires; en foy de çe que dessus, nous avons fait depescher la presente, signée de nostre main, seellée de nostre seel secret, et contresignée de nostre secretaire d'estat. Fait à Madrid le premier de mars, del'an mil six cent quarante huict.

PHILIPPE.
Par ordonnance de Sa Ma[jes]té.
GER[ONY]MO DELA TORRE.

INDEX.

3- 17- 11-

CPSIA information can be obtained
at www.ICGtesting.com
Printed in the USA
LVHW030706191121
703680LV00020B/355

9 789353 703967